Sustaining the Law

Joseph Smith's Legal Encounters

Edited by
Gordon A. Madsen, Jeffrey N. Walker, and John W. Welch

BYU Studies
Provo, Utah

Opinions expressed in this publication are the opinions of the authors, and their views should not necessarily be attributed to The Church of Jesus Christ of Latter-day Saints, Brigham Young University, or BYU Studies. All revenues from this book will help fund future publications.

Library of Congress Cataloging-in-Publication Data

Sustaining the law : Joseph Smith's legal encounters / edited by Gordon A. Madsen, Jeffrey N. Walker, and John W. Welch.
    pages cm.
  Includes bibliographical references and index.
  ISBN 978-1-938896-70-5 (hardcover : alk. paper)
1. Smith, Joseph, Jr., 1805–1844—Trials, litigation, etc. 2. Mormons—Legal status, laws, etc.—United States—History—19th century. I. Madsen, Gordon A., 1929– editor of compilation. II. Walker, Jeffrey N., editor of compilation. III. Welch, John W. (John Woodland) editor of compilation.

  KF228.S5528S87 2014
  342.7308'52893092--dc23

                    2013047246

Contents

Preface   v
Jeffrey N. Walker

Introduction   ix

1   Joseph Smith and the Constitution   1
    John W. Welch

2   The Smiths and Religious Freedom:
    Jesse Smith's 1814 Church Tax Protest   39
    John W. Welch

3   Standing as a Credible Witness in 1819   51
    Jeffrey N. Walker

4   Being Acquitted of a "Disorderly Person" Charge in 1826   71
    Gordon A. Madsen

5   Securing the Book of Mormon Copyright in 1829   93
    Nathaniel Hinckley Wadsworth

6   Organizing the Church as a Religious Association in 1830   113
    David Keith Stott

7   Winning against Hurlbut's Assault in 1834   141
    David W. Grua

8   Performing Legal Marriages in Ohio in 1835   155
    M. Scott Bradshaw

9   Looking Legally at the Kirtland Safety Society   179
     Jeffrey N. Walker

10   Tabulating the Impact of Litigation on the Kirtland Economy   227
     Gordon A. Madsen

11   Losing Land Claims and the Missouri Conflict in 1838   247
     Jeffrey N. Walker

12   Imprisonment by Austin King's Court of Inquiry in 1838   271
     Gordon A. Madsen

13   Protecting Nauvoo by Illinois Charter in 1840   297
     James L. Kimball Jr.

14   Suffering Shipwreck and Bankruptcy in 1842 and Beyond   309
     Joseph I. Bentley

15   Serving as Guardian under the Lawrence Estate, 1842–1844   329
     Gordon A. Madsen

16   Invoking Habeas Corpus in Missouri and Illinois   357
     Jeffrey N. Walker

17   Defining Adultery under Illinois and Nauvoo Law   401
     M. Scott Bradshaw

18   Legally Suppressing the *Nauvoo Expositor* in 1844   427
     Dallin H. Oaks

Legal Chronology of Joseph Smith   461

Lawyers and Judges in the Legal Cases of Joseph Smith   515

Glossary of Early Nineteenth-Century Legal Terms   546

Contributors   555

Index   557

Preface

In October 2006, a group of Church historians went on a tour of early Church history sites. This two-week trip took us from Sharon, Vermont, to Carthage, Illinois. As we travelled, there was lots of time to share ideas and stories. During one of those long afternoons, John W. (Jack) Welch and I talked about the possibility of combining the Joseph Smith Papers Project's Legal and Business Series with his teaching of a course on Joseph Smith and early American law at the J. Reuben Clark Law School at Brigham Young University. Teaming up in this way seemed like a perfect fit, and so it has been.

Church Historian Elder Marlin K. Jensen has called the Joseph Smith Papers Project "the single most significant historical project of our generation."[1] When completed, it will present to the world a monumental collection of documents relating to Joseph Smith, including his diaries, journals, revelations, correspondence, as well as administrative, business and legal documents. The print version will be approximately twenty-four volumes, and the web version will include an even broader array. A cadre of several dozen scholars, researchers, archivists, transcribers, copyeditors, and other professionals staff the project. Made possible through the generosity of the Larry H. Miller family, the project provides a unique opportunity to gather, analyze, and publish these papers that future generations of writers will use to write more factually accurate histories of the life of Joseph Smith Jr. and the foundation of The Church of Jesus Christ of Latter-day Saints and the Mormon people.

Gordon Madsen, Sharalyn Howcroft, and I, as the original members of the Joseph Smith Papers legal team, have spent much of the past decade gathering and creating case files for each of the identified lawsuits involving Joseph

---

1. R. Scott Lloyd, "'Historian by Yearning,' Collects, Preserves," *Church News of The Church of Jesus Christ of Latter-day Saints*, May 28, 2005.

Smith. Initial estimates were that he had been involved in about fifty lawsuits. As we collected, organized and compiled these legal records, the number kept increasing, topping now at more than 220 cases. These lawsuits range from simple collection cases to complex actions involving sophisticated legal theories, and Joseph retained scores of attorneys to both bring and defend these actions. They include both civil and criminal matters. The case files we created include indexes, documents, transcripts, and secondary materials—almost like pleading files that one would find in law firms today. To these files are added editorial and footnote annotations to give background and context.

While the annotations coincide in many respects with the work being done in presenting documents in the other parts of the Joseph Smith Papers, the documents going into the legal series require additional analysis to provide the reader with an understanding of the applicable laws and judicial procedures. Such legal analysis presents modern lawyers and readers with a number of challenges. For example, all of the cases involving Smith predate the first enactment of modern American civil procedure in 1848. Consequently, working with Joseph Smith's legal papers—just like working with the legal papers of John Adams, John Marshall, Daniel Webster, Andrew Jackson, Abraham Lincoln, or Oliver Cowdery—requires an understanding of early nineteenth-century law in America that blended both the British and American systems.

At the same time that the legal papers team was doing research, a growing series of articles about Joseph Smith's legal experiences was being published in *BYU Studies*. Professor Welch, the editor-in-chief of *BYU Studies*, planned to use those articles as a main part of the curriculum for his law school course. As he and I, during our tour, discussed the possibilities of combining our efforts, the basic contours of this groundbreaking class and this book began to take shape. Using theses lawsuits as collected and organized for the Joseph Smith Papers Project, the course could explore the broader contextual dimensions of the emergence of the American legal system in the frontiers of early American Republic in which Smith and his people lived in the 1820s to 1840s. From his early trials in New York, to land, banking, and collections cases in Ohio, to the criminal prosecutions arising from the Mormon War of 1838 in Missouri, to his activity as a politician (first as mayor of Nauvoo and then as a candidate for the presidency), to his murder while in custody on other charges following his court appearance in Carthage concerning lawsuits filed after the destruction of the press used to print *The Expositor*, Smith's legal experiences largely parallels and in many respects epitomizes the American justice system of his day.

Upon arriving home from our trip, Jack sought and readily received permission to teach the course. It has now been taught for eight years. This reader is substantively a result of these classes. Many have assisted Jack, Gordon, and me in running this course, including Joseph Bentley, Morris Thurston, Ross Boundy, and Kelly Schaeffer-Bullock, who have served as guest lecturers and professional contributors. Each year our teaching materials have been improved and developed, based on new discoveries, classroom experiences, student feedback, and the ongoing work of research assistants too numerous to name and to whom a great debt of gratitude is owed.

I have been overwhelmed at the capacity and dedication of the students who have taken our course. They have each produced research papers, memoranda, and personal reports of their findings and impressions. On many occasions they have taken the preliminary drafts of transcripts in the case files and have made significant contributions to preparing those materials for future publication in the Joseph Smith Papers Legal and Business Records series. This has included not only doing excellent historical legal research, but also assisting in creating glossaries, chronologies, and annotations. Our law students have also delved into historical records and early American legal treatises and judicial opinions. The groundbreaking research papers by Nathaniel Wadsworth and David Stott were so good that they were published in *BYU Studies* and now appear in this reader.

Most gratifying has been the interest of our students in the life of the Prophet Joseph Smith and how studying his legal involvement provides unique insights into his character and world. It has been and continues to be an exciting process to explore something that has been often misunderstood, if not completely overlooked, by historians and readers of all persuasions. But undeniably, Joseph Smith was intimately, actively, and consistently involved in the American legal system. To ignore these important activities is to miss much of how he spent his time and energies, brilliantly and effectively—so much so that Daniel H. Wells, himself a lawyer, judge, and attorney general, who was well acquainted with Smith, would opine: "I have known legal men all my life. Joseph Smith was the best lawyer that I have ever known in my life."[2] Our studies continue to prove that Wells was right.

Jeffrey N. Walker
December 2013

---

2. Daniel H. Wells, as quoted in *The Journal of Jesse Nathaniel Smith: Six Decades in the Early West: Diaries and Papers of a Mormon Pioneer, 1834–1906* (Salt Lake City: Jesse N. Smith Family Association, 1953), 456.

Introduction

This book is a first of its kind. Although hundreds of volumes and articles have been written about Joseph Smith, the prophet and organizer of The Church of Jesus Christ of Latter-day Saints, no book before has ever been dedicated exclusively to assembling materials pertaining to his legal encounters.[1] Those numerous incidents were serious and significant developments in his life personally as well as in the history of his people institutionally. Throughout his life, the courtroom became a familiar setting to him, and resulting judicial outcomes had enormous impacts. One cannot come to grips with the life of Joseph Smith without studying his more than two hundred encounters with judges, lawyers, judicial procedures, legal transactions, and legal principles. And yet no book written about Joseph Smith adequately features or takes this dimension of his life into account. This book is a first step in the direction of allaying that deficiency.

Joseph Smith took the law seriously. In 1835 the first edition of the Doctrine and Covenants, which he approved and published, set forth a statement of beliefs regarding governments and laws in general. It included, "We believe that all men are bound to sustain and uphold the respective governments in which they reside, while protected in their inherent and inalienable rights by the laws of such governments" (D&C 134:5). In 1842 Joseph succinctly declared, "We believe in obeying, honoring, and sustaining the law" (Article of Faith 12). In an editorial penned on February 17, 1844, he wrote, "The constitution expects every man to do his duty; and when he fails the law urges him; or should he do

---

1. One study, Edwin Brown Firmage and Richard Collin Mangrum, *Zion in the Courts: A Legal History of the Church of Jesus Christ of Latter-day Saints, 1830–1900* (Urbana: University of Chicago Press, 1988), chs. 3–5, discusses some of Joseph Smith's lawsuits in the context of the legal experiences of the Saints as a whole.

too much, the same master rebukes him."[2] Although some have questioned if Joseph Smith and his people observed these beliefs in practice—and he was not entirely perfect as a man, as he himself admitted—this collection of materials demonstrates in fascinating detail how he gave much more than mere lip service to obeying, honoring, and sustaining the law. Scrupulously and resourcefully, he walked the rough-and-not-so-ready paths of the still-developing American legal system just one generation before the calamitous U.S. Civil War.

By all measures, Joseph Smith led an amazingly extraordinary life. His accomplishments and endeavors in the face of formidable odds are bewildering. While people may variously agree or disagree with his theology, politics, management style or sociality, few would disagree with the strong consensus that emerged from a prestigious panel of speakers at his bicentennial celebration at the Library of Congress in 2005,[3] that Joseph Smith was a remarkable American, with wide ranging visions and goals for people all over the face of the earth. He was inspired by extraordinary means and insights that were magnetically attractive to many people who came in close contact with him, while others of an opposite pole were equally repulsed by that magnetism. Those diametrically opposed reactions, which came along with his prophetic calling—that his name "should be had for good and evil ... among all people"[4]—often played themselves out in the arenas of courtrooms, from his youth until the day he was murdered.

Joseph Smith was born a simple American farm boy in 1805 in a remote cabin in Vermont, but from this humble background, he would rise to become a national figure. Near the end of his life, in 1844, he announced his campaign for the presidency of the United States. His frequent contacts with judges, legislators, governors, and even President Martin Van Buren gave him firsthand experiences with the strengths and weaknesses of the legal and political processes of his day. While he may not have had a serious chance of winning the 1844 national election, he ran shrewdly as a third-party candidate who was definitely serious about encouraging legal reforms in the United States. He hoped and worked to improve public opinions on momentous issues including slavery, religious freedom, prisons, and public lands. He and Robert F.

---

2. Joseph Smith Jr., *History of The Church of Jesus Christ of Latter-day Saints,* ed. B. H. Roberts, 2d ed., rev., 7 vols. (Salt Lake City: Deseret Book, 1971), 6:220 (hereafter cited as *History of the Church*).

3. John W. Welch, ed., *The Worlds of Joseph Smith: A Bicentennial Conference at the Library of Congress* (Provo, Utah: BYU Press, 2006).

4. *The Joseph Smith Papers: Histories, Volume 1: Joseph Smith Histories, 1832–1844,* ed. Karen Lynn Davidson et al. (Salt Lake City: Church Historian's Press, 2012), 222; see also Joseph Smith—History 1:33.

Kennedy remain the only two Americans to be assassinated while they were candidates for the office of United States president. Long after visiting Nauvoo and Joseph Smith in mid-May, 1844, Josiah Quincy, who was the son of a president of Harvard University and later mayor of Boston, wondered out loud, "What historical American of the nineteenth century has exerted the most powerful influence upon the destinies of his countrymen?" The answer, he allowed, may well be: "Joseph Smith, the Mormon prophet."[5]

Though not trained in the law, Joseph Smith impressed people of other faiths as having naturally a keen legal mind. He associated with many lawyers and judges, some of them being the best and brightest in his day. He was readily attracted to good legal talent. The appendix at the end of this volume (pp. 545–45) identifies, for the first time, over sixty lawyers and judges who were involved with Joseph Smith in one way or another, as his advocates, consultants, or adjudicators. He paid well for their services and worked closely with many of them. Joseph Smith consistently followed the law as carefully as he could. He sought and followed the advice of the best lawyers he could find. In response to Governor Ford's letter on June 22, 1844, charging that actions of the Mormons had been an affront to the Constitution, Smith replied that whatever has been done "was done in accordance with the letter of the [Nauvoo] charter and Constitution as we confidently understood them, and that, too, with the ablest counsel; but if it be so that we have erred in this thing, let the Supreme Court correct the evil. We have never gone contrary to constitutional law, so far as we have been able to learn it. If lawyers have belied their profession to abuse us, the evil be upon their heads."[6]

It has always been known that Joseph Smith accomplished an absolutely amazing amount before he was murdered in Carthage, Illinois, in 1844.[7] He translated and published the Book of Mormon in New York; organized the Church in New York, and then resettled it in Ohio, Missouri, and Illinois; founded cities, including Kirtland, Far West, and Nauvoo; called and trained hundreds of church leaders; studied Hebrew and the Bible; founded the Relief Society of Nauvoo; ran businesses, alone and with partners; developed real estate and built temples; wrote and published articles and editorials; had a large family and embraced a wide circle of friends; and served in several civic capacities, including commander-in-chief of a large legion of militia men,

---

5. Josiah Quincy, *Figures of the Past*, new edition (1883; reprint, Boston: Little, Brown, 1926), 317. See Jed Woodworth, "Josiah Quincy's 1844 Visit with Joseph Smith," *BYU Studies* 39, no. 4 (2000): 71.

6. *History of the Church*, 6:535.

7. For John Taylor's statement in this regard, made shortly after Joseph's martyrdom, see Doctrine and Covenants 135:3.

as well as the mayor and chief judge for the city of Nauvoo. He spoke regularly in weekly worship services, dedications, and at all-too-frequent funerals; he attracted tens of thousands of followers, prompting waves of converts to immigrate to the United States. On top of that, astonishingly, he was also party to or participant in at least 220 lawsuits. Some were minor matters, but many demanded and consumed great time and attention.

To fathom all of this, the long legal chronology at the back of this book (pp. 461–514) should be regularly consulted. It lists month by month, and often day by day, the incessant barrage of litigation and legal proceedings that Joseph Smith encountered throughout his lifetime.[8] This one-of-a-kind chronicle is an important tool for understanding the contents of this book. For ease of reference, case names appear in bold type the first time they appear, and cross references are given to chapters which discuss particular entries. The chronology gives an overview of many legal matters, as well as many other activities and roles that Joseph cared for while simultaneously handling these legal matters. Seeing this legal web, which overlays everything else he was doing allows readers to know what else was going on at the same time as these terribly distracting legal troubles. For most mere mortals, enduring two or three lawsuits per lifetime is considered stressful enough. For Joseph Smith, all that stress was subsumed by his positive character and absolute commitment to the mission with which he had been repeatedly entrusted by his God.

Much of this legal complexity has only recently been found, organized, and analyzed. This book is an outgrowth of the widely acclaimed Joseph Smith Papers project, as all remote corners have been scoured to locate every possible document relating to Joseph Smith. As a result, thousands of pages of new materials have been catalogued and transcribed, with the possibility of discovering even more. From all of this new information, one may well imagine, much will be learned about Joseph Smith as a person, prophet, and citizen. Currently, three volumes in the Joseph Smith Papers Legal and Business Records series are underway, making this a burgeoning area of historical research.

As work on the legal papers of Joseph Smith has unfolded, a class has been offered at the J. Reuben Clark Law School at Brigham Young University on Joseph Smith and early nineteenth-century American law, taught by the three editors of this volume. Of course, a wide range of regularly published legal history textbooks and reference works are used in this class. In addition to those

---

8. This chronology of Joseph Smith's legal history has been compiled by the editors with assistance from Joseph Bentley, Sharalyn Howcroft, Ronald Esplin, members of the Joseph Smith Papers team, and BYU law students. Supporting documents will be published in the forthcoming Joseph Smith Papers Legal and Business Records series.

Readings on Law, Culture, and Politics in Joseph Smith's Era

Bailyn, Bernard. *The Ideological Origins of the American Revolution*. Cambridge, Mass.: Belknap Press, 1992.

Banner, Stuart. *Legal Systems in Conflict: Property and Sovereignty in Missouri, 1750–1860*. Norman, Okla.: University of Oklahoma Press, 2000.

Bushman, Richard L. *The Refinement of America*. New York: Vintage Books, 1993.

Friedman, Lawrence. *A History of American Law*. New York: Simon and Schuster, 2006.

Grossberg, Michael, and Christopher Tomlins, eds. *The Cambridge History of Law in America*. 3 vols. New York: Cambridge University Press, 2007.

Hall, Kermit L., Paul Finkelman, and James W. Ely Jr. *American Legal History: Cases and Materials*. 4th ed. New York: Oxford University Press, 2011.

Hall, Kermit L., and Peter Karsten. *The Magic Mirror: Law in American History*. 2d ed. New York: Oxford University Press, 2009.

Hoeflich, Michael H., ed. *Sources of the History of the American Law of Lawyering*. Clark, N.J.: Lawbook Exchange, 2007.

Holmes, David L. *The Faiths of the Founding Fathers*. New York: Oxford, 2006.

Horwitz, Morton J. *The Transformation of American Law, 1780–1860*. New York: Oxford University Press, 1992.

Hutson, James H. *Forgotten Features of the Founding*. Lanham, Md.: Lexington Books, 2003. And *Church and State in America: The First Two Centuries*. Cambridge: Cambridge University Press, 2008.

Howe, Daniel Walker. *What Hath God Wrought: The Transformation of America, 1815–1848*. New York: Oxford University Press, 2007.

Lambert, Frank. *The Founding Fathers and the Place of Religion in America*. Princeton, N.J.: Princeton University Press, 2003.

Morison, Samuel Eliot, Henry Steele Commager, and William E. Leuchtenburg, *A Concise History of the American Republic*. New York: Oxford University Press, 1977.

Lutz, Donald, *The Origins of American Constitutionalism*. Baton Rouge: Louisiana State University Press, 1988.

Noll, Mark A., and Luke E. Harlow, eds. *Religion and American Politics: From the Colonial Period to the Present*. 2d ed. New York: Oxford University Press, 2007.

Novak, Michael, *On Two Wings: Humble Faith and Common Sense at the American Founding*. San Francisco: Encounter Books, 2002.

Presser, Stephen B., and Jamil S. Zainaldin. *Law and Jurisprudence in American History: Cases and Materials*. 8th ed. St. Paul, Minn.: West, 2013.

Urofsky, Melvin I., and Paul Finkelman, eds. *Documents of American Constitutional and Legal History*. 3d ed. 2 vols. New York: Oxford University Press, 2008.

Wood, Gordon S. *The Creation of the American Republic, 1776–1787*. Chapel Hill: University of North Carolina Press, 1969. And *Empire of Liberty: A History of the Early Republic, 1789–1815*. New York: Oxford University Press, 2009.

Zunz, Oliver, and Alan S. Kahan. *The Tocqueville Reader: A Life in Letters and Politics*. Malden, Mass.: Blackwell, 2002.

referred to in the footnotes in this book, readers may want to peruse the items on the accompanying list of useful books about law, culture, and politics in Joseph Smith's era. For primary sources, including statutes and treatises from the early nineteenth century, numerous legal books are now available online.[9] But in addition, a specialized set of readings about Joseph Smith's legal experiences was needed for use in that course, and hence this collection originated.

This book is published with several audiences in mind: general readers, law students, lawyers, legal scholars and historians. It brings together a dozen of the best articles published on several of the main legal cases in which Smith was personally involved. Each chapter tells a fascinating story in which controlling legal documents have survived, allowing detailed comprehension and extensive analysis. For helping to bring this book together and making this publication possible, special recognition and appreciation go to Ross Boundy, Jennifer Hurlbut, Marny Parkin, Chase Walker, Kelly Schaeffer-Bullock, Malory Hatfield, Sarah Hampton, the Joseph Smith Papers Project, the Mormon Historic Sites Foundation, and the J. Reuben Clark Law School and its Law Society.

In addition to the substantive appendices, published here for the first time are the four new chapters on Joseph Smith and the Constitution, the formation and legal aftermath of the Kirtland Safety Society, the results of litigation on the Kirtland economy, and the legal definition of adultery under Illinois and Nauvoo law. Eleven of the other chapters have been published in *BYU Studies,* while two have appeared in the *Journal of Mormon History,* one in *Mormon Historical Studies,* and one in the *Utah Law Review,* with a first printing of another having appeared in the *Brigham Young University Law Review,* as indicated at the end of each chapter respectively. To make this material as conveniently understandable as possible, each of these articles has been shortened, substantively updated, edited, and illustrated, while nonessential footnotes have been trimmed and sidebar texts of primary sources added. The more fully documented versions of these articles can be found in their original publications. To reflect these significant changes, the titles of these articles have all been adjusted.

By now it should be obvious that the study of Joseph Smith and the law is as fascinating as it is complicated. This book aims to make the task of understanding this material a bit simpler. Here are some key points to keep in mind while reading this book.

First, it is important to understand that the law in early nineteenth-century America was markedly different from the present. Going into that world is almost like traveling to a foreign country. One might anticipate that the

---

9. See such digital collections as Google.books; HeinOnline; LexisNexis; Westlaw; Making of Modern Law: Legal Treatises, 1800–1926; Making of Modern Law: Primary Sources, 1626–1926.

nineteenth-century American legal and judicial system was different from the American system today, but the degree of that difference will probably come to most readers as a shock. Juries reigned almost supreme and in all kinds of cases. Lawyers did not go to law schools—which did not exist—and they could wear many hats, which professionals today would consider conflicts of interest. Promissory notes were circulated instead of currency, which was hard to find in frontier economies—paper money was not issued by the United States until the 1860s. Even the legal vocabulary was much different in those days than it is today (hence the glossary at the end of this volume).

More substantively, it may come as a surprise to many readers that during Joseph Smith's time, the Bill of Rights (the first ten amendments to the Constitution) was not binding on the states, only on the federal government. As such, the establishment clause of the First Amendment[10] and the due process clause in the Fifth Amendment—which prohibits state and local governments from depriving persons of life, liberty, or property without meeting certain fairness requirements—did not apply to actions of the individual states. Further, the Fourteenth Amendment had not yet been added to the U.S. Constitution, and thus, the equal protection clause, which requires each state to provide equal protection of law to all people within its jurisdiction, was merely a political ideal in Smith's day,[11] not the law of the land.

In addition, the court system itself was also much different than it is today. Typically, cases were filed either in a justice court or in a court of common pleas, depending on their nature. For example, in New York, cases in a justice court were heard by a single justice of the peace. Such justices were not required at all to have been trained in law and were elected by citizens of the district. Appeals from the justice courts were heard in courts of common pleas, presided over by three justices, all of whom were required to be trained in the law. Litigants had the option of appealing a case to an even higher judicial level, if a justice made a decision they believed was unfair. Joseph either lodged an appeal, or threatened to appeal, in many instances, but judges were not always available, since most courts were only in session certain months of the year and the higher judges often traveled on a circuit covering several counties.

---

10. Realizing this makes sense of the need for Doctrine and Covenants 134:9 to speak against states mingling religious influence with civil government, "whereby one religious society is fostered and another proscribed."

11. Expressed in the Declaration of Independence, that "all men are created equal." Equality, of course, is not a self-defining concept; see Hugo A. Bedau, *Justice and Equality* (Englewood Cliffs, N.J.: Prentice-Hall, 1971). Nor did the U.S. Constitution of 1787 treat all men, let alone women, equally. Joseph Smith's political campaign pamphlet, however, spoke of the Constitution as "so high a charter of equal rights" and advocated "more equality through the cities, towns and country ... [to] make less distinction among the people."

It is important to realize that Smith's legal experiences arose in many juris-dictions—New York, Pennsylvania, Ohio, Missouri, Iowa, and Illinois, as well as federal—and that each had its own system and types of laws. Few laws operated uniformly from state to state, making it hard to generalize about what the law was in those days. As Smith moved from one state to another, he may well have expected the laws that he had known in the previous jurisdic-tion to apply to his situation in the new jurisdiction.

Did he obey the law? The first step in objectively answering that question must be to determine what the law was in those days. Was it against New York law to use a seer stone as an instrument in dictating the text of a book? Was it unlawful under Ohio law for a religious leader who was not ordained as a Protestant minister to perform marriages within his religious community? How was treason defined under Missouri or United States law? What was the normal procedure in the 1830s for invoking the writ of habeas corpus to resist arrest, imprisonment, and the deprivation of liberty? What evidentiary and procedural standards should apply in a constitutional case of first impression when the governor of Missouri demands that the governor of Illinois extra-dite a citizen of Illinois back to stand trial in Missouri? Was it objectionable under federal or state constitutional law for a legally constituted commander to mobilize militiamen in a well-regulated fashion to protect the streets of Nauvoo from conspiring mobs that were threatening to move into the city? Was it unusual, let alone illegal, for a duly elected city council to determine that a newspaper was a public nuisance and authorize the city police to abate that nuisance? Was it criminal under Illinois law in the early 1840s for a person to commit adultery if that conduct was kept private and was neither open nor notorious?

Answering such questions is not easy today. It was not easy even in those days, for law in the early nineteenth century was undergoing seismic trans-formations, and the law of the time was often uncertain and continuously developing, especially as settlers broke ground across the central parts of the United States. By Joseph Smith's day, the disestablishment movement held sway, separating church matters and state affairs, and power was being shifted in many regards from church congregations to state and local govern-ments; but that transition was still far from complete, and variations existed from state to state in such matters as the enforcement of Sabbath laws, sexual mores, marriage, divorce, women's rights, and the meaning of free speech and the free exercise of religion. The transformation from English common law to state statutory laws was in process and was by no means settled. As the nation and American law was still moving into the industrial age, the laws of torts, crimes, treason, federalism, contracts, public nuisance, property, corporations, banking, women, and slavery were all in great transition.[12] This time period provided creative frontiers for American law in nearly every field, and that transition fueled opportunities for change and progress of many kinds, but also created discrepancies, disagreements, and even led all too frequently to violence. Courts could do little to establish continuity in their judicial decisions, making legal opinions undependable and justice difficult to come by.

With his heavy involvement in the legal system, Smith quickly learned the rules of the game and legally used those rules to his full lawful advantage, striving to make full use of the new opportunities and protections afforded by the young nation's laws. His legal choices and conduct make it clear that he was well informed about legal matters and that he took explicit steps to make every appropriate use allowed by the law, whether he was obtaining the copyright for the Book of Mormon under federal law, performing marriages under Ohio law, shaping Nauvoo city ordinances, invoking the full protections of religious freedom, making effective use of new laws that governed the sale of federal land, asserting his right of habeas corpus, demanding proper venue, or applying for coverage under the newly adopted federal bankruptcy law. In his spare time, he studied law books. He knew the precise wording of the Constitution and the specific language of state statutes. No doubt he was well aware of many current legal developments at state and federal levels throughout his lifetime.

Further complicating the picture, Joseph appears in these cases in various social and political roles as well as church and fiduciary positions. While some of the cases revolved around religious issues, the majority did not. Joseph appeared in disputes involving business, property, municipal, martial, and constitutional law. While Joseph Smith usually found himself on the defensive, he was occasionally a plaintiff, witness, and judge. Though he often suffered legal wrongs, he usually chose not to take them to court. For example, he was tarred and feathered in Ohio and subjected to libel and slander in Illinois but did not seek judicial vindication. When he sued or petitioned for redress, he typically was concerned more with justice and protection for his people, rather than himself.

As a defendant, he was never convicted of any criminal offense. Whenever he was given a fair hearing, he was found to be an upstanding and honest

---

12. See Stephen B. Presser and Jamil S. Zainaldin, *Law and Jurisprudence in American History: Cases and Materials.* 8th ed. (St. Paul, Minn.: West, 2013), chs. 2–4; Morton J. Horwitz, *The Transformation of American Law, 1780–1860* (New York: Oxford University Press, 1992), passim.

citizen. Of his involvement with legal prosecutions, Brigham Young—who knew Joseph as well as anyone—testified in 1852, "Joseph Smith was not killed because he was deserving of it, nor because he was a wicked man; but because he was a virtuous man. I know that to be so, as well as I know that the sun now shines … I know for myself that Joseph Smith was the subject of forty-eight law-suits, and the most of them I witnessed with my own eyes; but not one action could ever be made to bear against him. No law or constitutional right did he ever violate. He was innocent and virtuous; he kept the law of his country and lived above it; … He was pure, just and holy, as to the keeping of the law. Now this I state for the satisfaction of those who do not know our history."[13]

In civil courts, judgments were often entered in favor of creditors against him and his partners, but often these obligations were not even contested and were simply being entered into the public record as a regular step in the ordinary debt collection process of that day. As far as one can tell, Joseph eventually paid his debts virtually in full, even when they were enormous, as was the case in the collapse of the ill-starred Kirtland Safety Society.

Even though Joseph consistently lived within the boundaries of the law, he lost much due to the unevenness of frontier opinions that sometimes prevailed in court. He was constantly distracted by lawsuits brought against him and suffered both physically and financially. He was held in state custody several times, sometimes under the watch of cruel and designing captors. He was denied bankruptcy claims while all others were approved, and he suffered many other financial blows from legal fees, demands for bail, and judgments, due to the lawsuits filed against him.

The law students who have used previous iterations of this book as their textbook have consistently come to the opinion that Joseph was responsible, accountable, loyal, prudent, merciful, cautious, meticulous, law-abiding, patient, positive, resourceful, astute, savvy, a good judge of character, and even legally brilliant (to use some of their own words), especially when it came to protecting the religious and civil rights of others or carrying out the duties with which he had been entrusted. He did not always win in civil actions regarding debt collection, and the rule of law sometimes worked for him, while other times it failed utterly. But Joseph Smith never lost faith in the Constitution and strived to work solidly under its aegis, even though he was often frustrated, disappointed, and wary of people administering it.

Occasionally, he pushed the envelope, finding himself on the cutting edge or testing the technical limits of the often unsettled law, but this is hardly

---

13. Brigham Young, *Journal of Discourses*, 26 vols. (Liverpool: F. D. Richards, 1855–86), 1:40–41 (July 11, 1852).

surprising for a man who was breaking new ground theologically and politically, frequently taking issue with the dominant culture, and trying to move quickly to meet the urgently pressing needs of his devoted circle of friends and followers who were so vulnerable and depended upon him so hopefully. Consequently, he understood that there were different sides to legal arguments, and he did not shy away from debating legal issues with the best legal minds around him.

Overall, Joseph Smith' involvement with the law of early nineteenth-century America impacted his life to a significant extent—much more than historians have typically recognized. Many biographical works have been produced about Joseph Smith, but those works have mostly focused on his personality, psyche, or religious and social achievements. Recognizing all the new information that legal developments have only recently brought to the table, one biographer lamented that old conclusions needed to be reconsidered and much of his book needed to be rewritten. For example, people have typically acquiesced that Joseph Smith was guilty of the crime of being a disorderly person in New York, that he illegally performed marriages in Ohio, that he was financially irresponsible in Kirtland, that provisions in his Nauvoo Charter were illegal, that he abused the right of habeas corpus in Illinois, that he did not discharge his financial duties as guardian, that he was properly charged with treason in Missouri and Illinois, and that he violated the Constitution when the *Nauvoo Expositor* press was destroyed. Readers may now read the primary documents behind such legal issues and see for themselves what the facts in these cases were, and how it might change some such conclusions, as they come to understand how the laws of the time applied to those situations, and what actually happened or legally should have happened in each of these cases.

This book does not begin to tell the entire story of Joseph Smith's legal history, but it is a step in that direction. This study is a still work in progress. Further research is ongoing about the application of early American law to the many lawsuits, legal transactions, and legal responsibilities that colored Joseph Smith's daily life. As there are many more cases to consider, a sequel volume is already taking shape. We regret any mistakes of fact or errors of law which may have occurred in spite of our best efforts. We will gladly correct those defects in subsequent printings of this material, especially as we continue to move toward the publication of the legal volumes in the Joseph Smith Papers. But as things stand at the moment, this book is an engaging point of departure for all readers interested in understanding the laws behind Joseph Smith's many encounters with the law.

The first page of an early copy of the United States Constitution beginning with the Preamble.

Chapter One

Joseph Smith and the Constitution

John W. Welch

Throughout his public life, Joseph Smith spoke frequently, insightfully, and supportively about the Constitution of the United States. He understood the importance of its general principles as well as its specific language. He appealed to it in various ways, on differing occasions, both affirmatively to advance the building of the kingdom of God on earth and also defensively to seek protection and reparation for injuries and deprivations. By looking at this material carefully, it becomes clear that Joseph read the Constitution meticulously and that he thoughtfully invoked many of its sections and phrases regularly and effectively.

In order to situate Joseph Smith's understanding of constitutional law within the legal and political context of the early American republic, this overview will (1) discuss what the Constitution was and was not during Joseph Smith's lifetime, (2) examine briefly the four revelations in the Doctrine and Covenants that relate most directly to the U.S. Constitution, (3) argue that when Joseph Smith referred to the "principles" of the Constitution, much of what he had in mind are the legal purposes found in the Preamble to the Constitution, and (4) present, as far as possible, every known explicit statement by Joseph Smith regarding the Constitution in chronological order with a few details about their historical contexts. This discussion lays a foundation for analyzing the ways in which Joseph Smith utilized constitutional law for legal and political purposes in the context of how the Constitution was understood in his day.

The United States Constitution in the 1840s

"In a revolution, as in a novel, the most difficult part to invent is the end," said Alexis de Tocqueville.[1] During Joseph Smith's lifetime (1805–1844), the American people were still trying to invent the end of the American Revolution. In those years, the United States was growing into a new vision of a country governed by the rule of law, premised upon new legal theories and sustained by state and federal constitutions. The United States Constitution was still a new and relatively untried experiment, and many political and social forces were forming the foundation of constitutional law in Joseph Smith's day. Religious groups claimed their traditional role in teaching and inculcating civic virtues that were thought to be essential in taming the desultory human tendencies of greed, folly, factionalism, power-mongering, and mobocracy.[2] The Industrial Revolution was transforming life in America economically, socially, and legally.[3] Expanding frontiers and the implimentation of Manifest Destiny were opening up new vistas and venues never before contemplated. America had been in a state of developmental flux since the days of the Revolution in 1776, but that burgeoning tide became even more dynamic with what Robert Remini has called the "revolutionary age of Andrew Jackson."[4]

In order to understand Joseph Smith in terms of early American political and legal theory, it is critical to be aware of what the Constitution was and what it was not during his lifetime.[5] Growing out of the Declaration of

---

1. Alexis de Tocqueville, *The Recollections of Alexis de Tocqueville* (1896), 71.

2. Daniel Walker Howe, *What Hath God Wrought: The Transformation of America, 1815–1848* (Oxford: Oxford University Press, 2007).

3. See generally, Morton J. Horwitz, *The Transformation of American Law: 1780–1860* (New York: Oxford University Press, 1992).

4. Robert Remini, *The Revolutionary Age of Andrew Jackson* (New York: Harper and Rowe, 1976). See further Robert V. Remini, *The Jacksonian Era* (Arlington Heights: Harlan Davidson, 1989); Robert V. Remini, ed., *The Age of Jackson* (Columbia: University of South Carolina Press, 1972); Arthur M. Schlesinger, Jr., *The Age of Jackson* (Boston: Little, Brown and Company, 1945); Howe, *What Hath God Wrought*.

5. See the reprint of the 1803 edition of Blackstone by St. George Tucker, *Blackstone's Commentaries: Volume 1* (New Jersey: Rothman Reprints, 1969), appendix D, 140–377, an extended discussion of the Constitution of the United States. Several treatises were published in Joseph Smith's lifetime on the Constitution, including William Rawle, *A View of the Constitution of the United States*, 2d ed. (Philadelphia: Philip H. Nicklin, 1829); Thomas Sergeant, *Constitutional Law*, 2d ed. (Philadelphia: Philip H. Nicklin, 1830); James Kent, *Commentaries on American Law*, 2d ed. (New York: Halsted, 1832), vol. 1, part 2, "Of the Government and Constitutional Jurisprudence of the United States"; and the most celebrated, Joseph Story, *Commentaries on the Constitution of the United States; with a*

Independence and the Articles of Confederation, by 1805 the Constitution of 1787 had its preamble, six articles, the 1789 Bill of Rights, and only two amendments. We tend to think of the political axiom that God endowed all men with inalienable rights to life, liberty, and the pursuit of happiness as a constitutional proposition, when in fact those words are found only in the Declaration of Independence. We also tend to think of the separation of powers established by the three branches of federal government as the most distinctive "principle" of the Constitution, but that does not appear to be what Joseph Smith had in mind when he spoke of the "principles" of the Constitution.

Many of the Constitution's most important amendments were adopted long after the Prophet's life. They have defined the national government's relationship with the individual citizen and with the states as we know it now, but in Joseph Smith's lifetime it was unclear to what extent the federal government could prevent states from denying citizens religious freedom,[6] from abusing their entitlement to due process, or even from withdrawing from the Union.

In 1865, the Thirteenth Amendment abolished slavery. Three years later, the Fourteenth Amendment for the first time required the states to guarantee all American citizens "equal protection of the laws." In 1920, the Nineteenth Amendment gave women the right to vote in federal elections. Before that time, while state constitutions guaranteed their citizens certain civil rights and liberties, the state constitutions differed markedly from each other, and their meanings were subject to various interpretations by each state's courts. It was not until after the Civil War that the divisive issue of states' rights on these issues was settled. In all, twenty-seven amendments have been added to the original Constitution since its ratification; in Joseph's day there were only twelve.

Moreover, those twelve amendments were understood somewhat differently then than they are today. For example, the First Amendment has always read, "Congress shall make no law respecting an establishment of religion, or prohibiting the free exercise thereof; or abridging the freedom of speech, or of the press; or the right of the people peaceably to assemble, and to petition the Government for a redress of grievances." While each phrase in this amendment was obviously very important to Joseph Smith and to most Americans

---

Preliminary Review of the Constitutional History of the Colonies and States, before the Adoption of the Constitution, 3 vols. (Boston: Hilliard, Gray, and Co., 1833).

6. Many states had a religious tax until the 1830s. Massachusetts was the last to abolish the religious tax in 1833. See the discussion in James H. Hutson, "Nursing Fathers: The Model for Church-State Relations in America from James I to Jefferson," in *Lectures on Religion and the Founding of the American Republic,* ed. John W. Welch (Provo, Utah: BYU Studies, 2003), 15–17; James H. Hutson, *Church and State in America: The First Two Centuries* (New York: Cambridge University Press, 2008).

of his day,[7] many people today do not realize that the First Amendment originally applied only to the Federal government and did not apply to the *states*
until well into the twentieth century. The Bill of Rights originally limited only
what Congress could do, as the Supreme Court clearly held in the 1833 case of
Barron v. Baltimore.[8] States had provisions in their individual laws and constitutions protecting religion or defining the extent to which local laws could
support or establish religion, but each state interpreted the idea of religious
liberty as it saw fit, and laws regarding religious matters, such as Sunday closing laws or punishments for adultery, varied measurably from state to state.

In addition, while the word "constitution" had been around since ancient
times, it was not clear in Joseph Smith's day how the American Constitution
would be different from its predecessors. The Founding Fathers, in drafting
the Constitution, were aware of the Greek writings of Aristotle and Polybius
as they grappled with the appropriate scope of federal powers and the rights
of individual states[9] and as they embraced a formal distinction between constitutional and ordinary law.[10] However, while many of the Greek city-states

---

7. For example, as early as 1833 and again in 1839, the right "to petition the Government for a redress of grievances," the final part of the First Amendment, was mentioned in
revelations regarding the troubles the Saints encountered in Missouri. For statements by
John Adams, John Jay, Thomas Jefferson, James Madison, and George Washington regarding the rights afforded here, see James H. Hutson, ed., *The Founders on Religion: A Book of
Quotations* (Princeton: Princeton University Press, 2005), 134–38.

8. In Barron v. Baltimore, 32 U.S. 243, 1833, the Court held that while the Bill of Rights
applied to the actions of federal government, it did not similarly restrict local and state
government. As the city of Baltimore grew, sand and earth began to accumulate in the
harbor, which made the previously deep waters shallower and diminished the value of
the wharf. The wharf owner brought a case against the city of Baltimore claiming that this
decrease in both land and value constituted a taking under the Fifth Amendment. Under
the Fifth Amendment, the government cannot "take" an individual's property without
just compensation. The Court determined that the Fifth Amendment did not apply in this
case because the legal cause of action related to state, not federal, action.

9. R. A. Ames, and H. C. Montgomery, "The Influence of Rome on the American Constitution," *Classical Journal* 30, no. 1 (1934): 19–27 (the Framers clearly turned to Rome for
inspiration, including the framework of three interdependent but sovereign ruling bodies); Gilbert Chinard, "Polybius and the American Constitution," *Journal of the History of
Ideas* 1 (1940): 35–58 (the Framers turned to Rome for resolving the competing interests
of large and small states). A scan of the Federalist Papers shows how much of the discussion involved Roman and Greek political history; for example, Paper no. 63 discusses how
Roman legislative houses were elected and operated.

10. "A constitution may be defined as an organization of offices in a state, by which
the method of their distribution is fixed, the sovereign authority is determined, and the
nature of the end to be pursued by the association and all its members is prescribed. Laws,

had adopted rules and regulations, termed constitutions, these documents did not have the legal stature or authority of modern constitutions as fundamental law, but were primarily guiding regulations for how a city-state would be run. Or, as Aristotle used the term, a constitution "is the way of life of the citizen-body."[11]

Notably, the British Constitution, which emerged from Cromwell's Puritan Revolution in the 1640s, was never reduced to a written document. The English Compromise of 1688 resulted in an agreement that established parliamentary sovereignty, but those changes were never codified in a written constitution that defined the separation of powers or ensured fundamental rights. Instead, these British legal provisions were simply codified over time.

Although the American Constitution had the innovative advantage of being a written document, it still needed to be interpreted. Even with its Supremacy Clause in Article VI, which made all federal laws "the law of the land," it was far from settled in the 1830s how the rules regarding federal statutory preemption, the reach of federal authority, and the rights reserved by the individual states should be interpreted.[12]

For such reasons, many were initially skeptical about the viability of the American dream, especially as other attempts to establish democracies failed. The French Revolution (1789) quickly deteriorated into the Reign of Terror, and the French returned to a monarchy under Napoleon. Most South American countries underwent wars of independence in the 1820s and 1830s, and a few of them created constitutions, but most struggled for decades to establish stable constitutional republics. It was not until 1849 that another country—Denmark—would adopt an American-style constitution. In these years, most of Europe saw only the strengthening of imperialism and the corresponding distrust of democracy and demagogues. It was still an open question whether the American experiment would succeed or fail.

Although early Americans were willing to take on the challenge of forming a new nation, they strongly disagreed among themselves about the proper role of national and local governments. As is well known, Joseph Smith

---

as distinct from the frame of the constitution, are the rules by which the magistrates should exercise their powers, and should watch and check transgressors." Aristotle, *Politics* III (350 BC).

11. Aristotle himself analyzed at least 150 constitutions. Aristotle, *Politics,* trans. E. Barker (Oxford: Oxford University Press, 1958), 180.

12. Cristian G. Fritz, *American Sovereigns: The People and America's Constitutional Tradition before the Civil War* (New York: Cambridge University Press, 2008), 15; Christopher R. Drahozal, *The Supremacy Clause: A Reference Guide to the United States Constitution* (Westport: Praeger, 2004).

himself challenged the establishment on several occasions, especially as he ran for the United States presidency, but these public debates were conducted within the framework of a strong national commitment to the Constitution of the United States as America's principal source of hope to maintain law, order, civility, and progress in an otherwise untamed and scarcely even explored new world.

In this context, Joseph Smith, like most of his American contemporaries, strongly believed in the Constitution. Even if others did not always agree with him, he stood resolutely loyal to the principles upon which the Constitution was founded. Joseph Smith made at least a score of statements regarding the Constitution as identified below. They show that Joseph keenly understood the Constitution, that he had a very high level of faith in it, and that he believed it would endure forever.

Joseph Smith's Early Revelations Mentioning the Constitution

Although the word "constitution" appears in Joseph Smith's writings for the first time in 1833, he had already become legally aware in New York of many provisions in the United States Constitution well before that time, including the right to a trial by jury in 1819 (Amendment 6), the freedoms of speech, religion, assembly, and of the press in 1826–30 (Amendment 1), and the federal right to secure a copyright in 1829 (Article I, Section 8).[13] Then, from 1831 to 1839, the Mormons in Missouri and Illinois suffered tremendous persecution and depredation, bringing several other constitutional issues to the fore. This difficult time thrust Joseph Smith into the political sphere and affected his views on the roles of government:

> The conflict in Missouri changed Joseph's politics dramatically. For the first time, government figured in his thought as an active agent.... The Jackson County attacks made government an essential ally in recovering the Saints' lost lands.... From then on, Joseph was never far removed from politics.[14]

Four early statements canonized in the Doctrine and Covenants reveal the unique importance of civil obedience to the laws of the land, to the Constitution, its language, and the principles that it embodies. The first such revelation, received on **August 1, 1831**. D&C 58:21 reads, "Let no man break the laws of

---

13. See chapters 2–6 below.

14. Richard Lyman Bushman, *Joseph Smith: Rough Stone Rolling* (New York: Knopf, 2005), 226.

the land, for he that keepeth the laws of God hath no need to break the laws of the land."[15] Although not specifically mentioning the Constitution, this revelation uses language similar to a key phrase found in the Supremacy Clause (Article VI, Section 2), which defines the Constitution and all federal laws made in pursuance thereof to be "the supreme law of the land." This revelation affirms that God approves of human laws and requires his people to obey them, and Joseph believed the Constitution to be a tool in the hand of God to promote divine purposes and to protect all who live his laws.

Second, on **August 6, 1833,** the Lord spoke to Joseph, now recorded as D&C 98:5–7:

> And that law of the land, which is constitutional, supporting that *principle* of freedom, in maintaining rights and privileges belongs to all mankind and is justifiable before me. Therefore I the Lord, justify you, and your brethren of my church, in befriending that law which is the constitutional law of the land: And as pertaining to law of man, whatsoever is more or less than this cometh of evil.[16]

Thus, the Constitution bore a divine imprint and was much more than merely a document to be used for good or political ends. It embodied principles that supported freedom in maintaining human rights and privileges, which should not be either expanded or contracted.

Third, only four troubled months later, on **December 16, 1833,** following the Saints' expulsion from Jackson County, Missouri, and only five days before Joseph Smith filed suit against Doctor Philastus Hurlbut in Kirtland Ohio (see chapter 7 below) another revelation reaffirmed the divine source of the universal rights, protections, and freedom provided by the Constitution. It invoked the language of the First Amendment's provision of the right to petition for redress and declared God's direct involvement in the establishment of the Constitution and its principles for legal and doctrinal purposes:

---

15. Aug. 1, 1831. See also Robin Scott Jensen, Robert J. Woodford, and Steven C. Harper, eds., *Manuscript Revelation Books,* facsimile edition, first volume of the Revelations and Translations series of *The Joseph Smith Papers,* ed. Dean C. Jessee, Ronald K. Esplin, and Richard Lyman Bushman (Salt Lake City: Church Historian's Press, 2009), 163.

16. Aug. 6, 1833, as punctuated in the first edition (1835) of the Doctrine and Covenants, p. 216, v. 2; emphasis added. See also Jensen, Woodford, and Harper, *Manuscript Revelation Books,* facsimile edition, 549. Notably, the revelation infers that not all enacted laws are necessarily constitutional. Remarkably, it also proclaims that the constitutional principle of individual freedom "belongs to all mankind," not just to American citizens.

> It is my will that [the Saints] should continue to importune for redress … according to the laws and constitution of the people, which I [God] have suffered to be maintained for the rights and protection of all flesh, according to just and holy *principles*; that every man may act in doctrine and *principle* pertaining to futurity, according to the moral agency which I have given unto him, that every man may be accountable for his own sins in the day of judgment. Therefore, it is not right that any man should be in bondage one to another. And for this purpose have I established the Constitution of this land, by the hands of wise men whom I raised up unto this very purpose, and redeemed the land by the shedding of blood. (D&C 101:76–80)[17]

In this revelation, Joseph and the Saints were assured that God approved of using the law to fight injustice and that God had ordained the establishment of the Constitution of the United States by the hands of wise men, in order that people might act as agents "pertaining to futurity" and thus be held accountable for their sins before the judgment of God. Here, the notion of "futurity" encapsulates the principle behind the early American idea that civic virtue required people to believe in some state of "future rewards and punishment."[18] Many Americans felt the same way—or at least that the Constitution could not have come into being without the influence of divine Providence—including Benjamin Franklin, James Madison, Benjamin Rush, and George Washington.[19]

Fourth, on **March 27, 1836**, in the dedicatory prayer of the Kirtland Temple, Joseph again referenced the holy principles that stood behind the formation of the United States government. He prayed that "those *principles*, which were so honorably and nobly defended, namely, the Constitution of our land, by our fathers, be established forever" (D&C 109:54). While Joseph Smith never expressly defined what he meant by the word "principles," it would appear that the Preamble to the Constitution encapsulate Joseph's conceptual and practical understanding of the term.

---

17. December 16, 1833. See also Jensen, Woodford, and Harper, *Manuscript Revelation Books*, facsimile edition, 579; emphasis added.

18. James Hutson, "'A Future State of Rewards and Punishment': The Founders' Formula for the Social and Political Utility of Religion," in his *Forgotten Features of the Founding* (Lanham, Maryland: Lexington Books, 2003), 1–44.

19. Hutson, *Founders on Religion*, 76–78.

Principles in the Preamble to the Constitution

In D&C 101:77, the revelation referenced "holy principles" and the Lord's will concerning the United States, and in D&C 109:54 Joseph prayed that "those principles" might "be established forever." These formative statements speak of principles embedded in the Constitution, and while this word may refer to many things,[20] one should look first to the Preamble to find what Joseph meant by the "principles" of the Constitution. The Preamble stands as the first part of the Constitution and reads: "We the People of the United States, in Order to form a more perfect Union, establish Justice, insure domestic Tranquility, provide for the common defense, promote the general Welfare, and secure the Blessings of Liberty to ourselves and our Posterity, do ordain and establish this Constitution for the United States of America." In 1844, Joseph's presidential campaign pamphlet quoted the complete text of the preamble.[21]

When Joseph and others in his day spoke of the principles of the Constitution, it seems that the Preamble was never far from their minds. The Preamble has the pride of place in the Constitution, and the word *principle* comes from the Latin words *principalis* and *principium,* meaning the "first," the "origin," the "groundwork," or the "chief" or "guiding" part; that is, through which everything else must pass. These principles were both religious and legal. As the following exploration shows, Joseph was intimately guided by the Preamble's principles in his legal and ecclesiastical roles. These basic ideals constitute the underpinnings of the constitutional and political views of the Prophet just as much as they operated in his religious goals for the establishment of the Church and the building of Zion. In the Preamble are found the headlines of seven key principles. Whether using the same words or reflecting the same ideas, many of Joseph Smith's teachings are consonant with these seven principles.

"We the People." In his *Views of the Powers and Policy of the Government,* the Prophet stated that the power of government rests with the people. He

---

20. The word "principles" was used in Joseph Smith's day to describe the provisions of the Constitution "without which the republican form [of government] would be impure and weak." This term was particularly associated with the just and liberal principles that promote the "general welfare" and "internal peace," while protecting "individual rights" and insuring "reasonable safeguards of society itself." See Rawle, *View of the Constitution,* 121–25.

21. *General Smith's Views of the Powers and Policy of the Government of the United States* (Nauvoo, Ill., 1844), 1–2, reprinted in Joseph Smith Jr., *History of The Church of Jesus Christ of Latter-day Saints,* ed. B. H. Roberts, 2d ed., rev., 7 vols. (Salt Lake City: Deseret Book, 1971), 6:197–98 (hereafter cited as *History of the Church*).

said, "In the United States the people are the government, and their united voice is the only sovereign that should rule, the only power that should be obeyed." Thus, he admonished, "The aspirations and expectations of a virtuous people, environed with so wise, so liberal, so deep, so broad, and so high a charter of equal rights as appears in said Constitution, ought to be treated by those to whom the administration of the laws is entrusted with as much sanctity as the prayers of the Saints are treated in heaven."[22]

Likewise, the business of the Church was to be done by common consent of the people: "All things shall be done by common consent in the church."[23] As Joseph explained, "No official member of the Church has authority to go into any branch thereof, and ordain any minister for that church, unless it is by the voice of that branch."[24] The unanimous voice of the people was always the ideal, and in some cases it was explicitly required.[25]

"In Order to form a more perfect Union." In 1787 John Jay wrote an essay on the unity of the United States, saying, "Providence has been pleased to give this one connected country to one united people."[26] But by 1840, the natural unity that had bound the colonies together in the eighteenth century, resulting from their common cultural heritage and the shared experience

---

22. *General Smith's Views of the Powers and Policy of the Government of the United States,* 8, 3, reprinted in *History of the Church,* 6:208, 198.

23. D&C 26:2; see also D&C 28:13 ("For all things must be done in order, and by common consent in the church, by the prayer of faith"); D&C 104:71 ("And there shall not any part of it be used, or taken out of the treasury, only by the voice and common consent of the order"), D&C 72 (explaining the way in which the poor and the needy should be cared for), D&C 85 (providing information about the law of consecration).

24. Joseph Fielding Smith, comp., *Teachings of the Prophet Joseph Smith* (Salt Lake City: Deseret Book, 1972), 75; see also page 23.

25. D&C 102:3 ("Joseph Smith, Jun., Sidney Rigdon and Frederick G. Williams were acknowledged presidents by the voice of the council; and Joseph Smith, Sen., John Smith, Joseph Coe, John Johnson, Martin Harris, John S. Carter, Jared Carter, Oliver Cowdery, Samuel H. Smith, Orson Hyde, Sylvester Smith, and Luke Johnson, high priests, were chosen to be a standing council for the church, by the unanimous voice of the council"); 107:27 ("And every decision made by either of these quorums must be by the unanimous voice of the same; that is, every member in each quorum must be agreed to its decisions, in order to make their decisions of the same power or validity one with the other"); Smith, *Teachings of the Prophet Joseph Smith,* 108 ("That no one be ordained to any office in the Church in this stake of Zion, at Kirtland, without the unanimous voice of the several bodies that constitute this quorum, who are appointed to do Church business in the name of said Church, viz., the Presidency of the Church; the Twelve Apostles of the Lamb; the twelve High Councilors of Zion; the Bishop of Kirtland and his counselors; the Bishop of Zion and his counselors; and the seven presidents of Seventies; until otherwise ordered by said quorums").

26. John Jay, Federalist Papers no. 2.

of the Revolutionary War, was frayed. Joseph praised politicians who could lay aside "all party strife" and "like brothers, citizens, and friends" mingle together with "courtesy, respect, and friendship,"[27] and as a candidate for the Presidency he sought a unity that would transcend party squabbling and sectional politics. He boldly asserted,

> Unity is power; and when I reflect on the importance of it to the stability of all governments, I am astounded at the silly moves of persons and parties to foment discord in order to ride into power on the current of popular excitement.... Democracy, Whiggery, and cliquery will attract their elements and foment divisions among the people, to accomplish fancied schemes and accumulate power, while poverty, driven to despair, like hunger forcing its way through a wall, will break through the statutes of men to save life, and mend the breach in prison glooms.... We have had Democratic Presidents, Whig Presidents, a pseudo–Democratic-Whig President, and now it is time to have a *President of the United States.*[28]

Joseph subscribed to the divine command for unity: "I say unto you, be one; and if ye are not one ye are not mine."[29] He often extolled the blessings available through unity: "Unity is strength. 'How pleasing it is for brethren to dwell together in unity!' Let the Saints of the Most High ever cultivate this principle, and the most glorious blessings must result, not only to them individually, but to the whole Church."[30] Unity, he taught, also brought significant progress: "The greatest temporal and spiritual blessings which always come from faithfulness and concerted effort, never attended individual exertion or

---

27. Letter to the Editor, *Times and Seasons* (May 6, 1841), speaking of the admirable conduct of Stephen A. Douglas and Cyrus Walker who were "champions of the two great parties" in Illinois at the time.

28. *General Smith's Views,* 3, 6, 8, reprinted in *History of the Church,* 6:198, 204, 207.

29. D&C 38:27 ("I say unto you, be one; and if ye are not one ye are not mine"); see further D&C 42:36 ("That my covenant people may be gathered in one in that day when I shall come to my temple. And this I do for the salvation of my people"); 45:65 ("And with one heart and with one mind, gather up your riches that ye may purchase an inheritance which shall hereafter be appointed unto you"); 51:9 ("And let every man deal honestly, and be alike among this people, and receive alike, that ye may be one, even as I have commanded you"); Moses 7:18 ("And the Lord called his people Zion, because they were of one heart and one mind, and dwelt in righteousness; and there was no poor among them").

30. Smith, *Teachings of the Prophet Joseph Smith,* 174.

enterprise. The history of all past ages abundantly attests this fact."[31] Joseph also believed that partisanship had no place in the church and that members should be unified in purpose: "Party feelings, separate interests, exclusive designs should be lost sight of in the one common cause, in the interest of the whole."[32] Joseph clearly felt the principle of unity was paramount in all religious and civic realms.

"Establish justice." Law, justice, and liberty were Joseph's constant watch-cries. In an 1843 sermon given in Nauvoo, the prophet proclaimed, "It is a love of liberty which inspires my soul, civil and religious liberty—were diffused into my soul by my grandfathers, while they dandled me on their knees."[33] He readily invoked the right to appeal to the Constitution in establishing justice and protecting rights. Commenting on his run for the office of President of the United States, Joseph stated, "As the world have used the power of Government to oppress & persecute us it is right for us to use it for the protection of our rights."[34]

"Insure domestic tranquility." While Joseph Smith admired the Constitution's noble provisions of freedom, he suggested the U.S. Constitution did not go far enough in insuring protection of individual freedom and religious liberty:

> Although [the Constitution] provides that men shall enjoy religious freedom, yet it does not provide the manner by which that freedom can be preserved, nor for the punishment of Government Officers who refuse to protect the people in their religious rights, or punish those mobs, states, or communities who interfere with the rights of the people on account of their religion. Its sentiments are good, but it provides no means of enforcing them.[35]

Diverging sharply from the more limited constitutional interpretations embraced by the federal judiciary and prominent political thinkers of his day, Joseph's critique of the national political system would soon prove to be prophetic in several ways.

---

31. Smith, *Teachings of the Prophet Joseph Smith*, 183.

32. Smith, *Teachings of the Prophet Joseph Smith*, 231.

33. Andrew F. Ehat and Lyndon W. Cook, comps. and eds., *The Words of Joseph Smith: The Contemporary Accounts of the Nauvoo Discourses of the Prophet Joseph* (Orem, Utah: Grandin Book, 1991), 229. See also Joseph's "political motto" in *History of the Church*, 3:9; and "The Mormons," *New Yorker* 6 (October 13, 1838): 59, both cited below in this article.

34. Ehat and Cook, *Words of Joseph Smith*, 326.

35. *History of the Church*, 6:56–57; see more of this quotation below under October 15, 1843.

"**Provide for the common defense.**" Doctrine and Covenants 134:11 enjoins people to "appeal to the civil law for redress of all wrongs and grievances, where personal abuse is inflicted or the right of property or character infringed," and it assumes that law should exist "as will protect the same." Joseph felt strongly that the government had failed to defend the Saints in Ohio and Missouri.[36] He maligned the armies of history that had gained the glory of men at the cost of human bloodshed and misery, claiming that, rather than protecting their people, they had instead oppressed them.[37]

"**Promote the general Welfare.**" Joseph spoke strongly in favor of the general welfare and liberty that should be extended to all, especially in matters of faith. In 1839 he wrote: "This principle [of liberty] guarantees to all parties, sects, and denominations, and classes of religion, equal, coherent, and indefeasible rights; they are things that pertain to this life; therefore all are alike interested … Hence we say, that the Constitution of the United States is … like a great tree under whose branches men from every clime can be shielded from the burning rays of the sun."[38]

Joseph wanted all people, not just the Saints, to enjoy the blessings of laws to protect their general welfare. In 1843, he said, "If it has been demonstrated that I have been willing to die for a Mormon I am bold to declare before heaven that I am just as ready to die for a Presbyterian, a Baptist or any other denomination."[39] In 1841, as mayor of Nauvoo, Joseph Smith sponsored "An Ordinance on Religious Liberty in Nauvoo" providing that all "religious sects and denominations whatever, shall have free toleration, and equal privileges,

---

36. See, for example, D&C 123:7 ("It is an imperative duty that we owe to God, to angels, with whom we shall be brought to stand, and also to ourselves, to our wives and children, who have been made to bow down with grief, sorrow, and care, under the most damning hand of murder, tyranny, and oppression, supported and urged on and upheld by the influence of that spirit which hath so strongly riveted the creeds of the fathers, who have inherited lies, upon the hearts of the children, and filled the world with confusion, and has been growing stronger and stronger, and is now the very mainspring of all corruption, and the whole earth groans under the weight of its iniquity").

37. Smith, *Teachings of the Prophet Joseph Smith*, 248–49; *History of the Church*, 5:61, July 1842.

38. *History of the Church*, 3:304. A true transcription and analysis of this letter from Liberty Jail, with original spelling, grammar, and punctuation, is published in Dean C. Jessee and John W. Welch, eds. "Revelations in Context: Joseph Smith's Letter from Liberty Jail, March 20, 1839," *BYU Studies* 39:3 (2000): 125–45, and images of the letter are available at http://josephsmithpapers.org/paperSummary/letter-to-the-church-and-edward-partridge-20-march-1839.

39. Ehat and Cook, *Words of Joseph Smith*, 229.

in this city."[40] In January 1844, Joseph wrote: "I would strive to administer the government according to the Constitution and the laws of the union; and that as they make no distinction between citizens of different religious creeds I should make none."[41]

"Secure the Blessings of Liberty to ourselves and our Posterity." The Preamble ends, "And secure the Blessings of Liberty to ourselves and our Posterity." Likewise, Joseph sought that the principles of the Constitution might be "established forever,"[42] for now and for the benefit of future generations. He saw the benefits of the principles established by the Constitution of the United States flowing to all peoples. He expressed the hope that "all nations [will adopt] the God-given Constitution of the United States as a palladium of Liberty & equal Rights."[43] In Liberty Jail in 1839, Joseph pled for the blessings of life, liberty, and property to be championed for the benefit of future generations: "It is an imperative duty that we owe to all the rising generation, and to all the pure in heart" (D&C 123:11).[44]

While the word "principles" was used in Joseph Smith's day to describe the many provisions of the Constitution "without which the republican form [of government] would be impure and weak," this term was particularly associated with the just and liberal principles that promote the "general welfare" and "internal peace," while protecting "individual rights" and insuring "reasonable safeguards of society itself." Thus, in William Rawle's 1829 treatise on the Constitution, this term refers most prominently to the broad principles set forth in the Preamble that define the purposes of constitutional government generally and that are to be protected specifically by the constitutional restrictions on that government.

The Legal Status of the Preamble in Antebellum America

While likely the best-known section of the Constitution, the Preamble remains largely neglected in the study of American constitutional law today. Questions about the legal force and vitality of the Preamble are not typically

---

40. *History of the Church,* 4:306, discussed below under March 1, 1841.

41. *History of the Church,* 6:155–56, discussed below under January 1844.

42. D&C 109:54: "Have mercy, O Lord, upon all the nations of the earth; have mercy upon the rulers of our land; may those principles, which were so honorably and nobly defended, namely, the Constitution of our land, by our fathers, be established forever."

43. Benjamin F. Johnson, *I Knew the Prophets: An Analysis of the Letter of Benjamin F. Johnson to George F. Gibbs, Reporting Doctrinal Views of Joseph Smith and Brigham Young,* ed. Dean R. Zimmerman (Bountiful, Utah: Horizon Publishers, 1976), 31, spelling regularized.

44. Jessee and Welch, "Revelations in Context," 143.

even raised in academic literature or judicial opinions today. The current state of the Preamble is fairly clear: it is not considered a decisive element in constitutional interpretation and does not enjoy binding legal status. The 1938 annotated Constitution states, "No power to enact any statute is derived from the preamble. The Constitution is the only source of power authorizing action by any branch of the Federal Government."[45] The current official annotated Constitution likewise affirms, "The preamble is not a source of power for any department of the Federal Government."[46] But for Joseph Smith, the Preamble was the very foundation of the whole system of American government.

A preamble is an introduction that states the document's purpose. Prefatory statements such as the Preamble serve an important role in statutory interpretation. The Founding Fathers would have been intimately familiar with preambles, which predated the United States Constitution. Similar prefatory statements are found in the Petition of Rights of 1628, the Habeas Corpus Act of 1679, the Bill of Rights of 1689, the Act of Settlement of 1701, the Articles of Confederation of 1777, and a number of state constitutions. Ancient writings give examples of the importance of prefatory statements. For example, in Plato's *Laws*, the Athenian asks his interlocutor, "Then is our appointed lawmaker to set no such prefatory statement in front of his code?" He suggested that the lawmaker should do more than "curtly tell us what we are to do, add the threat of a penalty, and then turn to the next enactment." Also, he advised the drafter to include a "word of exhortation," and "advice."[47] Thomas Hobbes, the influential English political philosopher, explained the importance of including exhortation and advice in a prefatory statement:

> The Perspicuity, consisteth not so much in the words of the Law it selfe, as in a Declaration of the Causes, and Motives, for which it was made. That is it, that shewes us the meaning of the Legislator; and the meaning of the Legislator known, the Law is more easily understood by few, than many words. For all words, are subject to ambiguity; and therefore multiplication of words in the body of the Law, is multiplication in ambiguity: Besides it seems to imply,

---

45. The Constitution of the United States of America (annotated): Annotations of Cases Decided by the Supreme Court of the United States to January 1, 1938, S. Doc. No. 74-232 (1938), citing Dorr v. United States, 195 U.S. 140 (1904). Courts have consistently held that the governing portion of the Constitution is in the text of the body of the Constitution.

46. The Constitution of the United States: Analysis and Interpretation: Analysis of Cases Decided by the Supreme Court of the United States to June 28, 2002, S. Doc. No. 108-17 (2004), citing Jacobson v. Massachusetts, 197 U.S. 11, 22 (1905).

47. Plato, *Laws,* 4:723d–e.

(by too much diligence) that whosoever can evade the words, is without the campasse of the Law. And this is a cause of many unnecessary Processes. For when I consider how short were the Lawes of ancient times; and how they grew by degrees still longer; me thinks I see a contention between the Penners, and Pleaders of the Law; the former seeking to circumscribe the later; and the latter to evade their circumscriptions; and that the pleaders have got the Victory. It belongeth therefore to the Office of a Legislator, (such as is in all Commonwealths the Supreme Representative, be it one Man, or an Assembly,) to make the reason Perspicuous, why the Law was made; and the Body of the Law it selfe, as short, but in as proper, and significant termes, as may be.[48]

Following in Hobbes's tradition, the Preamble was created to determine the origin, scope, and purpose of the Constitution.[49] In fact, it appears that many of the Founding Fathers fully expected the Preamble to be binding.[50] On the other hand, many anti-Federalists who attended the Constitutional Convention feared that the Preamble possessed too much power. An unnamed anti-Federalist argued that the Preamble of the Constitution, which embodied the "spirit" of the document, would be used by courts to interpret the clauses of the Constitution: "The courts ... will establish as a principle in expounding the constitution, and will give every part of it such an explanation, as will give latitude to every department under it, to take cognizance of every matter, not only that affects the general and national concerns of the union, but also of such as relate to the administration of private justice, and to regulating the internal and local affairs of the different parts." He feared that the Preamble would infringe upon states' rights because it was by "the people," rather than the states.[51]

Alexander Hamilton, on the other hand, argued that the Preamble is the "Key of the Constitution." As such, "Whenever federal power is exercised, contrary to the spirit breathed by this introduction, it will be unconstitutionally

---

48. Thomas Hobbes, *Leviathan*, ch. 30, p. 182.

49. Sturges v. Crowninshield, 17 U.S. 122 (1819).

50. See William W. Crosskey, *Politics and the Constitution in the History of the United States* (Chicago: University of Chicago Press, 1953), 365–66, 374–79; Eric M. Exler, *The Power of the Preamble and the Ninth Amendment: The Restoration of the People's Unenumerated Rights*, 24 Seton Hall Legis. J. 431, 435–37 (1999–2000); Raymond Marcin, *'Posterity' in the Preamble and Positivist Pro-Position*, 38 Am. J. Juris 273, 281–88 (1993).

51. Brutus, Essay XII, in *The Anti-Federalist Papers and the Constitutional Convention Debates*, ed. Ralph Ketcham (New York: Mentor, 1986), 300.

exercised and ought to be resisted."[52] It is clear that Hamilton believed that the Preamble would be binding and that even the Bill of Rights was not necessary because the Preamble secured the same basic rights.[53]

No less a legal giant than Chief Justice John Marshall of the United States Supreme Court also suggested that the Preamble deserves the same respect as the rest of the Constitution. In 1819 he explained that the Preamble provides the spirit of the Constitution, which "is to be respected not less than its letter; yet the spirit is to be collected chiefly from its words."[54]

William Rawle's treatise on the Constitution (first edition in 1825; second edition in 1829) spoke of the Preamble as a "distinct exposition of principles" which reveals the motives and intentions that guide readers "in the construction of the instrument," which he insisted "can only mean the ascertaining the true meaning of an instrument." Rawle stressed the importance of deducing the meaning of each provision in the Constitution by taking cognizance of "its known intention and its entire text, and to give effect, if possible, to every part of it, consistently with the unity, and harmony of the whole."[55] Joseph Smith, a contemporary of Rawle, likewise approached the Constitution holistically.

Supreme Court Justice Joseph Story, whose monumental 1833 commentary on the Constitution dominated American jurisprudence for much of the nineteenth century, began his analysis of "the actual provisions of the constitution" with a fifty-page exposition of the Preamble, arguing that "the importance of examining the preamble, for the purpose of expounding the language of a statute, has been long felt, and universally conceded in all judicial discussions. ... the preamble ... is a key to open the minds of the makers, as to the mischiefs, which are to be remedied, and the objects, which are to be accomplished."[56] From the common law, he cited the Latin maxim, *cessante legis proemio, cessat et ipsa lex* (where the preamble [the Latin *proemio,* also means reason, purpose] for a law ends, there also the law itself ends), concluding that "there does not seem any reason why, in a fundamental law or constitution of government, an equal attention should not be given to the intention of the framers, as stated in the preamble. And accordingly we find, that it has been constantly referred to by statesmen and jurists to aid them in the exposition of its provisions." He continued, "The preamble never can be resorted to, to enlarge

---

52. James Monroe, *The Writings of James Monroe,* ed. Stanislaus Murray Hamilton, 7 vols. (New York: AMS, 1969), 3:356, citing Alexander Hamilton.

53. Federalist Papers no. 84.

54. See Sturges v. Crowninshield, 17 U.S. 122, 202.

55. Rawle, *View of the Constitution,* 29, 30, 31.

56. Story, *Commentaries on the Constitution,* 1:443.

the powers confided to the general government"; but interpreters are not at liberty "to adopt a restrictive meaning [of expressly granted powers], which will defeat an avowed object of the constitution, when another equally natural and more appropriate to the object is before us."[57] Justice Story's admonition notwithstanding, between the years of 1825 and 1990, the sections of the Preamble that reference justice, general welfare, and liberty were mentioned only twenty-four times by the U.S. Supreme Court, and then mostly in dissenting opinions,[58] as the legal influence of the Preamble waned over time.

In 1905 the Preamble was decisively stripped of any binding legal status. In *Jacobsen v. Massachusetts,* after rejecting the argument that constitutional rights could be derived from the Preamble, Justice Harlan went on to say:

> Although that Preamble indicates the general purposes for which the people ordained and established the Constitution, it has never been regarded as the source of any substantive power conferred on the Government of the United States, or any of its Departments. Such powers embrace only those expressly granted in the body of the Constitution, and as such may be implied from those so granted.[59]

Justice Harlan may have rightly recognized that the Preamble of the Constitution does not confer express powers, but his dismissal of it as lacking any substantive power whatsoever ignores the important guiding role that the Framers intended for the Preamble. Whether reading the provisions of the Constitution restrictively or expansively, as the case might require, in order to value, comprehend, and give proper effect to its intended purposes the Preamble ought to be the starting place for subsequent analysis. However, as a consequence of Justice Harlan's dicta, from 1905 onward the Preamble has only rarely been cited in judicial opinions.

By contrast, in Joseph Smith's day, the Preamble was highly regarded, and the common view was that it was a significantly compelling part of the Constitution. Consistent with that prevailing view, Joseph saw the Preamble's fundamental principles as functioning conceptually at the head of all political, legal, and constitutional theory and practice, as the following statements bear out.

---

57. Story, *Commentaries on the Constitution,* 444–45.

58. Milton Handler, Brian Leiter, and Carole E. Handler, "A Reconsideration of the Relevance and Materiality of the Preamble in Constitutional Interpretation," *Cardozo L. Rev.* 12 (1990–91): 117, 120–21, n. 14.

59. Jacobson v. Massachusetts, 197 U.S. 11, 13–14 (1905).

Joseph's Statements Concerning the Constitution, 1836 to 1844

Through the course of his leadership, Joseph increasingly addressed political and legal topics. These statements came by way of letters, sermons, and official Church pronouncements about law and the Constitution. This section provides a list and brief discussion of each of these statements.

During the Missouri period, Joseph held no political or governmental positions, but as the situation in Missouri worsened, Joseph's involvement in political affairs became more pronounced, as did his statements on the subject of the Constitution and the role of government. The Mormons suffered serious loss during the persecutions in Missouri, which regularly occurred under color of state law. Ultimately, they would file 678 petitions and claim damages totaling $2,275,789.[60] This financial claim was independent of the emotional and physical sufferings caused by the persecutions.

On **July 25, 1836,** as their spiritual leader, Joseph counseled members of the Church in Missouri to "Be wise; let prudence dictate all your counsels; preserve peace with all men, if possible; stand by the Constitution of your country; observe its principles; and above all, show yourselves men of God, worthy citizens."[61] Joseph stressed that government works only when citizens obey the law. Any law imposed from the top down will result in tyranny. He also wanted the Saints to be blameless in their dealings with their Missouri neighbors. Around this same time, Joseph expressed the hope that "All nations [will adopt] the God-given Constitution of the United States as a palladium of Liberty & equal Rights."[62]

In **March 1838,** Joseph's journal reports the following thoughts as he arrived near Far West, Missouri, after traveling from Kirtland, Ohio:

> After being [at Far West] two or three days, my brother Samuel arrived with his family and shortly after his arrival while walking with him and certain other brethren the following sentiments occurred to my mind:
>
> Motto of the Church of Latter-day Saints
>
> The Constitution of our country formed by the Fathers of liberty. Peace and good order in society. Love to God, and good will to man. All good and wholesome laws, virtue and truth above all things, and aristarchy, live for ever! But woe to tyrants, mobs,

---

60. Clark V. Johnson, *Mormon Redress Petitions: Documents of the 1833–1838 Missouri Conflict* (Provo, Utah: Religious Studies Center, 1992), xxviii.

61. *History of the Church,* 2:455; *Messenger and Advocate* 2 (August 1836): 358.

62. Johnson, *I Knew the Prophets,* 31, spelling regularized, no date given.

aristocracy, anarchy, and toryism, and all those who invest or seek out unrighteous and vexatious law suits, under the pretext and color of law, or office, either religious or political. Exalt the standard of Democracy! Down with that of priestcraft, and let all the people say Amen! That the blood of our fathers may not cry from the ground against us. Sacred is the memory of that blood which bought for us our liberty.

Signed Joseph Smith, Thomas B. Marsh, David Patten, Brigham Young, Samuel Smith, George Hinkle, John Corrill, and George Robinson.[63]

It is notable that the motto for the Church begins with the foundation of the Constitution. It may be that "the motto reflects Joseph's experience with dissent and persecution in Kirtland and signaled his determination to vigorously assert the Latter-day Saints' right to establish themselves in Missouri and to pursue their goals without harassment."[64] But it quickly becomes evident that the motto applied just as much to the situation in Missouri, where the persecution became even more intense, especially at Gallatin, Haun's Mill, and Far West just a few months later.

As events turned violent, Joseph invoked and affirmed his commitment to the Constitution. In Gallatin, Missouri, a greatly out-numbered group of Mormons fought to defend their civil rights, and on **August 7, 1838,** Joseph wrote: "Blessed be the memory of those few brethren who contended so strenuously for their constitutional rights and religious freedom, against such an overwhelming force of desperadoes!"[65] As had been articulated in 1835, Latter-day Saints "believe that all men are bound to sustain and uphold the respective governments in which they reside, while protected in their inherent and inalienable rights," and that "all men are justified in defending themselves ... in times of exigency" (D&C 134:5, 11). Then, in the face of growing tensions, on **October 13, 1838,** Joseph gave this statement to a New York newspaper: "We are friendly to the Constitution and laws of this State and of the United States, and wish to see them enforced."[66] Only three weeks later, Joseph and many others were arrested at Far West and imprisoned in Liberty

---

63. About March 16, 1838. Dean C. Jessee, Mark Ashurst-McGee, and Richard L. Jensen, eds., *Journals, Volume 1: 1832–1839,* vol. 1 of the Journals series of *The Joseph Smith Papers,* ed. Dean C. Jessee, Ronald K. Esplin, and Richard Lyman Bushman (Salt Lake City: Church Historian's Press, 2008), 237–38; *History of the Church,* 3:9.

64. Jessee, Ashurst-McGee, and Jensen, *Journals* 1:229 (commentary).

65. *History of the Church,* 3:59.

66. "The Mormons," *New Yorker* 6 (October 13, 1838): 59.

Jail, even though he was confident that the Mormon militia of the country of Caldwell, acting under the general orders of General Doniphan, had been well regulated and had been "very careful in all their movements to act in strict accordance with the constitutional laws of the land."[67] In vain Joseph invoked his right to be heard and released under the constitutionally guaranteed rights of due process and writ of habeas corpus.[68] Underlying all of this was a deep division over the meaning of constitutional rights. Joseph later recounted a conversation he had with General Wilson, one of the Missouri militia leaders, upon his arrest at Far West: "I inquired of him why I was thus treated. I told him I was not aware of having done anything worthy of such treatment; that I had always been a supporter of the Constitution and of democracy. His answer was, 'I know it, and that is the reason why I want to kill you, or have you killed.'"[69]

On **March 20, 1839,** after more than five months in Liberty Jail, Joseph called upon the Saints to "present" their evidence and grievances "to the heads of government." In this letter, he invoked the right guaranteed by the First Amendment to petition the government for redress, which Joseph called "the last effort which is enjoined on us by our Heavenly Father [including the exhaustion of their legal and constitutional rights], before we can fully and completely claim that promise which shall call him forth from his hiding place; and also that the whole nation may be left without excuse" (D&C 123:6). Even under these dire circumstances, Joseph stood by his constant faith in the Constitution. Relying again on his metaphor of the Constitution as a protecting tree, Joseph wrote:

> The Constitution of the United States is a glorious standard; it is founded in the wisdom of God. It is a heavenly banner; it is to all those who are privileged with the sweets of liberty, like the cooling shades and refreshing waters of a great rock in a thirsty and weary land. It is like a great tree under whose branches men from every clime can be shielded from the burning rays of the sun.... We say that God is true; that the Constitution of the United States is true; that the Bible is true, that the Book of Mormon is true; that the Book of Covenants is true; that Christ is true; that the ministering angels sent forth from God are true.[70]

---

67. *History of the Church,* 3:162.

68. See chapter 16 below, discussing habeas corpus in Missouri.

69. *History of the Church,* 3:191.

70. *Millennial Star* 1, no. 8 (December 1840): 197; *History of the Church,* 3:304; Jessee and Welch, "Revelations in Context," 144–45.

If there were any doubt as to Joseph's personal feelings toward the Constitution, his letter unambiguously grants it divine status, on par with his conviction as to the truthfulness of latter-day scripture and his role as a modern prophet. But what did Joseph mean by "the Constitution is true"? Since he was never outspokenly impressed by the separation of powers in Articles 1, 2, and 3, which define the duties of the three branches of government, he more likely had in mind the foundational principles expressed in the Preamble and the Bill of Rights, as discussed above, which called upon the United States government to secure the blessings of liberty and justice to all.

Managing to get out of Missouri and arriving in Quincy, Illinois, the Prophet summarized the depredations the Saints had suffered and noted: "I ask the citizens of this Republic whether such a state of things is to be suffered to pass unnoticed, and the hearts of widows, orphans, and patriots to be broken, and their wrongs left without redress? No! I invoke the genius of our Constitution. I appeal to the patriotism of Americans to stop this unlawful and unholy procedure; and pray God may defend this nation from the dreadful effects of such outrages."[71]

On **November 28, 1839,** a few months after settling at Nauvoo, Illinois, Joseph carried a letter to Congress, excercising his constitutional right to petition the federal government for redress[72] for the Missouri persecutions, basing his claim on the rights that Mormon settlers in Missouri should have been extended under Article IV, Section 2, of the U.S. Constitution:

> Your constitution guarantees to every citizen, even the humblest, the enjoyment of life, liberty, and property. It promises to all, religious freedom, the right to all to worship God beneath their own vine and fig tree, according to the dictates of their conscience [Amendment 1]. It guarantees to all the citizens of the several states the right to become citizens of any one of the states, and to enjoy all the rights and immunities of the citizens of the state of his adoption [Article IV, Section 2]. Yet of all these rights have the Mormons been deprived.... They have applied to the state of Missouri, courts of Missouri, federal courts.[73]

The following day, **November 29, 1839,** Joseph obtained an audience with the president during which he continued his petition for redress. After

---

71. *History of the Church,* 3:332.

72. Amendment 1 concludes by granting "the right of the people ... to petition the Government for a redress of grievances."

73. *History of the Church,* 4:37.

reading Joseph's letter of introduction, Van Buren responded, "What can I do? I can do nothing for you! If I do anything, I shall come in contact with the whole state of Missouri."[74] A second visit a few months later brought the same result. Van Buren responded, "Gentleman, your cause is just, but I can do nothing for you."[75] Joseph learned from this that the president saw himself as powerless in the face of states' rights. Van Buren was a Whig and an advocate of states' rights who "consistently opposed any extension of federal power."[76] For the rest of his life, Joseph campaigned to encourage federal officials to take action under the authority granted to them by the Constitution. To this effect, he sent personal letters to all the potential presidential candidates in 1843.[77] In the wake of all the Missouri persecutions, Joseph often expressed frustration with the lack of protection to general citizens. Joseph ardently believed that one of the responsibilities of the United States president was to provide for the general welfare, as well as the protection of property and the right to petition the federal government for redress, all as expressly provided in the Preamble to the Constitution and the First Amendment.

Once back in Nauvoo, Joseph was fully engaged in the legal system. In a time when conflicts of interest were underdeveloped, He was elected by the people and appointed by the city council as mayor, chief judge of the municipal court, lieutenant-general of the Nauvoo Legion, and a member of the city council.[78] If the voice of the people had functioned properly, as it did in Joseph's case under the provisions of the Nauvoo Charter, then "we the people" could elect or appoint whomever they wished, which officers then had solemn duties to act for the equal benefit of all, which Joseph

---

74. *History of the Church,* 4:40.

75. *History of the Church,* 4:80; Roll of History, Church History Library; see also *History of the Church,* 6:157; New York *Herald,* January 26, 1844.

76. James B. Allen, "Joseph Smith v. John C. Calhoun: Presidential Politics and the States' Rights Controversy," 21, paper delivered in the Joseph Smith Exhibit Lecture Series at BYU's Harold B. Lee Library, March 8, 2006; James B. Allen, "Joseph Smith vs. John C. Calhoun: The State's Rights Dilemma and Early Mormon History," in *Joseph Smith Jr.: Reappraisals after Two Centuries,* ed. Reid L. Neilson and Terryl L. Givens (Oxford: Oxford University Press, 2009), 82.

77. Joseph sent personal letters to President Van Buren, John C. Calhoun, Lewis Cass, Henry Clay, and Richard M. Johnson. Each of these individuals was considered an 1844 presidential hopeful. *History of the Church,* 6:64–65.

78. Similarly, lawyers could represent a client on one day and then represent that client's competitor or accuser the next day. It appears that, especially in a public setting, it was left to the populace to decide how many offices they would elect a person to hold. The text of the Nauvoo Charter is reprinted in *History of the Church,* 4:239–45. For a study of the provisions of the Nauvoo Charter, see chapter 13 below.

did. For example, in **March 1, 1841,** Joseph attended Nauvoo City Council meetings and presented several bills aimed at creating a civic order in the city. One of these was the Ordinance on Religious Liberty in Nauvoo: "Be it ordained ... that ... all ... religious sects and denominations whatever, shall have free toleration, and equal privileges, in this city."[79] The ordinance provided that religious persecution within the city limits was punishable by a fine of up to five hundred dollars, imprisonment for up to six months, or both. Joseph passionately believed in expansive rights for all religions, including his own.

On **March 30, 1842,** Joseph taught the women of the newly formed Relief Society, "We must ... observe the Constitution that the blessings of heaven may rest down upon us—all must act in concert or nothing can be done."[80] Quite emphatically, Joseph insisted here on unity, citing the constitutional model.

On **May 22, 1842,** in Nauvoo, when accused of an attempted assassination of Lilburn Boggs, Joseph said, "I am tired of the misrepresentation, calumny and detraction, heaped upon me by wicked men; and desire and claim, only those principles guaranteed to all men by the Constitution and laws of the United States and of Illinois."[81] Again he expected others to "establish justice," to uphold such rights as respecting the right of habeas corpus and due process as established by the Constitution.[82]

On **February 25, 1843,** the Nauvoo city council heard from Joseph about a "sound currency for the city," again expressly premised upon the Constitution. As provided in Article I, Section 10, "No state may coin money or make any thing but gold and silver coin a tender in payment of debts." Based on the Tenth Amendment's reservation of powers to the states, Joseph opined that Article I, Section 10 did not bar the City of Nauvoo from adopting a city ordinance making only gold and silver legal tender. As presented in the *History of the Church,* he reasoned at length:

> The city council assembled. The subject of a sound currency for the
> city having previously arisen, I addressed the council at consider-
> able length...

79. *History of the Church,* 4:306; Roll of History, March 1, 1841, Church History Library.

80. Nauvoo Relief Society Minute Book, March 30, 1842, 22, at http://josephsmith papers.org/paperSummary/nauvoo-relief-society-minute-book.

81. Letter to Bartlett, *History of the Church,* 5:15; Rough Draft Notes of the History of the Church, 1842a-014, Church History Library.

82. On Joseph's exercise of this right of habeas corpus under Article I, Section 9, of the Constitution, in quashing the three attempts by the Governor of Missouri, in 1841, 1842, and 1843, to extradite Joseph as a fugitive from that state, see chapter 16 below.

Situated as we are, with a flood of immigration constantly pouring in upon us, I consider that it is not only prudential, but absolutely necessary to protect the inhabitants of this city from being imposed upon by a spurious currency. Many of our eastern and old country friends are altogether unacquainted with the situation of the banks in this region of country; and as they generally bring specie with them, they are perpetually in danger of being gulled by speculators. Besides there is so much uncertainty in the solvency of the best of banks, that I think it much safer to go upon the hard money system altogether. I have examined the Constitution upon this subject and find my doubts removed. The Constitution is not a law, but it empowers the people to make laws.

For instance, the Constitution governs the land of Iowa, but it is not a law for the people. The Constitution tells us what shall not be a lawful tender. The 10th section declares that nothing else except gold and silver shall be lawful tender, this is not saying that gold and silver shall be lawful tender. It only provides that the states may make a law to make gold and silver lawful tender. I know of no state in the Union that has passed such a law; and I am sure that Illinois has not. The legislature has ceded up to us the privilege of enacting such laws as are not inconsistent with the Constitution of the United States and the state of Illinois; and we stand in the same relation to the state as the state does to the Union. The clause referred to in the Constitution is for the legislature—it is not a law for the people. The different states, and even Congress itself, have passed many laws diametrically contrary to the Constitution of the United States.

The state of Illinois has passed a stay law making property a lawful tender for the payment of debts; and if we have no law on the subject we must be governed by it. Shall we be such fools as to be governed by its laws, which are unconstitutional? No! We will make a law for gold and silver; and then the state law ceases and we can collect our debts. Powers not delegated to the states or reserved from the states are constitutional. The Constitution acknowledges [Amendment 10] that the people have all power not reserved to itself. I am a lawyer; I am a big lawyer and comprehend heaven, earth and hell, to bring forth knowledge that shall cover up all lawyers, doctors and other big bodies. This is the doctrine of the Constitution, so help me God. The Constitution is not law to us, but it makes provision for us whereby we can make laws. Where it provides that no one shall be hindered from worship[p]ing God according to his own conscience, is a law. No legislature can enact a law to prohibit it. The Constitution provides to regulate bodies of men and not individuals.[83]

Based on his persuasive reasoning in light of the law at that time, the Nauvoo City Council passed an ordinance on March 4, 1843, that only gold and silver coin would be accepted as legal tender in payment of city taxes, debts, and fines imposed under the ordinances of the city, while City Scrip would no longer be issued or used as moneyed currency in the city. Anyone passing counterfeit bills, coins, or copper coins would be subject to fine or imprisonment, and anyone passing paper currency would be fined one dollar for each dollar thus passed (letting the punishment equal the crime). Joseph's constitutional law analysis here about the powers of local government was sound. At the same time, he continued to press for a national bank and a national currency as a part of his presidential political platform, which was something the Whigs favored but the Democrats opposed.[84]

When Joseph said on that occasion that the "Constitution is not a law, but it empowers the people to make laws," he saw the Constitution as a foundation document that authorizes people (through their representatives or states) to enact laws within the scope of the powers granted to them. Perhaps he selected Iowa as a way to illustrate this point because Iowa at that time was simply a territory, governed directly only by the U.S. Constitution and such laws as the federal government may have adopted. Article 1 Section 10 of the Constitution limits the scope of powers granted to states; among those

---

83. *History of the Church,* 5:289–90; Roll of History, Church History Library.

84. The Whig platform of 1844 stood for a well-regulated currency, a tariff for revenue, the distribution to the states of proceeds from the sales of public lands, a single term for president, reform of executive usurpations, and improving governmental efficiency. The Democratic party platform for 1844 advocated limited federal powers, frugality in government, states rights, separation of federal money from private banking, liberty, asylum for the oppressed, use of sales proceeds from public lands only for national objectives, maintaining the president's veto power, and keeping title to the whole territory of Oregon. Thomas Hudson McKee, *The National Conventions and Platforms of All Political Parties: 1789 to 1905* (Baltimore: The Friedenwald Company, 1906); J. M. H. Frederick, *National Party Platforms of the United States Presidential Candidates Electoral and Popular Votes* (Akron: J. M. H. Frederick, 1896); Wilfrid E. Binkley, *American Political Parties* (New York: Alfred A. Knopf, 1959); Felice A. Bonadio, ed., *Political Parties in American History: 1828–1890* (New York: G. P. Putnam's Sons, 1974); Daniel Walker Howe, ed., *The American Whigs: An Anthology* (New York: John Wiley & Sons, 1973); Chandos Fulton, *The History of the Democratic Party From Thomas Jefferson to Grover Cleveland* (New York: P. F. Collier, 1892).

limitations, no state may coin money, issue bills of credit, or make anything except gold and silver coin legal tender for the payment of debts. Thus the Constitution provides bounds within which the states could enact authorized statutes, as they might see fit. Iowa had no legal tender law, because no federal tender law had been adopted and the Constitution did not provide otherwise. Moreover, although no state had seen a need to pass a law making gold and silver coin legal tender, this was not because the Constitution had in any way abrogated that right.

On **June 30, 1843,** the Prophet took yet another occasion to assert the rights and powers given by the state of Illinois to the city of Nauvoo, when he became entangled in yet another wave of attempts the state of Missouri to arrest him. On June 10, a letter was sent from Missouri to Illinois Governor Thomas Ford, informing Ford that Joseph Smith had been indicted for treason. A special agent, Joseph Reynolds, was sent to apprehend Joseph. A week later, Governor Ford issued an arrest warrant for Joseph, who was then arrested on June 23. The next day he obtained a writ of habeas corpus from the Nauvoo municipal court, despite the efforts of the officials to prevent him from doing so. Still under arrest, but having been carried to Nauvoo for the hearing, he was greeted with a band and a procession. He spoke to the assembled crowd with words of comfort regarding the status of their city charter, saying: "It has been asserted by the great and wise men, lawyers and others, that our municipal powers and legal tribunals are not to be sanctioned by the authorities of the state." But, Joseph countered,

> If there is not power in our charter and courts [which granted Nauvoo the right to issue writs of habeas corpus], then there is not power in the state of Illinois, nor in the congress or constitution of the United States; for the United States gave unto Illinois her constitution or charter, and Illinois gave unto Nauvoo her charters, ceding unto us our vested rights, which she has no right or power to take from us.[85]

He went on to speak of Article I, Section 9, of the Constitution, which provides: "The privilege of the writ of habeas corpus shall not be suspended." Joseph asserted,

> The Constitution of the United States declares that the privilege of the writ of Habeas Corpus shall not be denied. Deny me the right of Habeas Corpus, and I will fight with gun, sword, cannon, whirlwind, and thunder, until they are used up like the Kilkenny

---

85. *History of the Church,* 5:466.

cats.... The benefits of the Constitution and Laws are alike for all; and the great Eloheim has given me the privilege of having the benefits of the Constitution, and the writ of Habeas Corpus.[86]

His view in this regard was legally appropriate in his day and his argument proved successful.[87]

On **October 15, 1843**, Joseph Smith preached a Sunday sermon at the stand east of the unfinished temple in Nauvoo. He spoke on the limitations he saw in the Constitution:

It is one of the first principles of my life, and one that I have cultivated from my childhood, having been taught it by my father, to allow every one the liberty of conscience. I am the greatest advocate of the Constitution of the United States there is on the earth. In my feelings I am always ready to die for the protection of the weak and oppressed in their just rights. The only fault I find with the Constitution is, it is not broad enough to cover the whole ground.

Although it provides that all men shall enjoy religious freedom, yet it does not provide the manner by which that freedom can be preserved, nor for the punishment of Government officers who refuse to protect the people in their religious rights, or punish those mobs, states, or communities who interfere with the rights of the people on account of their religion. Its sentiments are good, but it provides no means of enforcing them. It has but this one fault. Under its provision, a man or a people who are able to protect themselves can get along well enough; but those who have the misfortune to be weak or unpopular are left to the merciless rage of popular fury.

The Constitution should contain a provision that every officer of the Government who should neglect or refuse to extend the protection guaranteed in the Constitution should be subject to capital punishment; and then the president of the United States would not say, *"Your cause is just, but I can do nothing for you,"* a governor issue exterminating orders, or judges say, "The men ought to have the protection of law, but it won't please the mob; the men must die, anyhow, to satisfy the clamor of the rabble;

---

86. *Journal of Discourses* 2:167; *History of the Church,* 5:470–71. The term "Kilkenny cat" refers to a tenacious fighter.

87. See chapter 16 below.

they must be hung, or Missouri be damned to all eternity." Executive writs could be issued when they ought to be, and not be made instruments of cruelty to oppress the innocent, and persecute men whose religion is unpopular.[88]

Thus, Joseph expressed his deep frustration with the failure of the federal judicial system to provide justice for him and his people. Also expressing similar disappointments and concerns, Joseph may have said the following about this time: "This nation will be on the very verge of crumbling to peices [*sic*] and tumbling to the ground and when the constitution is upon the brink of ruin this people will be the Staff up[on] which the Nation shall lean and they shall bear the constitution away from the very verge of destruction."[89]

In **November, 1843,** Church leaders decided to "seize whatever influence they could to achieve redress for the crimes committed against them in Missouri by appealing to the precepts of equality and human rights guaranteed to American citizens."[90] Among this series of appeals was a letter, ghostwritten in November 1843 by W. W. Phelps, in which Joseph appealed to citizens of Vermont, his native state, for help.

> Must we, because we believe in the fullness of the Gospel of Jesus Christ, the administration of angels, and the communion of the Holy Ghost, like the Prophets and Apostles of old,—must we be mobbed with impunity, be exiled from our habitations and property without remedy, murdered without mercy, and Government find the weapons and pay the vagabonds for doing the jobs, and give them the plunder into the bargain? Must we, because we believe in enjoying the constitutional privilege and right of worship[p]ing Almighty God according to the dictates of our own consciences, and because we believe in repentance, and baptism for the remission of sins, the gift of the Holy Ghost by the laying on of hands, the resurrection of the dead, the millennium, the day of judgment, and the Book of Mormon as the history of the aborigines of this continent,—must we be expelled from the institutions of our country, the rights of citizenship and the graves of our friends

88. *History of the Church*, 6:56–57.

89. Howard and Martha Coray notebook, in Ehat and Cook, *Words of Joseph Smith*, 416; on the uncertainties of the date of this discourse, see 418–19 n. 1; and Dean C. Jessee, "Joseph Smith's 19 July 1840 Discourse," *BYU Studies* 19 (Spring 1979): 390–94.

90. Brent M. Rogers, "To the 'Honest and Patriotic Sons of Liberty': Mormon Appeals for Redress and Social Justice, 1843–44," *Journal of Mormon History* 39, no. 1 (Winter 2013): 37.

and brethren, and the Government lock the gate of humanity and shut the door of redress against us? If so, farewell freedom![91]

On **December 21, 1843,** the Nauvoo City Council invoked the Tenth Amendment and other constitutional provisions as its legal basis in proposing a bill to be adopted by the U.S. Senate and House of Representatives to empower the mayor of Nauvoo to call to his aid a sufficient number of U.S. troops to repel the invasion of mobs, keep the public peace, protect the innocent from lawlessness, and preserve the power and dignity of the Union.[92]

Joseph believed that the powers of the federal executive and legislative branches had been overly restricted. When Joseph petitioned presidential hopeful John C. Calhoun, who was nominally a Democrat but flirted with the Whig party in 1842 and 1844, Calhoun told Joseph that the type of relief the Mormons requested was outside the scope of the federal government. In response to Calhoun, the Prophet explained his own reading of the Constitution:

> I would admonish you ... to read the 8th section and 1st article of the Constitution of the United States, the *first, fourteenth and seventeenth* "specific" and not very "limited powers" of the Federal Government, what can be done to protect the lives, property, and rights of a virtuous people, when the administrators of the law and law-makers are unbought by bribes.... And God, who cooled the heat of Nebuchadnezzar's furnace or shut the mouths of lions for the honor of a Daniel, will raise your mind above the narrow notion that the General Government has no power, to the sublime idea that Congress, with the President as Executor, is as almighty in its sphere as Jehovah is in his.[93]

---

91. *History of the Church,* 6:92.

92. *History of the Church,* 6:124–32; see also 6:84–88.

93. *History of the Church,* 6:160; New York *Herald,* January 26, 1844. Article I, Section 8 deals with taxing powers, Section 14 grants military powers to regulate a land force, and Section 17 give Congress power over lands purchased by the federal government. By arguing to Senator Calhoun that Congress and the President of the United States have broad powers, under Article I, Section 8, paragraph 1, to collect taxes, duties, imposts, and excises, and spend money however they deem in furtherance of "the common defense and general welfare of the United States," Joseph Smith was advancing a view similar to Joseph Story's interpretation of this constitutional taxing clause. See Jeffrey T. Renz, "What Spending Clause? (or the President's Paramour): An Examination of the Views of Hamilton, Madison, and Story on Article I, Section 8, Clause 1 of the United States Constitution," *John Marshall Law Review* 33 (1999): 83–144; lucidly showing that Hamilton saw "an independent grant of power [to tax] in the General Welfare Clause," 103; whereas Madison saw a power "to spend beyond the powers enumerated in Article I, Section 8," and "admitted

Calhoun (like the Whig leader Van Buren) did not initially agree with Joseph on this point, but by 1847 Calhoun would end up agreeing that the Union was endangered by a totally corrupt party system and bribes, and in 1848–49 he would unite the South against Northern political abuses on some of the same grounds that Joseph had raised in his letter to him in 1843.[94]

In **January 1844,** Joseph declared himself a candidate for president of the United States.[95] In running for president, he sought to strengthen the federal government's ability to ensure justice for all the citizens, and to insure the Constitution was upheld equally in all the states. Indeed, it would appear that Joseph's major motivation in running for national office was to re-enthrone the constitution as the supreme law of the land. In a statement to the New York *Herald* he wrote:

> If I should be elected, I would strive to administer the government according to the Constitution and the laws of the union; and that as they make no distinction between citizens of different religious creeds I should make none. As far as it depends on the Executive department, all should have the full benefit of both, and none should be exempt from their operation.[96]

A few days later, on **February 8, 1844,** he reiterated his stance on strengthening the federal government to uphold the Constitution:

---

a limited spending power in the General Welfare Clause, but argued that this power was applicable only to the enumerated powers," 108–9. Joseph Story, *Commentaries on the Constitution,* 3:373–82 §§911–18, "competently" criticized Madison's views (Renz, "What Spending Clause?" 119); and in United States v. Butler, 297 U.S. 1 (1936), Madison's view was finally rejected (Renz, "What Spending Clause?" 123). Nevertheless, as Renz argues, the Welfare Clause in Article I, Section 8, paragraph 1, was probably originally included only "as a limitation on the power to raise revenue," 129, for "Section 8 is, in effect, a limitation on the plenary grant of power in Section 1," 101. The meaning of the federal power to tax continues to raise perplexing interpretive issues, as in National Federation of Independent Business v. Sebelius, 132 S. Ct. 2566 (2012).

94. Irving H. Bartlett, *John C. Calhoun: A Biography* (New York: W.W. Norton, 1994). Calhoun worked on his treatise, *Disquisition on Government,* beginning in 1843 and completing it in 1849, presenting his ideas on these subjects.

95. For Joseph Smith's presidential campaign generally, see Robert S. Wicks and Fred R. Foister, *Junius and Joseph* (Logan: Utah State University Press, 2005); Timothy L. Wood, "The Prophet and the Presidency: Mormonism and Politics in Joseph Smith's 1844 Presidential Campaign," *Journal of the Illinois State Historical Society* 93, no. 2 (2000): 167–93; Margaret C. Robertson, "The Campaign and the Kingdom: The Activities of the Electioneers in Joseph Smith's Presidential Campaign," *BYU Studies* 39, no. 3 (2000): 147–80.

96. *History of the Church,* 6:155–56; New York *Herald,* January 26, 1844.

I would not have suffered my name to have been used by my friends on anywise as President of the United States, or candidate for that office, if I and my friends could have had the privilege of enjoying our religious and civil rights as American citizens, even those rights which the Constitution guarantees unto all her citizens alike. But this as a people we have been denied from the beginning. Persecution has rolled upon our heads from time to time, from portions of the United States, like peals of thunder, because of our religion; and no portion of the Government as yet has stepped forward for our relief. And in view of these things, I feel it to be my right and privilege to obtain what influence and power I can, lawfully, in the United States, for the protection of injured innocence; and if I lose my life in a good cause I am willing to be sacrificed on the altar of virtue, righteousness and truth, in maintaining the laws and Constitution of the United States, if need be, for the general good of mankind.[97]

In the early months of 1844, missionaries were called to go forth to both preach the gospel and promote Joseph Smith's candidacy for president. Joseph's platform was laid out in a pamphlet, *General Smith's Views of the Powers and Policy of the Government of the United States,* and copies were printed by the thousands for the missionaries to distribute. As one might expect, constitutional issues were central to his platform. Unlike other party platforms, this one quoted the Preamble in full, and it spoke throughout of "the people," "unity" and "union." It further praised George Washington for promoting the "common welfare" and "providing for the common defense," repeatedly advocated peace and "tranquility," extolled the blessings of "liberty" for all, and promised to administer government "with an eye single to the glory of the people." This pamphlet spoke directly of the Constitution: "We are friendly to the Constitution and laws and wish to see them enforced."

In his famous King Follett discourse, on **April 7, 1844,** Joseph boldly claimed his freedom of religious belief, asserting that "every man has a right to be a false prophet as well as a true prophet,"[98] that "there is no law in the heart of God that wo[ul]d allow any one to interefere with the rights of man,"[99]

---

97. *History of the Church,* 6:211; Wilford Woodruff, *Wilford Woodruff's Journal, 1833–1898, Typescript,* ed. Scott G. Kenney, 9 vols. (Midvale, Utah: Signature Books, 1983–84), 2:349, February 8, 1844.

98. Willard Richards, Diary, in Ehat and Cook, *Words of Joseph Smith,* 341; see also 349.

99. Thomas Bullock, Report, in Ehat and Cook, *Words of Joseph Smith,* 349; see also D&C 134:2, 4.

and that "no man is authorized to take away life in consequence of their religion. All laws and governments ought to tolerate [all expressions of religious belief] whether right or wron[g]."[100]

By **June 18, 1844,** Nauvoo was in an uproar over the actions of apostate Mormons who created a slanderous newspaper, the *Nauvoo Expositor*. The City Council had found legal grounds to have this printing press destroyed as a public nuisance, but that action brought on the city the wrath of the state. Joseph responded by calling out the Nauvoo Legion to defend the city and declared martial law: "I have good reason to fear a mob is organizing to come upon this city.... The officers of the Nauvoo Legion will see that no one passes in or out of the city without due orders."[101] In his last address to the Nauvoo Legion, Joseph defended this action as a privilege granted by the Constitution:

> We have never violated the laws of our country. We have every right to live under their protection, and are entitled to all the privileges guaranteed by our state and national constitutions. We have turned the barren, bleak prairies and swamps of this state into beautiful towns, farms and cities by our industry; and the men who seek our destruction and cry thief, treason, riot, &c., are those who themselves violate the laws, steal and plunder from their neighbors, and seek to destroy the innocent, heralding forth lies to screen themselves from the just punishment of their crimes by bringing destruction upon this innocent people. I call God, angels and all men to witness that we are innocent of the charges which are heralded forth through the public prints against us by our enemies; and while they assemble together in unlawful mobs to take away our rights and destroy our lives, they think to shield themselves under the refuge of lies which they have thus wickedly fabricated.[102]

---

100. William Clayton, Report, in Ehat and Cook, *Words of Joseph Smith*, 357, assuming, one might add, that in all such cases "a regard and reverence are shown to the laws" and that "such religious opinions do not justify sedition nor conspiracy" (D&C 134:7). On the constitutionality of the civil abatement of printing presses as public nuisances under the law in ante-bellum America, particularly in Illinois, see chapter 18 below.

101. *History of the Church*, 6:497.

102. *History of the Church*, 6:498. He also spoke against "all those who trample under foot the glorious Constitution and the people's rights," swearing to spill his blood if necessary so that "this people shall have their legal rights, and be protected from mob violence." *History of the Church*, 6:499.

On **June 22, 1844,** just five days before his death, Joseph wrote to Illinois Governor Ford, "I am ever ready to conform to and support the laws and Constitution, even at the expense of my life. I have never in the least offered any resistance to law or lawful process, which is a well-known fact to the general public."[103] In response to this volatile situation, Governor Ford accused Nauvoo magistrates of "having committed a gross outrage upon the laws and liberties of the people,"[104] and he called for the end of martial law and for the Nauvoo city council to submit to the arrest warrants that had been issued regarding the destruction of the *Nauvoo Expositor.* As part of his response, Joseph wrote,

> As to martial law, we truly say that we were obliged to call out the forces to protect our lives; and the Constitution guarantees to every man that privilege [Amendment 2]; and our measures were active and efficient, as the necessity of the case required; but the city is and has been continually under the special direction of the marshal all the time. No person, to our knowledge, has been arrested only for violation of the peace, and those some of our own citizens, all of whom we believe are now discharged. And if any property has been taken for public benefit without a compensation, or against the will of the owner, it has been done without our knowledge or consent, and when shown shall be corrected, if the people will permit us to resume our usual labors....
>
> "The Constitution also provides that the people shall be protected against all unreasonable search and seizure" [Amendment 2]. True. The doctrine we believe most fully, and have acted upon it; but we do not believe it unreasonable to search so far as it is necessary to protect life and property from destruction....
>
> We do not believe in the "union of legislative and judicial power," and we have not so understood the action of the case in question.
>
> Whatever power we have exercised in the habeas corpus has been done in accordance with the letter of the charter and Constitution as we confidently understood them, and that, too, with the ablest counsel; but if it be so that we have erred in this thing, let the Supreme Court correct the evil. We have never gone contrary to constitutional law, so far as we have been able to learn it.

---

103. *History of the Church,* 6:526.
104. *History of the Church,* 6:534.

If lawyers have belied their profession to abuse us, the evil be on their heads.[105]

As he had consistently done throughout his life, Joseph asserted the right to stand on his legal and constitutional rights and privileges. His letter to Ford demonstrates a keen awareness of the Second Amendment, asserting that the Nauvoo Legion has been "active and efficient." The Second Amendment states, "A well regulated militia being necessary to the security of a free State, the right of the People to keep and bear arms shall not be infringed," and it was generally understood that the corollary to this constitutional language was that "the right of people to keep and bear arms shall not be infringed. The prohibition is general."[106] He also invoked protection under the Constitution's Fifth Amendment against double jeopardy.[107]

On **June 26, 1844**, the day before his death, Joseph had an interview with Governor Ford regarding a constable who had refused Joseph's request to be protected from the mob (as later reported by John Taylor):

> This very act was a breach of law on his part—an assumption of power that did not belong to him, and an attempt, at least, to deprive us of our legal and constitutional rights and privileges. What could we do under the circumstances different from what we did do? We sued for, and obtained a writ of habeas corpus from the Municipal Court, by which we were delivered from the hands of Constable Bettisworth, and brought before and acquitted by the Municipal Court.... After our acquittal, in a conversation with Judge Thomas, although he considered the acts of the party illegal, he advised, that to satisfy the people, we had better go before another magistrate who was not in our Church.... In accordance with his advice we went before Esq. Wells, with

---

105. *History of the Church,* 6:538–39.

106. Rawle, *View of the Constitution,* 121–22, emphasizing that local militias "should be well regulated.... A disorderly militia is disgraceful to itself, and dangerous not to the enemy, but to its own country. The duty of the state government is to adopt such regulations as will tend to make good soldiers with the least interruptions of the ordinary and useful occupations of civil life." To the same effect, see also Story, *Commentaries on the Constitution,* 3:746–47. The prevailing jurisprudence of his day explains why Joseph went out of his way to attest that the Nauvoo Legion had acted efficiently, under strict supervision, and without arrests or interference with the lives or property of the citizens. See also Tucker, *Blackstone's Commentaries* (1803), which called the right to bear arms "the true palladium of liberty," the right of self defense being "the first law of nature."

107. *History of the Church,* 6:540.

whom you are well acquainted; both parties were present, witnesses were called on both sides, the case was fully investigated, and we were again dismissed.[108]

Joseph's summary of these events shows not only his respect for constitutional law but also his intimate knowledge of its workings.

Not all Americans in the highly charged political climate of the Mississippi valley in the 1830s and 1840s held the same high for the Constitution as did Joseph. In 1837 in the city of Alton, on the Illinois side of the Mississippi River fifteen miles north of St. Louis, mobs destroyed the abolitionist newspaper that the Reverened Elijah P. Lovejoy had moved to Alton, following the similar destruction of his press by a mob in St. Louis and his expulsion from that city. After promising the citizens of Alton that the *Observer* would not agitate in favor of the abolitionist cause, his paper soon became a partisan abolitionist newspaper "of the fiercest sort, and religion was pressed into its service."[109] On October 26, 1837, a convention assembled, which soon became violent, aroused mainly by a violent harangue against slavery by Reverend Beecher, then president of Illinois College. In his diatribe, Beecher "contended that slavery was wrong, sinful, and morally wrong, and ought not to be borne with an instant. No Constitution could protect it. If the Constitution sanctioned iniquity, the Constitution was wrong in the sight of God and could not be binding upon the people of this country. For his part, he did not sanction the Constitution. It was not binding on him."[110] Only two years later in Missouri and seven years later just upstream in Illinois, Joseph encountered the same type of hostilities which were likewise unrestrained by the rule of constitutional law.

Conclusion

Throughout Joseph Smith's many legal encounters, public statements, and private correspondence, he sustained the law, in spirit, word, and deed. Many of his statements throughout his short life confirm that Joseph Smith believed in the unique and divinely inspired importance of the American Constitution.

He spoke often of principles that can be found in the Preamble. Quite remarkably, he made arguments based explicitly on Article I, Section 8 (federal powers, including taxing, regulating armies, and recognizing copyrights);

---

108. *History of the Church*, 6:582.
109. Thomas Ford, *A History of Illinois* (Chicago: S. C. Griggs, 1854), 235.
110. Ford, *History of Illinois*, 237–38.

Section 9 (the right of habeas corpus); and Section 10 (gold and silver as legal tender); Article IV, Section 2 (becoming full citizens of another state and the extradition power); Article VI, Section 2 (the Supremacy clause); as well as the provisions enshrined in the Bill of Rights' First Amendment (prohibiting state establishment of religion, guaranteeing rights of religious worship, speech, press, assembly, and petitioning for redress), and also the Second (a well-regulated militia and the right to bear arms), Fourth (search and seizures), Fifth (due process), Sixth (speedy trial, right to confront accusers), Eighth (no excessive bail or cruel punishments), Ninth (federal powers shall not deny rights retained by the people), and Tenth (rights reserved by the states) Amendments. He encountered charges of treason (Article III, Section 3). He availed himself of the constitutional right to secure his copyright in published works (Article I, Section 10).

His statements about the Constitution arose in a variety of settings: out of legal and political problems in Missouri, in connection with the establishment of Nauvoo as a municipality under the Nauvoo Charter, in response to efforts by Missouri or Illinois to arrest him, during his campaign for the Presidency, and in his defense of actions taken by the city council of Nauvoo. His fervent and constant defense of the Constitution is most remarkable in light of all he and the early Saints were forced to endure. Even if prevailing legal views did not always agree with him, Joseph stood resolutely loyal to the principles upon which the Constitution was founded. Notably, Joseph found no conflict between God and government, and he sincerely strived to honor and obey both.

While Joseph never developed and articulated a systematic explanation of constitutional law, one can infer key jurisprudential and constitutional law principles from his many legal encounters and statements. It is clear that Joseph believed in order and the rule of law. The free exercise of religion was one of his central beliefs. He taught that order required limits to what the majority or vocal interest groups could say and do at the expense of constitutionally protected liberties. He expected federal officers to use powers they had been given to ensure the enjoyment of rights guaranteed by the Constitution. Joseph was willing to fight, and even die, for fairness, freedom from oppression, equity, and unity. He repeatedly denounced false imprisonment and mob violence. He also believed that the people, as the voice of the sovereign, should be unified. It is clear, however, that Joseph's definition of unity did not require homogenization. He was certainly not a conformist, and he never required people to conform to his beliefs. Even so, Joseph believed that nonconformists must be respectful in their actions and not jeopardize the well-being and peace of the whole. In the face of opposition and prejudice, Joseph strove to accommodate the people in Ohio, Missouri, and Illinois. He was willing to give respect and demanded that his rights also be respected.

Many questions remain over what Joseph would have said and done if he had been involved in the debates of the late 1840s and 1850s about slavery and states rights. Would he have proposed constitutional amendments to strengthen the Constitution where he saw its deficiencies and failings? Would he have supported Lincoln's efforts to preserve the union through the lengthy Civil War? Would he have issued the Emancipation Proclamation and promoted the extension of civil rights to African Americans and Native Americans? Would he have been able to compensate slave owners in taking slaves from them, as his 1844 platform proposed to do? While we have no answers to many such questions, one can be confident that any answers to such questions would be consistent with his actions, his reliance on revelation, and his core commitment to the principles of the Constitution expressed in the Preamble.

To the end, Joseph upheld the Constitution and its principles, for himself and all others. As he said to Governor Ford, on **June 26, 1844,** the day before his murder: "If there is trouble in the country, neither I nor my people made it, and all that we have ever done, after much endurance on our part, is to maintain and uphold the Constitution and institutions of our country, and to protect an injured, innocent, and persecuted people against misrule and mob violence."[111]

---

111. *History of the Church,* 6:581.

Chapter Two

The Smiths and Religious Freedom: Jesse Smith's 1814 Church Tax Protest

John W. Welch

From the beginning, Vermont and its Green Mountain tradition placed prominence on freedom. Born in Sharon, Vermont, and describing himself in the opening line of his campaign literature as he ran in 1844 for President of the United States as having been "born in a land of liberty,"[1] Joseph Smith carried with him throughout his life a high regard for religious freedom. While he was still at an impressionable age, as young as eight or nine, his first lesson concerning the jarring pressures and legal practicalities that composed the free exercise of religion and the disestablishment of state involvement in church affairs probably came through the eyes of his uncle Jesse.

Over a period of about fifty years, the new American Republic cut official ties between church and state. This was a step by step process, known as disestablishmentarianism.[2] Separating church and state was not simply a matter of expelling the King of England (the head of the Church of England) from the thirteen American colonies. Even after the Revolution, state taxes continued to support all kinds of schools, including church run schools, and local taxes also paid for church buildings and the salaries of ministers, to say nothing of so-called state "Blue Laws" that prohibited such religious offenses as

---

1. *General Smith's Views of the Powers and Policy of the Government of the United States* (Nauvoo, Ill., 1844), 1, reprinted in Joseph Smith Jr., *History of The Church of Jesus Christ of Latter-day Saints*, ed. B. H. Roberts, 2d ed., rev., 7 vols. (Salt Lake City: Deseret Book, 1971), 6:197.

2. As an example of this process, see appendix 3, "Disestablishment and the Right to Perform Marriages," at the end of M. Scott Bradshaw, "Joseph Smith's Performance of Marriages in Ohio," *BYU Studies* 39 no. 4 (2000): 61–69.

blasphemy, idolatry, or not attending church on the Sabbath. Joseph Smith's immediate family experienced firsthand numerous changes during this invigorating time of separation.

Illustrating one phase of this transition is the following 1814 document, which was handed down from generation to generation among the descendants of Silas Sanford Smith, brother to Jesse Smith (1768–1853), the eldest brother of Joseph Smith's father. This document, donated to The Church of Jesus Christ of Latter-day Saints by George Smith Dibble in the early 1990s, provides several interesting insights into the character of Jesse Smith as well as perspectives on the religious background of this member of the extended family of the Prophet Joseph Smith.

Uncle Jesse was the first son of Mary Duty and Asael Smith, the paternal grandparents of Joseph Smith Jr. These people were strong-willed individuals who stood by their convictions. In his certificate of 1814, Jesse stated that he stood alone as the only one opposed to an action taken in 1813 by the Presbyterian congregation to which he belonged.[3] Being the eldest in his family, Jesse naturally commanded considerable respect from his siblings, and this document evidences a skillful Smith family ability to state opinions clearly and forcefully.

What was Jesse's objection? His controversy with his fellow church members in Tunbridge, Vermont, arose over a set of resolutions that they had adopted on June 5, 1813, voting to return to congregational autonomy and to employ Jacob Allen, a Congregationalist, as their minister.[4] In the process, as Jesse objected, they had "assume[d] the right to bind and loose" and had dissolved "the government and dicipline [*sic*] of the [central] church." In addition, they had rejected "the idea of infant or minor membership."

Sharing some of his father's "desire to test all religious opinions by the holy scriptures and sound reason," he objected to these resolutions primarily on scriptural grounds. For example, in Jesus' blessing of the children, Jesse found evidence that all family members should be allowed to partake of the blessings of the church directly. He recoiled at the idea of membership in a church congregation where his entire family could not participate.

---

3. The Tunbridge community church operated under the Presbyterian form of church government for eight years, deciding in 1813 to return to Congregationalism. James Ramage, *Centennial Celebration of the Congregational Church, Tunbridge, Vermont* (Montpelier, VT.: Watchman, 1892, 25–26).

4. Under the Plan of Union, Presbyterian and Congregationalist churches could hire ministers from either faith. Albert E. Dunning, *Congregationalists in America* (Boston: Pilgrim, 1894), 321–33; Gaius Glenn Atkins and Frederick L. Fagley, *History of American Congregationalism* (Boston: Pilgrim, 1942), 142–46.

Likewise, concerning "the right to bind and loose," Jesse also found in the New Testament clear evidence that church authority "to bind or loose, to make laws or administer government or discipline" or "to transfer this power to others by the Imposition of their hands" was given only to the apostles and elders; authority could not be reconstituted in a mere determination of "the body of the church." Jesse cited the apostolic council in Acts 15 and the procedures of Deuteronomy 17 as examples that only a representative body of central church leaders "having jurisdiction over lesser bodies" had exclusive authority to decide issues of church governance, such as the adoption of the local resolutions to which Jesse objected. Accordingly, Jesse rejected the action taken by these local citizens because they were acting outside the "mode of government" authorized for the church by Jesus Christ.

While his protest certificate itself contains no information about the immediate circumstances that finally provoked Jesse Smith, on November 18, 1814, to memorialize his religious convictions and reasons for disagreeing with his Presbyterian brethren in Tunbridge, he had waited long enough. For seventeen months, he had hoped for a change, but at length "imperious necessity" compelled him to action. Perhaps his position had been misunderstood or misrepresented in the congregation; he probably had been subjected to social criticism; he was eventually excommunicated.

How did Vermont law get involved in this religious matter? In several ways. First off, well-meaning state laws had inserted themselves into the configuration of church government. The Articles of Agreement, by which the local congregation in Tunbridge had been organized, were constituted under the laws of the state of Vermont, particularly under a law entitled An Act for the Support of the Gospel.[5] This law and these articles gave the

---

5. Jesse Smith refers here to a series of Vermont laws dealing with the establishment of churches in Vermont. As the following sequence demonstrates, many issues in this regard were regularly discussed, contested, and modified in the early years of Vermont history. Initially, the 1777 Constitution of Vermont, section 41, provided: "All religious societies or bodies of men, that have or may be hereafter united and incorporated, for the advancement of religion and learning, or for other pious and charitable purposes, shall be encouraged and protected in the enjoyment of the privileges, immunities and estates which they, in justice, ought to enjoy, under such regulations as the General Assembly of this State shall direct." In 1783, the basic act was passed "to Enable Towns and Parishes to erect proper Houses for public Worship, and support Ministers of the Gospel." See *Acts and Laws of Vermont* (Oct. 1783). This law was modified in 1787 as An Act for supporting Ministers of the Gospel. See *Acts and Laws of Vermont* (Oct. 1787), restated a decade later as An act for the support of the Gospel (Oct. 26, 1797). In 1801, this law was modified in a bill entitled An act in addition to, and alteration of an act, entitled "An Act for the support of the gospel." See *Acts and Laws of Vermont* (passed Nov. 3, 1801), 17–20. In 1807, a bill was

local populace (not the church hierarchy) considerable control over "every attempt of the church to call and settle [employ] a minister." Moreover, these legal provisions and instruments gave the state courts power to foreclose on a person's "houses or lands or both as surety" for the collection of any delinquent salaries owed by a local congregation to a minister of the gospel. Thus, it is even possible that Jesse had refused to pay his share of the salary of Jacob Allen, the minister whose hiring he had opposed, and someone was threatening legal action to compel Jesse to pay. In the end, Jesse followed the procedure outlined in Vermont law by which an objector could secure exemption from that local assessment.

By way of legal background, in 1783 the general assembly of Vermont had passed a law enabling towns and parishes to build churches and to provide for the support of ministers of the gospel. By a majority vote, a town or parish could levy a tax sufficient to cover the costs of hiring a minister, "to be assessed on the Polls [individual persons] and rateable Estates [appraised property] of Persons Living [residing], or Estates lying, within the Limits of such Town or Parish." In addition, the statute recognized that many people within the town or parish might be of different sentiments in respect to their religious duties, "whose conscience this act is not to control: and likewise some, perhaps, who pretend to differ from the Majority with a Design only to escape Taxation." Therefore, the act provided that a person who belonged to a different church could dissent from the majority view and be exempt from the tax, but only if "he, she, or they, shall bring a Certificate, signed by some Minister of the

---

passed entitled "an act to repeal a certain act, and parts of an act"; it repealed sections 2–6 of the 1797 act. See *Vermont Laws* (passed Oct. 24, 1807), 22. In 1812, an explanatory act clarified that all contracts made before the 1807 repeals were still enforceable. See *Vermont Laws* (passed Nov. 6, 1812), 159–60. The resolution of Jesse's Tunbridge Presbyterian congregation were adopted June 5, 1813; later that year an act was passed authorizing voluntary associations to enter into binding agreements to hire a minister, even though "it is not agreeable to the principles or practice of people of the Presbyterian denomination, to make such contracts with particular ministers." See *Vermont Laws* (passed Oct. 28, 1813), 5. And in 1814, an act "in addition to an act, for the support of the gospel" empowered a voluntary association to become "a body corporate and politic ... to carry into effect any agreement by them made, for the settlement or support of a minister ... and have all the powers incident and necessary to corporations," having "full power to make their own by-laws, and regulations concerning the times and places of holding their meetings, and the mode of warning such meetings, the election and duties of the several officers, the manner of admitting and discharging member, and managing all other interests and concerns of said associations or societies, which shall not be repugnant to the constitution and laws of this state." *Vermont Laws* (passed Nov. 10, 1814), 112–14. Jesse's protest was dated eight days later, November 18, 1814.

Gospel, Deacon, or Elder, or the Moderator in the Church of Congregation to which he, she or they, pretend to belong, being of a different Persuasion."

Over time, the law changed concerning the procedures to be followed and the contents to be required in filing a certificate of dissent. In 1787 a law entitled An Act for Supporting Ministers of the Gospel (restating the 1783 law) required that the "certificate shall make known … the religious sentiments of the signer thereof." In 1801 the Act for the Support of the Gospel was amended to provide simply that any person "who was either in the minority of said vote, or who was not at the meeting, at the time of passing such vote, … shall have liberty to enter his dissent, in writing, on the records of the town or parish," without stating any particular religious sentiments, but only after "paying up all taxes and assessments until that time, and for the whole of the year in which such dissent is made," and this shall release the person "from any further taxation, for the support of such minister."[6] Although the law of 1801 did not expressly require the townsperson to state any particular religious grounds for his dissent, Jesse Smith's statement followed the earlier convention, setting forth at great length his beliefs and making known his religious sentiments with respect to the entire issue.

A copy of this legal document was written into the Tunbridge town records. That recorded version begins, "Protest of Brother Jesse Smith against a Vote of the Ch[urc]h passed June 25$\underline{th}$ 1813."[7] There, Jesse declared himself unable to continue in fellowship with the church so long as the offending resolutions remained in force. Nevertheless, he went out of his way in the end to affirm his open-mindedness, his eagerness to be convinced otherwise should he be in error, his willingness to assume personal responsibility for any public harm he might have caused by any such error, and his community spirit and goodwill toward those of the opposing view.

Other traits of character are revealed in Jesse's certificate. For example, it confirms that the Smiths were very family oriented. Jesse insisted, on scriptural authority, that admitting a man to the privileges of the church required

---

6. 1801 *Vermont Laws,* November 3, 1801, Section 3, Proviso 2. Also pursuant to this law, Joseph Smith Sr., like several other citizens of Randolph, Vermont, recorded a protest in the Randolph town records on July 1, 1802, stating, "I Do not agree in Religious opinion With a Majority of the Inhabitants of this Town." *Randolph Liber Primus,* miscellaneous records (commencing 1790), 71.

7. The private text published below conforms with the public document in almost all substantive respects, and the recorded version has been used to clarify obscure places and torn edges in the private document with those words shown in brackets. Some punctuation has also been added in the transcript below.

also the admission of all or any of his household. He objected to membership in any society "where my family could not partake of the benefit directly."

Moreover, this document shows Jesse Smith as a God-fearing, religious man, even though he was not satisfied with the events in his church. He questioned unauthorized church acts and hoped that his church brethren would return to the "former vows" they had made, which he understood to be more in harmony with the practices of the New Testament church, or if change was in order, God would spiritually confirm the decision of his congregation. Until such spiritual guidance was forthcoming, Jesse was willing to leave one church and look elsewhere for religious affiliation. While he comes across as very conservative in his Presbyterian views, uncompromisingly entrenched as he was in Calvinistic theology throughout his life, here in 1814 he also shows himself to be willing to change his stance if shown by God or scripture to be wrong.

Interestingly, and in several ways, this legal document can readily be seen as part of the background for the Restoration of the gospel of Jesus Christ through the Prophet Joseph Smith. It illustrates the intensity of religious debates and study occurring during the period shortly before the youthful Joseph entered the grove where he received his first vision six years later in 1820. In articulating his religious persuasions, Jesse here discusses doctrinal issues with a remarkable scriptural facility. He quotes the Bible extensively, accurately, and readily; he has given considerable thought to the practical implications of several passages in the Bible. For example, he realized the importance of being led by apostles and elders, of conferring authority by the laying on of hands, and of applying the divine instructions and institutions of the Old Testament even in the new age under Christ.

Even more specifically, in 1813, the seven-year-old Joseph underwent a searing leg-saving operation following an infection that had resulted from typhoid.[8] As part of his recovery from this surgery, he traveled with his uncle Jesse to Salem, Massachusetts, where the sea air was thought to be therapeutic. Although no evidence exists of what these two traveling companions talked about as they passed the long hours coming and going over the remote buggy roads, it is not hard to imagine that topics of religion often came up. Their conversations could well have turned to the subjects that Jesse felt so strongly about at this very time and which he expressed so clearly in his 1814 protest. One can well imagine the impact Jesse's bold action might have had on the young Joseph's views of many matters concerning religious freedom and doctrinal necessity.

---

8. See LeRoy S. Wirthlin, "Nathan Smith (1762–1828): Surgical Consultant to Joseph Smith," *BYU Studies*, 17 no. 3 (1977): 319–37.

Jesse Smith's certificate legally opting out of the Tunbridge congregation reads as follows:

On the 30ᵗʰ of July 1809 I was admitted to the fellowship and Communion of the Ch[urc]h in this Town organised and officered with ruling elders in Presbyterian form, but destitute of a stated Gospel ministry: we had a teaching Elder who was by profession a presbyterian having charge of a congregational Church in this vicinity whose steadfast belief and uniform declaration was that Presbyterian church government and decipline was (in his opinion) the only form recognized in scripture. The Church having no teaching Priest was not united to any particular Presbytery. being but few in number I believe all expected to make slow progress, but as far as I understood anything of the matter no one thot of going back or returning like the dog to his vomit or like the sow that was washed to her wallowing in the mire [2 Pet. 2:22]. For we are assured that no one putting his hand to the plow and looking back is fit for the kingdom of heaven [Luke 9:62] undoubtedly meaning the Church. It was also understood that every baptised child was a member of the church and thus acknowledged by by [sic] receiving the seal of the covenant which ordinance, say the Assembly of divines, doth signify and seal our ingrafting into Christ and our engagement to be the Lords; this is true otherwise I know of no meaning to the command the Lord is said to have given concerning the poor debtor who owed ten thousand talents (viz) that he his wife and children of all that he had should be sold and payment should be made [Matt. 18:24–25]........ Thus encouraged by the prospect that I and mine might walk in the light of the church be ruled and diciplined by men in the vineyard of the Lord elected for the purpose set apart and qualified for the office and they with him who should labor in word and doctrine if God should favor us with a wat[c]hman on this part of the wall together with the whole body of the church each in their station should come forward with mutual endeavor for the instruction of our children in the ways of thrut [truth] and righteousness teaching them to mind the same things for the edification of themselves and others and of building them up in the most holy faith according to those precepts (and those only) which are laid down in that gospel thro which life and immortality are brot to light.... This appeared to me and still does appear like building again the Tabernacle of David together with the ruins thereof that the residue of men might seek the Lord [Acts 15:16]...... These are some of my reasons for joining the church and such was the Ch[urc]h when I did join it.. I came forward I trust under the Influence of the Holy Ghost. I still hope I did not trust in a vain thing. the vanity of the Gentiles or an arm of flesh but I think I had and still have some reason to believe that my cheif hope and dependance was and is on him who inhabits the praises of Israel before whom the nations are counted as the small dust of the balamce [*sic*] and who taketh up the Isles as very little thing. Lebanon is not sufficient to burn nor the beasts thereof for a burnt offering [Isa. 40:15–16]... before whom all nations are counted as nothing yea less than nothing and vanity [Isa. 40:17]..... Notwithstanding my remaining corruptions which at times seem to be carrying me away as with a whirlwind, my motives were good. My object was and is to come up to the help of the Lord against the mighty [Judg. 5:23].... The church remained in this situation till the memorable 5ᵗʰ of June 1813 about which time Mr Jacob Allen appeared as a candidate for the ministry of the congregational order so called, the members of the church generaly esteemed the man and finally sett[l]ed him as their minister ..... but as a preliminary the then government and discipline of the church must be abolished, for it seems the man was honest he would not act contrary to his own understanding of the scripture as he had been taught ... at this time the members of the church in general meeting for the purpose did, to my astonishment and in opposition to all I could say or do, assume the right to bind and loose [Matt. 16:19; 18:18], passed a decree dissolving the government and dicipline of the church together with the Idea of infant or minor membership and to my understanding the church also .... I was then in the minority with only one other person who has sinse gone with the multitude so far as to attend for the present on the ministry and the ordinances .. I now stand alone the only opposer to the decree and the maner of passing the same ..

I have waited more than 17 months hoping and praying that the church would return to their former vows as I understood them or that God would open the eyes of my understanding so as to see them in the right if they were so .. but neither of these have as yet come to pass and the time has arrived when imperious necessity compells me to enter solemnly my protest against this unprecedented act of the church in decreeing its own disolution as I understand the measure .... I now therefore declare in presence of these men whom I have considered as my brethren who were mine acquaintance with whom I took sweet council and with whom I walked to the house of God in company feeling willing to appeal to that God who trieth the reins and searches the hearts of the children of men. for the purity of my motives. that I cannot (with grief do I reflect on the causes that have led to this) in consience subscribe to this decree or consider myself bound by this act of the church of the said 5$^{\underline{th}}$ of June, neither can I fellowship the church while under the guidance of this decree and the subsequent proceedings arising therefrom so as statedly or occasionaly to commune with them in the ordinance of the Lords super [*sic*] [or] attend on the ministry supported in the ^present form ... for the following reasons 1$^{\underline{st}}$ I never did agree to any such thing .. 2$^{\underline{nd}}$ I cannot find in the scriptures any precepts or example for admiting a man to the priviliges of the church and [ex]cluding all or any of his houshold. Our Lord said suffer little children and forbid them not to come unto me for of such is the kingdom of heaven [Matt. 19:14] meaning the church. he took them up in his arms put his hands upon them and blessed them. I never had a serious wish to become a member of the church or any other society where my family could not partake of the benefit directly. 3$^{\underline{rd}}$ because I find no warrent in the scripture for the church collectively to make laws or decrees to bind any either themselves or others. the great head of the church gave to his Apostles the keyes of the kingdom of heaven [Matt. 16:19] or church . and to no other[.] he authorized them to bind & loose ^& to transfer this power to others by the Imposition of their hands & says upon this rock will I build my church and the gates of hell shall not prevail against it [Matt. 16:18], meaning by the rock I believe the mode of government. I do not believe that Jesus Christ in any instance has authorized the whole body of the church to bind or loose to make laws or administer goverment or discipline. The church is called the kingdom of heaven and a kingdom cannot exist acording to the common aceptation of the term without rulers and ruled, kings and subjects. The first disputation which arose in the christian church in the Apostolic age was not determined by the members or brotherhood, but Paul & Silas and certain others went up to Jerusalem unto Apostles and elders about this question [Acts 15:22–29]. this I understand was a representative body when convened having jurisdiction over lesser bodies. this was not an advisory council, there is there no advice offered. but they utter their sentence and the assembly agree to lay no greater burden than these nesessary things &c [Acts 15:28] (this burden these rulers did lay & bind upon the subjects of the kingdom) in what country Soever they might reside. This mode of procedure was in strict conformity to the plain command of God in the 17$^{\underline{th}}$ chapter of Deuteronmy. If there arise a matter too hard for the[e] in Judgement between blood and blood between plea and plea and between stroke and stroke being matters of controversy within thy gates. then shalt thou arise and get thee up unto the place which the Lord thy God shalt choose and thou shalt come unto the p[r]eists the Levites and unto the judge that should be in those days and enquire and they shall shew thee the sentence of judgment and thou shalt do according to the sentense which they of that place which the Lord shall choose shalt show thee and thou shalt observe to do according to all that they inform the[e] according to the sentencs of the law which they shall teach thee and according to the judgment which they shall tell the[e] thou shalt do thou shalt not decline from the sentence which they shall shew the[e] to the right hand or to the left [Deut. 17:8–11]... I am aware some will say this was in another age and a new order of things have suceeded. I reply we have the same Lawgiver under the new as under the old dispensation. I state also that this command has never been repealed again I understand Jerusalem to be the only place God had at that time made known as the place of his chosen for the seat of Judgment and it seems the Apostles and elders together with a representation of the whole church thought of going to no other place for a decision about this controversy between plea and plea. much scripture I believe might be brot in support of this mode of procedure but I am not allowed to be lengthy-. my 4$\underline{th}$ and last re[a]son for absenting myself from the church is the manner of settling and supporting the minister. I am not able to learn from the scriptures of the old and new testament that the church of Christ in any age of the world had any right to form any connection with those without concerning the calling settling suporting or dismising their pastor or teacher but in looking over the ground work of the call settlement and support of the minister & also provision for his dismision if need be. I do find the whole predicated upon a legislative act of the state of Vermont which by the authority of the s[ai]d state is declared to be an act entitled an for the support of the Gospel.[9] Here are articles of agreement called the constitution of the first congregational or Presbyterian church and society in Tunbridge. These articles are fourteen in number signed if I mistake not by nearly all the male members of the church and a number of others & declared to be binding on them and those who shall come after them except the eighth article .... In these articles there is pointed out and defined the right of the church and the colatteral rights of the society or those without as relates to the call settlement and support of the minister so long as he lives or till he is dismised in the transaction of all this business. The people without the church by these articles of agreement or this constitution have in their power if they please to defeat every attempt of the church to call and settle a minister. There is no higher authority quoted in all or any of these articles than that of the state of Vermont. There is not a single expression in this whole instrument which is copied from the word of God or anything which alludes to divine revelation, there is no law recognized for the collection even amoung the [Saints for] the suport of the ministry but the political code of our country which is [ever varying its course and object.] The church or as many of them and others as have signed this instrument

---

9. See note 5 above.

have bound themselves to mortgage their houses or lands or both as surety for the fullfillment of their contracts with the minister and one another which mortgage is liable to forclosure by order of a political court of Judicature at any time on the failure of the mortgagor to pay the interest of the money he has funded .... Therefore considering as I do this constitution as it is called to be, to say the least, not in conformity to the word of God I must I am constrained to protest against the measure in all its bearings. I cannot I dare not proceed on this ground, the consequences to myself and family notwithstanding I fear God and not man and wish to worship him in the beauty of holiness and in conformity to his own appointment. I cannot subscribe to this mode of procedure. I must now commit my character to the mercy of that God who knows my motives & to the impartial judgement of the church so far as it by them may be known at the period when the greatness of the kingdom under the whole heaven shall be given to the people of the saints of the most High.

Arise O God plead thine own cause [Ps. 74:22] O let not the oppressed return ashamed let the poor and needy praise thy name [Ps. 74:21] blessed be the Lord God the God of Isreal who only doth wondrous things [Ps. 72:13] and let the whole earth be filled with his glory [Ps. 72:19]......... I now subscribe this my protest with some reasons which have opperated to [produce it, with mine own hand] and in presense of the Lord of all the earth promising his grace assisting, that if ever I should be convinced that I ought not to have done this thing, I will use of all the means which may then be in my power to retract and that in the most suitable public manner if I continue to think I am right I feel a determination, God willing, to use my best endeavor to bring the church back to a sense of their duty and to this purpose I mean to employ my influence if any I have and to these purposes I mean to devote myself either to be convinced myself or to convince my opposers done this 18th day of Nov. in the year of our Lord Christ 1814.

Jesse Smith

This article was originally published as "Jesse Smith's 1814 Protest," BYU Studies *33, no. 1 (1993): 131–44.*

Chapter Three

Standing as a Credible Witness in 1819

Jeffrey N. Walker

Joseph Smith Jr.'s introduction to the legal system came at an early age. In January 1819, his father, Joseph Sr., and oldest brother, Alvin, initiated a lawsuit against Jeremiah Hurlbut arising from his sale of a pair of horses to the Smiths for $65. During the previous summer, the Smith boys had been working for Hurlbut to both pay down the $65 obligation and for other goods. Twelve witnesses were called during the trial, including Hyrum and Joseph Jr. Under New York law, being just thirteen, Joseph Jr.'s testimony about the work he had performed was admissible only after the court found him competent. His testimony proved credible, as the court record indicates that every item he testified about was included in the damages awarded to the Smiths. Although Hurlbut appealed the case, no records have survived noting the final disposition of the appeal, leading one to speculate that perhaps it was settled outside of court. The significance of this case is not limited to the fact that a New York judge found the young Joseph Jr., just a year prior to his First Vision, to be competent and credible as a witness. Additionally, the fact that the suit was brought against a prominent Palmyra family and involved two other prominent community leaders as sureties on appeal may have contributed to Joseph Jr.'s memory of his estrangement from much of the Palmyra community.

Background

The Smith family moved to Palmyra during the winter of 1817–18, after both crop and business failures in Vermont. Joseph Sr. first arrived in the area in

1816, initially working as a merchant in Palmyra. Shortly after the arrival of his family, he and Alvin decided to turn their energies to farming. To pursue their farming interests, on March 27, 1818, they executed a promissory note in the amount of $65 in favor of Jeremiah Hurlbut for the purchase of a pair of horses. The promissory note was payable the following January to be paid in "good merchant grain," evidencing the Smiths' plans to farm. By summer 1818, the Smith boys were working as farmhands on Hurlbut's and likely his mother's Palmyra farms.

The town of Palmyra, founded in 1789, was originally called "Swift's Landing" and "District of Tolland." The name was changed to Palmyra in 1796. In the year 1800 the town's population was about 1,000. By 1820 it had grown to 3,124. The Erie Canal, which runs through Palmyra, was proposed in 1807. It was under construction from 1817 through 1825, reaching Palmyra in 1822.

The Hurlbuts were a prominent founding family of Palmyra. They were part of a group of founding settlers coming from the Wyoming Valley in Pennsylvania. In the 1780s, this group of Wyoming Valley residents appointed fellow residents John Swift and John Jenkins to find them a new settlement. Swift and Jenkins would ultimately purchase property including the land that would be organized as Palmyra in 1790.[1] While the Court of General Sessions of Ontario County created Palmyra on January 16, 1789, it was not formally organized until 1796 with John Swift being elected as the town's supervisor.[2] Jeremiah Hurlbut was four years old when his family moved to Palmyra in 1795.[3] His father had operated a distillery in Palmyra and had built a home and barn in town. He was called "Captain," an apparent reference to his service in the Revolutionary War. His death in 1813 left Jeremiah, the oldest son of ten, responsible for the family and his widowed mother, Hannah Millet Hurlbut.

By January 1819, when the promissory note became due, the Smiths and the Hurlbuts disagreed on several fronts. First, although the promissory note had become due, the Smiths had found the pair of horses to be "unsound." Second, the Smith boys had been working for Hurlbut, and with the failure of the horses they sought payment for their labor. Finally, Hurlbut claimed

1. *The First Settlement and Early History of Palmyra, Wayne County, N.Y.: Embracing Some Incidents and Anecdotes Hitherto Unpublished* (Palmyra, NY: Wayne Democratic Press, 1858), 4–5.

2. *First Settlement and Early History of Palmyra*, 8.

3. King's Daughters' Library. "Genealogy and Palmyra Standing Files." Manuscript; Microform edition: "Genealogy H–L," *Genealogy and Palmyra Standing Files*. Provo, Utah: BYU Library, 1970. FHL US/CAN Film 833182. Family History Library, Salt Lake City.

that the Smiths owed him money for using some of his farm equipment and for other goods they had received from him.

The Dispute

On January 12, 1819, Joseph Sr. and Alvin filed with the local Justice of the Peace, Abraham Spears, a summons and declaration against Hurlbut. As justice courts were not "courts of record," no record of these proceedings would have been created if the matter had not been appealed. Once the case was appealed, Justice Spears was required to prepare a record of the trial and forward it to the court of common pleas, the next highest court. It is that record and the pleadings attached thereto that provide us with the details of this trial.

Three documents delineate the competing claims between the parties: (1) the "Promissory Note"; (2) the "List of Services" detailing the work that the Smiths claimed to have provided to Hurlbut; and (3) the "List of Goods" detailing the goods Hurlbut claimed to have given the Smiths.

1. The promissory note, dated March 27, 1818, appears to be written by Joseph Sr. and includes both his and Alvin's signatures. It reads in full:

> For value Received I Promise to Pay to Jeremiah Hurlbut Or Barer the sum Of Sixty five Dollars to be Paid in good Merchant Grain at the market Price by the first January next with use for value Received March the 27th—1818
>
> Jo[s] Smith
> Alvin Smith

The signatures of both Joseph Sr. and Alvin have remained on the promissory note, evidencing that the note was not fully satisfied. During this period, promissory notes were often treated as currency, being exchanged, transferred, and sold. Consequently, when a note was paid in full, the signatures were torn off so the note would not be subsequently used in commerce.

On the back of the promissory note, additional information pertained to the status of the obligation. First, the notation on the back, "rec[d] on the within Note—fifty three Dollars by the Corps on the ground—~~which the~~ Aug[t] 210th 1818—," appears to be in accord with the agreement between the parties that the Smiths would be paying the note by "good Merchant Grain," although the amount credited for the grain was less than the face amount of the note. Second, calculations show the balance due on the note. These calculations appear to be in the handwriting and signature of Justice Spears, and are included as follows:

Note	65.00
Int.	1.50
	66,50
Deduct	53.00
	13,50
	39
Balance	13.89

Judgment entered on the within note Feby 6th 1819

A.Spear JP

The words "with use" in the text of the promissory note justified the inclusion of interest in this calculation, and thus interest of $1.50 is included. Also, $0.39 was likely charged for court costs, as both parties were required to pay their own costs during this era.

2. The list of services appears to be in the handwriting of Joseph Sr., and it details the work the Smiths had performed for Hurlbut. The two most likely explanations for the list of services are either: (1) the document was prepared concurrent to the work being performed by the Smiths; or (2) in anticipation of trial in the justice court. It is unlikely that it was prepared as part of the appeal process because on appeal, the court record noted that an interlocutory judgment accompanied by a writ of inquiry was entered. An interlocutory judgment and a writ of inquiry indicate that a judgment was awarded in an amount to be determined in a later proceeding.[4] Thus, if this list was prepared for the hearing in the court of common pleas, there would have been no reason for the writ of inquiry to be ordered.

The following is a transcription of the list of services. The date at the top likely indicates the date the Smiths started working for Hurlbut. This is further supported by the date noted on the list of goods (see further below), which notes at its top: "10 May-Aug 1818." The next line references "hanah," which is likely a reference to Hannah Millet Hurlbut, Jeremiah Hurlbut's widowed mother, who also had a farm in Palmyra. Such a reference likely indicates the Smiths may have worked at both Jeremiah and Hannah Hurlbut's farms during summer 1818. The X's on this document appear to have been placed by either Judge Spears or members of the jury, as the judgment rendered in the Smith's favor included these items as damages.

The following is a transcription of this document (bold type indicates different and heavier handwriting):

---

4. J. Bouvier, *A Law Dictionary* (Philadelphia, PA: T. & J. W. Johnson, 1839), s.c. "interlocutory judgment," "writ of inquiry," 550–51.

May the 8th 1818

hanah jer Hulbert D^r

X to work moveing fence next |.| oc^t white	$0.75 X
X to plowing garden	X 0,50 X
X to work with teem & boys	X 1.50 X
to Dressing veal	~~0.25 X~~
X to hyrum half Day fenceing	X 0.50
X to my Self & Hyrum & teem one Day	X 3.00
X to making fence one Day	X 1.00
half Day	
X to Hyrum & horses Drawing Rales	X 1.50
up to the 22nd May	
X July the 10th D^r to half Day mowing	X 0.50
X to one Day mowing &c.	X$1.00
X to part of two Days my self & Boys <hayers>	X 0.75
X to Joseph half Day Drawing hay	X 0.25
X to Hyrum & teem part of a Day Drawing hay	X 1.00
to horses & waggon one & half Days Drawing	
X hay & Rye in the South field –	X$2.25
to horses & waggon two & half Days	
X Drawing hay & grain in the north field	X 3.75
X to horses & waggon to pitsfields	X 0.75 X
to horse to Onterio	X 1.00
8 to takeing horse without Leave	
to go to the Ridge	X 4 00
X to horses & waggon one Day Drawing wood	X 1.50
to horses & waggon three Days Drawing	
X Stocks ponkins Buckwheat Rales & wood	X 4.50 [p. 1]
to one Day of the horses & waggon	
X Drawing Corn & wheet	X$1.50
X to horse to go to quaker meeting	X 0.50
to takeing horse without leave	X 1 00 X
to go after peaches	
Dr |..| after feed admitted	$5.00 X
to two Bushels of Seed wheat (1.25)	2.50 X
X 2 bus Rye	X|.| 75
Damages sustained by means of warranty &	
fraud or ducet in the Sale of Horses &c	80.00
To not performing contra|.|y	25 00 [p. 2]

A review of these entries allows for several conclusions. First, references to "self" appear to be referring to Joseph Sr. as the itemization also refers to "myself & Boys." The "boys" would include Alvin, Hyrum, and Joseph Jr. Consequently, references to "Joseph" would be for Joseph Smith Jr. With this understanding, one can then determine which items each Smith testified about. These entries for work performed by the Smiths totaled $41.25.

The final two entries on the list appear to be connected with the filing of the lawsuit as additional damages that Joseph Sr. and Alvin asserted based on the failure of the horses and the obligation under the promissory note. The first seeks damages due to the failure of the horses for $80, while the second for $25 is based on a breach of contract with the only written contract between the parties being the promissory note.

While this exhibit may have been helpful in identifying what services the Smiths claimed were performed, rules of evidence require a party to produce actual testimony from a witness to establish what services had been provided. Such testimony would be used at the trial, including that of Hyrum and Joseph Jr.

3. The list of goods appears to list the goods and services allegedly provided by Hurlbut to Joseph Sr. for which Hurlbut sought payment or offset. This interpretation is supported internally with notations of "Joseph Smith to Jeremiah Hurlburt Dr"[5] and one item notes, "to be paid by Smith." On the following pages are a transcription and image of this document (fig. 1). Bold type indicates different and heavier handwriting. Additional markings on this document appear to have been made either by the judge or by a member of the jury. The markings include "X," "proved," "admitted," and so forth. These notations appear to track the testimony and evidence presented at the trial. In addition, they could assist in determining how the justice court calculated and rendered their final judgment.

---

5. The "Dr" is a bit confusing as there is no evidence that Hurlbut was a doctor. Perhaps the "Dr" could be an abbreviation for "debtor" as Hurlbut was the debtor to the Smiths for the labor to which the lists seek as an offset.

Joseph Smith

To Jeremiah Hurlburt Dr

May 10th 1818 **X** To two bushels of oats @3/		$0.75 **X**
" 15 " **X** To 2 bushels of Rye & chess		0 75 **X**
" 20 " <**admitted ½**> To 2 ½ bushels of oats @3/		0.93
" 24 " **X** Planting corn one day @6/		0.75 **X**
" " ½ bushel of seed corn **proved**		0.37
" ½ bushel of flax seed **proved**		0.43
" (**admits half**) 10 bushels of Potatoes – Ruff & br		3.75
June **proved** To 300 Rails the |.|/c to be paid by Smith @2|.|		3.75
" To hoing corn 1 ½ days @ @ 6/ **proved**		1.12
" **proved** To hoing corn 2 days in the west lot		1.50

May 10th 1818 **X** To two bushels of oats @3/ $0.75 **X**

" 15   "   **X** To 2 bushels of Rye & chess   0 75 **X**

" 20   "   <**admitted ½**> To 2 ½ bushels of oats @3/   0.93

" 24   "   **X** Planting corn one day @6/   0.75 **X**

"   "   ½ bushel of seed corn **proved**   0.37

"   ½ bushel of flax seed **proved**   0.43

" (**admits half**) 10 bushels of Potatoes – Ruff & br   3.75

June **proved** To 300 Rails the |.|/c to be paid by Smith @2|.| 3.75

" To hoing corn 1 ½ days @ @ 6/ **proved**   1.12

" **proved** To hoing corn 2 days in the west lot   1.50

July – To 3^d days works hoing corn on the
east lot & Renting myself **proved**   3.00

" To sowing Buckwheat   ½ **day**   0.37

August   To ½ Ton of hay @56/ **admitted**   3.50

" **proved** To slveing a hern   0.37

one week   To use of a plow most of the summer **proved**   1.25

To paid Smith half of Tax on land   1.62 ½

To damage for not working land according
to agreement   25.00 <|-|>

To 28 dollars damage sustaned in the
wrong apprisal of crops   28 00

$76.89 ½ [p. 1]

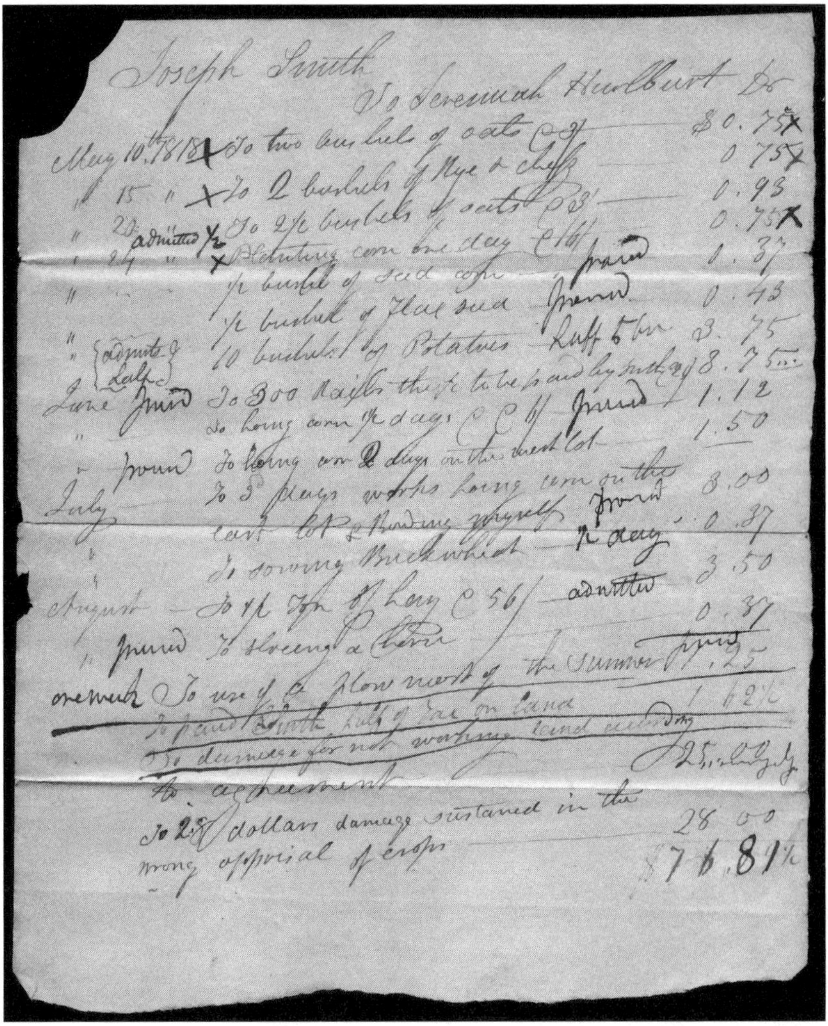

Figure 1. Hurlbut's list of goods. Ontario County, New York, May 10–August 1818, 1 p., MS, Ontario County Records Center, Canandaigua, New York.

The Justice Court Trial

The record of this jury trial in the justice court is found in the pleading captioned as the "Judgment Roll,"[6] which was prepared by Justice Spears when Hurlbut appealed the judgment to the court of common pleas. The Ontario Court of Common Pleas adopted the "Rules to Regulate the Practice in Cases of Appeals," which notes:

> A plaintiff of the term next after the appeal was lodged with the Justice, shall file a memorandum shortly stating that the cause had been commenced tried & determined before the Justice and the bringing the appeal according to the Statute the appearance of the parties in this court and the joining of issue, or the default of either party in appearing as the case may be, the return of the Justice verbatim, the demand of a trial by Jury if there is such a demand, the award of a venire returnable immediately, the trial either by a Jury or the Court, the continuances if any and the other proceedings and judgment according to the nature of the case said usages of law.[7]

Consequently, the judgment roll (see transcription on following page) provides a detailed description of the justice court's jury trial.

On January 12, 1819, Joseph Sr. and Alvin filed *pro se* a summons and declaration against Hurlbut in the local justice court. A justice court was the lowest level of the court system in early nineteenth-century New York. It was similar to today's small claims court. The justice court had limited jurisdiction with civil cases limited to $50 at issue.[8] After filing in the local justice court, the local constable served the summons and declaration on Hurlbut the following day. A declaration was the equivalent of a complaint today. This case was brought before the enactment of the Field Code of 1848, which first

---

6. Ontario County, N.Y., February 9, 1819, 1 p., MS, Ontario County Records Center, Canandaigua, N.Y. Endorsed: " On Appeal / Jeremiah Hurlburt / vs / Joseph Smith / Return"; "Filed Feby. 17th 1819."

7. Ontario County Court of Common Pleas, Court Minutes, vol. 8 (August 1819–August 1820), 19, MS, Ontario County Records Center, Canandaigua, New York.

8. As explained in a New York 1829 Justice Manual, "Suits may be brought before a Justice when the debt or balance due, or the damages claimed, shall not exceed fifty dollars." Thomas G. Waterman, *Justice's Manual: Summary of the Powers and Duties of Justices of the Peace, in the State of New York: containing a Variety of Practical Forms, adapted to Cases Civil and Criminal,* 2d ed. (Albany, N.Y.: Websters and Skinners, 1829), 2.

Justices Court

Joseph Smith
vs
Jeremiah Hurlbutt

The jury Drawn and sworn were:

James White
Lemuel Spear
Zebulon Reeves
Th P Baldwin
Thomas Rogers
Alva Uandee
John Russel
Timothy C Strong
Stephen Spear
Levi Jackson
Dorastus Cole
Denison Rogers

The names of the witnesses sworn & examined were as follows, plaintiffs witnesses:

Hyrum Smith
Joseph Smith Junr
Silas Shirtliff
George Proper
Ara Canfield

Defendants wit:

Fanny Lee
Lemuel Lee
Ephraim Huntly
Jared D Ainsworth
Henry Stodard
Solomon Tice
James Cole

Summons issued January 12th 1819

Returnable the 22d inst at 2 oclock PM at my office in Palmyra, personally servd January 13th 1819 by D Uandee Constable January 22d parties were called and present plaintiffs Declaration was for several articles of account and one item was for Damages which Plaintiff sustained in the purchase of a span of horses of Defendant which horses was said to be unsound. Defendant Denies the Charge and Pleads a set off of a balance Due on a note and several articles of account Court adjourned till the 30th inst to Ara Lilly at the request of the parties. January 30th parties presant plaintiff requests that the cause should be tried by a jury venira issued January 30th and for want of a constable to serve it the Court adjourned till the 6th of Febuary 1819 at 1 oclock P.M at the request of the Plaintiff and by consent of the Defendant February 6th parties presant, Jury summond by Daniel Uandee Constable and Drawn and after hearing the proof and alagations of Both parties they found for the plaintiff $40.78

Judgment against Defendant for $40.78

Cost of suit 4 76
$45 54

N:B the summons issued in the above suit was for trespass on the Case for fifty Dollars or under, This May certify that the above is a correct return which has been before me and that the Defendant in the above e[n]titled suit appeals to the court of Common pleas for the County of Ontario

Given under my hand at palmyra this 9th day of February 1819 Abraham Spear JP

introduced the modern system of civil procedure in America.[9] Accordingly, this 1819 action was based on a "Writ of Trespass on the Case," as originated under British common law and procedure.[10]

This form of action, commonly referred to simply as the "case," was a catchall procedure when no other specific writ corresponded with the circumstances of a plaintiff's injury. These claims typically involved an indirect injury to the plaintiff's character, health, quiet, or safety; to personal rights; or to personal property.[11] In contrast, a claim brought under "writ of trespass" normally dealt with real property. While breach of contract was not grounds for an action of trespass on the case, the action could be based on injuries indirectly (consequential damages) resulting from performance or non-performance of a contract, and therefore was commonly used for mixed contract and tort actions.[12]

In the Smiths' situation, it appears that this was the correct writ to commence the present action by the Smiths. Their claims centered on recovery for personal services, as well as being excused for performance on the promissory note based on Hurlbut's misrepresentations of the horses' nature or condition. Consequently, the Smtihs' claims included contract claims (which could have been brought as a writ of assumption) and tort claims for misrepresentation or fraud. The writ of trespass on the case allowed both claims to be brought under this single writ.

As shown on the judgment roll, a week after the summons and declarations were served on January 13, both parties appeared *pro se* on January 22 before Justice Spears. Neither party had retained counsel. It appears that the parties discussed their respective claims at this hearing. The Smiths explained that they were seeking payment for the labor they had performed for Hurlbut (itemized on the list of services), for the damages they sustained as a result of the "unsound" nature of the span of horses[13] they had purchased from him

---

9. Lawrence M. Friedman, *A History of American Law* (N.Y.: Touchstone, 2001), 293–301.

10. John H. Baker, *An Introduction to English Legal History* (London: Butterworth, 2002), 61.

11. Thorne v. Deas, 4 Johns. 84 (N.Y. Sup. Ct. 1809).

12. Bouvier, *Law Dictionary*, s.v. "Breach of contract," 449–50.

13. A span of horses consists of "two of nearly the same color, and otherwise nearly alike, which are usually harnessed side by side. The word signifies properly the same as *yoke,* when applied to horned cattle, from buckling or fastening together. But in America, *span* always implies resemblance in color at least; it being an object of ambition with gentlemen and with teamsters to unite two horses abreast that are alike." Noah Webster, *American Heritage Dictionary of the English Language,* 1st ed. (1828), s.v. "Span."

and for payments of grain they had made on the promissory note. Hurlbut countered that the Smiths still owed on the promissory note for the horses, as well as for goods that he had sold them (itemized on the list of goods). Judge Spears continued the case for a week, at which time the parties appeared and the Smiths requested a jury. Apparently, Judge Spears had not anticipated the jury request because he had not arranged for a constable to secure one. Therefore, the judge continued the case for another week, until February 6, 1819.

The law provided that a twelve-man jury was available even in a justice court. The record notes that the Smiths requested a *jury venire*, the process whereby a sheriff is commanded by writ to "come from the body of the county; before the court from which it issued, on some day certain and therein specified, a certain number of qualified citizens who are to act as jurors in the said court."[14] Under applicable New York law "qualified citizens" at that time were limited to male inhabitants of the county where the trial was being held between the ages of twenty-one and sixty and who at the time had personal property in the amount of not less than $250 or real property in the county with a value of not less than $250.[15] In the rural community of Palmyra, this effectively meant those qualified to be on the jury would be the more affluent and prominent men of the area. Ironically, none of the Smiths would have qualified to be a juror.

The trial was finally held on February 6, 1819. Twelve jurors were impaneled, all men and property owners. A total of twelve witnesses were called at trial, with the Smiths calling five and Hurlbut calling seven. Both Joseph Jr. and Hyrum were called to testify. This was Joseph Jr.'s first direct interaction with the judicial process. He had turned thirteen years old a month and a half prior to the trial. New York law and local practice permitted the use of child testimony, subject to the court's discretion to determine the witness's competency. The test for competency required a determination that the witness was of "sound mind and memory." A New York 1803 summary of the law for justices of the peace notes that "all persons of sound mind and memory, and who have arrived at years of discretion, except such as are legally interested, or have been rendered infamous, may be improved as witness."[16] This determination as to competency rested within the discretion of the judge. The general criteria were articulated in Bouvier's *Law Dictionary*:

---

14. Bouvier, *Law Dictionary*, s.v. "jury venire," 466.

15. Charles Edwards, *The Juryman's Guide throughout the State of New York* (New York: O. Halsted, 1831), 54.

16. *A Conductor Generalis: being A Summary of the Law Relative to the Duty and Office of Justice of the Peace . . .* (Albany, N.Y.: E. F. Backus, 1819), 129.

The age at which children are said to have discretion is not very accurately ascertained. Under seven years, it seems that no circumstances of mischievous discretion can be admitted to overthrow the strong presumption of innocence, which is raised by an age so tender. Between the ages of seven and fourteen, the infant is, prima facie, destitute of criminal design, but this presumption diminishes as the age increases, and even during this interval of youth, may be repelled by positive evidence of vicious intention; for tenderness of years will not excuse a maturity in crime, the maxim in these cases being, *malitia supplet aetatem*. At fourteen, children are said to have acquired legal discretion.[17]

The application of these principles is articulated in a New York 1829 justice's manual, noting that "there is no particular age at which children are to be admitted to testify—but it is to be determined by their apparent sense and understanding. The court may examine a child, or other person of weak intellect, to ascertain his capacity, and the extent of his religious and other knowledge. After such examination the matter must rest, in a great measure, in the discretion of the court."[18]

The New Jersey Supreme Court similarly ruled in *Van Pelt v. Van Pelt*, 3 N.J.L. (N.J. 1810) 236, at 236:

If it has appeared to the justice at the time of the trial, that the witness was fourteen years of age, and that he was possessed of ordinary understanding; that is, was not uncommonly deficient in mental qualifications, the justice ought to have taken his testimony, and left it to the jury to judge of the credit due to it. But as it did not appear to the justice that the boy was fourteen years of age at the trial, we incline to think that his capacity as a witness was a proper subject of discretion in the justice; and therefore, that the judgment must be affirmed.

From the record, it appears that Judge Spears found Joseph Jr. competent and that he did indeed testify during the trial. This is evident by reviewing the list of services that was part of the court file. Joseph Jr.'s testimony would have been required to admit those services that he personally performed. Further, it is interesting to note that all the services Joseph Jr. testified about were included in the damages awarded to the Smiths.

---

17. Bouvier, *Law Dictionary*, s.v. "competency," 329.
18. Waterman, *Justice's Manual*, 73.

Based on the judgment roll, the jury found in favor of the Smiths in the amount of \$40.78 in damages and \$4.76 in court costs. Unfortunately, the record does not articulate how the court derived this damage award. Examining the respective claims is helpful but not determinative. There are several scenarios that may have resulted in this judgment in favor of the Smiths. The following is a likely explanation based on these documents and pleadings:

Rationale for Ruling	Source	Amount
Re: Sale of Horses:		
• The Smiths are liable for amount of the Promissory Note for the horses, plus interest of \$1.50.	Promissory Note [front]	<\$66.50>
• The Smiths had paid in grain a portion of the obligation owed on the Promissory Note.	Promissory Note [back]	\$53.00
• The horses were not as sound as promised and so Hurlbut was guilty of breach of contract as alleged by Smiths	List of Services [p. 2]	\$25.00
Re: List of Services:		
• Hurlbut was obligated to pay the Smiths for the work performed on his and his mother's farms as delineated by the Smiths and awarded by the jury.	List of Services [p. 1]	41.25
Re: List of Goods:		
• The Smiths owed Hurlbut for goods. Hurlbut claimed that there was \$76.89 owed. However, his adding was off and based on the List of Goods, \$77.21 was owed. The judge or jury noted on this exhibit the items that were owed by an X or noted "admitted" or "proved."	List of Goods [p. 2]	<\$13.50>
Re: Reconcile the judgment:		
• This could be for interest.	Judgment Roll	\$1.53
Total Judgment to Smith		\$40.78

Although the court did not award the Smiths the entire claim they had brought before the court, the Smiths had, for all practical purposes, won their case.

The Appeal

On February 7, 1819, the day following the trial, Hurlbut retained legal counsel to initiate both a new case, as well as an appeal in the court of common pleas. Hurlbut's attorney, Frederick Smith, was a familiar figure in the Palmyra legal community. He was not only an attorney but also a sitting justice of the peace for Ontario County. Frederick Smith was first elected as a justice in 1814 and continued to serve in that capacity until 1827.[19]

That same day, Hurlbut's counsel had a writ of *capias ad respondendum*[20] issued against Joseph Sr. and Alvin. This was an alternative process for initiating a lawsuit in the Ontario Court of Common Pleas. This action was brought in the court of common pleas because it sought damages of $140 and therefore exceeded the $50 jurisdictional limit of the justice court. While the writ of *capias* does not delineate the basis of the damages, it does note that it was brought under the same writ as was used in the prior justice court trial—"plea of trespass on the case." The $140 damage claim is likely the $65 owed under the promissory note and the $76 that Hurlbut claims the Smiths owed him for goods. The following is the text of this writ:[21]

> Ontario County. SS, — The people of the state of New-York, by the Grace of God, Free and Independent- to our Sheriff of our county of Ontario, Greeting:[22]
>
> We command you to take Joseph Smith & Alvin Smith if they may be found in your bailiwick, and them safely keep, so that you have their bodies before our Judge ~~and Assistant Justices~~, at our next Court of Common Pleas, to be holden at the Court-House in the town of Canandaigua, in and for our county of Ontario, on the third Tuesday of May next, to answer unto Jeremiah Hurlbut

---

19. Edgar A. Werner, *Civil List and Constitutional History of the Colony and State of New York* (Albany, N.Y.: Weed, Parson & Co., 1884); Registers of Government Appointments, vol. A, Records Series A0006-78, Box 32 of 33, "List of Appointed State Officers, 1823–29" (New York Archives).

20. A "writ of capias" is commonly used to command the sheriff to "take the body of the defendant, and to keep the same to answer, *ad respondendum*, the plaintiff in a plea." Bouvier, *Law Dictionary*, s.v. "writ of capis,"329.

21. Ontario County, N.Y., February 7, 1819, 2 pp., hybrid, Ontario County Records Center, Canandaigua, New York. Endorsed: "Ont Com Pleas / Jeremiah Hurlburt / v / Joseph Smith & / Alvin Smith / Dr $140 – / F Smith Atty"; "Filed 25th May 1819."

22. Small caps represent printed text.

IN A PLEA OF TRESPASS ON THE CASE TO HIS DAMAGE OF ONE
HUNDRED AND FORTY DOLLARS

AND HAVE YOU THEN THERE THIS WRIT —WITNESS, ~~JOHN
NICHOLAS~~, <NASH> ESQUIRE, FIRST JUDGE OF OUR SAID
COURT, AT CANANDAIGUA, THE 7ᵀᴴ DAY OF FEBRUARY 1819.

PER CURIAM.   H. NW NAIR, CLERK.

F. SMITH ATTORNEY. [p. 1].

On the back of this writ, Sheriff Phineas P. Bates noted "Cepi Corpus to
Joseph Smith. None as to A. Smith." *Cepi corpus* confirms that the sheriff
made the arrest pursuant to the *capias*.[23] It appears the sheriff found Joseph Sr.
but not Alvin, and indeed this is confirmed in the statement of issues filed by
Hurlbut on June 19, 1819, a few months later as part of his appeal.

On the following day, February 8, 1819, Hurlbut's attorney filed an appeal,
including the requisite "appeal bond" of the justice court judgment. The
appeal bond in this case[24] deserves special attention for a couple of reasons. First, the amount of the appeal bond was $81.56, twice the amount of
the justice court judgment ($40.78). At first blush, this amount appears in
accord with applicable New York law. However, a closer examination reveals
a fatal problem. The New York Supreme Court ruled, on both the 1818 and
1824 acts pertaining to appeal bonds, that the amount of the bond was to be
double the judgment *and* the court costs, not just the judgment.[25] In *Latham
v. Edgerton,* the court found that because the appellant had failed to submit
a bond that was double the amount of the judgment *and* the court costs, as
awarded by the justice court, the court of common pleas lacked jurisdiction
and reversed the judgment.

Based on the judgment roll, the justice court judgment included damages of $40.78 and court costs of $4.76. The bond proffered by Hurlbut only
covered the damages and did not include the court costs. This failure, under
the *Latham* court's ruling, would have voided the court of common pleas'
jurisdiction over the appeal altogether. Unfortunately, there is no evidence
that the Smiths ever raised this issue, which is likely due to the fact that while
Hurlbut retained counsel for the appeal, the Smiths did not. Consequently,
they were probably never even aware of this potentially fatal mistake.

---

23. Bouvier, *Law Dictionary*, s.v. "capias," 161.

24. Ontario County, N.Y., February 8, 1819, 2 pp., MS, Ontario County Records Center,
Canandaigua, New York. Endorsed: "Jeremiah Hurlbut / & / To / Joseph Smith / Bond."

25. Latham v. Edgerton, 9 Cow. (1828), 227, at 229, citing Ex parte Harrison, 4 Cow.
(1825) 61, at 63–64.

Second, pursuant to statute, Hurlbut was required to secure the bond with two sureties. Hurlbut had Solomon Tise and William Jackway sign as sureties on the bond. Solomon Tice was Hurlbut's brother-in-law, having married Hurlbut's sister, Anna, in 1808 in Palmyra.

William Jackway's family was among Palmyra's earliest settlers, having arrived in 1787. Jackway was a veteran of the Revolutionary War and owned a five-hundred-acre farm in Palmyra. Hurlbut's appeal may have been the first skirmish of what would be years of conflict between the Smiths and the Jackways. In 1831, Joseph Jr. would mention a son of William Jackway in a letter to his brother, Hyrum, noting: "David Jackways [*sic*] has threatened to take father with a supreme writ in the spring."[26] It appears that the Smiths' lawsuit against Hurlbut may have aligned some of the founding families of Palmyra in opposition to the Smiths. These actions predate Joseph Jr.'s heavenly experiences and the seeming fall-out within the Palmyra community.

Once the court certified the appeal bond, the justice court prepared the judgment roll, a document delineating the proceedings of the case, including the claims brought, the members of the jury, the witnesses and the judgment, and the Ontario Court of Common Pleas adopted "Rules to Regulate the Practice in Cases of Appeals" noting that "the party noticing a cause for trial shall previous to the term serve a notice of issues on the Clerk."[27] Accordingly, Hurlbut's attorney prepared and filed a Statement of Issues[28] with the court of common pleas as part of the appeal. In this statement, Hurlbut claimed, in part:

> They the said Defendants[29] would pay to the said Jeremiah Hurlbert or bearer the sum of Sixty five Dollars to be paid in good merchantable grain in one year from the date thereof with use for value received-
>
> BY means of which said promise and undertaking, the said defendants [The Smiths] became liable to pay and deliver, and ought to have paid and delivered to the said Plaintiff on the day last

---

26. Joseph Smith to Hyrum Smith, March 3, 1831, 3pp. MS, Joseph Smith Collection, Church Archives, Salt Lake City.

27. Ontario County Court of Common Pleas, Court Minutes, volume 8 (August 1819–August 1820), 19, MS, Ontario County Records Center, Canandaigua, New York.

28. Ontario County, New York, March 27, 1818, 1 p., hybrid, Ontario County Records Center, Canandaigua, New York. Endorsed: "Ontario Com. pleas. / Jeremiah Hurlbert / vs / Joseph Smith im- / pleaded with / Alvin Smith / F Smith Atty / Narr-"; "De |-| cpa"; "To file"; "Filed 26th June 1819."

29. As Hurlbut filed the appeal, as well as initiated a new action in the Court of Common Pleas, he became noted as the plaintiff in these pleadings with the Smiths as the defendants.

aforesaid, the said sum of money in said note mentioned according to the tenor and effect of the said note- Yet the said Defendants although requested by the said Plaintiff [Jeremiah Hurlbut] on the day last aforesaid, and often since that day, to wit, at Palmyra aforesaid have not paid said note or any part thereof to the said Plaintiff not have otherwise paid and satisfied to the said Plaintiff the said sum of money or any part thereof, but they to do the same have hitherto wholly refused, and still do refuse, to the damage of the Plaintiff of one hundred and Forty Dollars and therefore he brings his suit & c.

Hurlbut's position is very similar to the one he took during the justice court trial. Interestingly, he makes no reference to the $53 the Smiths had paid in "crops on the ground" as identified on the promissory note. Rather, he treats the promissory note as being owed in full. One can only surmise that this approach was one of strategy and not of oversight.

The caption to the statement of issues further confirms that Alvin Smith had most likely not been served with the *capias* (equivalent to a summons). It notes:

Ontario Com. Pleas
Jeremiah Hurlbut
Vs
Joseph Smith
impleaded with
Alvin Smith

The term "impleaded" indicates that a person who was not named as a party in the action as originally instituted has been brought into the action. The purpose of an impleader is to promote judicial economy, in that it permits two cases to be decided at once. While Alvin had not been served in the new suit commenced by Hurlbut in the Ontario Court of Common Pleas, he was already a co-plaintiff in the justice court suit from which Hurlbut had appealed the resulting judgment. Alvin was therefore impleaded into the new case. Some have speculated that during this time Alvin had taken work on the Erie Canal,which could explain why he was not around to be served with the *capias*.

The final reference to this case comes in a docket entry[30] in the Ontario Court of Common Pleas dated August 1819. It simply states:

---

30. Ontario County Court of Common Pleas, Court Minutes, vol. 8 (August 1819– August 1820), 19, MS, Ontario County Records Center, Canandaigua, New York.

Jeremiah Hurlbut
vs   The like as 2ᵈ above.
Joseph Smith impleaded
with Alvin Smith

Unfortunately, if the "2d above" refers to two entries above this entry, the notation there simply also reads "the like." The entry immediately above this entry contains the following ruling:

> "The like having been duly ordered on motion of F. Smith Plain-
> tiffs Atty interlocutory judgment & that a writ of inquiry issue."

This may be what the court intended to reference, as both matters were being handled on appeal by Frederick Smith. If this is the case, then to make sense of this, one needs to understand the relationship between an "interlocutory judgment" and a "writ of inquiry."

An interlocutory judgment is

> one given in the course of a cause, before final judgment. When the action sounds in damages, and the issue is an issue in law, or when any issue in fact not tried by a jury is decided in favor of the plaintiff, then the judgment is that the plaintiff ought to recover his damages without specifying their amount; for, as there has been no trial by jury in the case, the amount of damages is not yet ascertained. The judgment is then said to be interlocutory. To ascertain such damages it is the practice to issue a writ of inquiry.[31]

And a writ of inquiry is "a writ directed to the sheriff of the county where the facts are alleged by the pleadings to have occurred, commanding him to inquire into the amount of damages sustained 'by the oath or affirmation of twelve good or lawful men of his county;' and to return such inquisition, when made, to the court."[32]

It would appear that the "plaintiff" would be Hurlbut, as indicated by the caption on the Docket Entry and in the *capias*. There is no evidence that the Smiths ever appeared during the appeal. This would have resulted in a default being entered in favor of Hurlbut. If that is the case, then it appears that the court of common pleas reversed the jury's finding for the Smiths in the justice court. However, unlike modern default judgments in which damage awards are based on the complaint, the successful party in this case

---

31. Bouvier, *Law Dictionary*, s.v. "interlocutory judgment," 550.
32. Bouvier, *Law Dictionary*, s.v. "writ of inquiry," 502.

would have been required to establish the amount of damage by admissible evidence. Hence, after receiving a reversal, the court of common pleas effectively remanded the case back to the local level to have the amount of damages determined. There is no record of any subsequent events related to this matter.

Conclusion

This case could be viewed as nothing more than an example of the frontier legal system in the early nineteenth century. The facts are not terribly compelling or important—the sale of some horses, a demand of payment for labor by some farmhands, and some offsetting claims for grain and seeds. These events were undoubtedly commonplace in early agricultural America. As such, this case might have remained in obscurity because of its commonness. But this is no ordinary case; its importance rests not only on its facts, but also on who its participants were.

Ironically, this case does not reveal as much about the Smith family as it does about how sympathetically, credibly, and reasonably Joseph Jr. and the Smith family may have been viewed in the eyes of their Palmyra neighbors in 1819. The case provides a window into a period of time that is rarely viewed, namely those early years when the Smiths lived in upstate New York, just a year or so before the profoundly complicating religious events that would result in estrangement of the Smiths and disbelief in the minds of many locals.

One might ask whether this case would have been treated differently if it had arisen even a year later, after the First Vision, or after any of Moroni's visits. Would Abraham Spears have hesitated before finding this young boy competent? Would the jurors, representing the Palymra community, have found his testimony less than credible?

This case stands as an undisputed account of how Joseph Jr., and his family, were regarded in Palmyra in 1819. The jurors, composed of the more affluent members of the community, found in favor of the Smiths' claims against a much more prominent family. Even more important, this same jury, in conjunction with the local justice of the peace, found the young boy Joseph Smith to be both a credible and competent witness—something that some dispute today. Yet, there it is. Found recently and nearly two centuries after it was decided, this case provides a judicial estimate of Joseph Jr.'s character, and that finding alone makes the case significant.

This article, in a different form, was published as "Joseph Smith's Introduction to the Law," Mormon Historical Studies 11, *no. 1 (Spring 2010).*

Chapter Four

Being Acquitted of a "Disorderly Person" Charge in 1826

Gordon A. Madsen

Was Joseph Smith Jr. ever convicted of a crime? With one exception, historians agree that the Prophet was cleared or never convicted in all cases in which criminal charges were laid against him. That one exception, a "disorderly person" charge made when Joseph was twenty years old, has been shrouded by partial and unclear historical documentation. Since the 1826 trial of Joseph Smith has been extensively commented upon, one might wonder what else is to be said about this blip in Mormon history. However, little has been done to put that trial into the legal context of that day and to examine the applicable statutory, procedural, and case law in force in New York in 1826. This chapter will attempt to do that and then reexamine the conclusions drawn by earlier writers.

In March 1826, upon the sworn complaint of one Peter Bridgeman, Joseph Smith was brought before Justice of the Peace Albert Neely in South Bainbridge, New York, on the charge of being a "disorderly person." The earliest-known reference to the trial appeared in an article written five years later in 1831 by A. W. Benton.[1] Forty-one years later, William D. Purple claimed to have generated his version from his memory and notes; he had been asked by Judge Neely to act as scribe for the trial.[2] Other accounts written

---

1. A. W. Benton, "Mormonites," *Evangelical Magazine and Gospel Advocate* 2 (April 9, 1831). Benton wrote from his purported memory, implying he was a witness to the proceedings.

2. W. D. Purple, "Joseph Smith, the Originator of Mormonism Historical Reminiscences of the Town of Afton," *The Chenango Union*, May 3, 1877, as quoted in Francis W. Kirkham, *A New Witness for Christ in America: The Book of Mormon*, 2 vols. (Independence,

by Charles Marshall and Daniel S. Tuttle were derived from some pages purportedly severed from Judge Neely's docket book by his niece, Miss Emily Pearsall.[3] Neither the "docket book" or the Purple or Pearsall notes have survived. The disparities and inconsistencies among these accounts were later analyzed by Fawn Brodie, Francis Kirkham, and Hugh Nibley, the latter two expressing skepticism about their authenticity.[4]

Then in 1971, the Reverend Wesley P. Walters discovered two bills in the basement of the Chenango County Sheriff's building in Norwich, New York.[5] These bills were among a cache of some 8,000 "Audits" or bills paid by Chenango County during the 1820–30 decades. The first was submitted by Justice Neely to Chenango County for his services for a series of trials he conducted in 1826. There are seven trials listed on Neely's bill, running from some time prior to March 20 through November 9. The page is age-worn and illegible in part.[6] Figure 1 is a partial reproduction with some names approximated. Figure 2 is the text of the bill submitted by the constable in the case, Philip De Zeng, which lists more than thirty lines of billed services, presumably rendered during 1826. Before considering the meaning of these two bills and what Wesley Walters (their discoverer) claims they tell us, let us first consider the relevant New York laws in 1826 and the charge alleged against Jospeh Smith in this matter.

The Charge

With what exactly was Joseph Smith charged? Judge Neely's bill simply indicates "misdemeanor," but Oliver Cowdery wrote that Joseph Smith was charged more specifically on this occasion with being a "disorderly person."[7]

Mo.: Zion's Printing and Publishing Co., 1959), 2:364. Purple appears as a party or witness in other Bainbridge cases: Benton does not.

3. C[harles] M[arshall], "The Original Prophet," *Fraser's Magazine* 7 (February 1873): 225–35 (published in London); republished in New York in *Eclectic Magazine* 17 (April 1873): 479–88, and again in the *Utah Christian Advocate,* January 1886. See Kirkham, *New Witness,* 2:474. The Tuttle account was first published in 1883 in *Schaaf-Herzog Encyclopedia of Religious Knowledge,* 2:1576–77.

4. Kirkham, *New Witness,* 1:475–92; 2:354–68, 370–500; Hugh Nibley, *The Myth Makers* (Salt Lake City: Bookcraft, 1961), 139–58.

5. W[esley] P. Walters, "Joseph Smith's Bainbridge, N.Y., Court Trials," *The Westminster Theological Journal* 36 (Winter 1974): 123; Marvin S. Hill, "Joseph Smith and the 1826 Trial: New Evidence and New Difficulties," *BYU Studies* 12 (Winter 1972): 224.

6. Copies of the originals are in the possession of the author.

7. Oliver Cowdery, "Letter VIII to W. W. Phelps," *Messenger and Advocate* 2 (October 1835): 201.

Figure 1: From Chenango County to Albert Neely, Jr.

People	Assault & Battery
vs.	

—— Brazee
Trial at G. A. Leadbetter's

Same	Justices
vs.	James Humphrey
Peter Brazee	Zechariah Tarbil [Tarbel]
	Albert Neely
Same	
vs.	To my fees in trial
John Sherman	of above cause 3.68

Same	Misdemeanor
vs.	
Joseph Smith	
The Glass Looker	To my fees in examination
March 20, 1826	of the above cause 2.68

. . .

Figure 2: Bill for Services by Constable Philip De Zeng

. . .
Serving Warrant on Joseph Smith & travel . . 1.25
Subpoenaing 12 Witnesses & travel 2.50
Attendance with Prisoner two days &
   1 night 1.75
Notifying two Justices . . . . 1.—
10 miles travel with Mittimus to take him . . . . 1.—
. . .

Benton agreed but characterized the basis for the charge as "sponging his living from [the public's] earnings."[8] Purple claimed that Joseph was charged with being a "vagrant, without visible means of livelihood."[9] Marshall and Tuttle called him a "disorderly person and an imposter."[10]

The statute that would seem to apply, enacted in 1813 by the New York State Legislature, reads as follows:

> That [1] all persons who threaten to run away and leave their wives or children to the city or town, and [2] all persons who shall unlawfully return to the city or town from whence they shall respectively have been legally removed by order of two justices of the peace, without bringing a certificate from the city or town whereto they respectively belong; and also [3] all persons who not having wherewith to maintain themselves, live idle without employment, and also [4] all persons who go about from door to door, or place themselves in the streets, highways or passages, to beg in the cities or towns where they respectively dwell, and [5] all jugglers [those who cheat or deceive by sleight of hand or tricks of extraordinary dexterity], and [6] all persons pretending to have skill in physiognomy, palmistry, or like crafty science, or pretending to tell fortunes, or to discover where lost goods may be found; ... and [7] all persons who run away and leave their wives and children whereby they respectively become chargeable to any city or town; and [8] all persons wandering abroad and lodging in taverns, beer-houses, out-houses, market-places, or barns, or in the open air, and not giving a good account of themselves, and [9] all persons wandering abroad and begging, and ... [10] all common prostitutes, shall be deemed and adjudged disorderly persons.[11]

Several of these ten provisions came from the classic definitions of a vagrant; however, in this statute vagrants are not classed separately, but are rather included with all the other people who are considered "adjudged disorderly persons." So there is no reason to conclude that the twenty-year-old Joseph was accused of being a vagrant. He had not made himself a financial burden to the community, wandered homelessly, begged, deceived by sleight

---

8. Kirkham, *New Witness,* 2:467.

9. Kirkham, *New Witness,* 2:364.

10. Kirkham, *New Witness,* 2:360.

11. *Revised Laws of New York* (1813), 1:114, sec. I.

of hand, or refused to work. By all accounts, he was employed by Josiah Stowell, which largely precludes a charge of vagrancy.

The two bills, however, provide little help in determining the nature of the charge brought against Joseph, beyond specifying that the offense was a misdemeanor. It is true that the judge, on the first bill, identifies Joseph as "the Glass Looker," but that entry is below Joseph's name rather than opposite where "Misdemeanor" appears, and in each of the other cases itemized, the offense is always listed opposite the accused's name rather than below it. Since this bill was a summary of fees for seven trials, the last of which is dated November 9, 1826, it was undoubtedly written some time after Joseph Smith's trial, and so this identifier may reflect perceptions outside of the trial itself. Indeed, there was no statutory or common law crime of "glass looking" then on the books, unless, of course, the wording in item 6 in the statute— "pretending to tell fortunes, or to discover where lost goods may be found"— was understood to include "glass looking." But even at that, being a "glass" looker might not have included the use of a seer "stone." Moreover, such practices were common enough that these activities would not, in and of themselves, have been considered criminal; only "pretending" or deceptively using such practices could give rise, under the statute, to a charge of disorderly conduct. Thus, "Glass Looker" is more likely a phrase of identification than the statement of a criminal charge in Judge Neely's bill. Similarly, the word "imposter" was not used in the statute to describe any criminal offense. So we are left with the charge of somehow being a disorderly person.

The Court

Was this trial conducted by a single justice of the peace or by a three-judge court of special sessions? If it was the latter, it is reasonable to assume this was a felony charge. Walters infers from the item in Constable De Zeng's bill, which lists "notifying two justices," that the trial was conducted before a Court of Special Sessions.[12] This brings us to an examination of the court system that existed in New York in the 1820s, and ample evidence suggests that this was a misdemeanor charge presided over by a single justice of the peace. Three courts are relevant to our purposes: justice courts, courts of special sessions, and courts of general sessions.

Four Justices of the Peace operated in Bainbridge in 1826: Albert Neely, James H. Humphrey, Zechariah Tarbel (sometimes Tarbell or Tarble) and Levi Bigelow. The first case shown on the Neely bill names three defendants

---

12. Walters, "Joseph Smith's Bainbridge Trials," 133.

The State Court System (NY)

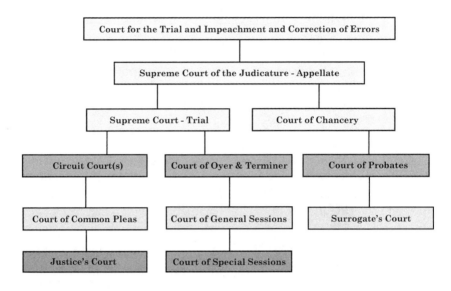

charged with Assault and Battery and also names the two additional Justices (Humphrey and Tarbel) who tried the case with him. The Joseph Smith case shows no co-Justices sitting in on his trial. All the other cases on the bill likewise name no fellow Justices joining in the trials. That Joseph Smith's name appears *only* on the Neely bill, which is prima facie evidence that his case was not heard before a three justice Court of Special Sessions.

Justice courts, or courts presided over by a single justice of the peace, were then (as such courts generally are today) the bottom rung on the legal ladder. A widely used treatise titled *The Justice's Manual*, first published in 1825, described the role of a justice of the peace.[13] Justices of the peace were not generally trained in law, but were appointed or elected from the more affluent gentlemen of a community and had limited original jurisdiction in criminal matters to literally "keep the peace"—to hear cases regarding trespass against persons and property, breaches of the peace, and misdemeanors (including vagrancy and disorderly persons). In criminal matters, justices of the peace could sentence offenders to "the bridewell, or house of correction, there to be kept at hard labour, ... for a term not exceeding sixty days, or until

---

13. Thomas Gladsby Waterman, *The Justice's Manual, or, A Summary of the Powers and Duties of Justices of Peace in the State of New York* (Binghamton, N.Y.: Morgan & Canoll, 1825).

the next general sessions [of the peace],"[14] with the provisos that a "common gaol [jail]" could be used in a county that had no bridewell or work house, and that any two justices (one being the committing justice) could discharge any offender if "they see cause."[15] They were also empowered to conduct bail hearings or in some instances preliminary examinations or preliminary hearings in certain felony cases. Where appropriate, the justice court could *bind over* such accused felons to the court of general sessions to stand trial.

On the rung above justice courts were the courts of special sessions, which were comprised of three justices of the peace sitting as one court. The statutes of 1813 redefined the jurisdiction of these courts and granted them power to try criminal offenses "under the degree of grand larceny," except where the accused posted bail within forty-eight hours of being charged and elected to be tried at the next session of the court of general sessions in the county, and special sessions courts could impose fines not exceeding twenty-five dollars and jail terms not exceeding six months.[16] These notions of limited jurisdiction are corroborated in the *Justice's Manual*. It says regarding courts of special sessions:

> This court is composed of three Justices, associated for the particular purpose of trying some person accused of an offense under the degree of grand larceny.
>
> The jurisdiction of this court is limited, by the statute, to cases of "petty larceny, misdemeanor, breach of the peace, or other criminal offence under the degree of grand larceny." The only point of difficulty, relative to jurisdiction, is, in determining what offences are under the degree of grand larceny. And I know of no rule by which the different degrees of criminality may be determined, except by the punishments directed. I therefore conclude that this court has not jurisdiction of any offence the punishment whereof *may be* imprisonment in the state prison; nor, where the term of imprisonment in the common gaol is fixed to exceed six months; nor where a fine is fixed to exceed $25.... If this rule be correct, the jurisdiction of a court of special sessions may be readily determined, in any supposable case, by reference to the punishment prescribed for the offence in question.[17]

---

14. Waterman, *Justice's Manual*, 116.

15. *Revised Laws of New York* (1813), 1:114–15, secs. I and II.

16. *Revised Laws of New York* (1813), 2:507–8, sec. IV.

17. Waterman, *Justice's Manual*, 200–1; italics in original.

The third and top-tier trial court was the court of general sessions and with the language of the *Justice's Manual* in mind, sometimes called county court. These courts were the general professional courts of the state, presided over by trained, full-time judges. They tried felony cases and reviewed and retried those cases appealed from either justice-of-the-peace courts or courts of special sessions.

Now, understanding the New York court system in 1826 and with the language of the *Justice's Manual* in mind, we return to Justice Neely's bill, where we see that the first item listed concerned a court of special sessions and the other two justices were James Humphry and Zechariah Tarbil. It was an "Assault & Battery" case, involving three defendants, two named Brazee, and a Sherman. Special-session court jurisdiction was probably invoked because the case involved multiple defendants and was a misdemeanor "under the degree of grand larceny."[18]

The provision in the disorderly persons statute states: "It shall and may be lawful for any justice of the peace to commit such disorderly persons (being thereof convicted before him by his own view, or by the confession of such offenders, respectively, or by the oath of one or more credible witness or witnesses) to the bridewell or house of correction."[19] Here, the *Justice's Manual* rightly speaks in the singular—"*a* justice of the peace *is* authorized to commit to the bridewell"—and the forms to be used that follow are all couched in first person singular and provide for a single signature. Conversely the forms suggested by the *Manual* to be used by courts of special sessions speak in the plural and require three signatures.[20] Since the statute limits the sentence to sixty days and speaks of the matter being tried before "him," and since the Neely bill shows no additional justices listed under "Misdemeanor" similar to their listing in the first case itemized on the bill, it follows that Joseph Smith's case was tried by Neely alone.

In light of all this information, what is the meaning of the De Zeng entry "Notifying two Justices"? I frankly do not know. Walters infers from this that the trial was conducted before a court of special sessions.[21] However, it is possible that De Zeng confused this case with the earlier three-justice court of special sessions. Or perhaps Neely first thought the Joseph Smith case needed to be heard by three justices and later changed his mind. In any event, the record is clear that no other justices are mentioned in Joseph's trial, either

---

18. Waterman, *Justice's Manual*, 200.

19. *Revised Laws of New York* (1813), 1:114, sec. 1.

20. Waterman, *Justice's Manual*, 116–20, 203–8; italics added.

21. Walters, "Joseph Smith's Bainbridge Trials," 133.

in the Neely bill, or the Pearsall notes, or the Purple account. Moreover, several other of Constable de Zeng's bills to Chenango County for both prior and subsequent years, shows the same "notifying Justices" or "notifying two Justices" wording when the cases to which the "notifying" language applied were in fact tried by a single Justice of the Peace. Whether de Zeng in those instances summoned several Justices before one agreed to take the case, or whether he assumed those cases were to be three justice hearings, when in fact they proved to be handled by a single Justice, as in the Joseph Smith case, who can say? All that can be said with certainty is that de Zeng charged the County for notifying two Justices, but none of the other Justices billed Chenango County for trying Joseph Smith. And finally, there is no indication that a jury trial was requested or waived, or any fee billed for summoning or swearing a jury. It thus appears safe to conclude that Joseph was tried by Neely in a simple justice court—indicating the charge was a mere misdemeanor, as the Neely bill on its face indicates.

The Meaning of the Term *Recognizance*

What is meant by the term *recognizances* found at the end of the Marshall rendering of the Pearsall notes? The full Neely bill of $2.68 in the Joseph Smith case is itemized as follows: "Costs: Warrant, 19c. Complaint upon oath, 25½c. Seven witnesses, 87½c. Recognisances [*sic*], 25c. Mittimus, 19c. Recognisances of witnesses, 75c. Subpoena, 18c.—$2.68."[22]

Recognizance or *recognize* was used interchangeably with *examination* or *examine* in the early 1800s, in much the same synonymous fashion as were the words *warrant* and *mittimus*. *To recognize* meant then (and sometimes even today) "to try; to *examine* in order to determine the truth of a matter."[23] On the other hand, the plural *recognizances* referred to types of bonds or undertakings. Sometimes it referred to bail used by nineteenth-century courts to guarantee attendance at court at a later time or more frequently used by justices of the peace to bond or "recognize" someone to keep the peace or to maintain good behavior. Walters, in his analysis of the trial, relies upon this meaning of the word. But *recognizance* or *recognize* meant "to examine." Indeed, other justice-of-the-peace bills scrutinized by Walters refer

---

22. C[harles] M[arshall], "The Original Prophet," 230.

23. John Bouvier, *Bouvier's Law Dictionary and Concise Encyclopedia,* 8th ed, by Francis Rawle, 3 vols. (St. Paul, Minn.: West Publishing, 1914), 3:2842; italics added.

to "recognizing two witnesses 0.50" (meaning a fifty-cent fee for examining two witnesses) or "recognizing three witnesses 0.75."[24]

Walters assumes that "Recognizance 25" on the Neely itemization refers to the fee for an appearance bond by Joseph Smith guaranteeing his coming to court and that "Recognisances of witnesses, 75c." refers to the fee for putting three witnesses under similar bond or recognizance to also appear at the future trial. Since by Walter's own reckoning the trial supposedly took place the very next day (the De Zeng entry states, "Attendance with Prisoner two days & 1 night"), there would be little need to bond witnesses for twenty-four hours and no opportunity for the prisoner to be "recognized" in the bail sense of the word.

It seems more reasonable to assume, therefore, that *recognizance* in Neely's bill refers to the fees for the examination of the defendant and witnesses. This is further corroborated by *The Justice's Manual*, which specifies the forms of such recognizances and requires that the accused and two sureties sign the same, that a transcript or summary of the testimony be reduced to writing, and that additional orders of transmittal to the next session of the court of general session be executed.[25] No such bonds or recognizances with additional signatures, or at least the naming of co-signing sureties, appear in the record.

None of the reports hints that the proceeding against Joseph Smith was a preliminary examination for a felony or other offense beyond Justice Neely's jurisdiction (as has been advanced by Dan Vogel as an alternative analysis[26]), and Neely's bill fits a fact situation suggesting he tried the matter himself. Therefore, "recognizance" as used in the bill must mean "examining" the witnesses and defendant, rather than binding them over for a trial to be conducted in a court of general sessions at a later time.

The Trial

Wesley Walters reconstructed the trial in these terms:

> When Joseph was arrested on the warrant issued by Albert Neely, he would have been brought before Neely for a preliminary examination to determine whether he should be released as innocent of the charges or, if the evidence seemed sufficient, brought to trial. During the examination Joseph's statement would be taken (probably not under oath), and witnesses for and against the

24. Walters, "Joseph Smith's Bainbridge Trials," 138 n. 28.

25. Waterman, *Justice's Manual*, 190–95.

26. Dan Vogel, "Rethinking the 1826 Judicial Decision," Mormon Scripture Studies, http://mormonscripturestudies.com/ch/dv/1826.asp (accessed December 5, 2013).

accused were sworn and examined. Both before and during the examination Joseph remained under guard, with Constable De Zeng in "attendance with Prisoner two days & 1 night," referring to the day of examination and the day and night preceding. Since the evidence appeared sufficient to show that Smith was guilty as charged, he was ordered held for trial. In such situations, if the defendant could not post bail the justice at his discretion could either order the arresting officer to continue to keep the prisoner in his custody, or he could commit him to jail on a warrant of "commitment for want of bail," sometimes referred to as a "mittimus." The latter appears to have been the fate of young Joseph since De Zeng's bill records "10 miles travel with Mittimus to take him"—and the wording should probably be completed by adding "to gaol." Shortly after this Joseph's bail was posted as the entry "recognizance 25" cents would indicate. The material witnesses, three in this instance, were meanwhile also put under recognizances to appear at the forth-coming Court of Special Sessions (Neely's "recognizances of witnesses 75" cents). The Court was summoned to meet by Justice Neely through Constable De Zeng's "notifying two Justices." At this point the course of events becomes somewhat difficult to trace, mainly because we lack the other two justices' bills which might clarify the trial proceedings. Probably what happened was that the Court of Special Sessions found young Smith guilty, as Neely records, but instead of imposing sentence, since he was a minor "he was designedly allowed to escape," as the Benton article expresses it. Perhaps an off-the-record proposition was made giving Joseph the option of leaving the area shortly or face sentencing, and it would explain why no reference appears in the official record to the sentencing of the prisoner. Another possibility, of course, is that Joseph jumped bail and when the Court of Special Sessions met they may have decided not to pursue the matter further, hoping the youth had learned his lesson. Dr. Purple, in any event, carried away the impression that "the prisoner was discharged, and in a few weeks left the town."[27]

In this reconstruction, Walters assumes a number of unsupported or unwarranted facts and procedures. First, he posits a preliminary hearing *and* a trial occurred on two successive days, the first before Justice Neely and the

---

27. Walters, "Joseph Smith's Bainbridge Trials," 139–41.

second before Neely and two unnamed additional justices. There are at least five reasons to reject that possibility:

(1) The court of special sessions' jurisdictional prerogatives exceeded the sentence limit prescribed by the Disorderly Persons statute, suggesting that such cases were rather tried by single justices of the peace.

(2) As noted previously, the Disorderly Persons statute speaks of a trial in language of a single justice. This is corroborated by the language in *The Justice's Manual,* prescribing the forms to be used, for example from the warrant form: "command you to take the said John Stiles, and him bring before *me.*"[28] That language left no room for a three-justice court.

(3) Both Dr. Purple and whoever made the notes ultimately delivered by Miss Pearsall to Marshall and Tuttle refer to one hearing only, and none of them suggests multiple justices sitting to hear the matter. Nor is there any purported transcript or notes of a second hearing.

(4) No additional justices of the peace are noted in the Neely bill opposite the Joseph Smith heading, as they were in the first assault-and-battery case.

(5) Courts of special session were to try those cases coming before them to a jury unless that right was waived by the accused. There is no hint in the bills, notes, or commentaries that a jury was either impaneled or waived.

Further, there is no basis for Walters's assumption that Neely found that "since the evidence appeared sufficient to show that Smith was guilty as charged, he was ordered held for trial," or for his assumption that "Recognizance 25" meant bail, posted after Joseph was first jailed. In a footnote, Walters himself appears to abandon that jail-and-bail notion by noting that the fee for constables to take prisoners to court was nineteen cents and to take them to jail was twenty-five cents. Constable De Zeng in this instance billed nineteen cents.[29] It should here be observed that the phrase *to take* meant "to arrest" or "to capture"; hence, "to take prisoner" could more probably mean the act of arresting rather than transporting him somewhere, especially since no place is mentioned.

---

28. Waterman, *Justice's Manual,* 117–18; italics added.
29. Walters, "Joseph Smith's Bainbridge Trials," 140 n. 36.

Walters assumes that the three witnesses were first examined and then put under "recognizance" to appear later at the supposed second hearing. But if that theory were to be reflected in Justice Neely's bill, there would be a charge for examining the witnesses *and* a charge for taking their bond to appear at a future time for trial. Only one such charge of twenty-five cents for the defendant and seventy-five cents for the three witnesses is listed. Also missing is any reference to the minimal bonds or recognizance forms signed either by the witnesses or by witnesses and their sureties. The far safer conclusion, as I maintain, is that "recognizance" as used in Neely's bill means "examining" defendant and witnesses.

From this point on, Walters's "reconstruction" is all admittedly supposition. He admits the "course of events becomes somewhat difficult to trace," largely, he speculates, because the "other two justices' bills" are missing—missing, as we have shown above, because there were no other justices.

Notwithstanding Walters's claim that the Pearsall notes were originally written by Purple and his acknowledgment that Purple's published account states that Smith was "discharged," Walters nonetheless declares that Smith was "probably" found guilty "as Neely records." Thereafter, Walters continues, Smith was either "designedly" allowed to escape because of his youth or given an "off-the-record" invitation to leave the county, or he jumped bail. And when the three justices convened a special session court, they forgot the whole matter, recognizance bonds and all, hoping the boy had "learned his lesson." This chain of unsupported hypotheses stretches credulity further at every link.[30]

Moreover, it cannot be maintained having abandoned the three justice court theory, argued instead that the trial was in reality a "Court of Inquiry," or what would be called today a "Preliminary Hearing" and that Joseph was "bound over" or ordered to appear in the Court of General Sessions (the Court of Common Pleas, when it is sitting on a criminal matter), but that he never appeared before that court. The threshold problem with that suggestion is that the New York Statute[31] together with the instructions in the

---

30. For example, it would make no sense whatever that Joseph appeared in Bainbridge within a matter of months after this trial to have Squire Tarbill marry him to Emma Hale on January 18, 1827, if, as Walters posits, Tarbill was one of the judges who supposedly gave Joseph "the option of leaving the area shortly or face sentencing." It makes even less sense if, as alternately suggested, Joseph had "jumped bail." Walters, "Joseph Smith's Bainbridge Trials," 139–41.

31. *Laws of New York,* vol. 2 (1813), 507, sec. II spells out the preliminary examination procedure for felonies or crimes, and sec. III explains the direct trial procedure for misdemeanors..

Justice's Manual[32] (a widely used instructional manual for New York Justices of the Peace) expressly provided that such hearings are available only in felony or "crimes" prosecutions—not misdemeanors.

The Pearsall and Purple Notes

So, what really happened? What can we draw from the statutory and case law, the bills, the admittedly incomplete and inconsistent "reports" of the note-takers, and the even more inconsistent conclusions of the commentators? Let us first resort to *The Justice's Manual* as a basis for judging the reliability of the Pearsall and Purple notes and their pretensions at being official. Purple claimed that Justice Neely was his friend and asked him to make notes of the trial. He also admitted telling the story repeatedly over the more than forty years before he submitted his article to the *Chenango Union* in May 1877.[33] Miss Pearsall, according to Tuttle, had torn her notes from her Uncle Albert Neely's docket book.[34]

How close does either come to meeting the requirements of a transcript of testimony required of a justice of the peace at that time? The statute provides that

> in all cases where any conviction shall be had before any court of special sessions, in pursuance of the act hereby amended, it shall be the duty of the justices holding such court of special sessions, to make a certificate of such conviction, *under their hands and seals,* in which shall be briefly stated the offence, conviction and judgment thereon; and the said justices shall within forty days after such conviction had, cause such certificate to be filed in the office of the clerk of the county in which the offender shall be convicted, and such certificate, *under the hands and seals of such justices,* or any two of them, and so filed, or the exemplification thereof by such clerk, under his seal of office, shall be good and legal evidence in any court in this state, to prove the facts contained in such certificate or exemplification.[35]

---

32. Waterman, *Justice's Manual,* 192–95.

33. Quoted in Kirkham, *New Witness,* 2:362–64.

34. Quoted in Walters, "Joseph Smith's Bainbridge Trials," 134.

35. *Laws of New York, Forty-third Session* (1820), 235–36, sec. II; italics added.

The Justice's Manual states that in implementing this statute

> upon this judgment, the court are [*sic*] required to make a certificate of the conviction, under their hands and seals, "in which shall be briefly stated the offence, conviction and judgment thereon"; and within 40 days thereafter cause this certificate to be filed in the office of the clerk of the county.

The *Manual* then goes on to add this significant language:

> Before the passing of this act, the record of conviction, before a court of special sessions, was required to be drawn with much particularity and precision; to show not only the jurisdiction of the court, but also the regularity of their proceedings.[36]

So if Walters is correct, and a court of special sessions convened, and the Pearsall notes were "The Official Trial Record" (as he maintains), where is the certification "under their hands and seals" wherein is "briefly stated the offence, conviction and judgment thereon"? The Purple notes are equally lacking such certification. On the other hand, if (as I maintain) Justice Neely alone tried the matter, and if a conviction resulted, far more particularity would have been needed in such notes demonstrating jurisdiction, the regularity of the proceedings, the conviction, and the sentence. In either event, the record of conviction would have needed to be filed with the county clerk within forty days. No such record has to date been unearthed in the office of the Clerk of Chenango County.

But what can be learned from the two accounts? Both suggest that some sort of proceeding took place. The Pearsall account lists Peter Bridgeman as complainant; the Purple notes say the complainants were Josiah Stowell's "sons." Both accounts begin with Joseph Smith being examined. Purple's account is a first-person narrative with observations interspersed. The Pearsall notes purport to be summaries of testimony. Two witnesses, Josiah Stowell and Jonathan Thompson, together with the accused, are common to both accounts. Purple adds Joseph Smith Sr., and Pearsall adds Horace Stowell, Arad Stowell, and a Mr. McMaster as witnesses. Since the Neely itemization at the end of the Pearsall account notes the presence of the defendant and "three witnesses," modern readers are left to conjecture as to who testified besides Joseph Smith, Josiah Stowell, and Jonathan Thompson.[37]

---

36. Waterman, *Justice's Manual*, 204–5.
37. Kirkham, *New Witness*, 2:361, 365.

Clearly, then, the Purple and Pearsall accounts do not pass muster as reproductions of court transcripts of testimony. Moreover, there are several inconsistencies and discrepancies between them. Is there anything in them that might help to clarify the charge of disorderly person?

The Elements of the Crime

What were the elements of proof that Justice Neely would have to find in order to rule Joseph Smith guilty of being a disorderly person? From the common law, or accumulated "case law" as it sometimes is called, there are some fundamental elements required in any criminal prosecution. Case law is comprised of opinions of appellate courts, but one would not expect to find a large number of disorderly person convictions reaching the Court of Appeals of New York, or other appellate courts, for that matter, for the simple reason that the class of people charged with this offense are unlikely to be able to pay for appeals. Even so, a few cases of a related nature do appear in the early New York casebooks, called *Reports,* that do shed some light on the subject.

For example, the 1810 case of *People v. Babcock* has some relevance, establishing that private frauds were not criminal. In that case, the accused obtained by false pretenses from one Rufus Brown a release of an eighteen-dollar judgment on the representation that he would pay ten dollars cash and give his promissory note for the remaining eight dollars. Having received the release, he absconded without paying the cash or giving his note. The trial court convicted him of the crime of "Cheat." The Court of Appeals of New York, reversing the conviction, said:

> The case of the *King v. Wheatley* (2 Burr. 1125) established the true boundary between frauds that were, and those that were not indictable at common law. That case required such a fraud as would affect the *public;* such a deception that common prudence and care were not sufficient to guard against it as the using of false weights and measures, or false tokens, or where there was a conspiracy to cheat.[38]

This case was repeatedly cited in later New York rulings and stood for the proposition that private frauds were not criminally indictable. This rule was expressly repeated in *The Justice's Manual.* For example, "*Fraud* is an offence at common law. To constitute this offence, however, the act done must effect

---

38. 7 *Johnson's Reports,* 201–5 (1810), 204; italics added.

the public—and be such an act as common prudence would not be sufficient to guard against; as the using of false weights and measures, or false tokens, or where there has been a conspiracy to cheat."[39]

An earlier and equally often cited case, *People v. C. & L. Sands,* establishes another principle—that in order to be actionable the crime must be "mischief already done."[40] In this case, the accuseds were charged with the offense of being a nuisance for keeping fifty barrels of gunpowder in a certain building near the dwelling houses of "diverse good citizens, and near a certain public street," and also of "transporting 10 casks of gunpowder through the streets of Brooklyn in a cart." After conviction in the court below, the defendants appealed. The Court of Appeals reversed the decision and adopted the holding of an English case that ruled "a powder magazine was not itself a nuisance, but that to render it such, there must be 'apparent danger or mischief already done.'"[41]

Another relevant principle is familiar to most judges and attorneys under the Latin phrase *mens rea,* meaning "criminal state of mind." This principle is succinctly stated in *The Justice's Manual* also: "To constitute a crime against human laws, there must be, first, a vicious [*sic*] will; and, secondly, *an unlawful act* consequent upon such vicious will."[42]

Applying the principles of these three cases just cited, then, Justice Neely was obliged to find that some public rather than private fraud or harm had taken place; that implicit in Joseph Smith's activities there was either some apparent danger or mischief already done; and that the acts complained of were willful or done with a "vicious" or criminal state of mind.

The Evidence

With that measure, what did the evidence show? Joseph Smith was reputed to be able to look into a stone and discover lost treasure. Let us assume, for argument's sake, that this is close enough to come within the statute's reference to "where lost or stolen goods may be found." The Pearsall notes state that

> at Palmyra he had frequently ascertained in that way where lost property was, of various kinds; that he has occasionally been in the habit of looking through this stone to find lost property for three years, but of late had pretty much given it up on account

---

39. See, for example, People v. Miller, 14 *Johnson's Reports,* 371 (1817).

40. 1 *Johnson's Reports,* 78 (1806).

41. 1 *Johnson's Reports,* 85 (1806).

42. Waterman, *Justice's Manual,* 167; italics in original.

[of] its injuring his health, especially his eyes—made them sore; that he did not solicit business of this kind, and had always rather declined having anything to do with this business.[43]

Purple quotes no testimony directly but rather gives a lengthy recital of how Joseph obtained his stone. He claims Joseph exhibited the stone to the court. Earlier in his narrative, he alludes to Joseph's use of the stone as a means of bilking Stowell and others, but it is far from clear that those remarks pretend to be a summary of Joseph Smith's testimony and makes them a sort of preamble.[44]

The pivotal testimony, in my view, was that of Josiah Stowell. Both accounts agree on the critical facts. The Pearsall account states: "[Joseph Smith] had been employed by him [Stowell] to work on [the] farm part of [the] time; … that he positively knew that the prisoner could tell, and professed the art of seeing those valuable treasures through the medium of said stone."[45] The Purple account states:

> Justice Neely soberly looked at the witness and in a solemn, dignified voice, said, "Deacon Stowell, do I understand you as swearing before God, under the solemn oath you have taken, that you *believe* the prisoner can see by the aid of the stone fifty feet below the surface of the earth, as plainly as you can see what is on my table?" "Do I *believe* it?" says Deacon Stowell, "do I believe it? No, it is not a matter of belief. I positively know it to be true."[46]

From the array of the other witnesses there was no testimony that any of them parted with any money or other thing of value to Joseph Smith. Only Josiah Stowell did so, and then for part-time work on his farm in addition to services rendered in pursuit of treasure. More to the point, he emphatically denied that he had been deceived or defrauded. On the contrary, he "positively" knew the accused could discern the whereabouts of subterranean objects. In short, only Josiah Stowell had any legal basis to complain, *and he was not complaining.* Hence Purple's concluding comment, "It is hardly necessary to say that, as the testimony of Deacon Stowell could not be impeached, the prisoner was discharged, and in a few weeks he left the town."[47] Indeed, following the law, Justice Neely had no other choice.

---

43. Kirkham, *New Witness*, 2:360.
44. Kirkham, *New Witness*, 2:364–65.
45. Kirkham, *New Witness*, 2:360.
46. Kirkham, *New Witness*, 2:366.
47. Kirkham, *New Witness*, 2:368.

The Outcome

It could be argued that Justice Neely may have had no training in law and therefore that the precedents and principles I have advanced were not part of his training or experience. Even if that were so, and that all he had as a minimum were the statutes under which the charge was tried together with *The Justice's Manual*, the same result of acquittal would have been mandated.

As confirmation that this was in fact the outcome, and as noted previously, the statute required the justice upon conviction to commit the defendant "to the bridewell, or house of correction, of such city or town, there to be kept at hard labour, for any time not exceeding sixty days, or until the next general sessions of the peace to be holden in and for the city or county in which such offence shall happen."[48] And, as also noted, such a sentencing would have needed to be certified by Judge Neely and filed in the county clerk's office within forty days. Moreover, Neely's bill requesting payment would have had an additional item under a heading of "Warrant for commitment—$1.00," which is not there, and Constable De Zeng's bill for taking Joseph Smith to jail would have been increased by twenty-five cents. The "bridewell" or poor house was located in MacDonough, a town some 17 miles north and west of Bainbridge, and thus the trip there would have added $3.50 to his bill. All those additions are missing from the bills. Moreover, the database of the names of all the people who were sentenced to the poor house in the 1820s mentions eight so sentenced in 1826. The twenty-year-old Joseph Smith was not among that number. There is additional statutory language following that last quote that places a continuing duty on the justice to discharge convicted disorderly persons from the house of corrections earlier than the maximum sixty days. So unless Judge Neely did, in fact, discharge the prisoner, Neely had a continuing responsibility regarding Smith, about which the record is silent. Indeed, an argument could be advanced that the absence of these many formalities shows that Justice Neely, knowing that he acquitted the prisoner, also knew that there was no need to formalize a record.

Against these strong indications that Joseph Smith must have been acquitted, there remains only the concluding statement of the Pearsall record, "And thereupon the Court finds the defendant guilty."[49] I believe this statement is an afterthought supplied by whoever subsequently handled the notes and is not a reflection of what occurred at the trial. This view is buttressed by the curious fact that all through the Pearsall notes, Joseph Smith is referred

---

48. Waterman, *Justice's Manual*, 116.
49. Kirkham, *New Witness*, 2:360–62.

to only as the "prisoner." Then for the first time, in this final sentence, he is called the "defendant."

Conclusion

What can be inferred about this experience? The foregoing considerations lead me to conclude that in 1826 Joseph Smith was indeed charged and tried for being a disorderly person and that he was acquitted. Whatever the gist of that charge, he was found guilty of no crime. Indeed, perhaps Oliver Cowdery, who either served as a justice of the peace or practiced as a lawyer from 1837 until his death in 1848, had it just about right. He wrote in 1835, "While in that country, some very officious person complained of him as a disorderly person, and brought him before the authorities of the county; but there being no cause of action he was honorably acquitted."[50]

This updated article was originally published as "Joseph Smith's 1826 Trial: The Legal Setting," BYU Studies 30, no. 2 (1990): 91–108.

---

50. *Messenger and Advocate* 2 (October 1835): 201.

Postscript: Joseph Acquitted Again in 1830

In June/July 1830, Joseph was again charged with being a disorderly person in two cases, the first in South Bainbridge, Chenango County, and the second in Colesville, Broome County, on successive days.

The first case is described by Richard Bushman as follows:

> Doctor A. W. Benton of Chenango County, whom Joseph Knight called a "catspaw" of a group of vagabonds, brought charges against Joseph as a disorderly person. On June 28, he was carried off to court in South Bainbridge by constable Ebenezer Hatch, trailed by a mob that Hatch thought planned to waylay them en route. When a wheel came off the constable's wagon, the mob nearly caught up, but, working fast, the two men replaced it in time and drove on....
>
> The nature of the charges brought against Joseph in the court of Justice Joseph Chamberlain of Chenango County is not entirely clear. Joseph Smith said it was for "setting the country in an uproar by preaching the Book of Mormon," ... but Joseph Knight Sr. said Benton swore out the warrant for Joseph's "pretending to see under ground," going back to the old money-digging charges of the 1826 trial....
>
> Joseph Knight hired James Davidson to defend the Prophet, but Davidson ... advised engaging John Reed as well, a local farmer noted for his speaking ability. Reed later said that Joseph "was well known for truth and uprightness; that he moved in the first circles of community, and he was often spoken of as a young man of intelligence, and good morals." ... The hearing dragged on until night, when Justice Chamberlain, whom Reed considered a man of "discernment," acquitted Joseph.[51]

The bills of Justice of the Peace Joseph P. Chamberlain and Constable Ebenezer Hatch were among the Audits of Chenango County noted in footnote 6 above. Chamberlain's bill shows no reference to a commitment to the bridewell nor an item showing he required a Peace Bond of

---

51. Richard Lyman Bushman, with Jed Woodward, *Joseph Smith: Rough Stone Rolling* (New York: Alfred A. Knopf, 2005), 116–17.

the Defendant. Hatch's bill shows no mileage to transport Joseph to the bridewell at MacDonough. There is considerable other reminiscence and corroborating material to reconstruct those trials, which again supports the conclusion that Joseph was acquitted.

The second case was tried before a three justice of the Peace court—a Court of Special Sessions. Bushman continues his description of this second proceeding with these words:

> Joseph had no sooner heard the verdict than a constable from neighboring Broome County served a warrant for the same crimes. The constable hurried Joseph off on a fifteen-mile journey without a pause for a meal....
>
> At ten the next morning, Joseph was in court again, this time before three justices who formed a court of special sessions with the power to expel him from the county.... Reed said witnesses were examined until 2 a.m., and the case argued for another two hours.[52]

One of the judges in that court was Joel K. Noble, who wrote his memory of that trial on several occasions. The first known publication was in 1832, quoting from a letter from a "gentleman in Windsor, Broome Co., N. Y.," dated August 30, 1832.[53] Here, the warrant was for "breach of the peace against the state of New York, by looking through a certain stone to find hid treasures." In the newspaper article, Noble reports some of the statements by witnesses and at other points summarizes or interprets their testimony. Because the lawyers began their case by trying to show that Joseph had taken money from widows and Church members, it appears that they understood that the crime of being a "disorderly person" needed to involve direct evidence of fraud on the public. Nevertheless, their argument still failed because there was testimony that Joseph had not looked "in the glass within the space of two years last past." Noble's conclusion thus reads: "Joseph Smith, jr. was discharged; he had not looked in the glass for two years to find money, &c.,—hence it was outlawed," or in other words, the cause of action was barred by the statue of limitations and was dismissed completely.

---

52. Bushman, *Rough Stone Rolling*, 17.

53. "Mormonism," *New England (Boston) Christian Herald*, November 7, 1832, 22–23; and reprinted in *(Limerick, Maine) Morning Star*, December 16, 1832.

Chapter Five

Securing the Book of Mormon Copyright in 1829

Nathaniel Hinckley Wadsworth

By the beginning of July 1829, Joseph Smith had completed his translation of the Book of Mormon.[1] One year removed from the harrowing loss of the initial 116 pages of the translation in 1828,[2] he was determined to not lose this work again, in any sense. On June 11, 1829, Joseph deposited, with or had delivered to the clerk of the Northern District Court of New York, a single, printed page (fig. 2) that resembled what would become the title page of the 1830 Book of Mormon, in order to secure a copyright to the work.[3] The court clerk, Richard Ray Lansing, generated the official executed copyright form, which he retained; his record book was eventually deposited in the Library of Congress and was discovered by researchers in December 2004 (fig. 3).

A perfected copyright—the legal evidence of a property right in a creative work—would ensure that Joseph alone had the authority to publish the Book of Mormon. Securing the copyright protected the text of this book of scripture and was seen as a validation of the impending appearance of this work. In October 1829, Joseph wrote from Pennsylvania to Oliver Cowdery concerning the

---

1. David Whitmer stated that the translation was completed on July 1, 1829. *Kansas City Daily Journal,* June 5, 1881, cited in Larry C. Porter, "A Study of the Origins of The Church of Jesus Christ of Latter-day Saints in the States of New York and Pennsylvania, 1816–1831" (PhD diss., Brigham Young University, 1971; BYU Studies and Joseph Fielding Smith Institute for Latter-day Saint History, 2000), 96.

2. Lucy Mack Smith, *Lucy's Book: A Critical Edition of Lucy Mack Smith's Family Memoir,* ed. Lavina Fielding Anderson (Salt Lake City: Signature Books, 2001), 408–19.

3. Copyright Records, June 11, 1829, U.S. District Court for the Northern District of New York 1826–1831, volume 116, Rare Book and Special Collections Division, Library of Congress.

Book of Mormon: "There begins to be a great call for our books in this country. The minds of the people are very much excited when they find that there is a copyright obtained and that there is really a book about to be produced."[4]

Joseph may have also seen the copyright as a help in recouping the considerable costs of producing the book. Another publisher could have cut into sales, but a copyright would help prevent such problems.

Most historians have treated Joseph's June 11 filing as the sole event necessary to vest in him all legal rights to the Book of Mormon.[5] Indeed, in January 1830, he successfully asserted his rights against Abner Cole, an opportunistic editor who pirated selections from the Book of Mormon and printed them in his newspaper.[6] However, more than the mere filing of the title page with the clerk of the court was required to vest full copyright protection in Joseph, and his efforts to secure a federal copyright are probably not why Joseph succeeded against Cole. Indeed, the young prophet probably did not meet all five of the federal law's requirements for a valid copyright, as discussed below. Joseph's legal victory over Cole was more likely premised on common law rights that Joseph held in the *unpublished* manuscript simply by virtue of having created the work.

Copyright Laws in Nineteenth-Century America

Before turning to Joseph Smith's clash with Abner Cole, readers need a general understanding of the copyright laws in the United States during the early nineteenth century. That understanding requires one to know the difference between statutory law and common law.

Statutory law is defined as "the body of law derived from statutes rather than from constitutions or judicial decisions." It consists of all the written laws created by the legislative bodies of governments. *Common law* is "the body of law derived from judicial decisions, rather than from statutes or constitutions."[7] Historically, common law was believed to consist of legal

---

4. Joseph Smith Jr. to Oliver Cowdery, October 22, 1829, in Michael Hubbard Mackay et al., ed., *Documents, Volume 1: July 1828–June 1831,* vol. 1 of the Documents series of *The Joseph Smith Papers,* ed. Dean C. Jessee, Ronald K. Esplin, and Richard Lyman Bushman (Salt Lake City: Church Historian's Press, 2013), 97.

5. See, for example, Richard Lyman Bushman, *Joseph Smith: Rough Stone Rolling* (New York: Alfred A. Knopf, 2005), 80; Edwin Brown Firmage and Richard Collin Mangrum, *Zion in the Courts: A Legal History of The Church of Jesus Christ of Latter-day Saints, 1830–1900* (Chicago: University of Illinois Press, 1988), 50.

6. Smith, *Lucy's Book,* 470–75.

7. *Black's Law Dictionary,* 8th ed. (St. Paul, Minn.: Thomson/West, 2004), 1452, s.v. "statutory law," 293, s.v. "common law."

truths that existed independently but were considered inarticulate until put into words by a judge. Where statutory law did not answer a question in a particular case, a judge might turn to common law and could decide the issue "in accordance with morality and custom," and later judges would regard this decision as precedent. In 1829 both statutory law and common law provided copyright protections to an author's work—statutory law applied to both published and unpublished works, and common law applied only to unpublished works.

As with most areas of U.S. law, the antecedents of these copyright laws can be traced back to England. The first copyright act, passed in England in 1709, was the Statute of Anne. Prior to the Statute of Anne, the Stationers' Company, a guild of printers, held perpetual copyrights in the works it published.[8] The new act reversed that and vested the copyright in the authors of the works. In addition, rather than preserving the perpetual nature of copyrights, the Statute of Anne granted authors the sole right to print and sell their works, subject to certain conditions, for a period of only fourteen years.[9] Many authors and publishers took the position that this statute was merely an appendage to a common law right that gave authors lifetime ownership in their creative works. In 1774, however, the House of Lords ruled against this argument in the case *Donaldson v. Beckett*, declaring that no common law right of copyright existed. The statute alone granted authors rights in their published works. A similar statutory scheme was later adopted in America.

In 1783, the Continental Congress, lacking the authority to make a federal copyright law, recommended that each state establish its own copyright law. Following the pattern set forth in the Statute of Anne, Congress recommended that authors be given rights to their works for at least fourteen years. Most states complied with the request of Congress, including New York in 1786. Trouble soon arose, however, because copyright protection in one state could not guarantee an author's protection in another state. Moreover, inconsistencies from one state to another demonstrated that the states could not "separately make effectual provision for [copyrights]."[10] Solving this problem was important enough that copyright law was covered in the United States

8. John Tehranian, "Et Tu, Fair Use? The Triumph of Natural-Law Copyright," *University of California at Davis Law Review* 38 (February 2005): 465, 467–68.

9. An Act for the Encouragement of Learning by Vesting the Copies of Printed Books in the Authors or Purchasors of such Copies during the Times Therein Mentioned, 1709, 8 Ann., c. 21 (Eng.).

10. James Madison, No. 43, in Alexander Hamilton, John Jay, and James Madison, *The Federalist*, ed. George W. Carey and James McClellan, Gideon edition (Indianapolis: Liberty Fund, 2001), 222.

Constitution, ratified in 1789, through the granting of power to the United States Congress to enact federal copyright law.

Under the Constitution, the states ceded to the federal government the power "to promote the Progress of Science and useful Arts, by securing for limited Times to Authors and Inventors the exclusive Right to their respective Writings and Discoveries."[11] Under this authority, Congress enacted the first federal copyright statute in 1790 (see fig. 1).[12] The Copyright Act of 1790 granted to "the author and authors of any map, chart, book or books ... the sole right and liberty of printing, reprinting, publishing and vending such map, chart, book or books, for the ... term of fourteen years from the time of recording the title thereof in the [district court] clerk's office."[13] The copyright was renewable for an additional fourteen years, provided the author met certain conditions. The disparate state copyright statutes were preempted as the federal government exercised full authority to create statutory copyright law.

The protections afforded by this federal statute went further than some state protections.[14] Under the new law, after an author or proprietor (a person who had acquired the rights from the author) had secured the copyright to a book, any other person who printed or published the work without consent of the author or proprietor, or who knowingly sold unauthorized copies, was required to forfeit all such copies to the author or proprietor.[15] The offender was also required to "pay the sum of fifty cents for every sheet which shall be found in his or their possession," with one-half of the payment going to the copyright holder and the other to the federal government.[16] If an author failed to do all that was necessary to secure a copyright in a book, he or she could still print and sell it, but the statute would not preclude others from likewise printing and selling the work.

Some lawyers argued that this federal statute functioned concurrently with the common law in protecting an author's rights in his or her creative

---

11. U.S. Constitution, art. 1, sec. 8, par. 8.

12. An Act for the Encouragement of Learning, by Securing the Copies of Maps, Charts, and Books, to the Authors and Proprietors of Such Copies, during the Times Therein Mentioned (May 31, 1790), 1st Cong., 2d sess., ch. 15, in *Statutes at Large of United States of America, 1789–1873*, 17 vols. (Washington, D.C.: [various publishers], 1845–73), 1:124 (hereafter cited as 1790 Act).

13. 1790 Act, ch. 15, sec. 1, *Stat.*, 1:124.

14. The New York law, for example, would permit another to publish an author's work if the author refused to publish a sufficient number of copies or charged an unreasonably high price for his books. An Act to Promote Literature (April 29, 1786), sess. 9, ch. 54. *Laws of New York*, 299.

15. 1790 Act, ch. 15, sec. 2, *Stat.*, 1:124–25.

16. 1790 Act, ch. 15, sec. 2, *Stat.*, 1:125.

Figure 1. Provisions from the U.S. Copyright Law in Effect in 1829

1790 SEC. 1. Any person or persons, being a citizen or citizens of these United States, or residents therein, his or their executors, administrators or assigns, who hath or have **purchased or legally acquired** the copyright of any such map, chart, book or books, in order to print, reprint, publish or vend the same, shall have the sole right and liberty of printing, reprinting, publishing and vending such map, chart, book or books for the term of **fourteen years** from the recording the title thereof in the clerk's office, as is herein after directed: And that **the author** and authors of any map, chart, book or books, for the like term of fourteen years from the time of recording the title thereof in the clerk's office as aforesaid. And if, at the expiration of the said term, the author or authors, or any of them, be living, and a citizen or citizens of these United States, or resident therein, the same exclusive right shall be continued to him or them, his or their executors, administrators or assigns, for the **further term** of fourteen years: *Provided*, he or they shall cause the title thereof to be a second time recorded and published in the same manner as is herein after directed, and that within six months before the expiration of the first term of fourteen years aforesaid.

SEC. 2. If any other person or persons, from and after the recording the title of any map, chart, book or books, and publishing the same as aforesaid, and within the times limited and granted by this act, shall print, reprint, publish, or import, or cause to be printed, reprinted, published, or imported from any foreign kingdom or state, any copy or copies of such map, chart, book or books, **without the consent** of the author or proprietor thereof, first had and obtained in writing, signed in the presence of two or more credible witnesses; or knowing the same to be so printed, reprinted, or imported, shall publish, sell, or expose to sale, or cause to be published, sold or exposed to sale, any copy of such map, chart, book or books, without such consent first had and obtained in writing as aforesaid, then such offender or offenders shall **forfeit all and every copy** and copies of such map, chart, book or books, and all and every sheet and sheets, being part of the same, or either of them, to the author or proprietor of such map, chart, book or books, who shall forthwith destroy the same: And every such offender and offenders shall also forfeit and **pay** the sum of fifty cents for every sheet which shall be found in his or their possession, either reprinted or printing, published, imported or exposed to sale, contrary to the true intent and meaning of this act, the one moiety [half] thereof to the author or proprietor of such map, chart, book or books who shall sue for the same, and the other moiety [half] thereof to and for the use of the United States, wherein the same is cognizable.

SEC. 3. No person shall be entitled to the benefit of the act, in cases where any map, chart, book or books, hath or have been already printed and published, unless he shall first deposit, and in all other cases, unless he shall before publication **deposit a printed copy** of the title of such map, chart, book or books, in the clerk's office of the district court where the author or proprietor shall reside: And the clerk of such court is hereby directed and required to **record the same** forthwith, in a book to be kept by him for that purpose, in the words following, (giving a copy thereof to the said **author or proprietor**, under the seal of the court, if he shall require the same.) "District of ____ to wit: *Be it remembered,* That on the ____ day of ____ in the ____ year of the independence of the United States of America, A.B. of the said district, hath deposited in this office the title of a map, chart, book or books, (as the case may be) the right whereof he claims as author or proprietor, (as the case may be) in the words following, to wit: [here insert the title] in conformity to the act of the Congress of the United States, intituled 'An act for the encouragement of learning, by securing the copies of maps, charts, and books, to the authors and proprietors of such copies, during the times therein mentioned.' C.D. clerk of the district of _____." For which the said clerk shall be entitled to receive **sixty cents** from the said author or proprietor, and sixty cents for every copy under seal actually given to such author or proprietor as aforesaid. And such author or proprietor shall, within two months from the date thereof, cause a copy of the said record to be **published in one or more of the newspapers** printed in the United States for the space of four weeks.

SEC. 4. The author or proprietor of any such map, chart, book or books, shall, within six months after the publishing thereof, **deliver**, or cause to be delivered to the Secretary of State **a copy** of the same....

SEC. 6. That any person or persons who shall print or publish any manuscript, without the consent and approbation of the author or proprietor thereof, ... shall be liable to suffer and pay to the said author or proprietor all damages occasioned by such injury, to be recovered by a special action on the case founded upon this act, in any court having cognizance thereof.

1802 Supp., SEC. 1.... In addition ... he shall ... give information by causing **the copy of the record**, which, by [the 1790 act] he is required to publish in one or more of the newspapers, **to be inserted at full length** in the title-page or in the page immediately following the title of every such book or books. **[Boldings added.]**

works. But, the United States Supreme Court rejected that argument in 1834 in the case *Wheaton v. Peters,* holding that no common law copyright existed in *published* works.[17] At the same time, the Supreme Court accepted the commonly held position that common law copyright protection existed for *unpublished* works:

> That an author, at common law, has a property in his manuscript, and may obtain redress against any one who deprives him of it, or by improperly obtaining a copy endeavors to realise a profit by its publication, cannot be doubted; but this is a very different right from that which asserts a perpetual and exclusive property in the future publication of the work, after the author shall have published it to the world.[18]

Thus, in affirming an author's property interest in his unpublished manuscript, the *Wheaton* decision established a principle of copyright law under the common law, according to which Joseph Smith could have successfully asserted copyright protection regarding the Book of Mormon before, but not after, the book's publication. After publication, Joseph would have had to rely on compliance with the federal statute.

Obtaining a Federal Statutory Copyright

To secure a copyright under the federal statute, Joseph Smith would have had to meet all the statute's requirements. The 1790 copyright law, as amended in 1802, granted an author the copyright in a work commencing at the time the title was filed in the clerk's office, but more than that initial step was required. No person was "entitled to the benefit of this act" unless that person satisfied the following five requirements:[19]

(1) Give notice to the clerk: "Deposit a printed copy of the title of such map, chart, book or books, in the clerk's office of the district court where the author or proprietor shall reside."[20]

(2) Pay the clerk: "Sixty cents" for the clerk's preparation of the copyright certificate and "sixty cents for every copy under seal actually given to such author or proprietor."[21]

---

17. Wheaton v. Peters, 33 U.S. 591 (Supreme Court of the United States 1834).
18. Wheaton v. Peters, 657.
19. 1790 Act, ch. 15, sec. 3, *Stat.,* 1:125.
20. 1790 Act, ch. 15, sec. 3, *Stat.,* 1:125.
21. 1790 Act, ch. 15, sec. 3, *Stat.,* 1:125.

(3)   Give full notice in the book: "Give information by causing the copy of the record [the clerk's certificate] ... to be inserted at full length in the title-page or in the page immediately following the title of every such book or books."[22]

(4)   Give notice to the public: "Within two months from the date [of the certificate], cause a copy of the said record to be published in one or more of the newspapers printed in the United States for the space of four weeks."[23]

(5)   Provide a public copy of the book: "Within six months after the publishing [of the book], deliver, or cause to be delivered to the Secretary of State a copy of the same, to be preserved in his office."[24]

Evidence Relevant to Joseph Smith's Compliance with the Statutory Requirements

Joseph Smith clearly satisfied the first and third requirements, and presumably the second. However, he may well have fallen short regarding the fourth and fifth requirements.

Requirement 1. Richard Ray Lansing, clerk of the United States District Court for the Northern District of New York, processed Joseph's filing for the Book of Mormon copyright in June 1829. He gave to Joseph a signed office copy of the copyright application, which has been held for many years in the archives of the Church in Salt Lake City and published on occasion. The official court-executed copy of the copyright form and the accompanying "title" page were recently located in the Library of Congress (see figs. 2, 3).[25] Requirement 1 was fully met.

It would be interesting to know more about how and where the filing with Lansing was accomplished. Joseph Smith's personal record simply states that he went to Palmyra, New York; secured a copyright; and agreed to pay Egbert Grandin three thousand dollars to print five thousand copies of the

---

22. An Act Supplementary to an Act, Intituled "An Act for the Encouragement of Learning, by Securing the Copies of Maps, Charts, and Books to the Authors and Proprietors of Such Copies during the Time Therein Mentioned," and Extending the Benefits Thereof to the Arts of Designing, Engraving, and Etching Historical and Other Prints (April 29, 1802), 7th Cong., 1st sess., ch. 36, sec. 1, in *Statutes at Large of United States of America,* 2:171 (hereafter cited as 1802 Act).

23. 1790 Act, ch. 15, sec. 3, *Stat.,* 1:125.

24. 1790 Act, ch. 15, sec. 4, *Stat.,* 1:125.

25. See note 3 above.

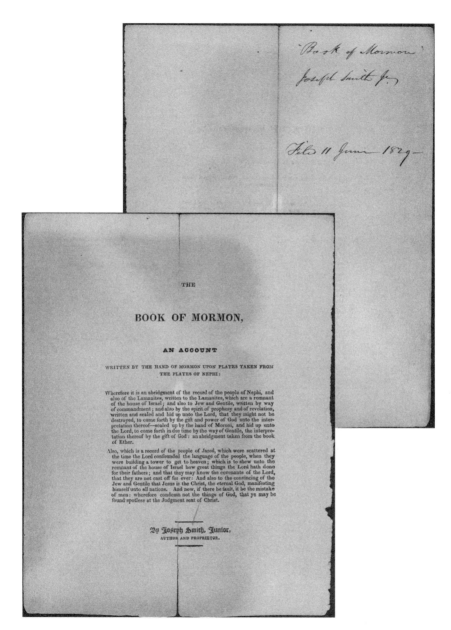

Figure 2. Front and reverse sides of the preliminary printing of the title page to the Book of Mormon, dated and filed on June 11, 1829. Courtesy Rare Book and Special Collections, Library of Congress.

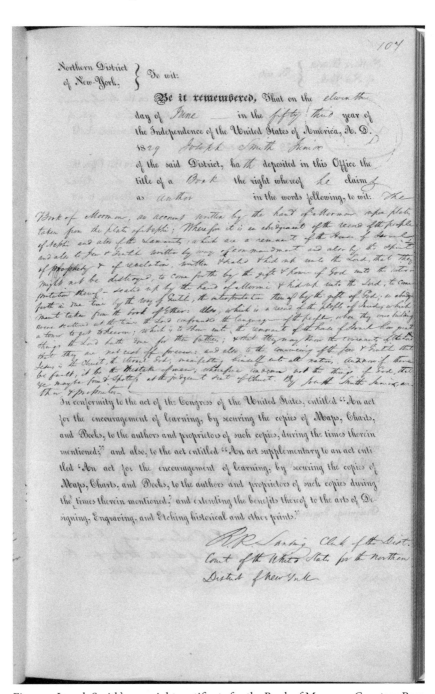

Figure 3. Joseph Smith's copyright certificate for the Book of Mormon. Courtesy Rare Book and Special Collections, Library of Congress.

book.[26] It is unlikely that the copyright form was filed in Palmyra, since the law required applicants residing in Palmyra or Fayette to file in the federal district court located in Utica. Still, a filing in or near Palmyra is not out of the question, for the clerk of the court may have been there for some function of the court, but no evidence to that effect has been found.

Also unknown is how the title page was delivered to Richard Lansing. Church historian Larry C. Porter writes, "It is not certain whether Joseph Smith simply submitted his title entry by mail to Lansing at Utica, New York, or whether it was delivered by hand."[27] Alternatively, Joseph may have made the difficult trip to Utica, about one hundred miles each way from Fayette, or another person may have carried the signed forms on Joseph's behalf. Alternatively, the title page may have been simply submitted to Lansing by mail. In a letter to Hyrum Smith from St. Lawrence County, New York, dated June 17, 1829, Jesse Smith, Hyrum's uncle, refers to a visitor he received, as a "fool" who "believes all [about the golden plates] to be a fact."[28] Richard Lloyd Anderson suggests that the man referred to in Jesse's letter was Martin Harris, who, on his way to St. Lawrence County, could have stopped in Utica to deposit the title page of the Book of Mormon in the district court.[29]

Regardless of where, or by whom, the form was submitted, Lansing signed the copyright certificate, which identified Joseph Smith as "author and proprietor" of the work. This wording came from the federal statute, which made copyrights available to authors or proprietors of books or other works. Furthermore, as John W. Welch has pointed out, "A *translator* was qualified, for copyright purposes, as the author of a book he had translated."[30]

Requirement 2. Together with this filing, Joseph must have paid the requisite fee, or he would not have received the certificate in return. The fees probably totaled $1.20: sixty cents for recording the official copy and another sixty cents for giving a copy of the certificate to Joseph.[31] Presumably, this fee was paid.

---

26. Joseph Smith Jr., *History of The Church of Jesus Christ of Latter-day Saints*, ed. B. H. Roberts, 2d ed. rev., 7 vols. (Salt Lake City: Deseret Book, 1971), 1:71.

27. Larry C. Porter, "Egbert Bratt Grandin," in *Book of Mormon Reference Companion*, ed. Dennis L. Largey (Salt Lake City: Desert Book, 2003), 308.

28. Jesse Smith to Hyrum Smith, June 17, 1829, Joseph Smith Letterbook (1837–43), Church History Library, published in Dan Vogel, comp. and ed., *Early Mormon Documents*, 5 vols. (Salt Lake City: Signature Books, 1996), 1:553.

29. Richard L. Anderson, interview by author, March 2005, Provo, Utah.

30. John W. Welch, "Author and Proprietor," in Welch, *Reexploring the Book of Mormon*, 156, citing an 1814 English case and an 1859 district court case.

31. The sum of $1.20 would equal about $70 in today's dollars.

The restored E. B. Grandin & Co. printing press, where the first copies of the Book of Mormon were printed. Photo courtesy John W. Welch.

Requirement 3. Joseph met the third requirement by having the full wording of the certificate received from Lansing printed on the back of the title page of the 1830 edition of the Book of Mormon.

Requirement 4. Less certain is whether Joseph completely satisfied the statutory requirement of publishing the court's certificate in a local newspaper for four weeks within the two months after filing the book's title. On June 26, 1829, Egbert B. Grandin, with whom Joseph contracted to print the Book of Mormon, published the text of the book's title page in his Palmyra newspaper, the *Wayne Sentinel*. This text was again published in August by two other local papers: in the *Palmyra Freeman* on August 11, and in the *Niagara Courier* on August 27.

While publishing the text of the title page was probably an attempt to follow the law, the law technically required the publication of the entire copyright certificate. Furthermore, the title page did not appear in a newspaper "for four weeks" before August 11, 1829, the two-month date before which the publishing requirement was to be met.

On March 26, 1830, Grandin again published the title page of the Book of Mormon in the *Wayne Sentinel* and announced that the book was available for purchase. This was followed by publication of the book's title page in the

Wayne Sentinel on April 2, 9, 16, and May 7. These consecutive notices may have been a second attempt on the part of Grandin and Joseph Smith to satisfy the legal requirements for obtaining a copyright. Richard Lloyd Anderson notes that Joseph and his associates "may have thought they were complying with the intent of the law by printing just what they had originally submitted to the clerk of the court—the title page."[32] While the notices in Grandin's newspaper could have merely been advertisements for the sale of the book, the fact that there were four of them within two months, the time period mentioned as required by the statute, might indicate otherwise. Still, these notices, coming almost a full year following Joseph's original filing with R. R. Lansing, would not appear to satisfy the technical requirements of the law.

Requirement 5. Given the evidence of Joseph's efforts to comply with the foregoing statutory requirements, it is quite possible that he or Grandin sent a copy of the published Book of Mormon to the U.S. Secretary of State, who at the time was Martin Van Buren. However, no record has survived indicating that a copy was submitted to Van Buren, as required, within six months of the book's publication, which should have occurred by September 26, 1830.[33]

Based on all available evidence, Joseph Smith did not satisfy all five federal requirements to secure a copyright in the Book of Mormon. But he was not alone in his shortcomings. An extensive examination of several New York and Pennsylvania newspapers printed in the 1820s revealed very few occasions on which an author published the full copyright certificate from any federal district court.[34] At the same time, advertisements for the sale of newly published books are numerous. Moreover, several books published in the early nineteenth century claimed to be copyrighted but did not include a copy of the court's certificate printed in the book.[35] Though some authors no doubt complied with every aspect of the federal copyright statute, it may still be true that Joseph Smith did more than most.

---

32. Richard L. Anderson, interview, quoted in Porter, "Egbert Bratt Grandin," 308.

33. A search of the records in the Library of Congress containing the lists of books submitted to Martin Van Buren as Secretary of State by the district courts for copyright yields no entry showing that a copy of the Book of Mormon ever made its way to Washington following its publication in March 1830. The author thanks James H. Hutson and Barbara Cramer for checking volumes 342, 343, and an unnumbered volume, catalogued as Copyright Records, Department of State, covering submissions from September 24, 1827, through January 7, 1832.

34. After thoroughly searching several contemporary newspapers, Don Enders and research assistants for John W. Welch have concluded that authors generally did not publish their copyright certificates in newspapers.

35. For example, Washington Irving's *A History of New York*, published in New York in 1809, contains only the words "Copy-right secured according to Law."

Legal Consequences of
Failing to Meet All of the Statute's Requirements

In light of these shortcomings, one wonders: would these defects have compromised Joseph's full copyright protection of the Book of Mormon? Court opinions from the time indicate that Joseph's actions would have been insufficient to uphold statutory copyright protection in court, despite his good-faith efforts and partial compliance.

In 1824, Judge Bushrod Washington of the United States Supreme Court, sitting on the Circuit Court in the Eastern District of Pennsylvania, ruled that an author must comply strictly with all the provisions of the copyright act to receive its benefits.[36] In light of the language in the 1802 amendment, Judge Washington held that a person seeking copyright protection must perform all of the acts prescribed by the copyright law "before he shall be entitled to the benefit of the act." Under this analysis, Joseph Smith would not have been entitled to copyright protection for the Book of Mormon. The United States Supreme Court, in its 1834 *Wheaton* decision, agreed with Judge Washington, declaring that compliance with all of the provisions of the copyright act was necessary to secure the statutory rights.[37] But, as mentioned previously, common law would have prevented others from publishing the Book of Mormon before the book's public release, and this is the strongest legal explanation for Joseph's success against Abner Cole in January 1830.

Abner Cole's Infringement

Joseph Smith did not leave a record of his encounter with Cole. The only account of the dispute comes from Joseph's mother, Lucy Mack Smith, who recorded the incident several years after its occurrence. The conflict arose while Joseph was spending most of winter 1829–30 in Harmony, Pennsylvania, with his wife, Emma. During this time, Hyrum Smith, Oliver Cowdery, and Martin Harris oversaw the printing of the Book of Mormon in Palmyra.[38] Egbert B. Grandin handled the publishing of the book at his print shop and gave Hyrum and Oliver access to the shop every day except Sunday.

---

36. Ewer v. Coxe, 8 Federal Cases 917, 919–20 (Circuit Court, Eastern District Pennsylvania, 1824).

37. Wheaton v. Peters, 591.

38. See John W. Welch, "The Miraculous Translation of the Book of Mormon," in *Opening the Heavens: Accounts of Divine Manifestations, 1820–1844,* ed. John W. Welch (Provo, Utah: Brigham Young University Press; Salt Lake City: Deseret Book, 2005), 98–99; Richard L. Bushman, *Joseph Smith and the Beginnings of Mormonism* (Chicago: University of Illinois Press, 1984), 108–9.

Lucy reports that one Sunday, probably in December, "Hyrum became very uneasy" and felt "something was going wrong at the printing Office."[39] Oliver at first resisted Hyrum's suggestion to go to Grandin's shop on Sunday, but soon the two men were on their way to the office. There they found Abner Cole busily printing a newspaper.[40]

Hyrum asked Cole why he was working on Sunday. Cole responded by saying that evenings and Sundays were the only times when he was able to use the printing press. Hyrum and Oliver soon discovered that Cole was violating more than the religious law of the Sabbath—Cole was copying passages from the Book of Mormon to include in his newspaper, the *Reflector*.[41]

Oliver Cowdery. Courtesy of the Church Archives, The Church of Jesus Christ of Latter-day Saints.

In fact, Cole had begun writing about Joseph Smith and his work in the first issue of the *Reflector* on September 2, 1829: "The Gold Bible, by Joseph Smith Junior, author and proprietor, is now in press and will shortly appear. Priestcraft is short lived!"[42] Three months later, on December 9, Cole, who wrote under the pseudonym of Obadiah Dogberry, announced in his paper that he would soon begin to provide his readers with selections from the Book of Mormon. Cole likely had no difficulty in procuring printed sheets of the Book of Mormon, discarded or otherwise, conveniently located at Grandin's shop. The first selection, 1 Nephi 1:1–2:3 in the current edition of the Book of Mormon, appeared in the January 2, 1830, issue of the *Reflector*.[43]

Hyrum informed Cole that a copyright had been secured for the book, but Cole indignantly refused to stop his work. After a lengthy debate, Hyrum and Oliver left the print shop after they were unable to dissuade Cole from his course.[44]

39. Smith, *Lucy's Book*, 470.

40. Smith, *Lucy's Book*, 470–71.

41. Smith, *Lucy's Book*, 471; Porter, "Study of the Origins," 32.

42. Larry C. Porter, "'The Field Is White Already to Harvest': Earliest Missionary Labors and the Book of Mormon," in *The Prophet Joseph: Essays on the Life and Mission of Joseph Smith*, ed. Larry C. Porter and Susan Easton Black (Salt Lake City: Deseret Book, 1988), 84.

43. Andrew H. Hedges, "The Refractory Abner Cole," in *Revelation, Reason, and Faith: Essays in Honor of Truman G. Madsen*, ed. Donald W. Parry, Daniel C. Peterson, and Stephen D. Ricks (Provo, Utah: FARMS, 2002), 461.

44. Smith, *Lucy's Book*, 472.

Impressed with the seriousness of the circumstances, Hyrum and Oliver determined that Joseph needed to be notified of Cole's actions. Accordingly, Joseph Smith Sr. went to Harmony and returned with his son on the following Sunday.[45] That night, probably January 3, 1830,[46] the Prophet went to Grandin's shop, where he found Cole and examined his paper. Joseph asserted his ownership of the book and the right to publish it and demanded that Cole cease his "meddling." Instead of refuting Joseph's publishing right, Cole sought a fight, but Joseph refused. In Lucy's reconstruction of the events, Joseph declared, "I know my rights and shall maintain them." Then, "in a low significant tone," Joseph stated, "there is Law—and you will find that out if you did not know it before."[47] This bold statement by Joseph is all the more remarkable considering that Cole was nearly twice as old as Joseph and was probably much more familiar with the law, having worked as a lawyer and justice of the peace.[48] Perhaps recognizing the inferiority of his position and not wanting to litigate the matter, Cole ultimately assented to an arbitration to determine Joseph's rights to the Book of Mormon. The arbitration was settled in Joseph's favor, and Cole agreed to stop printing the Book of Mormon passages but was apparently not assessed the damages allowed by the statute. After settling the affair with Cole, Joseph returned home to Pennsylvania.[49]

Arbitration in New York in 1830

Although nothing more is known about the arbitration agreed to by Cole, an examination of general arbitration rules and procedures from the time sheds light on what may have occurred.

Prior to Smith and Cole's arbitration, the legislature in New York had passed two bills relating specifically to arbitration. First, in 1791, the legislature passed "An act for determining differences by arbitration."[50] Second, an amendment to this act was added in April 1816.[51]

---

45. Smith, *Lucy's Book,* 473–74.

46. Hedges, "Refractory Abner Cole," 463.

47. Smith, *Lucy's Book,* 474–75.

48. Hedges, "Refractory Abner Cole," 450–51. Cole was born between June 2, 1780, and August 6, 1784.

49. Smith, *Lucy's Book,* 475.

50. An Act for Determining Differences by Arbitration (February 28, 1791), 14th sess., ch. 20, *Laws of New York,* 219–20 (hereafter cited as 1791 Act).

51. An Act to Amend the Act, Entitled "An Act for Determining Differences by Arbitration," and for Other Purposes (April 17, 1816), 39th sess., ch. 210, *Laws of New York,* 242 (hereafter cited as 1816 Amendment).

The three-paragraph 1791 act had the stated purpose of "promoting trade, and rendering the awards of arbitrators the more effectual in all cases." To these ends, the act made it lawful for parties to an arbitration to agree that the outcome of their controversy "be made a rule of any court of record in this State." If a party thereafter refused to abide by the ruling of the arbitrator or umpire, the person would be subject to all penalties that would apply if the person had resisted the order of a court. However, the person could escape penalty if he could show, by oath, "that the arbitrators or umpire misbehaved themselves, and that such award, arbitration or umpirage, was procured by corruption, or other undue means." Any arbitration found to be "procured by corruption or undue means" would be "void and of none effect."[52] In summary, an arbitration would be treated as binding as a ruling of the court if the parties so agreed.

The amendment to this law, passed in 1816, allowed "any justice of the peace, residing in any city or county in this state, in which any dispute, controversy or difference whatsoever, may have been submitted to arbitration . . . to swear or affirm the several witnesses required to give testimony before said arbitrator or arbitrators." The amendment also made witnesses in an arbitration proceeding subject to the perjury laws of the state.[53]

Besides these statutes, several contemporary New York cases commented on the nature of arbitrations. Arbitration, as defined by a New York court in 1830, was "a submission by parties of matters in controversy to the judgment of two or more individuals." Those who decided the dispute, the arbitrators, were chosen by the parties.[54] Apparently a common practice was for each party to choose his own arbitrator and have those two arbitrators select a third arbitrator, or umpire, for the case.[55] The arbitrators were to act as "jurors to determine facts, [and as] judges to adjudicate as to the law; and their award when fairly and legally made, is a judgment conclusive between the parties, from which there is no appeal." As demonstrated by the statutory provisions, arbitrations could be treated as a ruling of a court and were binding on the parties. One judge even stated that an arbitration "ought to be of a more binding force between the parties" than a jury verdict.[56]

---

52. 1791 Act, ch. 20, *Laws of New York*, 219, 220.

53. 1816 Amendment, ch. 210, *Laws of New York*, 242–43.

54. Elmendorf v. Harris, 5 Wend. 516, 522 n. 1 (Supreme Court of Judicature of New York 1830).

55. *Webster's 1828 Dictionary*, s.v. "arbitration," available at http://65.66.134.201/cgi-bin/ webster/webster.exe?search_for_texts_web1828=arbitration.

56. Story v. Elliot, 8 Cow. 27, 31 (Supreme Court of Judicature of New York 1827) (citations omitted).

A person's choice to submit to arbitration rather than litigate a case in a courtroom was often money-driven. Arbitration offered an end to dispute "with very little expense to the parties." Still, arbitration did not offer the same prospects for justice as an official courthouse. Arbitrators, though chosen for their impartiality, would "frequently mingle in their decisions their own knowledge of the matters in dispute." "Their ends are mainly honest," but their decisions, "though intelligible, are not drawn up with technical accuracy."[57]

If an arbitrator's decision was not consistent with the law, it would still be binding on the parties,[58] and an arbitration decision could not be appealed to a court except in the case of an arbitrator's misconduct.[59] And while an arbitrator's decision would be binding on the parties involved, the decision would not be binding on third parties.[60]

The Smith-Cole Arbitration

With all of these legal norms in place, we can imagine what might have occurred between Joseph and Abner Cole. The date of their arbitration is unknown, but it did not occur on the Sunday of Joseph's visit, for that would have violated the Sabbath law, and the two men also needed time to procure witnesses and arbitrators. Further extracts of the Book of Mormon appeared in the *Reflector* on January 13 and 22, suggesting the arbitration might have concluded several days after Joseph arrived in Palmyra.[61]

Given Cole's legal experience, the two parties probably first would have agreed on the question to be arbitrated, namely, whether Joseph's claim to property rights or copyright in the book were sufficient to prohibit Cole's publishing of part of its text. Joseph also may have wanted to recover monetary damages or to confiscate Cole's printed pages as granted under the federal copyright statute.

Next, the two may have agreed on arbitrators. Possibly each chose a man to act as an arbitrator, and those two men then chose a third. In accordance

---

57. Jackson v. Ambler, 14 Johns. 96, 103 (Supreme Court of Judicature of New York, 1817).

58. Mitchell v. Bush, 7 Cow. 185, 187 (Supreme Court of Judicature of New York, 1827).

59. Cranston, et al. v. The Executors of Kenny, 9 Johns. 212, 213 (Supreme Court of Judicature of New York, 1812) (citations omitted).

60. Vosburgh v. Bame, 14 Johns. 302, 304 (Supreme Court of Judicature of New York, 1817).

61. Hedges, "Refractory Abner Cole," 463. For an alternate suggestion of the dating and order of events with Cole, see Vogel, *Early Mormon Documents*, 2:407–8.

with the statute, the local justice of the peace may have sworn in any witnesses who would testify before the arbitrators.

The arbitrators apparently ruled against Cole. Their decision, whether legally sound, was binding on Cole, and no known claim was ever made that the arbitrators' decision was corrupt and therefore void. Lucy Mack Smith did not specify the premise of Joseph's defense—whether he relied on the statutory copyright law or on the common law. If the arbitrators based their decision on the federal statutory copyright law, they must have concluded that Joseph's actions had been sufficient to acquire that protection. After all, Joseph could not have been expected to have complied yet with the statutory requirement of delivering a copy of the book to the secretary of state, since copies were still not available. But his failure to give public notice of his copyright within two months of receiving his certificate would have been more problematic. Thus, what is more likely, and also more consistent with the law, is that the arbitrators' decision in Joseph's favor was based on the common law protection of authors' rights in unpublished manuscripts, not on Joseph's unperfected copyright filing.

For legal purposes, one would need to ask: Was the Book of Mormon published or unpublished in January 1830? When Cole was copying portions of the Book of Mormon, many of the work's pages had been printed. But printing alone did not constitute publishing, for the copyright statute distinguished the two, granting authors the right of "printing, reprinting, publishing and vending" a book covered by the statute.[62] Simply because portions of the Book of Mormon had been printed under Joseph's authorization does not mean they had been published.

The 1828 *Webster's Dictionary* defines "publish" as meaning "to send a book into the world; or to sell or offer for sale a book, map or print."[63] As is well known, the Book of Mormon was not available for purchase until March 26, 1830,[64] but at least portions of it had been distributed before then. In 1829, Thomas B. Marsh obtained the proof sheet of the first sixteen pages of the book and used it to teach others about the book. Solomon Chamberlain also obtained sixty-four pages of the unbound book from Hyrum Smith and used them in his preaching. Oliver Cowdery gave his brother Warren some pages

---

62. 1790 Act, ch. 15, sec. 1, *Stat.*, 1:124.

63. *Webster's 1828 Dictionary*, s.v. "publish."

64. In the May 26, 1830, issue of the *Wayne Sentinel*, notice was given that the Book of Mormon had been published.

of the book, which Warren showed to others. Even Joseph Smith apparently used proof sheets to promulgate the work.[65]

If Cole had been aware of those events, he might have argued that the Book of Mormon (or at least portions of it) had indeed been published, or sent forth to the world. Still, Joseph could have answered that the distributions of a few proof sheets were limited and private in nature. If the arbitrators based their decision on the common law, they believed the Book of Mormon had not been published. This result is consistent with Joseph's words to Cole where he asserted his ownership of the book and his right yet to publish it.

Whatever Abner Cole's and Joseph Smith's arguments may have been, and whatever the basis was for the arbitrators' decision, the decision was more binding upon the parties than a judgment in court. Joseph apparently received no damages, and Cole apparently never contested the judgment. Joseph Smith was never again involved in any other legal disputes regarding the copyright to the Book of Mormon.

Conclusion

The episode with Abner Cole is perhaps the first instance where Joseph Smith asserted legal rights that had a direct impact on the religious work to which he devoted his life. Convinced of the justice of his cause, the twenty-four-year-old prophet confidently told Cole that he knew the law and that it would protect him; Joseph did not hesitate to dispute the older and more experienced editor. Even though Joseph may have been somewhat overconfident in his knowledge of statutory copyrights, he correctly realized the protection of the law. Possibly because of his efforts to secure a copyright for the Book of Mormon, or more likely even without the need to invoke those efforts, Joseph was successful in this legal defense of the work God had called him to do.

This article was originally published as "Copyright Laws and the 1830 Book of Mormon," BYU Studies 45, no. 3 (2006): 77–99.

---

65. Porter, "'Field Is White,'" 79–83.

Chapter Six

Organizing the Church
as a Religious Association in 1830

David Keith Stott

While much has been written about the organization of The Church of Jesus Christ of Latter-day Saints in upstate New York, questions remain regarding the events of April 6, 1830. This article examines the organizational events of the Church from a legal perspective. In the nineteenth century, individuals desiring to form a church had two legal alternatives: forming a religious corporation or organizing a religious society. Understanding the requirements of each and considering which legal entity Church leaders would have preferred provide new insights into the organizational events.

Historical Background

In June 1829, shortly after Joseph Smith and Oliver Cowdery received the Aaronic Priesthood, they were commanded by revelation to organize a church.[1] Received ten months before the organization, this revelation outlined a

---

1. Dean C. Jessee, ed., *The Papers of Joseph Smith*, 2 vols. (Salt Lake City: Deseret Book, 1989–92), 1:302: "Whilst the Book of Mormon was in the hands of the printer, we ... made known to our brethren, that we had received commandment to organize the Church And accordingly we met together for that purpose, at the house of the above mentioned Mr Whitmer (being six in number) on Tuesday the sixth day of April, AD One thousand, eight hundred and thirty."

No contemporary documentation or minutes of the April 6, 1830, meeting exist, making a precise accounting of the organizational events difficult. The most detailed source is Joseph Smith's Manuscript History, as set forth in Jessee, *Papers of Joseph Smith*. This account is an 1839 transcript recorded by one of Smith's scribes, James Mulholland, nine years after the organization of the Church.

rough agenda for the future meeting and commanded Joseph and Oliver to defer this organization until those who had been or would be baptized could meet together and sanction such an event.[2]

Around noon on Tuesday, April 6, 1830, over fifty persons gathered in the small, two-room farmhouse of Peter Whitmer Sr. to witness the organization of the Church of Christ.[3] After opening the meeting with prayer, the

---

2. Larry C. Porter, "Organizational Origins of the Church of Jesus Christ, 6 April 1830," in *Regional Studies in Latter-day Saint Church History: New York*, ed. Larry C. Porter, Milton V. Backman Jr., and Susan Eastman Black (Provo, Utah: Brigham Young University Press, 1992), 152, quoting Joseph Smith Jr., *History of The Church of Jesus Christ of Latter-day Saints*, ed. B. H. Roberts, 2d ed., rev., 7 vols. (Salt Lake City: Deseret Book, 1971), 1:60–61: "We had not long been engaged in solemn and fervent prayer when the word of the Lord came unto us in the chamber, commanding us that I should ordain Oliver Cowdery to be an Elder in the Church of Jesus Christ; and that he also should ordain me to the office; and then to ordain others, as it should be made known unto us from time to time. We were, however, commanded to defer this our ordination until such times as it should be practicable to have our brethren, who had been and who should be baptized, assembled together, when we must have their sanction to our thus proceeding to ordain each other, and have them decide by vote whether they were willing to accept us as spiritual teachers or not; when also we were commanded to bless bread and break it with them; and then attend to the laying on of hand for the gift of the Holy Ghost, upon all those whom we had previously baptized, doing all things in the name of the Lord." David Whitmer was also present during this revelation.

3. The Lord possibly commanded that the specific date of April 6 be used for organization. See the introduction to Doctrine and Covenants 20: "We obtained of him [Jesus Christ] the following, by the spirit of prophecy and revelation; which not only gave us much information, but also pointed out to us the precise day upon which, according to his will and commandment, we should proceed to organize his Church once more here upon the earth." This statement is curious in light of the Book of Commandments and Revelations, which dates Section 20 as recorded on April 10, 1830, suggesting that the revelation was written, or at least recorded, after the organizational meeting. Robin Scott Jensen, Robert J. Woodford, and Steven C. Harper, eds., *Revelations and Translations, Volume 1: Manuscript Revelation Books*, vol. 1 of the Revelations and Translations series of *The Joseph Smith Papers*, ed. Dean C. Jessee, Ronald K. Esplin, and Richard Lyman Bushman (Salt Lake City: Church Historian's Press, 2011), 60.

Larry C. Porter has thoroughly examined prospective individuals who attended the organizational meeting. David Whitmer estimated the number at fifty, although as many as seventy-three could have been in attendance. See Porter, "Organizational Origins," 153–55. Some scholars have recently called into question the location of the organizational meeting. It is generally accepted that the meeting took place in the home of Peter Whitmer Sr. in Fayette, New York. However, until 1834 the *Evening and Morning Star* referred to the Church being organized in Manchester, New York. See, for example, "Prospects of the Church," *Evening and Morning Star* 1 (March 1833): 76; and "Rise and Progress of the Church of Christ," *Evening and Morning Star* (April 1833): 84. For advocates of the Manchester site, see H. Michael

twenty-four-year-old Joseph Smith called on the brethren present to show whether they accepted him and Oliver Cowdery as their "teachers in the things of the Kingdom of God" and whether they should be organized as a church.[4] After a unanimous vote, Joseph ordained Oliver by the laying on of hands to the office of elder, after which Cowdery in turn ordained Smith to the same office.[5] They then oversaw the administration of the sacrament and confirmed those present who had previously been baptized, conferring upon them the gift of the Holy Ghost.[6] Joseph also received a revelation and ordained others to priesthood offices.[7] Joseph states that "we dismissed with the pleasing knowledge that we were now individually, members of, and acknowledged of God, 'The Church of Jesus Christ,' organized in accordance with commandments and revelations."[8]

Laws Regarding the Formation of Nineteenth-Century Religious Corporations

Not only were the events of that day spiritually meaningful to members of the Church, but the actions taken were legally significant. The early leaders of the Church apparently were aware of these legal implications as they tried to

---

Marquardt and Wesley P. Walters, *Inventing Mormonism: Tradition and the Historical Record* (Salt Lake City: Smith Research Associates, 1994), 154–56; and Dan Vogel, comp. and ed., *Early Mormon Documents*, 5 vols. (Salt Lake City: Signature Books, 1996), 1:92 n. 82.

4. Jessee, *Papers,* 1:302–3: "Having opened the meeting by solemn prayer to our Heavenly Father we proceeded, (according to previous commandment) to call on our brethren to know whether they accepted us as their teachers in the things of the Kingdom of God, and whether they were satisfied that we should proceed and be organized as a Church."

5. Jessee, *Papers,* 1:303: "To these they consented by an unanimous vote. I then laid my hands upon Oliver Cowdery and ordained him an Elder of the 'Church of Jesus Christ of Latter Day Saints.' after which he ordained me also to the office of an Elder of said Church." Oliver Cowdery later described ordaining Joseph Smith as "Prophet, Seer, Revelator, and Translator just as [Doctrine and Covenants 21] says." *True Latter Day Saints' Herald,* August 1, 1872, 473. This article recounts an 1847 interview of Oliver Cowdery by William E. McLellin in Elkhorn, Wisconsin.

6. Jessee, *Papers,* 1:303: "We then took bread, blessed it, and brake it with them, also wine, blessed it, and drank it with them. We then laid our hands on each individual member of the Church present that they might receive the gift of the Holy Ghost, and be confirmed members of the Church of Christ." It is unclear whether only the six original members of the Church or all in attendance who had been previously baptized were confirmed.

7. See Doctrine and Covenants 21; Jessee, *Papers,* 1:303.

8. Jessee, *Papers,* 1:303.

obey the laws of the land in organizing a church.[9] In seeking out what legally took place on April 6, 1830, historians have assumed that Church leaders attempted to incorporate, and they cite an 1813 New York statute entitled An Act to Provide for the Incorporation of Religious Societies.[10] But upon closer examination, the historical evidence, as well as the purposes and benefits of religious corporations fails to align with the act of incorporation, suggesting that the Church never incorporated in New York.

In nineteenth-century New York, a corporation was a legal entity "composed of individuals united under a common name, the members of which succeed[ed] each other" so that the entity continued unchanged despite an evolving membership.[11] Various types of corporations existed,[12] including

---

9. See Doctrine and Covenants 20:1: "The rise of the Church of Christ in these last days, … it being regularly organized and established agreeable to the laws of our country"; see also notes 95–96 below and accompanying text.

10. See, for example, Porter, "Organizational Origins," 155–58; Larry C. Porter, *A Study of the Origins of the Church of Jesus Christ of Latter-day Saints in the States of New York and Pennsylvania* (Provo, Utah: Joseph Fielding Smith Institute for Latter-day Saint History and BYU Studies, 2000), 100, 155; see also John K. Carmack, "Fayette: The Place the Church Was Organized," *Ensign* 19 (February 1989): 15; Larry C. Porter, "Organization of the Church," in *Encyclopedia of Latter-day Saint History*, ed. Arnold K. Garr, Donald Q. Cannon, and Richard O. Cowan (Salt Lake City: Deseret Book, 2000), 877–81; Daniel H. Ludlow, "Organization of the Church, 1830," in *Encyclopedia of Mormonism*, ed. Daniel H. Ludlow, 4 vols. (New York: Macmillan, 1992), 3:1049; and W. Jeffrey Marsh, "The Organization of the Church," in *Joseph: Exploring the Life and Ministry of the Prophet*, ed. Susan Easton Black and Andrew C. Skinner (Deseret Book, 2005), 120.

11. J. Bouvier, *A Law Dictionary*, rev. 6th ed. (1856), 2 vols., accessed at http://inclusion .semitagui.gov.co/Publications/Bouviers/bouvier.htm, s.v. "Corporation." A corporation thus maintained "a perpetual succession" and enjoyed a "sort of immortality." John Holmes, *The Statesman, or Principles of Legislation and Law* (Augusta, Maine: Severance Dorr, Printers, 1840), 226. To understand the benefits of this corporate immortality, compare corporations to partnerships which would necessarily dissolve after the death or departure of one of the partners. See Bouvier, *Law Dictionary*, s.v. "Partnership": "The law will not presume that it shall last beyond life." See also note 19 below for the typical headaches surrounding a nonincorporated entity's property succession.

Throughout this article, no contemporary histories regarding the law of incorporating churches in the 1830s are cited because none exist. Thus, the author focuses strictly on early statutes and primary sources. Broad histories that detail the development of the laws of the incorporation or organization of business associations are largely irrelevant to the incorporation of churches, which faced a dissimilar developmental path.

12. In the nineteenth century, corporations were divided into private and public categories, public corporations being those owned and operated by the government. Bouvier, *Law Dictionary*, s.v. "Corporation." Private corporations were further categorized into religious and lay categories. Holmes, *Statesman*, 226; James Kent, *Commentaries on American*

religious corporations, which were composed of "spiritual persons"[13] who took "a lively interest in the advancement of religion"[14] and who took the steps to incorporate.

The literature of that era refers to three main benefits that flowed to a church by being incorporated. First, religious corporations maintained a perpetual succession with trustees carrying out the original purpose of the church despite an ever-changing membership or the passage of time.[15] Second, this "immortality" allowed for the religious corporation to manage "with more facility and advantage, the temporalities belonging to the church or congregation."[16] Without corporate status, the property of the church was owned by individual members, and the church did not possess "the power to transfer the privileges given to it to other persons" when the owning members died.[17] Alternatively, a corporation was "considered as *one person,* which has but one will"[18] and could transfer property upon death with relative ease.[19] Third, religious corporations had various

---

Law, 4 vols., 14th ed. (Boston: Little, Brown, 1896), 2:274; Joseph K. Angell and Samuel Ames, *A Treatise on the Law of Private Corporations Aggregate* (Boston: Hilliard, Gray, Little and Wilkins, 1832), 25.

13. Holmes, *Statesman,* 226.

14. Angell and Ames, *Treatise on the Law,* 25. Religious corporations must have "created [the corporation] with a view of promoting religion and perpetuating the rights of the church." Holmes, *Statesman,* 226. Also, the purpose of religious corporations must have been entirely ecclesiastical. See Angell and Ames, *Treatise on the Law,* 26, providing the example that even if Dartmouth College was composed entirely of ecclesiastical persons, because the object of a school was not "entirely ecclesiastical," it could not be a religious corporation and was thus an eleemosynary (charitable) corporation.

15. See Holmes, *Statesman,* 226. This perpetual succession was a main function of all corporations. In the United States Supreme Court case *Dartmouth College v. Woodward,* Justice Marshall commented that corporations allow for "a perpetual succession of individuals [which] are capable of acting for the promotion of the particular object, like one immortal being." 4 Wheaton, (U.S.) R. 636 (1819). In a subsequent case, Justice Marshall further stated, "The great object of an incorporation is to bestow the character and properties of individuality on a collective and changing body of men." Providence Bank v. Billings, 4 Peters, (U.S.) R. 562 (1830). Religious corporations were no different; the church could exist indefinitely and continue long after any one member passed on while maintaining the purpose and integrity of the original institution.

16. Kent, *Comentaries,* 2:275.

17. Angell and Ames, *Treatise on the Law,* 7.

18. Angell and Ames, *Treatise on the Law,* 7, emphasis in original.

19. Angell and Ames, *Treatise on the Law,* 7, emphasis in original: "If, for example, a grant of land should be made to twenty individuals not incorporated, the right to the land cannot be assured to their successors, without the inconvenience of making frequent and numerous conveyances. When, on the other hand, any number of persons are

legal rights, including the power to make contracts, to have a common seal, and to use the corporate name,[20] all allowing for easier property management.

State laws varied on how a congregation could form a religious corporation.[21] New York updated its incorporation statute in 1813, entitled An Act to Provide for the Incorporation of Religious Societies, which detailed how a church could self-incorporate.[22] Section Three of the Act stated that to form a religious corporation, the congregation should gather to elect between three and nine trustees:

> It shall be lawful for the male persons of full age … to assemble at the church, meeting-house, or other place where they statedly attend for divine worship, and, by plurality of voices, to elect any number of discreet persons of their church, congregation or society, not less than three, nor exceeding nine in number, as trustees, to take the charge of the estate and property belonging thereto, and to transact all affairs relative to the temporalities thereof.[23]

---

consolidated and united into a corporation, they are then considered as *one person*, which has but one will,—that will being ascertained by a majority of votes."

20. Angell and Ames, *Treatise on the Law*, 277–92.

21. Churches could form a religious corporation in two ways. R. H. Tyler, *American Ecclesiastical Law: The Law of Religious Societies* (Albany: William Gould, 1866), 58: "Sometimes religious societies are incorporated here by special charters, but more frequently, under general incorporating laws." First, the government granted a "special charter" which incorporated a church. The British government employed this method in the American colonies, granting special privileges of incorporation to specific state-sponsored churches. See generally Paul G. Kauper and Stephen C. Ellis, "Religious Corporations and the Law," *Michigan Law Review* 71 (1973): 1499, 1505–9, describing the influence of "the English notion that a corporation could exist only with the express prior approval of the state" (1505). This idea was adopted by the early colonies which used specific corporate grants for certain state-endorsed churches. After the American Revolution, this method fell into disfavor, and the United States adopted a more widespread method of incorporation—the enactment of "general" state incorporation laws giving churches the ability to incorporate without legislative mandate. Kauper and Ellis, "Religious Corporations and the Law," 1509–10: "The difficulties inherent in any system that grants special favors to a few led to the downfall of incorporation by special charter. It seems probable that the spirit of separation and pluralism that swept the country at the time of the American Revolution lent aid to the enactment of general incorporation laws."

22. Religious Incorporations, An Act to Provide for the Incorporation of Religious Societies, in *The Revised Statutes of the State of New York* (1836, enacted Feb. 5, 1813), at 206; hereafter cited as New York Religious Incorporation Statute.

23. New York Religious Incorporation Statute §3. Other sections of the statute set forth detailed obligations such as requiring the board of trustees to serve three-year terms and

Trustees played a key role in a religious corporation. Similar to directors of present-day corporations, trustees were managing officers responsible for the temporal affairs of the church.[24] The church vested all property in these trustees, who held it for the use and benefit of the congregation.[25]

The main event at incorporation meetings was the election of these trustees. New York's statute described the formalities of this election:

> And that at such election, every male person of full age ... shall be entitled to vote, and the said election shall be conducted as follows: the minister of such church ... shall publicly notify the congregation of the time when, and place where, the said election shall be held ... ; that on the said day of election, two of the elders ... to be nominated by a majority of the members present, shall preside at such election, receive the votes of the electors, be the judges of the qualifications of such electors, and the officers to return the names of the persons who, by plurality of voices shall be elected to serve as trustees for the said church, congregation or society.[26]

The minister of the religious society gave notification of the upcoming election at least fifteen days beforehand, including two successive Sabbaths.[27] The notice was very simple, merely requiring that the time and place of the election

---

be re-elected to stay in office (§6), limiting trustee powers (§8) and the number of trustees who could serve (§§3, 9), and mandating certain administrative responsibilities (§§7, 9).

24. Sandford Hunt, *Laws Relating to Religious Corporations* (New York: Nelson and Phillips, 1876), iv: "The relation which the trustees bear to the corporation is not that of private trustees to the *cestuis que trust,* but that of directors to a civil corporation. They are managing officers of the corporation, invested, as to its temporal affairs, with such particular powers as are specified in the statute."

25. See Kauper and Ellis, "Religious Corporations and the Law," 1511: "The trustee form [of general incorporation statutes] was initially adopted in most eastern states. It consisted of a body of trustees, usually elected by the congregation, which was incorporated as a unit. All church property was vested in the corporate body, which held it for the use and benefit of the church, congregation, or society involved. This form grew out of the common law practice of using trustees to hold property for a voluntary association incapable of taking or holding property in its own name."

26. New York Religious Incorporation Statute, §3.

27. Tyler, *American Ecclesiastical Law,* 85: "This notification must be given for two successive Sabbaths, or days on which such church, congregation or society shall statedly meet for public worship," or in other words, "at least fifteen days before the day of such election."

be given.[28] By a voting majority, the congregation was to elect two elders to preside over the election, tally votes, and announce the winning trustees.

The statute also required certification with the county clerk:

> And the said returning officers shall immediately thereafter certify, under their hands and seals, the names of the persons elected to serve as trustees ... in which certificate the name or title by which the said trustees and their successors shall forever thereafter be called and known, shall be particularly mentioned and described; which said certificate, being proved or acknowledged as above directed, shall be recorded as aforesaid; and such trustees and their successors shall also thereupon, by virtue of this act, be a body corporate, by the name or title expressed in such certificate; and the clerk of every county for recording every certificate of incorporation by virtue of this act, shall be entitled to seventy-five cents, and no more.[29]

The trustees were required to certify the incorporation by filing a document containing the names of the trustees, giving the official title by which the corporation would be known, and paying a fee. Upon the certificate being recorded, the organizing church officially became a religious corporation.

Evidence That the Church Probably Did Not Incorporate

Three reasons become apparent as to why leaders of the early Church probably did not incorporate it on April 6, 1830: (1) incorporation would have required an organizational structure incompatible with that of the Church; (2) the early Church would not have received any tangible benefits for which other churches would have traditionally sought incorporation; and (3) historical evidence does not align with several of the statute's main requirements.

First, the trustee system of incorporated churches would have forced an organizational framework that was not in accordance with the preferred leadership structure of the early Church. In religious corporations, power was disbursed between three to nine trustees, who led by democratic majority vote. This system did not comport with the single office of a prophet who was to lead the Church. According to at least one account, on April 6, 1830, Joseph Smith was ordained *the* prophet, seer, and revelator for the Church,

---

28. Tyler, *American Ecclesiastical Law,* 85: "This notice is a very simple one, and no form of it need be given."

29. New York Religious Incorporation Statute, §3.

plainly the sole leader of the new organization.[30] Oliver Cowdery was likewise Joseph's unequivocal second-in-command. These two men, with Joseph foremost, were to lead the Lord's Church through revelation, not three to nine trustees who governed by majority vote.[31]

Second, most of the benefits of forming a religious corporation would not have enticed the early Church. As mentioned above, religious corporations primarily formed to enjoy perpetual succession and easier property management.[32] Such benefits would not have concerned Church leaders in 1830 due to the Church's financial state. The Church did not own any property, such as a building or land. Rather, the Saints used public lands such as creeks and rivers to perform baptisms and members' homes, schools, or other churches as meetinghouses.[33] Perpetuity and simplified property management are of little advantage when a church holds no assets. The minimal tangible benefits combined with a forced organizational structure likely would have dissuaded the early Church leaders from incorporating.

Third, the eyewitness accounts of the organizational meeting and descriptions of subsequent Church operation only modestly resemble the statutory requirements of New York's law. While the early Saints followed a few of the

---

30. See note 5 above. The earliest recorded revelation we have in which the Lord unequivocally states that Joseph Smith alone was the Lord's mouthpiece came in the summer of 1830. See Doctrine and Covenants 28:1–7. Until then, Oliver Cowdery could arguably have been considered a joint-holder of the Melchizidek Priesthood keys with Joseph. See, for example, Joseph Fielding Smith, *Doctrines of Salvation*, 3 vols., comp. Bruce R. McConkie (Salt Lake City: Bookcraft, 1954), 1:212: "Oliver Cowdery's standing in the beginning was as the 'Second Elder' of the Church, holding the keys jointly with the Prophet Joseph Smith." Even this two-person organization would not comport with the trustee requirements of the statute.

31. Additionally, incorporation did not come without strings attached. Fulfilling New York's incorporation requirements invited government regulation, although the enforcement of such requirements is questionable in that area of the state. Because corporations enjoyed perpetual succession, the legislature placed a limit on the amount of property that churches could hold each year. New York Religious Incorporation Statute, §12, states that religious corporations could "have, hold, and enjoy lands, tenements, goods and chattels of the yearly value of three thousand dollars." Incorporated churches were also required to get state approval before any purchase of property. New York Religious Incorporation Statute, §11; see also Angell and Ames, *Treatise on the Law*, 183: "No religious corporation can sell any real estate without the Chancellor's order." If Church leaders were aware of such restrictions, they might have been reluctant to invite such oversight without significant benefits from incorporation.

32. See notes 15–20 above.

33. See Porter, "Study of the Origins," 100–101; see also note 38 below and accompanying text.

New York Religious Incorporation Statute	Fulfilled on April 6, 1830?	
Congregation assembles at the church, meetinghouse, or other place where church meets to worship	Yes	The Whitmer home could qualify, although the Whitmers had never hosted a formal Church meeting before April 6, 1830.
Minister gives notice of meeting to congregation	Yes	Joseph Smith gave notice of the upcoming meeting to the Saints.
Two elders elected to preside at election of trustees, judge the trustees' qualifications, and return the names of winners	No	While Joseph Smith and Oliver Cowdery were sustained as leaders of the Church, there is no record that they ever presided over the election of any trustees.
Three to nine trustees elected to take over church's property and transact church's affairs	No	Documents list six elders as original members, but there is no record that the congregation voted on them, and they did not perform trustee-like duties afterward.
Certificate filed with county clerk	No	No such certificate has been found.

following minor requirements, the more essential portions of the statute appear to not have been followed on April 6, 1830.

The statute required that "male persons of full age ... assemble at the church, meeting-house, or other place where they stately attend for divine worship."[34] The Saints met in the home of Peter Whitmer Sr., a locally influential farmer residing in Fayette, New York.[35] Despite not being an actual church, the home of a member appears to be a valid setting for an ecclesiastical election; other churches during that time period likewise chose to incorporate in the house of a member.[36] But the Whitmer home does not appear to be where the Saints "stately attend[ed]" for divine worship. The Church held no formal meetings there before April 6, 1830,[37] and after organization

---

34. New York Religious Incorporation Statute, §3.

35. See note 3 above.

36. Porter, "Study of the Origins," 159, citing a Seneca County Courthouse record book recording the incorporation certificate of the Methodist Episcopal Society "held at the House of Benjamin Kenny in the Village of Seneca Falls ... on the 6th day of January 1829."

37. The Church held its first public discourse (by Oliver Cowdery) on April 11, 1830, and held the first conference of the Church two months after organization, on June 1, 1830, both at the Peter Whitmer Sr. home. See Jessee, *Papers*, 304, 307.

the Church met at various locations, including two different schoolhouses, various churches, and other members' homes.[38] However, the Whitmer home was the location of three subsequent general conferences, which implies that when the early members needed a formal meeting place, they chose the Whitmer home. Additionally, Joseph Smith resided there at the time of organization, and it was essentially the headquarters of the Church.[39] Such a setting would probably qualify as an appropriate location for incorporation under the statute.

The statute further required that the minister "publicly notify the congregation of the time when, and place where, the said election shall be held."[40] Joseph Smith's manuscript history states, "[We] made known to our brethren, that we had received commandment to organize the Church And accordingly we met together for that purpose, at the house of Mr Whitmer."[41] Joseph states that he gave such notification, which is also evidenced by the sizable number in attendance at the organizational meeting.

The location and notice requirements constitute the extent of clear similarities between the statute and the accounts of the Church's organization. Additional requirements only tangentially align with the descriptions given of the meeting.

For example, the statute requires the election of two elders to preside over the election. "Two of the elders ... [shall be] nominated by a majority of members present ... [to] preside at such election, receive votes of the electors, ... and the officers to return the names of the [elected trustees]."[42] A seemingly parallel event is found when the congregation on April 6, 1830, voted on Joseph Smith and Oliver Cowdery: "[Joseph] proceeded ... to call on our brethren to know whether they accepted us as their teachers in the things of the Kingdom of God.... To these they consented by an unanimous vote."[43] But such an election was not for Joseph and Oliver to be temporary officers who would preside, run, and tally an election of a board of trustees. The congregation sustained Joseph and Oliver as the leaders of the Church. There is no record of any electoral judges being chosen.

---

38. Porter, "Study of the Origins," 100.

39. See, for example, Keith W. Perkins, "From New York to Utah: Seven Church Headquarters," *Ensign* 31 (August 2001): 52, which states, "*Wherever the prophet of the Lord was, there was the headquarters of the Church.*"

40. New York Religious Incorporation Statute, §3.

41. See Jessee, *Papers,* 302.

42. New York Religious Incorporation Statute, §3.

43. See Jessee, *Papers,* 302–3.

Perhaps of most significance is the absence of any actual election of trustees. The statute states that "male persons of full age ... [shall elect three to nine] trustees, to take the charge of the estate and property belonging thereto, and to transact all affairs relative to the temporalities thereof."[44] In the accounts of April 6, 1830, there is no mention of any election of trustees. Since the central purpose of an incorporation meeting was to elect these trustees, this silence is informative. Scholars point to the six original members of the Church as evidence of statutory compliance with this requirement.[45] But the accounts refer to them simply as "members," not trustees. Further, these six original members played a minimal role in the organizational meeting; in fact, their names were only recorded several decades afterward.[46] Also, after the organization these six original members do not appear to collectively perform any typical trustee duties such as the buying and selling of property or the creation of bylaws for the Church.[47] The statute clearly demonstrates that the decision-making power of a religious corporation should lie *in the trustees* after incorporation, while in reality, Joseph Smith maintained sole decision-making power as prophet.

Finally, the statute required that the officers "certify, under their hands and seals, the names of the persons elected to serve as trustees, ... [and] the name or title by which the said trustees and their successors shall forever thereafter be called and known."[48] No one has ever found the Church's incorporation certificate that was to be filed with the county clerk. Two historians in particular have meticulously searched to no avail for the certificate of incorporation in several government offices and courthouses in upstate New York.[49] While it is not unusual for historical documents to go missing and never be found again, historians not only have failed to find the actual certificate,

---

44. New York Religious Incorporation Statute, §3.

45. See, for example, Porter, "Study of the Origins," 159: "The writer would again like to emphasize that in a majority of the accounts referring to the organization of the LDS Church, the number six is stressed as the automatic number required by New York State Law to incorporate.... It appears that Joseph Smith arbitrarily selected six individuals to assist in meeting the requirements of the law."

46. See, for example, Porter, "Study of the Origins," 98–99, citing lists of the original six members by Joseph Knight Jr. in 1862 and David Whitmer in 1887. Note the discrepancy between the two lists, one citing Samuel H. Smith and the other John Whitmer, lending further evidence to the minimal role the original six members played. See generally Richard Lloyd Anderson, "Who Were the Six Who Organized the Church on April 6, 1830?" *Ensign* 10 (June 1980): 44–45.

47. New York Religious Incorporation Statute, §3.

48. New York Religious Incorporation Statute, §3.

49. Porter, "Study of the Origins," 155–60; Carmack, "Fayette," 15.

but also have not found any record that the county clerk ever received such certification or the requisite fee—separate notations that the clerk would have made in addition to filing the certificate.[50] This absence comes despite records of several other churches filing certificates during the time period.[51]

In summary, the only clear similarities between the statute and the events of April 6, 1830, appear to be Joseph Smith giving notice to the members of the Church to meet at the Whitmer home, a place where the Saints would typically gather. Otherwise, there are only seeming coincidences in the numbers of elders and electoral judges and of original members and trustees. While this could merely show a lack of awareness or compliance with the statute, it is more likely the Saints were simply not trying to incorporate, and perhaps were even unaware of the statute.

Seeing the Church as an Unincorporated Religious Society

Stronger evidence suggests that on April 6, 1830, Joseph Smith organized the Church as an unincorporated "religious society." First, in the nineteenth century, formation of a religious society often preceded incorporation. Second, the organizational events of the Church closely align with the customary methods that other churches followed for creating new religious societies. Third, early statements regarding the organization of the Church support the creation of a religious society. These facts lead to the likely conclusion that Church leaders did not incorporate the institution in New York but instead formed an unincorporated religious society.

Religious societies were regularly operating churches that did not hold corporate status. The legal definition of a religious society was "a voluntary association of individuals or families ... united for the purpose of having a common place of worship, and to provide a proper teacher to instruct them ... and to administer the ordinances of the church."[52] Essentially, religious societies comprised all unincorporated churches.

A religious society could be created by anyone wishing to form one's own church. Unlike religious corporations, in 1830 no federal or state statutes

---

50. Porter, "Study of the Origins," 156. Dr. Porter speculates that either the founders submitted the certificate and it was lost and never recorded or that "the initial press of business and the increasing opposition locally somehow stayed them from executing the document formally in a court of law."

51. Porter, "Study of the Origins," 155–56.

52. Tyler, *American Ecclesiastical Law*, 54. See also Bouvier, *Law Dictionary*, s.v. "Society": "A society is a number of persons united together by mutual consent, in order to deliberate, determine, and act jointly for some common purpose."

regulated the formation of religious societies. Rather, formation was deter-mined "by usage"; in other words, according to the policies and customs of each church.[53] In the 1830s, it was the common practice to create a religious society before incorporating.[54] In fact, nineteenth-century incorporation statutes were drafted with the presumption that such a statute would be applied to a pre-existing religious society.[55] If early Church leaders were aware of such a practice, they would have opted to form a religious society and not a corporation.

---

53. William Lawrence, "The Law of Religious Societies and Church Corporations," *American Law Register* 21 (June 1873): 537: "It is a general rule that every person of proper intellectual capacity, may unite with others assenting thereto, in perfecting the organiza-tion of a religious society according to the forms required by the ecclesiastical faith and church government which may be adopted." See also Lawrence, "The Law of Religious Societies," 362–63: "A particular religious society may be organized with an appropriate number of members as a new and original congregation.... In all such cases there are in many of the different denominations proceedings or forms to be observed, in obedience to regulations prescribed or resulting from usage." See also Lawrence, "Law of Religious Societies," 541: "There can be but little practical necessity for any legal provision by statute to authorize or regulate this form of organization. It is created as at common law by such written articles of association as religious societies may adopt or may rest in parol." This aligns with religious societies' legal similarities to partnerships, which could be formed by any express act of the partners. See Bouvier, *Law Dictionary*, s.v. "Partnership": "Part-nerships are created by mere act of the parties; and in this they differ from corporations which require the sanction of public authority, either express or implied."

54. The organization of the Church occurred before a larger movement developed to incorporate churches throughout the United States. Colonial churches seldom incor-porated, primarily because the use of general statutes of incorporation did not yet exist. Joseph Stancliffe Davis, *Essays in the Earlier History of American Corporations* (Cam-bridge: Harvard University Press, 1917), 79–80; see also note 21 above. Into the 1870s, a "large proportion of all the religious societies in many of the states [were still] unincorpo-rated," Lawrence, "Law of Religious Societies," 540. By the turn of the twentieth century, the majority of churches in America incorporated. See "Incorporation of Religious Soci-eties," *Columbia Law Review* 5 (February 1905): 154: "At present a majority of the religious societies in this country conduct their affairs under a franchise [civil corporation]." The LDS Church organized before this movement to incorporate gained momentum, and organizing without incorporation would have been common for a church in 1830.

55. Note the very title of New York's incorporation statute: An Act to Provide for the Incorporation of Religious Societies. See also Lawrence, "Law of Religious Societies," 548, emphasis in original: "The statutes [authorizing incorporation] generally contemplate a prior *ecclesiastical* organization." The statute's requirements also presume the incorpora-tion of a preexisting religious society. It called for the election to be held at the typical place of worship, and the minister was to publish notice to the congregation at least two Sundays in advance. New York Religious Incorporation Statute, §3. Also, the trustees were active males chosen from the general body of the church and were to take charge of the church's

The organizational events of the Church align with customary methods that other churches followed for creating new religious societies (see fig. 1). Unlike religious corporations, in 1830 the formation of a religious society was regulated by the individual policies and customs of each church, not by legislative statutes.[56] Most new societies formed local branches of larger existing religions, such as the Presbyterian, Methodist, Baptist, and Episcopal faiths, whose mother churches had detailed policies that the new religious societies were to follow in order to effectively organize. Alternatively, a new church not being formed as a branch of an existing denomination had no restrictions on how they could form. By examining the instruction that other churches gave regarding how to form new congregations, one can understand the customary method for forming a religious society with which Joseph Smith possibly employed. The events of the organization of the LDS Church align in several ways with the guidelines of these other churches.

One of the leading faiths in upstate New York was Presbyterianism.[57] To guide the growth of the church in new communities like Palmyra, the General Assembly of the Presbyterian Church printed pamphlets and treatises specifying how to form new congregations.[58] The organization of a new Presbyterian religious society occurred as follows. Individuals were to send a petition to the presbytery that would appoint two ruling elders to organize the church.[59] The two ruling elders, "having given due notice to the persons

---

estate and property. New York Religious Incorporation Statute, §3. These requirements only seem sensible if a previously operating church was applying for incorporation.

56. See note 53 above and accompanying text.

57. Milton V. Backman, *Joseph Smith's First Vision: The First Vision in its Historical Context* (Salt Lake City: Bookcraft, 1980), 66–69. Due to the renewed religious interest incited by the Second Great Awakening, the Presbyterian Church in Palmyra divided into two congregations in 1817. Several members of Joseph Smith's family, including Lucy, Hyrum, and Samuel, regularly attended one of these congregations, the Western Presbyterian Church, during Joseph's youth. Backman, *Joseph Smith's First Vision*, 69.

58. See, for example, *Report of a Committee of the General Assembly, Appointed for Revising the Form of Government, and the Forms of Process of the Presbyterian Church, in the United States of America* (Philadelphia: Thomas and William Bradford, 1819), including on the title page, "Ordered to be Printed for the Consideration of the Presbyteries"; see also Lawrence, "Law of Religious Societies," 363 n. 56; Benjamin F. Bittinger, *Manual of Law and Usage* (Philadelphia: Presbyterian Board of Publication, 1888), 30–35; W. H. Workman, *Presbyterian Rule, Embracing the Form of Government, Rules of Discipline, and Directory for Worship, in the Presbyterian Church in the United States* (Richmond, Va.: Presbyterian Committee of Publication, 1898), 21–27.

59. Lawrence, "Law of Religious Societies," 363 n. 56, quoting *Prescribed Rules for Organizing a United Presbyterian Congregation*.

who are to compose the new congregation of the time and place of meeting ... [would] converse with all who propose[d] to unite in forming the congregation; and being satisfied with their religious attainments and character, ... on the day appointed for the organization, [would] publicly receive them."[60] The organizational meeting was to begin with the "usual exercises of public worship,"[61] or "devotional exercises, conducted by the presiding minister,"[62] followed by the election of the ruling elders.[63] Only "male communicating members" in the church could be elected as elders, who after election were ordained to their offices.[64] This was accomplished when one of the elders asked the congregation, "Do you the members of this congregation acknowledge and receive this brother as a Ruling Elder ... in this church?"[65] The members then responded "in the affirmative, by holding up their right hands" and then witnessed the setting apart of the elder by prayer.[66] Baptisms also commonly played a role in such events.[67]

The Methodist Church published similar guidelines. Methodists were among the earliest to organize in the Palmyra area and enjoyed tremendous growth during Joseph Smith's youth due to the success of Methodist circuit riders.[68] In rural areas, these itinerant preachers rotated through different areas of the country, opting for camp meetings in forest groves or barns rather than formal meetinghouses.[69] The actual formation of a congregation often had to wait until a preacher was willing to permanently minister to a congregation. The church counseled that "persons desiring to organize themselves ... [should] apply to a Methodist preacher, having regular pastoral charge near them, who receives them as members of the church ... on a profession of their faith. The preacher then enrolls their names in the general register of his charge" and "when these steps have been taken, the society is duly constituted, and becomes an organic part of the church, and has regular pastoral care."[70]

---

60. Lawrence, "Law of Religious Societies," 363 n. 56.

61. Lawrence, "Law of Religious Societies," 363 n. 56.

62. Bittinger, *Manual of Law and Usage*, 31.

63. *Report of a Committee of the General Assembly*, 10; Workman, *Presbyterian Rule*, 23.

64. *Report of a Committee of the General Assembly*, 10.

65. *Report of a Committee of the General Assembly*, 10.

66. *Report of a Committee of the General Assembly*, 10.

67. Bittinger, *Manual of Law and Usage*, 32; Workman, *Presbyterian Rule*, 22.

68. Backman, *Joseph Smith's First Vision*, 57, 70.

69. Backman, *Joseph Smith's First Vision*, 70–71.

70. Lawrence, "Law of Religious Societies," 364 n. 56.

Figure 1. Excerpts from Pamphlets and Rules Regarding the Formation of Local Congregations

Presbyterian: Form of Government and General Administration: *Prescribed Rules for Organizing a United Presbyterian Congregation.*

When a congregation becomes too numerous to meet conveniently in one place for public worship, or when for any other reason it would promote the general interests of the church to organize a new congregation, the persons so judging shall make application to the Presbytery, within whose bounds they reside, setting forth the necessity or propriety of such organization. Whenever application for this purpose is made, notice shall be given by the Presbytery to the session of the congregation, that may be affected by the new organization, before the petition is granted.

If after hearing the reasons, the Presbytery determines to grant the application, it shall appoint a minister and two ruling elders, if practicable, to carry the object into effect; and they having given due notice to the persons who are to compose the new congregation of the time and place of meeting for said purpose, shall, after the usual exercises of public worship, proceed to hold an election for the proper officers.

When the persons who are to compose the new congregation are already members of the church in full communion, the election of officers shall be conducted as in congregations already organized.

But when the applicants are not in communion, the minister shall converse with all who propose to unite in forming the congregation; and being satisfied with their religious attainments and character, he shall, on the day appointed for the organization, publicly receive them by proposing the questions usually proposed to applicants for membership. The election shall then be conducted in the prescribed way.

When the election is over, the minister shall announce to the congregation the names of the persons elected; and on their agreeing to accept the office, and having been examined by him as to their qualifications for, and their views in undertaking it, a day shall be appointed for their ordination, the edict served, and the ordination conducted as in other congregations.

The presiding minister shall report to the Presbytery his procedure in the case, with the names of the officers who have been chosen and ordained. And these with the name of the congregation shall be entered on the Presbytery's list.

Methodist: *Mode of Organizing a New Society of the Methodist Episcopal Church as determined by Usage.*

If in a certain neighborhood there are persons desiring to organize themselves into a Christian Society in accordance with the rules and usages of the M. E. Church, how is such organization effected?

They apply to a Methodist preacher, having regular pastoral charge near them, who receives them as members of the church, either by written certificate of their good standing in some other society, or on profession of their faith. The preacher then enrolls their names in the general register of his charge, and in a class-book which he gives to one of them whom he appoints as leader of the class. The leader represents them in the Quarterly Conference.

When these steps have been taken, the society is duly constituted, and becomes an organic part of the church, and has regular pastoral care. And this care is perpetuated from year to year by the appointment of a pastor by the bishop at the session of the Annual Conference in whose bounds such society is situated.

If this society have a house of worship, or propose to erect one, a board of trustees must be created in accordance with the laws of the state or territory to hold the property in trust for said society. These trustees must be approved by the Quarterly Conference of the Circuit of which such society is a part. And to be admitted, the charter, deed or conveyance of such house of worship, must contain the trust required by the discipline of the church.

Baptist: Edward T. Hiscox, *The Baptist Directory: A Guide to the Doctrines and Practices of Baptist Churches.*

When a number of Christians, members of the same or of different churches, believe that their own spiritual improvement, or the religious welfare of the community so requires, they organize a new church.

This is done by uniting in mutual covenant, to sustain the relations and obligations prescribed by the Gospel, to be governed by the laws of Christ's house, and to maintain public worship and the preaching of the Gospel. Articles of faith are usually adopted, as also a name by which the church shall be known, and its officers elected.

Episcopal: Murray Hoffman, *A Treatise on the Law of the Protestant Episcopal Church in the United States.*

Whenever any number of persons shall associate to form an Episcopal congregation, they shall ... acknowledge and accede to the constitution, canons, doctrine, discipline, and worship of the Protestant Episcopal Church in the United States ...; they shall assume a suitable name by which their church or parish shall be designated, and appoint not less than three nor more than eleven vestrymen and two wardens....

The form of organization of a parish is this: "We the subscribers, assembled for the purpose of organizing a parish of the Protestant Episcopal Church in the town of _____ ..., after due notice given, do hereby agree to form a parish, to be known by the name of _____ church, and as such do hereby acknowledge and accede to the constitution and canons of the Protestant Episcopal Church in the United States of America, and the constitution and canons of the same Church in the diocese.

The Baptist Church was also prominent in the Palmyra area and had a membership of several hundred in the 1820s.[71] They grew quickly, "primarily by converting unchurched americans," and relied on uneducated lay ministers to staff their congregations.[72] A key tenet of the Baptist faith focused on the independence of each congregation.[73] The method for organization of a Baptist society was thus, not surprisingly, free of many formalities and could differ from society to society. One treatise describes the loose requirements as follows: "When a number of Christians, members of the same or of different churches, believe that their own spiritual improvement, or the religious welfare of the community so requires, they organize a new church. This is done by uniting in mutual covenant to sustain the relations and obligations prescribed by the Gospel.... Articles of faith are usually adopted, as also a name by which the church shall be known, and its officers elected."[74]

The Episcopal Church in the United States, formerly known as the Church of England, also instructed new members on how to form a congregation.[75] Like the Baptist Church, the Episcopal Church gave general instructions for formation without any rigid formalities. The congregation was to give notice of an upcoming organizational meeting and at such meeting adopt articles of association, assume a suitable name, elect officers, and agree to the beliefs and practices of that church.[76]

Comparability to the Organization of the LDS Church

While a significant difference exists between organizing an entirely new church and forming a new congregation under an existing denomination, the organizational events of April 6, 1830, align quite closely with various elements in the customary methods for organizing local congregations as prescribed by these other churches.

---

71. Backman, *Joseph Smith's First Vision*, 64–65.

72. Backman, *Joseph Smith's First Vision*, 56.

73. Milton V. Backman Jr., *Christian Churches of America: Origins and Beliefs* (New York: Charles Scribner's Sons, 1976), 136.

74. Edward T. Hiscox, *The Baptist Directory: A Guide to the Doctrines and Practices of Baptist Churches* (New York: Sheldon and Company, 1876), 17.

75. Episcopalian preachers only taught sporadically in western New York at the beginning of the nineteenth century, and consequently a permanent Episcopalian congregation did not take hold in Palmyra until 1823. Backman, *Joseph Smith's First Vision*, 74–75.

76. Murray Hoffman, *A Treatise on the Law of the Protestant Episcopal Church in the United States* (New York: Stanford and Swords, 1850), 237–38.

Notice was given to the membership. Joseph Smith informed his brethren of the revelation commanding him to organize a church.[77] Both the Presbyterian and Episcopalian churches required notice be given to the prospective membership of a religious society. The prospective leadership gave "due notice to the persons who [were] to compose the new congregation of the time and place of meeting."[78]

Ruling or leading elders were elected. Joseph Smith called on the brethren present to know whether they accepted him and Oliver Cowdery as "their teachers in the things of the Kingdom of God."[79] Each of the four other churches elected their officers at their organizational meetings. The April 6 election of Joseph and Oliver is most similar to the Presbyterians' subscribed meeting, which included the election of two "ruling elders." Oliver and Joseph respectively ordained one another as elders on April 6, 1830,[80] with Joseph being the "first elder" and Oliver the "second elder."[81] Compare also the question asked at a Presbyterian service ("Do you the members of this congregation acknowledge and receive this brother as a Ruling Elder?"[82]) with Joseph Smith's description of the election ("[We called] on our brethren to know whether they accepted us as their teachers in the things of the kingdom of God"[83]). Presbyterians then answered in the affirmative by raising their right hands,[84] a practice similar to that of the LDS Church.

The organization was accompanied by usual exercises of public worship. The April 6 meeting opened with prayer and, after the election of elders, included the administration of the sacrament as well as "time spent

---

77. See note 41 above and accompanying text.

78. Lawrence, "Law of Religious Societies," 363 n. 56, quoting *Prescribed Rules for Organizing a United Presbyterian Congregation*; see also Hoffman, *Treatise on the Law of the Protestant Episcopal Church*, 246: "We the subscribers, assembled for the purpose of organizing a parish of the Protestant Episcopal Church ..., after due notice given, do hereby agree to form a parish."

79. Jessee, *Papers*, 302–3.

80. See note 5 above and accompanying text.

81. Doctrine and Covenants 20:2–3. Early versions of the Articles and Covenants of the Church read simply "an elder." See Scott H. Faulring, "An Examination of the 1829 'Articles of the Church of Christ' in Relation to Section 20 of the Doctrine and Covenants," *BYU Studies* 43, no. 4 (2004): 72 n. 52. Reference to Joseph Smith as "first elder" came in the 1835 Doctrine and Covenants. Note that priesthood licenses issued at the first conference of elders on June 9, 1830, specifically designated that Joseph was the First Elder and Oliver Cowdery was the Second.

82. *Report of a Committee of the General Assembly*, 10.

83. Jessee, *Papers*, 302–3.

84. *Report of a Committee of the General Assembly*, 10.

Customary Elements of Other Churches' Organizational Meetings		Similar Element Found in Organization of LDS Church?
Notice given to membership	Yes	Joseph Smith notified the brethren that he "had received commandment to organize the Church."
Election of ruling elders	Yes	A sustaining vote was taken as to whether the congregation accepted Joseph and Oliver as their leaders.
Usual exercises of public worship	Yes	Members oversaw the administration of the sacrament, prophesied, and witnessed.
Ordinations, baptisms and confirmations	Yes	Joseph and Oliver ordained elders and others to priesthood offices, confirmed members, and performed baptisms.
Official church name, membership and constitution	Yes	D&C 20 was received prior to organization, the "Church of Christ" was adopted as the official name, and a commandment was received to keep a record.

in witnessing."[85] Each of these portions of the meeting could be considered parts of a normal worship service, similar to the Presbyterian organizational meeting that began with the "usual exercises of public worship" and "devotional exercises."[86]

Ordinations, baptisms, and confirmations were then performed. In addition to Joseph Smith and Oliver Cowdery being ordained to the office of elder by the laying on of hands, others were called and ordained to priesthood offices. The leaders then confirmed members of the Church and gave them the gift of the Holy Ghost.[87] After the meeting, "several persons who had attended ... [became] convinced of the truth, came forward shortly after, and were [baptized]."[88] This coincides with the practice of the Baptist and Episcopal churches, who similarly ordained other officers and accepted additional members into their church through baptism on the days of organization.

An official church name was given, membership recorded, and articles of regulation were soon put in place. After the organizational meeting, the

---

85. Jessee, *Papers,* 303.
86. *Report of a Committee of the General Assembly,* 10.
87. See notes 4–7 above and accompanying text.
88. Jessee, *Papers,* 303.

Church was officially known as "The Church of Christ."[89] Similarly, the Baptist and Episcopal churches both required that the congregation designate a suitable name for each church that organized.[90] Also, at the organizational meeting, Joseph Smith received a revelation that called for a record to be kept among the Church (D&C 20:82).[91] The Methodist Church likewise kept a record after organizing that included a "general register" of the members of the church. Note also the role of the Articles and Covenants of the Church, which represent a declaration of the doctrine and practices that the newly organized Church would follow—in essence a constitution or bylaws for the new church.[92] Correspondingly, the Episcopal Church required the reading and adoption of articles of association at their organizational meetings, and the Baptist Church required that articles of faith be adopted. While it is unknown how much, if any, of the Articles and Covenants was read at the organizational meeting,[93] they were accepted by the Church in a June conference, and the focus of early Church leaders on composing these articles aligns with the customary practice of other denominations. In summary, the events of the LDS organizational meeting aligned with the custom of coexisting churches seeking to form a religious society.

Historical Statements in Context

Finally, viewing the organization of the Church from the perspective of a religious society aligns well with the historical statements made by its earliest members. Indeed, the absence of any historical reference to incorporation in any of the accounts of April 6, 1830, is revealing. There exists no statement from any eyewitness or early Church member describing the event as an act of "incorporation." The events were instead consistently referred to as the

---

89. See Doctrine and Covenants 20:1; 21:11; David Whitmer, *An Address to All Believers in Christ* (Richmond: 1887), 73: "In June, 1829, the Lord gave us the name by which we must call the church, being the same as He gave the Nephites. We obeyed His commandment, and called it the church of christ."

90. Hiscox, *Baptist Directory*, 17; Hoffman, *Treatise on the Law of the Protestant Episcopal Church*, 246.

91. See note 7 above and accompanying text; Doctrine and Covenants 21:1.

92. Composing these articles was a principal goal of early leaders. Oliver Cowdery penned an early version of the Articles and Covenants in 1829 (entitled "the articles of the Church of Christ") and Church membership ratified the Articles and Covenants of the Church of Christ at the first conference in June 1830. See Faulring, "An Examination of the 1829 'Articles of the Church of Christ.'"

93. See note 3.

"organization" or "organizing" of the Church, terms typically used to describe a formation of a religious society.[94] If the leaders of the Church were familiar with the statutory difference between incorporation and organization, their use of the word "organization" is significant.

While Church members did not refer to the incorporation statute, they did refer to the organization being done according to the laws of the land. The Articles and Covenants describe the organization being done "agreeable to the laws of our country."[95] Additionally, in 1887 David Whitmer stated that the Church was formed according to the "laws of the land":

> The reason why we met on that day was this; the world had been telling us that we were not a regularly organized church, and we had no right to officiate in the ordinance of marriage, hold church property, etc., and that we should organize according to the laws of the land. On this account we met at my father's house in Fayette, N.Y., on April 6, 1830, to attend to this matter of organizing according to the laws of the land.[96]

These statements have motivated scholars to look for a statute that the Saints were trying to comply with and implement—a specific "law of the land." But reference to the organization being accomplished "according to the laws of the land" can just as well be construed as a declaration that the organization was done "legally" or "in a customary manner," not necessarily according to a specific statute.[97] Whitmer's overall concern appears to have been that

---

94. Nearly every example that the author found of instructions to new congregations regarding the formation of religious societies in the nineteenth century used "organization" or "organize" to describe the act of creation. See, for example, Lawrence, "Law of Religious Societies," quoting Presbyterian instructions for creating a religious society that stated, "When a congregation becomes too numerous ... it would promote the general interests of the church to organize a new congregation" (363); and quoting Methodist instructions for creating a religious society, which stated that a group could be formed "if in a certain neighborhood there are persons desiring to organize themselves into a Christian Society" (364).

95. See Doctrine and Covenants 20:1: "THE RISE of the Church of Christ ... being regularly organized and established agreeable to the laws of our country."

96. Whitmer, *Address to All Believers,* 33; see also David Whitmer, *Kansas City Daily Journal,* June 5, 1881: "On the 6th of April, 1830, the church was called together and the elders acknowledged according to the laws of New York" (Church History Library, The Church of Jesus Christ of Latter-day Saints, Salt Lake City.)

97. An act may be consistent with the common law (the unwritten, judge-made law which derives its force from the consent and practice of the governed) and be done according to the laws of the land without any specific statute explicitly governing the action.

community members were criticizing their lack of any legal organization whatsoever. Forming a religious society would have quelled such criticism.[98]

Further, Whitmer specifically mentions the Church lacking the authority to marry and hold church property. Both of these acts could be done by a religious society. The ability to perform marriages was not exclusively held by religious corporations but could be performed by a minister of any religious society,[99] and the members of an organized religious society could hold property on the congregation's behalf.[100]

A number of statements by subsequent members show a misunderstanding of New York's legal requirements for organizing a church.[101] These statements have since caused confusion regarding the Church's formation, most notably the reason for having six original members. As an example of one of these statements, the Apostle Erastus Snow stated the following in 1873:

> At that time there existed in the State of New York a legal statute forbidding anybody to minister in spiritual things, except a regularly recognized minister, and which also provided, that any six believers had the right to assemble to organize a religious body. After inquiring of the Lord, and to enable him to minister lawfully, the Prophet Joseph was commanded to enter into an organization; it was therefore on the 6th of April, 1830, that this

---

98. The critics pointed to a lack of formal church organization, not that the Church had failed to incorporate.

99. Nineteenth century legal treatises declared that "no peculiar ceremonies are requisite by the common law to the valid celebration of the marriage. The consent of the parties is all that is required." Kent, *Commentaries*, 2:87. "It can be done by ministers of the gospel and priests of every denomination.... When performed by a minister or priest, it shall be according to the forms and customs of the society to which he belongs." Member of the New York Bar, *The Citizen's Law Book* (New York: Henry Ludwig, 1844), 412.

100. Religious societies were treated as "quasi-partnerships" and members of such societies could acquire, lease, and sell property on behalf of the congregation. See Tyler, *American Ecclesiastical Law*, 55, emphasis in original: "It has however been held that property may be granted to individuals for the *use* of a church not incorporated." Lack of incorporation limited the transfer of property after death, and the property needed to be kept in the members' names and not that of the church, but a religious society was not forbidden from holding property. Before April 6, 1830, the Church was not even an unincorporated religious society. By "organizing," they obtained the right to perform marriages and hold property, and they satisfied the concerns outlined by Whitmer.

101. See, for example, Porter, "Study of the Origins," 159: "In a majority of the accounts referring to the organization of the LDS Church, the number six is stressed as the automatic number required by New York State Law to incorporate."

statute was complied with, and the Church became recognized by the laws of the State of New York.[102]

A number of problems exist in this statement regardless of whether the Church incorporated or not. No portion of the religious incorporation statute, or any statute for that matter, forbade the exercise of "spiritual things" by nonministers. Additionally, the thought that there must be six believers to organize a religious body is also mistaken. There was no numerical requirement to form a religious society, and the incorporation statute required between three and nine, not six exactly.[103] Statements like Elder Snow's have led historians to believe that the number of original members held legal significance.[104] Such was not the case. Unfortunately, understanding the Church's organization as that of a religious society rather than a corporation fails to shed light on why Joseph chose to recognize six men as members, other than that it was probably not because any statute or law required it.

Conclusion

In the nineteenth century, church members could legally form a new congregation through two methods: the creation of a religious corporation or the organization of a religious society. While historians have long assumed Joseph Smith created a religious corporation on April 6, 1830, it is more likely he created a religious society when he organized the Church. Considering the Church's condition in 1830, forming a religious society clearly met the Church's needs and avoided an undesirable leadership structure. Additionally, the recorded accounts of the organizational meeting lack conformity with the incorporation statute's requirements but strongly resemble the customary methods of how other churches formed religious societies.

Understanding the legal status of the newly organized Church places the events of April 6, 1830, in a clearer context. Nearly every aspect of the Church's organizational meeting was a typical practice of the Baptist, Episcopalian, Methodist, or Presbyterian churches.[105] This not only shows that

---

102. "Discourse by Erastus Snow," *Latter-day Saints' Millennial Star* 35 (April 22, 1873): 249–50.

103. Elder Snow did not join the Church until 1833 at the age of fourteen and was not an eye-witness to any of the events in New York. See generally Andrew Karl Larson, *Erastus Snow: The Life of a Missionary and Pioneer for the Early Mormon Church* (Salt Lake City: University of Utah Press, 1971), 17–18.

104. See, for example, note 101 above.

105. The sole exception to this is Joseph Smith's receipt of a revelation.

the early Church members did comply with the law in organizing, but also possibly explains why they chose certain actions during the meeting.[106]

After the meeting, Joseph records that he felt "acknowledged of God, 'The Church of Jesus Christ,' organized in accordance with commandments and revelations."[107] Not only did Joseph organize the Church according to the laws of the land, but he obeyed God's commandments in doing so. The Church's organization was thus done according to both the laws of God and man.

First published with more extensive analysis under the title "Legal Insights into the Organization of the Church in 1830," BYU Studies 49, no. 2 (2010): 121–48.

---

106. The author wishes to emphasize that this article focuses solely on the legal analysis of a single event in Church history. This article was not intended to participate in any ongoing debate regarding the history of priesthood organization, Church hierarchy, and later unfolding developments. Such issues go beyond the scope of this deliberately limited article.

107. Jessee, *Papers,* 303.

Chapter Seven

Winning against Hurlbut's Assault in 1834

David W. Grua

Joseph Smith became well acquainted with the legal system in Ohio during his seven years there. Through encounters, he seems to have developed a guarded view of the law's prospect for delivering justice. At first, he had a firm belief that, through faith and God's assistance, he could obtain justice through the judicial process. He was willing to go before the courts to present his complaints with confidence that he would ultimately prevail against all challenges. But after 1837, when those who opposed him began assailing him with what he called "vexatious lawsuits,"[1] he learned he could not rely on courts for his protection and rights.

Important in Joseph Smith's legal experience was the April 1834 case of *Ohio v. Doctor Philastus Hurlbut*. This was his first appearance in the courts of Ohio and a rare occasion on which he took the initiative in a judicial action. In December 1833, Hurlbut, an excommunicated Latter-day Saint, had threatened publicly to kill Smith in Kirtland, Ohio. Coming in the midst of a season of persecution of the Saints in Ohio and Missouri, this threat was one that the young President of the Church was not willing to let pass. He filed an official complaint with the Geauga County authorities, requesting them to prevent Hurlbut from carrying out his threat. As the prosecution proceeded during the first four months of 1834, Smith recorded his prayers to the Lord that the courts would be filled with the spirit of justice.

---

1. Dean C. Jessee, ed., *The Papers of Joseph Smith*, 2 vols. (Salt Lake City: Deseret Book, 1989–92), 2:214.

Events Leading to This Legal Action

Although the case itself began on December 21, 1833, events occurred nine months earlier that set it in motion. In March 1833, the newly baptized Doctor

Philastus Hurlbut (Doctor was his given name) arrived in Kirtland, Ohio. Joseph Smith recorded that Hurlbut visited the Smith home on March 13 to discuss the Book of Mormon.[2] Five days later, Sidney Rigdon ordained Hurlbut an elder, and on March 19 Hurlbut was called to serve a mission in Pennsylvania.[3]

Shortly after establishing himself in Pennsylvania, Hurlbut's fellow missionary Orson Hyde accused Hurlbut of immorality before a church council in Kirtland, which excommunicated him on June 3, 1833, for "unchristian conduct with the female sex."[4] Hurlbut, however, was not present at this hearing and appealed the decision. He traveled to Kirtland, confessed his offense, and the council reinstated him on June 21, 1833. It was soon evident that his repentance was not sincere, as two days later the council excommunicated Hurlbut for claiming to outsiders that he had "deceived Joseph Smith's God."[5]

Orson Hyde. Courtesy of the Church Archives, The Church of Jesus Christ of Latter-day Saints.

Hurlbut determined to pursue the matter by lecturing against Joseph Smith and the Church. While delivering his anti-Mormon lectures in Pennsylvania, Hurlbut sensationalized the ill-founded theory that the Book of

---

2. Joseph Smith, Journal, January 11, 1834, Church History Library, The Church of Jesus Christ of Latter-day Saints, Salt Lake City; Dean C. Jessee, *Papers of Joseph Smith,* 2 vols. (Salt Lake City: Deseret Book, 1989-92), 2:19. Most of the documents cited here from Church History Library are available in *Selected Collections from the Archives of The Church of Jesus Christ of Latter-day Saints,* 2 vols. (Provo, Utah: Brigham Young University Press, 2002), DVD 20.

3. "Kirtland Council Minute Book," 12, 14, 16, Church History Library; Benjamin Winchester, *The Origin of the Spalding Story* (Philadelphia: Brown, Bicking, and Guilbert, 1840), 6.

4. "Kirtland Council Minute Book," 12; Orson Hyde to George G. Adams, June 7, 1841, in Benjamin Winchester, *Plain Facts* (England, 1841).

5. "Kirtland Council Minute Book," 21–22.

Mormon was based on an unpublished manuscript written several years earlier by Solomon Spalding entitled *Manuscript Found*. Hurlbut also accused Joseph Smith of "lieing in a wonderful manner" so that "people are running after him and giving him mony."[6] After gathering financial support from anti-Mormons in the area around Kirtland, Hurlbut embarked in the summer of 1833 on a journey through Ohio, Massachusetts, Pennsylvania, and New York, generating evidence against Joseph.[7]

In late November and early December 1833, word reached Kirtland that a mob had expelled the Latter-day Saints from Jackson County, Missouri.[8] Geauga County anti-Mormons, emboldened by this news, began to threaten Smith and his followers in Ohio with a similar expulsion. Tensions were high. On December 5, 1833, Smith wrote to Edward Partridge and others in Missouri that "the inhabitants of this county threaten our destruction and we know not how soon they may be permitted to follow the examples of the Missourians."[9] George A. Smith later said of this time period: "In consequence of the persecution which raged against the Prophet Joseph and the constant threats to do him violence it was found necessary to keep continual guard to prevent his being murdered by his enemies, who were headed by Joseph H. Wakefield and Dr. P. Hurlbert ... during the fall and winter I took part of this service going 2½ miles to guard at President Rigdon's."[10] Wakefield and his fellow anti-Mormons left no account of their involvement in these persecutions.

In mid-December 1833, Hurlbut returned to Kirtland and began to lecture on his material. How and when Hurlbut threatened to kill Smith remains unknown, but George A. Smith later stated that "in delivering lectures he [Hurlbut] had said he would wash his hands in Joseph Smith's blood."[11] Joseph felt constrained to take his complaint before the county officials.[12]

---

6. Joseph Smith to William W. Phelps and others, August 18, 1833, Church History Library.

7. Winchester, *Origin of the Spalding Story*, 7–11.

8. On Kirtland's reaction to the Missouri troubles, see Milton V. Backman Jr., *The Heavens Resound: A History of the Latter-day Saints in Ohio, 1830–1838* (Salt Lake City: Deseret Book, 1983), 162–74.

9. Joseph Smith to Edward Partridge and others, December 5, 1833, Joseph Smith Letterbook 1, 68-69, Church History Library.

10. George A. Smith, "Memoirs," 12, George A. Smith Collection, Church History Library.

11. George A. Smith, in *Journal of Discourses*, 26 vols. (Liverpool: F. D. Richards, 1855–86), 11:8, November 15, 1864.

12. "Mormon Trial," *Chardon Spectator and Geauga Gazette*, April 12, 1834, page 3.

The Justice Court

On December 21, 1833, Joseph Smith went to the office of John C. Dowen, justice of the peace for Kirtland Township, and filed a complaint against Hurlbut, stating that there was "reason to fear that Doctor P. Hurlbut would Beat wound or kill him or injure his property." The complaint asked the court to compel Hurlbut to keep the peace.[13] The Ohio statute relevant to the case reads:

> It shall be lawful for any person to make complaint on oath or affirmation, before a justice of the peace, stating, amongst other things, that the person making such complaint has *just cause to fear, and does fear,* that another *will beat, wound, or kill him* or her, or his or her ward, child, or children; or will commit some other act of personal violence upon him, her or them; or will burn his or her dwelling house, or out-house, or will maliciously injure, or *destroy his or her property,* other than the buildings aforesaid.[14]

On December 27, 1833, Justice Dowen issued an arrest warrant directing that Hurlbut be apprehended and brought before Painesville Justice of the Peace William Holbrook.[15] Oddly, the warrant issued by Dowen did not direct that Hurlbut be brought before Dowen himself; but the Ohio statue allowed this.[16] He may have done this because Hurlbut was residing in, or close to, Painesville at the time, or Justice Dowen may have felt that Hurlbut would receive a more impartial hearing in Painesville than in Mormon Kirtland.

On January 4, 1834, Kirtland Constable Stephen Sherman brought Hurlbut to Justice Holbrook's office in Painesville. Justice Holbrook postponed the hearing until January 6, 1834, during which time Hurlbut remained in the

---

13. Record Book P, 431–32. Geauga County Archives and Records Center, Chardon, Ohio. This legal action was used as a preventive measure to impede individuals from acting out threats.

14. An Act Defining the Powers and Duties of Justices of the Peace and Constables, sections 9 and 33.1 (passed March 1831 and took effect June 1) (hereafter cited as Justices of the Peace Act), *Acts of a General Nature, Enacted, Revised, and Ordered to be Reprinted,...* (Columbus: Olmsted and Bailhache, 1831), emphasis added; J. R. Swan, *Statutes of the State of Ohio, of a General Nature,...* (Columbus: Samuel Medary, 1841), 502–535.

15. John C. Dowen, Statement, January 2, 1885, p. 3, Chicago Historical Society. See Justices of the Peace Act, section 33.4. Justices of the Peace Act, section 10, states that warrants may be returned before any justice of a county. Dowen, a Methodist, had moved to Kirtland in 1832 and was elected justice of the peace in 1833. Holbrook was a justice of the peace in Painesville at least from 1831 to 1834.

16. Justices of the Peace Act, section 10, at 196, and section 33.2, at 199–200.

custody of Constable Sherman.[17] A probable reason for the delay was that witnesses needed to be subpoenaed and prepared to give testimony concerning the threat. By statute, a justice of the peace could delay the hearing while material witnesses were found and prepared.[18] By statute, postponements could occur "from time to time … until the cause of delay be removed" as long as the defendant was not in jail for more than a total of thirty-six hours. Thus, it is probable that Hurlbut was not kept in jail during the postponement, but simply remained in the custody of the constable.[19] In the meantime, word of the arrest quickly spread throughout the county.

Constable Sherman brought Hurlbut before Justice Holbrook on January 6, 1834, only to be turned away again. The court record states that "not being yet ready for the examination on the part of the State this cause is again postponed to the 13th of January 1834, at 9 o'clock a.m."[20]

The preliminary hearing determined if the prosecution had sufficient evidence to send the case to the county court. The county prosecuting attorney did not attend these preliminary hearings,[21] thus requiring Joseph Smith as the aggrieved party to retain a lawyer. He hired Benjamin Bissell, who had a reputation as one of Ohio's ablest attorneys. He served as the ad hoc prosecuting attorney for this hearing, calling all witnesses for the state and presenting the state's case.[22]

---

17. Record Book P, 431–32.

18. Justices of the Peace Act, section 22.

19. Upon postponement of a civil case, if the defendant did not give bail for his later appearance, the justice had to commit him to jail, "there to remain until the time appointed for the trial, which shall not exceed three days from the return of such capias; or the justice may order the constable to hold such defendant in custody, until the plaintiff shall have notice and time to attend and proceed to trial." Justices of the Peace Act, sections 19 and 20. Swan, *Statutes of the State of Ohio* 509.

20. Record Book P, 431–32. The civil act provided that trial could be postponed for up to twenty days as a matter of right and longer if both parties consented. Justices of the Peace Act, section 23, at 510. If a material witness resided in another state or county, or was otherwise absent, continuance could be extended, "on good cause shown, by affidavit, and on payment of the costs of such continuance" for up to ninety days. Justices of the Peace Act, section 23, p. 510.

21. Swan, *Statutes of the State of Ohio*, 738a.

22. It was not part of the legal duty of a county prosecuting attorney to attend to prosecutions on behalf of the state before individual justices of the peace; his duties were confined to the county court of common pleas and the state supreme court. An Act to Provide for the Election of Prosecuting Attorneys (January 29, 1833), section 2; Swan, *Statutes of the State of Ohio*, 738. Justices of the Peace Act, section 11, specifies only that the justice conducts an examination. A nineteenth-century commentary on Ohio law explained how

Excerpt from Joseph Smith's Ohio "Book of Record," January 11, 1834, spanning pages 44 and 45: "Thirdly, that the Lord would grant that our brother Joseph might prevail over his enemy, even Doctor P. Hurlbut, who has threatened his life, whom brother Joseph has caused to be taken with a precept; that the Lord would fill the heart of the court with a spirit to do justice, and cause that the law of the land may be magnified in bringing him to justice." Courtesy of the Church Archives, The Church of Jesus Christ of Latter-day Saints.

As a defendant, Hurlbut was entitled to engage a lawyer on his behalf. He retained James A. Briggs, who was admitted to the bar only three months earlier. Briggs, despite his inexperience, was familiar with the situation because of his association with anti-Mormons who funded Hurlbut's research.[23] Although this hearing was designed to allow the prosecution to present its case, Briggs took advantage of the opportunity to make arguments for his client and cross-examined the state's witnesses.

On January 13, 1834, Smith traveled the twelve miles from Kirtland to Painesville for the preliminary hearing. Although only Justice of the Peace William Holbrook was identified in the court record, eyewitnesses reported that two Painesville justices presided at the hearing.[24] The identity of the second justice remains unknown. The Methodist church on the southeast corner of the public square served as the courthouse and was filled to overflowing.[25]

Bissell called sixteen witnesses over the next three days to testify concerning the alleged threat.[26] Most of these witnesses were members of the LDS community or people who had relatives who had joined the Mormons. The majority of the witnesses gave evidence against Hurlbut, while four apparently testified in Hurlbut's defense.[27] Justice Holbrook allowed the lawyers to discuss at length topics unrelated to Hurlbut's guilt or innocence. The trial became something of an inquest concerning the merits of Mormonism, especially the Book of Mormon. Joseph Smith himself was on the witness stand on two of the three days. Briggs asked Smith to give the court his account of finding the plates used to translate the Book of Mormon. Bissell objected, since that topic

---

these lawyers were to examine the witnesses. See John J. Manor, *A Treatise on the Criminal Law of the State of Ohio* (Toledo: Commercial Book and Job Steam-Printing House, 1857), 524–26.

23. James A. Briggs, letter to the editor, *Cleveland Leader and Morning Herald,* January 1884; James A. Briggs to John Codman, March 1875, in John Codman, "Mormonism," *International Review* 11 (September 1881): 222.

24. James A. Briggs, letter to the editor, *New York Tribune,* January 31, 1886. Howe said that two magistrates of Painesville Township heard the case. Eber D. Howe, *Mormonsim Unvailed [sic]: or, a Faithful Account of That Singular Imposition and Delusion, from Its Rise to the Present Time* (Painesville, Ohio: By the author, 1834), 276.

25. Briggs to Codman.

26. Record Book P, 431–32.

27. Journal M, p. 193, Geauga County Archives and Records Center, Chardon, Ohio; Mark Staker, "'Thou Art the Man': Newel K. Whitney in Ohio," *BYU Studies* 42, no. 1 (2003): 116–17; Samuel F. Whitney, statement, March 6, 1885, pp. 17–19, microfilm, Church History Library; George A. Smith, in *Journal of Discourses,* 7:112, November 15, 1864. That Wakefield funded Hurlbut's research, see *Painesville Telegraph,* January 31, 1834; Joseph Smith, Journal, April 1, 1836.

had nothing to do with Hurlbut's guilt or innocence. He then withdrew the objection because everyone in the room wanted to hear the account.[28]

At the conclusion of these testimonies, Justice Holbrook gave his ruling:

> It is the opinion of the Court that the Complainant had reason to fear that Doctor P. Hurlbut would Beat wound or kill him or injure his property as set forth in his complaint and it is the consideration of the Court that the defendant enter into a recognizance to keep the peace generally and especalley towards the Complainant, and also to appear before the Court of Common Pleas on the first day of the term thereof next to be holden in and for said County and not depart without leave, or stand committed till the judgement of the Court be complied with.[29]

Unfortunately, the court record did not state the dollar amount of the recognizance (that is, the bond Hurlbut was required to post). The amount required by law was to be between $50 and $500.[30] A 1837 leading Ohio law treatise states:

> The recognizance should be for such an amount, as will be likely to insure a compliance with its conditions. The justice ought, therefore, in determining its amount, to take into consideration the nature of the offense, and the character and property of the defendant. . . . The amount should not be oppressive, but never so small as to hold out an inducement to the accused to forfeit his recognizance.[31]

It is likely that the prosecution witnesses whose testimonies were deemed material were also recognized to appear at the trial before the Geauga County Court of Common Pleas.[32]

Holbrook's unwillingness to dismiss the charges turned the tide of public opinion momentarily, and hostilities receded immediately. The Church leaders wrote: "There is not quite so much danger of a mob upon us as there has been. The hand of the Lord has thus far been stretched out to protect

---

28. James A. Briggs, *Naked Truths about Mormonism,* January 1888, 4.

29. Record Book P, 431–32.

30. Justices of the Peace Act, section 12.

31. Swan, *Statutes of the State of Ohio,* 482–83.

32. An Act Directing the Mode of Trial in Criminal Cases (March 7, 1831), section 2, *Acts of a General Nature, Enacted, Revised, and Ordered to be Reprinted, . . .* , 155.

MORMONISM UNVAILED :

OR,

A FAITHFUL ACCOUNT OF THAT SINGULAR IMPOSITION AND

DELUSION,

FROM ITS RISE TO THE PRESENT TIME.

WITH SKETCHES OF THE CHARACTERS OF ITS

PROPAGATORS,

AND A FULL DETAIL OF THE MANNER IN WHICH THE FAMOUS

GOLDEN BIBLE

WAS BROUGHT BEFORE THE WORLD.

TO WHICH ARE ADDED,

INQUIRIES INTO THE PROBABILITY THAT THE HISTORICAL PART

OF THE SAID BIBLE WAS WRITTEN BY ONE

SOLOMON SPALDING,

MORE THAN TWENTY YEARS AGO, AND BY HIM INTENDED TO HAVE

BEEN PUBLISHED AS A ROMANCE.

BY E. D. HOWE.

PAINESVILLE :

PRINTED AND PUBLISHED BY THE AUTHOR.

1834.

Mormonism Unvailed, published in 1834 in Painesville, Ohio, seven months after the D. P. Hurlbut trial. While Eber D. Howe is listed as author, the book contains many of Hurlbut's anti-Mormon materials. On the frontispiece are two images showing an interpretation of events Joseph Smith related at the January 1834 preliminary hearing. Courtesy L. Tom Perry Special Collections, Harold B. Lee Library, Brigham Young University.

us. . . . Since the trial the spirit of hostility seems to be broken down in a good degree but how long it will continue so we cannot say."[33]

Six days later, on January 28, 1834, with Frederick G. Williams as scribe, Joseph Smith continued dictating the Hurlbut story from where they left off on January 11, 1834. He said that Hurlbut "saught the distruction of the saints in this place and more particularly myself and family" (a vague reference to Hurlbut's lectures and the threat). Smith then recorded that "as the Lord has in his mercy Delivered me out of his hand till the present and also the church that he has not prevailed viz the 28 day of Jany 1834 for which I off[er] the gratitud[e] of my heart to Allmighty God for the same." The brethren then

---

33. The Presidency of the High Priesthood to the Brethren scattered from Zion, January 22, 1834, Joseph Smith Letterbook 1, p. 81.

knelt and prayed that God would continue to deliver them in the pending law suit and ended with a plea to soften the hearts of wealthy Geauga County land owners, including one who had funded Hurlbut's research.[34]

In the following months, speculation arose in Geauga County concerning the impending trial. Hurlbut's supporters claimed that the whole proceeding was a sham brought about by the judge so that the lawyers could continue to harass Joseph Smith before the county court. In this heightened state of rumor, prediction, and speculation, the April trial approached. Activity also continued in the courts. Assistant Prosecuting Attorney for Geauga County Reuben Hitchcock met with Justice Holbrook and made the required copy of the proceedings of the preliminary hearing, as well as a copy of the recognizance to keep the peace.[35]

The County Court

On March 31, 1834, Smith traveled 9–10 miles to appear before the Geauga County Court of Common Pleas in Chardon.[36] Although Hurlbut had been ordered to appear before the court on that day, several cases were being heard, meaning that the Hurlbut case would not be held for several more days. Who served as counsel for Hurlbut remains unknown. Briggs made no mention of representing him beyond the January hearing. The prosecuting attorney, although not named in the court record, was probably Stephen Mathews.[37]

On April 1, 1834, Smith recorded that he spent the day making subpoenas for witnesses.[38] He must have then given the subpoenas to the clerk, who had authority to serve them.[39] In preparation for the trial, Smith wrote his

---

34. Joseph Smith, Journal, January 28, 1834; Jessee, *Papers of Joseph Smith*, 2:20. See also *Painesville Telegraph*, January 31, 1834.

35. "It shall be the duty of every justice of the peace, in criminal proceedings, to keep a docket thereof …: and when the party accused shall be recognized, or committed for the want of such recognizance, he shall transmit or deliver a transcript of such proceedings to the clerk of the court, or prosecuting attorney …; which transcript shall contain an accurate bill of all the costs that have accrued, and the items of charge composing the same." Justices of the Peace Act, section 21, at 197.

36. Joseph Smith, Journal, March 31, 1834; Jessee, *Papers of Joseph Smith*, 2:27.

37. Matthews served as prosecuting attorney of Geauga County from 1828 to 1835. *Pioneer and General History of Geauga County* (Burton, Ohio: Historical Society of Geauga County, 1880), 70. Reuben Hitchcock was his assistant prosecuting attorney.

38. Joseph Smith, Journal, April 1, 1834; Jessee, *Papers of Joseph Smith*, 2:28.

39. Actually, the clerk would then give them to the constable, who would deliver them. An Act Directing the Mode of Trial in Criminal Cases (March 7, 1831), section 22, *Acts of a General Nature, Enacted, Revised, and Ordered to be Reprinted,* ….

feelings about the Lord's goodness and prophesied concerning Hurlbut's fate: "My soul delighteth in the Law of the Lord for he forgiveth my sins and will confound mine Enimies the Lord shall destroy him who has lifted his heel against me, even that wicked man Docter P. H[u]rlbut he will deliver him to the fowls of heaven and his bones shall be cast to the blast of the wind for he lifted his arm against the Almity therefore the Lord shall destroy him."[40]

On April 2 and 3, 1834, Smith attended court. Presiding Judge Matthew Birchard[41] listened to the examination of seventeen witnesses for the prosecution and seven witnesses for the defense.[42] Judge Birchard then adjourned the case for the weekend on Friday, April 4, 1834. On Monday testimony resumed, and on Tuesday "the court house was filled, almost to suffocation, with an eager and curious crowd of spectators, to hear the Mormon trial, as it was called."[43]

The official court record no longer exists. The *Chardon Spectator and Geauga Gazette* is the only surviving contemporary source to give an account of the testimony. By combining this source with a late reminiscence of Hurlbut's witness Samuel Whitney, we can reconstruct some of what the witnesses said. First, testimony was heard concerning Hurlbut's reputation. It was determined that Hurlbut had once been a member of the Mormon society but had been excommunicated for misconduct. Whitney stated, "Jo testified in court that Hurlbut was expelled for base conduct with lude women."[44] According to the *Chardon Spectator and Geauga Gazette,* other witnesses testified, "After this, he [Hurlbut] discovered, that Joe was a false prophet, and the Book of Mormon a cheat;—began lecturing against it, and examining and collecting proof that the story of the Book of Mormon was taken from a manuscript romance, written by one Spalding, who formerly lived at Conneaut, and who died before publication."[45] These statements set the stage for testimony concerning the threat on Smith's life.

The *Chardon Spectator and Geauga Gazette* stated, "Many witnesses testified to threats of revenge from Hurlburt." Justice of the Peace John C. Dowen, who testified in Hurlbut's behalf, said this concerning the nature of the threat:

---

40. Joseph Smith, Journal, April 1, 1834; Jessee, *Papers of Joseph Smith,* 2:28.

41. Birchard was elected to the Common Pleas bench in 1832 and served as Presiding Judge from 1833 to 1837. *History of Portage County* (Chicago: Warner, Beers and Co., 1885), 332. The nature of this legal action did not allow for trial by jury.

42. 1831–1835 Execution Docket, p. 110, Geauga County Archives and Records Center, Chardon, Ohio.

43. "Mormon Trial," 3.

44. Whitney, Statement, 17.

45. "Mormon Trial," 3.

"Hurlbut said he would 'kill' Jo [Smith]. He meant he would kill Mormonism."[46] This argument was probably Hurlbut's main defense. It is true that Hurlbut posed a serious threat to the Church as an entity, but most other witnesses gave evidence in support of the claim that Hurlbut indeed intended to physically enact violence upon Smith.

Dowen's statement shifted the testimony from the actual nature of the threat to the question of whether or not Smith had reason to fear bodily injury, considering the fact that he was in a predominantly Mormon community. A female witness, when asked on cross-examination why she did not immediately inform Smith of the threat, said "that she did not believe Hurlburt, or any other human being, had the power to hurt the prophet." Smith, however, in his own three-hour-long testimony, stated that he actually did fear for his life.[47]

According to Samuel Whitney (younger brother of Newel K. Whitney and a minister in the Methodist church in Kirtland), Smith "testified that he had no arms and that his house was not guarded." It appears that the attorneys were attempting to reconstruct the violent atmosphere in Kirtland in order to provide context to the threat and to determine if Smith really had reason to fear for his life, for when Whitney took the stand, he was asked about the ominous atmosphere in Geauga County. "I was a witness and supposed I was to testify about the firing of guns in Kirtland which had brought together the Mormon men under arms several times; they were in constant fear of being mobbed."[48] Soon, however, the attorneys began to question Whitney about the character of Joseph Smith:

> I was asked if I believed Jo. S. the M prophet was a man of truth and veracity.... I said I did not for Jo knew he had sworn to things which he was well aware I knew were not true. Jo had told me a short time previous, while I was painting my bro's store (he at that time was living in the dwelling part of it), that he had a sword and pistol, and that his house was guarded by six men every night.[49]

No other surviving source sheds further light on the Prophet's testimony about guards. Whitney's memory of these events was recorded fifty years later and, therefore, cannot be accepted without reservation. George A. Smith and others confirmed that they guarded Smith's home during the winter of 1833–34.[50]

---

46. Dowen, Statement, 3.
47. "Mormon Trial," 3.
48. Whitney, Statement, 18.
49. Whitney, Statement, 17–19.
50. George A. Smith, "Memoirs," 12.

After hearing the concluding testimony on Wednesday, April 9, 1834, Judge Birchard ruled that the court was "of opinion that the said complainant had ground to fear that the said Doctor P. Hurlbut would wound, beat or kill him, or destroy his property as set forth in said complaint."[51] Hurlbut was then ordered to enter into new recognizance for $200 to keep the peace and be of good behavior toward the citizens of Ohio generally and especially toward Smith for six months.[52] Hurlbut, as the losing party, was also ordered to pay the court costs of $112.59, as was normal.[53] If a defendant lost a case, the court of common pleas was required to "render judgment against him or her for the costs of prosecution, to be taxed, and award execution therefore."[54] The total number of trial days remains unknown, but Smith, along with several other witnesses, was paid $3.00 at $.50 per day, suggesting that the trial lasted six days, split between two weeks.[55]

Smith recorded in his journal a statement summarizing the court's decision that illustrated his belief that he could receive a fair trial in the American courts as well as his humility and gratitude. "On the 9 [April 1834] after an impartial trial the Court decided that the said Hurlbut was bound over under 200 dollars bond to keep the peace for six month[s] and pay the cost which amounted to near three hundred dollars all of which was in answer to our prayer for which I thank my heavenly father."[56] Over the next two years, Geauga County sheriffs failed to collect the court costs.[57]

However, Hurlbut found other, ultimately more damaging ways to continue his attack against Smith. Although defeated in court, Hurlbut soon saw to the publication of his arguments against Smith by selling his research to

---

51. Record Book P, 432.

52. The terms of the recognizance set forth by the court mirror the statutory language, which required that the defendant "keep the peace, and be of good behavior generally, and especially towards the person complaining." Justices of the Peace Act, section 12, at 196. The law regarding the time period for the recognizance simply stated that the recognizance be "for such term of time as the court may order." Justices of the Peace Act, section 15, at 196.

53. Justices of the Peace Act, section 17; Record Book P, 432.

54. Justices of the Peace Act, section 17, at 196.

55. 1831–1844 Order Book, April 9, 1834, Geauga County Archives and Records Center, Chardon, Ohio; An Act Directing the Mode of Trial in Criminal Cases (March 7, 1831), section 24, *Acts of a General Nature, Enacted, Revised, and Ordered to be Reprinted,* . . . .

56. Joseph Smith, Journal, April 7–9, 1834; Jessee, *Papers of Joseph Smith,* 28–29. The court costs of $112.59, combined with the $200 recognizance, would account for the figure of $300.

57. Execution Docket F, p. 82, Geauga County Archives and Records Center, Chardon, Ohio.

editor Eber D. Howe, publisher of the *Painesville Telegraph,* who agreed to publish the research in book form. The book was first advertised in November 1834, in that newspaper, under the title of *Mormonism Unvailed.*[58] At that point, Hurlbut himself dropped out of the picture of Church history. He later joined the United Brethren Church, and on various occasions found himself embroiled in controversy with that church's leaders, indicating that Smith was not the only religious figure with whom Hurlbut had trouble.[59]

Conclusion

Ohio v. Hurlbut hinged on the legal definitions of threats and fear, two things that would follow Smith throughout his life. Smith learned how the law of the land could prevent his enemies from acting out their threats and how he could lessen his own fears. Smith also came away from the case with a distinct belief that he could receive impartial treatment from the American court system. Although after 1837 Smith expressed his displeasure with "vexatious suits," *Ohio v. Hurlbut* shows that at least as late as 1834 he believed strongly that justice could be found in the courts.

An earlier version of this article, with further documentation, appeared as "Joseph Smith and the 1834 D. P. Hurlbut Case," BYU Studies 44, no. 1 (2005): 33–54.

---

58. *Painesville Telegraph,* November 28, 1834.

59. Dale W. Adams, "Doctor Philastus Hurlbut: Originator of Derogatory Statements about Joseph Smith, Jr.," *John Whitmer Historical Association Journal* 20 (2000): 86–87.

Chapter Eight

Performing Legal Marriages in Ohio in 1835

M. Scott Bradshaw

During the 1830s, ministers from a wide range of Christian denominations performed marriages in Ohio. Attempting to compile a comprehensive list of such churches would be a mammoth task, but a sampling of the court records from several Ohio counties shows that representatives from at least a dozen religious denominations were actively solemnizing marriages. These denominations included Anabaptists, Baptists, Congregationalists, Disciples of Christ, Episcopalians, Evangelicals, German Reformed, Mennonites, Methodists, Presbyterians, Unitarians, Universalists and, of particular interest to readers here, Latter-day Saints.[1]

Most of these ceremonies were performed under a provision of Ohio law that prescribed procedures through which any ordained minister could be

---

1. County records in Ohio sampled for this article include Champaign County Court of Common Pleas, Minutes, October 1835–October 1836, Ohio State Historical Society, Columbus, Ohio (hereafter cited as OSHS); Tuscarawas County Court of Common Pleas, Journal, November 1835, OSHS; Cuyhahoga County Court of Common Pleas, Journal Books F and G, April 1832–October 1835 microfilm, Family History Library, The Church of Jesus Christ of Latter-day Saints, Salt Lake City, Utah (hereafter cited as FHL); Geauga County Court of Common Pleas, Final Record Book T, and Journal Book M, March 1833–October 1837, microfilm, FHL; Jackson County Court of Common Pleas, Journal Book D, 1834, microfilm, FHL; Wayne County Court of Common Pleas, Journal Book 6, March 1833–October 1835, microfilm, FHL; Portage County Court of Common Pleas, Journal, September 1830–May 1837, County Microfilming and Records Center, Ravenna, Ohio; Medina County Court of Common Pleas, Journal Books B and C, 1831–1837, and Book E, June 1835–October 1837, Medina County Courthouse, Medina, Ohio.

Sidney Rigdon. Courtesy Church History Library, The Church of Jesus Christ of Latter-day Saints.

licensed to solemnize marriages. The county courts of common pleas issued licenses to perform marriages, and the granting of these licenses was a routine matter. According to law, a minister merely needed to appear before a county court and produce "credentials of his being a regular ordained minister of any religious society or congregation."[2] The statute provided that, once granted, such licenses were to be valid for as long as the minister continued serving the same denomination.

My survey of Ohio county court records revealed only one denial of a request for a license to perform marriages. In March 1835, Sidney Rigdon made a motion for a license before the judge of his county court, Presiding Judge Matthew Birchard of the Geauga County Court of Common Pleas, which had jurisdiction over the Kirtland area. Even though Rigdon held the priesthood in the LDS Church and was a counselor to Joseph Smith in the presidency of the Church, the judge still refused Rigdon's motion, holding that he was not a "regularly ordained minister of the gospel within the meaning of the Statute."[3] Whether or not intentional, the judge's denial, which seems to reflect mostly local hostilities, as discussed further below, must have signaled to other Mormon elders not to bother applying. Geauga County court records do not contain any evidence that other Saints either requested or were denied licenses to solemnize marriages.

The denial of Rigdon's motion was not the only problem he had with the court over the marriage issue. Court records show that Rigdon was indicted in June 1835 and tried in October for illegally solemnizing the 1834 marriage of Orson Hyde and Marinda Johnson.

---

2. An Act Regulating Marriages, January 6, 1824 (hereafter cited as 1824 Act), in *Acts of a General Nature, Enacted, Revised, and Ordered to be Reprinted,...* (Columbus: Olmsted and Bailhache, 1831), 429–31, section 3 (hereafter cited as *1831 Acts*). This act is also found in J. R. Swan, *Statutes of the State of Ohio, of a General Nature,...* (Columbus: Samuel Medary, 1841), 582–84 (hereafter cited as *1841 Statutes*).

3. Geauga County Court of Common Pleas, Journal Book M, 380–81.

Again, Geauga Court of Common Pleas Judge Matthew Birchard presided, not only over the grand jury that issued the indictment against Ridgon, but the ensuing trial as well. The court record cryptically recounts the trial:

> And now at this term of Said Court that is to say, at the term there of first aforesaid comes the Prosecuting Attorney for the County, and also the defendant in person, and thereupon a Jury were empanelled and Sworn. – Whereupon the said Prosecuting Attorney Says he will no further prosecute this Indictment – Whereupon it is ordered that the said Sidney Ridgon be discharged from said Indictment and go thereof without day.[4]

A contemporary news report on October 30, 1835, provides further details pertaining to this trial:

> The performance of the marriage ceremony by Ridgon having been proven, on the part of the prosecution, Ridgon produced a license of the Court, which had been granted to him several years ago, as a minister of the gospel of that sect usually called Campbellites, but who call themselves disciples, to continue so long as he remained a minister in regular standing in that denomination. The prosecution then undertook to prove by parol[5] that he had abandoned that church, and joined the Mormons, and held principles inconsistent with his former faith. It appeared that the society of disciples kept minutes of their proceedings, and no church record of his dismissal being offered, the Court rejected the testimony,[6] and a *nolle prosequi*[7] was entered.[8]

---

4. Geauga County Court of Common Pleas, Criminal Record, Final Record Book T, 4, MS, Geauga County Courthouse, Chardon, Ohio. "Without day" meant without delay.

5. *Parol evidence* is oral rather than written. John Bouvier, *A Law Dictionary*, 6th ed. (Philadelphia, PA: Childs & Peterson, 1856).

6. Under the "parol evidence rule," a party cannot present oral evidence to contradict unambiguous written documentation. In this case, the prosecutor was attempting to contradict the Campbellite church records that never noted Rigdon's dismissal by testimony. Judge Birchard rejected this attempt.

7. *Nolle Prosequi* means that "an entry made on the record, by which the prosecutor or plaintiff declares that he will proceed no further"; the effect of a nolle prosequi is to release the defendant, "but it does not operate as an acquittal; for he may be afterwards reindicted, and even upon the same indictment, fresh process may be awarded." Bouvier, *Law Dictionary*.

8. *Chardon Spectator and Geauga Gazette*, October 30, 1835, p. 3, col. 1, cited in *Contemporary Accounts of the Latter-day Saints and Their Leaders Appearing in Early Ohio*

This newspaper report is helpful. First, it explains that at least a partial trial took place. This clarifies why a jury was empanelled, as noted in the court record. Second, it indicates that Ridgon tried to use his 1826 Campbellite license to marry to justify his performing the marriage of Hyde and Johnson. Third, it confirms that the prosecutor knew that Ridgon was no longer a Campbellite minister and in fact was a Mormon minister. The prosecutor clearly understood that the Ohio Marriage Act specifically provided that a license issued by a court of common plea based on a minister's credential was only valid, "so long as he shall continue a regular minister in *such* society or congregation."[9] While the prosecutor was not successful, Ridgon (and Smith) would understand that another legal avenue for marrying was necessary.

While Judge Birchard's refusal of Rigdon's motion may have dissuaded LDS elders from making similar requests in Geauga County, at least one elder was not deterred from performing marriages—even without a license. County marriage records show that on November 24, 1835, Joseph Smith solemnized the marriage of Newel Knight and Lydia Goldthwaite Bailey. These records also show that during the next two months, Joseph performed an additional ten weddings. By June 1837, he had married a total of nineteen couples in Kirtland.[10]

Joseph's decision to perform marriages apparently surprised some of the Saints. This is evident from the accounts of the Knight-Bailey wedding. Lydia's history states that Joseph's brother Hyrum was "astonish[ed]" when he learned that Joseph intended to personally marry her and Newel. Probably referring to Sidney Rigdon's legal troubles, Lydia's history explains that Ohio law "did not recognize the 'Mormon' Elders as ministers" and that LDS elders had been arrested and fined for performing marriages.[11] Newel was also amazed. He noted in his journal that Joseph did not have a license to perform marriages and that without this the authorities could impose a penalty.[12]

Joseph was not timid in announcing his intent to solemnize marriages. During the Knight ceremony, he stated that LDS elders had been "wronged" in connection with the marriage license issue and explained that from this

Newspapers, comp. Milton V. Backman, 3 vols. (Provo, Utah: Brigham Young University, 1976), 2:n.p.

9. 1824 Act, section 3 (emphasis added).

10. Geauga County Marriage Records, Book C, microfilm of holograph, 141–42, 144, 165, 188–89, 233–34, FHL. Other Latter-day Saint elders also performed marriages.

11. Homespun [Susa Young Gates], *Lydia Knight's History* (Salt Lake City: Juvenile Instructor Office, 1883), 30.

12. Newel Knight, Autobiography and Journal, folder one, [45–46], Church History Library, The Church of Jesus Christ of Latter-day Saints, Salt Lake City.

time forth he intended to marry couples whenever he saw fit.

Joseph also predicted that his enemies would never be able to use the law against him.[13]

Nor was the Prophet silent with respect to the uncertainty over his authority to solemnize marriages. In comments made during a Sunday sermon, just days after the Knight wedding, Joseph justified his action by explaining that he had done as God commanded him. He further stated that it was his right, or "religious privilege," as he put it, to perform marriages. Not even the U.S. Congress, he said, had "power to make a law that would abridge the rights of [his] religion."[14]

Lydia Goldthwaite Bailey Knight. Courtesy Church History Library, The Church of Jesus Christ of Latter-day Saints.

Not surprisingly, Newel's and Lydia's comments regarding Ohio law and Mormon elders have led some historians to assume that Joseph Smith acted without legal authority when he married couples in Kirtland. These writers have used the term "illegal" quite freely in describing these weddings, also noting that, in the case of the Knight wedding, Lydia had not obtained a divorce from her previous spouse, Calvin Bailey, an abusive husband who had abandoned Lydia several years earlier.

No historian has been more direct in questioning the propriety of Joseph's performance of marriages than Michael Quinn:

> [I]n November 1835 he [Joseph] announced a doctrine I call "theocratic ethics." He used this theology to justify his violation of Ohio's marriage laws by performing a marriage for Newel Knight and the undivorced Lydia Goldthwaite without legal authority to do so.[15]

Quoting Newel's surprise at Joseph's performance of the marriage, Quinn continues:

---

13. Homespun [Susa Young Gates], *Lydia Knight's History,* 31.

14. Quoted in Newel Knight, Autobiography and Journal, folder three, page 6.

15. D. Michael Quinn, *The Mormon Hierarchy: Origins of Power* (Salt Lake City: Signature Books, 1994), 88.

In addition to the bigamous character of this marriage, Smith had no license to perform marriages in Ohio. . . .

Two months later Smith performed marriage ceremonies for which neither he nor the couples had marriage licenses, and he issued marriage certificates "agreeable to the rules and regulations of the Church of Jesus Christ of Later-day Saints." Theocratic ethics justified LDS leaders and (by extension) regular Mormons in actions which were contrary to conventional ethics and sometimes in violation of criminal laws.[16]

Others, such as Richard Van Wagoner, have likewise accused Joseph Smith of disregarding the law:

Smith's performance of this marriage was one of his earliest efforts to apply heavenly guidelines on earth despite legal technicalities. Not only was Smith not a lawfully recognized minister, but Lydia Bailey, whose non-Mormon husband had deserted her, was never formally divorced.[17]

Although these and other historians have concluded that the Prophet was acting illegally in marrying the Knights, no writer to date has tested this assertion.[18] In view of the negative spin that Quinn and Van Wagoner put on Joseph's actions, it seems appropriate to study this issue and related circumstances in greater detail. The results of this research may surprise some readers. As is detailed in this chapter, Joseph was indeed within his statutory rights in assuming the authority to solemnize marriages. Moreover, he was correct when he stated that performing marriages was his "religious privilege." Ohio's marriage statute and history provided clear grounds for these conclusions.

The Knight-Bailey Marriage

As is evident from the previous quotes, much of the controversy surrounding Joseph's decision to solemnize marriages stems from his performance

---

16. Anson Phelps Stokes and Leo Pfeffer, *Church and State in the United States* (New York: Harper and Row, 1964), 71–72.

17. Richard S. Van Wagoner, *Mormon Polygamy: A History,* 2nd ed. (Salt Lake City: Signature Books, 1989), 7.

18. The story of the Newel Knight–Lydia Bailey wedding is retold and reinterpreted by William G. Hartley in "Newel and Lydia Bailey Knight's Kirtland Love Story and Historic Wedding," *BYU Studies* 39, no. 4 (2000): 6–22; see also other retellings in the sources cited there and in the original version of the article in *BYU Studies.*

of the Knight-Bailey wedding. While some of the primary sources do seem to cast doubt on the Prophet's legal authority, they also contain facts that attest to a general concern for legal compliance on the part of all parties involved. Newel in particular exhibited a grasp of legal issues that, though flawed, seems to have set the tone for events leading to his marriage.

According to Lydia's account, when Newel proposed, he attempted to persuade Lydia that her prior marriage to Calvin Bailey was not a legal impediment. Newel explained that "according to the law she was a free woman, having been deserted for three years with nothing provided for her support." Lydia seems to have been unimpressed with these arguments based on human law. She was more concerned with the "law of God," apparently fearing the moral implications of this second marriage.[19]

None of the accounts clarify exactly what Newel meant when he assured Lydia that the law made her "free"; however, a review of Ohio statutes shows what he likely had in mind. According to a definition of the crime of bigamy adopted in Ohio in 1831, individuals previously married could legally remarry, without any necessity of obtaining a divorce, if the prior spouse had been "continually and willfully absent for the space of three years."[20] Newel may also have had in mind a provision of state divorce law, which allowed abandonment for three years to serve as grounds for divorce, though this alternative seems less likely.[21] Divorces require time-consuming judicial action, a fact that would have been common knowledge even in the nineteenth century.

Judging by the terms of the 1831 bigamy statute, Newel's assessment of Lydia's rights was unquestionably correct. Lydia could indeed have remarried without fear of prosecution and without first obtaining a divorce. The exact date Bailey left her is unknown, but facts contained in her history and Newel's journal suggest that she had been abandoned for at least three years and possibly four.[22] Nevertheless, Newel seems to have been unaware that

---

19. Homespun [Susa Young Gates], *Lydia Knight's History, 27–28*.

20. An Act for the Punishment of Crimes, 1831, section 7, *1831 Acts*, 136.

21. An Act concerning Divorce and Alimony, January 6, 1824, section 1, in *1831 Acts*, 431–32; An Act to Amend the Act, Entitled An Act concerning Divorce and Alimony, December 31, 1827, section 1, *1831 Acts*, 433.

22. Available evidence is contradictory as to when Calvin Bailey abandoned Lydia. Her history suggests that it was "about three years" after her marriage in 1828, thus suggesting an 1831 date. *Lydia Knight's History*, 11. His journal states that Calvin left Lydia shortly after the birth of her second child, a son. Genealogical sources show that this child was born on February 12, 1832, making an early 1832 date the most likely one. In either case, at the time of Newel's proposal to her, Lydia would have met the three-year requirement

earlier in 1835 the state legislature adopted a new bigamy statute.[23] This law lengthened to five years the time required to constitute abandonment—a requirement Lydia would not have met. Of course, the terms of that bigamy statute still required that, in order to be convicted, a married person had to have "a husband or wife living," which Lydia probably did not have.

While Newel may have been mistaken in his understanding of the three-year-abandonment provision under the prevailing Ohio bigamy statute, his reference to Lydia being "free" under the law establishes an important part of the context for subsequent events. After Lydia rebuffed Newel's proposal, Newel turned to God in fasting and prayer and then decided to seek the advice of the Prophet Joseph.[24] Lydia's account describes what happened next:

> Accordingly, Joseph presented his petition to the Lord, and the reply came that Lydia was free from that man. God did not wish any good woman to live a life of lonliness [*sic*], and she was free to marry. Also that the union of Newel and Lydia would be pleasing in His sight.[25]

Joseph's use of the precise word that Newel employed—free—would seem to tie his response to Newel's initial legal argument. The Prophet's confident response also laid to rest the moral concerns Lydia had. The Prophet assured her that she would not lose her salvation in remarrying; in fact, God would be pleased with her marriage to Newel.

Trusting in Joseph's word, the couple made immediate plans to marry. Lydia's history reports that their confidence in the Prophet was soon vindicated. Shortly after their marriage on November 24, 1835, the couple learned that Calvin Bailey, Lydia's previous husband, had died, a fact they took as convincing proof of the inspiration in Joseph's reply.[26] Oddly, Quinn and Brooke characterized this union as "bigamous," yet omitted Lydia's highly significant mention of Bailey's actual death. The death of Lydia's former husband prior to her remarriage would have made bigamy a nonissue if it had been raised, for without proof that his death occurred after the marriage, the

---

for remarriage but not the newer, five-year requirement. The birth date of Lydia's second child is found under "Lydia Goldthwait," b. 1832, Ancestral File 4.19, AFN:2SPB-TR. Newel's account is found in Knight, Autobiography and Journal.

23. An Act Providing for the Punishment of Crimes (1835), sections 7 and 42, *1841 Statutes*, 230, 239.

24. *Lydia Knight's History*, 28.

25. *Lydia Knight's History*, 28.

26. The death date of Calvin Bailey is unknown. Several researchers have searched extensively for it, as yet unsuccessfully.

state could not have borne its burden of proof in prosecuting Lydia for big-amy. Consequently, any liability that Joseph otherwise might have incurred for solemnizing such a marriage—if in fact it had been bigamous—thereby probably became a moot issue.[27]

Newel's journal shows that he was concerned with another legal issue besides Lydia's right to remarry, namely compliance with the Ohio marriage statute. Newel reports having gone by horse to the county clerk to obtain a marriage license (not to be confused with a license to solemnize marriages), returning by 3 P.M. on the day of the marriage.[28] A search of county records confirms that Newel did indeed comply with sections 6 and 7 of the Ohio statute and received a license for his marriage to Lydia.[29]

Joseph Smith's Compliance with the Ohio Marriage Statute

While the accounts of marriages that Joseph Smith later performed are not as detailed as those of the Knight-Bailey wedding, they contain important facts evidencing Joseph Smith's compliance with the Ohio marriage statute. However, some of these later accounts contain important facts. For example, an entry in Joseph's journal contains a transcription of a marriage certificate he issued in January 1836 to William Cahoon and his bride, Nancy Miranda Gibbs.[30] This is the same certificate that Quinn refers to (quoted previously), seemingly suggesting there was something improper in the issuance of these certificates. In reality, the wording of this certificate and of the Ohio mar-riage statute helps prove the legality of Joseph's performance of this marriage. A brief examination of Ohio marriage law will demonstrate this point.

The Ohio marriage statute in force during Joseph Smith's Ohio years was entitled An Act Regulating Marriages. Passed by the Ohio legislature on January 7, 1824, this act specified rules for marriage age, consanguinity, and licensing and specified who could solemnize marriages (see fig. 4). It also

---

27. Under section 9 of the 1824 Act, a fine could be imposed on anyone solemnizing a marriage "contrary to the true intent and meaning" of the act. How this provision might theoretically have applied to Joseph's actions is not clear. Determining the "intent" of a statute is an imprecise process, especially with older statutes for which few judicial prec-edents or legislative history materials are available.

28. Knight, Autobiography and Journal, folder one, [45].

29. This license, dated November 25, 1835, is located in Geauga County Marriage Licenses, 1833–1841, microfilm of holograph, FHL. Joseph's journal and county records place the date of the actual marriage on November 24.

30. Scott H. Faulring, ed., *An American Prophet's Record: The Diaries and Journals of Joseph Smith* (Salt Lake City: Signature Books, 1987), 116 (January 19, 1836).

prescribed when and how records of marriages were to be filed, and it stipulated penalties for various violations.[31] The crucial language in section 2 of the act provides:

> It shall be lawful [1] for any ordained minister of any religious society or congregation, within this State, who has, or may hereafter, obtain a license for that purpose, as hereinafter provided, *or* [2] for any justice of the peace in his county, *or* [3] for the several religious societies, agreeably to the rules and regulations of their respective churches, to join together as husband and wife, all persons not prohibited by this act.[32]

Accordingly, the language of this act specifies that "ordained ministers" could receive licenses to solemnize marriages from the local courts of common pleas. But even if Judge Birchard were not inclined to grant these licenses to Latter-day Saint elders, the Mormons still had other avenues open to them under this statute. According to this same section, a justice of the peace could also perform marriages. Indeed, the Mormons elected several justices of the peace in Geauga County during their stay in Kirtland. This included Oliver Cowdery, Horace Kingsbury, Frederick G. Williams, and Seymour Brunson, all of whom performed marriages in Kirtland specifically noting that it was done under color of that office. Records indicate that they married a total of 34 couples between 1835 and 1837. Other than Joseph Smith (who married 20 couples while in Kirtland), these were virtually the only other Mormons performing marriages in Kirtland. The only other person to do so was Sidney Rigdon, who not only married Orson Hyde and Marinda Johnson in September 1834 that resulted in his indictment, but also two other marriages prior to the Hyde/Johnson marriage, including marrying Brigham Young to Mary Ann Angel in March 1834, and two other couples after the litigation over the Hyde/Johnson marriage in late 1836.

But the statute also provided that marriages could also be performed by the "several religious societies, agreeably to the rules and regulations of their respective churches." For those acting under the second half of section 2, there was no requirement for the person or religious society performing the marriage to hold a license from a county court.[33]

An examination of entries in Joseph Smith's journal suggests that he intended the marriages he performed to be valid under this latter category.

---

31. The provisions of the 1824 Act stood virtually unchanged for decades.
32. 1824 Act, section 2, italics added.
33. See 1824 Act, section 2.

The Cahoons's marriage certificate, for example, shows that Joseph explicitly used the precise language of the Ohio statute. The Prophet stated that he married the Cahoons "agreeably to the rules and regulations of the Church of Christ of Latter-Day Saints on matrimony."[34] Likewise, a marriage Joseph performed in January 1836 included similar language: his journal states that he married John Boynton and Susan Lowell "according to the rules and regulations of the church of the Latter-day Saints."[35] The use of statutory wording on these two occasions would not seem to have been coincidence. Rather, Joseph seems to have intended to show unequivocally that the marriage was valid under the third clause of section 2 of the state of Ohio's marriage statute.[36]

While the case for the legality of these later marriage ceremonies may be clear, what of the Knight-Bailey marriage? The accounts contain no evidence that the Prophet used the language of the statute on this occasion. Such language, however, was not necessary. No provision of the law required such a reference, and other denominations, such as the Quakers, performed marriages in Ohio under the "rules and regulations" clause without making explicit reference to the statute in their marriage certificates.[37] Thus, under the law, Joseph needed only to act according to the rules and regulations of the Church. If he did this, then the Knight-Bailey marriage would have been legally performed, regardless of whether Joseph knew of his statutory authority or made any explicit reference to it.

The Church's rules for marriage were included in the section entitled "Marriage" near the end of the 1835 Doctrine and Covenants (see fig. 1).[38] These rules were drafted earlier in 1835 and adopted in August of that year at an assembly of Saints in Kirtland.[39] The Church rules likely were the "rules … on matrimony," that Joseph followed in marrying the Cahoons in January 1836, as it may well have served as Joseph's guide in marrying the Knights in November 1835.[40] This likely possibility is suggested by a comparison of the

---

34. Faulring, *American Prophet's Record*, 116 (January 19, 1836).

35. See Dean C. Jessee, ed., *The Papers of Joseph Smith*, 2 vols. (Salt Lake City: Deseret Book, 1989–92), 2:153–54 (January 20, 1836).

36. See 1824 Act, section 2.

37. For an example of a Quaker marriage certificate, see H. E. Smith, "The Quakers, Their Migration to the Upper Ohio: Their Customs and Discipline," *Ohio Archaeological and Historical Society Publications* 28 (1928): 35–85.

38. *Doctrine and Covenants of the Church of the Latter Day Saints* (1835), section 101 (hereafter cited as Doctrine and Covenants [1835]).

39. See Robert J. Woodford, "The Historical Development of the Doctrine and Covenants," 3 vols. (Ph.D. diss., Brigham Young University, 1974), 3:1784–85.

40. Faulring, *American Prophet's Record*, 116 (January 19, 1836).

rules to the accounts of the Knight event. In this document, one finds the substance of the actual ceremony and the procedures to be followed.[41]

Even if Joseph Smith had deviated from these rules set forth in the 1835 Doctrine and Covenants, his status as prophet of the Church would arguably have qualified his wording per se as "rules and regulations" under the statute. This follows from passages in the Doctrine and Covenants that established Joseph as a revelator and a "Moses" to his people and passages that instructed the people to be obedient to Joseph's word (D&C 21:1; 28:2–3). Thus, the Knight wedding would again have been valid because Joseph, the recognized revelator for the Church, performed it under a claim of divine authority.

While it is evident that Joseph acted in accordance with Ohio's marriage statute when he married the Knights, Joseph's account is silent on the issue of legality of this particular action. Newel and Lydia seem to have been worried about something, perhaps the question of whether Lydia's former husband was still alive. Perhaps they were unsettled by the wording of printed marriage license forms used by the clerk of the court in Geauga County. Those forms contained a blank for the names of the parties intending to marry and stipulated that the ceremony was to be performed either by a justice of the peace or a minister of the gospel holding a license to solemnize marriages issued by any Ohio county court. Once the names were filled in and the clerk signed and dated the form, the marriage license became valid. What these forms did not state is that "religious societies" also had authority to perform marriages.[42] Lest the mention of this omission raises doubts as to Joseph's authority under the "religious societies" clause, it must be pointed out that these forms did not hold the force of law. The wording on the forms was not prescribed by Ohio statute.[43] Rather, forms seem to have been printed locally, in the case of Geauga County, creating a time-saving convenience for county clerk D. D. Aiken (see fig. 2).[44]

---

41. Doctrine and Covenants [1835], section 101. Joseph's accounts are found in Jessee, *Papers of Joseph Smith*, 1:145–46 (November 24, 1835); and 2:88–89 (November 24, 1835); "Manuscript History of The Church of Jesus Christ of Latter-day Saints," November 24, 1835, Church History Library; and Joseph Smith Jr., *History of The Church of Jesus Christ of Latter-day Saints*, ed. B. H. Roberts, 2d ed., rev., 7 vols. (Salt Lake City: Deseret Book, 1971), 2:320 (hereafter cited as *History of the Church*).

42. See marriage license of James D. Davis and Roxana Davis, dated January 13, 1831, Davis Family Papers, Church History Library; and marriage license of Robert B. Thompson and Mercy R. Fielding, dated June 4, 1837, Mercy F. Thompson Papers, 1837–45, Daughters of Utah Pioneers Collection, Church History Library.

43. S.v. "Forms," index, *1831 Acts*.

44. The marriage license for Robert and Mercy Thompson bears a small notation in the lower left corner, partially obscured, which indicates that the form was printed in Cleveland.

Figure 1. 1835 Doctrine and Covenants, Section 101

MARRIAGE

According to the custom of all civilized nations, marriage is regulated by laws and ceremonies: therefore we believe, that all marriages in this church of Christ of Latter Day Saints, should be solemnized [1] in a public meeting, or feast, prepared for that purpose: and [2] that the solemnization should be performed by a presiding high priest, high priest, bishop, elder, or priest, not even prohibiting those persons who are desirous to get married, of being married by other authority. [3] We believe that it is not right to prohibit members of this church from marrying out of the church, if it be their determination so to do, but such persons will be considered weak in the faith of our Lord and Savior Jesus Christ. Marriage should be [4] celebrated with prayer and thanksgiving; and [5] at the solemnization, the persons to be married, standing together, the man on the right, and the woman on the left, shall be addressed, by the person officiating, as he shall be directed by the holy Spirit; and [6] if there be no legal objections, he shall say, [7] calling each by their names: "You both mutually agreed to be each other's companion, husband and wife, observing the legal rights belonging to this condition; that is, keeping yourselves wholly for each other, and from all others during your lives." And [8] when they have answered "Yes," he shall [9] pronounce them "husband and wife" in the name of the Lord Jesus Christ, and by virtue of the laws of the country and authority vested in him: [10] "may God add his blessings and keep you to fulfill your covenants from henceforth and forever. Amen." [11] The clerk of every church should keep a record of all marriages, solemnized in his branch. [12] All legal contracts of marriage made before a person is baptized into this church, should be held sacred and fulfilled. Inasmuch as this church of Christ has been reproached with the crime of fornication, and polygamy: we declare that we believe, that [13] one man should have one wife; and one woman, but one husband, except in case of death, when either is at liberty to marry again. [14] It is not right to persuade a woman to be baptized contrary to the will of her husband, neither is it lawful to influence her to leave her husband. All children are bound by law to obey their parents; and to influence them to embrace any religious faith, or be baptized, or leave their parents without their consent, is unlawful and unjust. We believe that all persons who exercise control over their fellow beings, and prevent them from embracing the truth, will have to answer for that sin. [**Numbers indicate rules and regulations to be observed.**]

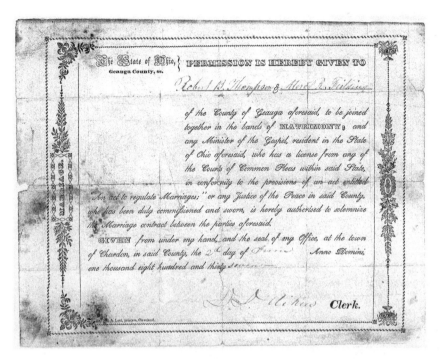

Figure 2. Marriage license of Robert B. Thompson and Mercy R. Fielding, the last recorded couple Joseph Smith married in Kirtland, Ohio. Courtesy Daughters of Utah Pioneers Museum, Salt Lake City.

Moreover, other facts clearly attest to the legality of the marriages he performed. For example, he submitted the certificates for marriages he performed to the county clerk for recording. Section 8 of the Ohio marriage act required that a certificate be submitted, within three months of each wedding, signed by the minister or justice who had performed the ceremony. Joseph's journal and county marriage records show that the Prophet complied with this requirement, as he submitted records for several marriages. The first of these was the certificate for the Knight-Bailey marriage, recorded by Aiken on February 22, 1836, two days prior to the deadline. That Joseph made this filing deadline and at the same time submitted several other marriage certificates shows that this submission was not an almost-belated afterthought (see fig. 3).[45] Furthermore, the county clerk could not have recorded these certificates if they were invalid or illegal on their face.

---

45. See Jessee, *Papers of Joseph Smith*, 2:178 (February 22, 1836); *History of the Church*, 2:398; Geuga County Marriage Records, Book C, 141–42, 144, 165, 188–89, 233–34.

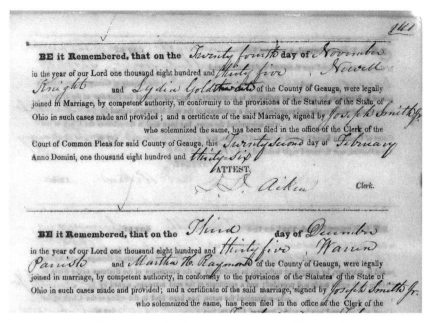

Figure 3. Geauga County records of marriages solemnized by Joseph Smith in Kirtland, Ohio, from November 1835 through January 1836. These records were filed in Geauga County within the ninety-day term prescribed by law. The records contain a record of the marriage of Newel Knight and Lydia Goldthwaite Bailey. Courtesy Judge Charles E. Henry, Geauga County Probate Court.

Evidence of scrupulous adherence to legal standards can also be seen in the case of at least one person whom Joseph married, William Cahoon. Unlike Newel Knight, who rode miles to obtain a marriage license for his wedding, Cahoon's autobiography recounts that he found a legal way to avoid this trip. Section 6 of the Ohio marriage act specified that the parties did not need a marriage license if the event was properly announced in advance and if the ceremony was held in public (see fig. 4), and Cahoon's autobiography states that these requirements were met.[46]

The propriety of Joseph Smith's open performance of the Knight-Bailey marriage and several later marriages is further demonstrated by the fact that he was never prosecuted for these actions.[47] With charges against Rigdon

---

46. William F. Cahoon, *Autobiography,* 44, Church History Library.

47. Any indictment of Joseph for illegally solemnizing marriages would be found in the records of the Geauga County Court of Common Pleas. This is because the potential fine for this offense exceeded the jurisdictional amount of justices of the peace yet was

having been dropped only on a legal technicality just weeks prior to the Knight-Bailey marriage, Joseph could have expected to be prosecuted himself, if indeed he had acted in violation of the law. This assumption is buttressed when one considers that some citizens in the region advocated using the law as a way of challenging the influence of the Latter-day Saints.[48]

---

not high enough to bring the case within the original jurisdiction of the supreme court. 1824 Act, section 9; An Act to Organize the Judicial Courts, February 7, 1831, section 4, *1841 Statutes,* 222–23; An Act Defining the Powers and Duties of Justices of the Peace, and Constables, in Civil Cases, March 14, 1831, section 1, *1841 Statutes,* 505–6. Likewise, as bigamy was a noncapital offense, any indictment of Lydia for this crime would also be found in these same records.

48. See, for example, Eber D. Howe, *Autobiography and Recollections of a Pioneer Printer* (Painesville, Ohio: Telegraph Steam Printing House, 1878), 44–45; "New Bible— a Hoax," *Observer and Telegraph* [Huron, Ohio], February 10, 1831, 3.

Figure 4. Selections from the 1824 Ohio Statute on Marriage

Sec. 1. *Be it enacted by the General Assembly of the State of Ohio,* That male persons of the age of eighteen years, female persons of the age of fourteen years, not nearer of kin than first cousins, and not having a husband or wife living, may be joined in marriage: *Provided, always,* That male persons under the age of twenty-one years, female persons under the age of eighteen years, shall first obtain the consent of their fathers, respectively; or in the case of the death or incapacity of their fathers, then of their mothers or guardians.

Sec. 2. That it shall be lawful for any ordained minister of any religious society or congregation, within this State, who has, or may hereafter, obtain a license for that purpose, as hereinafter provided, or for any justice of the peace in his county, **or for the several religious societies, agreeably to the rules and regulations of their respective churches,** to join together as husband and wife, all persons not prohibited by this act.

Sec. 3. That **any minister of the gospel,** upon producing to the court of common pleas of any county within this State, in which he officiates, credentials of his being a regular ordained minister of any religious society or congregation, shall be entitled to receive, from said court, a license, authorizing him to solemnize marriages within this State, so long as he shall continue a regular minister in such society or congregation.

Sec. 6. That previous to persons being joined in marriage, notice thereof shall be published, (in the presence of the congregation,) on two different days of public worship, the first publication to be at least ten days previous to such marriage, within the county where the female resides; **or a license shall be obtained** for that purpose, from the clerk of the court of common pleas in the county where such female may reside.

Sec. 7. That the clerk of the court of common pleas, as aforesaid, may inquire of the party, applying for marriage license, as aforesaid, upon oath or affirmation, relative to the legality of such contemplated marriage; and **if the clerk shall be satisfied** that there is no legal impediment thereto, then he shall grant such marriage license: … and the clerk is hereby authorized to administer such oath or affirmation, and thereupon issue and sign such license, and affix thereto the seal of the county: … and if any clerk shall in any other manner issue or sign any marriage license, he shall forfeit and pay a sum not exceeding one thousand dollars, to and for the use of the party aggrieved.

Sec. 8. That a certificate of every marriage hereafter solemnized, signed by the justice or minister solemnizing the same, shall be transmitted to the clerk of the county wherein the marriage was solemnized, **within three months thereafter,** and recorded by such clerk: every justice or minister, (as the case may be,) failing to transmit such certificate to the clerk of the county, in due time, shall forfeit and pay fifty dollars; and if the clerk shall neglect to make such record, he shall forfeit and pay fifty dollars, to and for the use of the county.

Sec. 9. That if any justice or minister, by this act authorized to join persons in marriage, shall solemnize the same contrary to the true intent and meaning of this act, the person so offending shall, upon conviction thereof, forfeit and pay any sum not exceeding one thousand dollars, to and for the use of the county, wherein such offence was committed: and if any person not legally authorized, shall attempt to solemnize the marriage contract, such person shall, upon conviction thereof, forfeit and pay five hundred dollars, to and for the use of the county wherein such offence was committed.

[Boldings added]

The Additional Argument of Religious Privilege

Joseph Smith actually did have legal authority to perform marriages in Ohio. He seems to have known this by January 1836, when his journal records that he performed marriages according to the "rules and regulations of the Church." However, he may not have been certain of these rights at the time of the Knight wedding in November 1835.[49] If not, then the further question arises: what was his rationale for asserting his authority to perform this marriage? When Joseph insisted during his Sunday sermon that marrying the Knights was his right, or "religious privilege," was he correct, or was he just using a hyperbole to create a legal fig leaf to cover his actions? As with the case of his statutory rights under Ohio marriage law, a study of this question also provides clear vindication for the Prophet. Although the issue of which ministers could solemnize marriages had been a contentious one in a number of states, by 1835 this controversy was a thing of the past. Previous legal restrictions had been lifted, and all Christian ministers enjoyed this right, even in former "establishment states," where constitutional and statutory provisions had existed favoring particular denominations.[50] In Ohio, religious freedom had always been granted under state law. Ohio's first constitution protected "rights of conscience" in matters of religion.[51]

Ohio's marriage law always reflected the notion of religious freedom. Beginning with the state's first marriage law in 1803 up until the passage of the 1824 marriage act (in force during the Church's Ohio years; see fig. 4), the provisions of Ohio marriage law allowed not just ordained ministers to perform marriages but also religious groups according to their own rules. While the 1803 statute granted this latter right only to Mennonites and Quakers, later revisions extended this right to all "religious societies." This new wording effectively granted authority for all Christian faiths to solemnize their own matrimonial contracts without the necessity of obtaining licenses from the county courts. Accordingly, Joseph was well within his rights, as a citizen of the state of Ohio, to claim his "religious privilege" under this basic rubric of Ohio jurisprudence. Indeed, the organizational status of the Church during this time would not have affected the right of its clergy to marry. Ohio law recognized unincorporated religious societies;[52]

---

49. Faulring, *American Prophet's Record*, 116 (January 19, 1836).

50. For a lengthy discussion of the history of the disestablishment of religion in America, see the original version of this article in *BYU Studies*.

51. See "Third Article in the Declaration of Rights," *Spirit of the Pilgrims* 4 (December 1831): 648.

52. In Methodist Episcopal Church of Cincinnati v. Wood, 5 Ohio 283 (Ohio Supreme Court, December 1831 term), the court recognized an unincorporated splinter group from

the Marriage Act does not refer to "incorporated religious societies;" and the Ohio incorporation statute for religious societies, which was enacted principally for the purpose of owning or conveying real and personal property, never references marriage.[53] No evidence has been found that his performance of marriages in Ohio was ever a subject of public concern during his lifetime.[54]

The Prejudicial Denial of Sidney Rigdon's Motion for a License

In view of the abundant statutory and historical evidence supporting Joseph Smith's performance of marriages, one wonders why Sidney Rigdon specifically, and the Saints generally, experienced difficulties in this regard. Previous scholarship has assumed that the Kirtland Saints generally received fair treatment at the hands of the county court. While this conclusion still seems valid, a number of facts related to the marriage issue invite us to take a deeper look at this assumed impartiality. Considerable evidence points toward discrimination against Rigdon and the Saints in Geauga County.

Conspicuously, other LDS elders successfully obtained licenses outside Geauga County. Elder Seymour Brunson already held such a license at the time that Elder Rigdon's motion for a license was denied. Brunson obtained his license in Jackson County, in southern Ohio (not to be confused with the Missouri county by the same name), a place where, according to Lydia Knight, "prejudice did not run so high."[55] A March 21, 1836, entry in Joseph's

---

the incorporated Methodist Episcopal Church of Cincinnati, noting: "The body of persons, thus separated, agreed upon articles of association, differing essentially from the rules governing the Methodist Episcopal Church. By these articles of association they have since conducted their affairs, and conducted worship as a distinct church, denying all accountability, alike in the spiritual and corporate power of the Methodist Episcopal Church." However, while it recognized the legitimacy of this separated church, the court held that it could not make a claim to any of the property of the Methodist Episcopal Church, as it was not incorporated.

53. Ch. 97, in *1841 Statutes*.

54. Milton V. Backman Jr., *The Heavens Resound* (Salt Lake City: Deseret Book, 1983), 337, states that critics continued to raise such questions after the Rigdon litigation; this statement is based on secondary sources, and they in turn reference only an affirmation of equal priesthood privilege in *Messenger and Advocate* 3, no. 7 (April, 1837), 496, and a "vexatious writ" sworn out but not further prosecuted against Joseph Smith Sr. in 1838 as reported in "History of Luke Johnson, by Himself," *Millennial Star* 27, no. 1 (January 7, 1865), 6. Joseph Smith Jr. performed a number of marriages in Ohio, the last on June 4, 1837.

55. *Lydia Knight's History*, 30; see also Jackson County Ohio Court of Common Pleas, Journal Book D, 49; and Ferron Allred Olson, *Seymour Brunson: Defender of the Faith* (Salt Lake City: By the author, 1998), 62.

journal records that he "prepared a number of Elders licinces, to send by Elder [Ambrose] Palmer to the court [in] Medina County in order to obtain licenses to marry, as the court in this county will not grant us this privilege."[56] Even though Joseph had already been performing marriages under, as we suppose, the "rules and regulations" clause for several months, some LDS elders probably wanted the additional assurance of holding actual licenses to solemnize marriages. Court records from Medina County confirm that two elders received licenses, though not until the June 1836 term of court.

In light of counties outside Geauga granting licenses to Mormon elders, Geauga's refusal of Rigdon's motion seems problematic. Why might Judge Birchard of Geauga County have refused? Birchard's refusal cannot have been for any lack of assertiveness on Rigdon's part. Court records show that Rigdon took the unusual step of using the services of an attorney in making his motion.[57] Evidently, Rigdon did not want to risk a refusal.

The most plausible explanation for Judge Birchard's apparent discrimination can be found in political and religious differences that set the Saints apart from other Geauga County residents. Politically the Kirtland Saints typically voted for Democratic candidates, whereas the other residents of the county generally voted for Whig candidates.[58] Birchard himself was a Democrat and was not a church-going man.[59] One would not expect a judge to be prejudiced against any group; however, this judge may have reflected the political or religious biases of powerful local constituencies whom he would not have wanted to alienate.[60] Presbyterian Whigs virtually dominated Geauga County politics at this time and were prominent in state politics.[61] Birchard's chances for reappointment by the Ohio General Assembly at the end of his

---

56. Jessee, *Papers of Joseph Smith,* 2:190 (March 21, 1836).

57. Geauga County Court of Common Pleas, Journal Book M, 380–81.

58. Max H. Parkin, "Mormon Political Involvement in Ohio," *BYU Studies* 9, no. 4 (1969): 489.

59. *The Biographical Cyclopaedia and Portrait Gallery: With an Historical Sketch of the State of Ohio,* 6 vols (Cincinnati: Western Biographical Publishing, 1884), 3:626–27. At Peter Hitchcock's funeral, Judge Birchard spoke, even though the two were of "opposite politics." Since the Hitchcocks were Whigs, this would imply that Judge Birchard was a Democrat. *Pioneer and General History of Geauga County with Sketches of Some of the Pioneers and Prominent Men,* 2 vols. (n.p.: Historical Society of Geauga County, 1880), 2:514.

60. A newspaper from a nearby county reported that Birchard had won favor with local citizens despite initial misgivings over his appointment that had been expressed in the press. "Judge Birchard," *Elyria Ohio Atlas,* April 25, 1833, n.p.

61. See "Church and State," *Painesville Republican,* September 28, 1837, 2; "Church and State," *Painesville Republican,* October 19, 1837, 2; "Equal Rights," *Painesville Republican,* October 19, 1837, 2.

seven-year term, or for appointment to the state supreme court bench, could have hinged to a considerable degree on the opinion local constituencies held of him.[62]

Moreover, Judge Birchard may have denied Sidney Rigdon's application for a license in an attempt to court the favor of influential Presbyterian Whigs, although this cannot be known for sure. However, one might infer that these Presbyterians in Geauga County held views similar to other Presbyterians in the region. The tone of articles printed in the local Presbyterian press may be an indicator. Typical of many papers, the *Hudson Observer and Telegraph,* located about thirty miles south of Kirtland in Summit County, ran articles expressing skepticism or even ridiculing the spiritual claims at the root of the LDS Church. For example, in 1834, this paper commented that some of the "good people" of the area had converted to Mormonism. The paper then suggested that a few good nights of sleep should be enough to straighten out their thinking.[63] The editor also eagerly anticipated the publication of Eber Howe's *Mormonism Unvailed* and ran a series of unfavorable articles on the Church.[64] Similarly, at least some of the local Presbyterian clergy also seem to have taken a dim view of Mormonism. One minister in Painesville commented in a letter to his sponsoring organization that the Book of Mormon was a "mixture of fallacy & profaneness." He passed on second-hand reports of "alleged licentiousness" among Mormons and of their "annulling the marriage covenant."[65]

Regardless of Judge Birchard's motives for rejecting Sidney Rigdon's motion for a marriage license, the judge's decision is not justifiable from a legal point of view. The practice in Ohio courts was to freely grant requests for marriage licenses, provided the requester presented appropriate credentials. Examples can even be found where licenses were granted to representatives of groups whose members traditionally had solemnized marriages under their own rules without licenses. Such a case occurred in Wayne County, where a Mennonite minister was granted a license to perform marriages.[66] This

---

62. According to the Ohio constitution, judges were appointed for seven-year terms by a joint ballot of both houses of the General Assembly. *Ohio Constitution* (1802), art. 3, section 8.

63. "Mormonism," *Hudson Observer and Telegraph,* April 3, 1834.

64. Eber D. Howe, *Mormonism Unvailed: or, A Faithful Account of That Singular Imposition and Delusion, from Its Rise to the Present Time* (Painesville, Ohio: By the author, 1834); "From the Junior Editor," *Hudson Observer and Telegraph,* May 22, 1834, 3; and the three-part series "From the Junior Editor … Mormonism," *Hudson Observer and Telegraph,* May 29, June 5, and June 12, 1834, 3.

65. William M. Adams to Absalom Peters, May 14, 1831, AHMSA.

66. Wayne County Court of Common Pleas, Journal Book 6, 16.

denomination had historically been categorized with Quakers and given special authority to solemnize marriages "agreeable" to its own rules.[67]

Conclusions

It appears obvious that Joseph Smith was aware of the legal issues surrounding performing marriages in Kirtland. This included the reality that the local Geauga Court of Common Pleas judge was not issuing licenses to Mormons to perform marriages and the local prosecutor's propensity to prosecute Mormons if he believed they violated the Marriage Act. With the adoption of the section on Marriage in the 1835 Doctrine and Covenants, the Mormons provided a way to qualify to perform marriages under the third category of Ohio's Marriage Act without a license. The Prophet's personal reliance on this understanding is supported by at least two relevant facts: First, he never sought to obtain a license to marry from any Court of Common Pleas in Ohio, as far as can be determined; and yet, second, he caused each of the twenty marriages he performed in Ohio to be recorded with the court in accordance with the requirements of the Marriage Act. If he was uncertain whether such marriages were legal, why would he risk heavy penalties to have them officially recorded? Further, if there was a claim that such marriages were illegal, why were no prosecutions ever brought? The inescapable answer to both questions is that they were accepted as legal marriages.

At the same time, he did not go out of his way to explain the legality of this to others. As the spiritual leader, it would seem more appropriate for him to discuss these marriages in religious rather than legal terms. Thus, one record reports that he explained his marriage of Newel Knight to Lydia Bailey as follows:

> Our Elders have been wronged and prosecuted for marrying without a license. The Lord God of Israel has given me authority to unite the people in the holy bonds of matrimony. And from this time forth I shall use that privilege and marry whomsoever I see fit. And the enemies of the Church shall never have power to use the law against me.[68]

Unfortunately, this emphasis has led some to question the legality of the marriages Joseph performed. Such concerns had some basis, as Rigdon's

---

67. 1824 Act, section 2.

68. *Lydia Knight's History: The First Book of the Noble Women's Lives Series* (Salt Lake City, UT: Juvenile Instructor Office, 1883), 31. See also Hartley, "Newel and Lydia Bailey Knight's Kirtland Love Story," 7–22.

indictment certainly was not a secret. But the Prophet's explanation was simple and based on faith that God had provided a way through the third clause of section 2 of the Ohio Marriage Act.

As frustrating as Joseph Smith may have found all of these difficulties, the Prophet ultimately suffered little inconvenience as a result. Consistent with his prediction, Joseph was never arrested or prosecuted for performing the Knight-Bailey marriage or any of the subsequent marriages he solemnized in Ohio. Ironically, the most serious outcome of his decision has been the unnecessary damage to his reputation done by historians who have assumed that he acted in violation of the law. In making this assumption, these writers not only have made a mistake, but they also have missed some of the deeper meaning in the event. Joseph's performance of the Knight-Bailey marriage was not the illegal act of an unethical man. Rather, this act was a bold assertion of the rights that he believed his followers were entitled to as American citizens.

Joseph Smith's action invokes the memory of earlier "dissenting" ministers who also struggled against prejudices and whose efforts helped bring about greater religious freedom in the United States. Just as he later would personally seek redress for the Saints' wrongs in Missouri, even pleading their cause in Washington, Joseph insisted in Ohio that Latter-day Saints be accorded their privileges and protections under state marriage law. Consistent with his strong protection of individual religious liberties,[69] the Prophet acted squarely in harmony with the prevailing legal attitudes and regulations of the day in solemnizing marriages.

A longer version of this article was originally published as "Joseph Smith's Performance of Marriages in Ohio," BYU Studies 39, no. 4 (2000): 23–69.

---

69. See also J. Keith Melville, "Joseph Smith, the Constitution, and Individual Liberties," *BYU Studies* 28, no. 2 (1988): 65–74.

Chapter Nine

Looking Legally at the Kirtland Safety Society

Jeffrey N. Walker

The Kirtland Safety Society has been the source of much debate within the historical community.[1] Most commentators agree that the Kirtland Safety Society was an imprudent venture. Some have even argued that its failure marked an almost fatal blow to Joseph Smith's leadership.[2] Charges of personal gain and illegality are often included in their critique. Unfortunately, those debating

1. Dale W. Adams, "Chartering the Kirtland Bank," *BYU Studies* 23 (Fall 1983): 467–82; Karl R. Anderson, *Joseph Smith's Kirtland: Eyewitness Accounts* (Salt Lake City: Deseret Book, 1989), 193–207; Ronald K. Esplin, "Joseph Smith and the Kirtland Crisis," in *Joseph Smith, the Prophet and Seer,* ed. Richard Neitzel Holzapfel and Kent P. Jackson (Provo, Utah: Religious Studies Center, Brigham Young University; Salt Lake City: Deseret Book, 2010), 261–90; Edwin Brown Firmage and Richard Collin Mangrum, *Zion in the Courts: A Legal History of the Church of Jesus Christ of Latter-day Saints, 1830–1900* (Urbana: University of Illinois Press, 2001), 54–58; Marvin S. Hill, C. Keith Rooker, and Larry T. Wimmer, "The Kirtland Economy Revisited: A Market Critique of Sectarian Economics," *BYU Studies* 17 (Summer 1977): 391–475; Larry T. Wimmer, "Kirtland Economy," in *Encyclopedia of Mormonism*, 4 vols. (New York: Macmillan, 1992), 2:792–93; Scott H. Partridge, "The Failure of the Kirtland Safety Society," *BYU Studies* 12 (Summer 1972): 437–54; D. Paul Sampson and Larry T. Wimmer, "The Kirtland Safety Society: The Stock Ledger Book and the Bank Failure," *BYU Studies* 12 (Summer 1972): 427–36; Mark L. Staker, *Hearken, O Ye People* (Salt Lake City: Greg Kofford Books, 2009), 463–543; Mark L. Staker, "Raising Money in Righteousness: Oliver Cowdery as Banker," MS in possession of author, an edited version of which appeared in *Days Never to Be Forgotten: Oliver Cowdery*, ed. Alexander L. Baugh (Provo, Utah: Religious Studies Center, Brigham Young University, 2009), 143–254.

2. Adams, "Chartering the Kirtland Bank," 467; Firmage and Mangrum, *Zion in the Courts,* 58; J. H. Kennedy, *Early Days of Mormonism* (Charles Scribner's Sons, 1888),

this matter offer little or no legal analysis to support their position. This article is a starting point to rectify this omission. To do so this article will be separated into three parts. The first will provide a brief background of the economy in nineteenth-century America that gave rise to the organization of the Kirtland Safety Society and how it fit into the broader national financial landscape. The second examines the events—nationally, locally, and internally—that led to the failure of the Kirtland Safety Society. And the third examines the law and the lawsuit that was filed in connection with its demise.

The Rise of the Kirtland Safety Society

The organization of the Kirtland Safety Society, known formally at its inception as the Kirtland Safety Society Banking Company, must be viewed within the broader context of banking practices, legal definitions, and the national economy in the 1830s. Although the organizers of this company gave their best efforts in following available legal and accepted business practices, the venture was met with overwhelming difficulties and challenges on several fronts.

With the election of Andrew Jackson in 1828 came the inevitable demise of America's second effort to establish a central banking system.[3] True to his reelection campaign promise in 1832, Jackson successfully caused the second bank to prematurely become ineffective by withdrawing government funds in 1833. It would finally close in 1836. With this closure and the corresponding lack of a national currency, the only available money remaining was specie. Specie, often referred to as "hard currency," included gold, silver, and copper

164–66; Dean A. Dudley, "Bank Born of Revelation: The Kirtland Safety Society Anti-Banking Company," *Journal of Economic History* 30, no. 4 (1970): 848–53.

    3. Alexander Hamilton under George Washington established the first national or central bank in 1791. It had a twenty-year charter. The second central bank of the United States was established in 1816, six years after the charter of the first national bank had expired. It also had a charter for twenty years to expire in 1836. Andrew Jackson not only fought to prevent a renewal, but also to close it early by executive order, ending the deposits of government funds into it. Bray Hammond, "Jackson, Biddle, and the Bank of the United States," *Journal of Economic History* 7, no. 1 (1947), 1–23; Hugh T. Rockoff, "Money, Prices and Banks in the Jacksonian Era," in *The Reinterpretation of American Economic History,* ed. R. W. Fogel and Stanley Engerman (New York: Harper and Row, 1971), ch. 33; Harry N. Scheiber, "The Pet Banks in Jacksonian Politics and Finance, 1833–1841," *Journal of Economic History* 23, no. 2 (1963): 196–214; George R. Taylor, *Jackson versus Biddle: The Struggle over the Second Bank of the United States* (Boston: D.C. Heath, 1949); Peter Temin, *The Jacksonian Economy* (New York: W. W. Norton, 1969), 196; Donald B. Cole, *The Presidency of Andrew Jackson* (Lawrence: University Press of Kansas, 1993), 95–120, 188–200; Harry L. Watson, *Liberty and Power: The Politics of Jacksonian America* (New York: Hill and Wang, 1990), 132–72.

minted into coins by the government. Specie, by its very nature, was inherently and chronically in short supply,[4] particularly in Ohio.[5] Such shortages restricted economic growth, especially in frontier America.[6] To fill this growing vacuum came a rapid increase use of bank notes. Bank notes are essentially promissory notes.[7] Promissory notes are negotiable debt instruments. However, when between individuals the ability to use them as transferrable currency is very limited.[8] As Scott Partridge aptly explained:

> Banks were able and willing to meet the demand for money by the simple process of exchanging the notes of a bank for the promissory note or bill of exchange of a firm or individual, i.e., by exchanging one kind of debt for another. The evidence of a bank's debt had general acceptability as a medium of exchange; the evidence of a firm's or individual's debt did not. Thus, by monetizing private debt, the growing demand for money was met.[9]

4. Herman E. Krooss, *American Economic Development* (Englewood Cliffs, N.J.: Prentice-Hall, 1955), 206 ("As a general proposition, the American economy was characterized by a chronic shortage of capital and capital funds"); Partridge, "Failure of the Kirtland Safety Society," 442. Indeed the very scarcity of gold, silver and other precious metals is the very reason for their value. William M. Gouge, *A Short History of Paper Money and Banking in the United States* (Philadelphia: T. W. Ustick, 1833), part 1, 8–10.

5. George W. Knepper, *Ohio and Its People: Bicentennial* (Kent, Ohio: Kent State University Press, 2003), 133.

6. "The attitude was, essentially, that 'the East won't finance us and if they do, they will kill us with interest.' The conclusion that frontier communities should finance themselves, whatever their hard equity, was not unique to Kirtland." Firmage and Mangrum, *Zion in the Courts,* 54. "Two things that were holding back the development of the [Western] Reserve were transportation and a medium of exchange—money and credit. It would have been out of character for these pioneering Americans to fail to overcome these obstacles." Harlan Hatcher, *The Western Reserve: The Story of New Connecticut in Ohio* (Cleveland, Ohio: World Publishing Co., 1966), 118.

7. "Although a promissory note, in its original shape, bears no resemblance to a bill of exchange [a banknote]; yet, when indorsed, it is exactly similar to one; for then it is an order by the indorser of the note upon the maker to pay to the indorsee. The indorser is as it were the drawer; the maker, the acceptor; and the indorsee, the payee. Most of the rules applicable to bills of exchange, equally affect promissory notes." John Bouvier, *A Law Dictionary* (Philadelphia: T. & J. W. Johnson, 1839), s.v. "promissory note."

8. The ability to exchange banknotes for specie was considered "one of the greatest practical improvements which can be made in the political and domestic economy of any State, and that such convertibility was a complete check against over issue." Gouge, *Short History of Paper Money,* ix. For a detailed examination of banking practices at the time, see George Tucker, *The Theory of Money and Banks Investigated* (Boston: Charles C. Little and James Brown, 1839).

9. Partridge, "Failure of the Kirtland Safety Society," 444.

Not only did bank notes increase the supply of money, it created greater liquidity. While money is the most liquid of assets, land, crops, and equipment are some of the least. As America in the early nineteenth century was predominately agrarian, specifically in the Ohio valleys,[10] farmers, while not being poor *per se*, were in a very illiquid position. The use of bank notes backed by farms allowed them to participate to a far greater extent in the local economies. In this manner local banks issuing bank notes became a principal vehicle to allow more people to participate in the growth of the economy. However, without the protections, regulations, or governance of a central banking system, these local banks were fragile financial institutions.[11]

It is within this environment that the boom years of Kirtland in the early to mid 1830s occurred.[12] With the significant influx of Mormons arriving in Kirtland throughout this time,[13] Kirtland experienced unprecedented economic growth.[14] A full array of agricultural products was being generated, including sheep, cattle, dairy, grains, and maple sugar. Manufacturing products in Kirtland included tanned goods, lumber, ash, bricks, and even cast iron products. The connection to Cleveland in 1833 by the Ohio Canal only further enhanced the economic opportunities in Kirtland.[15] Yet,

---

10. Charles C. Huntington, "A History of Bank and Currency in Ohio before the Civil War," *Ohio Archaeological and Historical Quarterly* 24 (1915): 235–539.

11. As Paul B. Trescott summarized, "During the 1830s boom-and-bust banking was particularly prevalent in two regions, one bounded by upstate New York, Ohio and Michigan, and the other on the southern frontier." *Financing American Enterprise* (New York: Harper and Row, 1963), 24; Gouge, *Short History of Paper Money*, part 1, 133.

12. In providing their analysis of the rise and fall of the Kirtland Safety Society, Hill, Rooker, and Wimmer opined: "Previous historical accounts of the Kirtland Economy have overlooked the fact that Smith provided his creditors with assets, that he was buying and selling land at market prices, and that the economic reversals in the Kirtland economy involved a change in economic conditions that 'reasonably prudent' economic men probably would not have anticipated." Hill, Rooker, and Wimmer, "Kirtland Economy Revisited," 394.

13. Hill, Rooker, and Wimmer, "Kirtland Economy Revisited," 408–9, concludes that the population growth in Kirtland started at "approximately 1,000 inhabitants in 1830 to a peak of 2,500 in 1837 (an increase of 150 percent)."

14. Oliver Cowdery reported in the January 1837 *Messenger and Advocate*: "Our streets are continually thronged with teams loaded with wood, materials for building the ensuing season, provisions for the market, people to trade, or parties of pleasure to view our stately and magnificent temple. Although our population is by no means as dense as in many villages, yet the number of new buildings erected the last season, those now in contemplation and under contract to be built next season, together with our every day occurrences, are evincive of more united erection, more industry and more enterprise."

15. Hill, Rooker, and Wimmer, "Kirtland Economy Revisited," 397, notes that with the opening of the Ohio Canal in 1833, by 1840 the population of then existing towns had nearly tripled and the increase in volume of trade in wheat and flour increased tenfold.

accompanying such growth came significant inflation. Land prices increased in Kirtland 500 percent between 1830 and 1837.[16] In one year alone (1836–37) food prices increased by 100 percent.[17] Such inflation was further aggravated by a shortage of money.[18] Access to banking services in Kirtland was severely limited to the Bank of Geauga headquartered in Painesville, Kirtland's economic competitor. Mormons found that such financial services were generally inaccessible as anti-Mormons were controlling them.[19] Further, the Mormons were struggling with carrying the debt associated with the building of the Kirtland Temple,[20] coupled with the closure of the United Firm in October 1836 with the various businesses being returned or given to its members. The Church had few avenues to generate income to fund its growing financial needs and obligations. These dynamics led Church leaders to look at creating their own local bank in Kirtland to alleviate these problems. Opening a local bank reasonably appeared to be a viable solution. And such a solution made good economic sense, as a local newspaper about the announcement of the opening of the Kirtland Safety Society noted: "It is said they have a large amount of specie on hand and have the means of obtaining much more, if necessary. If these facts be so, its circulation in some shape would be beneficial to community, and sensibly relieve the pressure in the market so much complained of."[21]

As Joseph Smith, Hyrum Smith, Sidney Rigdon, and Oliver Cowdery returned from Salem, Massachusetts, in September 1836, it appears that they had finalized their decision to open a bank in Kirtland.[22] By mid-October the venture was organized to accept money from initial shareholders in exchange for stock. To facilitate greater participation stock prices were kept at the unusual low price of $50 per share,[23] in contrast to other local

16. Hill, Rooker, and Wimmer, "Kirtland Economy Revisited," 411.

17. Anderson, *Joseph Smith's Kirtland,* 210.

18. Firmage and Mangrum, *Zion in the Courts,* 54.

19. Rich McClellin, "The Kirtland Economy, a Broader Perspective," prepared for Mormon History Association Annual Meeting, Killington, Vermont, May 2005, 10–11, copy in possession of author.

20. Estimates on the debt on the Kirtland Temple range from $20–30,000 (Truman Cole, "Mormonism," *Cincinnati Journal and Western Luminary,* August 25, 1835, 4) to more than $100,000 (George A. Smith, "Gathering and Sanctification of the People of God," *Journal of Discourses,* 26 vols. [Liverpool: F. D. Richards, 1855–86], 2:213, March 18, 1855); Staker, "Raising Money in Righteousness," 1, 38.

21. *Painesville Republican,* January 19, 1837.

22. Joseph Young to Lewis Harvey, November 6, 1880, Church History Library, The Church of Jesus Christ of Latter-day Saints, Salt Lake City (hereafter cited as CHL) ("The prophet had conceived a plan of instituting a Bank, with a view of relieving their financial embarrassment").

23. Sampson and Wimmer, "Kirtland Safety Society: The Stock Ledger Book," 427–29.

banks offering shares for between $100 and $400 per share. Small quarterly installment payments ($0.13 per share) further allowed more to participate.[24] Among the earliest investors were Brigham Young, who invested $150,[25] and Sidney Rigdon, who bought 3,000 shares.[26] By the end of October 1836, the venture had attracted 36 subscribers or investors contributing more than $4,000.[27] Joseph Smith and his household would become the largest investors in the Kirtland Safety Society, owning collectively 12,800 shares.[28] In this manner the venture was funded through private investors who in return received stock in the company. The venture then would make loans documented by banknotes. Most often, the borrower collateralized these loans with land.

An organizational meeting was held on November 2, 1836. The original organization of the Kirtland Safety Society Banking Company (the "Kirtland Safety Society") included 32 directors[29] with a Committee of the Directors of six members. This initial committee included Sidney Rigdon, President; Joseph Smith, Cashier; Frederick G. Williams, Chief Clerk; and David Whitmer, Reynolds Cahoon, and Oliver Cowdery as members. A "Constitution" for the organization was also adopted at this initial meeting. This Constitution was published as a *Messenger* extra in early December 1836. The Constitution included the following fourteen articles:

Article I: Authorized capital stock of $4,000,000, Shares at $50 par value

Article II: Managed by 32 directors

Article III: Officers: President, Cashier and Chief Clerk

Article IV: Six directors to oversee discounting

Article V: $1 per day paid to the officers and six directors

Article VI: Adoption of Constitution and election of officers

Article VII: Books open for inspection

Article VIII: Dividends every six months

Article IX: Installment payments

Article X: Notice for payments of installments

---

24. Staker, "Raising Money in Righteousness," nn. 43–45.

25. Brigham Young, Account Book, 1836–46, October 15, 1836, 1, CHL.

26. Sampson and Wimmer, "Kirtland Safety Society: The Stock Ledger Book," 427–28.

27. Sampson and Wimmer, "Kirtland Safety Society: The Stock Ledger Book," 427–28.

28. Stock Ledger of the Mormon Bank at Kirtland, Ohio, 1836–37, p. 173–74, CHL.

29. Who exactly comprised these thirty-two directors is not know. Based on the records available most of the members of the Quorum of the Twelve Apostles were included. For a discussion on this matter see Staker, "Raising Money in Righteousness," n. 47.

Article XI: President empowered to call meetings

Article XII: Quorum is ⅔ of directors; meetings with officers

Article XIII: Bylaws

Article XIV: Amending this constitution

With the corporate organization of the Kirtland Safety Society in place, the next step was to have the organization recognized or chartered as a bank by the Ohio legislature. The political climate seemed to dictate the Church's decision to send Orson Hyde to Columbus, Ohio, to seek a charter for the Kirtland Safety Society.[30] While the country was heavily Democratic with the elections of Presidents Jackson and then Van Buren, Geauga County, Ohio, where Kirtland was located, was a Whig stronghold in an otherwise Democratic state. And Hyde was a Whig. Hyde briefly met with Joseph Smith and others returning from Salem, where he was most likely advised about the anticipated banking venture. However, upon his return to Kirtland he did not become involved in the Kirtland Safety Society as either a member or subscriber.[31] Hyde's efforts in Columbus with the legislature were less than successful. Bad weather resulted in his late arrival, and the backroom negotiations, giving political favors, and lack of any political alliances proved fatal.[32] While one might expect that, at a minimum, he could look to his state representatives from Geauga County for assistance, these representatives were actually in competition with the Mormons from Painesville. In the end, the proposal for

---

30. In retrospect, most would argue that sending Oliver Cowdery might have proven more successful securing the charter as he had been significantly involved in Democratic politics in Ohio. Hyde's selection appears to have been made principally on party affiliation and not capacity or connections or even interest. Adams, "Chartering the Kirtland Bank," 471–72; Marvin S. Hill, "An Historical Study of the Life of Orson Hyde, Early Mormon Missionary and Apostle from 1805–1852" (master's thesis, Brigham Young University, 1955), 106. Cowdery's political activities as a Democrat included publishing a weekly political newspaper, the *Northern Times*, whose prospectus had it originally called the *Democrat*. He was active in both local and state Ohio politics. Cowdery had previously been the point person for Mormon politics in Ohio, having attended the state convention and served on several committees. However, instead of being sent to Columbus, Cowdery was tasked to obtain the printing plates for the Kirtland Safety Society. Leonard J. Arrington, "Oliver Cowdery's Kirtland, Ohio, 'Sketch Book,'" *BYU Studies* 12, no. 4 (1972): 414.

31. Hyde was occupied during this time assisting Jacob Bump open a merchant store in Kirtland from merchandise Bump had acquired from Joseph Smith. Jacob Bump to Joseph Smith Jr., Geauga County Property Deeds, December 5, 1836, Book 22, 568; Jacob Bump Merchant Capital, Geauga County Tax Duplicates, Kirtland Chattel Tax 1837, Geauga County Courthouse, Chardon, Ohio.

32. Howard Bodenhorn, *State Banking in Early America: A New Economic History* (New York: Oxford University Press, 2003), 12–18.

a charter for the Kirtland Safety Society was never even read on the floor of the legislature as hoped before the Christmas break.[33]

By January 2, 1837, the leadership of the Kirtland Safety Society, in recognition that the chances to obtain a charter looked doubtful, decided to legally reorganize the Kirtland Safety Society from a corporate entity with a state charter to a private joint stock company. This change is often overlooked but is legally significant. Joint stock companies had existed for centuries.[34] A joint stock company is an unincorporated business entity that trades upon joint stock or partnership interests. They are business entities "assuming a common name, for the purpose of designating the society, the using of a common seal, and making regulations by means of commodities, boards of directors, or general meetings."[35] Three distinctions typically differentiate a joint stock company

---

33. Staker, "Raising Money in Righteousness," 13. In contrast, at least two other ventures designed to issue notes in Geauga County were both read and introduced during this first legislative session, including the Ohio Rail Road Company in Painesville that was approved by both the House and Senate to circulate notes, and the Fairport and Wellsville Railroad Company, Grandison Newell's project. This company also received a charter and was approved to circulate notes. This railroad venture was in apparent result of having the Ohio Canal bypass Painesville. In an effort to overcome this perceived slight, Newell and his colleagues determined that having a railroad connection would eclipse the canal. Newell's plan was to build a railroad from Fairport Harbor through Painesville to Wellsville on the Ohio River. McClellin, "Kirtland Economy," 6–7. Newell was already one of the founders and a director of the Bank of Geauga headquartered in Painesville. County prosecutor Reuben Hitchcock and his father, Peter Hitchcock, a judge on the Ohio Supreme Court, also served as directors to the Bank of Geauga. Reuben Hitchcock would prosecute the case against Joseph Smith and others for operating the Kirtland Safety Society without a state charter.

34. "Companies, not trading upon a joint stock, or, in other words, regulated companies, have existed from very early times . . . The East India Company, which was established in 1599, was one of the first which traded upon a joint stock." John Collyer, *A Practical Treatise on the Law of Partnership* (London: S. Sweet, 1840), 721.

35. Collyer, *Practical Treatise on the Law of Partnership*, 730. "By an institution of this sort is meant a company having a certain amount of capital, divided into a greater or smaller number of transferable shares, managed for the common advantage of the shareholders by a body of directors chosen by and responsible to them. After the stock of a company of this sort has been subscribed, no one can enter it without previously purchasing one or more shares belonging to some of the existing members. The partners do nothing individually; all their resolutions are taken in common, and are carried into effect by the directors and those whom they employ." J. R. McCullough, *A Dictionary, Practical, Theoretical and Historical of Commerce* (Philadelphia: Thomas Wardle, 1840), 1:455; Rianhard v. Hovey, 13 Ohio 300, 301 (1844) ("[T]he company was intended to be a joint stock company. . . . Among these, provision was made for the annual election of three directors, on the first Monday of November, who were to have power to make all contracts and arrangements

from a corporation (other than a lack of legislative approval) in the early nineteenth century. The first is the reliance by the members of a joint stock company on contractual terms rather than statutory provisions to articulate their rights and duties.[36] The amended Articles of Agreement for this new entity were prepared and published in the *Messenger and Advocate*,[37] delineating the contractual rights and duties of its members. The second is the removal of limited liability as found in corporate entities, thereby making its members jointly and severally liable for the obligations of the venture.[38] In this manner a joint stock company operates like a partnership for liability purposes. Article 14 articulates this change, providing "All notes given by said society, shall be signed by the Treasurer and Secretary thereof, and we the individual members of said firm, hereby hold ourselves bound for the redemption of all such notes."[39] And third, the members' ownership cannot be freely transferrable, as with a corporation's stock. Rather, transferability is subject to contractual agreement, not statutory or even common law rights.[40]

---

necessary to effect the objects of the company, to appoint officers and agents, and to make such rules and regulations as they should see fit. The stock of the company was to be transferable by assignment, by permission of the directors at one of their regular meetings, and dividends to be declared when the funds of the company should justify.").

36. Collyer, *Practical Treatise on the Law of Partnership*, 731. "[C]orporate bodies have the power of binding their members by the acts resolved upon in the manner prescribed by their charters, which power they derive from their corporate character, and not from contract and agreement between themselves; on the other hand, voluntary associations are governed entirely by the rules which the parties have themselves agreed to."

37. *Messenger and Advocate* (January 1837): 441–43.

38. "According to the common law of England, all the partners in a joint stock company are jointly and individually liable, to the whole extent of their fortunes, for the debts of the company. They may make arrangements amongst themselves, limiting their obligations with respect to each other; but unless established by an authority competent to set aside the general rule, they are all indefinitely responsible to the public." McCullough, *Dictionary*, 1:455.

39. Article 16 further provided that "[a]ny article in this agreement may be altered at any time, annulled, added unto or expunged, by the vote of two-thirds of the members of said society; except the fourteenth article, that shall remain unaltered during the existence of said company." In 1816 the legislature in Ohio passed an act to provide penalties for issuing bank notes without a charter. As part of that act, all such unauthorized bank shareholder or partner was made "jointly and severally answerable" (or liable). *Acts Passed at the First Session of the Fourteenth General Assembly of the State of Ohio* (Chillicothe, Ohio: Nashee and Denny, 1816), sec. 11, 12.

40. "Where the shares are not transferable at the mere unrestricted option of the holder, the association, as far as relates to that matter, will be legal. In the case of *The King* v. *Webb*, which has been so often referred to, the shares could not be transferred to any person who would not enter into the original covenants: nor could more than twenty be held by the

The official name of the venture was also changed to the Kirtland Safety Society *Anti*-Banking Company in an apparent effort to further evidence and give full public notice of this change in the structure and legal form of the company.[41] With these changes in place, the leaders worked to open the Kirtland Safety Society in early January 1837.[42] Within a week of opening, the venture had loaned its first installment of notes, totaling approximately $10,000 in $1s, $2s, and $3s.[43] The loans evidenced by the notes were for 90 days, the typical length for notes during this time. These initial efforts generated the exact result hoped for—increased economy activity in Kirtland. This included the funding for the construction of a road, Joseph Street, fronting the Kirtland Temple; increased sales at the Newel K. Whitney store; and the acquisitions of additional farmland. Yet, with such positive results also came the beginning of concerted

---

same person, unless they came to him by operation of law; and the object of the society, which was to supply the inhabitants of Birmingham, being shareholders, with bread and flour, virtually limited the transfer of shares to persons residing in the neighbourhood. And the Court of King's Bench gladly availed themselves of these circumstances, in order to hold the association legal." Collyer, *Practical Treatise on the Law of Partnership*, 733. This component is not in the Articles of Agreement. For a comparable Ohio case, see Wells v. Wilson, 3 Ohio 425, 438 (1828) ("It seems to me incontrovertible that this is a joint stock company, or public partnership; and as such, its stock is subject to the general law operating upon such companies, where the articles of association make no distinction. It is usually a provision of the articles of association of all public joint stock companies, that the stock shall be assignable. Where this is part of the compact, it would follow, as of course, that this absolute power or right to sell the stock, agreed upon by all as a fundamental rule, could not be limited or controlled by a part. I apprehend, therefore, that this doctrine is only applicable to such public companies as have made their stock transferable by their original and fundamental compact. In such case it is a just and necessary doctrine.")

41. The preamble to the Articles of Agreement states this distinct purpose from banking: "We, the undersigned subscribers, for the promotion of our temporal interests, and for the better management of our different occupations, which consist in agriculture, mechanical arts, and merchandising; do hereby form ourselves into a firm or company for the before mentioned objects, by the name of the 'Kirtland Safety Society Anti-Banking Company,' and for the proper management of said firm, we individually and jointly enter into, and adopt, the following Articles of Agreement." *Messenger and Advocate,* January 1837, 441.

42. These efforts included crossing out "Cashier" and "President" replacing them with "Treasurer" and "Secretary," respectively. Joseph Smith and Sidney Rigdon continued to execute notes with Newel K. Whitney and Fredrick Williams also signing notes as "pro tempore," *latin* for "for the time." Also, a stamp "Anti" was made and they started inserting the "Anti" into the name on the notes. This practice appears to have been shortly thereafter discontinued.

43. At this point the Kirtland Safety Society had collected approximately $21,000 cash. Banking practices at the time permitted leveraging the specie to cover 5–10 percent of the notes. The Kirtland Safety Society, therefore, could have extended notes totaling between $20,000 and $40,000 and remain in compliance with such practices.

attacks on the venture. Grandison Newell led such activities by buying Kirtland Safety Society notes and then taking them to the Kirtland Safety Society to be redeemed for specie in order to deplete its capital reserves.[44] Wilford Woodruff recorded on January 24, 1837, that "We had been threatened by a mob from Panesville to visit us that night & demolish our Bank & take our property."[45] The *Painesville Telegraph,* an anti-Mormon newspaper, also started publishing aggressive articles about the dangers and alleged illegalities of the newly launched Kirtland Safety Society.[46]

Both the success of and challenges to the Kirtland Safety Society resulted in the Kirtland Safety Society leaders deciding to undertake two additional efforts to secure a state corporate charter for the Kirtland Safety Society. The first was to instruct Hyde to make additional efforts to get the proposed charter sponsored before the end of the second legislative session. Hyde made contact with Samuel Medley, a Democratic senator who was proposing banking reform.[47] Such efforts did result in getting the proposed charter read on the floor of the Senate, but the proposal failed on a 24 to 11 vote. That vote, closing this first door, came on the same day that Joseph Smith and others arrived in Monroe, Michigan,[48] seemingly opening a second door.

The second effort was to acquire a controlling interest in an out-of-state chartered bank and make the Kirtland Safety Society a branch or subsidiary of that already chartered bank.[49] This business and legal approach had been done

---

44. Newell would later boast how he had "run the Mormons out of the country." Kennedy, *Early Days of Mormonism,* 168; James Thompson's Statement, *Naked Truths about Mormonism* (Oakland, Calif.: Deming, 1888), 3. Grandison Newell was a farmer, businessman, and banker from Painesville. Whether based on religious, financial, or political motives, Newell was one of the most well known and active antagonists against the Church, especially Joseph Smith and his leadership. This included providing financing for Doctor Philastus Hurlbut's 1833 trip to Palmyra to collect affidavits that were published in Eber D. Howe's anti-Mormon book *Mormonsim Unvailed [sic]: or, a Faithful Account of That Singular Imposition and Delusion, from Its Rise to the Present Time* (Painesville, Ohio: By the author, 1834).

45. Dean C. Jessee, "The Kirtland Diary of Wilford Woodruff," *BYU Studies* 12, no. 4 (1972): 383–84.

46. "A New Revolution—Mormon Money," *Painesville Telegraph,* January 20, 1837; "How the Mighty Have Fallen," *Painesville Telegraph,* February 7, 1837; "Bank of Monroe," *Painesville Telegraph,* February 10, 1837; "Monroe Bank," *Painesville Telegraph,* February 24, 1837; "For the Telegraph," *Painesville Telegraph,* March 31, 1837.

47. Hyde's contact to Samuel Medley likely came through Oliver Cowdery and his prior political efforts.

48. Adams, "Chartering the Kirtland Bank," 477–79; Ohio General Assembly, *Journal of the Senate of the State of Ohio,* 35th General Assembly, 1836–37, 360–66.

49. When the Kirtland Safety Society opened for business in January 1837, Ohio law did not prevent a bank properly chartered in one state to open a branch in Ohio. The closest

numerous times by large banking institutions in the East as they acquired banks as branches or affiliates in various states throughout the country. The leaders of the Kirtland Safety Society selected the Bank of Monroe, located in Monroe, Michigan, as its target for such a merger or acquisition. The Bank of Monroe was one of the oldest banks in Michigan, having been chartered in 1827. Monroe, Michigan, was only 150 miles from Kirtland. By February 10, 1837, Joseph Smith, Hyrum Smith, Sidney Rigdon, and Oliver Cowdery arrived in Monroe to close on the deal. Previously, to avoid a possible conflict of interest, Oliver Cowdery had resigned from the Kirtland Safety Society[50] and disposed of his other business interests in Kirtland. The owners of the Bank of Monroe sold their controlling interest in that bank to the Kirtland Safety Society, with the Society paying upfront $3,000 in Cleveland drafts and receiving notes totaling more than $20,000 from principals of the Bank of Monroe.[51] As a part of the deal Cowdery was appointed as a director and vice president of the Monroe Bank.[52] Cowdery stayed in Monroe when the others returned to Kirtland.

---

applicable law was enacted on March 14, 1836, by the Ohio General Assembly entitled, "an act to prohibit the establishment, within this State, of any branch, office, or agency of the Bank of the United States, as recently chartered by the Legislature of the Commonwealth of Pennsylvania." *Acts of a General Nature, passed at the First Session of the Thirty-Fourth General Assembly of the State of Ohio* (Columbus: James B. Gardiner, 1836), 37–39. This act was enacted to prohibit anyone to open a branch in Ohio of the Bank of the United States whose twenty-year charter expired on April 10, 1836. M. St. Clair Clarke and D. A. Hall, *Legislative and Documentary History of the Bank of the United States: Including the Original Bank of North America* (Washington, D.C.: Gales and Seaton, 1832), 713. Three years later, in 1839, the Ohio General Assembly enacted a law that expanded the scope of the 1836 act to include "any bank, or other association or company incorporated by the laws of any other State, or by the laws of the United States." An act to prohibit the establishment within this State of any branch, office, or agency of the United States Bank of Pennsylvania, or any other bank or corporation incorporated by the laws of any other State, or by the laws of the United States, and for other purposes, *Acts of a General Nature, Passed by the Thirty-Seventh General Assembly of Ohio, At Its First Session Held in the City of Columbus* (Columbus: Samuel Medary, 1839), sec. 2, 10 (passed February 9, 1839). As anticipated by the directors of the Kirtland Safety Society, through the Bank of Monroe's charter the Kirtland Safety Society could become a branch office.

50. This resignation was apparently done due to the legal questions as to whether Ohio law permitted someone to be a director of an out-of-state bank while being a director of the Kirtland Safety Society.

51. The acquisition was announced in the *Monroe Times,* February 16, 1837; reprinted in "Bank of Monroe," *Painesville Republican,* February 23, 1837.

52. Staker, "Raising Money in Righteousness," 21–24; "Kirtland Safety Society to Bank of Monroe," reprinted in *Painesville Republican,* February 23, 1837.

Notes issued by the Kirtland Safety Society, February 10 and March 1, 1837, signed by Joseph Smith and Sidney Rigdon. Courtesy J. Reuben Clark Law School.

Note issued by the Bank of Monroe, September 1, 1837, signed by Oliver Cowdery. Courtesy Jeffrey N. Walker.

The Fall of the Kirtland Safety Society

Despite these efforts that appeared to have resolved the Kirtland Safety Society's charter issue, the national Panic of 1837 ultimately thwarted all efforts to create a viable banking venture. The panic started in New York City in mid-February 1837. Banks across the nation began to close in March 1837. Rioting and looting was widespread throughout the country—starting in the East. Many have pointed to President Jackson's policy change requiring all federal land acquisition to be made in specie rather than notes as a catalyst to the panic.[53] The federal government sought to stem the panic by releasing more specie into the economy, totaling more than $9,000,000. Such efforts did little to improve the situation. The panic was devastating to the Bank of Monroe, resulting in its temporary closure. In fact, all the banks in Michigan would close.[54] This financial setting resulted in Michigan enacting what would be the nation's first "free banking" laws.[55] Enacted on March 15, 1837, this act removed the requirement that a bank needed a state-approved charter.[56] This innovation undermined those banks already having charters in Michigan. With the closure, albeit temporary, of the Bank of Monroe, Cowdery resigned as a director and returned to Kirtland.[57] Banks throughout

---

53. Peter Rousseau, "Jacksonian Monetary Policy, Specie Flows and the Panic of 1837," *Journal of Economic History* (June 2002): 457–88.

54. Carter H. Golembe, *State Banks and the Economic Development of the West, 1830–44* (New York: Arno Press, 1978), 440–56.

55. Kevin Dowd, *The Experience of Free Banking* (New York: Routledge, 1992), 211–12; Howard Bodenhorn, "Banking Chartering and Political Corruption in Antebellum New York: Free Banking as Reform," in *Corruption and Reform: Lessons from America's Economic History,* ed. Edward Glaeser and Claudia Goldin (Chicago: University of Chicago Press, 2006), 231–55; Gerald P. Dwyer, "Wildcat Banking, Banking Panics, and Free Banking in the United States, *Economic Review* 81 (December 1996): 6–9; Larry J. Sechrest, *Free Banking: Theory, History and a Laissez-Faire Model* (London: Quorum Books, 1993), 3.

56. An Act to organize and regulate banking associations, in *Acts of the Legislature of the State of Michigan; Passed at the Annual Session of 1837* (Detroit: John S. Bagg, 1837), sec. 1, 76 (passed March 15, 1837). The fatal blow resulting in abandoning the Bank of Monroe came when the Michigan legislature enactment on March 15, 1837, that provided that "any person could form an association for banking business," thereby removing the need for a charter to operate a bank in Michigan, making chartered banks in Michigan like the Bank of Monroe, meaningless. Harvey J. Hollister, "Bank and Banking," in *History of the City of Grand Rapids, Michigan* (Grand Rapids, Mich.: Munsell, 1891), 671–72.

57. Cowdery's return to Kirtland marked the abandonment of having the Bank of Monroe act as the "parent" bank for the Kirtland Safety Society. Cowdery was elected a justice of the peace in Kirtland on May 25, 1837. "Oliver Cowdery," *Painesville Republican,* May 25, 1837 ("Oliver Cowdery, late printer at Kirtland, has been elected a Justice of the Peace in that place, without opposition").

Ohio were similarly decimated. Even the Bank of Geauga closed. The Kirtland Safety Society was similarly affected. With the hope of its survival diminishing, Joseph Smith and Sidney Rigdon stopped issuing any notes and instead looked to collect on the loans that were starting to come due in April 1837. The discount and loan book for the Kirtland Safety Society evidences that some notes were indeed redeemed.[58]

The final and decisive blow to the Kirtland Safety Society came in May 1837 with disagreement (and disaffection and even excommunication in some cases) with various Mormon leaders,[59] including Orson and Parley Pratt, Luke and Lyman Johnson, Frederick G. Williams, John Boynton, Warren Parrish, and, most importantly for the Society, John Johnson. John Johnson had acquired 3,000 shares in the Kirtland Safety Society, the maximum number of shares allowed. He had pledged much of his real property as collateral for this purchase. This collateral was essential in keeping the Kirtland Safety Society solvent. However, with his departure from the Church, Johnson took with him his property, transferring much of it to family members.[60] While Johnson's actions appear to have been in violation of the terms and conditions of the Kirtland Safety Society, no legal action was ever taken against him.[61] With such defections and financial

---

58. Kirtland Safety Society, Discount and Loan Book, CHL.

59. In fact, as Ronald Esplin explained, "The 1837 Kirtland crisis, or Kirtland apostasy as it is sometimes known, cost us perhaps a third of the leadership—not a third of the members, but some of the elite, some of the well-educated, some of the more prosperous." Esplin, "Joseph Smith and the Kirtland Crisis," 262. This apostasy reached its full strength by the end of May 1837. Charges were brought against some of these leaders before the Kirtland High Council on May 29. At the same time, Lyman and Luke Johnson, Orson Pratt, and Warren Parrish countered with charges of their own delivered to Bishop N. K Whitney against Joseph Smith and Sidney Rigdon. John Boynton joined in the charges against Smith and Rigdon. Most of the charges involved the operations of the Kirtland Safety Society. Wilford Woodruff, *Wilford Woodruff's Journal, 1833–1898, Typescript*, ed. Scott G. Kenney, 9 vols. (Midvale, Utah: Signature Books, 1983–84), May 28, 1837; Fred C. Collier and William S. Harwell, eds., *Kirtland Council Minute Book* (Salt Lake City: Collier's Publishing Co., 2002), May 29, 1837; Charges submitted by L. E. Johnson, Orson Pratt, Warren Parrish, and Luke Johnson, May 29, 1837, Newel K. Whitney Collection, L. Tom Perry Special Collections, Harold B. Lee Library, Brigham Young University.

60. John Johnson, primarily through his son-in-law John Boynton, was heavily involved in land speculation that was rampant in Kirtland during this time.

61. While the other members of the Kirtland Safety Society undoubtedly would have had a claim against John Johnson for unilaterally taking his real property out of the venture, under joint stock company law, Johnson may have had a defense. As explained in Rianhard v. Hovey, 13 Ohio 300, 302 (1844), "How far are the stockholders liable for debts contracted by the directors? It may be admitted that, as to many persons parties to this suit, the acts of the directors in departing from the original objects of the association, and engaging in

reversals, both Joseph Smith and Sidney Rigdon resigned and withdrew from the institution in June 1837.[62] Yet, even with their resignations, Warren Parrish and Frederick G. Williams, now disaffected from the Church, took control of the Kirtland Safety Society and continued to make loans by issuing more banknotes.[63] Parrish in particular abused his position as the president of the Society, replacing Sidney Rigdon.[64] Parrish was accused of massive malfeasance during his tenure as president including forgery[65] and embezzlement.[66]

With such improprieties mounting, in August 1837 Smith published a public notice in the *Messenger and Advocate* captioned as "Caution," noting:

> To the brethren and friends of the church of Latter Day Saints, I am disposed to say a word relative to the bills of the Kirtland Safety Society Bank. I hereby warn them to beware of speculators, renegades and gamblers, who are duping the unsuspecting and the unwary, by palming upon them, those bills, which are of no worth, here. I discountenance and disapprove of any and all such

---

hazardous undertakings foreign to and adverse to it, was such a violation of their rights as gives them, in a court of equity, no just claim to contribution; and yet, as to creditors, the case may be quite different. Had such stockholders seen proper to step forward and assert their own rights at the time, and given notice to the public, they could not have been made responsible for any debts subsequently contracted. They neglected, however, to take any measures to inform the public, and left the directors in the sole management of their property, in the exercise of their name as a firm, and of the credit of the firm."

62. The Stock Ledger for the Kirtland Safety Society contained entries to July 2, 1837, which effectively matched the withdrawal by Smith and Rigdon. While some have argued that the bank stopped issuing notes in February, these references clarify the matter. Sampson and Wimmer, "Kirtland Safety Society: The Stock Ledger Book," 429.

63. *Elder's Journal* 1 (August 1838): 58.

64. This change likely took place on May 1, 1837, at the semiannual meeting of the Kirtland Safety Society.

65. Claims of forgery were based on the issuance of new banknotes with the signatures of Joseph Smith and Sidney Rigdon. Brigham Young recalled: "Warren Parrish was the principal operator in the business [Kirtland Safety Society]. He had his partners, and they did not stop until they had taken out all the money there was in the bank, and also signed and issued all the notes they could." Andrew Jenson, *The Historical Record*, 6 vols. (Salt Lake City, 1887), 5:433–34.

66. Many claimed that Parrish stole more than $20,000 from the Kirtland Safety Society. Orson F. Whitney, *Life of Heber C. Kimball* (Salt Lake City: Tevens and Wallis, 1945), 100; Staker, *Hearken, O Ye People*, 547, n. 98; Brigham H. Roberts, comp., *A Comprehensive History of The Church of Jesus Christ of Latter-day Saints: Century I*, 6 vols. (Salt Lake City: Deseret News, 1930), 1:405. Frederick G. Williams was appointed president after Joseph withdrew. *Elders' Journal* (August 1838): 58; Frederick G. Williams, *The Life of Dr. Frederick G. Williams, Counselor to the Prophet Joseph Smith* (Provo, UT: BYU Studies, 2012), 454–73.

practices. I know them to be detrimental to the best interests of society, as well as to the principles of religion.

JOSEPH SMITH Jun.

Such "Caution" effectively ended the Kirtland Safety Society. Yet the fallout was yet to be fully felt. One expected a plethora of litigation to result from the failure of the Kirtland Safety Society, as it is estimated that more than two hundred individuals had bought stock in the venture suffered losses[67] in addition to the numerous parties who held Kirtland Safety Society notes.[68] Yet only one case was filed against Joseph Smith, and that was by his nemesis, Grandison Newell.[69]

---

67. Anderson, *Joseph Smith's Kirtland,* 193; Hill, Rooker, and Wimmer, "Kirtland Economy Revisited," specifically appendix C for a list of the stockholders on the Kirtland Safety Society's ledger book. For a discussion about the ledger book, see Sampson and Wimmer, "Kirtland Safety Society: The Stock Ledger Book." The Smith household (including Joseph Sr. and Lucy, Hyrum and Jerusha, Joseph Jr. and Emma, Samuel, Sophronia Stoddard, Katherine Salisbury, and Lucy Jr., not to mention uncles, aunts, and other relatives) suffered the greatest losses, having owned 12,800 shares of stock (approximately 33 percent of the outstanding stock) in the Society. Their losses were followed, in size, by the Rigdon family (including Sidney, Phebe, and Sidney's mother, Nancy), who owned 4,400 shares of stock (approximately 11 percent of the outstanding stock). The John Johnson family losses would have been between the Smiths and the Rigdons, having owned 8,200 shares of the outstanding stock (approximately 13 percent) had John Sr. not withdrawn his collateral in an obvious effort to mitigate his potential losses. Staker, *Hearken, O Ye People,* 524–25. Wilford Woodruff recounted, "Warren Parrish, who was a clerk in the Bank, afterwards acknowledged he took 20,000 dollars, and there was strong evidence that he took more." Jessee, "Kirtland Diary of Wilford Woodruff," 398 n. 77.

68. As Hill, Rooker, and Wimmer observed, estimating the number of notes in circulation has proven difficult with some arguing that there were no notes to others claiming that as much as $150,000 in notes had been placed in circulation. Using a mathematical methodology that used the serial number of extant notes, these authors estimated that $85,000 of notes is the most reasonable estimate. Hill, Rooker, and Wimmer, "Kirtland Economy Revisited," 444–48. Indeed there were a significant number of notes in circulation.

69. In April 1837, Newell filed a complaint with Painesville Justice of the Peace Edward Flint claiming that he had "just cause to fear and did fear, that Joseph Smith, Jr. would kill him or procure other persons to do it." Based on Newell's complaint, Justice Flint issued a warrant for the arrest of Smith. Joseph Smith was arrested and brought before Justice Flint on May 30, 1837, to respond to these allegations. Because of the limited jurisdiction of justices of the peace, Justice Flint could only hold a hearing to determine whether there was sufficient evidence to establish probable cause that a crime had been committed. If Justice Flint so found, he would require the accused to enter into a recognizance, thereby agreeing to appear at the next term of the Court of Common Pleas, where the charges

The Aftermath of the Kirtland Safety Society

Banking began in Ohio in 1803 during its first legislative session[70] with the granting of a corporate charter to the Miami[71] Exporting Company on April 15, 1803, for the purpose of exporting agricultural products and banking, including the right to issue notes.[72] Other privately chartered banks soon dotted Ohio, including the Bank of Marietta and Bank of Chillicothe in 1808, Bank of Steubenville in 1809, Western Reserve Bank and Bank of Muskingum in 1812, Farmers' & Mechanics' Bank in 1813, and the Dayton Manufacturing Company in 1814.[73] During this same time, various other businesses in Ohio began carrying on banking operations without charters. For example, in 1807 the Alexandrian Society of Grantsville, which was chartered for literary purposes, began issuing bank notes. The Bank of Marietta and Farmers' & Mechanics' Bank began operations as a bank before they had received their charters from the legislature. "Many other unauthorized banks were established in the state [Ohio] during the years 1811 to 1814, and by the

---

would be tried and to keep the peace during the interim. Justice Flint postponed this preliminary hearing until June 3, 1837, at the request of the defendant for additional time to prepare. On June 3, 1837, Joseph Smith appeared with his attorneys Benjamin Bissell and William Perkins. James Paine appeared with Newell. During this hearing Justice Flint heard the testimony of nearly a dozen witnesses after which he determined that probable cause existed to place Smith under a $500 recognizance bond to appear on the first day of the next term of the Geauga Court of Common Pleas on the charge and to keep the peace. Justice Flint also put three of the witnesses, Sidney Rigdon, Orson Hyde and Solomon Denton, under recognizance of $50 each to appear and testify at the next term of the Geauga Court of Common Pleas in this matter. He then prepared a transcript of his actions and forwarded it to the Geauga Court. The June term of the Geauga Court commenced the following Monday, June 5, 1837. The Geauga Court of Common Pleas heard the case on Friday, June 9, 1837, where the evidence was again presented. At the conclusion of this trial the court discharged Joseph Smith and ordered the state to pay all court costs.

70. Ohio enacted its Constitution on November 29, 1802, and was admitted as a state on February 19, 1803.

71. Miami is in reference to the Miami Valley located in the southwest portion of Ohio, a fertile area in the early nineteenth century containing more than a quarter of the total population of Ohio. Daniel Drake, *Natural and Statistical View; Or Picture of Cincinnati and the Miami Country* (Cincinnati: Looker and Wallace, 1815), 169–70.

72. *Acts of the State of Ohio: First Session of the General Assembly, Held Under the Constitution of the State* (Chillicothe, Ohio, 1803), 126–36, specifically sec. 6; Report of Judiciary Committee (January 7, 1837) on the resolution on allowing Miami Exporting Company to have the powers of a bank. *Ohio House of Representative Journal* (Columbus, Ohio, 1837), 188–95.

73. Huntington, "History of Bank and Currency," 260–64.

close of the latter year the large amount of notes issued by these institutions had become a matter of concern to the legislature."[74]

The Ohio General Assembly formally addressed this public problem by passing its first act prohibiting the unauthorized issuing of bank notes on February 8, 1815.[75] As one commentator in 1896 noted, "In 1815, Ohio commenced a war which she carried on longer and more vigorously, because apparently with less success, than any other State, against unauthorized bank notes."[76] In the next session, the Ohio legislature strengthened its attack on unauthorized banking activities by enacting on January 27, 1816, "An act to prohibit the issuing and circulating of authorized bank paper" (the "Act of 1816"). The Act of 1816 provided for a $1,000 penalty against any "officer, servant, agent or trustee" of an unincorporated "bank or money association."[77] The Act of 1816 also provided that an "informer" could bring an action of debt (a civil action) against violators of the Act and receive 50 percent of the recovery, with the other 50 percent "going to aid to the public revenue of the state."[78] The Act of 1816 further made all shareholders or partners in any such banking venture jointly and severally liable "in their individual capacity, for the whole amount of the bonds, bills, notes and contracts of such bank."[79] As these provisions indicate, the Act of 1816 was focused at punishing the bank, its officers, and owners—the direct and indirect *suppliers* of unauthorized bank note in circulation.[80]

In 1823, during the Twenty-First General Assembly of the State of Ohio, a three-person committee was formed to revise the laws of Ohio.[81] The rational was explained by resolution that the frequent revisions of the laws of

---

74. Huntington, "History of Bank and Currency," 266.

75. *Acts Passed at the First Session of the Thirteenth General Assembly of the State of Ohio* (Chillicothe, Ohio: Nashee and Denny, 1815), 152–56.

76. William Graham Sumner, *A History of Banking in the United States* (New York: Journal of Commerce and Commercial Bulletin, 1896), 91.

77. *Acts Passed at the First Session of the Fourteenth General Assembly of the State of Ohio*, sec. 1, 10.

78. *Acts Passed at the First Session of the Fourteenth General Assembly of the State of Ohio*, sec. 5, 11.

79. *Acts Passed at the First Session of the Fourteenth General Assembly of the State of Ohio*, sec. 11, 12–13.

80. The following cases were brought under the Act of 1816: Bonsal v. State, 11 Ohio 72 (1841); Brown v. State, 11 Ohio 276 (1842); Bartholomew v. Bentley, 15 Ohio 659 (1846); Johnson v. Bentley, 16 Ohio 97 (1847); Lawler v. Walker, 18 Ohio 151 (1857); Kearny v. Buttles, 1 Ohio St. 362 (1853); Lawler v. Burt, 7 Ohio St. 340 (1857).

81. *Acts of a General Nature Passed at the First Session of the Twenty-First General Assembly of the State of Ohio* (Columbus, Ohio: P. H. Olmsted, 1823), 37–40.

the state have resulted in "an unavoidable consequence, [of] our statutes become in short order, so voluminous and complicated, that it is difficult for officers of our government, and still more so for those less conversant with our statute books, to determine what is the law, by which they are regulate their conduct."[82] During previous sessions when laws were enacted, revised, amended or repealed, the legislature had concurrently worked to reconcile such changes with the then existing laws. This process resulted in the General Assembly having "revise[d] the laws of a general nature, three times in a period of thirteen years."[83] Yet such efforts proved problematic, taking up much of the time and energy of legislature and even then the "revised laws have not therefore, presented to the public, that definite and concise, that simple and uniform code, which is so desirable."[84] The remedy was to appoint a three-person committee tasked with the responsibility

> to digest and compile a code of laws, containing the principles of the laws now in force, expunging therefrom such acts and parts of acts, as have been repealed, have expired by limitation, or have been superseded and rendered nugatory by subsequent acts; … to draft separate bills containing such new principles as they may be directed by the General Assembly to adopt; or such as they may think proper to recommend; and also separate bills containing the necessary amendments of such other acts as will be affected by such new principles, so that those principles may be adopted or rejected by the General Assembly without destroying the harmony of the code.[85]

As a result this committee proposed a new Act to regulate judicial proceedings where banks and bankers are parties, and to prohibit bank bills of certain descriptions (the "Act of 1824").[86] Section 23 of this Act specifically addressed unauthorized entities issuing bank notes:

---

82. *Acts of a General Nature Passed at the First Session of the Twenty-First General Assembly of the State of Ohio*, 38.

83. *Acts of a General Nature Passed at the First Session of the Twenty-First General Assembly of the State of Ohio*, 38.

84. *Acts of a General Nature Passed at the First Session of the Twenty-First General Assembly of the State of Ohio*, 38.

85. *Acts of a General Nature Passed at the First Session of the Twenty-First General Assembly of the State of Ohio*, 39.

86. *Acts of a General Nature, Enacted, Revised and Ordered to be Re-Printed at the First Session of the Twenty-Second General Assembly of the State of Ohio* (Columbus, Ohio: P. H. Olmsted, 1824), 358–66.

That no action shall be brought upon any notes or bills hereafter issued by any bank, banker or bankers, and intend for circulation, or upon any note, bill, bond or other security given, and made payable to any such bank, banker or bankers, unless such bank, banker, or bankers shall be incorporated and authorized by the laws of this state to issue such bills and notes, but that all such notes, and bills, bonds, and other securities shall be held and taken in all courts as absolutely void.[87]

Section 23 of the Act of 1824 effectively superseded the Act of 1816. Its aim was not to stop the *supply* of unauthorized bank notes, as the Act of 1816 had tried to do, but rather aim at stopping the *demand* for such unauthorized bank notes by declaring such notes to be void and unenforceable in court.[88] This shift in focus remained the law in Ohio until 1840, when the General Assembly of Ohio repealed Section 23 of the Act of 1824.[89] Thus, the Act of 1824, and not the Act of 1816, was the operable law at the time when the notes of the Kirtland Safety Society were being circulated. Not only did the General Assembly in 1840 repeal Section 23, it also reaffirmed that with its repeal the Act of 1816 was no longer suspended.[90]

---

87. *Acts of a General Nature, Enacted, … at the First Session of the Twenty-Second General Assembly of the State of Ohio,* 365–66.

88. The suspension of the Act of 1816 by section 23 of the Act of 1824 did not prevent actions to be brought by the state under its criminal code. In Cahoon v. State, 8 Ohio 537 (1838) brought during the time that the Act of 1816 was suspended: Cahoon was indicted for circulating banknotes from a nonexistent corporation. Cahoon's counsel objected to the jury instruction arguing that the jury should have been charged that "if they found the note offered in evidence was issued by an *existing* bank or company, they should acquit, whether the bank was incorporated or not." Cahoon v. State, 8 Ohio 537 (1838) (emphasis in original). In remanding the case, the Ohio Supreme Court held that the "offence is the uttering of such note, knowing it to be of a non-existing bank or company, and not the uttering a note knowing it to have been issued by an existing unincorporated bank." Cahoon v. State, 8 Ohio 538 (1838). Criminal charges were never brought against any of the directors of the Kirtland Safety Society. Under the analysis the court used in Cahoon v. State, any such charge would have proven ineffective, as the Kirtland Safety Society was indeed in existence when it opened for business.

89. *Acts of a General Nature by the Thirty-Eighth General Assembly of the State of Ohio* (Columbus, Ohio: Samuel Medary, 1840), sec. 8, 117.

90. *Acts of a General Nature by the Thirty-Eighth General Assembly of the State of Ohio,* 113–17. A new act "to prohibit unauthorized Banking, and the circulation of unauthorized Bank paper" was enacted in 1845 (hereafter cited as the "Act of 1845"). The Act of 1845 was similar to the Act of 1816 in that it provided for a $1,000 penalty to officers, directors or owners of an unauthorized bank, but broadened those subject to the penalty to include

The legal effects of the suspension of the Act of 1816 with the enactment of Section 23 of the Act of 1824 and then the repeal of Section 23 and the reinstatement of the Act of 1816 in 1840 was discussed by the Ohio Supreme Court in *Johnson v. Bentley*, 16 Ohio 97 (1847). The defendants in that case interposed a general demurrer (a demurrer being an attack on the legal sufficiency of an action) over a judgment entered against them under the Act of 1816 for being officers of an unauthorized bank issuing bank notes. The defendants argued that the enactment of Section 23 of the Act of 1824 effectively repealed the Act of 1816. Consequently, when Section 23 itself was repealed in 1840 and the General Assembly did not reenact the Act of 1816, any claims brought under the Act of 1816 were rendered invalid. In affirming the judgment against the alleged bankers, Justice Nathaniel C. Reed[91] unequivocally held that

> [t]he act of 1824 did not repeal the act of 1816, it only suspended its action. If it had repealed it, the repeal of the repealing act would not have revived it.... Under the act of 1816, suits could be maintained upon the notes and bills of unauthorized bankers. The 23d section of the act of 1824 declared that the courts should no longer entertain such suits. The 11th section of the act of 1816, which fixed the liability of illegal bankers upon their bills and notes, remained unaffected. But the 23d section of the act of 1824, forbid the courts to entertain any suit or action upon such liability. Then, after the passage of the act of 1824, there was a liability without a right of action to enforce it. The remedy was denied,— it has been restored by a repeal of the act denying it. This is, then, a mere case of suspending remedy, and the legislature has the full power to restore it.[92]

"every person who ... become[s] in any way interested" in an authorized bank. The Act of 1845 eliminated the provision whereby a citizen could bring a suit and share in 50 percent of the recovery. Act of 1816, sec. 5.

91. Justice Reed was one of four sitting Ohio Supreme Court Justices in 1847. The other three justices were Reuben Wood, Matthew Birchard and Peter Hitchcock. An act to organize the judicial courts, *Statutes of the State of Ohio* (1841) sec. 1, 222 (passed February 7, 1831) ("That the supreme court shall consist of four judges).

92. Johnson v. Bentley, 16 Ohio 97, 99–100 (1847); Lewis v. McElvain, 16 Ohio 347, 356 (1847) (By the act of March 23, 1840, this provision of the act of 1824 was repealed. And the court held in the before-cited case of Johnson v. Bentley et al., "that inasmuch as this provision was repealed, the bills and notes were left as under the law of 1816, and that although void by the law of 1824, still that the plaintiffs could recover—in other words,

Justice Reed further discussed that the policy behind the enactment of Section 23 of the Act of 1824 that precluded the remedies under the Act of 1816 was aimed at "alarming the people, and refusing a remedy upon such paper ... [with the] evident intention to create distrust in the public mind."[93] However, "after a trial of the policy of the 23d section of the act of 1824 for sixteen years, it was found that it did not check illegal banking.... To have protected such men in their ill-gotten wealth, by the 23d section of the act of 1824, would have been a species of legalized robbery. The legislature [in 1840], therefore, repealed that clause of the [1824] act, which forbid suits to be brought by the holders of such paper."[94]

Thus, during the period that the Kirtland Safety Society operated (November 1836–November 1837), the Act of 1816 was suspended and replaced by the Act of 1824. Section 23 of the Act of 1824 provided that no claims could be brought under the Act of 1816 and that no holder of a bank note from an unauthorized bank could bring an action against any of the officers, directors or owners of such bank.

However, there was one large exception: *Rounds v. Smith,* the only piece of litigation actually pursued in this regard against Joseph Smith. On February 9, 1837, slightly over a month after the bank had opened on January 3, 1837, Samuel D. Rounds[95] initiated six suits against each of the then Committee of Directors of the Kirtland Safety Society Anti-Banking Co., including Joseph Smith, Sidney Rigdon, Warren Parrish, Frederick G. Williams, Newel K. Whitney, and Horace Kingsbury.[96] Samuel Rounds sued as a straw man for

---

that the repeal of the law of 1824 set up or gave validity to notes and bills which were uncollectible when issued. Such, at least, is the effect of the decision").

93. Johnson v. Bentley, 16 Ohio 97, 102 (1847).

94. Johnson v. Bentley, 16 Ohio 97, 102–3 (1847); Porter v. Kepler, 14 Ohio 127, 138 (1846) (recognizes that the Act of 1824 superseded the Act of 1816); Lawler v. Walker, 18 Ohio 151, 158 (1849) (notes that the Act of 1816 was back in force by 1841, when the claims in the case were brought).

95. Samuel D. Rounds "played only a small role in Kirtland's history. He was born in Boston about 1807, lived for a time in Lewis County, New York, then moved to Painesville, Ohio about 1834 ... Samuel and his two sons ... laid brick for a living." Dale W. Adams, "Grandison Newell's Obsession," *Journal of Mormon History* 30 (Spring 2004): 173–74. There are no known documents that explain the connection between Rounds and Samuel. Perhaps Rounds work as a mason and Newell's interests in various building ventures, including railroading, connected them.

96. Horace Kingsbury (ca. 1798–1853) was a jeweler and silversmith. He was born in New Hampshire and moved to Painesville, Ohio, in 1827. He joined the LDS Church and was ordained an elder in 1832. He was elected a Painesville trustee in 1847 and mayor in 1848.

Grandison Newell. Newell later reportedly said that he paid Rounds $100 to bring the cases.[97] Newell's involvement is beyond dispute, as he even starts to appear in the court pleadings themselves shortly after judgment is entered in October 1837.[98] These suits were specifically brought under the Act of 1816, alleging damages as provided under Section 1 of $1,000[99] in each case. These suits were also brought as *qui tam*[100] suits as provided for in Section 5 of the Act of 1816[101] that allowed the informer, here Rounds, to recover 50 percent of

97. Mary A. Newell Hall, a Newell family historian, quoted Grandison Newell as saying, "Samuel D. Rounds, the complainant, I bought off, and gave him $100. I have been to all the vexation and troubles and paid all costs from the first commencement." Mary A. Newell Hall, "Thomas Newell and His Descendants" (Southington, Conn., 1878), 132–38, as cited in Adams, "Grandison Newell's Obsession," 173.

98. See for example, collection efforts on the judgment entered against Rigdon noted on the Bill of Goods that the sale of property owned by Rigdon that was appraised for sale on January 29, 1838, "remained unsold by direction of Grandison Newell," as well as paying to Newell the $604.50 that was recovered by the sheriff over the same personal property of Rigdon. Bill of Costs, October 24, 1837, Geauga County Court of Common Pleas, Execution Docket G, 106, Geauga County Courthouse.

99. Section 1 of the Act of 1816 provided: "That if any person shall, within this state, act as an officer, servant, agent or trust to any bank or monied association ... except a bank incorporated by a law of this state, he shall, for every such offence, forfeit and pay the sum of one thousand dollars."

100. Sometimes abbreviated as Q.T., *qui tam* comes from the Latin phrase *qui tam pro domino rege quam pro se ipso in hac parte sequitur,* meaning "who as well for the king as for himself sues in this matter." Giles Jacob, *The Law-Dictionary: Explaining the Rise, Progress and Present State, of the English Law,* corrected and enlarged by T. E. Tomlins, 6 vols. (Philadelphia: I. Riley, 1811), s.v. "qui tam." John Bouvier explains a *qui tam* action occurs "when a statute imposes a penalty, for the doing or not doing an act, and gives that penalty in part to whosoever will sue for the same, and the other part to the commonwealth." Bouvier, *Law Dictionary,* s.v. "qui tam." The various pleadings in this case are captioned for example as "Samuel D. Rounds, qui tam v. Joseph Smith" (or other defendants) or sometimes simply "Samuel D. Rounds, q.t. v. Joseph Smith."

101. Section 5 of the Act of 1816 provided: "That all fines and forfeitures imposed by this act, may be recovered by action of debt or by indictment, or presentment of the grand jury, and shall go one half to the informer where the action is brought, and the other half in aid of the public revenue of this state; but where the same is recovered by indictment or presentment, the whole shall be to the use of the state." This language parallels similar acts enacted by Congress shortly after the enactment of the Constitution. For example, a 1791 act of Congress provided that "One half of all penalties and forfeitures incurred by virtue of this act shall be for the benefit of the person or persons who shall make the a seizure, or shall first discover the matter ... And any such penalty and forfeiture shall be recoverable with costs of suit, by action of debt, in the name of the person or persons entitled thereto." Harold J. Krent, "Executive Control over Criminal Law Enforcement: Some

the fine imposed. Rounds retained Reuben Hitchcock[102] to represent him in this action.[103] Hitchcock was also the state prosecutor for Geauga County.[104] Consequently, Hitchcock was the attorney for Rounds, as well as the State of Ohio. Each suit was captioned "Samuel D. Rounds v. [Defendant]."[105]

Lessons from History," *American University Law Review* 38 (1989): 296–97. This relationship between the state and the informer creates a quasi-criminal situation, criminal in that if the state itself pursued the matter it squarely is a criminal matter. However, when a private citizen brings the suit it is civil in nature. Krent notes, in this regard, "Through the qui tam actions, private citizens helped enforce the criminal laws. Such actions were long considered quasi-criminal. Indeed, during the nineteenth and early twentieth centuries, civil qui tam actions represented the functional equivalent of criminal prosecution." Krent, "Executive Control," 397. This relationship clearly existed in the Act of 1816 with the distinction that if the state itself brought the action it would have been criminal via indictment from a grand jury with the entire amount going to the state. This being the case, the law in such quasi-criminal actions requires a higher standard for proof. As noted by the 1835 United States Supreme Court in United States v. The Brig Burnett, 34 U.S. 682, 691 (1835) that held "no individual should be punished for violation of a law which inflicts forfeiture of property, unless the offense shall be established beyond a reasonable doubt."

102. Reuben Hitchcock (1806–83) was an attorney, judge, banker and railroad executive. He was born in Burton, Geauga Co., Ohio, and son of Peter Hitchcock, also an attorney and justice on the Illinois Supreme Court. Reuben attended Yale College, 1823–26. He was admitted to Ohio bar about 1831. Moved to Painesville, Geauga (now Lake) Co., Ohio, about 1831.

103. Reuben Hitchcock wrote his father, Peter Hitchcock, on June 26, 1837, from Painesville, noting, "Last winter I was employed by Saml D. Rounds." Reuben Hitchcock to Peter Hitchcock, June 26, 1837, Western Reserve Historical Society, Cleveland, Ohio.

104. Reuben Hitchcock was the prosecuting attorney for Geauga County from 1837 to 1839.

105. Reuben Hitchcock in a letter to his father dated February 6, 1837, asks: "I wish to ascertain the practice in this State, when it is provided that the penalty may be recurred by action of debt or indict— on half to the informed + the other half to the State, but if recovered by indictment the whole goes to the State— In case an action of debt is brought at the instance of an informer should the suit be in the name of the State of Ohio for of the informer qui tam— I have examined considerably I can find nothing in our decisions on the subject, and know not what the old fashioned qui tam actions are in this State— If consistent with your duty will you inform me on this point." Reuben Hitchcock to Peter Hitchcock, February 6, 1837, Western Reserve Historical Society, Cleveland, Ohio. While we do not have Peter Hitchcock's reply, Reuben determined to bring the case in the name of the informer, Rounds, and not the State of Ohio. Joseph R. Swan, *A Treatise on the Law Relating to the Powers and Duties of Justices of the Peace and Constables in the State of Ohio* (Columbus: Isaac N. Whiting, 1839), 487 ("Where a statute creates a penalty, and authorizes a recovery before a justice by an action in debt, but is silent as to the person or corporation in whose name the penalty shall be prosecuted, the action should, in general, be brought in the name of 'The State of Ohio' ... But if part be given to him, or to any other informer who shall sue, and part to some other person, or corporation, then the suit should be brought by the party aggrieved, or by the informer;

Rounds had writs of summons[106] ordered by Presiding Judge Van R. Humphrey[107] and issued by the court clerk, David D. Aiken,[108] against each defendant on February 9, 1837. These summons commanded that the various defendants appear before the Geauga County Court of Common Pleas on March 21, 1838, to answer the action of a plea of debt[109] for $1,000, each. Describing the claim, the Summons was endorsed noting,

> Suit brot to recover of deft a penalty of $1000 incurred by acting on the 4th day of Jan.y 1837, as an officer of a Bank not incorporated by law of this State and denominated "The Kirtland Safety Society Anti Banking Co." contrary to the Statute in such case made and provided. Amt. claimed to be "due $1000.[110]

---

who, with the person or corporation entitled to a portion of the penalty should be named in the process") (hereafter cited as Swan, *Duties of Justice of the Peace*).

106. Writs of summons are writs prepared by the court and given to a constable or sheriff to serve on a party commanding them to come to court to answer a complaint on a specific date. After serving the defendant(s), the officer would then return the original copy of the summons to the court with an endorsement on the back indicating when and how they performed the service, or that they could not find the defendant within their bailiwick after searching for them. Jacob, *Law-Dictionary*, 6:137, s.v. "writ of summons"; Bouvier, *Law Dictionary*, s.v. "summons"; *Statutes of the State of Ohio* (1841), ch. 66, sec. 14, 15, 16 114(8); ch. 86, sec. 1, 3, 5, 6; ch. 97, sec. 3.

107. Van Rensselaer Humphrey (1800–1864) was a teacher, lawyer, and judge born in Goshen, Connecticut. He moved to Hudson, Ohio in June 1821 and in 1824 was elected Hudson Township justice of the peace. He was a member of the Ohio House of Representatives in 1828 and 1829 and elected by the Ohio Legislature as president judge of the Court of Common Pleas for the Third Judicial District in 1837. A position he would hold until 1844.

108. David Dickey Aiken (1794–1861) was the Geauga County clerk from 1828 to 1841. He was made an associate justice of the Geauga County Court of Common Pleas in 1846.

109. A plea of debt is the name of an action used for the recovery of a debt. The non-payment is an injury, for which the proper remedy is by action of debt, to compel the performance of the contract and recover the specific sum due. Action of debt is a more extensive remedy than assumpsit, as it is applicable for recovery of money due upon a legal liability, as for money lent, paid, had and received, due on an account, for work and labor, etc. Jacob, *Law-Dictionary*, s.v. "debt"; Bouvier, *Law Dictionary*, 1:290–91, s.v. "plea of debt"; Carey's Adm'r v. Robinson's Adm'r, 13 Ohio 181 (1844); Bank of Chillicothe v. Town of Chillicothe, 7 Ohio 31 (1836).

110. Each Writ of Summons was identical in this regard. See Transcripts of Proceedings for each defendant each dated October 24, 1837, Geauga County Court of Common Pleas, Final Record Book U, Geauga County Courthouse: 353–54 for Warren Parrish (hereafter cited as "Parrish Transcript"), 354–56 for Frederick G. Williams (hereafter cited as "Williams Transcript"), 356–57 for Newel K. Whitney (hereafter cited as "Whitney Transcript"), 358–59 for Horace Kingsbury (hereafter cited as "Kingsbury Transcript"),

Sheriff Abel Kimball[111] served the Summons on the defendants.[112] The returns of the Summons were reviewed by the Geauga County Court of Common Pleas on March 21, 1837, during its March term and the court continued the case until the June term.[113]

On April 24, 1837,[114] Rounds, by his counsel, Reuben Hitchcock, filed his declaration ("Declaration") with the court. A declaration is roughly the equivalent of the filing of the complaint today.[115] The Declaration, using the pleadings from the case brought against Joseph Smith as illustrative, in pertinent part, stated (paragraph numbers and emphasis added):

1. Samuel D. Rounds who sues as well for the State of Ohio as for himself complains of Joseph Smith Junior in a plea of debt.

2. For that the said Joseph Smith Junior on the fourth day of January in the year of our Lord one thousand eight hundred and thirty seven at Kirtland township in said County of Geauga **did act as an officer,**

359–62 for Sidney Rigdon (hereafter cited as "Rigdon Transcript"), 362–64 for Joseph Smith (hereafter cited as "Smith Transcript"). Collectively cited as "Trial Transcripts."

111. Sheriff Abel Kimball (1800–1880) was a farmer born in Rindge, New Hampshire, and moved to Madison, Geauga County, Ohio, in August 1813. He served as Geauga County second Sheriff beginning in 1835 and as Sheriff from 1838 to 1841.

112. Sheriff Abel Kimball's service was as follows: Joseph Smith: left a copy with his wife at his home on February 10, 1837 (Smith Transcript); Sidney Rigdon: left a copy with his wife at his home on February 10, 1837 (Rigdon Transcript); Frederick G. Williams: left a copy with his wife at his home on February 10, 1837 (Williams Transcript); Horace Kingsbury: personally served on February 10, 1837 (Kingsbury Transcript); Newel K. Whitney: personally served undated (Whitney Transcript); Warren Parrish: personally served on March 17, 1837 (Parrish Transcript).

113. The Ohio General Assembly enacted An Act to Regulate the Times of Holding the Judicial Courts on February 4, 1837. This act delineated the schedule for the Court of Common Pleas for Geauga County, that was then part of the Third Circuit, noting that it would hold court during the following three terms: A March term commencing on March 21; June term, commencing on June 5; and an October term, commencing on October 24. *Act of a General Nature Passed at the First Session of the Thirty-Fifth General Assembly of the State of Ohio* (Columbus: S. R. Dolbee, 1837), sec. 4, 13.

114. Only in the Kingsbury Transcript is the date of the filing of the Declaration noted. In the rest of the Transcripts the date is literally left blank.

115. The declaration is a document filed by the plaintiff in a Court of Law (as opposed to Chancery) that sets forth the names of the parties, facts from the view of the plaintiff, the legal basis under which the cause of action arises (described as a writ), and the relief sought. Jacob, *Law-Dictionary*, s.v. "declaration"; Bouvier, *Law Dictionary*, s.v. "declaration"; Nichols v. Poulson, 6 Ohio 305 (1834); Belmont Bank of St. Clairsville v. Walter B. Beebe, 6 Ohio 497 (1834); Headington v. Neff, for the use of Neff, 7 Ohio 229 (1835).

servant, agent and trustee of a Bank called "The Kirtland Safety Society Anti Banking Co." which said Bank was not then and there **incorporated by law;** contrary to the Statute in such case made and provided whereby and by the force of the said statute the defendant has forfeited for said offence the sum of one thousand dollars and thereby and by force of said statute an action hath accrued to the plaintiff who sues as aforesaid to have and demand of and from the defendant for the said State of Ohio and for himself, the said sum of one thousand dollars one half for the said State of Ohio and the other half for the plaintiff.

3. And also for that the said defendant afterwards to wit; on the day and year last aforesaid at Kirtland township aforesaid in the County of Geauga aforesaid did act as an officer of a certain other Bank called and denominated "The Kirtland Safety Society Anti Banking Co." which said last mentioned Bank was not then and there incorporated by law by then and there **assisting in the discounting of paper and lending money for said Bank contrary to the Statute** in such case made and provided, whereby and by force of the said statue the said defendant has forfeited for said last mentioned "offence" the further sum of one thousand dollars; and thereby and by force of said statute an action hath accrued to the plaintiff who sues as aforesaid to have and demand of and from the said defendant for the said State of Ohio and for himself the said last mentioned sum of one thousand dollars; one half for the said State of Ohio and the other half for the plaintiff.

4. And also for that the said defendant afterwards to wit; on the day and year last aforesaid at Kirtland township aforesaid in the County of Geauga aforesaid did **act as an officer of a certain other Bank not incorporated by law;** contrary to the Statute in such case made and provided whereby and by the force of the said statute the defendant has forfeited for said last mentioned offence the further sum of one thousand dollars and thereby and by force of said statute an action hath accrued to the said plaintiff who sues as aforesaid to have and demand of and from the defendant for the said State of Ohio and for himself said last mentioned sum of one thousand dollars, one half for the said State of Ohio and the other half for the plaintiff:

5. Yet the said defendant though often requested so to do has not paid the said several sums of one thousand dollars nor any nor either of them to the said State of Ohio and to the plaintiff who sues as

aforesaid; but has always neglected and refused so to do; which is to the damage of the plaintiff the sum of one thousand dollars, and therefore he brings this suit &c.[116]

The Declaration demarcated that the claims brought were based on Act of 1816 for unauthorized banking. The allegations were drafted to squarely fit within the language of the Act of 1816. Paragraph 2, above, alleged a claim for a $1,000 penalty for being a principal in an unauthorized bank. This claim and penalty had been provided in Sections 1 and 2 of the Act of 1816. Paragraph 3, above, alleged a claim for a $1,000 penalty as a result of said person identified in paragraph 1, above, for "the discounting of paper and lending money." This claim and penalty used the exact language of "discounting of paper and lending money" that had been found in Section 3 of the Act of 1816.

Paragraph 4, above, alleged a claim for a $1,000 penalty for being a principal in "a certain other Bank" that was also unauthorized. As previously noted, the Kirtland Safety Society was originally formally as "The Kirtland Safety Society Banking Company" on November 2, 1837. This name was changed in January 1837 to "The Kirtland Safety Society Anti-Banking Company." This change was further evidenced by replacing "President" with "Secretary" and "Cashier" with "Treasurer" on the notes that had been already executed in anticipation of opening the bank. Also, a stamp was made with the word "Anti" and was used on some of the executed notes to indicate the name change. However, the majority of notes distributed did not have "Anti" stamped on them.[117] Consequently, the allegations in paragraph 4, above, may be making reference for notes that were lent and discounted under the name "The Kirtland Safety Society Banking Company," instead of "the Kirtland Safety Society Anti-Banking Company." Finally, each of the paragraphs in the Declaration made reference to a 50/50 split between Rounds, as the plaintiff, and the State of Ohio. These references are in accord with Section 5 of the Act of 1816 that had provided that the penalty "shall go one half to the informer where the action is brought, and the other half in aid of the public revenue of this state."

Based on the foregoing, it is clear that the Declaration is squarely, indeed, exclusively based on the Act of 1816. Rounds's attorney, Reuben Hitchcock, further confirmed this in a letter to his father dated June 26, 1837, in which he describes the lawsuits as "qui tam suits vs the Mormons under the act prohibiting the circulation of unauthorized Bank paper to recover the penalty

---

116. Trial Transcripts.
117. Staker, *Hearken O Ye People*, 479.

William Perkins. From *History of Geauga and Lake Counties, Ohio* (1878).

one half of which goes to the informer & the other half 'in aid of the public revenue of the State,'" actually quoting the Act of 1816.[118] The problem with Hitchcock's action, however, is that Section 23 of the Act of 1824, as discussed above, had suspended the Act of 1816. Consequently, regardless of the veracity of factual allegations made in the Declaration, as a matter of law Rounds had not stated a viable cause of action. And it appears that that is what Joseph Smith and his fellow defendants' attorneys, William Perkins[119] and Salmon S. Osborn,[120] rightly understood as they filed demurrers in each case to be heard during the June 1837 term.[121] As explained by Giles Jacob:

---

118. Reuben Hitchcock to Peter Hitchcock, June 26, 1837. See Act of 1816, sec. 5.

119. William Lee Perkins (1799–1882) moved to Painesville, Ohio, in 1828. He formed the law firm of Perkins & Osborn with Salmon S. Osborn on February 18, 1834 and became the Lake County (divided from Geauga County) prosecuting attorney in 1840.

120. Salmon Spring Osborn (1804–1904) opened a law office in Chardon, Geauga Conty, Ohio, in partnership with R. Giddings in 1828. He moved to Painesville, Ohio, in about 1833 and formed the law firm of Perkins & Osborn the following year.

121. Perkins & Osborn were retained by Joseph Smith and the other defendants in March 1837, who paid to the law firm a $5.00 retainer each. See Bill for Attorney Fees from Perkins & Osborn to Joseph Smith, CHL (hereafter cited as Perkins & Osborn Billings). Joseph Smith had retained Perkins & Osborn on several matters noted in this bill that accounts for services provided from March through December 1837. From a letter dated October 29, 1838, from William Perkins to Joseph Smith that was a cover letter to a billing statement, we can conclude that Perkins provided most of the legal services in this case. William L. Perkins to Joseph Smith, October 29, 1838, Joseph Smith Collection and Joseph Smith Office Papers, CHL. This letter notes:

Painesville Oct 29. 1838

Joseph Smith Jr Esq
    Dear Sir
    At suggestion of our friend Mr. Granger we sent your statement of our amt & demands—You know I threw my whole influence, industry & whatever talents I have faithfully into your affairs—do something for me. "The labourer is worthy of his hire"

For in every action the point of controversy consists either in *fact* or in *law*; If in *fact,* that is tried by the jury; but if in *law,* that is determined by the court. A *demurrer,* therefore, is as issue upon matter of law. It confesses the facts to be true, as stated by the opposite party; but denies that by the law arising upon those facts, any injury is done to the plaintiff; or that the defendant has made out a lawful excuse; according to the party which first demurs, rests or abides in the law upon the point in question. As, in the matter of the declaration be insufficient in law then the defendant demurs to the declaration.[122]

In the Qui tam suits of Rounds, we have charged the different individuals according as we thought was about right in proportion to our services—I spent a great deal of time & labor in my office in those suits & though unsuccessfully it was no fault of ours you know. Parrish's billed & we have a judgt against him for his proportion & presume it will be collected—

I have heard much of you troubles & take an interest in your welfare & believe you must prevail, not withstanding all persecutions—

I read Mr. Rigdons elegant & spiritual 4th of July address for mail, please present my compliments to him & wish him well for his prosperity—We have a small amount against Mr. Marks, which he will recognize, He escaped our collection when he left—

Yours truly
W[m] Perkins

P.S. We also sent an amount against Mr George W Robinson & a __ G.W. Robinson

Joseph Smith assumed responsibility for his legal fees, as well as those of Sidney Rigdon, Frederick G. Williams, and Newel K. Whitney over the Rounds case. He did not assume responsibility for either Warren Parrish or Horace Kingsbury. By October 1838 when the bill was sent by Perkins to Smith, Parrish had left the church and was under suspicion of embezzling money from the Kirtland Safety Society. It appears that Horace Kingsbury left the LDS Church prior to or just after these events but was a resident in Painesville both before and after the Mormons arrived and were then driven out of Kirtland. It would therefore make sense that Smith would not assume his obligations. Kingsbury was elected mayor of Painesville in 1847. From this letter it appears that Perkins provided these legal services.

122. Jacob, *Law-Dictionary,* s.v. "demurrer" (emphasis in original); Bouvier, *Law Dictionary,* s.v. "demurrer"; Green v. Dodge and Cogswell, 6 Ohio 80, 84 (1833) (Facts are taken as true in the demurrer and court only looks at the application of the law); Belmont Bank of St. Clairsville v. Beebe, 6 Ohio 497, 497–498 (1834) ("This case stands before the court on a demurrer to the declaration … The omission of this averment makes the count bad"); Pennsylvania and Ohio Canal Co. v. Webb, 9 Ohio 136, 138 (1839) ("The first question arising upon the demurrer is upon the sufficiency of the declaration").

Perkins's use of demurrers appears both appropriate and fatal to the declarations filed by Hitchcock. Such an argument would be straightforward: For purposes of the demurrers the facts alleged in the declarations would be taken as true. However, even when taken as true, Hitchcock had failed to allege a legally viable claim in the declaration as each and every claim is made under the Act of 1816, which had undisputedly been suspended by the Act of 1824. Consequently, the Declaration, and each claim asserted therein, should be dismissed.

Unfortunately, the demurrers that would confirm that this was the legal argument actually raised by Perkins have not survived. Rather, the court record merely notes: "This cause came on to be heard upon a demurrer to the declaration of the plff. & was argued by counsel[123] on consideration thereof whereof it is adjudge that the said demurrer be overruled with costs on motion of the def. leave is given him to amend—on payment of the costs—and this cause is continued until the next term [in the fall of 1837]."[124] However, after the trial of this case, Perkins & Osborn prepared bills of exceptions that included the argument "that the statute upon which the suit was founded was not in force."[125] The importance of this argument was certainly not lost on them. The *Painesville Republican* even wrote about the problems with the Act of 1816 in the context of the Kirtland Safety Society in an article dated January 19, 1837, noting,

> a law of this state passed February 22, 1816, "to prohibit the issuing and circulating of unauthorized Bank Paper," published in the Telegraph last week, if now in force, might subject persons who give these bills a circulation, to some trouble. It is doubted however, by good judges, whether the law to which we have alluded, is now in force, or if in force, whether it is not unconstitutional, and therefore not binding upon the people.[126]

---

123. It appears that Perkins & Osborn charged an additional $5.00 to each defendant for preparing and arguing these demurrers for a total of $30.00. Perkins & Osborn Billings.

124. Overruled Demurrer in Rounds v. Smith, June 10, 1837, Common Pleas Journal, Book N, 223, Geauga County Courthouse; Overruled Demurrer in Rounds v. Rigdon, June 10, 1837, Common Pleas Journal, Book N, 223; Overruled Demurrer in Rounds v. Kingsbury, June 10, 1837, Common Pleas Journal, Book N, 222; Overruled Demurrer in Rounds v. Williams, June 10, 1837, Common Pleas Journal, Book N, 223; Overruled Demurrer in Rounds v. Parrish, June 10, 1837, Common Pleas Journal, Book N, 223; Overruled Demurrer in Rounds v. Whitney, June 10, 1837, Common Pleas Journal, Book N, 222 (collectively the "Overruled Demurrers").

125. Perkins & Osborn Billings.

126. "Anti-Banking Company," *Painesville Republican*, January 19, 1837.

In a February 16, 1837, article entitled "For the Republican," the *Painesville Republican* further articulated the problems with the Act of 1816:

The law of 1816, under which these suits are instituted, has long since become obsolete and inoperative. In the year 1824, the legislature appointed by joint resolution, a committee to revise generally the laws of the State. That committee, in their sound discretion, adopted such laws as were suited to the genius and spirit of the age, and rejected such as were not; but which were made upon the spur of the occasion without much reflection or deliberation.[127]

With the denial of the demurrers and the conditional granting of leave to amend, thereby continuing the case, the court accessed costs against the defendants for $1.05 each that included court costs and the opposing counsel's legal fees.[128] Payment of the costs was a condition to allow the defendants

---

127. "For the Republican," *Painesville Republican*, February 16, 1837. The article further noted: "The law of '16 against private banking, was of the latter description—it was rejected by the committee and was not republished by the legislature; but instead, a general law regulating banks and bankers was passed, containing amongst other provisions, a section making all notes, bonds, &c. issued by unauthorized banking companies null and void, without, however, annexing any penalty.... It is the duty of the legislature (and has hitherto been their practice) to promulgate or publish their laws. It then (and not before) becomes the duty of any citizen to obey the laws. We must suppose the legislature regarded the law of 1816 as not in force, and hence they did not publish it with their revised code; unless indeed we suppose the intended purposely to adopt the policy of the Athenian tyrant Draco, who, the more easily to ensnare his people, wrote his laws in small characters and hung them up high in the market places, that they might not read them. If the legislature makes their decrees and lock[s] them up in their own bosoms, or in the archives of the State, and then punish the people for not obeying laws they never saw or heard of, they are greater tyrants than ever disgraced the age of a Nero or Calagula. What man of common information thinks of looking beyond the statute books which is published and distributed by authority of the legislature, for a rule of civil conduct? And who expects to be punished as a criminal for not conforming to laws of which he has never heard. The administration of criminal justice is a matter of the highest importance to a people proud of and boasting of their liberties, and in proportion to its importance, (says a great lawyer) should be the care and attention of the legislature, in properly forming and enforcing it. It should be founded on principles that are permanent, uniform and universal, and always conformable to the dictates of truth and justice, the feelings of humanity and the indelible rights of mankind. If this law be still in force there has been on the part of those high in office, a great dereliction of duty, and probably Mr. Servantes would come in for a share of the odium."

128. Bill of Costs in Rounds v. Smith, June 5, 1837, Geauga County Court of Common Pleas, Execution Docket G, 15, notes that it was paid, but no date of payment; Bill of Costs in

to amend their responses to the declarations—essentially to file answers. This requirement was in accord with the practice and law of the time.[129] The answers filed by the defendants are also not extant.[130] However, from the trial transcripts, one can derive from the bills of exceptions prepared by defendants' counsel, the answers included the following:

1. That the Kirtland Safety Society Anti-Banking Company was not engaged in operating as a bank, but as a joint stock company.

2. That the Act of 1816 upon which the case was brought was not literally in force after the enactment of Section 23 of the Act of 1824 or that even if the Act of 1816 was enforceable that the practice in Ohio was not to enforce it.

3. That the making of loans by the Kirtland Safety Society Anti-Banking Company was not the circulation of paper money.

The trial of these cases took place during the October term of the Geauga County Court of Common Pleas, commencing on October 24, 1837, the first

---

Rounds v. Rigdon, June 5, 1837, Geauga County Court of Common Pleas, Execution Docket G, 15, notes that it was paid on July 19, 1837; Bill of Costs in Rounds v. Kingsbury, June 5, 1837, Geauga County Court of Common Pleas, Execution Docket G, 15, notes that $1.00 was paid; Bill of Costs in Rounds v. Williams, June 5, 1837, Geauga County Court of Common Pleas, Execution Docket G, 15, notes that it was paid on August 5, 1837; Bill of Costs in Rounds v Parrish, June 5, 1837, Geauga County Court of Common Pleas, Execution Docket G, 15, notes that it was paid, but no date of payment; Bill of Costs in Rounds v. Whitney, June 5, 1837, Geauga County Court of Common Pleas, Execution Docket G, 15, notes that it was paid, but no date of payment.

129. Leave to amend as requested by the defendants was typically granted on payment of costs, as required by statute. An act to regulate the practice of the judicial courts, *Statutes of the State of Ohio* (Columbus: Samuel Medary, 1841), sec. 51, 662 (passed March 8, 1831) (hereafter cited as *Statutes of the State of Ohio* (1841); and the act as Practice of the Courts Act). For example, in Headley v. Roby, 6 Ohio 521, 522 (1834), "on overruling the demurrer, the court gave the plaintiff in error leave to amend. The plaintiff in error then filed a plea of payment to the declaration and a notice of set-off." In addition to having to pay the costs associated with the demurrer, an affidavit may also be required to justify the motion to amend. This issue was discussed in Manley v. Hunt and Hunt, 1 Ohio 257, 257 (1824) where the trial court overruled a demurrer. "The defendants then moved for leave to answer, but not having produced an affidavit of merits, and that the demurrer was not filed for delay, as the statute requires, the court were on the point of overruling the application, when, by consent of the complainant, defendants were permitted to file their answers."

130. Perkins & Osborn did not bill for the preparation of these answers. One may assume it was part of the fees they charged for the preparation and arguing the demurrers or taken out of the initial retainers. Perkins & Osborn Billings.

day of the term.[131] They were argued before a four-judge bench,[132] including presiding judge Van R. Humphrey, and associate judges John Hubbard,[133] Daniel Kerr[134] and Storm Rosa.[135] The first matter of business when these cases were called was Rounds's decision to not pursue the actions against four of the six defendants, namely Warren Parrish, Frederick G. Williams, Newel K. Whitney, and Horace Kingsbury. The trial transcripts of Williams, Whitney, and Kingsbury each note: "And now at this term of said court, comes the defendant, and the plaintiff being three times demanded to come and prosecute his suit, comes not but makes default."[136] Entering default to dismiss these actions conformed to Ohio law.[137]

In contrast, the trial transcript regarding the action against Warren Parrish stated: "And now at this term of said Court … comes the said plaintiff and discontinues his suit."[138] No reason is given in the record why the case against Parrish is treated differently. A possible rationale for the difference may be found in a letter sent by Reuben Hitchcock to his father, Peter Hitchcock, dated June 26, 1837, where he asked the following question:

---

131. Trial Transcripts.

132. An act to organize the judicial courts, *Statutes of the State of Ohio* (1841), sec. 4, 222 (passed February 7, 1831) ("That the court of common pleas shall consist of a president and three associate judges.").

133. John Hubbard (1780–1854) was a farmer and judge born in Sheffield, Massachusetts. He moved to Madison, Geauga County, Ohio, by 1812. He was elected as an associate judge for Geauga County Court of Common Pleas in 1827.

134. Daniel Kerr (1791–1871) was a farmer, postmaster, and judge born in Fallowfield, Pennsylvania. He moved to Painesville, Ohio, before 1816. He then moved to Mentor, Ohio, where he became postmaster in 1819. Kerr returned to Painesville, where he was elected as an associate judge for the Geauga County Court of Common Pleas by 1831.

135. Storm Rosa (1791–1864) was a doctor, judge, teacher, and newspaper editor. Born in Coxsackie, New York, he moved to Painesville, Ohio, in 1818. He was a teacher at the Medical College of Willoughby University in 1834, located in Chagrin, Ohio. He was elected as an associate judge of Court of Common Pleas for Geauga County in 1836. Rosa was also the editor of the *Painesville Telegraph* from September 1838 to July 1839.

136. Williams Trial Transcript; Whitney Trial Transcript; Kingsbury Trial Transcript. The case against the defendants was dismissed, and the plaintiff was required to pay the court fees.

137. Spencer v. Brockway, 1 Hammond 257 (Ohio 1824) ("That such proceedings were had, that the said Elias being three times solemnly called, came not, but made default, and that judgment was thereupon rendered"); Flight v. State, 7 Ohio 180, pt.1, 180 (1835) ("The said Charles Fight was three times called to come into court, but made default, and his recognizance was forfeited").

138. Parrish Trial Transcript.

I wish your advice in the following matter. Last winter I was employed by Sam¹ D. Rounds & commence w|..|rat <u><qui tam></u> suits vs the Mormons under the act prohibiting the circulation of unauthorized Bank paper to recover the penalty one half of which goes to the informer & the other half "in air of the public revenue of the State"—Under the decisions Rounds has no right to discontinue the suits, but Kingsbury who is one of the Defts is anxious to get out of the difficulty & perhaps Rounds would let him off if he could—Under these circumstances have I as <u>prsecuting Atty</u> any ~~the~~ control over the suits? Have I any authority, where the <u>County</u> is not directly interested in the collection of money? If Rounds should ~~not~~ direct me not to prosecute the suit any fa[r]ther, should I be under any obligation to carry it on?— Please advise me on these points.¹³⁹

Reuben Hitchcock. From *History of Geauga and Lake Counties, Ohio* (1878).

Perhaps Hitchcock got Warren Parrish and Horace Kingsbury confused. If that were the case, Parrish may have paid something to Rounds to get out of the case. However, neither defaulting nor dismissing these defendants fully resolved the cases, and the Geauga County Court of Common Pleas surely understood that.¹⁴⁰ The following judgments were entered in each of these four cases: "The pl[ainti]ff being called to come into court and prosecute this suit comes not, Ordered that the plaintiff becomes non suit,¹⁴¹ and that

---

139. Reuben Hitchcock to Peter Hitchcock, June 26, 1837.

140. By statute, by dismissing this kind of case, Rounds was obligated to pay all costs. "That if any informer on a penal statute, to whom a penalty, or any part thereof, if recovered, is directed to accrue, shall discontinue his suit or prosecution, or shall be nonsuited in the same ... such informer shall pay all costs accruing on such suit or prosecution." Practice of the Courts Act, sec. 61, 665.

141. Nonsuit is the "name of a judgment given against a plaintiff, when he is unable to prove his case, or when he refuses or neglects to proceed to trial of a cause after it has been put at issue, without determining such issue. It is either voluntary or involuntary. A voluntary nonsuit is an abandonment of his cause by a plaintiff, and an agreement that a

the def[endan]t recov[e]r against him his costs."[142] In each case, costs were assessed against Rounds, as follows:

Case	Court Costs	Attorney's Fees
Rounds v. Parrish:	$2.15	$5.00[143]
Rounds v. Williams:	$2.15	$5.00[144]
Rounds v. Whitney:	$2.15	$5.00[145]
Rounds v. Kingsbury:	$3.53	$5.00[146]
Total:		$30.28

The court records do not show whether or not any of these costs were ever paid.

With these four cases dismissed, Rounds moved forward to try the two remaining cases. The record does not identify which case went first. A twelve-man jury tried both.[147] None of the jurors appear to be Mormons. As

---

judgment for costs be entered against him. An involuntary nonsuit takes place when the plaintiff on being called, when his case is before the court for trial, neglects to appear, or when he had given no evidence upon which a jury could find a verdict." Bouvier, *Law Dictionary*, s.v. "nonsuit"; Jacob, *Law-Dictionary*, s.v. "nonsuit." There are no appeals from a nonsuit, unless the nonsuit was ordered by or proceed from the action of the court; for, if the voluntary act of the party, he cannot appeal from it. Bradley v. Sneath, 6 Ohio 490, 496 (1834).

142. Record of Judgment in Rounds v. Parrish, Geauga County Court of Common Pleas, Journal N, 242; Record of Judgment in Rounds v. Williams, Geauga County Court of Common Pleas, Journal N, 242; Record of Judgment in Rounds v. Whitney, Geauga County Court of Common Pleas, Journal N, 241–42; Record of Judgment in Rounds v. Kingsbury, Geauga County Court of Common Pleas, Journal N, 241.

143. Bill of Costs in Rounds v. Parrish, Geauga County Court of Common Pleas, Execution Docket G, 127. This Bill of Costs also notes that Rounds owed $3.22 in his own court costs; Parrish Trial Transcript.

144. Bill of Costs in Rounds v. Williams, Geauga County Court of Common Pleas, Execution Docket G, 126. Perkins & Osborn billed Joseph Smith $10 for Williams's portion of the trial. This Bill of Costs also notes that Rounds owed $3.36 in his own court costs; Williams Trial Transcript.

145. Bill of Costs in Rounds v. Whitney, Geauga County Court of Common Pleas, Execution Docket G, 127 (actually notes $8.53 owed, but itemization only totals $7.15 and that amount matches his Trial Transcript). Perkins & Osborn billed Joseph Smith $10 for Whitney's portion of the trial. This Bill of Costs also notes that Rounds owed $3.22 in his own court costs; Whitney Trial Transcript.

146. Bill of Costs in Rounds v. Kingsbury, Geauga County Court of Common Pleas, Execution Docket G, 126. This Bill of Costs also notes that Rounds owed $3.46 of his own court costs; Kingsbury Trial Transcript.

147. Juries were governed by statute. Only white males over the age of twenty-one living in the county qualified as prospective jurors. An act relating to juries, *Revised Statutes*

both Joseph Smith's and Sidney Rigdon's trials occurred on the same day, one could assume that each trial took about a half day. From the trial bill of costs, $2.50 was charged for witnesses in Smith's trial,[148] and $2.25 for witnesses in the Rigdon's trial.[149] Witnesses subpoenaed and/or sworn to appear were paid $0.75 per day, as of June 1837, an increase from $0.50 per day.[150] The statute noted that this amount is a "daily" rate not per trial. One might reason that the witnesses testified in both trials during the same day and therefore the fees were split between the two trials. Thus, either 6⅓ witnesses testified at the $0.75 rate or 9½ testified at the $0.50 rate—an odd number either way.

---

of Ohio (Columbus: Olmstead and Bailhache, 1831), sec. 2, 94 (passed February 1, 1831) (hereafter cited as *Revised Statutes of Ohio* (1831)). Jurors were selected thirty days prior to the start of the court's term. From those qualified to serve, twenty-seven were randomly selected by the sheriff—fifteen to serve on the grand jury and twelve to serve on the petit jury. Act relating to juries, sec. 4, 95. By statute, jurors were paid $1.00 per day. An act to regulate the fees of officers in civil and criminal cases, *Statutes of the State of Ohio* (1841), sec. 15, 401 (passed March 22, 1837, and became effective on June 1, 1837). The prior act paid the same daily amount. *Revised Statutes of Ohio* (1831), sec. 14, 225. The Smith Trial Bill of Costs notes a $6.00 charge for the jury while the Rigdon Trial Bill of Costs combined the jury and attorney's fees totaling $11.00. However, the Smith Trial Bill of Costs clarifies this combined number as it notes $6.00 for jury fee and $5.00 for attorney's fees. It is reasonable to suppose that $6.00 was charged in both cases for the jury fee. Thus, it appears that trial only lasted half a day. The jury in Joseph Smith's trial included Guy Wyman, Caleb E. Cummings, John A. Ford, William Crafts, David Smith, George Patchin, Ira Webster, Stephen Hulbert, William B. Crothers, Jason Manley, Joseph Emerson, and Thomas King. Smith Trial Transcript. Sidney Rigdon's jury included Amos Cunningham, John McMackin, Erastus Spencer, Gerry Bates, George D. Lee, William C. Mathews, William Graham, Benjamin Adams, Harrison P. Stebbins, Jonathan Hoyt, Heman Dodge, and Thaddeus Cook. Rigdon Trial Transcript.

148. Trial Bill of Costs in Rounds v. Smith, Geauga County Court of Common Pleas, Execution Docket G, 105 (hereafter cited as "Smith Trial Bill of Costs").

149. Trial Bill of Costs in Rounds v. Rigdon, Geauga County Court of Common Pleas, Execution Docket G, 106 (hereafter cited as "Rigdon Trial Bill of Costs").

150. An act fixing the fees of witnesses in civil and criminal cases, *Statutes of the State of Ohio* (1841), sec. 1, 390 (passed March 22, 1837, and became effective on June 1, 1837). The fee was the same whether the witness was testifying in a civil or criminal case. Act fixing the fees of witnesses in civil and criminal cases, sec. 2, 390. This is an increase from the $0.50 per day fee previous to this act. *Revised Statutes of Ohio* (1831), sec. 9, 224 ("That witnesses shall be allowed the following fees: For going to attending at, and returning from court, under a subpoena, per day, to be paid by the party at whose instance he is summoned (on demand), and taxed in the bill of costs, fifty cents"); Swan, *Duties of Justice of the Peace,* 103 ("Witnesses are, in general, allowed fifty cents per day, in each case in which they are subpoenaed, or sworn and examined, whether subpoenaed or not").

The testimony solicited or the evidence introduced at the trials can only be generally surmised. The bills of exception, as noted in the Smith and Rigdon trial transcripts, filed by their counsel offer some insight as to testimony and evidence, some of which was objected to, but introduced over the objections, including:

1. Witnesses testified about the existence of the Kirtland Safety Society Anti-Banking Company on January 4, 1837, the second day that the venture was open.

2. Introduced "articles of association," alleging the creation of the Kirtland Safety Society Anti-Banking Company.

3. Introduced various "bank bills of various denominations" that were allegedly issued by the Kirtland Safety Society Anti-Banking Company.[151]

4. Testimony that Smith and Rigdon were each "a director in said 'Society' and that he assisted in issuing and loaning the same."

From these bills of exception it does not appear that their counsel put on any witnesses or introduced any evidence after the plaintiff rested. Instead, once plaintiff had rested, Smith and Rigdon's counsel "moved the Court" as follows:

1. "To charge the Jury that the statute upon which the suit was founded was not in force";

2. "That the loaning of said paper or bills was not a loaning of money if the statute was in force"; and

3. "That there was no evidence which would authorize them [the jury] to return a verdict for the Pl[ainti]ff."

The court refused to grant these requests, and instead charged the jury as follows:

1. "Charged the Jury that said Statute [the Act of 1816] was in force;

2. "That a lending of the paper or bills was a lending of money within the statute"; and

---

151. Both the Smith and Rigdon trial transcripts had Kirtland Safety Society notes. The note attached to the Smith trial transcript has since been stolen. A photocopy copy of the Smith trial transcript in the Family History Library, The Church of Jesus Christ of Latter-day Saints, Salt Lake City (hereafter cited as FHL), includes the note.

3. "That if they found that the def[endan]t was a director in said society and assisted in issueing and lending said paper or bills it would constitute him an 'officer' within the meaning of the statute; and

4. "That for the purpose of coming to a conclusion they might take the whole testimony as well the appearing of the def[endan]ts names on the same [the notes]."

The jury returned a "true verdict"[152] finding that the defendant "is indebted to the plaintiff in the sum of one thousand dollars. It is therefore considered by the Court that the plaintiff recover against the defendant his debt aforesaid so found as aforesaid, and also his costs and charges by him in and about the prosecuting of this suit in that behalf expended." This could not have been a surprise to Joseph Smith, Sidney Rigdon, or their counsel. Their counsel immediately prepared and submitted a bill of exceptions[153]

---

152. A "true verdict" references the juror's oath to only make their decision based on the evidence. "The fact only is in evidence, and, consequently, the law not being in evidence is not before them. Thus in the clearest terms does the oath limit and define their duty." Jacob, *Law-Dictionary*, s.v. "jury" (emphasis in original).

153. Ohio law provided: "And when a party to a suit, in any court of common pleas within this state, alleges an exception to any order or judgment of such court, it shall be the duty of the judges of such court, concurring in such order or judgment, if required by such party during the term, to sign and seal a bill containing such exception or exceptions as heretofore, in order that such bill or exceptions may, if such party desire it, be made a part of the record in such suit." Practice of the Courts Act, sec. 96, 676. This bill of exceptions was the first step in having a judgment examined by the Ohio Supreme Court. "The bill of exceptions is in practice, and by law, to be signed and sealed only, not to be prepared by judges; the only obligation upon the judges is to sign and seal a true bill of exceptions." State ex rel. Atkins v. Todd, 4 Ohio 351, 351 (1831); Baldwin v. State, 6 Ohio 15, 16 (1833) ("In civil cases, the bill of exceptions is made part of the record only on the application of the party.... If the clerk omit to perform this duty, the party is not without remedy, in the court where the omission takes place. But this court, upon a writ of error, can only notice matter inserted in the record. It cannot look at that which ought to have been, but which is not so inserted"); Acheson v. Western Reserve Bank, 8 Ohio 117, 119 (1837) ("Our *practice act*, section 96, provides that in civil cases the bill of exceptions may be made part of the record, if the excepting party request it. The court have repeatedly ruled that if a party would avail himself, upon error, of exceptions taken, at the trial in the common pleas, he must cause such exceptions to be made part of the record"); Osburn v. State, 7 Ohio 212, pt. I, 215 (1835) ("We find nothing in the record to sustain the second assignment of error as a matter of fact. No notice is taken of any refusal to sign a bill of exceptions, or of any judge erasing his name after having signed it. The record only is before us, on this writ of error, and we can examine no allegation, in respect to facts, not embodied in it"). Perkins & Osborn charged Joseph Smith $25.00 for the trial noting "Oct. T[erm]—trial Rounds Qui Tam against you."

that was signed by them and "sealed" or entered onto the record of the court. Joseph Smith's remedy would have to come from the Ohio Supreme Court.[154]

While a bill of exceptions is required to create an appealable record, it was only the first of several steps to appeal a final judgment.[155] Within thirty days following the trial of the case, the party appealing (the appellant) "shall enter into a bond to the adverse party,[156] with one or more good and sufficient sureties, to be approved of by the clerk of such court,[157] in double the amount of the judgment ... and costs, in case a judgment or decree should

---

They charged another $10.00 for "drawing bill of Exceptions for writ of Error." They also billed Smith for their representation of Sidney Rigdon, charging him $25.00 for the trial and $10 for the bill of exceptions. Billings of Perkins & Osborn.

154. Section 2 of the Act to organize the judicial court (passed on February 7, 1831), provided that the Ohio Supreme Court had "appellate jurisdiction from the court of common pleas, in all civil cases in which the court of common pleas has original jurisdiction." *Statutes of the State of Ohio* (1841), 222. Section 103 further explained: "That final judgments in the courts of common pleas, may be examined and reversed or affirmed, in the supreme court holden in the same county, upon a writ of error, whereto shall be annexed and returned therewith, at a day and place therein mentioned, an authenticated transcript of the record and assignment of error, and prayer for a reversal, with a citation to the adverse party, or his attorney." Act to organize the judicial court, 222, 678–79. Practice of the Courts Act, sec. 108, 681 ("That in civil cases an appeal shall be allowed, of course, to the supreme court, from any judgment or decree rendered in the court of common pleas, in which such court had original jurisdiction").

155. Act to organize the judicial court, sec. 109, 682 provided that "the party desirous of appealing his cause to the supreme court, shall, at the term of the court of common pleas in which judgment or decree was rendered, enter on the records of the court, notice of such intention."

156. If the adverse party collects on the judgment, hence no stay of execution was granted by the trial court, the appeal bond becomes unnecessary. Cass v. Adams, 3 Ohio 223, 223–224 (1827) (Court held that an execution on goods by a *fieri facia* thereby put property in the hands of the sheriff pending the appeal made the requirement for an appeal bond as an unnecessary "cumulative remedy").

157. In Stanbery v. Mitten, 6 Ohio 546, 547 (1828) the court held that section 109 of the Act to Regulate the Practice of the Judicial Courts "provides that the bond required to perfect an appeal from that court shall be approved by its clerk. It is his duty to judge of the sufficiency of the bond and of the security. This is a ministerial act of his, and this court has in the way no control over it. When the appeal bond is approved by the clerk and filed, the rights of the appellant and the obligations of the appellee are fixed, and a majority of this court are of opinion such rights are beyond the power of this court, upon a mere question of expediency or convenience. A party should reflect upon the effect of his steps before he takes them, and not the court to permit him to retrace them. This court is careful not to interfere with the exercise of such duties, so clearly vested in the clerk and the party, in order to substitute its own discretion."

be entered in favor of the appellee."[158] During this thirty-day period, on motion of the party appealing the court may stay execution on the judgment. Once the appeal bond is entered, thereby perfecting the appeal,[159] the appellant would prepare a writ of error[160] based on the bill of exceptions[161] to be issued by the supreme court.[162] The clerk of the court of common pleas then makes "an authenticated transcript of the docket or journal entries, and of the final judgment or decree made and rendered in the case; which transcript, together with the original papers and pleadings filed in the cause" and delivers it to the office of the clerk of the supreme court, on or before the first day of the next term.[163]

---

158. Stanbery v. Mitten, 6 Ohio 546, 547 (1828).

159. Work v. Massie, 6 Ohio 503, 503 (1834) ("Section 109 of the practice act directs the mode of perfecting an appeal").

160. A writ of error "is a writ issued out of a court of competent jurisdiction, directed to the judges of a court of record in which final judgment has been given, and commending them ... to send it to another court of appellate jurisdiction, therein named, to be examined in order that some alleged error in the proceedings may be corrected.... Its object is to review and correct an error of law committed in the proceeding." Bouvier, *Law Dictionary*, s.v. "writ of error"; Jacob, *Law-Dictionary*, s.v. "error."

161. Duckwall v. Weaver, 2 Ohio 13, 13 (1825) ("The defendants objected to the whole of the evidence offered; the objection was overruled, and a bill of exceptions taken. A verdict was found for the plaintiff. Judgment entered, and a writ of error taken"); Moore v. Beasley, 3 Ohio 294, 294 (1827) ("He then moved the court to instruct the jury that the case was within that statute, which was also refused, and bills of exception were taken. A verdict and judgment were rendered for the plaintiff, and a writ of error taken to reverse it, on the matters stated in the bills"); King v. Kenny, 4 Ohio 79, 80 (1829) ("Upon this bill of exceptions the writ of error was founded"); Trustees of Cincinnati Tp. v. Ogden, 5 Ohio 23, 23 (1831) ("This cause came before the court on a writ of error to the court of common pleas of Hamilton county. The case was this, as presented in a bill of exceptions"); Eldred v. Saxton, 5 Ohio 215, 2115 (1831) ("The defendant took his bill of exceptions. There was a verdict and judgment for the plaintiff for fifty-one dollars and five cents and costs, to reverse which this writ of error was brought"); James v. Richmond, 5 Ohio 337, 338 (1832) ("To this decision of the court, the defendant, by his counsel, excepted, and his bill of exceptions was sealed. A judgment having been rendered against the defendant, this writ of error is prosecuted to reverse that judgment").

162. Practice of the Courts Act, sec. 3, 651.

163. Practice of the Courts Act, sec. 112, 683. "That when any cause is removed by appeal into the supreme court, the appeal shall be tried on the pleadings made up in the court of common pleas, unless for good cause shown, and on the payment of costs, the said court should permit either or both parties to alter their pleadings; in which case, such court shall lay the party under such equitable rules and restrictions as they may conceive necessary, to prevent delay." Practice of the Courts Act, sec. 114, 684. Either party to the appeal can request a copy of this transcript that the clerk of the court of common pleads can provide at the parties' "own proper costs and charges." Practice of the Courts Act, sec. 112, 683.

However, in the present two cases (*Rounds v. Smith* and *Rounds v. Rigdon*) nothing in the record evidences that appeal bonds were ever secured, motions were ever made to stay execution on the judgments, or writs of error ever requested. The court entered the judgments in both cases on October 25, 1837.[164] Consequentially, while the bills of exceptions delineate the legal basis for an appeal of the judgments, the appeals were never perfected or further pursued. Their lawyers, Perkins & Osborn, stopped billing after the trial and preparations of the bills of exceptions.

One can only speculate as to why these appeals were not further pursued by Joseph Smith or Sidney Rigdon. Neither the litigants nor their attorneys left an explanation. Legally the appeal should have been considered very strong. Yet, while the law appears clear now, at the time the courts had yet to rule on this issue and public opinion was indeed split.[165] Smith and Rigdon would have to consider that the four-judge court had expressly refused to apply the law as argued by their counsel that the Act of 1816 was suspended. It would not be until 1840 that the Ohio Supreme Court ruled on this matter affirming their position.[166] Consequently, the appeal must have looked more problematic then than it does today.

Collection efforts against Smith and Rigdon were commenced on November 6, 1837—exactly two weeks after the trials and judgments. Judgment against Smith totaled $1,024.10, comprised of the $1,000 penalty under the

---

164. The judgment in Rounds v. Smith, Geauga Court of Common Pleas, Journal N, 237, noted: "Debt—This day came the parties and thereupon came a Jury to wit: Guy Wyman, Caleb E. Cummings, John A. Ford, William Coafts, David Smith, George Patchin, Ira Webster, Stephen Hulbert, William B. Crothers, Jason Manley, Joseph Emerson and Thomas King, who being duly empannelled & sworn, will & truly to try the issue joined between the parties, do find that the deft is indebted to the plff in the sum of one thousand dollars. It is therefore considered by the Court that the plff recover against the deft. the said sum of one thousand dollars his deft aforesaid and also his costs." The judgment in Rounds v. Rigdon, Geauga Court of Common Pleas, Journal N, 237, noted: "Debt— This day come the parties & thereupon came a Jury to wit: Amos Cunningham, John McMackin, Erastus Spencer, Gerry Bates, George D. Lee, Wm C. Matthews, William Graham, Benjamin Adams, Harrison P. Stebbins Jonathan Hoyt, Heman Dodge and Thaddeus Cook, who being duly empanelled and sworn well and truly to try the issue joined between the parties, do find that the deft is indebted to the plff in the sum of one thousand dollars. It is therefore considered by the Court that the plff recover against the deft. his debt aforesaid, and also his costs."

165. See above, pp. 211–12.

166. See above, pp. 196–201.

Act of 1816, $23.35 in plaintiff's costs[167] and $0.75 in defendant's costs.[168] Judgment against Rigdon totaled $1,023.58, comprised of the $1,000 penalty under the Act of 1816, $22.77 in plaintiff's costs[169] and $0.81 in defendant's costs.[170]

Amidst these collection efforts Joseph Smith received the following revelation on January 12, 1838: "Thus Saith the Lord, let the Presidency of my Church, take their families as soon as it is practicable, and a door is open for them, and moove to the west, as fast as the way is made plain before their faces, and let their hearts be comforted for I will be with them."[171] Smith and Rigdon would leave that night for Missouri.[172] Their families would follow shortly thereafter.

Collecting on judgments was governed by statute.[173] Once a judgment was entered, a judgment lien was automatically placed on all real property of the debtor in the county where the judgment was rendered "from the first day of the term at which judgment shall be rendered."[174] Personal property was only encumbered upon seizure.[175] By statute the court initiated the collection process by issuing a writ of fieri facias.[176] This writ directs usually the

---

167. The plaintiff's costs were broken down as follows: $5.31 in clerk costs, $4.54 in sheriff costs, $2.50 in witness fees, $6.00 in jury fees and $5.00 in attorney's fees. Smith's Trial Bill of Costs.

168. Smith's costs of $0.75 were for clerk costs. Smith's Trial Bill of Costs.

169. The plaintiff's costs were broken down as follows: $5.04 in clerk costs, $4.48 in sheriff costs, $2.25 in witness fees, $6.00 in jury fees and $5.00 in attorney's fees. Rigdon's Trial Bill of Costs.

170. Rigdon's costs of $0.81 were for clerk costs. Rigdon's Trial Bill of Costs.

171. Dean C. Jessee, Mark Ashurst-McGee, and Richard L. Jensen, eds., *Journals, Volume 1: 1832–1839*, vol. 1 of the Journals series of *The Joseph Smith Papers*, ed. Dean C. Jessee, Ronald K. Esplin, and Richard Lyman Bushman (Salt Lake City: Church Historian's Press, 2008), 283.

172. Joseph Smith Jr., *The History of the Church of Jesus Christ of Latter-day Saints*, ed. B. H. Roberts, 2d ed. rev., 7 vols. (Salt Lake City: Deseret Book, 1971), 3:1 ("On the evening of the 12th of January, about ten o'clock, we left Kirtland, on horseback, to escape mob violence, which was about to burst upon us under the color of legal process to cover the hellish designs of our enemies, and to save themselves from the just judgment of the law").

173. An act regulating judgments and executions, *Statutes of the State of Ohio* (1841), sec. 1, 467 (passed March 1, 1831) (hereafter cited as Judgment and Execution Act).

174. Judgment and Execution Act, sec. 2, 468.

175. Judgment and Execution Act, sec. 2, 468.

176. Fieri facia "is the name of the writ of execution. It is so called because when writs were in Latin, the words directed to the sheriff, were, *quod fieri facias de bonis et catallis, &c*, that you cause to be made of the goods and chattels &c. The foundation of this writ is a judgment for debt or damages, and the party who has recovered such a judgment is

local sheriff, or other officer, to first pursue the collection on any personal property of the debtor. If no personal property was located, or if after the sheriff's sale of such personal property the judgment was not fully satisfied, the sheriff was authorized to move for the sale of the real property of the debtor.[177] Before the sheriff could proceed to sell any personal property of the debtor, he "shall cause public notice to be given of the time and place of the sale, for at least ten days before the day of sale; which notice shall be given by advertisement, published in some newspaper published in the county."[178] If land thereafter was to be sold to satisfy the judgment, the sheriff was required to obtain appraisal as to the value of the land from "three disinterested freeholders, who shall be resident within in the county where the lands taken in execution are situated."[179] Thirty-day notice of the sale of land was also required.[180]

While it does not appear from the record that Sheriff Kimball was successful in collecting anything from Joseph Smith,[181] his efforts against Rigdon proved successful. The record notes three efforts to sell the personal property of Sidney Rigdon. The first recovered $604.50 from the sale of such personal property. The second effort indicated that the personal property seized was "claimed by a third person and awarded to the claimant." The third effort resulted in the sale of additional personal property that was sold for $111.75.[182] The record is not clear as to what all was levied or sold during these three collection efforts. Yet, the record does include one published notice for a

---

generally entitled to it, unless he is delayed by the stay of execution which the law allows in certain cases after the rendition of the judgment, or by proceeding in error." Bouvier, *Law Dictionary*, s.v. "fieri facias"; Jacob, *Law-Dictionary*, 3:43, s.v. "fieri facias."

177. Judgment and Execution Act, sec. 3, 469–70.

178. Judgment and Execution Act, sec. 9, 472.

179. Judgment and Execution Act, sec. 10, 473. These appraisers were put under oath affirming to their impartiality to perform the appraisals. The appraisals of "an estimate of the real value in money, of said estate, upon actual view of the premises" were signed by the appraisers and then returned to the sheriff. Judgment and Execution Act, sec. 10, 473. Copies of the appraisals were then filed with the clerk of the court from which the writ was issued. Judgment and Execution Act, sec. 11, 473. At the sale, the property could not be sold for less than two-thirds of appraised value. Judgment and Execution Act, sec. 12, 474.

180. Notice of the sale of such property had to take place at least thirty days before the sale in the same manner as the notice for personal property. Judgment and Execution Act, sec. 14, 474.

181. Interestingly, the collection efforts against Rigdon as delineated on his Trial Bill of Costs were also duplicated on Smith's Trial Bill of Costs, although it is clear by reading the notations that the efforts were solely against Rigdon.

182. Rigdon Trial Bill of Costs.

sheriff's sale of Rigdon's personal property. Published in the *Painesville Tele-graph* on February 22, 1838, it noted:

SHERIFF'S SALE

BY Virtue of an Execution issued by the Clerk of the Court of Common Pleas of Geauga county, and to me directed, I shall expose to sale at the Inn of John Johnson in Kirtland, on Monday, the 5th day of March next, between the hours of 10 o'clock A M. and 4 P.M. of said day, the following described property, to wit: 2 Bureaus, 1 cupboard, 1 box stove, 1 table, 3 stands, 1 clock and case, 1 cradle, 3 looking glasses, 4 chairs, 4 window sashes, part box glass, 5 trunks and contents, 1 barrel dried fruit, 1 basket of clothing, a quantity of zinc, 1 pail, glass bottles, bedsteads, several rolls of paper, ribbons, hearth rug, carpeting; 1 bed & bedding, 2 waiters, quantity of books, 6 tin pans, 2 castors, knives and forks, 1 inkstand, 1 urn, 2 globes, 2 brass pin setts, 2 brass candlesticks; glass ware and crockery, and sundry other articles. Taken at the suit of S.D. Rounds vs. Sidney Rigdon.

ABEL KIMBALL, 2d, Shff.

Feb. 20, 1838.[183]

Sheriff Kimball forwarded the $604.50 to Grandison Newell. And the $92.00[184] of the $111.75 was apparently used to pay the fees incurred on these two executions on Rigdon's personal property. It is unclear what happened to the balance of $19.75.

In addition to executing on Rigdon's personal property, Sheriff Kimball also started the process to sell an acre lot purportedly owned by Rigdon.[185] Rigdon's Trial Bill of Costs notes that by January 20, 1838, Sheriff Kimball had such real property appraised at $666.00. However, this lot remained unsold "by direction of Grandison Newell."[186]

Why would Newell direct that this lot not be sold? Clearly the court understood that the judgments belonged to Newell and not to Rounds. Thus, perhaps the answer has to do with the fact that Newell was at that point

---

183. *Painesville Telegraph*, February 22, 1838, 3.

184. These fees included $91.50 to the sheriff and $0.50 to the clerk of court. Rigdon Trial Bill of Costs.

185. The Rigdon Trial Bill of Costs identifies this real property as follows: "part of lots five & six on Block 114 in Kirtland City Plat in Kirtland township Geauga County Ohio supposed to contain one acre of land more or less."

186. Rigdon Trial Bill of Costs.

negotiating the settlement of the judgments with William Marks[187] and Oliver Granger,[188] as agents for Joseph Smith and Sidney Rigdon.[189] On March 1, 1838, he would assign the Judgments to Marks and Granger for $1,600, as follows:[190]

---

187. William Marks (1792–1872) was a farmer, printer, publisher, and postmaster. Marks was born at Rutland, Vermont. He lived at Portage, New York, where he was baptized into the LDS Church by April 1835. He moved to Kirtland, Ohio, by September 1837, appointed a member of the Kirtland high council on September 3, 1837, and agent to Bishop Newel K. Whitney on September 17, 1837. Marks was made president of the Kirtland stake in 1838.

188. Oliver Granger (1794–1841) was born at Phelps, New York. He was the Sheriff of Ontario Co. and colonel in the militia. Granger was baptized into the LDS Church and ordained an elder by Brigham and Joseph Young, ca. 1832–1833. He moved to Kirtland, Ohio, in 1833 and was appointed to the Kirtland high council on October 8, 1837.

189. On September 27, 1837, Joseph Smith and Sidney Rigdon appointed Oliver Granger as their "agent and attorney" relating to the Kirtland Safety Society. The full appointment stated:

Kirtland Ohio Set 27-1837

Know all men by these present that we Joseph Smith Jr. and Sidney Rigdon hereby appoint and constitute Oliver Granger our proper agent and attorney to act in our name to all interests and purposes as we ourselves could act if we were personally present: to manage conduct and bring to settlement a business which we had with J. F. Scribner of Troy City in the state of New York in relation to the paper of Kirtland Safety Society

Given under our hand at Kirtland Geauga County Ohio the day and date above written.

Sidney Rigdon
Joseph Smith Jr

Power of Attorney from Sidney Rigdon and Joseph Smith Jr. to Oliver Granger, September 27, 1837, Joseph Smith Collection, CHL. William Marks was never made agent or given power of attorney by either Smith or Rigdon. However, Marks was appointed as agent for Newel K. Whitney on September 17, 1837. Kirtland High Council Minutes, September 17, 1837, CHL. Further, Smith and Rigdon deeded land to Marks starting in April 1837 for Marks to use to settle debts in Kirtland against them and/or the Church. See Deed from Rigdon to Marks, April 7, 1837, FHL, 20240, vol. 23, 535; Deed from Smith to Marks, April 7, 1837, FHL, 20240, vol. 23, 538; Deed from Smith to Marks, April 10, 1837, FHL, 20240, vol. 23, 535-536; Deed from Smith to Marks, April 10, 1837, FHL, 20240, vol. 23, 536-537; Deed from Smith to Marks, April 10, 1837, FHL, 20240, vol. 23, 538; Deed from Smith to Marks, April 10, 1837, FHL, 20240, vol. 23, 539; Deed from Smith to Marks, April 10, 1837, FHL, 20240, vol. 24, 189.

190. Grandison Newell to William Marks and Oliver Granger, March 1, 1838, Whitney Collection.

For and in consideration of Sixteen hundred dollars to me in hand paid by William Marks and Oliver Granger I do hereby sell assign and set over to the Said William Marks and Oliver Granger two Judgments in favor of Samuel D. Rounds and assigned to me by said Rounds against Joseph Smith jr and Sidney Rigdon of one thousand dollars each which Judgments were obtained at the Court of Common Pleas holden at Chardon in and for the County of Geauga, to wit, on the 24$^{\underline{th}}$ day of October 1837, and I do agree to pay all costs that has accrued on said Judgments up to this date.

G. Newell

Kirtland March 1st 1838
Attest Lyman Cowdery[191]

With acceptance of this payment, Grandison Newell had been paid a total of $2,204.50.[192] Pursuant to the assignment of claims, Newell assumed the costs incurred in the cases totaling $24.10 for Smith and $23.58 for Rigdon. The record does not show that Newell ever paid these costs to the court. Thus, Newell netted from these lawsuits $2,156.82, which is $156.82 more than the total of the judgments. Moreover, of that amount, Newell was only supposed to receive 50 percent with the other 50 percent going to the state of Ohio. Newell never forwarded any of this recovery to the state, as will be evidenced by his revival of these two judgments in 1859. A full discussion of these later developments is a matter to be continued at another time. At this point in this litigation, however, it is already clear that Grandison Newell had collected more than 100 percent of the judgments, and under any ethical or legal analysis, this should have more than ended this lawsuit. Grandison Newell, however, had no ethical boundaries in this matter, and in reviving these judgments in 1859 he would use the law to commit a fraud on the state of Ohio long after the death of Joseph Smith in Illinois.[193]

---

191. Lyman Cowdery (1802–1881) was a lawyer, constable, and probate judge. He was born at Wells, Vermont. He was the older brother of Oliver Cowdery.

192. $1,600 from the Assignment of Claims and $604.50 from the sale of Rigdon's personal property.

193. For further information, see the end of ch. 10 below.

Chapter Ten

Tabulating the Impact of Litigation on the Kirtland Economy

Gordon A. Madsen

From the time Joseph and Emma Smith arrived at the doorstep of Newel K. Whitney in Kirtland, Ohio, on February 4, 1831, until they closed the door to their own home and departed that city on January 12, 1838, Joseph was involved in 50 lawsuits either as plaintiff or defendant. At least, that is the number located thus far; there may be more. Of the 50, five were criminal actions, treated briefly below. In the 45 civil matters, Joseph Smith Jr. was plaintiff or co-plaintiff in 7, and defendant or co-defendant in 38 (27 of which were collection cases, see fig. 1). All this litigation, with three exceptions treated at the end of this chapter, occurred between March 1834 and November 1839. During that five and a half years, Joseph was "in court" for an average of 9 cases a year. This article focuses on the financial impact that this litigation had on the Kirtland economy.

The court records for 20 of these cases are found in the Courts of Common Pleas, as they were and are called in Ohio, which are known as courts "of record"—that is, the dockets of these courts are public records kept by the county clerk and which are still retained in the Geauga County Archives and the Lake County Clerk's Office. Kirtland and its neighboring town to the northeast, Painesville, were part of Geauga County, Ohio, in 1831. In 1840, Geauga County was split, and its northern portion became Lake County. Kirtland and Painesville were part of Geauga until 1840 and have belonged to Lake County since then. I have also included 18 cases from courts of Justices of the Peace that have thus far been located or identified. Those courts were not courts of record, and we are dependent on finding Justice of the Peace dockets in various repositories or in the possession of descendants of those Justices of the Peace living in the environs of Kirtland in the 1830s.

In addition to the cases brought against Joseph, 13 more (fig. 2) were brought against Reynolds Cahoon, Jared Carter, and Hyrum Smith, who were the committee charged with building the Kirtland Temple and were partners in the mercantile business as well. They are also included here because they were closely connected with Joseph. In those actions, where all or one of them is named (often in company with other individual Latter-day Saints), these men are always defendants, never plaintiffs. Because the cases in which Joseph is named together with the Temple Committee are so intertwined, and most of the Kirtland litigation stems from debt incurred in connection with the construction of the Kirtland Temple, all of them are included in this study. Some of the cases that name the Temple Committee also include Joseph Smith, and they have been included in the 45 identified above. One final case involving the Temple Committee that is both civil and criminal is also treated. This paper thus summarizes 58 civil and 7 criminal actions.

Five Criminal Cases Involving Joseph Smith in Ohio

1. State of Ohio v. Hurlbut. This case, the most famous of the criminal cases in Kirtland, was tried March 31, 1834. Joseph Smith was the complaining witness in that action. Doctor Philastus Hurlbut ("Doctor" was his first given name, not a professional title) had publicly threatened Joseph's life. A jury found Hurlbut guilty, and the Court of Common Pleas ordered him to keep the peace, and in particular, to leave Joseph Smith undisturbed. Hurlbut was also ordered to post a $200.00 bond guaranteeing such good behavior for six months (called a peace bond), and to pay the court costs of $112.59. He left town without paying the costs and leaving the sureties on his peace bond stranded for six months (the term of the bond). This nineteenth-century criminal procedure was the forerunner of today's restraining orders.[1]

2. State of Ohio v. Smith. In June 1835 in the Court of Common Pleas, Calvin Stoddard, brother-in-law to the Prophet, accused Joseph of assault and battery. Justice of the Peace Lewis Miller of Painesville, after hearing (a preliminary hearing) some evidence, bound Joseph over to the Court of Common Pleas, where a grand jury issued an indictment against Joseph for assault and battery. The matter was tried before the Court of Common Pleas without jury on June 16, 1835. The decision reads in part: "and the said Joseph Smith Junior Pleaded to the foregoing Indictment, and said thereof

---

1. For an analysis of this case, see ch. 7 in this volume.

he is guilty, unless the Court on hearing the evidence adduced shall be of opinion that he is not guilty—. And the Court having heard the evidence do adjudge that the said Joseph Smith Jun' is not guilty as he stands charged in said Indictment.—Wherefore it was ordered that he be discharged from said Indictment and go thereof without day."² The phrase "without day" meant the defendant had no further court day scheduled—he was free.

3. State of Ohio on complaint of Newell v. Smith. On April 13, 1837, Grandison Newell claimed Joseph Smith had threatened to kill him and initiated an action under the same criminal statute that was used by Joseph against Hurlbut discussed first above. After hearing eleven witnesses for the prosecution and ten for the defense, Justice of the Peace Flint (who was conducting a similar preliminary hearing) ruled in favor of Newell and put Joseph under recognizance (or bond) to appear at the next term of the Court of Common Pleas. The record of the proceedings before Justice Flint was transmitted to the Court of Common Pleas, and a trial was held on June 5, 1837. At the conclusion of the trial, the court held: "the Court having heard the evidence adduced, are of the opinion that the complainant had no cause to fear as set forth in his said complaint—it is therefore adjudged by the court, that the said Joseph Smith Junior be discharged, and go thereof without day—at the cost of the State taxed at [blank]."³ More about Grandison Newell will appear below.

4. State of Ohio v. Smith. Joseph was cited for contempt in the spring of 1837 for failing to appear as a subpoenaed witness in a criminal case pending in Ravenna, Portage County (about thirty miles south of Kirtland). In his response, Joseph stated that he was only a character witness for the defendant, knowing nothing about the facts of the case, and that he had been notified that the defendant was not going to be in court on the day of trial, which proved to be true. Joseph was excused of any contempt and discharged.

5. State of Ohio v. Ritch. Finally, on September 12, 1837, Joseph was the complaining witness against one Abram Ritch in an action for "oppression by color of office." Ritch was a constable in Kirtland and incidentally was the constable who served subpoenas and summonses and made arrests in the *Hurlbut* case noted above. Seven witnesses testified. The Justice of the Peace ruled: "The charge is not made out against the said Abram Ritch, and he go hence without day."⁴ The Justice of the Peace who made that ruling was Oliver Cowdery, who

---

2. Copy of case document in possession of the author, forthcoming in the Joseph Smith Papers Legal and Business Records series.

3. Copy of case document in possession of the author, forthcoming in the Joseph Smith Papers Legal and Business Records series.

4. Copy of case document in possession of the author, forthcoming in the Joseph Smith Papers Legal and Business Records series.

by 1837 had become one of Kirtland's Justices of the Peace. Cowdery did not detail in his decision what the official oppressive act(s) of Ritch were about which Smith complained.

Three Cases Not Directly Involving Joseph Smith

Three other cases should here be mentioned, two of them criminal and one civil. Though not counted above, they also impacted the Kirtland economy.

State of Ohio v. Smith [Joseph Smith Sr.] et al. On August 15, 25, and 26, 1837, Joseph's father, Joseph Smith Sr., and 18 others including Joseph's brothers William, Samuel, and Don Carlos, were charged with the crimes of riot and of assault and battery on the complaint of Warren Parrish. Parrish had become leader of a splinter group, and one Sabbath prior to August 15 he with a party of his followers, armed with pistols and Bowie knives, attempted to take possession of the Kirtland Temple on August 14. Joseph Sr. and the 18 other named defendants removed them. A total of 48 witnesses gave testimony in the two-day hearing. Justice of the Peace Oliver Cowdery determined, "After mature deliberation upon the law and the evidence, it was considered that the charge against them was not sustained, and they were therefore discharged."[5]

Benjamin Bissel v. Joseph Smith Sr. et al. As a civil case footnote to the criminal one just cited, on January 26, 1838, Benjamin Bissell, who had represented all the defendants in that case, sued them all for his legal fees incurred in the case.[6] Before he filed his declaration, he asked for a continuance, and then dropped the case. A declaration would be called a complaint in today's usage. More about the procedure will be explained hereafter.

State of Ohio v. Zebedee Coltrin, Lyman Sherman, John Sawyer, Harlow Redfield, and Willard Woodstock. The final case here involved a criminal charge arising out of the burning of the printing office and book-bindery located just west of the Kirtland Temple on January 15, 1838. The trial was held on January 17 and 19 before Justice of the Peace Warren Cowdery (who had succeeded his brother Oliver). The defendants were charged with arson. Zebedee Coltrin had left Ohio and was not arrested. Thirty witnesses testified. The prosecutor early in the presentation of the evidence dropped his

---

5. Oliver Cowdery, Justice of the Peace Docket, p. 226, Huntington Library, San Marino, California. Eliza R. Snow, one of the witnesses who testified, left a record of these events in Eliza Roxey Snow, *Biography and Family Record of Lorenzo Snow* (Salt Lake City: Deseret News, 1884), 20–22.

6. Copy of case document in possession of the author, forthcoming in the Joseph Smith Papers Legal and Business Records series.

claim against Harlow Redfield and made him one of the thirty witnesses. At the conclusion of the evidence, Justice of the Peace Cowdery ruled: "No facts were elicited that went to indict the prisoners of the crime charged in the complaint, either as principles [*sic*] or accessories."[7] They were therefore discharged.

These two criminal cases, together with the five discussed above, account for the full extent of the criminal actions involving Mormon leaders in Ohio.

Seven Civil Cases Involving Joseph Smith as Plaintiff in Kirtland

Seven civil actions in which Joseph was plaintiff (or co-plaintiff) were generally small collection matters and had little impact on the Kirtland economy. They are included in the totals above but are not listed in the accompanying figures.

Eight Miscellaneous Cases Involving Joseph Smith as Defendant in Kirtland

1. Lake v. Smith. Dennis Lake had marched in Zion's Camp, and upon his return to Kirtland became disappointed with the march or disenchanted with the church or both. On December 10, 1834, he sued Joseph Smith to be paid for his time and effort in making the march. Two Justices of the Peace, J. C. Dowen and Arial Hanson, granted judgment to Lake for $63.67. Joseph appealed to the Court of Common Pleas, which on June 16, 1835, reversed the judgment and ordered Lake to pay Smith's court costs as well as his own, which totaled $35.50.

2. George Metcalf Paymaster of 1st Brigade, 2nd Regiment, 9 Division Ohio Militia v. Samuel H. Smith. This case was an appeal from the assessment of two fines of $.75 and $1.00 levied on Samuel H. Smith, Joseph's younger brother, for failure to appear at two musters of the Ohio Militia to which he had been assigned. The fine was ordered by a Militia Court of Inquiry, affirmed by a military Court of Appeals, and transferred to Justice of the Peace Dowen for collection. Dowen's 1885 reminiscence states: "I issued a writ for Jo and his brother Sam Smith, for non-attendance at training. I decided that as Rev. Coe, the Presbyterian minister was exempt, I excused Joe because he was a preacher … Sam I fined $1.75. He appealed."[8] While

---

7. Oliver Cowdery, Justice of the Peace Docket, p. 342.

8. Copy of case document in possession of the author, forthcoming in the Joseph Smith Papers Legal and Business Records series.

Joseph was initially involved in the action, he was excused by Dowen. Samuel appealed on the basis that he was a "minister of the gospel" like his brother. The Court of Common Pleas affirmed the judgment of Justice Dowen against Samuel and added "damages" of $.20 plus the costs of court from both courts, totaling $32.40. What started out as a $1.75 fine mushroomed into $34.35. Samuel was compelled to sell a cow to make payment.

3. Six claims before an unnamed Justice of the Peace in Painesville. On July 27, 1837, while Joseph Smith, Sidney Rigdon, Brigham Young, and others were en route to Canada, they were intercepted in Painesville and taken before a Justice of the Peace, and six different civil matters or claims were presented. Five were dismissed that day. In the sixth, a trial date was set five weeks later, and bail was posted by Anson Call. The trial occurred on said date, and Joseph was discharged. No court documents have surfaced regarding those cases. Only references to them from journals of Joseph, Brigham Young, and Anson Call corroborate the fact that they occurred.[9]

Twenty-Seven Collection Cases Involving Joseph Smith

Three other civil actions will be dealt with in some detail further below, but the 27 civil collection matters (fig. 1) will now be addressed as a block. But first, some foundation needs to be established. Promissory notes in frontier America were more than memoranda of debt. They were frequently exchanged or circulated (by the process of endorsing the back of the note) almost as if they were legal tender or specie. Moreover, it was far easier to bring a lawsuit based on a promissory note than a contract, written or oral, or on an open account of a business. When such promissory note was ultimately presented to its maker to be redeemed, the maker after paying the note would tear off his signature at the bottom, thus preventing it from being circulated further, and it would constitute a convenient receipt of payment. If the obligor did not tear off the signature, and the note came into other hands, it could be recirculated and ultimately brought back to him and he would have to pay it a second time.

Of the 326 promissory notes still extant executed by Joseph Smith, the Joseph Smith Legal Papers team has not yet matched each of the lawsuits described below, all of which were based on promissory notes, with the appropriate notes, assuming they are extant.

---

9. Joseph Smith Jr., *History of The Church of Jesus Christ of Latter-day Saints,* ed. B. H. Roberts, 2d ed., rev., 7 vols. (Salt Lake City: Deseret Book, 1971), 2:502 (hereafter cited as *History of the Church*); "History of Brigham Young," *Millennial Star* 25 (August 8, 1863): 503–4.

Next, it will be helpful to list the prominent Mormon business firms or entities that were doing business in Kirtland during the 1830s:

Printing Firm, sometimes called **United Firm.** Printing and other businesses. Included Joseph Smith, Sidney Rigdon, Frederick G. Williams, William W. Phelps, Oliver Cowdery, Newel K. Whitney, John Johnson Sr., and others temporarily in and out.

F. G. Williams & Co. Successor to the Printing Firm, with some of the above named partners in and out over the time period, ultimately concluding with Williams and Cowdery as partners.

N. K. Whitney & Co. N. K. Whitney's sole proprietorship. Whitney store, ashery, saw mill, and other businesses.

Smith, Cowdery & Co. Joseph and Oliver as partners operated what was called "Joseph's Variety Store."

Smith, Rigdon & Co. Joseph and Sidney Rigdon's store in Chester.

Carter, Cahoon & Smith. Jared Carter, Reynolds Cahoon, and Hyrum Smith, the Temple Committee. Also operated a store sometimes alternately under the name of **Cahoon, Carter & Co.**

Boynton & Johnson. John Boynton and Luke Johnson's store.

Pratt, Young & Smith. Parley P. Pratt, Brigham Young, and Hyrum Smith's stone quarry.

Kirtland Safety Society. An attempted corporation that became a joint stock company. Joseph Smith, Sidney Rigdon, Frederick G. Williams, Newel K. Whitney, Horace Kingsbury, and Warren Parrish were directors at time of the Rounds suit referred to hereafter.

All the individuals named in the various businesses above are co-defendants, in various combinations, together with a number of other co-signers on the assorted promissory notes sued on in the cases below.

Tabulated in figure 1 are the records of the Joseph Smith cases and the entries in the execution docket for those cases, which is the history of collection efforts and payments made. Not all payments were reported to the county clerk, keeper of the execution docket. There is evidence of payments which were not listed in the execution docket. The docket is dependent on the conscientiousness of the creditors or the insistence of the debtors to require the creditor to go to the courthouse after the debt is paid and record it. To date, from secondary sources, not from cancelled notes or recorded admissions of payment, a little over $8,000.00 in such undocketed payments to creditors have been uncovered, not all of which are traceable to litigating creditors.

The columns on figure 1 show the plaintiffs' names; date of the action; amount sued for (the claim); if discontinued (meaning presumably abandoned before a declaration, known today as the complaint, was filed); if

Figure 1. Collection Cases against Joseph Smith Jr.

Plaintiffs	Date Filed	Claim	Discontinuted	Settled	Satisfied	Balance
1. Holmes & Dayton	June 1837	$183.30			$183.30	0
2. Bank of Geauga	June 1837	$3,018.00		$3,018.00		0
3. T. Martindale	June 1837	$6,000.00		$6,000.000		0
4. H. Kelly	June 1837	$2,083.47			$541.41	$1,542.06
5. Pattersons	June 1837	$610.37			$610.37	0
6. Cyrus Lake	July 1837	$53.24			$53.24	0
7. Unshur	August 1837	$39.96			$39.96	0
8. Newbold	October 1837	$400.00		$400.00		0
9. Eaton	October 1837	$1,185.66				$1,185.66
10. Barker & Bump	October 1837	$214.34	$214.34			0
11. Seymour & Griffith	October 1837	$150.00	$150.00			0
12. J. Wright	October 1837	$1,055.31		$1,055.31		0
13. W. Foster	December 1837	$100.45		$100.45		0
14. Jacob Bump	January 1838	$45.14		$45.14		0
15. Jacob Bump	January 1838	$854.28			$854.28	0
16. M. Allen	January 1838	$120.56			$120.56	0
17. Wm. Spencer	January 1838	$56.41	$56.41			0
18. Ray Boynton & Harry Hyde	April 1838	$881.15				$881.15
19. C. Stannard	April 1838	$256.40	$256.40			0
20. Com'l Bank of Lake Erie	April 1838	$1,230.00		$1,230.00		0
21. Bailey & Reynolds	April 1838	$1,000.00		$1,000.00		0
22. Holmes & Holmes	April 1838	$10,000.00		$10,000.00		0
23. M. Allen	June 1838	$0.00				0
24. Halstead & Haines	April 1838	$2,337.35			$948.00	$1,389.35
25. Underwood	April 1838	$1,685.55			$1,685.55	0
26. Joseph Coe	June 1839	$900.00	$900.00			0
27. J. Bump	October 1842	$0.00				0
Totals		$34,460.94	$1,577.15	$22,848.90	$5,036.67	$4,998.22

Figure 2. Collection Cases against Temple Committee

Plaintiffs	Date Filed	Claim	Discontinuted	Settled	Satisfied	Balance
1. I. Goodman	October 1836	$237.40			$237.40	0
2. S. Corning	October 1836	$592.47				$592.47
3. Goodman & Goodman	October 1836	$645.17			$645.17	0
4. Dockstader	March 1837	$500.00	$500.00			0
5. H. Kelly*	March 1837	$2,093.80			$506.73	$1,587.07
6. J. Newbold	October 1837	$469.00		$469.00		0
7. R. Boynton*	April 1838	$890.97				$890.97
8. Leavitt & Lord	?	$729.78	$729.78			0
9. J. Scribner	April 1838	$956.80				$956.80
10. Thompson, Phelps, & Douglas	June 1838	$958.11	$958.11			0
11. Keeler, McNiel, & Rosseter	June 1838	$4,000.00	$4,000.00			0
12. Otis Eaton	November 1838	$539.00		$539.00		0
13. Chancy J. Caulkins	November 1838	$678.00			$678.00	0
Totals		$13,290.50	$6,187.89	$1,008.00	$2,067.30	$4,027.31

*These debts are duplicated in the list in figure 1. The debt due to H. Kelly is the same as figure 1, line 4. The debt due to R. Boynton is the same as Ray Boynton and Harry Hyde in figure 1, line 18. These people sued both Joseph Smith and the Temple Committee for the same debt, which was incorrect procedure. The variation in amounts is due to different court fees involved.

settled (meaning paid before the trial); if satisfied (meaning paid after judgment); and balance (cases where no record of payment appears in the execution docket, and presumably the amount still owing at the time accounts were turned over to Oliver Granger, as explained below).

The list of creditors is composed of two banks (creditors 2 and 20); five New York City merchants (creditors 4, 9, 18, 21 and 24); two Buffalo merchants (creditors 5 and 8); one Painesville merchant (creditor 11); two Kirtland landowners (creditors 3 and 22, whose claims [$6,000.00 and $10,000.00] were the two largest filed, both of which were paid or "settled" prior to trial); the engraver who made the plates for the printing of the Kirtland Safety Society banknotes (creditor 25); a farmer who supplied one-third of the money to purchase the Egyptian papyri (creditor 26); and an assortment of smaller claimants.

Figure 2 relates to the Temple Committee with the same columns and data. In two instances the same creditor sued Joseph and associates and the Temple Committee on the same debt. The first, Hezekiah Kelly (#4 in fig. 1 and #5 in fig. 2) obtained a judgment against Joseph et al. for $2,083.47 and against the Committee in the same amount. A partial payment of $541.41 is reflected in the judgment docket, leaving an unpaid balance of $1,542.06. While Joseph and associates and the Temple Committee were individually jointly liable for the whole debt, the creditor (Kelly) under the law then (as now) was not allowed to collect twice on the same promissory note or debt. So, in terms of arriving at a total remaining indebtedness, these entries amount to a duplication of the same debt. The same is true of Ray Boynton (creditor #18 against Joseph, et.al. and #7 against the Temple Committee). His judgment against Joseph was $881.15 and against the Committee is $890.97, the difference being reflected in the respective court costs assessed. No payment of record appeared in the respective execution dockets on this debt.

So, while the creditors could look to all the judgment debtors jointly and severally, the total debt of Joseph and the Committee needs to be reduced by the duplications. Taking the unpaid balance of the Kelly judgment of $1,542.06 and using the lower judgment in Boynton's cases of $881.15, the total unpaid debt of record from figures 1 and 2 of $9,025.53 is reduced by $2,423,21, leaving the actual Mormon litigated and unpaid debt of record at $6,602,32.

One case with its appeal, not included in figure 2, should be mentioned because it is neither a criminal nor a collection case and was appealed to the Ohio Supreme Court of Judicature. On August 11, 1836, Charles Morse sued the Temple Committee (Carter, Cahoon, and Hyrum Smith), plus Jacob Bump,

Orson Hyde, and William Barker in a civil action of trespass, but the nature of his claim was that these defendants had committed "false imprisonment" and "unlawful detention" of his body in the Kirtland Temple for a period of several hours, claiming $300.00 damages. Thus Morse brought a civil action claiming a criminal offense. A jury was empanelled in the Court of Common Pleas, and at the end of the plaintiff's testimony, the court ruled: "The Court are of the opinion that the same does not support the case set forth in the declaration (Plaintiff's Complaint), the Court therefore direct a non suit for that reason: And thereupon the jury are discharged from the further consideration of the premises. Therefore it is considered that the said defendants go hence without day, and recover of the said plaintiff their costs in this behalf expended to be taxed." Morse appealed. The Supreme Court of Judicature affirmed the lower court's decision and ordered Morse to pay the costs in both courts, which amounted to $78.[10]

To these totals in the previous tables needs to be added a mortgage on the Kirtland Temple signed by Joseph, Sidney Rigdon, and Oliver Cowdery plus the Temple Committee, in the amount $4,500.00, which was paid sometime around January 1841. While no release of the mortgage was recorded, neither was an action to foreclose the mortgage ever initiated.

The agent who accomplished most of this liquidating of debt was Oliver Granger, assisted for a period by William Marks, who were left behind in Kirtland when Joseph and Sidney departed on January 12, 1838. Many of the Saints deeded land (valued at $7,450.00) to Granger upon their departure from Kirtland for him to dispose of "for the debts of the church," and in exchange for corresponding land in Missouri (fig. 3). Those deeds and accompanying receipt/orders were the precursor and historical setting for the revelation received by Joseph Smith on July 8, 1838, in answer to the query, "O Lord, show unto thy servants how much thou requirest of the properties of thy people for a tithing."[11] The first two verses answer, "Verily, thus saith the Lord, I require all their *surplus* property to be put into the hands of the bishop of my church in Zion, For the building of mine house, and for the laying of the foundation of Zion and for the priesthood, and for *the debts of the Presidency of my Church*" (D&C 119:1–2, italics added). Certainly property in Kirtland being abandoned would qualify as "surplus" property.

---

10. Supreme Court Records (Geauga County), Book C, p. 139–41, Geauga County Archives, Chardon, Ohio.

11. "Revelation, 8 July 1838—C [D&C 119]," The Joseph Smith Papers, http://joseph smithpapers.org/paperSummary?target=x4756.

Figure 3. Property Transferred to Oliver Granger

Grantor	Grantee	Date Recorded	Amount
John Johnson	Oliver Granger	April 19, 1838	$600.00
William Barker	Oliver Granger	May 4, 1838	$1,000.00
John Smith	Oliver Granger	May 18, 1838	$400.00
Osmyn M. Deuel	Oliver Granger	May 18, 1838	$2,400.00
Sally Berman & others	Oliver Granger	May 18, 1838	$1,700.00
Levi Richards	Oliver Granger	April 24, 1839	$800.00
John P. Green	Oliver Granger	May 18, 1839	$100.00
Arza Judd Jr. & others	Oliver Granger	November 30, 1839 (1849?)	$450.00
		Total	$7,450.00

Figure 4. Property Transferred from Oliver Granger

Grantor	Grantee	Date Recorded	Amount
Oliver Granger	John W. Howden	May 18, 1838	$1,700.00
Oliver Granger	John W. Howden	May 18, 1838	$3,022.00
Oliver Granger	Lyman Cowdrey	October 22, 1838	$1,000.00
Oliver Granger	Henry W. Stoddard	April 27, 1839	$400.00
Oliver Granger	Roger Plaisted	April 27, 1839	$300.00
Oliver Granger	William Perkins	April 27, 1839	$100.00
Oliver Granger	Benjamin Goff	July 10, 1839	$7.41½
Oliver Granger	John Norton	June 3, 1840	$25.00
Oliver Granger	Harmon Orrin	August 1840	$?
Oliver Granger	Anna Burdick	March 3, 1841	$400.00
Oliver Granger	Isaac Dudley	August 17, 1841	$200.00
Oliver Granger	William M. Halstead	May 27, 1842	$461.00
Oliver Granger	John Howden	May 24, 1842	$400.00
		Total	$8,015.41½

It is difficult now to ascertain which of the debts of the Saints Granger paid, since no accounting or report from Granger to Smith has thus far been located. It is assumed, however, that those debts sued on after January 1838 and those beginning with the Patterson case (number 5 in fig. 1) that show payment dates after January 1838 were Granger settlements. However, one satisfaction after judgment was shown in the execution docket to have been paid by Almon W. Babbitt, who for a short time at a later period was head of the Kirtland Stake of the Church. The following statement gives some indication of Granger's work:

> To all whom it may concern.
>
> This may certify that during the year of Eighteen hundred and thirtyseven I had dealings with Messrs Joseph Smith Jr and Sidney Rigdon together with other members of the society, to the amount of about three thousand dollars, and during the spring of Eighteen Hundred and thirty eight, I have received my pay in full of Col Oliver Granger to my satisfaction. And I would here remark that it is due Messrs Smith & Rigdon & the society generally, to say that they have ever dealt honorable and fair with me, and I have received as good treatment from them as I have received from any other society in this vicinity: and so far as I have been correctly informed, and made known of their business transactions generally they have so far as I can judge been honorable and honest, and have made every exertion to arrange & settle their affairs; & I would further state that the closing up of my business with said society has been with their agent Col Granger appointed by them for that purpose; and I consider it highly due, Col Granger from me here to state that he has acted truly and honestly with me in all his business transactions with me, and has accomplished more than I could have reasonably expected. And I have also been made acquainted with his business in this section, and wherever he has been called upon to act, he has done so, and with good management he has accomplished and effected a close of a very large amount business for said society, and as I believe to the entire satisfaction of all concerned.
>
> John W Howden
> Painsville Geauga Co Ohio Oct 27th 1838[12]

---

12. "Certificate from John W. Howden, 27 October 1838," The Joseph Smith Papers, http://josephsmithpapers.org/paperSummary/certificate-from-john-w-howden-27-october-1838.

Howden was Clerk of the Court of Common Pleas, and thus likely the recipient of some of the Granger payments as agent for some of the litigation creditors.

Granger doubtless made payments to parties who did not sue, but from the incomplete record it appears that the overwhelming majority of Smith's and the Church's Kirtland debts were paid. Research is ongoing regarding the Granger property transactions and payments, but at present $8,015.41½ in payments to creditors (fig. 4), including, but not limited to the litigating creditors listed above, have been documented. Granger died in Kirtland on August 25, 1841. Reuben McBride succeeded him in the debt-paying assignment for a short time.

Accumulating the totals yields the following:

	Amount Claimed	Amount Discontinued, Settled, or Satisfied
Joseph Smith Cases	$34,460.94	$29,462.72
Temple Committee Cases	$13,290.50	$9,263.19
Adjustment for duplicate judgements		$2,423.21
Kirtland Temple Mtg	$4,500.00	$4,500.00
Totals	**$52,251.44**	**$45,649.12**

Thus, we can conclude that 87 percent of the litigated debt is shown to have been dropped, settled, or paid, with $6,602 ($4,998 plus $4,027 minus the duplications of $2,423) left outstanding. If amounts of undocketed payments may be attributed to those creditors, this percentage moves upward accordingly.

No consideration is given in this paper to the impact the Kirtland Safety Society's failure had on the Kirtland economy, for two principal reasons. First, there is no indication that any of the major creditors listed above ever took or traded in the bank's notes. Certainly no bank notes were alleged to be part of any of their claims sued on. Second, in this writer's opinion those who have written about the bank have made estimates about the total number and dollar value of banknotes actually circulated based on variable and unknown facts, the most glaring of which is that there is no hard evidence now extant of what dollar amount was actually issued or redeemed. Even Fawn Brodie admits that the bank's failure had little, if any, impact on the Kirtland economy.[13]

---

13. "The rise and fall of the bank brought very little actual change to Kirtland's economy." Fawn Brodie, *No Man Knows My History* (New York: Knopf, 1966), 199.

Three Special Cases

Now, to the consideration of the final three civil cases not yet discussed.

The Russell Farm. This was the only mortgage foreclosure action brought against Joseph in Kirtland. On October 10, 1836, Alpheus C. Russell sold his 132.4-acre farm to Joseph Smith, Reynolds Cahoon, and Jacob Bump for $12,904, taking as the purchase price six promissory notes which had staggered payment dates: five of the notes were for $1,000.00 each payable June 1, 1837, 1838, 1839, 1840, and 1841 and the sixth note for $6,904.00 payable June 1, 1842. The promissory notes and a mortgage for the purchase price were signed by the three purchasers and their wives, and the mortgage was filed with the Geauga County Recorder.

Apparently no payments were made on any of the notes. Russell waited until June 1843, one year after the due date on the sixth note, before he filed his action to foreclose the mortgage. Jacob Bump and his wife Abigail were the only purchasers then still in Kirtland, and the case was heard during the March 1844 term of court, when final judgment of foreclosure, which, with the accumulated interest, totaled $16,409.61, was entered. The farm was appraised, pursuant to the statutory requirements, at $2,376, and a sheriff's sale was conducted at which Russell was the only bidder. He bid $1,584, which was two-thirds of the appraisal, the statutory minimum acceptable bid. Russell made no effort thereafter to proceed against the Bumps, Smiths, or Cahoons on his deficiency judgment ($16,409.61 less $1,584.00). Russell retained the property until his death in 1860 and it remained in the family until 1876.[14]

Newell and the Kirtland Safety Society. The final two litigations both involve Grandison Newell, Samuel D. Rounds, and Henry Holcomb against Joseph Smith, Sidney Rigdon, Frederick G. Williams, Newel K. Whitney, Horace Kingsbury, and Warren Parrish, all directors of the Kirtland Safety Society. This drawn-out matter involves the bank, the Kirtland Temple, incorporating the Church in Ohio and the long-after-the-fact probating of the would-be Ohio portion of Joseph Smith's estate.

Before beginning, a quick primer on the mechanics of a civil action or lawsuit in 1830s Ohio is in order. A suit was commenced by a plaintiff or his attorney appearing at the county courthouse and requesting the clerk of the Court of Common Pleas to issue a writ of summons instructing the sheriff to hand or "serve" the written summons (which contained only a skeletal recital

---

14. Copy of case document in possession of the author, forthcoming in the Joseph Smith Papers Legal and Business Records series.

of the relief sought) on the defendant or defendants. After serving the summons, the sheriff would file a paper called a return of service stating the fact of delivery of the summons and the date and place of delivery. At the next term of court (terms of court were scheduled every three months), the plaintiff would file a declaration. This was a detailed outline of his claim against the defendant(s). Today that declaration is called a complaint. At the following term of court or any time prior thereto, the defendant(s) or their attorney would file a responsive document called a plea, sometimes named a demurrer. In today's usage that is called an answer. Procedural motions could be made and continuances could be granted, but ultimately a hearing or trial with or without a jury would be held and a judgment arrived at. Then either party could give notice of intent to appeal the decision and file a bill of exceptions, which outlined the issues of law or fact which the appellant claimed were erroneously dealt with by the trial court. If no appeal was pursued, the judgment would stand, and if it were for money damages in favor of the plaintiff, part of the judgment would order the sheriff to forthwith execute on (sell) the defendant(s)'s property to satisfy the judgment.

One month after the Kirtland Safety Society Anti-Bank (so named because it had failed to obtain a corporate charter from the Ohio legislature and thus could not be a bank) had opened its doors, on February 9, 1837, Samuel D. Rounds, who was in reality Grandison Newell's front man, suing *qui tam* (a legal phrase meaning "and for another") filed six requests for summons against the six directors of the Kirtland Safety Society.[15] This generated six cases, one each for Smith, Rigdon, Williams, Whitney, Kingsbury and Parrish. The Ohio banking statute provided that operating as a bank without a state charter was illegal and punishable by a fine of $1,000.00 and permitted any interested or affected citizen to bring a qui tam action on his own behalf and on the behalf of the state. "Behalf" is the right word because the law provided that the State and the litigant would split the resulting penalty equally, if any. After the declaration, plea, motions, continuances, and so forth, the two trials of Joseph and Sidney began on October 24, 1837. Separate juries and the full panel of all four judges of the court were in attendance at both trials, which were both concluded that same day. The other four cases were discontinued on the plaintiff's motion. The verdict was against each defendant, and the court imposed the fine of $1,000.00 against each. Joseph's and Sidney's attorney did file a bill of exceptions and a notice of intent to appeal.[16]

---

15. See ch. 9 for a full discussion of this litigation.

16. In a prosecution on a related criminal statute making it a felony to "make, alter, publish, pass, or put in circulation, any note or notes, bill or bills, of a bank, company, or association,

The appeal, however, was not pursued and the execution docket shows that the sheriff in January 1838 levied on and sold personal property of Sidney Rigdon amounting to $604.50, and some other personal property whose ownership (Sidney's or Joseph's) he does not indicate, which he also sold for $111.75. After deducting his and the clerk's fees, which total $111.75, the record discloses "Shff. Paid Grandison Newell $604.50." (Note that it was not paid to Samuel D. Rounds, the plaintiff of record). Then on March 1, 1838, Newell sold the judgments to William Marks and Oliver Granger:

> For and in consideration of Sixteen hundred dollars to me in hand paid by William Marks and Oliver Granger I do hereby sell assign & set over to the said William Marks and Oliver Granger two Judgements in favor of Samuel Rounds and assigned to me by said Rounds against Joseph Smith and Sidney Rigdon of one thousand dollars each which Judgements were obtained at the Court of Common Pleas holden at Chardon in and for the County of Geauga to wit on the 27th day of October 1837, and I do agree to pay all costs that has accrued on said Judgments up to this date.
>
> G. Newell
>
> Kirtland March 1ˢᵗ 1838
> Attest Lyman Cowdery[17]

So, after collecting $604.50 from the sheriff, Grandison Newell sold or assigned the two judgments to William Marks and Oliver Granger for $1,600. He neither paid the sheriff and clerk their fees, nor reimbursed Marks and Granger for them as agreed. Remember he was entitled to only half of the judgments. There was no accounting rendered to the court showing that he ever remitted to the State of Ohio its one-half.

---

which never did, in fact, exist" knowing the same to be the fact, the Ohio Supreme Court, in December 1838 in the case of Wilbur Cahoon v. State (1838), 8 Ohio Reports 538–9, overturned the conviction of Cahoon, because "The offense is the uttering of such note, knowing it to be of a non-existing bank or company, and not the uttering of a note knowing it to have been issued by an existing unincorporated bank" (italics added). That reasoning would suggest that had Joseph's and Sidney's appeals been perfected, the judgments against them would likely also have been overturned, if the Supreme Court, being consistent, felt the proscribed conduct was limited to those institutions which claimed to be banks without charters, as opposed to existing institutions not claiming to be banks.

17. G. Newell, Assignment of the Rounds Judgment by Grandison Newell to Oliver Granger and William Marks, N. K. Whitney Papers, L. Tom Perry Special Collections, Harold B. Lee Library, Brigham Young University.

In 1840, while Granger was still in Kirtland, Joseph, then in Nauvoo, wrote him that a possible buyer for the Kirtland Temple had surfaced and instructed him to incorporate the Church in Ohio, which meant, of course, getting a bill passed through the legislature. This time, unlike their previous attempt to get a charter for the Kirtland Safety Society, the Mormon lobbying effort was successful. So, a bank could not be chartered, but a church could. The sale of the temple, however, did not materialize.

Twenty years later, on October 22, 1860, Grandison Newell reappeared and moved the same court to revive the Rounds judgments, claiming that they had not been satisfied and that there was still real property belonging to Joseph Smith's estate situated in Kirtland which could be levied upon. The previous year, Newell had lobbied a special bill through the Ohio legislature granting him the state's "half." He then had his granddaughter's husband, Henry Holcomb, petition the Court of Common Pleas to be appointed administrator of the estate of Joseph Smith, claiming he was acting on behalf of creditors of the estate whom he represented. The purported estate property was the Kirtland Temple and a 13-acre parcel in the Kirtland flats. Holcomb was so appointed, and the full probate procedure was followed, including notices, appraisals, and so on. As a part of the probate process, Emma Smith, as surviving widow of Joseph Smith, had to be given written notice because she had a dower interest in the estate. That meant she was entitled to one-third of the income of the estate for the rest of her life. In the case of non-income producing property, as here, a computation of some simple interest formula on the appraised valuation of the estate property was used. The court determined Emma's dower interest to be $4.11 per year for the rest of her life, to be paid through the clerk of the court by all subsequent owners of the estate property. After the probate was completed on April 18, 1862, Holcomb used Newell's newly acquired state's half of the Rounds judgments to execute on all the property. He then sold the two parcels to William Perkins (Holcomb's attorney) the following day, who paid $217 for the temple and $163 for the 13 acres. Perkins the same day resold the temple piece to Russell Huntley, who, nearly nine years later on February 17, 1873, sold it to Joseph Smith III and Mark H. Forscutt (a member of the RLDS church's Quorum of Twelve Apostles). A quiet title lawsuit in 1879–80 and uninterrupted occupation by the Reorganized Church of Jesus Christ of Latter Day Saints finally vested title to the temple in today's Community of Christ church.

Grandison Newell—having sold the judgments to Marks and Granger, collected $204.50 more than the total judgments, failed to pay the costs of $111.75, and failed to remit to the state its half—got the legislature to cede its half to him. This action made him owner of what he had already sold. He then walked away with the temple plus thirteen acres, which he promptly sold.

Had Oliver Granger or William Marks taken the document of sale of the Rounds judgments to the county clerk and recorded it, all of Newell's machinations would have been prevented because Newell would no longer be the record owner of the judgments, and the fact that the judgments had been not only paid in full, but that the State's half remained unpaid, would have prevented his getting the legislation and frustrated the remaining events that followed. But in the end the court records in Ohio that have been recently found more than reveal his duplicitous conduct.

Conclusions

This truncated and still incomplete overview of Joseph's and the Temple Committee's legal experience in Ohio supports several tentative conclusions and reflections about both the legal and spiritual conditions in Kirtland.

On the criminal front, Joseph and his friends came off unscathed as defendants, and won a couple of cases as complaining witnesses.

Of the $52,251.44 reduced by duplications noted above to $49,828.23 recorded debt of Joseph and the Committee, $43,225.91 was paid. There were no defrauded creditors, but rather paid creditors, 87 percent of whose claims were satisfied in a reasonably prompt time frame. And that payment came largely after the Saints had abandoned Kirtland and the symbol of their sacrifice, the temple. I see here shades of the similar loss in Nauvoo.

While the payment of debts in Kirtland is a part of the focus of this study, it is important to note that the payment of those debts as detailed above was not done in a vacuum. During the same time, the Saints incurred the cost of settlement in Kirtland, expulsion, and resettlement in Missouri; the cost of Zion's Camp; the cost of building of the Kirtland Temple; the absorbing of immigrating poor converts; the printing enterprise which produced the second edition of the Book of Mormon, the Book of Commandments, the Doctrine and Covenants, a hymnbook, many tracts, and two newspapers; the destruction of a press; and more. Knowing of all these contemporary economic demands leaves one wondering how any economic viability was achieved at all.

Also not mentioned here is the sacrifice of those few somewhat well-off Saints who gave their all and left Kirtland essentially impoverished. One has to ask how in an eight-year-old church did Joseph persuade people to persist in what has to be viewed as a voluntary sharing and sacrificing of their temporal goods to the point of impoverishment. One could argue that they lived a near version of a law of consecration—if starting out at various levels of economic security and ending up in Missouri equally poor can be so called. And they did it in such numbers. One partial answer might be that they felt the spiritual rewards, particularly those tangibly experienced in the Kirtland Temple, were well worth the cost.

Joseph, in Nauvoo, looking back on those days and the additional crucibles of pain through which he and the Saints had thereafter passed, said, "These I have met in prosperity and they were my friends; and I now meet them in adversity, and they are still my warmer friends. These love the God that I serve; they love the truths that I promulge; they love those virtues, and those holy doctrines that I cherish in my bosom with the warmest feelings of my heart, and with that zeal which cannot be denied. I love friendship and truth; I love virtue and law."[18]

---

18. *History of the Church,* 5:108.

Chapter Eleven

Losing Land Claims and the Missouri Conflict in 1838

Jeffrey N. Walker

Persecution and the financial collapse in Kirtland in 1838 forced Joseph Smith to leave Ohio and headquarter the Church in Missouri, where thousands of Latter-day Saints had already settled. Once in Missouri, he and the other leaders faced the challenge of finding affordable places for these newcomers to settle, as they had previously contributed their lands and money to help satisfy debts arising from the construction of the Kirtland Temple. Daviess County, Missouri, became a strategic settlement area for the Ohio Saints.

Shortly after arriving in Missouri, Joseph and other leaders left Far West, Missouri, "to visit the north countries for the purpose of Laying off stakes of Zion, making Locations & laying claims [to land] for the gathering of the saints for the benefit of the poor."[1] The "north countries" had yet to be fully surveyed by the Federal government, and this allowed the Saints to settle on the land and obtain preemption rights that did not require them to pay for their land until the surveys were completed sometime in the future. As inspired as this solution to the land-less Mormons seemed to be, after the surveying was finished, these same rights were an impetus for non-Mormon land speculators to frantically force Mormons out of Missouri in late 1838. By examining the preemption rights and land surveying practices, this chapter explains why Mormons settled in certain parts of northern Missouri and shows how some Missourians manipulated the situation for their own

---

1. Joseph Smith Jr., Scriptory Book, May 18, 1838, MS, Church History Library, The Church of Jesus Christ of Latter-day Saints, Salt Lake City. See also Dean C. Jessee, *The Papers of Joseph Smith*, 2 vols. (Salt Lake City: Deseret Book, 1989–92), 2:243.

personal gain. While the causes of Mormons' expulsion from Missouri are multifaceted, this legal element is a crucial factor in this tragic story.

The Sale of Federal Lands

After the War of 1812 and a shift to nationalism emerged, Representatives Henry Clay, Daniel Webster, and John C. Calhoun led the postwar Congress to strengthen the national economy by improving infrastructure of the federal government. This included creating a new national banking system, improving roads, and selling public lands to fund the growing national government. These policies fractured the already fragile political parties and alliances, and opponents of federalism elected Andrew Jackson as president in 1828. As the voice for free enterprise, states' rights, and laissez-faire government, Jackson expanded executive powers that increased the effort to reduce the federal debt by selling federal lands.[2] Andrew Jackson recognized that the revenue generated by the sale of these public lands on the rapidly expanding western frontier could, in short order, eliminate the national debt. By his fourth annual report to Congress in 1832, Jackson was able to report that "the expenses of the [Revolutionary] war" had been met, and therefore public lands no longer needed to serve as a source of revenue, but rather could "be sold to settlers ... at a price barely sufficient to reimburse" the government for its costs.[3]

The power to sell public lands and the establishment of the process for such sales rested securely in the U.S. Constitution.[4] Already in 1812, the supervision of public land sales was placed in the General Land Office (GLO) within the Department of the Treasury,[5] which was authorized to subdivide the public domain into land sales districts. Under the direction of the president, the GLO created local land offices to carry out its mandate of aggressively

---

2. See James D. Richardson, ed., *A Compilation of the Messages and Papers of the Presidents, 1789–1897,* 10 vols. (By the author, 1899), 2:450–51.

3. Richardson, *Messages and Papers of the Presidents,* 2:600–601.

4. "The Congress shall have Power to dispose of and make all needful Rules and Regulations respecting the Territory or other Property belonging to the United States." U.S. Constitution, art. 4, sec. 3.

5. Opinions of the Attorney General (hereafter cited as Ops. Atty. Gen.), no. 66 (July 4, 1836), *General Public Acts of Congress, Respecting the Sale and Disposition of the Public Lands, with Instructions Issued, from Time to Time, by the Secretary of the Treasury and Commissioner of the General Land Office, and Official Opinions of the Attorney General on Questions Arising under the Land Laws,* 2 vols. (Washington, D.C.: Gales and Seaton, 1838), 2:103–4.

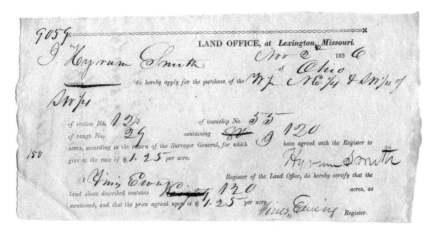

Hyrum Smith filed this preemption application in Missouri in 1836. Courtesy Church History Library, The Church of Jesus Christ of Latter-day Saints.

selling public lands.[6] But as waves of settlers moved west, these pioneers, often referred to as squatters, became an obstacle to the orderly sale of public lands. In response, the federal government severely limited the rights squatters could have to these frontier properties. The land policies adopted in 1785, and again in the Land Act of 1787, required competitive bidding on land in an attempt to discourage and often displace squatters. In an effort to protect themselves from these laws, squatters formed claim associations, whose primary purpose was to intimidate speculators, often referred to as claim jumpers, from bidding on land improved by a squatter.

Within this setting the first universal preemption laws were enacted in 1830.[7] Preemption was the process whereby individuals secured a preference right to purchase public land they had improved and inhabited, once the land was ready for sale to the public.[8] The Pre-emption Act of 1830 extended preemptive rights to "every settler or occupant of the public lands" who was in possession at the date of passage and had cultivated any portion of the land

---

6. An Act Authorizing the President of the United States to Remove the Land Office in the District of Lawrence County, in the Territory of Arkansas (March 2, 1821), *General Public Acts*, ch. 257, 1:339.

7. An Act to Grant Pre-emption Rights to Settlers on the Public Lands (May 29, 1830), 21st Cong., 1st sess., ch. 208, in *Statutes at Large of United States of America, 1789–1873*, 17 vols. (Washington, D.C.: [various publishers], 1845–73), 4:420–21.

8. W. W. Lester, *Decisions of the Interior Department in Public Land Cases, and Land Laws* (Philadelphia: H. P. and R. H. Small, 1860), 355.

not to exceed one hundred sixty acres.[9] This law was originally limited to one year, but it was extended by subsequent acts in 1832, 1833, 1834, 1838, 1840.[10] These renewals were necessary because Congress anticipated that preemptive claims could be granted and the final sale consummated within the span of the act or its extension, but this turned out not to be the case. Western expansion far outpaced the GLO's ability to manage the growth.

The Preemption Process

The implementation of the preemption process was designed to be a simple and straightforward way to manage the public land problem. Yet, implementation proved both complicated and time consuming.

First, a settler would go to the local district GLO and complete a short application that included an affidavit verifying that he was improving and occupying the land to which the preemption right was being claimed.[11]

Second, the president would set the sale date for all land sold under the act or its extension.[12] It was then the responsibility of the surveyor general over the subject area to have the land adequately surveyed and verified and the corresponding paperwork physically returned to the local land office.[13]

---

9. Pettigrew v. Shirley, 9 Mo. 683, 686 (1846).

10. Isaac v. Steel, 4 Ill. 97, 3 Scam. 97 (1841).

11. The individual who wanted to assert a preemptive right must do so by "producing his proof of such right at any time within *one year* from the date of the act." *General Public Acts,* GLO, Circular no. 495 (May 23, 1831).

12. Pettigrew v. Shirley, 9 Mo. 683, 687 (1846).

13. Surveying was a complicated process. Initial physical surveys were contracted out by the federal government to be done by trained surveyors. While this general survey gave enough detail to know what section and range a claim was being made in, the general survey did not provide sufficient detail about the particulars within the township where the land was located. Once the state legislature created a county, the responsibility to draw townships using these physical surveys fell to the surveyor general. See generally J. B. Johnson, *The Theory and Practice of Surveying* (New York: John Wiley and Sons, 1904), 176–79. Once completed, these township plats had to be verified and then certified by the surveyor general's office and sent to the local land office, referred to as the "return date." The land could not be sold until the local land office had received back the certified township plats. Importantly, if the surveys were not returned before the end of the term of the act under which the preemptive right was asserted, such rights would be tacked onto the successor act.

Then the local land office would publish notice that the surveys were complete and the scheduled sale would take place.[14] Such notice was required to be published within a reasonable time before the sale date.

Finally, if a settler failed to pay for the preemptive land by the specified sale date, his preemptive right lapsed, and the land could be sold to any other interested party.[15]

The implementation of this process proved to be thorny. The difficulty centered on the rapid influx of settlers on land for which the township surveys had not been completed and certified by the general surveyor's office. In these situations, the prospective settler chose the land he wanted to claim (up to one hundred sixty acres), began cultivating it, and then went to the local land office to complete a preemptive application. When such land had not been certified with a township survey (thereby determining to one-tenth of an acre the actual public land being purchased), the local land office registrar could verify only that the applicant had adequately occupied and cultivated the subject land and accept the application for it. This often was referred to as "proofing" the preemption claim.[16] The registrar could not accept payment, as the exact price could be determined only after the township plats were received. Therefore, preemptive claims were general rights (for example, 40 acres) until the surveys were completed, whereupon they became specific rights (for example, 39.2 acres). Once the verified survey was received by the local land office, the registrar published a notice of the receipt, thereby informing the settler that he must pay for the land by the predetermined sale date or be subject to having the land sold at public sale to any interested party. Unexpectedly, however, there was a persistent, and sometimes significant, delay in getting the verified township plat surveys back to the local land office. A settler could file an application for his land and then wait months, or sometimes even years, for the surveying process to be completed, thereby triggering the requirement to pay for the land. As one might imagine, this lengthy process caused untold complications. The failure of plats to arrive at the local land office, thus preventing a sale to proceed, was "the worst bottleneck in the administrative system.... The end result was the cancellation or postponement of a number of public sales that had been advertised."[17] The cancellation and postponements actually worked to the Mormon's advantage

---

14. When surveys were not returned in a timely fashion, such notice had to be cancelled or postponed.

15. *General Public Acts*, Circular No. 503, GLO (February 8, 1832).

16. See Gaines v. Hale, 16 Ark. 9 (1855).

17. Malcolm J. Rohrbough, *The Land Office Business: The Settlement and Administration of American Public Lands, 1789–1837* (New York: Oxford University Press, 1968), 260.

by giving them more time to raise the funds necessary to purchase the lands. Understanding these realities adds insight into Church leader's decision to explore areas in Missouri that had not been fully surveyed, especially the 1838 LDS expansion into Daviess County.

Mormons on the Missouri Frontier

By the summer of 1831, Mormons had settled in Jackson County, and, reinforced by prophetic decree, Church members sought to build Zion there. Joseph Smith laid out a city for the Saints, including a site on which to construct a temple. Throughout 1832, Mormons arrived to support the establishment of this new Church center, and by the end of that year nearly twelve hundred Latter-day Saints lived in Missouri.[18]

Such rapid growth proved dangerous, as the non-Mormon population feared losing political and economic power.[19] Competing religionists and early settlers fueled the simmering discontent, which erupted in violence in July 1833.[20] Such violence eventually led to the forced surrender and expulsion of virtually the entire Mormon community from Jackson County in November 1833.[21]

These displaced Saints found temporary refuge in nearby Clay County, immediately north and across the Missouri River. They sought help from the state government, and the Saints were advised to seek redress through legal channels.[22] Efforts to strengthen the Mormon community in Clay County were doomed as the initial kindness of the locals dissipated and was replaced by prejudice and enmity.

Desperate for a solution, Church leaders contemplated moving north to the unsettled Missouri frontier. Fearing the same persecutions might follow, they

---

18. Richard Neitzel Holzapfel and T. Jeffery Cottle, *Old Mormon Kirtland and Missouri: Historic Photographs and Guides* (Santa Ana, Calif.: Fieldbrook Productions, 1991), 162.

19. Richard L. Bushman, "Mormon Persecutions in Missouri, 1833," *BYU Studies* 3, no. 1 (1960): 11–20.

20. B. H. Roberts, *The Missouri Persecutions* (Salt Lake City: George Q. Cannon and Sons, 1900), 85–97.

21. Milton V. Backman Jr., *The Heavens Resound: A History of the Latter-day Saints in Ohio, 1830–1838* (Salt Lake City: Deseret Book, 1983), 170–72.

22. "History of Joseph Smith," *Times and Seasons* 6 (May 1, 1845): 880. The Mormons retained four attorneys—Alexander Doniphan, David Atchison, Amos Rees, and William Wood—to seek legal assistance to return to their homes in Jackson County. Roger D. Launius, *Alexander William Doniphan: Portrait of a Missouri Moderate* (Columbia: University of Missouri Press, 1997), 15.

sought legal help to establish a safe location to resettle. One of the Church's lawyers and also a member of the Missouri legislature representing Clay County, Alexander Doniphan agreed that moving into the unsettled areas might alleviate the tensions between the groups. Doniphan sponsored a bill during the late-1836 legislative session that would allow the Saints to settle in the entire unincorporated territorial northern portion of Ray County.[23] This bill met with stiff opposition by the representatives from Ray County, resulting in a substantive compromise—the creation of two new counties in Missouri, Caldwell and Daviess, by the end of 1836. Caldwell County was informally designed to accommodate Mormons. This compromise also enlarged Ray by four townships (giving Ray twenty townships rather than the typical sixteen) and left Caldwell County with only twelve townships.[24]

Anticipating the creation of these counties and seeking to avoid the vicissitudes of persecution, Mormons began moving northward even before the official creation of Caldwell or Daviess counties.[25] Mormons built their main settlement in Mirable Township (Caldwell County) and christened the town Far West. With the possibility of settling in northern Missouri and thereby avoiding further persecution, emigration to Caldwell County exploded. Between 1836 and 1838 "more than 4,900 of them lived in the county, along with a hundred non-Mormons." The Far West area boasted "150 homes, four dry goods stores, three family groceries, several blacksmith shops, two hotels, a printing shop, and a large schoolhouse that doubled as a church and a courthouse."[26] A second community emerged on Shoal Creek, sixteen miles east of Far West, called Hawn's Mill.[27] By 1838, Hawn's Mill was home to

23. Launius, *Alexander William Doniphan*, 39–40.

24. The History of Daviess County, Missouri (Kansas City, Mo.: Birsall and Dean, 1882), 235.

25. Copies of the "Original Entries for Lands in Caldwell County," Caldwell County Recorder's Office, Kingston, Missouri, as cited in Leland H. Gentry, "The Land Question at Adam-ondi-Ahman," *BYU Studies* 26, no. 2 (1986): 10 n. 14.

26. James B. Allen and Glen M. Leonard, *The Story of the Latter-day Saints* (Salt Lake City: Deseret Book, 1976), 116–17. See also Robert Allen Campbell, *Campbell's Gazetteer of Missouri* (St. Louis, Mo.: R. A. Campbell, 1874).

27. Named after Jacob Hawn (traditionally spelled "Haun," but a review of applicable land records, as well as the marker on his grave evidences that he spelled his name "Hawn"), who built a gristmill on Shoal Creek. Jacob Hawn settled on approximately forty acres on Shoal Creek and entered his claim for this property on December 7, 1835, more than a year before the creation of Caldwell County. See "Original Entries for Lands in Caldwell County," Caldwell County Recorder's Office, Kingston, Missouri. His mill site became the center of the community commonly referred to as Haun's Mill. Mormons settled along the east-west running Shoal Creek, building multiple mills around Hawn's own mill. Consequently, this area comprised some of the most valuable lands owned by Mormons.

approximately twenty families, with another forty or more families settling on farms in the vicinity.[28] The pace of emigration to these settlements accelerated following the economic problems in Kirtland and Smith's decision to move from Ohio to Missouri that spring.[29]

Ohio Saints Relocate to Northern Missouri

The exodus from Kirtland, Ohio, was costly. Significantly in debt from the construction of the Kirtland Temple, the failure of the Kirtland Safety Society, and the expense of defending lawsuits, the Church was on the edge of financial collapse. While many have argued that the Saints left Kirtland to escape their financial obligations, the facts demonstrate a concerted and largely successful effort by Church leaders to satisfy obligations before their departure. To meet these obligations the leaders sold most of the Church's properties. Many individuals also donated funds from the sale of their homes, farms, and businesses to pay Church debts.[30] The financial sacrifice by the Kirtland Saints was considerable.

Such sacrifice by the Saints also meant that most of these people arrived in Missouri without sufficient financial means to purchase property.[31] The plight of the Saints from Ohio, coupled with the ongoing emigration of new converts (most of whom also arrived without financial means), placed significant pressure on Church leaders to find an affordable place for them to

---

28. Alma R. Blair, "The Haun's Mill Massacre," *BYU Studies* 13, no. 1 (1972): 62–63; Beth Shumway Moore, *Bones in the Well: The Haun's Mill Massacre, 1838; A Documentary History* (Norman, Okla.: Arthur H. Clark, 2006), 29, 39; www.farwesthistory.com/haunsm.htm.

29. An account of this three-month journey is in Kirtland Camp, Journal, March–October 1838, MS, in the handwriting of Elias Smith, Church History Library.

30. "Of the $52,251.44 recorded debt of Joseph and the [Temple] Committee, $47,062.83 was paid. There were no defrauded creditors, but rather paid creditors, 90% of whose claims were satisfied in a reasonably prompt time frame. And that payment came largely after the Saints had abandoned Kirtland and the Symbol of their sacrifice, the Temple." Gordon A. Madsen, "The Impact of Litigation against Joseph Smith and Others on the Kirtland Economy" (presented at the Mormon Historical Society 2005, Killington, Vermont), 17, copy in author's possession.

31. "Typical of Saints who faced the uncertainties of the exodus from Kirtland with little or no money or means was Truman O. Angell, the skilled temple carpenter. He and his wife and two small children left in a one-horse wagon. Their first day out of Kirtland, he had to spend his last money to repair the wagon, leaving him with 'a rickety wagon, a balky horse, not a penny in my pocket, a family to feed and a thousand miles to go.'" Karl R. Anderson, *Joseph Smith's Kirtland: Eyewitness Accounts* (Salt Lake City: Deseret Book, 1989), 238.

settle. From this perspective it seems logical that leaders looked to unsurveyed counties in northern Missouri for new settlements, and on May 18, Smith and other key leaders, including Sidney Rigdon, David Patten, and Edward Partridge, left Far West "to visit the north countries for the purpose of Laying off stakes of Zion, making Locations & laying claims [to land] for the gathering of the saints for the benefit of the poor."[32]

Some claim that the basis for Mormons' expansion into Daviess County (the "north countries") was that Caldwell County was overflowing with Mormons.[33] A review of Missouri land sales, however, belies this conclusion. While Mirable Township, the location of Far West, had been substantially settled or claimed, most of the other eleven townships in Caldwell County remained almost entirely available through 1838. Consequently, the decision to settle the poor on unsurveyed land was not motivated by a lack of available real property in Caldwell; rather the decision stemmed from a need to find affordable land. By the time Smith arrived in Missouri in early 1838, Caldwell County had been completely surveyed, including the return of township plats. Therefore, property in this county was not ideal for the impoverished Saints because the land had to be paid for at the time of settlement.[34] It appears Smith's initiative to scout out communities in Daviess County was motivated by the realization that this land had not yet come onto the market because verified township surveys had not been completed. The law allowed impoverished Saints to secure preemption rights to their property without having to pay until the township plat surveys were completed. Because of the backlog on these surveys, new settlers anticipated working their land and generating the income necessary to purchase the property (at $1.25 per acre).

Mormons in Caldwell and Daviess counties actively participated in the federal program of preemption. Writing to her brother Levi on February 19, 1838, Hepzibah Richards, sister of Willard Richards, explained how this was to work:

> People who go from [Kirtland] to Missouri by water take passage
> at Wellsville [Columbiana Co., Ohio] about 100 miles south of
> here, on the Ohio river; you can find it on the Atlas; then follow

---

32. Smith, Scriptory Book, May 18, 1838. See also Jessee, *Papers of Joseph Smith*, 2:243.

33. See, for example, Sidney Rigdon, *An Appeal to the American People: Being An Account of the Persecutions of the Church of Latter Day Saints; and of the Barbarities Inflicted on Them by the Inhabitants of the State of Missouri*, 2d ed. (Cincinnati, Ohio: Shepard and Stearns, 1840), 15; *Elders' Journal* 1, no. 3 (July 1838): 33.

34. The township plat for Mirable Township (location of Far West) was completed on January 15, 1835. Township Plat for Mirable Township, Church History Library.

on down the Ohio and up the Missouri river quite to the western part of the State of Missouri. There are thousands of acres of good land which have never been in the market; people take up lots and settle on them, then petition for preemption rights, which are always granted. The probability is it will never come into the market, and if it does, it will be sold cheap.[35]

During his May 1838 trip to the "north countries," Joseph Smith met with Saints who already had moved into Daviess County and, under his direction, organized the city of Adam-ondi-Ahman. This location was to be a central gathering place for the anticipated influx from Kirtland as well as for converts from other areas. At its height, Adam-ondi-Ahman alone boasted a population of fifteen hundred and more than two hundred homes.[36] By fall 1838, Caldwell and Daviess counties had become home to roughly ten thousand Mormons.[37]

Missouri Land Sales in Late 1838

Although thousands of Mormons had settled new communities in Caldwell and Daviess counties in 1838, these inhabitants soon faced expulsion. The cause of that expulsion is multifaceted. From the uniqueness of Mormons' faith, both doctrinally and in practice, to their apparent disposition for allying with the Indians, their overall antislavery stance, and their rapidly growing political power and resulting voting blocs, the non-Mormon residents of Daviess and the surrounding counties grew increasingly uncomfortable with their Mormon neighbors. Much has been written in the defense of the motives of both groups.[38] Some have acknowledged that certain Missourians enjoyed an unin-

---

35. Selections from Letter of Hepzibah Richards, February 19, 1838, cited in Journal History of the Church, February 19, 1838, Church History Library, also available on *Selected Collections from the Archives of The Church of Jesus Christ of Latter-Day Saints,* 2 vols. (Provo, Utah: Brigham Young University Press, 2002), vol. 2, DVD 1, microfilm copy in Harold B. Lee Library, Brigham Young University, Provo, Utah.

36. Stephen C. LeSueur, *The 1838 Mormon War in Missouri* (Columbia: University of Missouri Press, 1987), 30, 101–11.

37. Modern historians put the number around ten thousand. See, for example, Susan Easton Black and Richard E. Bennett, eds., *A City of Refuge, Quincy, Illinois* (Salt Lake City: Millennial Press, 2000), 6, 24.

38. Alexander L. Baugh, "A Call to Arms: The 1838 Mormon Defense of Northern Missouri" (PhD diss. Brigham Young University, 1996; Provo, Utah: BYU Studies and Joseph Fielding Smith Institute for Latter-day Saint History, 2000); LeSueur, *1838 Mormon War in Missouri*; Bushman, "Mormon Persecutions in Missouri, 1833"; Roberts, *Missouri*

tended windfall of improved land from Mormons' removal.[39] However, a closer look at events leading to the infamous extermination order evidences that some Missourians carefully orchestrated the persecution in October and November 1838 specifically to gain control of Mormons' preemption rights. In fact, this appears to be central to the motives of these Missourians. They did not reap an unintended windfall; rather they orchestrated the deliberate taking of these rights.[40]

By presidential mandate, the date for the sale of surveyed property under the extended Act of 1830,[41] which included the land in Daviess County, was set for November 12, 1838. As previously discussed, this date could be extended only in the event the verified surveys (the "township plats") were not returned within a reasonable time of the sale date so appropriate notice could be given to the settlers who held pending preemption claims, requiring them to pay for their property. If the verified surveys were not returned, the preemptive rights were required to be extended to the next sale date pursuant to the anticipated next extension of the act. The citizens in Daviess County were aware of this sale date, as notice of the sale had been published in various local newspapers beginning in August 1838.[42] The only question

---

Persecutions. Suffice it to say that some commentators cast a broad net of blame on both Mormons and Missourians. Certainly blame can be found on both sides of the conflict. In terms of proportionality, however, the ultimate harm inflicted by Missourians on Mormons dwarfs any reasonable, comparable acts by Mormons. How can one compare the Battle of Crooked River with the Hawn's Mill Massacre? Or compare the burning of Jacob Stolling's store in Gallatin with the extermination order?

39. See, for example, LeSueur, *1838 Mormon War in Missouri*, 237–39.

40. Mormons living in Caldwell and Daviess counties were fully aware of the preemption rights to the lands they were occupying and cultivating. Pursuant to Smith's revealed direction (see D&C 123:1–6), the Saints prepared redress petitions after being expelled from Missouri. In late 1839 these petitions were taken to Washington, D.C., where 491 of them were presented. Additional efforts to obtain redress occurred in 1840 and 1842. A final attempt was made in fall 1843. More than 770 petitions were prepared. See Paul C. Richards, "Missouri Persecutions: Petitions for Redress," *BYU Studies* 13, no. 4 (1973): 520–43; Clark V. Johnson, ed., *Mormon Redress Petitions: Documents of the 1833–1838 Missouri Conflict* (Provo, Utah: BYU Religious Studies Center, 1992).

41. The 1830 act was extended by Congress on June 22, 1838. This extension granted preemption rights to all settlers who were occupying and cultivating land at the time the extension was passed.

42. Such notice to anyone with possible claims was published in the *Missouri* (St. Louis) *Argus* starting on August 5, 1838, and reprinted every week through August, September, and October. The *Southern Advocate* (Jackson) also carried a similar notice in September 1838 and then every week through November. Gentry, "The Land Question at Adam-ondi-Ahman," 55 n. 34.

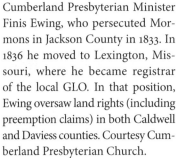

Cumberland Presbyterian Minister Finis Ewing, who persecuted Mormons in Jackson County in 1833. In 1836 he moved to Lexington, Missouri, where he became registrar of the local GLO. In that position, Ewing oversaw land rights (including preemption claims) in both Caldwell and Daviess counties. Courtesy Cumberland Presbyterian Church.

Daniel Dunklin, who resigned as Missouri governor to accept the federal position as surveyor general for Arkansas, Illinois, and Missouri. As surveyor general, Dunklin directed the completion of the surveying of Caldwell and Daviess counties in Missouri. Courtesy Church History Library, The Church of Jesus Christ of Latter-day Saints.

was whether the returned township surveys would arrive in time to allow for the proper conduct of the land sales.

In mid-September 1838, the surveyor general's office in St. Louis, Missouri, completed the township surveys for Daviess County subject to sale on November 12, 1838. These plats were certified and sent to that office by the surveyor general, Daniel Dunklin (former Missouri governor).[43] The plats were received by the local registrar, Finis Ewing, at the district office in Lexington, Missouri, on approximately September 24, but the public was not made aware of that receipt until it was published on October 21.[44] This,

---

43. Daniel Dunklin, as surveyor general, noted the surveys were "examined and approved" in St. Louis on September 15, 1838. These surveys were started by Joseph C. Brown and completed by Lisbon Applegate. See Township Surveys for Daviess County, September 15, 1838, Church History Library.

44. The delay in publishing this notice is somewhat suspect. While beyond the scope of this paper, evidence exists that Ewing helped orchestrate the taking of Mormons' preemptive rights in Daviess County. The returned surveys had been received by the local land office in

therefore, was the first date the Saints could have learned they would definitely be required to pay for their preemption claims by November 12. It appears more than a coincidence that A. P. Rockwood reported on October 24, 1838, that the Saints' mail had stopped coming to Far West.[45]

Before the publication of the October 21 notice, and as the predetermined sale date of November 12, 1838, moved perilously close, Mormons anticipated that the sale date likely would be moved to the following year. Consequently, by September 1838, Mormons in Daviess County had agreed to buy out their non-Mormon neighbors' preemptive rights and possessions. This option was confirmed by General H. G. Parks in writing to General David Atchison on September 25, 1838: "On to-morrow, a committee from Daviess county meets a committee of the Mormons at Adam-on-diahmon, to propose to them to buy or sell, and I expect to be there."[46] Joseph Smith wrote on September 26, 1838, "The mob committee met a committee of the brethren, and the brethren entered into an agreement to purchase all the lands and possessions of those who desired to sell and leave Daviess county."[47] Shortly thereafter allegations arose that Mormons were burning homes and farms in Daviess County. Hyrum Smith later testified, referring to the October burnings allegedly perpetrated by Mormons, that "the houses that were burnt, together with the pre-emption rights, and the corn in the fields, had all been previously purchased by the Mormons of the people and paid for in money and with waggons and horses and with other property, about two weeks before."[48]

The Land Grab

Yet some Missourians were not appeased by the purchase of their land and possessions (or commitment to do so) by Mormons. These Missourians had no apparent intention of leaving Daviess County. The tenuous peace Mormons thought they had brokered was violated before it could be fully consummated.

Lexington and published in the *Southern Advocate* (Jackson), October 21, 1838, 4. This notice informed the public that payment for preemption claims would be due by November 12, 1838.

45. Albert Perry Rockwood, Journal, October 24, 1838, in handwriting of Phinehas Richards, Church History Library.

46. *Document Containing the Correspondence, Orders, &C in Relation to the Disturbances with the Mormons* (Fayette, Mo.: Boon's Lick Democrat, 1841), 33.

47. Manuscript History of the Church, B-1, addendum note U, 7, Church History Library.

48. "Missouri vs. Joseph Smith," *Times and Seasons* 4 (July 1, 1843): 248. Hyrum Smith's entire testimony appears on pages 246–56.

By the third week in October these Missourians knew that the surveys had been properly returned and that Mormons' preemption rights probably would be paid, thereby giving Mormons title not only to their preemptive claims, but also to the newly acquired claims from their neighbors. Some Missourians were determined to thwart this outcome. For example, Sashel Woods,[49] a Presbyterian minister and a leader in the military attacks on DeWitt, Adam-ondi-Ahman, and Far West,

> called the mob together and made a speech to them, saying that they must hasten to assist their friends in Daviess county. The land sales (he said) were coming on, and if they could get the Mormons driven out, they could get all the lands entitled to pre-emptions, and that they must hasten to Daviess in order to accomplish their object; that if they would join and drive them out they could get all the lands back again, as well as all the pay they had received for them. He assured the mob that they had nothing to fear from the authorities in so doing, for they had now full proof that the authorities would not assist the Mormons, and that they might as well take their property from them as not.[50]

The ensuing weeks evidenced the implementation of Woods's strategy by the Missourians.[51] The siege of DeWitt, the Battle of Crooked River, and the Hawn's Mill Massacre proved that any peace Mormons thought they had purchased had been lost. According to Hyrum Smith, some Missourians were "doing every thing they could to excite the indignation of the Mormon people to rescue them, in order that they might make that a pretext of an accusation for the breach of the law and that they might the better excite the prejudice of the populace and thereby get aid and assistance to carry out their hellish purposes of extermination."[52] That goal was furthered significantly by Missouri Governor Lilburn W. Boggs's issuance of the infamous extermination

---

49. Sashel Woods was a Cumberland Presbyterian minister and considered Finis Ewing his mentor. Reverend Ewing's animosity toward Mormons propelled him to be one of the key players in orchestrating their expulsion from Jackson County in 1833. Ironically three ministers, Cornelius Gilliam, Samuel Bogart, and Sashel Woods, "led much of the opposition to the Saints." LeSueur, *1838 Mormon War in Missouri*, 247.

50. Rigdon, *Appeal to the American People*, 29–31.

51. Woods was not alone. Concurrent with his efforts, "Cornelius Gilliam was busily engaged in raising a mob in Platt and Clinton counties, to aid Woods in his effort to drive peaceable citizens from their homes and take their property." Rigdon, *Appeal to the American People*, 31.

52. "Missouri vs. Joseph Smith," 246–47.

order, on October 27, 1838, just six days after publication of the notice of sale.

The process of driving Mormons from Missouri is telling of Missourians' motives. By November 1, 1838, massive numbers of troops forced a Mormon surrender at Far West. "The city was surrounded with a strong guard, and no man woman or child was permitted to go out or come in, under the penalty of death."[53] Mormon travel throughout the northern counties was restricted from that point forward.[54]

In addition to the travel restrictions, General John B. Clark of the Missouri militia commenced the process of systematically arresting key Mormons. By early November, Clark had arrested over fifty Church members.[55] These men were not only ecclesiastical leaders, they also were the most prominent landowners in Daviess County. They were taken to Richmond to appear before Judge Austin A. King. A preliminary hearing, or "court of inquiry," as it was then called, was conducted over two weeks to determine whether there was sufficient evidence to bind over (hold for trial) any of the arrested men.[56] It hardly seems a coincidence that the hearing began on November 12—the exact day the

Judge Austin A. King, who presided over a "Court of Inquiry" against Mormon leaders to determine whether there was sufficient evidence to hold them for trial. This hearing began on November 12—the exact day the Daviess County preemption land sales started—and lasted two weeks, preventing the Mormons from completing their preemption claims. Library of Congress.

---

53. "Missouri vs. Joseph Smith," 250.

54. "On his [General John B. Clark's] arrival there [Far West], he placed guards around the town, so that no person might pass out or in without permission. All the men in town were then taken and put under guard, and a court of inquiry was instituted, with Adam Black on the bench." Rigdon, *Appeal to the American People*, 46.

55. Gordon A. Madsen, "Joseph Smith and the Missouri Court of Inquiry: Austin A. King's Quest for Hostages," *BYU Studies* 43, no. 4 (2004): 97.

56. At the conclusion of the preliminary hearing, twenty-nine people were released outright. Twenty-four of the remaining were bound over for trial. All but ten of these individuals were released on bail, leaving Smith and other Church leaders as the sole remaining prisoners. Madsen, "Joseph Smith and the Missouri Court of Inquiry," 98.

Daviess County preemption land sales started. These sales continued for the statutory two weeks, which ran exactly concurrently with the preliminary hearing. Those critical two weeks were the Mormons' final opportunity to exercise their preemption rights, in person, as the federal law required. But during those two weeks, all Mormons in northwest Missouri were either in the midst of their preliminary hearing or "fenced in by the gentiles"[57] at Far West—with travel and communication restricted.

One of the purposes behind the restriction on travel is revealed through its results. Although the import of this restriction has been obscured by time, the nineteenth-century Mormons understood what had happened. Parley P. Pratt stated:

> The Anti-Mormons were determined the Mormons should yield and abandon the country. Moreover the *land sales* were approaching, and it was expedient that they should be driven out before they could establish their *rights of pre-emption*. In this way their valuable improvements—the fruit of diligence and enterprise— would pass into the hands of men who would have the pleasure of enjoying without the toil of earning.[58]

---

57. Mormons used this phrase to describe the sieges to their cities, particularly Far West. This phrase appeared as commentary in some of the deeds Mormons were forced to execute in conveying their lands to the Missourians. For example, in a warranty deed dated November 15, 1838, with eight grantors—Austin Hammer, Samuel Zimmer, James Huntsman, Issac Ellis, John Pye, John York, David Norton, and Elias Benner—to Willis G. Casper as grantee contains the following language in the text of the deed: "All being Latterday Saints now living in Caldwell County in Missouri and being fenced in by the Gentiles commanded by John B. Clark who is murdering our People and so we are going to leave the County & State, we do for the good of the poor." Copy of this deed in Church History Library. Interestingly, three of the grantors, Austin Hammer, John York, and Elias Benner, had been killed sixteen days earlier at the Hawn's Mill Massacre. There was no signatory line for Elias Benner, while Austin Hammer's and John York's signatures were made by an "X." Signing with an "X" is a legally recognized signature for people who are illiterate, but neither Hammer nor York were illiterate, as they had filed applications for their land at the Lexington Land Office on November 26, 1836, and had signed their names on these applications. See Austin Hammer and John York, Preemption Applications, Church History Library.

58. Parley P. Pratt, *Late Persecution of the Church of Jesus Christ, of Latter Day Saints* (New York: J. W. Harrison, 1840), 149; italics in original. "If the Saints who fled DeWitt hoped they would escape their tormentors, they hoped in vain. Sashiel Woods urged the troops who had surrounded the town to hurry to Daviess County, because the preempted lands would soon go on sale and must be secured by Missourians." Marvin S. Hill, *Quest for Refuge: The Mormon Flight from American Pluralism* (Salt Lake City: Signature Books, 1989), 89.

Joseph Smith, Sidney Rigdon, and Elias Higbee also articulated this fact in their report to the United States Senate and House of Representatives on January 27, 1840. They acknowledged the persecution against the Saints, first in Jackson and then in Clay, Caldwell, and Daviess counties, was rooted in that

> they were a body of people, distinct from their fellow citizens, in religious opinions, in their habits, and in their associations; and withal sufficiently numerous to make their political and moral power a matter of anxiety and dread to the political and religious parties by which they were surrounded, which prejudices arose not from what the Mormons had done; but from the fear of what they might do, if they should see proper to exercise this power.

They continued:

> In addition to this, the Mormons had either purchased of the settlers or the General Government, or held by Pre-emption rights, what were regarded the best lands in that region of the Country. The tide of speculation during this period of time ran high; and the cupidity of many was thus unlawfully aroused to possess themselves of these lands, and add to their wealth by driving the Mormons from the country, and taking forcible possession of them; or constraining them to sell through fear and coercion at prices merely nominal and of their own fixing.[59]

Even those outside the Mormon community acknowledged this motive. In an article published in the *New Yorker* dated October 13, 1838, the editor succinctly wrote:

> The latest accounts from the Mormon neighborhood in Missouri directly assert that all the trouble is occasioned by the "world's people" about them, who covet the fine lands on which they have settled, or wish to frighten or drive them from the country before they have taken up any more in the fertile country surrounding their settlement. Of course, this interferes with the trade of the Preemptioners, who are determined to eject them, either by their own force, or by stirring up the State against them.[60]

---

59. Memorial, Joseph Smith, Sidney Rigdon, and Elias Higbee, Washington, D.C., to the Honorable Senate and House of Representatives of the United States, January 27, 1840, photocopy of the original in National Archives and Church History Library, 8–9.

60. The article continues: "The Columbia [Missouri] Patriot distinctly asserts that such are the true causes of all the trouble. A committee of the citizens of Chariton county have

William Aldrich, a Mormon resident in Daviess County, noted in his redress petition that he "was als[o] deprived of the privelege of Proveing if my Preemption being under the spetial order of General Clark which prohibited [them] from leaving Farwest in Caldwell Co."[61] Likewise, Joseph Younger, another Mormon resident in Daviess County, claimed loss for his "perremtions Rights five hundred dollars Being cept under gard whil the Land sales at Lexinton was going on."[62] Jabis Durfee similarly explained that he had gained a preemption right in Daviess County upon which he had built a house and mill: "I resided on said tract of land untill October AD. 1838 which—entitled me to a Preemtion right on said land: according to the laws of the United States: Whereas I was prevented from proving up said right and entering said tract of land in consequence of an order from Governor Boggs authorising an armed force to drive me with others from the State."[63] His brother, Perry Durfee, echoed this complaint that he was taken prisoner and "was prohibited from entering my preemption which I held in Davis Co"[64] (see fig. 1). Perhaps Willard Richards articulated it best, declaring the entire hearing at Richmond as nothing more than "a lie out of whole cloth."[65]

---

been among the Mormons, to investigate the truth of the accusations against them, and they declare them wholly unfounded. Jo. Smith and Rigdon have given bonds of $1,000 each to keep the peace [and have certified]: 'We are friendly to the Constitution and laws of this State and of the United States, and wish to see them enforced." See "The Mormons," *New Yorker* 6 (October 13, 1838): 59.

61. Johnson, *Mormon Redress Petitions*, 414.

62. Johnson, *Mormon Redress Petitions*, 386–87.

63. Johnson, *Mormon Redress Petitions*, 442. Dated January 18, 1840, Jabis Durfee's redress petition notes, in part, "I moved into Davies County State of Misouri in December in the year of 1837 and settled on the North West Quarter of Section No eighteen in Township fifty eight North and Range—twenty Seven West. I improved said Quarter by cultivating a portion of the soil and building a house in which I lived also a mill. I resided on said tract of land untill [*sic*] October AD. 1838 which—entitled me to a Preemtion right on said land: according to the laws of the United States: Whereas I was prevented from proving up said right and entering said tract of land in consequence of an order from Governor Boggs authorising an armed force to drive me with others from the State." From this description, Durfee's property can be found on the Original Entry Map for Daviess County, Missouri, Church History Library. As the foregoing maps document, Sashel Woods and Jon Cravens purchased Durfee's property on November 23, 1838. This undoubtedly was a strategic purchase, as no other property surrounding Durfee's was bought at that time. The reason for selecting this property by Woods and Cravens is obvious—the mill.

64. Johnson, *Mormon Redress Petitions*, 443.

65. Rough Draft, Manuscript History of the Church, 1838–39 draft history, 30, MS, Church History Library.

Once the time for the holders of preemption rights to exercise them had elapsed, the key actors in the preceding months' anti-Mormon activities immediately purchased nearly eighteen thousand acres of Daviess County land.[66] Based on estimates as to the number of Mormon families then living in Daviess County, it appears most of that land purchased previously had been settled and improved by Latter-day Saint occupants.[67] These were strategic purchases. For example, Adam-ondi-Ahman and many other tracts in the vicinity were purchased by Sashel Woods, his sons-in-law Jon Cravens and Thomas Calloway, and Woods's fellow Cumberland Presbyterian minister, George Houx.[68] Within two months the town's name was changed to Cravensville.[69] Other tracts also were strategically chosen. The Original Entry Map for Daviess County

Figure 1. Petition for redress submitted by Perry Durfee, brother of Jabis Durfee.

substantiates these Missourians' strategy to take the most valuable improved Mormon lands. For example, Cravens and Woods purchased Jabis Durfee's claim along with his home and a mill for $1.25 per acre on November 23, 1838, the first day following the lapse of Durfee's preemption rights.[70] Interestingly, Cravens and Woods purchased no property adjacent to the Durfee site (see fig. 2). The two men surgically purchased a mill site—the most valuable of all property in the frontier. This mill site was so ideal that it continued as such for

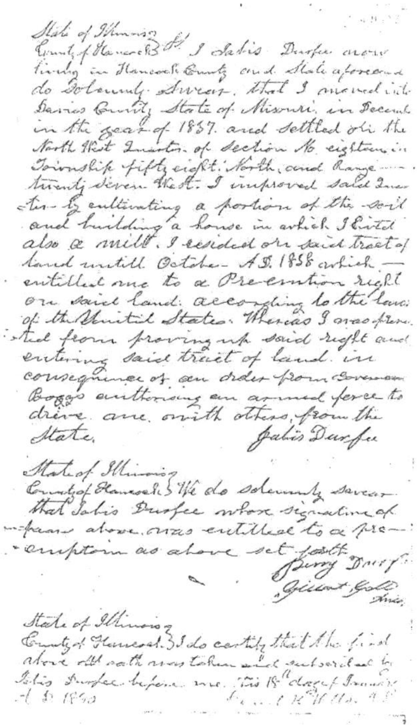

---

66. A review of the "Original Entries for Lands in Daviess County" shows that between November 21 and December 31, 1838, thousands of acres were bought. Mormons did not purchase a single acre. See "Original Entries for Lands in Daviess County."

67. *Document Containing the Correspondence, Orders, &C*, 27.

68. See "Original Entries for Lands in Daviess County." This document shows these men obtained the patent rights for most of Adam-ondi-Ahman on November 28, 1838, and the rest on December 18, 1838.

69. Cravensville, Missouri, Plat Records, Church History Library.

70. Johnson, *Mormon Redress Petitions*, 442, n. 103.

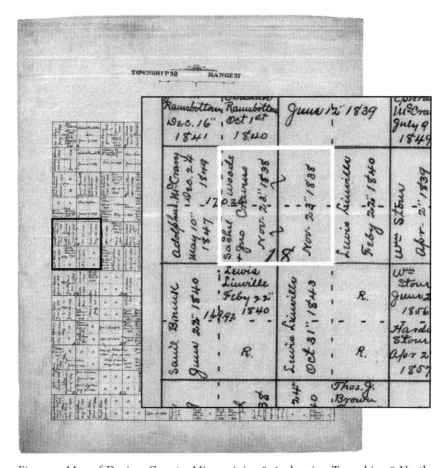

Figure 2. Map of Daviess County, Missouri, in 1876, showing Township 58 North Range 27 West and a close-up on section 18, where Jabis Durfee's property had been. Reverend Sashel Woods and his son-in-law Jon Cravens purchased Durfee's property on November 23, 1838—the day after the preemption rights lapsed. Courtesy Church History Library.

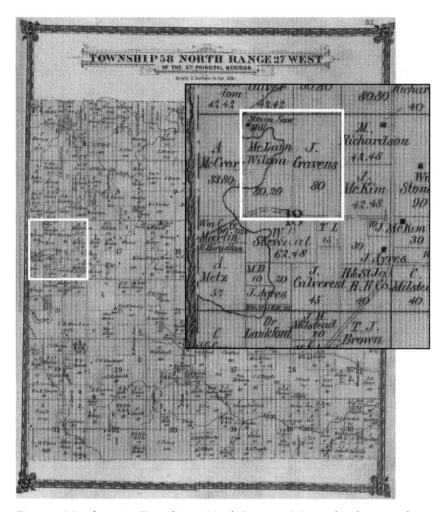

Figure 3. Map featuring Township 58 North Range 27 West and a close-up of section 18, showing Jabis Durfee's land that Sashel Woods and Jon Cravens bought in 1838. The mill Durfee had built on the land was shown as still in existence fifty years later. Courtesy Church History Library.

more than fifty years.[71] Cravens ultimately sold half (forty acres) of Durfee's property (eighty acres), which he purchased for $100, to McClain Wilson (see fig. 3) in 1866 for $1,225,[72] thereby reaping a very substantial profit.

Cravens and Woods were not alone. Other prominent figures in the Mormon War acquired significant property holdings in Daviess County, including Wiley C. Williams (aide to Governor Boggs), Amos Rees, William Mann, William O. Jennings, Jacob Rogers,[73] and others. Most of these individuals had not been residents of Daviess County prior to the land sales, indicating they were speculators who profited from the Mormons' misfortune.[74]

The *Daily Missouri Republican,* published in St. Louis, aptly summarized the effect of the Mormon conflict in its December 13, 1838, editorial:

> We have many reports here in relation to the conduct of some of the citizens of Daviess and other counties, at the recent Land Sales at Lexington—It is reported, said to be on the authority of a gentleman direct from Lexington, that at the recent land sales the lands of Caldwell and Daviess were brought into market, and that some of the citizens who have been the most active in the excitement against the Mormons, purchased a number of the Mormon tracts of land. Where the Mormons had made settlements and improvements, it is said, these citizens have purchased them for speculation. It is said, that the town of "Adamon Diamond," a Mormon town in Daviess, in which there are several houses,— a very valuable site for a town—was purchased at these sales for a dollar and a quarter an acre. It is further said, that there is a company formed, embracing a number of persons, for the purpose of speculating in the lands of these people.[75]

---

71. The maps are copies of the *Illustrated Historical Atlas of Daviess County Missouri* (Philadelphia, Pa: Edward Brother, 1876), 35 (copy in author's possession). The second document shows the existence of the mill that Durfee originally built in 1837.

72. John and Ruhama Cravens, Warranty Deed to McClain Wilson, December 7, 1866, Church History Library.

73. William Mann, William O. Jennings, and Jacob Rogers participated in the Hawn's Mill Massacre on October 30, 1838. Baugh, "A Call to Arms," 417, 418, 420.

74. See "Original Entries for Lands in Daviess County."

75. The editorial continued: "I should not have felt authorised to allude to these reports, for I know nothing of the source from whence they come, but for the fact, that the same matter was incidentally alluded to yesterday in the Senate. Many other things are said in connection with these sales, but for the present I do not feel authorised to give them. This matter should receive the attention of the committee on this subject, for it may lead to a better understanding of the causes of these disturbances. I look upon it as a matter of the

While the causes of the Mormon conflict in 1838 may be multifaceted, the result was not. Some Missourians enjoyed a financial windfall by getting clear title to the Mormons' lands in Daviess County. Whether this was the primary motive from the outset is still unclear, but it is an undisputable fact that key Missourians involved in the Mormon expulsion immediately seized a financial reward.

Conclusion

The nineteenth-century Mormons knew what had happened—and so did these Missourians who reaped the benefits. The Mormon tragedy in Missouri ended with a slow, painful walk to the Mississippi River, where the people crossed to Illinois to start rebuilding their lives. The optimism of Zion planted in Jackson County and the efforts to build refuge communities in Caldwell and Daviess counties were transferred to the founding of the "City of Joseph."

Yet Mormons did not forget the sorrows of Missouri. While popular history has painted the persecution as religiously motivated, the facts suggest a more base reason: greed, in its most ugly and insatiable form, to "have the pleasure of enjoying without the toil of earning."[76] Such efforts stain some of the earliest land records of northern Missouri. Nearly two years after their forced departure, Mormons petitioned the federal government for redress and put the reality of their losses into perspective:

> The Mormons, numbering fifteen thousand souls, have been driven from their homes in Missouri; property to the amount of two millions of dollars has been taken from them or destroyed; some of their brethren have been murdered, some wounded, and others beaten with stripes; the chastity of their wives and daughters inhumanly violated; all driven forth as wanderers; and many, very many, broken-hearted and penniless. The loss of property they do not so much deplore, as the mental and bodily sufferings to which they have been subjected; and, thus far, without redress. They are human beings, possessed of human feelings and human

---

greatest importance, how the committee on this subject may conduct this inquiry. The character of the State and the reputation of every citizen is involved in it, and it is due to all that a full investigation and impartial report should be made." Letter to the Editor, *Daily Missouri Republican*, December 13, 1838, 2.

76. Pratt, *Late Persecution of the Church of Jesus Christ*, 149.

sympathies. Their agony of soul for their suffering women and children was the bitterest drop in the cup of their sorrows.[77]

Examining the orchestrated loss of Mormon land as recorded on Daviess County abstracts is academically important, but it cannot provide an adequate understanding to the totality of these tragic events.

A more extensive version of this article was first published as "Mormon Land Rights in Caldwell and Daviess Counties and the Mormon Conflict of 1838: New Findings and New Understandings," BYU Studies 47, no. 1 (2008): 4–55.

---

77. "The Petition of the Latter-day Saints, commonly known as Mormons," 26th Cong., 2d sess., H. Doc. 22 (December 21, 1840), 12–13.

Chapter Twelve

Imprisonment by Austin King's Court of Inquiry in 1838

Gordon A. Madsen

On November 1, 1838, the Mormon settlement at Far West, Caldwell County, Missouri, was surrounded by state militia troops commanded by Generals Samuel D. Lucas and Robert Wilson. Mormon leaders Joseph Smith, Hyrum Smith, Sidney Rigdon, Parley P. Pratt, Lyman Wight, George Robinson, and Amasa Lyman were taken prisoner, and a court-martial was promptly conducted. General Lucas pronounced a sentence of death on all the prisoners, to be carried out the following morning, November 2, in the Far West town square. General Lucas contended that the infamous order of Missouri Governor Lilburn W. Boggs, issued to drive the Mormons from the state—or, in the alternative, to "exterminate them,"—granted him such authority. Brigadier General Alexander W. Doniphan, to whom the order pronouncing sentence was directed and who was an attorney by profession, refused the order, calling it "cold-blooded murder," and threatened to hold Major General Lucas personally responsible if it were carried out. It was not. Instead, Lucas and Wilson transported their prisoners first to Independence, Jackson County, and then to Richmond, Ray County.[1]

---

1. See Joseph Smith Jr., *History of The Church of Jesus Christ of Latter-day Saints*, ed. B. H. Roberts, 2d ed., rev., 7 vols. (Salt Lake City: Deseret Book, 1971), 3:187–206 (hereafter cited as *History of the Church*). See also Parley P. Pratt, *History of the Late Persecution* (Detroit: Dawson & Bates, 1839), reprinted in *Mormon Redress Petitions: Documents of the 1832–1838 Missouri Conflict*, ed. Clark V. Johnson (Provo, Utah: Religious Studies Center, Brigham Young University, 1992), 80–88.

On November 4, General John B. Clark, who was the overall commander of the Missouri militia, arrived at Far West. In his report to Governor Boggs, dated November 29, 1838, General Clark stated:

> I then caused the whole of the Mormons [except those seven leaders already removed by Lucas and Wilson] to be paraded, and selected such as thought ought to be put on their trial before a committing Magistrate, and put them in a room until the next morning, when I took up the line of march for Richmond, with the whole forces and prisoners, 46 in number ... and applied to the Hon. A. A. King to try them. He commenced the examination immediately after the defendants obtained counsel.... The inquiry, as you may well imagine, took a wide range, embracing the crimes of Treason, Murder, Burglary, Robbery, Arson and Larceny.[2]

Thus commenced the Criminal Court of Inquiry before Austin A. King in Richmond, Missouri, beginning November 12 through November 29. King was Judge of the Missouri Fifth Circuit Court, which included Livingston, Carroll, Ray, Clay, Clinton, Daviess, and Caldwell counties. It was this hearing that led to the imprisonment of Joseph Smith, Hyrum Smith, Lyman Wight, Alexander McRae, and Caleb Baldwin in the jail at Liberty, Clay County, on charges of treason.

At one end of the spectrum concerning the legitimacy of this November 1838 hearing, Hyrum Smith referred to it as a "pretended court."[3] At the other end, some writers have called it a reasonable hearing fairly reported that fully justified Judge King's order to hold the prisoners on charges of treason.[4] The Joint Committee of the Missouri Legislature later found that the evidence adduced

---

2. *Correspondence, Orders, &c. in Relation to the Disturbances with the Mormons; and the Evidence* (Fayette, Missouri: Missouri General Assembly, 1841), 90–91 (hereafter cited as *Missouri General Assembly Document*). See also *History of the Church*, 3:201–6. For notes on this and other Mormon documents from the Missouri period, see Stanley B. Kimball, "Missouri Mormon Manuscripts: Sources in Selected Societies," *BYU Studies* 14, no. 4 (1974): 458–87.

3. *History of the Church*, 3:420. Hyrum noted that he heard "the Judge say, whilst he was sitting in his pretended court, that there was no law for us, nor for the 'Mormons' in the state of Missouri; that he had sworn to see them exterminated and to see the Governor's order executed to the very letter; and that he would do so."

4. Gordon B. Pollock, "The Prophet before the Bar: The Richmond Court Transcript" (paper presented to the Mormon History Association, Annual Meeting, Logan Utah, May 17, 1988, copy in writer's possession), 18. See also, Stephen C. LeSueur, *The 1838 Mormon War in Missouri* (Columbia, Mo.: University of Missouri Press, 1987).

at trial was "in a great degree ex parte [one-sided], and not of the character which should be desired for the basis of a fair and candid investigation."[5]

To my knowledge, no one thus far has examined the transcript of the evidence in light of the law in force at the time to judge whether or not this Criminal Court of Inquiry met the legal standard of that day in charging the defendants with treason and referring them to a grand jury. This article is an effort to do just that. I will rely primarily upon two printed documents, both of which are records of the Criminal Court of Inquiry. The first, cited as *U.S. Senate Document,* was published by order of the U.S. Senate on February 15, 1841.[6] It contains only the testimony of the witnesses. The second, cited as *Missouri General Assembly Document,* was printed later that same year pursuant to a resolution of the Missouri Legislature.[7] It contains the testimonies but is prefaced by correspondence; orders between the militia generals and the governor and others leading up to the hearing; affidavits; and other documents related to subsequent proceedings.

Procedure in the 1838 Court of Inquiry

What was a court of inquiry? It would be known today as a preliminary hearing. It is the first hearing in a criminal case, conducted before a judge whose duty is to determine whether a crime has been committed and whether there is probable cause to believe that the person or persons brought before the court committed the crime.[8] The parties charged must be present during all stages of the proceeding[9] and are entitled to legal counsel, who may cross-examine the witnesses.[10] The prosecutor is obliged to present at least enough evidence to establish probable cause. He does not need to provide sufficient evidence to convince beyond a reasonable doubt. If the judge determines that probable cause has been shown and that the defendants are sufficiently connected to the alleged offense, he then "binds over" those defendants. If the offense is one for which the law permits bail, the defendants and their bondsmen are "recognized," which means to be put under oath and "bound over" to appear before a grand jury or to stand trial in the appropriate court. A written bond in a specified dollar amount is executed at

---

5. Missouri General Assembly Document, 2.

6. *Senate Document 189,* 26th Cong., 2d sess., 1841 (hereafter cited as *U.S. Senate Document*).

7. *Missouri General Assembly Document,* title page.

8. Practice and Proceedings in Criminal Cases, *The Revised Statutes of the State of Missouri, 1835* (Argus Office, 1835), art. 2, sec. 22, pp. 476–77.

9. Practice and Proceedings in Criminal Cases, art. 2, sec. 13, p. 476.

10. Practice and Proceedings in Criminal Cases, art. 2, sec. 14, p. 476.

that time by each defendant and his two bondsmen and filed with the court.[11] If the offense charged is not bailable, the defendants are committed to jail to await grand jury proceedings and/or trial.[12] The judge conducting the court of inquiry is required to reduce the testimony presented before him to writing, and the record is required to contain all the evidence, brought out on direct and cross-examination both tending to both innocence and guilt.[13]

The process used at the time for preserving and reducing to writing testimony at hearings and trials was by *recognizance*. The word had two meanings in the law. Both involved giving a sworn (usually written) statement before a judge. The first was a promise under oath given by a party or a witness in a civil or criminal action agreeing to appear at a future time set for the trial of the matter. The second was the reducing of testimony to writing, usually after the witness had given that testimony before the judge. The judge, or more often his clerk or designee, would write it, then the witness would read it or have it read to him, swear to its truthfulness, and sign it.[14]

In the case of the November 1838 court of inquiry, no testimony adduced from cross-examination and no questions from Judge King and answers thereto are in the record. Parley P. Pratt later testified of one such example of testimony not included in the record:

> During this examination, I heard Judge King ask one of the witnesses, who was a "Mormon," if he and his friends intended to live on their lands any longer than April, and to plant crops? Witness replied "Why not?" The judge replied, "if you once think to plant crops or to occupy your lands any longer than the first of April, the citizens will be upon you; they will kill you every one—men, women and children, and leave you to manure the ground without a burial. They have been mercifully withheld from doing this on the present occasion, but will not be restrained for the future."[15]

Originally, fifty-three Mormons, including Joseph and Hyrum Smith, were arrested and transported by Generals Wilson, Lucas, and Clark to Richmond. During the hearing, eleven more defendants were added.[16] Morris Phelps

---

11. Practice and Proceedings in Criminal Cases, art. 2, sec. 26, p. 477.

12. Practice and Proceedings in Criminal Cases, art. 2, sec. 27, p. 477.

13. Practice and Proceedings in Criminal Cases, art. 2, sec. 20 & 29, p. 476–77.

14. Practice and Proceedings in Criminal Cases, art. 2, sec. 20, p. 476, and sec. 29, p. 477.

15. *History of the Church*, 3:430

16. *U.S. Senate Document*, 19–20, 27, 34; *Missouri General Assembly Document*, 119, 132, 140.

and James H. Rollins never were named as defendants but were nonetheless bound over by Judge King's order.[17]

Forty-one witnesses for the prosecution are named, but both the *U.S. Senate* document and the *Missouri General Assembly* document contain testimony from only thirty-eight.[18] At the conclusion of the evidence, Judge King made the following order:

> There is probable cause to believe that Joseph Smith, jr., Lyman Wight, Hiram Smith, Alex. McRay and Caleb Baldwin are guilty of overt acts of Treason in Daviess county, (and for want of a jail in Daviess county,) said prisoners are committed to the jail in Clay county to answer the charge aforesaid, in the county of Daviess, on the first Thursday in March next. It further appearing that overt acts of Treason have been committed in Caldwell county, and there being probable cause to believe Sidney Rigdon guilty thereof, the said Sidney Rigdon (for want of a sufficient jail in Caldwell county) is committed to the jail in Clay county to answer said charge in Caldwell county, on the first Monday after the fourth Monday in March next.[19]

---

17. Rollins's name was spelled "Rawlins" and Morris's name was spelled "Maurice" in the order. *Missouri General Assembly Document,* 150.

18. *Missouri General Assembly Document,* 151, names them.

19. Missouri General Assembly Document, 150. "Lyman Gibbs" in the order was actually Luman Gibbs. *History of the Church* lists the names of all the prisoners with their correct spellings, *History of the Church,* 3:209. This paper focuses on Joseph Smith and the treason charges. The charges against Parley P. Pratt and his co-defendants for murder are only summarized as follows: Those charges arose from the "Battle of Crooked River." Upon receiving a report that Captain Samuel Bogart of the Missouri militia (mostly from Ray County and non-Mormon) had taken three Mormon prisoners and were camped on Crooked River in Ray County, just south of its border with Caldwell County, Judge Elias Higbee, a Mormon and the first District Judge of newly settled and predominantly Mormon Caldwell County, ordered Lieutenant Colonel George M. Hinkle, the commander of the state militia in that county, to call out a company to proceed to Crooked River to rescue the prisoners. Colonel Hinkle dispatched Captain David W. Patten and his men on that assignment. The Caldwell militia arrived at Crooked River just before dawn, and a short skirmish ensued. Moses Rowland of the Bogart company was killed, and Patten, Gideon Carter, and Patrick O'Banion of the Caldwell troops died. Several others on both sides were wounded. Pratt and his four co-defendants were in the Caldwell company. No evidence appears in the record that connects any of the five with Rowland's death. Indeed, without ballistic or forensic sciences as developed today, determining who fired a fatal shot in a pitched military battle would be nigh impossible to ascertain. The evidence does identify several other defendants who were also at Crooked River on that occasion

Judge King found probable cause to bind over twenty-three of the remaining defendants on charges of "Arson, Burglary, Robbery and Larceny" in Daviess County.[20] He then found no probable cause against six defendants, having earlier dismissed twenty-three of their fellow accuseds.

Trampling the Defendants' Right of Due Process

The procedural due process rights of Joseph and his associates were not protected in their hearing before Judge King. Under the Missouri law then in force, criminal actions were to be commenced by a party (the complainant) going before a magistrate (a judge or justice of the peace) and giving sworn testimony about a crime.[21] The magistrate then prepared a warrant "reciting the accusation" and issued it to an officer, directing him to arrest the defendant.[22] The arrested accused was then brought before the magistrate by the officer, and the warrant was endorsed and returned to the magistrate.[23]

In the case of Joseph Smith and his associates, none of this procedure was followed: no complainant appeared before a judge or magistrate; no warrant for arrest was ever issued or served on the sixty-four defendants; and no written warrant reciting the accusation was furnished to any of them. Sidney

---

who were not charged with murder. See *History of the Church,* 3:169–71; Baugh, "A Call to Arms," 99–113; and LeSueur, *Mormon War,* 137–42.

20. Missouri General Assembly Document, 150. Those bound over were: George W. Robinson, Alanson Ripley, Washington Voorhees, Sidney Turner ("Tanner" in the order), Jacob Gates, Jesse D. Hunter ("Jos." in the order), George Grant, Thomas Beck ("Rich" in the order and "Buck" in U.S. Senate Document, 1), John S. Higbee (*History of the Church,* 3:209; "Higbey" in both U.S. Senate Document, 1, and Missouri General Assembly Document, 97, 150), Ebenezer Page, Ebenezer Robinson, James M. Henderson, David Pettegrew (*History of the Church,* 3:209; "Pettegrew" in both U.S. Senate Document, 1, and Missouri General Assembly Document, 97, 150), Edward Partridge, Francis Higbee (*History of the Church,* 3:209; "Higby" in U.S. Senate Document, 1, and "Higbey" in Missouri General Assembly Document, 97, 150), George Kimball (*History of the Church,* 3:209; "Kimble" as charged in both U.S. Senate Document, 1, and Missouri General Assembly Document, 97, but "Kemble" in the order, Missouri General Assembly Document, 150), Joseph W. Younger, Daniel Garn (*History of the Church,* 3:209; "Carn" in both U.S. Senate Document, 1, and Missouri General Assembly Document, 97, 150), James H. Rollins (not originally charged, nor named as an added defendant in the record, but bound over as "James H. Rawlings" in the order, Missouri General Assembly Document, 150), Samuel Bent ("Lemuel" Bent in the order, Missouri General Assembly Document, 150), Jonathan Dunham, Joel S. Miles, and Clark Hallett.

21. Practice and Proceedings in Criminal Cases, art. 2, sec. 2, p. 474.

22. Practice and Proceedings in Criminal Cases, art. 2, sec. 3, p. 475.

23. Practice and Proceedings in Criminal Cases, art. 2, sec. 12, p. 476.

Rigdon reported, "No papers were read to us, no charges of any kind preferred, nor did we know against what we had to plead. Our crimes had yet to be found out."[24] Lyman Wight corroborated Sidney and said that it was General Clark and not a magistrate who "made out charges,"[25] not in writing, without sworn testimony, and without any warrant.[26]

Defendants, who were entitled to be present for all witnesses and to cross-examine those witnesses, were inserted into the hearing at several different points. Motions for separate trials were denied. Sidney Rigdon recalled, "At the commencement we requested that we might be tried separately; but this was refused, and we were all put on our trial together."[27]

Witnesses for the defendants were intimidated and driven off.[28] Hyrum Smith recounts the driving off of a defense witness named Allen from the courtroom in the midst of his testimony.[29] Cross-examination of witnesses[30] and objections by counsel and comments by Judge King are also missing. For example, Parley P. Pratt noted,

> This Court of Inquisition inquired diligently into our belief of the seventh chapter of Daniel concerning the kingdom of God, which should subdue all other kingdoms and stand forever. And when told that we believed in that prophecy, the Court turned to the clerk and said: "*Write that down; it is a strong point for*

---

24. *History of the Church,* 3:463. General Clark, who served as liaison between Governor Boggs and Judge King during the hearing, wrote the governor on November 10, 1838, two days before the hearing began: "I this day made out charges against the prisoners, and called on Judge King to try them as a committing court, and I am now busily engaged in procuring witnesses, and submitting facts." *Missouri General Assembly Document,* 67. He does not say that the "charges" were reduced to writing and accompanied by a warrant. Nor are there any such documents attached to the record in either *U.S. Senate Document* or *Missouri General Assembly Document.*

25. *History of the Church,* 3:206

26. *History of the Church,* 3:206–7, 348.

27. *History of the Church,* 3:463.

28. *History of the Church,* 3:212–13.

29. *History of the Church,* 3:419. Allen is not listed as a witness in either *Missouri General Assembly Document* or *U.S. Senate Document,* so no effort was made to reduce to writing what testimony he did give.

30. Peter H. Burnett, a non-Mormon journalist and attorney, was, as a journalist, covering the hearing and observed that Sampson Avard, the prosecution's first and principal witness, was "cross-examined very rigidly." Peter H. Burnett, *An Old California Pioneer* (Oakland, Calif.: Biobooks, 1946), 38. The record of Avard's testimony (*U.S. Senate Document,* 1–9, 21, *Missouri General Assembly Document,* 97–108) discloses no cross-examination.

treason." Our Lawyer observed as follows: "Judge, you had better make the Bible treason." The Court made no reply.[31]

Failure to record objections of counsel and comments of the court leaves an incomplete record to be examined on appeal (or by the Legislature, in this instance) and can lead to inferences on appeal that the evidence, not being objected to, was properly admitted into the record.

The right of defendants to be present for the testimony of all witnesses, the right to cross-examine all witnesses, the right to be tried separately, the right to be advised at the outset of the specific charges levied against them, the right to call witnesses to testify on their behalf without intimidation, and the right to make objections during the hearing were all established and guaranteed by *The Revised Statues of the State of Missouri, 1835,* as well as relevant provisions of the Missouri and U.S. constitutions.

When a judge elects to try sixty-four defendants on multiple charges, as Judge King did, the trampling of due process would seem inevitable. For example, Morris Phelps,[32] a Mormon, agreed to testify for the state. He was the prosecution's fifth witness, was excused, and then at the end of the hearing was charged with murder along with Parley P. Pratt and three others. Through the whole hearing he was never identified as a defendant, never afforded counsel, and never given opportunity to cross-examine a single witness. It would appear that his testimony was simply not satisfactory to the prosecutors.[33]

The report of the legislative committee, claiming that the hearing was "not of the character which should be desired for the basis of a fair and candid investigation"[34] has considerable basis in fact as disclosed by the record. It appears that fundamental due process was not afforded to those defendants.

Presentation of the Evidence

Sampson Avard was the founder and self-styled teacher of the Danites, a secret society of Mormons that came into being in the Missouri period. Their original purpose was to purge Caldwell County of Mormon dissidents. Danites did carry out some marauding raids in Daviess County. Avard was first arrested with the others in Far West but claimed to have become

---

31. *Autobiography of Parley P. Pratt* (Salt Lake City; Deseret Book, 1972), 211–12; italics in original.

32. Spelled "Morris" in *U.S. Senate Document,* 11–12, and "Maurice" in *Missouri General Assembly Document,* 109–10, 150.

33. *U.S. Senate Document,* 11–12; *Missouri General Assembly Document,* 109–10, 150.

34. *Missouri General Assembly Document,* 2.

disenchanted with Mormonism and "turned state's" evidence and was granted immunity.[35] He was a confessed active participant in the depredations about which he testified.

The main thrust of his testimony was to maintain that he was only acting under the direction of Joseph Smith and the First Presidency of the Church, who, he said, knew about and approved all his activities, thus implicating Joseph Smith, Hyrum Smith, and Sidney Rigdon. He was the prosecution's first and star witness.

Prosecution witness John Cleminson, a disenchanted Mormon and member of the Caldwell County militia, states that he "went in the expedition to Daviess in which Gallatin was burnt."[36] He then names who was "there" but continues:

> When we first went to Daviess, I understood the object to be to drive out the mob, if one should be collected there; but when we got there, we found none. I then learned the object was, from those who were actively engaged in the matter, to drive out all the citizens of Daviess and get possession of their property. It was understood that they [the Missourians] burnt Mormon houses, as well as the houses of the citizens.... It was said by some that the Mormons were burning their own houses, and by others, that the mob were burning them; and so much was said about it, that I did not know when I got the truth.[37]

Cleminson's testimony puts both Edward Partridge and David Pettegrew at Gallatin, but connects them with no specific criminal activity. No other witness puts those two at Gallatin or elsewhere in Daviess County. Both Partridge and Pettegrew were nonetheless bound over on the "Arson, Burglary, Robbery, and Larceny" charges. Moreover, much of what Cleminson says relates to what he had been told or understood, not what he saw.[38] Thus, much of Cleminson's testimony should have been exluded under the hearsay rule for lack of personal knowledge.

---

35. Avard is quoted as having told Oliver Olney prior to the Court of Inquiry that if Olney "wished to save himself, he must swear hard against the heads of the Church, as they were the ones the court wanted to criminate; ... 'I intend to do it,' said he, 'in order to escape, for if I do not they will take my life.'" *History of the Church*, 3:209–10.

36. Missouri General Assembly Document, 115. The phrase "in which Gallatin was burnt" implies that the whole village was burned down. Actually a store owned by Jacob Stollings in Gallatin was the only structure destroyed by fire.

37. U.S. Senate Document, 16; Missouri General Assembly Document, 115.

38. This testimony also brings to the fore the rule against hearsay. An out of court statement by someone other than a defendant or the testifying witness is by this rule

These illustrations point out the fundamental and pervasive problem with nearly all of the testimony at the trial. Virtually none of it connects any named defendant with any specific criminal act.

Analysis of the Charge of Treason against Joseph Smith and Others

We now come to the substantive law. To understand the charge of treason that was lodged in the Court of Inquiry, it is necessary to survey the governing laws, statutes, and cases that defined the crime of treason.

Joseph Smith, Lyman Wight, Hyrum Smith, Alexander McRae, and Caleb Baldwin were "bound over" to answer to the charge of treason committed in Daviess County. No date or specific set of facts appear in the court's order, and the only event in Daviess County on which testimony was admitted relating to criminal activities in that county was testimony which described the burning and looting of a store in Gallatin. Could such testimony support a charge of treason?

Both the constitutions of the United States and of the state of Missouri define the crime of treason and the evidence required to prove a charge of treason. The U.S. Constitution states:

> Treason against the United States, shall consist only in levying War against them, or in adhering to their Enemies, giving them Aid and Comfort. No Person shall be convicted of Treason unless on the Testimony of two Witnesses to the same overt Act, or on Confession in open Court.[39]

Likewise, the Missouri Constitution also states:

> That treason against the State can consist only in levying war against it, or in adhering to its enemies, giving them aid and comfort; that no person can be convicted of treason unless on the testimony of two witnesses to the same overt act, or on his own confession in open court.[40]

---

inadmissible because the party who purportedly made the statement is not available to be cross-examined as to the truth of his supposed statement.

39. *Constitution of the United States of America,* Article III, sec. 3.

40. "Missouri Constitution, 1820," in William F. Swindler, *Sources and Documents of United States Constitutions,* 10 vols. (Dobbs Ferry, N.Y.: Oceana, 1975), 5, Article XIII, sec. 15.

The Missouri statute in force at the time provided:

> Every person who shall commit treason against the state, by levy-
> ing war against the same, or by adhering to the enemies thereof,
> by giving them aid and comfort, shall, upon conviction, suffer
> death, or be sentenced to imprisonment in the penitentiary for a
> period not less than ten years.[41]

In addition, Missouri law required that "in trials for treason, no evidence shall be given of any overt act that is not expressly laid in the indictment, and no conviction shall be had upon any indictment for such offence, unless one or more overt acts be expressly alleged therein."[42]

The words "levying war" were defined by *Blackstone's Commentaries,* a four-volume summary treatise of the British and, in the American Editions, the U.S. case law. *Blackstone,* the proverbial Bible of frontier lawyers and judges, summarizes the case law definitions and expansions on that statute:

> The third species of treason is, "if a man do levy war against
> our lord the king in his realm." ... To resist the king's forces by
> defending a castle against them, is a levying of war: and so is an
> insurrection with an avowed design to pull down *all* inclosures,
> *all* brothels [original italics], and the like; the *universality* of the
> design making it a rebellion against the state, an usurpation of
> the powers of government, and an insolent invasion of the king's
> authority. But a tumult, with a view to pull down a *particular*
> house, or lay open a *particular* inclosure, amounts at most to a
> riot; this being no general defiance of public government. So, if
> two subjects quarrel and levy war against each other, ... it is only
> a great riot and contempt, and no treason.[43]

This treatise also emphasizes that for a person to be convicted of treason, he must have committed overt acts. After giving several examples, he concludes:

> But now it seems clearly to be agreed, that, by the common law
> and the statute of Edward III, *words* spoken amount to only a
> high misdemeanor, *and no treason....* As therefore there can be

---

41. Crimes and Punishments, *Revised Statutes of the State of Missouri, 1835,* article 1, sec. 1, p. 166.

42. Practice and Proceedings in Criminal Cases, art. 6, sec. 17, p. 491.

43. *Blackstone's Commentaries on the Laws of England,* 4 vols., reprint (Buffalo, N.Y., William S. Hein, 1992), 4:81–83, emphasis added.

nothing more equivocal and ambiguous than *words*, it would indeed be unreasonable to make them amount to high treason.[44]

Bollman and *Burr* and the Strict Definition of Treason

Although no Missouri courts had defined the meaning of treason under Missouri law in Joseph Smith's day, two pivotal U.S. Supreme Court cases involving Aaron Burr and his associates had addressed the law of treason in 1807.[45] These two cases, representing the law of the land under the supremacy clause in both the U.S. and Missouri constitutions, bear a number of contrasts and parallels to the Austin King hearing being here discussed.[46] In *Bollman*, the Court held that "to conspire to levy war and actually to levy war, are distinct offences," thereby foreclosing the argument that Joseph Smith was guilty of treason by having somehow conspired with others. In the *Burr* case, the Court held that "the presence of the party" is necessary as "a part of the overt act" that must be proved by the testimony of two witnesses, unaided by presumptive or circumstantial evidence, inferences or conjectures, thereby again making even a prima facie case of treason improper against Joseph Smith, who was not present at any scene of any relevant overt action. An underlying theme in these two opinions by Chief Justice Marshall is the need to define treason as narrowly as possible in order to protect the founding American principles of liberty and civic dissent.

Following the conclusion of his term as vice president of the United States in March 1805, Aaron Burr began an odyssey that became known as the "Burr conspiracy." In this plot, as inflated by the press, Burr allegedly intended to liberate or "revolutionize" Spanish-owned Mexico, sever and annex the states in the Mississippi valley from the Union, and rule over this grand empire.

Over a period of two years, he enlisted supporters, granted commissions in his proposed army, bought maps of Texas and Mexico, planned campaigns

---

44. *Blackstone's Commentaries*, 4:80, emphasis added.

45. United States v. Burr, 4 Cranch 470; 8 U.S. 281; 2 L. Ed. 684 (1807); and Bollman, 4 Cranch 75. Ex Parte Bollman and Ex Parte Swartwout, 8 U.S. (4 Cranch) 75 (1807).

46. I am relying primarily on three works for the information on the Burr conspiracy: Milton Lomask, *Aaron Burr: The Conspiracy and Years of Exile, 1805–1836* (New York: Farrar, Straus, Giroux, 1982); Albert J. Beveridge, *The Life of John Marshall*, 4 vols. (Boston: Houghton Mifflin, 1916, 1919); and David Robertson, *Trial of Aaron Burr for Treason*, 2 vols. (Jersey City, N.J.: Frederick D. Linn, 1879). Lomask authored an earlier companion work (*Aaron Burr: The Years from Princeton to Vice President, 1756–1805* [New York: Farrar, Straus, Giroux, 1979]) to which I referred but have not cited herein.

for invading first Texas and then Mexico, and bought arms and supplies.[47] He was betrayed by General James Wilkinson, his chief co-conspirator. Wilkinson sent a letter to President Thomas Jefferson exposing the plot (omitting, of course, his own involvement).[48]

Upon receiving Wilkinson's letter, Jefferson issued a proclamation that was circulated to all civil and military authorities and released to the press. It declared that a treasonous conspiracy was underfoot, ordered any and all conspirators or their supporters to cease on penalty of incurring "all the rigors of the law," and required all "officers, civil and military, of the United States, or any of the states or territories ... to be vigilant in searching out, and bringing to condign [deserved, merited] punishment, all persons ... engaged ... in such enterprize."[49]

Two of Burr's associates, Erick Bollman and Samuel Swartwout, who were both couriers of messages from Burr to Wilkinson, were arrested in the West by General Wilkinson; transported to Washington, D.C.; and charged with treason and "high misdemeanor," meaning in this case plotting war against a foreign government with which the U.S. was at peace. They were taken before the Circuit Court of the District of Columbia for their initial hearing (equivalent to Judge King's Court of Inquiry), at which they were "bound over" to stand trial. The men immediately thereafter obtained a writ of habeas corpus from the U.S. Supreme Court. The matter was reheard in that court. The lower court's bind-over order was reversed, and Bollman and Swartwout were discharged.

What Chief Justice John Marshall wrote in *Bollman* about treason is of principal importance. He first specified the charge: "The specific charge brought against the prisoners is treason in levying war against the United States." He then defined the crime.

> "Treason against the United States shall consist only in levying war against them, or in adhering to their enemies, giving them aid and comfort."
>
> To constitute that specific crime for which the prisoners now before the court have been committed, war *must be actually levied* against the United States. However flagitious [deeply criminal; utterly villainous] may be the crime of *conspiring* to subvert by force the government of our country, such conspiracy *is not*

---

47. Lomask, *Aaron Burr,* 33–35, 38–40, 50–51, 193–94.

48. Lomask, *Aaron Burr,* 164–68, 179.

49. Lomask, *Aaron Burr,* 180–81. Lomask cites Richardson, *Messages of the Presidents,* 1:404, as his source.

treason. To *conspire* to levy war and *actually* to levy war, are *distinct offences.* The first must be brought into operation, by the assemblage of men for a purpose treasonable in itself or the fact of levying war cannot have been committed. So far has this principle been carried, that ... it has been determined that the actual enlistment of men to serve *against the government,* does *not* amount to the levying of war.

He continued:

It is not the intention of the court to say that no individual can be guilty of this crime who has not appeared in arms against his country. On the contrary, *if war be actually levied,* that is, if a body of men be actually assembled for the purpose of effecting by force a treasonable purpose, all those who perform any part, however minute, or however remote from the scene of action, and *who are actually leagued in the general conspiracy,* are to be considered as traitors. But *there must be an actual assembling of men for the treasonable purpose, to constitute a levying of war.*[50]

He added that Congress and legislatures are at liberty to define and prescribe the punishments for related offenses, but whatever statutes were enacted, they could not rise to "constructive treason." That term refers to a doctrine created by the British jurists as an exception carved from the general classification of criminals as "accessories before the fact" (those who plotted and assisted in a crime before its commission, but who were not present at the time and place where it occurred), "principals" (those who actually committed the crime), or "accessories after the fact" (those who assisted or harbored the principals after the commission of the crime). In England, when a treason was charged, *all* accessories were by construction or definition deemed to be principals. Hence, Blackstone's phrase "in treason all are principals."

In Marshall's view, this doctrine was so repugnant that, to prevent it, the Founding Fathers inserted the definition of treason in the Constitution. Marshall wrote:

The framers of our constitution, who not only *defined and limited* the crime, but with jealous circumspection attempted to protect their *limitation* by providing that no person should be convicted of it, *unless on the testimony of two witnesses to the same overt*

---

50. *Bollman,* 4 Cranch 126; 8 U.S. 76–77; 2 L. Ed. 571, emphasis added.

act, or on confession in open court, must have conceived it more safe that punishment in such cases should be ordained by general laws, formed upon deliberation..., than that it should be inflicted under the influence of those passions which the occasion seldom fails to excite, and which a *flexible* definition of the crime, or a *construction which would render it flexible,* might bring into operation. It is therefore more safe as well as more consonant to the principles of our constitution, that the crime of treason should not be *extended by contruction* to doubtful cases; and that *crimes not clearly within the constitutional definition,* should receive such punishment as the legislature in its wisdom may provide.[51]

In a separate trial, Aaron Burr and six others were also arrested and ultimately taken to Richmond, Virginia, before Justice Marshall sitting as a circuit judge, joined by District Judge Cyrus Griffin.[52] These seven prisoners were also charged with treason and high misdemeanor and tried and acquitted of both charges. Repeatedly through the Burr trial, the defense counsel, claiming they were following the holding of the *Bollman* appeal, insisted that the "overt act" of making war must be proved *before* evidence of intent or conspiracy could be heard. The court frequently agreed and so instructed the government's attorneys, only to have them ask the court's indulgence promising that the next or soon-to-be-called witness would supply evidence of the overt acts. After some sixteen or seventeen witnesses had testified, the only testimony that smacked slightly of an "overt act" came from Jacob Allbright regarding Harmann Blennerhassett resisting arrest. That, however, was the only testimony of any overt act occurring in Virginia on which to hang a treason prosecution.[53] The court asked for argument that then went for days, involving as it did all eight attorneys as well as Burr, speaking as an attorney in his own behalf. During argument, the government's attorneys conceded that no witness had testified that Burr was at Blennerhassett Island, and that during all material times he was in Kentucky or Tennessee, but insisted under the doctrine of constructive treason, which they asserted *was* in effect in America as in England, that the acts of others were attributable to Burr.

---

51. *Bollman,* 4 Cranch 127; 8 U.S. 77; 2 L. Ed. 571, emphasis added.

52. Each of the Justices of the Supreme Court of that time also served as Circuit Court judge with fellow District Judges in one of the several circuits of states into which the country was divided.

53. The issue of jurisdiction should be explained here. "Crimes charged had to be *proved* to have occurred in the county of the circuit or district where they were charged in the state courts, and within the district charged in the federal court.

The court then ruled. It granted the motion terminating the taking of further evidence, instructed the jury as to the evidence thus far received. and invited them to retire to reach a verdict. The opinion was the longest one Marshall ever wrote. It took the whole of the three-hour afternoon session to read. The court adjourned. The following morning, the jury assembled and retired to deliberate. They quickly returned and announced: "'We of the jury say that Aaron Burr is not proved to be guilty under this indictment by any evidence submitted to us. We therefore find him not guilty.'"[54]

Marshall, in seeming contrast with his decision in *Bollman*, determined that "*whatever would make a man an accessary in felony makes him a principal in treason, or are excluded, because that doctrine is inapplicable to the United States* the constitution having declared that treason shall consist only in levying war, and having made the proof of *overt acts* necessary to conviction."[55]

Marshall then confronted the language he had written in the *Bollman* opinion, namely "all those who perform any part, however minute, or however remote from the scene of action." He acknowledged that counsel in the Burr trial had found this language ambiguous and after expanding and explaining that phrase for many pages he summarized:

> The presence of the party, where presence is necessary, being a part of the overt act, must be positively proved by two witnesses. No presumptive evidence, no facts from which presence may be conjectured or inferred, will satisfy the constitution and the law.
>
> … To advise or procure a treason is in the nature of conspiring or plotting treason, which is not treason in itself.
>
> The advising certainly, and perhaps the procuring, is more in the nature of a conspiracy to levy war, than of the actual levying of war. According to the opinion, it is not enough to be leagued in the conspiracy, and the war be levied, but it is also *necessary to perform a part*; that part is the act of levying of war. This part, it is true, may be minute: it may not be the actual appearance in arms, and it may be remote from the scene of action, that is, from the place where the army is assembled; but it must be a part, and that

---

54. Beveridge, *John Marshall,* 3:513; Lomask, *Aaron Burr,* 282. For the whole trial, in addition to Robertson, *Trial of Aaron Burr,* volumes 1 and 2, I have relied on Beveridge, *John Marshall,* 3:398–513, and Lomask, *Aaron Burr,* 233–98.

55. Appendix, Note (B) Opinion on the Motion to Introduce Certain Evidence in the Trial of Aaron Burr, for Treason, pronounced Monday, August 31 (1807) (more commonly cited as United States v. Burr), 4 Cranch, 473; 8 U.S., 284; 2 L. Ed., 685, emphasis added. Cited herein as United States v. Burr.

part must be performed by a person who is leagued in the conspiracy. This part, however minute or remote, constitutes the overt
act on which alone the person who performs it can be convicted.

... That overt act must be proved, according to the mandates of
the constitution and of the act of congress, by two witnesses.[56]

Thus, the controlling law relevant to Joseph Smith's case was fairly clear:
treason consisted "only in levying war" (not just riot or contempt), which
needed to be proved by "two witnesses to the same overt act" (and overt acts
did not include spoken words that even incited treason), and which overt act
or acts had been "expressly alleged" in the indictment. Beyond that, Missouri
statutes made it a crime, even if falling short of treason, to "interfere forcibly
in the administration of government" (acting in general defiance of public
government), or to "combine to levy war against any part of the people [of
Missouri]."

Moreover, with all their recital of facts and law, the *Bollman* and *Burr*
opinions clarify and refine what the law of treason was in America up to
and including 1838. The making of war must involve some minimal overt
act with "force and arms." While the overt act may be "minute" or of small
consequence, and at a distance from the scene of action, the party charged
must actually perform the act, and be "in league" with the other actors in
making the war. He cannot be legally said to be present if he is not actually
there and participating. Such "constructive treason" is not a part of U.S. law.
To advise or procure treason is in its nature conspiracy, and conspiracy alone
is *not* treason. The overt act must have occurred in the district or jurisdiction
where the crime is charged. Finally, the overt act must be proved *before* other
corroborating evidence may be received.

In addition, the 1835 criminal code of Missouri made it a crime against
the government of Missouri for any one person to conceal knowledge that
"any other person has committed, or is about to commit, treason against this
state," or for any two or more persons to make any "forcible attempt" within
the state to "interfere forcibly in the administration of the government, or
any department thereof," or for any twelve or more persons to "combine to
levy war against any part of the people of this state."[57] Not only are these
crimes not within the definition of treason, but as the following analysis will
show, none of these charges against Joseph were well founded, for he did not

56. United States v. Burr, 4 Cranch, 499–501, 505–6; 8 U.S., 304–305, 308; 2 L. Ed., 699–
700, 702–3, emphasis added.

57. Crimes and Punishments, *Revised Statutes of the State of Missouri, 1835,* article 1,
secs. 2, 4, 5, p. 166.

participate personally in any forcibly interference with government and no overt acts of levying war were expressly alleged or proved against him by the required two eye-witnesses.

The Case of Mark Lynch: Treason against a State

One final legal issue must be considered: Under the law in 1838, could treason be committed against a state, separate from the national government? The New York case of *People v. Lynch*,[58] while not standing expressly for the proposition that treason could never be committed against a state,[59] shows that the domains of state and federal treason laws, which had been vigorously debated in the early years of the American republic,[60] were still open to various interpretations and arguments.[61] In southern states such as Missouri, where states rights advocates were predominant, popular support probably favored the idea that states should be able to construe and enforce their own treason laws as broadly as federal law would allow. In northern states, such as New York, where federalist inclinations were stronger, deferring to United States interests would seem to have been more natural. Thus, in Joseph Smith's case, an argument by the defendants to the effect that treason could not be committed against an individual state might have gotten traction before a judge in a northern jurisdiction, but in the end probably would have been taken lightly by Judge Austin King.

Lynch arose during the War of 1812 between Great Britain and the United States. Mark Lynch, Aspinwall Cornell, and John Hagerman were indicted for treason against the *state* of New York, charging that they "did adhere to, and give, and minister aid and comfort to the subjects of the said king, … and his subjects, then, and yet being at war with, and enemies of the said state of *New-York*."[62]

---

58. People v. Mark Lynch, Aspinwall Cornell, and John Hagerman, Johnson Reports 11:549, Sup. Ct. New York (1814), hereafter cited as *Lynch*.

59. J. Taylor McConkie, "State Treason: The History and Validity of Treason against Individual States," *Kentucky Law Journal* 101, no. 2 (2012–13): 309, rightly shows that *Lynch* should not be interpreted overbroadly.

60. McConkie, "State Treason," 287–96.

61. The argument that treason could not be committed against a state was argued by Thomas Wilson Dorr in 1842 in Rhode Island, but ultimately to no avail. Although convicted of treason, Dorr was finally released from prison by a law passed by the state General Assembly. McConkie, "State Treason," 301–5.

62. *Lynch*, 549–50, emphasis in original.

The counsel for the defendants in that case argued that upon the creation of the union, individual states became components of the nation and treason could be committed only against the nation, otherwise the defendants could, for the same acts be in jeopardy to both the state and the nation. The prosecution argued that there was nothing in the federal constitution that prohibited states from having treason statutes, nor prohibiting them from exercising concurrent jurisdiction and prosecuting treasonous persons under their own statute.

Given the facts of this case, the New York court ruled:

> It has been attempted, on the part of the prosecution, to support this indictment under the statute of this state, (1 N. R. L. 145,) which declares treason against the people of this state to consist in levying war against the people of this state, within the state, or adhering to the enemies of the people of this state, giving to them aid and comfort in this state, or elsewhere.... *Great Britain* cannot be said to be at war with the state of *New-York,* in its aggregate and political capacity, as an independent government, and, therefore not an enemy of the state, within the sense and meaning of the statute. The people of this state, as citizens of the *United States,* are at war with *Great Britain,* in consequence of the declaration of war by congress. The state, in its political capacity, is not at war.
>
> ... [A]*dmitting the facts charged against the prisoners to amount to treason against the United States, they do not constitute the offence of treason against the people of the state of New-York, as charged in the indictment....* The offence not being charged as treason against the *United States,* the present indictment cannot be supported, even admitting this court to have jurisdiction.[63]

Thus, the court held that an allegation of treason against the United States does not automatically amount to an allegation of treason against one of its states.[64] In addition, the New York court followed the proposition that the U.S. Constitution, federal statutes, and U.S. court rulings controlled the sense and meaning of all treason laws within the United States.

---

63. *Lynch,* 549–50.

64. The concepts and holding of the *Lynch* case were mentioned in the petition of Joseph Smith, March 10, 1839, Church History Library, The Church of Jesus Christ of Latter-day Saints, Salt Lake City. See Gordon A. Madsen, "Joseph Smith and the Missouri Court of Inquiry: Austin A. King's Quest for Hostages," *BYU Studies* 43, no. 4 (2004): 121.

Evaluating the Evidence Presented to the Court of Inquiry

With the backdrop of law now in place, we can consider whether the evidence adduced at the court of inquiry justified Judge King's order binding over Joseph Smith and his associates for treason.

What happened in Daviess County in 1838? A store in Gallatin owned by Jacob Stollings (not a Mormon) and a home just outside of town were burned, and goods were taken from the store, a shop, and some homes. Livestock and household furnishings were seen being taken into Adam-ondi-Ahman. Later, several Missourians claimed that items stolen from them were found in Mormon homes in Daviess County. Two witnesses identified Alexander McRae and Caleb Baldwin as being in a group who took three guns and two butcher knives from them *four days after* the Gallatin incident.[65] Other witnesses saw David W. Patten (who all witnesses agreed was the commander of the Gallatin raid) and some of his "company" empty the Stollings store and heard Patten instruct someone to set it on fire. No witness claimed to see a person starting a fire in the store. Several stated that they later saw the store burning. No one claimed to see who set the Worthington home just outside Gallatin on fire or when that occurred.

Nine witnesses put Joseph Smith and Lyman Wight in the "expedition to Daviess."[66] Four name Hyrum Smith as also being in the expedition. Two put Caleb Baldwin in the expedition, and four name McRae. None of the nine witnesses who said Joseph, Hyrum, and Lyman were in the expedition said that any of the three was at Gallatin. One of the three who put Joseph at Adam-ondi-Ahman, Reed Peck (another disaffected Mormon), in his only direct reference concerning Joseph Smith in Daviess County added:

> I heard Perry Keyes, one who was engaged in the depredations
> in Daviess say that Joseph Smith, jr., remarked, in his presence,

---

65. *U.S. Senate Document*, 31, 32; *Missouri General Assembly Document*, 137.

66. The nine were: Sampson Avard (*U.S. Senate Document*, 3, 4, 21; *Missouri General Assembly Document*, 99, 100, 107), John Cleminson (*U.S. Senate Document*, 16; *Missouri General Assembly Document*, 115), Reed Peck (*U.S. Senate Document*, 18; *Missouri General Assembly Document*, 117), George M. Hinkle (*U.S. Senate Document*, 22; *Missouri General Assembly Document*, 126), Jeremiah Myers (*U.S. Senate Document*, 27; *Missouri General Assembly Document*, 132), Burr Riggs (*U.S. Senate Document*, 29; *Missouri General Assembly Document*, 134), Porter Yates (*U.S. Senate Document*, 36; "Porter Yale" in *Missouri General Assembly Document*, 143), Ezra Williams (*U.S. Senate Document*, 37; *Missouri General Assembly Document*, 144), William W. Phelps (*U.S. Senate Document*, 47; *Missouri General Assembly Document*, 125). Avard, Peck, and Yates are the ones who specifically place Joseph Smith and Lyman Wight at Adam-ondi-Ahman.

that it was his intention, after they got through in Daviess, to go down and take the store in Carrollton. This remark Smith made while in Daviess.[67]

Apart from the fact that Peck is reporting someone else's rendition of a purported statement of Joseph Smith, it is a quote of Joseph Smith's *intention*. It was not an observation of an *overt act*.

The second witness who said Joseph was at Adam-ondi-Ahman was Sampson Avard. He testified that at a "council" held at Far West (which is in Caldwell, not Daviess County)

> a vote was taken whether the brethren should embody and go down to Daviess to attack the mob. This question was put by the prophet, Joseph Smith, jr., and passed unanimously, with a few exceptions. Captains Patten and Brunson were appointed commanders of the Mormons by Joseph Smith, jr., to go to Daviess.... Mr. Smith spoke of the grievances we had suffered in Jackson, Clay, Kirtland, and other places; declaring that we must in future, stand up for our rights as citizens of the United states, and as saints of the most high God; ... [Joseph Smith] compared the Mormon church to the little stone spoken of by the Prophet Daniel; and the dissenters first, and the State next, was part of the image that should be destroyed by this little stone.... On the next day Captain Patten (who was called by the prophet Captain Fearnaught) took command of about one hundred armed men.... He then led the troops to Gallatin ... dispersing the few men there, and took the goods out of Stollings store, and carried them to 'Diahmon, and I afterwards saw the storehouse on fire.... Joseph Smith, jr., was at Adam-on-diahmon, giving directions about things in general connected with the war.... and these affairs were under the superintendence of the first presidency. [68]

There is simply no evidence here that connects Joseph Smith, Hyrum Smith, or Lyman Wight to any overt act or depredation at Gallatin or Adam-ondi-Ahman. The supposed inflammatory words he attributes to Smith were by his account all spoken in Caldwell County, not Daviess. Avard

---

67. *U.S. Senate Document,* 19; *Missouri General Assembly Document,* 118.

68. *U.S. Senate Document,* 3–4; *Missouri General Assembly Document,* 99–100. Porter Yates, the third witness who places Joseph Smith and Lyman Wight at Adam-ondi-Ahman, does no more than place them there.

acknowledged that Hyrum not only committed no overt act, he never even "made any inflammatory remarks."[69]

Lieutenant Colonel George M. Hinkle, the commander of the state militia at Caldwell County, both disputes and corroborates Avard's testimony regarding Joseph and Hyrum's "superintendence" and "giving direction" as follows: "Neither of the Mr. Smiths [Joseph and Hyrum] *seemed* to have any command as officers in the field, but *seemed* to give general directions." And, "I saw Colonel Wright start off with troops, *as was said,* to Millport; all this *seemed* to be done under the *inspection* of Joseph Smith, jr."[70] Such words are hardly direct evidence of giving an order, commanding troops, or any other overt act.

Under the standard of the *Bollman* and *Burr* decisions, what does that testimony, giving it full face value, establish? There may have been acts of arson, larceny, and destruction of property, possibly connected to Joseph Smith and the others, but not treason. There was no "making war"; indeed, no gunfire was reported by any witness at Gallatin; no "burning of all inclosures, all brothels"; no assault on the government; in short, no overt act of war—at Gallatin or elsewhere in Daviess County. Nor were Joseph Smith, Lyman Wight, or Hyrum Smith present at Gallatin during the putative acts, and they cannot have been "constructively present" for the purpose of charging treason because constructive treason is not part of American law.

Legal Conclusions

The order binding over Joseph Smith and the others for treason thus fails for at least six reasons:

First, the statutorily mandated minimums of due process of law to be afforded the defendants in the proceeding were pervasively disregarded or ignored.

Second, Reed Peck and others attributed to Joseph Smith an expression of an intention. The testimony upon which treason was charged used vague language such as that Joseph Smith and Hyrum Smith gave "directions about things in general" to troops.[71] Such statements are, at best, efforts to create a basis for "constructive treason." But constructive treason, was, in the *Burr* case, expressly rejected as a chargeable offense in the United States. Words, and words alone—even if they are conspiratorial in nature—are not treason.

---

69. *U.S. Senate Document,* 21; *Missouri General Assembly Document,* 107.

70. *U.S. Senate Document,* 22; *Missouri General Assembly Document,* 126; italics added.

71. See footnote 62.

Third, there was no armed assemblage making or levying war against the government at Gallatin: not a single gun was fired, there was no confrontation between armed camps.

Fourth, there was no overt act of making war.

Fifth, inflammatory language that Sampson Avard attributes to Joseph Smith was spoken in a county other than the one in which treason was charged, and words alone do not constitute treason.

Sixth, the testimony of two witnesses to the same act, as required by the United States and Missouri constitutions, was not produced. Indeed, as in the *Burr* case, no one testified of an overt act of making war at Gallatin.[72] This condition legally makes all the other testimony at the hearing as it relates to treason irrelevant.

One could argue that we could hardly expect Austin King to be familiar with the paticulars of laws of treason as well as the *Bollman, Burr,* and *Lynch* cases. Although King was living in frontier Missouri, he was one of the finest jurists in the state. At the beginning of the 1835 compilation of Missouri statues, A. A. King certified on October 10, 1835, the correctness of that massive compilation in behalf of the committee on which he served that assembled that volume. Thus it is unlikely that he was ignorant of these laws and cases. Moreover, it is likely he was specifically advised of the *Burr* case. In his first communication with Governor Boggs after arrival at Far West, General John B. Clark asked about the appropriate place to try the prisoners:

> The most of the prisoners here I consider guilty of *Treason,* and I believe will be convicted, and the only difficulty in law is, can they be tried in any county but Caldwell. If not they cannot be there indicted, until a change of population. In the event the latter view is taken by the civil courts, I suggest the propriety of trying Jo Smith and those leaders taken by Gen. Lucas, by a court martial for mutiny.... I would have taken this course with Smith at any rate; but it being doubtful whether a court martial has jurisdiction or not, in the present case—that is, whether these people are to be treated as in time of war, and the mutineers as having mutinied in time of war—and I would here ask you to forward to me the Attorney General's opinion on this point.[73]

---

72. The requirement of two corroborating witnesses for treason is unlike the probable cause needed for arson, larceny, burglary or receiving stolen property. That is, as shown in the *Bollman* and *Burr* opinions cited above, the two witness testimony of an overt act has to be provided *at the preliminary hearing stage.* Not so for other crimes.

73. *Missouri General Assembly Document,* 67.

The letter was written November 10, 1838. The governor replied on November 19, while the court of inquiry was in session:

> Sir:—You will take immediate steps to discharge all the troops you have retained in service as a guard, and deliver the prisoners over to the civil authorities. You will not attempt to try them by court martial, the civil law must govern. Should the Judge of the Circuit Court deem a guard necessary, he has the authority to call on the militia of the county for that purpose. In the absence of the Attorney General, I am unable to furnish you with his opinion on the points requested … but the crime of treason, whether it can be tried out of the county where the act was committed, we have no precedent, only that of the case of Aaron Burr, who was charged with the commission of that offence against the United States, at Blennerhassett's Island, in the State of Virginia, and he was tried at Richmond, Va.[74]

Boggs knew of the *Burr* decision and communicated its relevance, at least as he understood it on the question of jurisdiction, to Clark. And since Clark was Boggs's liaison to Judge King, it is reasonable to suppose that Governor Boggs's communication was transmitted to Judge King. However, there were, at the time, in print and widely distributed, sets of law reports that contained the *Bollman, Burr,* and *Lynch* opinions. What was available to King is now unknown, but it is significant that Joseph Smith's petition addressed to Justice George Thompkins of the Missouri Supreme Court, dated March 10, 1839, refers to each of the concepts and holdings of the *Bollman, Burr,* and *Lynch* cases. It therefore seems highly likely that the three cases were called to the judge's attention.

Synthesis and Aftermaths

Why did Judge King insist on binding over Joseph and his associates to be investigated by the grand jury for treason when he could more appropriately have charged them with the lesser offense of insurrection, or of arson, larceny, and receiving stolen goods, as he did the many other defendants?

The answer lies in the fact that both treason and murder are nonbailable offenses.[75] All the other chargeable offenses were bailable. Most, if not all,

---

74. *Missouri General Assembly Document,* 81–82.

75. *Blackstone's Commentaries,* 4:294–95; Habeas Corpus, *Revised Statutes of the State of Missouri, 1835,* sec. 12–13, p. 303; Practice and Proceedings in Criminal Cases, *Revised Statutes of the State of Missouri, 1835,* sec. 8–11, p. 475.

of the other defendants, shortly after being bound over, posted bail via the recognizance process noted earlier. They left the state and forfeited their bail. Not so for Joseph and the other co-defendants held for treason or murder. Sidney Rigdon succeeded after some months in being admitted to bail on a writ of habeas corpus.[76] Efforts by the others to obtain such writs and get a bail hearing fell on deaf ears.[77]

From the record of the court of inquiry, it thus appears that Austin A. King was determined to put Joseph Smith and those he perceived to be principal Mormon leaders in prison on some nonbailable charge and hold them there as hostages until the Mormons had all left the state. Hyrum Smith said as much:

> The next morning [after the hearing] a large wagon drove up to the door, and a blacksmith came into the house with some chains and handcuffs. He said his orders were from the Judge to hand-cuff us and chain us together. He informed us that the Judge had made out a mittimus and sentenced us to jail for treason. He also said the Judge had done this *that we might not get bail. He also said that the Judge declared his intention to keep us in jail until all the "Mormons" were driven out of the state.*[78]

Austin King was part of a quest for hostages. Due process and constitutional standards for probable cause were inconsequential in that quest. He allowed the rights of Joseph Smith and his associates to be violated. One need not be reminded that the same nonbailable treason gambit would be used again six years later at Carthage, Illinois, where Joseph and Hyrum Smith were martyred.[79]

The original version of this article was published as "Joseph Smith and the Missouri Court of Inquiry: Austin A. King's Quest for Hostages," BYU Studies 43, no. 4 (2004): 93–136.

76. *History of the Church,* 3:264.

77. *History of the Church,* 3:421.

78. *History of the Church,* 3:420, italics added; also printed in *Times and Seasons* 4, no. 16 (July 1, 1843), 4:255.

79. See Joseph I. Bentley, "Joseph Smith: Legal Trials of," in *Encyclopedia of Mormonism,* 3:1347. See also the discussion of the treason charge in Dallin Oaks's chapter on the suppression of the *Nauvoo Expositor* in this volume.

Chapter Thirteen

Protecting Nauvoo by Illinois Charter in 1840

James L. Kimball Jr.

From the inception of the Nauvoo Stake in October 1839, the Saints considered its officers to be the equivalent of a civil government of the area. Not only did the Nauvoo High Council pass resolutions regarding ferry usages, but it set standards and procedures for the cost and sale of town lots in Nauvoo (subject to the First Presidency's approval), contracted to erect a stone schoolhouse in the city, supervised the work of poor relief, and approved the establishment of businesses such as a water mill operated by Newel K. Whitney.[1] The Kingdom of God, however, was to function within the existing society and governmental structures and not apart from them, to honor, obey, and sustain the law (Article of Faith 12; D&C 134). Therefore, creating a legal government at Nauvoo was a vital link in the fulfillment of the Church's goals.

To this end, the Nauvoo High Council decided in December 1839 to send a petition to the Illinois State Legislature asking the state to define new boundaries for the cities of Nauvoo and Commerce and to "do all other needful acts relative to those cities."[2] This presumably called for the legal adoption of a city charter. The journals of the Illinois Senate and House for the legislative year beginning December 9, 1839, and ending February 1, 1840, however, do not reveal any such petition coming to the floor of either branch of the General Assembly. Whatever happened to circumvent it—whether the Illinois

---

1. Joseph Smith Jr., *History of the Church of Jesus Christ of Latter-day Saints,* ed. B. H. Roberts, 7 vols. (Salt Lake City: Deseret Book, 1948), 4:16–18, 46, 76 (hereafter cited as *History of the Church*).

2. *History of the Church,* 4:39.

John C. Bennett helped to draft the Nauvoo Charter and was instrumental in its passage by the Illinois legislature. Courtesy Church History Library, The Church of Jesus Christ of Latter-day Saints.

lawmakers did not envision the potential impact of the immigrants on their state, or were reluctant to commit themselves on a party basis to a question not yet fully explored—any initial attempts at that time to secure a charter were not successful.[3]

As the Tenth Semiannual Conference of the Church convened in Nauvoo on Saturday, October 3, 1840, after all the hardships and persecution in Missouri, every prospect for peace and stability seemed assured. The issue of a corporate city government came to the forefront during the morning session of the second day of the conference, when that body appointed a committee to draft a bill for the incorporation of the City of Nauvoo, and named as members of the committee Joseph Smith, John C. Bennett, and Robert B. Thompson. Another resolution authorized Bennett to superintend the bill through the legislature. After one hour's recess the conference resumed and, following a theological discourse by Joseph Smith, Bennett reported to the conference the "outlines" of a charter.

The speed with which the committee worked strongly suggests a prior agreement as to the contents of the document. How much detail Bennett presented to the congregation is unknown, but it is reasonable to assume that he set forth at least the main features of the charter. It is also reasonable to assume that Joseph Smith and John C. Bennett were the individuals most responsible for its final composition.[4]

The felicity with which this document moved through the adoption process also reflects the fact that most of the provisions in the Nauvoo Charter already existed in other city charters that had been recently granted by the Illinois legislature.[5] Indeed, the Nauvoo Charter incorporated by reference the thirty-nine

---

3. *Journal of the Senate of the Eleventh General Assembly of the State of Illinois* (Springfield: Wm. Walters, 1839); see also *Journal of the House of Representatives of the Eleventh Assembly of the State of Illinois* (Springfield: Wm. Walters, 1839).

4. *History of the Church*, 4:172, 178, 205–6.

5. At least five other city charters had been granted (Chicago, 1837; Alton, 1837; Galena, 1839; Springfield, 1840; and Quincy, 1840).

sections on legislative power previously conferred on Springfield, the Illinois capital, in February 1840. While the Nauvoo Charter was unique in its right to establish a university and in its definition of the mayor and aldermen as the chief justice and associate justices of the Nauvoo Municipal Court, its other key provisions were not unique. As in the Nauvoo Charter, the right to declare and remove nuisances was found in all Illinois city charters; the power of the mayor to call out the militia to carry into effect any city ordinance was granted by section 3 of the Galena Charter, adopted in 1839; and exclusive jurisdiction over all cases arising under municipal ordinances was extended to the mayor under article 6, section 8, of the Springfield Charter, adopted in 1840.[6]

The Illinois Twelfth General Assembly met on November 23, 1840. The forty senators met in the partially completed State House building, while the ninety representatives opened session in the nearby Methodist Church.[7] As the first item of business, John Moore, one of the chief spokesmen for the Democratic Party, introduced a bill to vacate the town plat of Livingston, which was read out loud and ordered to a second reading. Moore then obtained leave to introduce as the second bill of the session "an act to incorporate the City of Nauvoo,"[8] which was also read out loud and ordered to a second reading. On motion of Mr. William Richardson, a Democrat from Schuyler County, the rules of the Senate were dispensed and the bill was read a second time by its title, whereupon the Senate, on motion of Sidney H. Little, Whig senator from McDonough and Hancock Counties, sent the bill to the judiciary committee.

Eight days later, on Saturday, December 5, Adam W. Snyder, chairman of that committee, reported back the bill with an amendment to alter the boundaries of the city. The Senate concurred, and the bill was engrossed (that is, written plainly on parchment with all its amendments) for a third reading. On December 9, thirteen days after the introduction of the bill, the Nauvoo Charter was read the third time and passed.[9]

---

6. For extensive research on city charters in Illinois and surrounding states, see Christopher Crockett, "Nauvoo: A Historical and Comparative Analysis of the Nauvoo Charter from Passage to Repeal" (unpublished paper, BYU Law School, January 3, 2011), 51 pp.

7. Manfred Thompson, *Illinois Whigs before 1846* (Urbana: University of Illinois Graduate School, 1913), 76–79; *Journal of the Senate of the Twelfth General Assembly of the State of Illinois* (Springfield: Wm. Walters, 1840), 9, 23, 45, 61 (hereafter cited as *Senate Journal, Twelfth Assembly*).

8. *Laws of the State of Illinois Passed by The Twelfth General Assembly* (Springfield: William Walters, 1841), 52–57.

9. Thompson, *Illinois Whigs Before 1846*, 76–79; *Senate Journal, Twelfth Assembly*, 9, 23, 45, 61. A newspaper, *The Springfield Courier,* published only during the duration of the legislature, is consistently more detailed regarding legislative affairs during this session

The progress of the Nauvoo Charter Bill through the House of Representatives was much swifter than in the Upper House. On December 10, Daniel Turney's motion to have the bill read twice by its title only before sending the document to the judiciary committee evoked no comment. By December 12, the committee reported the bill to the floor of the House without amendment. On a motion, the rules were suspended and the bill read simply by title and passed. Bennett states there were only fifteen nays, but as the vote was probably by voice vote, there is no official record of it in any legislative source.[10]

Three days later the Senate delivered the bill to the Council of Revision. It passed that body on December 17 to become effective February 1, 1841 (see fig. 1). Altogether the bill lay before the Senate thirteen days, the House six days, and the Council of Revision two days, making the total elapsed time twenty-one days. The bill was never read completely before the House and only once before the Senate. However, many bills during the session were read by their titles only two times in either congressional body, but in every case the complete bill in question received at least one reading in each legislative chamber. Therefore, the difference between the passage of the Nauvoo Charter Bill and others in the session was one of time and procedure but was not really abnormal in either case.[11]

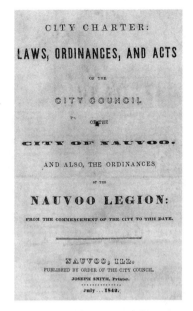

Figure 1. Publication of the Nauvoo Charter. Courtesy Church History Library, The Church of Jesus Christ of Latter-day Saints.

To guide such a document through the legislature required a purposeful hand. Some historians have ascribed to the leading Democrats Stephen A. Douglas and Sidney H. Little the responsibility for this management. However,

---

than the official minutes. See especially the issues for November 28, December 7, and December 10, 1840.

10. *Journal of the House of Representatives of the Twelfth General Assembly of the State of Illinois* (Springfield: Wm. Walters, 1840), 101, 110; *Illinois State Register*, July 15, 1842; Thomas Ford, *History of Illinois* (Chicago: S. C. Griggs, 1854), 263.

11. *Senate Journal, Twelfth Assembly*, 80, 89; *The Springfield Courier*, December 16 and 18, 1840.

the actual part that Douglas—who at the time was the Illinois Secretary of State—played in securing the charter remains elusive.[12]

Information about John C. Bennett's lobbying in the Assembly is also vague. To what extent he pleaded for sympathy, demanded satisfaction, or bargained for position is open to interpretation. One writer, tantalizingly suggesting Bennett was "a man of some sagacity and cunning but without principle," says that the Mormon delegate bargained "the whole Mormon vote in the future elections of the state."[13] Governor Ford asserted that Bennett "flattered both sides with the hope of Mormon favor; and both sides expected to receive their votes."[14] All seem to concede that Bennett played a major role in the passage of the charter.

Whatever the reasons behind the General Assembly passage of the Nauvoo Charter, the Mormons were overjoyed. The passage of the Charter of Nauvoo gave the budding city "a government within a government." With this charter, the Saints possessed a city government whose ordinances (according to the literal wording of section 11 of the charter; see fig. 2) needed only to be "not repugnant to the Constitution of United States or of this State." Not mentioned is any need to conform with other state laws or county regulations.[15]

By taking refuge in constitutions or charters, the Mormons illustrated they were but citizens of their age. In a nation whose various inhabitants in nationalist fervor had drawn up declarations of independence and constitutions for organizations as diverse as temperance societies and emigrating expeditions, the Saints were but participants in an American tradition.[16]

---

12. The Democrats, as the most organized party in the state, were in a better position to help the Saints. Douglas, as one of the leading spirits in the party, would naturally be one of the key men in this effort. Sidney Little represented Hancock and McDonough Counties (where large bodies of Mormons resided) in the Senate.

13. John Reynolds, *My Own Times* (Belleville, Ill.: B. H. Perryman and H. L. Davison, 1855), 576.

14. Ford, *History*, 263.

15. See James L. Kimball Jr., "The Nauvoo Charter: A Reinterpretation," *Journal of the Illinois State Historical Society* 64 (Spring 1971): 66–78. The breadth of this provision may or may not have been intended or understood. Section 30 of the Chicago charter (1837) gave the city the power to enact ordinances and regulations "not contrary to the laws of this state," while article 5, section 38, of the Peoria charter limited the city's power to enactments "not repugnant to, nor inconsistent with, the constitution of the United States or of this State." For the Peoria charter, see *Laws of the State of Illinois Passed at the Fourteenth General Assembly* (Springfield: Walters and Weber, 1845), 228. Read literally, the difference between these two formulations could on certain occasions be substantial.

16. See Ralph Henry Gabriel, *Course of American Democratic Thought* (New York: Donald Press, 1956), chaps. 1–3.

During the third and fourth decades in the nineteenth century, despite opinions of the United States Supreme Court to the contrary, several states— including Illinois—felt it was still an open question as to whether a corporate charter granted by government could ever be annulled or abrogated.[17] Fully aware of this situation and armed with ample, though not unanimous, legal precedent and opinion, LDS Church leaders opted to interpret the Nauvoo Charter as a veritable Magna Carta—a sacred, indestructible, inviolate instrument to be used for protection and power. In constitutionalism there was security; laws and resolutions were but water and sand. By invoking primary bases of law, Joseph Smith attempted to avoid what he termed rapacious and evil misuses of the law.

The broad provisions of the Nauvoo Charter were intended to enable the Mormons to establish a peaceful sanctuary, free from the kinds of violence and harassments they had experienced at the hands of Missouri officials. Nonetheless, it is a twist of historical irony, that while the Saints relied on their charter to be an unbreachable wall defending the rights of Zion, many of their non-Mormon neighbors came to view it as an offensive barrier.[18] The implementation of the constitutional provisions of the charter exacerbated the Mormons' problems by isolating and thereby alienating the affairs of the city from the rest of the county and state.[19]

Perhaps only in pre–Civil War America could Mormonism have been born. Perhaps only in the 1840s could the Nauvoo Charter have been framed.

---

17. The situation was in effect an historical spin-off of antebellum tensions over states' rights and special privilege. The issue was whether the state legislatures had the legal right to grant irrevocable basic charters (as the United States Constitution) as well as "special charters" to corporations which could favor one segment of society over another. While the United States Supreme Court in 1837 rendered a decision against special charters and thereby for free enterprise in the Charles River Bridge Case, the delicate political resolution of the issues was left to the discretion of the individual state legislatures. A helpful summary may be found in Stanley I. Kutler, *Privilege and Creative Destruction: The Charles River Bridge Case* (Philadelphia: Lippincott, 1971).

18. As early as January 1843, that Saints were aware that some members of the Illinois legislature had "long been trying to repeal the Charter of Nauvoo," but Joseph had received assurances from James Arlington Bennet that "the Legislature cannot repeal a charter where there is no repealing clause." Joseph Smith, Diary, March 4, 1843, quoted in Faulring, *American Prophet's Record*, 326; *History of the Church*, 5:296.

19. For a further consideration of the creation, contents, and consequences of the Nauvoo Charter, see Robert B. Flanders, *Nauvoo: Kingdom on the Mississippi* (Urbana, Ill.: University of Illinois Press, 1965); James L. Kimball Jr., "A Study of the Nauvoo Charter, 1840–1845," (master's thesis, University of Iowa, 1966); and Kimball, "Nauvoo Charter: A Reinterpretation," 66–78.

The coming of the Nauvoo Charter reflects for us, today, the time of America's coming of age; it illustrates the growing pains of a nation optimistically trying to mesh democratic and religious idealism in a world of economic difficulties and political realities. The charter demonstrates a meeting of the American notions of political and social experimentation, impelled by a belief in the perfectibility of the human condition, with the equally American qualities of eager opportunism and clannishness. To understand the coming of the Nauvoo Charter is not only to understand the people who lived at the head of the rapids on the Mississippi River but also to glimpse a nation at the headwaters of its history.

This article was originally published as "A Wall to Defend Zion: The Nauvoo Charter," BYU Studies 15, no. 4 (1975): 491–97.

Figure 2. Selected Sections from the Nauvoo Charter

An ACT to incorporate the City of Nauvoo, Illinois Laws 1840, 52–57. Effective February 1841.

Sec. 3. The inhabitants of said city, by the name and style aforesaid, shall have power to sue and be sued, plead and be impleaded, defend and be defended, in all courts of law and equity, and in all actions whatsoever; to purchase, receive and hold property, real and personal, in said city, to purchase, receive and hold real property beyond the city, for burying ground or for other public purposes for the use of the inhabitants of said city; to sell, lease, convey or dispose of property, real and personal, for the benefit of the city; to improve and protect such property, and to do all other things in relation thereto as natural persons.

Sec. 4. There shall be a city council to consist of a mayor, four aldermen, and nine councillors, who shall have the qualifications of electors of said city, and shall be chosen by the qualified voters thereof, and shall hold their offices for two years, and until their successors shall be elected and qualified. The City Council shall judge of the qualifications, elections and returns of their own members, and a majority of them shall form a quorum to do business, but a smaller number may adjourn from day to day, and compel the attendance of absent members under such penalties as may be prescribed by ordinance.

Sec. 5. The mayor, aldermen and councillors, before entering upon the duties of their offices, shall take and subscribe an oath or affirmation that they will support the Constitution of the United States, and of this State, and that they will well and truly perform the duties of their offices to the best of their skill and abilities.

Sec. 6. On the first Monday of February next, and every two years thereafter, an election shall be held for the election of one mayor, four aldermen, and nine councillors, and at the first election under the Act, three Judges shall be chosen *viva voce* by the electors present, the said judges shall choose two clerks, and the judges and clerks before entering upon their duties, shall take and subscribe an oath or affirmation such as is now required by law to be taken by judges and clerks of other elections; and at all subsequent elections, the necessary number of judges and clerks shall be appointed by the city council. At the first election so held the polls shall be opened at nine o'clock A. M., and closed at six o'clock P. M., at the close of the polls the votes shall be counted, and a statement thereof proclaimed at the front door of the house at which said election shall be held; and the clerks shall leave with each person elected, or at his usual place of residence within five days after the election, a written notice of his election, and each person so notified, shall within ten days after the election take the oath or affirmation hereinbefore mentioned, a certificate of which oath shall be deposited with the recorder, whose appointment is hereafter provided for, and be by him preserved, and all subsequent elections shall be held, conducted and returns thereof made as may be provided for by ordinances of the city council....

Sec. 11. The city council shall have power and authority to make, ordain, establish and execute all such ordinances, not repugnant to the Constitution of the United States or of this State, as they may deem necessary for the peace, benefit, good order, regulation, convenience and cleanliness of said city; for the protection of property therein from destruction by fire or otherwise, and for the health and happiness thereof, they shall have power to fill all vacancies that may happen by death, resignation or removal, in any of the offices herein made elective; to fix and establish all the fees of the office of said corporation not herein established; to impose such fines, not exceeding one hundred dollars for each offence, as they may deem just for refusing to accept any office in or under the corporation, or for the misconduct therein; to divide the city into wards; to add to the number of aldermen and councillors, and apportion them among the several wards as may be most just and conducive to the interests of the city....

Sec. 13. The city council shall have exclusive power within the city by ordinance, to license, regulate and restrain the keeping of ferries, to regulate the police of the city; to impose fines, forfeitures, and penalties for the breach of any ordinance, and provide for the recovery of such fines and forfeitures, and the enforcement of such penalties, and to pass such ordinances as may be necessary and proper for carrying into execution the powers specified in this Act: *Provided,* Such ordinances are not repugnant to the Constitution of the United States or of this State; and in fine to exercise such other legislative powers as are conferred on the city council of the city of Springfield, by an act entitled "An act to incorporate the city of Springfield, approved February third, one thousand eight hundred and forty."...

Selected Sections Incorporated into the Nauvoo Charter, Section 13, by Reference to the Springfield City Charter

Sec. 7. To make regulations to secure the general health of the inhabitants, to declare what shall be a nuisance, and to prevent and remove the same in the streets for the extinguishment of fires, and convenience of the inhabitants.

Sec. 11. To divide the city into wards, and specify the boundaries thereof, and create additional wards, as the occasion may require.

Sec. 34. To regulate the police of the city, to impose fines, and forfeitures, and penalties, for the breach of any ordinance, and provide for the recovery and appropriation of such fines and forfeitures, and the enforcement of such penalties.

Sec. 36. The City Council shall have power to make all ordinances which shall be necessary and proper for carrying into execution the powers specified in this Act, so that such ordinances be not repugnant to nor inconsistent with, the constitution of the United States or of this state.

Sec. 16. The mayor and aldermen shall be conservators of the peace within the limits of said city, and shall have all the powers of justices of the peace therein, both in civil and criminal cases, arising under the laws of the State; they shall as justices of the peace within the limits of said city, perform the same duties, be governed by the same laws, give the same bonds and security, as other justices of the peace, and be commissioned as justices of the peace in and for said city by the Governor.

Sec. 17. The mayor shall have exclusive jurisdiction in all cases arising under the ordinances of the corporation, and shall issue such process as may be necessary to carry said ordinances into execution and effect, appeals may be had from any decision or judgment of said mayor or aldermen, arising under the city ordinances, to the municipal court, under such regulation as may be presented by ordinance. Which court shall be composed of the mayor or chief justice, and the aldermen as associate justices, and from the final judgment of the municipal court to the circuit court of Hancock county, in the same manner of appeals are taken from judgments of the justices of the peace: *Provided,* That the parties litigant shall have a right to a trial by a jury of twelve men in all cases before the municipal court. The municipal court shall have power to grant writs of *habeas corpus* in all cases arising under the ordinances of the city council....

Sec. 23. In case the mayor shall at any time be guilty of a palpable omission of duty, or shall willfully and corruptly be guilty of oppression, malconduct or partiality in the discharge of the duties of his office, he shall be liable to be indicted in the circuit court of Hancock county, and on conviction he shall be fined not more than two hundred dollars, and the court shall have power on the recommendation of the jury, to add to the judgment of the court, that he be removed from office.

Sec. 24. The city council may establish and organize an institution of learning within the limits of the city for the teaching of the arts, sciences and learned professions, to be called the "University of the City of Nauvoo," which institution shall be under the control and management of a board of trustees, consisting of a chancellor, registrar, and twenty-three regents, which board shall thereafter be a body corporate and politic, with perpetual succession, by the name of the "Chancellor and Regents of the University of the City of Nauvoo," and shall have full power to pass, ordain, establish, and execute all such laws and ordinances as they may consider necessary for the welfare and prosperity of said university, its officers and students: *Provided,* That the said laws and ordinances shall not be repugnant to the Constitution of the United States or of this State, and *Provided, also,* That the trustees shall at all times be appointed by the city council, and shall have all the powers and privileges for the advancement of the cause of education which appertain to the trustees of any other college or university of this State.

Sec. 25. The city council may organize the inhabitants of said city subject to military duty into a body of independent military men, to be called the "Nauvoo Legion," the court martial of which shall be composed of the commissioned officers of said legion, and constitute the law making department, with full powers and authority to make, ordain, establish and execute all such laws and ordinances as may be considered necessary for the benefit, government, and regulation of said legion: *Provided,* Said court martial shall pass no law or act repugnant to, or inconsistent with the Constitution of the United States, or of this State, and, *Provided, also,* That the officers of the legion shall be commissioned by the Governor of the State. The said Legion shall perform the same mount of military duty as is now, or may be hereafter required of the regular militia of the State, and shall be at the disposal of the mayor in executing the laws and ordinances of the city corporation, and the laws of the State, and at the disposal of the Governor for the public defence, and the execution of the laws of the State or of the United States, and shall be entitled to their proportion of the public arms, and, *Provided, also,* That said legion shall be exempt from all other military duty.

[For a comparison of the powers granted under the Nauvoo Charter and other city charters in Illinois, see chapter 16, note 52, below.]

Chapter Fourteen

Suffering Shipwreck and Bankruptcy in 1842 and Beyond

Joseph I. Bentley

Although Joseph Smith was no stranger to accusations of fraud, one of the most serious began in the summer of 1842. Struggling to keep his head above financial water, he petitioned for bankruptcy under the new federal Bankruptcy Act, passed the year before. His petition was denied for reasons that went beyond the strict merits of the case and attacked him as an individual. The chief reason was Joseph's role in purchasing the steamboat *Nauvoo*, a symbol of the Mormons' bright economic hopes. When the *Nauvoo* ran aground in November 1840 after just two months of operation, a cascade of legal and financial calamities followed in its wake. These legal entanglements produced more than sixty court documents and generated serious consequences for Joseph Smith, his family, and the Church.

The Steamboat *Nauvoo*

The story begins with a physical obstacle: the Des Moines rapids. On August 31, 1840, the First Presidency urged all Latter-day Saints to gather yet again in a new place: Nauvoo, Illinois, which was established as the new Church headquarters.[1] Many Mormons, including most foreign immigrants, had to travel up the Mississippi River to reach their new Zion. The biggest obstacle to navigating this five-thousand-mile-long "Father of Waters" was

---

1. Joseph Smith, *History of The Church of Jesus Christ of Latter-day Saints,* ed. B. H. Roberts, 2d ed. rev., 7 vols. (Salt Lake City: Deseret News, 1932–51), 4:183–87, hereafter cited as *History of the Church.*

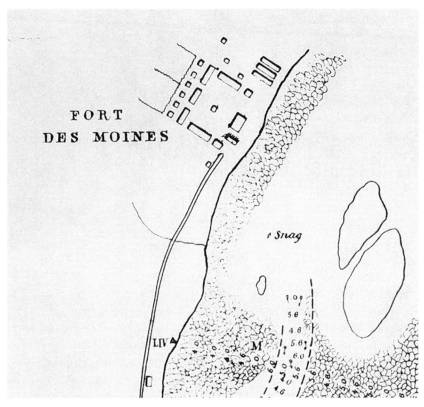

Des Moines Rapids. The narrow channel of the Mississippi River, with its depth measurements shown between the broken lines, flowed between the west bank and the two small islands. National Archives, Fortifications map file, Records of the Office of the Chief of Engineers, Record Group 77.

this eleven-mile-long limestone outcropping just below Nauvoo. Passage was possible only through a narrow channel along the Iowa side. It was so hazardous that large steamers had to off-load their cargo onto smaller boats or overland vehicles before navigating the outcropping. Wrecked steamers that had attempted to run these white-knuckle rapids and another fourteen-mile-long stretch above Nauvoo were strewn along both of these treacherous areas.[2] This obstacle presented both a challenge and a commercial opportunity for some industrious Latter-day Saints.

---

2. Joseph I. Bentley, "In the Wake of the Steamboat *Nauvoo*: Prelude to Joseph Smith's Financial Disasters, *Journal of Mormon History* (Salt Lake City, Winter 2009), 24–25, hereafter cited as "Joseph Smith's Financial Disasters."

Starting in 1836, Congress charged the U.S. Army Corps of Engineers with the challenging task of making the Mississippi River navigable, starting with the Des Moines rapids.[3] The officer placed in charge was First Lieutenant Robert E. Lee, age thirty, who would later become the commander of the Confederate army during the Civil War.[4] Lee began blasting and removing rock in the Des Moines rapids during 1838. By 1839, he had straightened and widened the channel from thirty to fifty feet and lowered it to a depth of five feet, removing more than two thousand tons of rock. However, the national depression that had begun in 1837 continued to worsen. In 1840, Congress ordered Lee to discontinue all operations and auction off his equipment, including his headquarters boat, the *Des Moines*.

Robert E. Lee, March 1864. Library of Congress.

Congress's decision proved a tempting opportunity for a group of five Mormon entrepreneurs, including Joseph Smith. At a public auction held at Quincy, Illinois, on September 10, 1840, the Mormons purchased the *Des Moines* and other river equipment from then-Captain Lee as the U.S. government's selling agent. The boat weighed 93 tons, was 120 feet long, and was about half the size of an average Mississippi steamer—hence, admirably suited to negotiate the rapids. It was designed to be one of the new city's first commercial enterprises, a fact its new owners underscored by naming it the *Nauvoo*.

The five Mormon purchasers were Peter Haws as principal, with four endorsers or guarantors: Joseph and Hyrum Smith, George Miller (later named the third bishop of the Church), and Henry W. Miller (unrelated to George). They came without cash but with letters of recommendation from Thomas Carlin, governor of Illinois, and Richard M. Young, U.S. Senator for

---

3. Mark Twain called this task of taming the Mississippi River "a job transcended in size by only the original job of creating it." *Id* at 25.

4. Later renowned for his role as commander of the Confederate military forces during the Civil War, this was Lee's first major military assignment after graduating from West Point in 1830. See Douglas S. Freeman, *Robert E. Lee: A Biography*, 4 vols (New York: C. Scribner's Sons, 1934–35), Vol. 1, Chaps. 9, 11.

Illinois. The purchase price was $4,866, and Lee accepted a promissory note due in eight months.[5]

Although the note is not clear, subsequent documents show that Peter Haws was the principal and the Millers and Smiths were only sureties for his obligation.[6] The sureties role, however, was essential, since the sale terms required "two approved endorsers." In addition, Robert E. Lee was very careful to obtain letters from prominent public figures authenticating the good character and financial integrity of the sureties.[7]

Concurrent with their purchase of the steamboat, the Mormons sold a five-sixth interest in the *Des Moines* to a consortium of two brothers (Charles and Marvin Street) and a third party as surety, Robert F. Smith (no relation to Joseph).[8] Ultimately Joseph, Hyrum, and the others sued the Streets and Robert F. Smith on February 7, 1844, to collect the balance of their unpaid note. That suit was dismissed the year after Joseph and Hyrum's deaths.[9]

As soon as the Mormons acquired their steamboat, they put it to work transporting passengers and freight up and down the Mississippi. One month earlier, on August 10, 1840, they had hired two river pilots, William and Benjamin Holladay. The *Nauvoo* had been plying the Mississippi for less than two months when it ran aground on November 14, only two months after the purchase. Apparently the damage was serious enough that the

---

5. The original promissory note for $4,866 and thirty-seven other documents comprise an eighty-seven-page collection of reports by and correspondence between the U.S. Treasury Department and various U.S. attorneys, marshals, and cabinet members, catalogued as Records of the Solicitor of the Treasury, Record Group 206, part 1, 1841–52, National Archives, Washington, D.C. (hereafter cited as "Treasury Papers").

6. See Register of Miscellaneous Suits in Which the United States Is a Party or Interested, 1834-1848 and Treasury Papers. The Treasury Papers specifically identify Peter Haws as the "Principal" and lists the other four signers as "sureties" in the transaction with Lee.

7. In a 10 September 1840 letter to Captain Lee, U.S. Senator Richard M. Young and D. G. Whitney, a Quincy merchant, state that the Smiths and Millers were all "good and sufficient for said amount [of the note] and that the Government [was] safe in accepting the same." "Treasury Papers."

8. Dallin H. Oaks and Joseph I. Bentley, "Joseph Smith and the Legal Process: In the Wake of the Steamboat *Nauvoo*," *Brigham Young University Law Review* 2, no. 3 (1976): 169, hereafter cited as "Joseph Smith and Legal Process." As justice of the peace and captain of the Carthage Grays in 1844, Robert F. Smith was later responsible for ordering Joseph and Hyrum Smith to jail, where they were murdered in June 1844. Bentley, "Joseph Smith's Financial Disasters," 28.

9. The dismissal date was May 22, 1846. See Bentley, "Joseph Smith's Financial Disasters," 28; see also Oaks and Bentley, "Joseph Smith and Legal Process," 171.

Nauvoo never operated again under Mormon control.[10] As a result, the Mormons sued the pilots as well. A complaint subsequently filed against them on April 23, 1841, alleged that the "defendants represented themselves to be skillful and competent pilots with understanding of the steam boat channel of the Mississippi River."[11]

Although he was on board the ship when it ran aground,[12] Joseph Smith certainly did not see himself as responsible for the wreck. On November 30, 1840, he and his co-owners hired counsel and had a writ issued in Carthage to arrest the Holladays for "taking possession of said Steam boat Nauvoo as pilots … but intending to injure the plaintiffs … willfully and with intent to destroy said boat ran the same upon rocks and sandbars out of the usual Steam boat channel of said river." They "greatly injured the hull and rigging"—more specifically, that "twelve or thirteen of the bottom timbers of said boat are cracked or split." The plaintiffs claimed $2,000 in damages to the boat plus $1,000 in lost profits. The Hancock County sheriff arrested both of the Holladays on November 30, 1840, but they were immediately released on bail and apparently fled from the state.[13] On April 23, 1841, the Mormons filed with the Hancock County Circuit Court in Carthage a civil action in "trespass on the case," a form of breach of contract against the Holladays. The case was dismissed on May 7, 1841, at plaintiffs' request, likely because the defendants had disappeared, along with any prospect of recovering damages.

This wreck dashed any hopes the operators had of paying off their note to the United States when it came due on May 10, 1841. When the default became apparent, Captain Robert E. Lee promptly asked the Solicitor of the Treasury (Charles B. Penrose) and the Secretary of War (John Bell) to sue the Mormons for collection. Since all signers of the note were then living in Illinois, Montgomery Blair, then U.S. Attorney for Missouri and later a member of Lincoln's first cabinet, transferred the case to Justin Butterfield,

---

10. Perhaps the Streets, who owned a majority interest in the enterprise, may have taken it over and rehabilitated it.

11. Complaint in Smith v. Holladay, Hancock County Circuit Court, May Term, 1841, Courthouse, Carthage, Ill.

12. Bentley, "Joseph Smith's Financial Disasters," 30.

13. See Bentley, "Joseph Smith's Financial Disasters," 31; see also Oaks and Bentley, "Joseph Smith and Legal Process," 170. Today's procedure is very different, but in the nineteenth century it was customary for the plaintiffs to have an arrest warrant issued, thus requiring the defendants to post bail (November 30, 1840). The witnesses were not subpoenaed until April 3, 1841, after a Samuel Hicks, possibly the plaintiffs' attorney, filed an affidavit. The actual suit was filed almost three weeks later on April 23.

U.S. Attorney for Illinois. Moving the paperwork took several months; but on April 3, 1842, Butterfield filed suit in Springfield to collect the debt. A month later on May 4, a summons was served on all four sureties; but the sheriff reported back that the actual principal, Peter Haws, was "not found." Federal judge Nathaniel Pope in Springfield called up the case three times on successive dates. No defendants appeared at any of the three dates, so on June 11, he entered a default judgment for $5,212—the original note principal plus interest and the costs of the suit.[14]

The U.S. Attorney, Justice Butterfield, was the driving force in the legal proceedings to collect the steamboat debt. One of the ablest attorneys in the state with a practice in Chicago and Springfield, he had been appointed to his current position by John Tyler's Whig administration, which took office in 1840. Although he later appeared as Joseph's attorney in the 1842 extradition hearing before Judge Pope, Butterfield vigorously pursued collection of the debt and obstructed Joseph's attempts to obtain a discharge in bankruptcy, which would have eliminated the debt.[15]

Why didn't the Mormons pay the $5,000 note owed to the U.S. government, or even appear in court to contest the suit or negotiate a settlement of the debt? First, from a legal perspective, Joseph Smith and the other three cosigners may have been only secondarily liable, and hence had a possible defense against collection, since the principal, Peter Haws, was not even served. But there is no record that the cosigners sought legal advice on the issue. Under the circumstances, a lawyer would have probably advised them to contest or settle the case, since the consequences of taking a default judgment were severe, including the possible seizure of real property.

Second, it seems likely that the four Mormons simply lacked the means to come up with even a partial payment. Times were hard in the United States, and nowhere harder than in Illinois. The Panic of 1837 and the resulting depression that had forced the sale of the *Des Moines* in the first place had strained everyone to his or her financial limits. In Illinois, the two largest banks failed in 1840 and 1841, and what little commerce existed was largely by barter. The Mormons were among the most cash-strapped in the state. They had incurred tremendous debts to Isaac Galland and Horace Hotchkiss in acquiring land to build up Nauvoo and were falling behind in making

---

14. Complete Record of the United States District Court for the District of Illinois, Vol. 1, no. 1600 (1819–27, Federal Records Center, Chicago), 529–31. This is the only case that lies outside the 1819–1827 time period covered by that volume and is the next-to-last entry in the volume. See also Oaks and Bentley, "Joseph Smith and Legal Process," 172–73.

15. Oaks and Bentley, "Joseph Smith and Legal Process," 184, 187.

payments on the obligations. Also, the very means they were counting on to enable payment—cash that would be generated by the *Nauvoo*—was wrecked with the steamboat.

Third, they probably attributed much of their financial pain to the federal government already. Up to fifteen thousand Saints had been driven from their homes in Missouri. In the process, they had lost huge sums of money, much of it paid to the federal government for homesteads in northern Missouri. In early 1840, Congress had rejected a mammoth "memorial" signed by 3,491 Saints.[16] Thus, at a time when there were many demands on their limited cash, it is easy to understand why Mormons lacked motivation to repay the federal government as a top priority.

Fourth, on May 6, 1842—one month before the default hearing and judgment on June 11, and two days after the sheriff served his summons for debt—ex-governor Lilburn W. Boggs was shot at his home in Missouri. Although seriously wounded, he survived. Joseph could prove that he was in Nauvoo on that day, and therefore not subject to extradition. Still, he was accused of being an accomplice and spent most of the summer in hiding to avoid being seized or extradited back to Missouri, a measure with which Illinois Governor Thomas Carlin was cooperating. Joseph therefore would have been hesitant to appear in an Illinois court at a time when the state was seeking his extradition.

Fifth, and perhaps most significantly, Joseph and Hyrum had just filed for bankruptcy. If their petition had been successful, the steamboat debt and all of their other financial obligations would have been discharged.[17] However, Joseph's petition was denied.

Bankruptcy

Declaring bankruptcy was a new option in American finance. To help relieve debtors from the nationwide depression that had begun with the Panic of 1837, Congress on August 19, 1841, passed a relatively simple bankruptcy act (see fig. 1)

---

16. U.S. Senate, Record Group 46 (1840–44), April 5, 1844.

17. Bankruptcy Act of 1841, chap. 9, 5 Stat., 440–49. See Oaks and Bentley, "Joseph Smith and Legal Process," 173–77. The act was only eight pages long. Its second sentence simply began as follows: "All persons whatsoever . . . owing debts who shall, by petition, set forth to the best of his knowledge and belief, a list of his or their creditors, their respective places of residence, and the amount due to each, together with an accurate inventory of his or his property . . . and therein declare themselves to be unable to meet their debts and engagements, shall be deemed bankrupts within the purview of this act, and may be so declared accordingly by a decree of such court."

Figure 1. Bankruptcy Act, Effective Feb. 1, 1842–Mar. 3, 1843

SEC. 1. All persons whatsoever, residing in any State, District or Territory of the United States, owing debts, which shall not have been created in consequence of a defalcation as a public officer; or as executor, administrator, guardian or trustee, or while acting in any other fiduciary capacity, who shall, by petition, setting forth to the best of his knowledge and belief, a list of his or their creditors, their respective places of residence, and the amount due to each, together with an accurate inventory of his or their property, rights, and credits, of every name, kind, and description, and the location and situation of each and every parcel and portion thereof, verified by oath, or, if conscientiously scrupulous of taking an oath, by solemn affirmation, apply to the proper court, as hereinafter mentioned, for the benefit of this act, and therein declare themselves to be unable to meet their debts and engagements, shall be deemed bankrupts within the purview of this act, and may be so declared accordingly by a decree of such court....

SEC. 3. All the property, and rights of property, of every name and nature, and whether real, personal, or mixed, of every bankrupt, except as is hereinafter provided, who shall, by a decree of the proper court, be declared to be a bankrupt, within this act, shall, by mere operation of the law, ipso facto, from the time of such decree, be deemed to be divested out of such bankrupt, without any other act, assignment, or other conveyance whatsoever; and the same shall be vested, by force of the same decree, in such assignee as from time to time shall be appointed by the proper court for this purpose.... *Provided, however,* that there shall be excepted from the operation of the provisions of this section the necessary household and kitchen furniture, and such other articles and necessaries of such bankrupt as the said assignee shall designate and set apart, having reference in the amount to the family, condition, and circumstances of the bankrupt, but altogether not to exceed in value, in any case, the sum of three hundred dollars; and, also, the wearing apparel of such bankrupt, and that of his wife and children; and the determination of the assignee in the matter shall, on exception taken, be subject to the final decision of said court.

SEC. 4. Every bankrupt, who shall bona fide surrender all his property, and rights of property, with the exception before mentioned, for the benefit of his creditors, and shall fully comply with and obey all the orders and direction which may from time to time be passed by the proper court, and shall otherwise conform to all the other requisitions of this act, shall (unless a majority in number and value of his creditors who have proved their debts, shall file their written dissent thereto) be entitled to a full discharge from all his debts, to be decreed and allowed by the court which has declared him a bankrupt, and a certificate thereof granted to him by such court accordingly, upon his petition filed for such purpose; ... and if any such bankrupt shall be guilty of any fraud or willful concealment of his property or rights of property, or shall have preferred any of his creditors contrary to the provision of this act, or shall willfully omit or refuse to comply with any orders or directions of such court, or to conform to any other requisites of this act, or shall, in the proceeding under this act, admit a false or fictitious debt against his estate, he shall not be entitled to any such discharge or certificate .... *Provided,* That no discharge of any bankrupt under this act shall release or discharge any person who may be liable for the same debt as a partner, joint contractor, endorser, surety, or otherwise, for or with the bankrupt. And such bankrupt shall at all times be subject to examination, orally, or upon written interrogatories in and before such court, or any commission appointed by the court therefor, on oath, or, if conscientiously scrupulous of taking an oath upon his solemn affirmation, in all matters relating to such bankruptcy and his acts and doings, and his property and rights of property, which, in the judgment of such court, are necessary and proper for the purposes of justice .... And if, upon a full hearing of the parties, it shall appear to the satisfaction of the court, or the jury shall find that the bankrupt has made a full disclosure and surrender of all his estate, as by this act required, and has in all things conformed to the directions thereof, the court shall make a decree of discharge, and grant a certificate, as provided in this act.

SEC. 5. All creditors coming in and proving their debts under such bankruptcy, in the manner hereinafter prescribed, the same being bona fide debts, shall be entitled to share in the bankrupt's property and effects, pro rata, without any priority or preference whatsoever, except only for debts due by such bankrupt to the United States, and for all debt due by him to persons who, by the laws of the United States, have a preference, in consequence of having paid moneys as his sureties, which shall be first paid out of the assets; and any person who shall have performed any labor as an operative in the service of any bankrupt shall be entitled to receive the full amount of the wages due to him for such labor, not exceeding twenty-five dollars....

SEC. 6. The district court in every district shall have jurisdiction in all matters and proceedings in bankruptcy arising under this act, and any other act which may hereafter be passed on the subject of bankruptcy; the said jurisdiction to be exercised summarily, in the nature of summary proceedings in equity, ... and the jurisdiction hereby conferred on the district court shall extend to all cases and controversies in bankruptcy arising between the bankrupt and any creditor or creditors who shall claim any debt or demand under the bankruptcy....

SEC. 7. All petitions by any bankrupt for the benefit of this act, and all petitions by a creditor against any bankrupt under this act, and all proceedings in the case to the close thereof, shall be had in the district court within and for the district in which the person supposed to be a bankrupt shall reside, or have his place of business at the time when such petition is filed, except where otherwise provided in this act....

SEC. 10. In order to ensure a speedy settlement and close of the proceedings in each case in bankruptcy, it shall be the duty of the court to order and direct a collection of the assets, and a reduction of the same to money, and a distribution thereof at as early periods as practicable, consistently with a due regard to the interests of the creditors, ... and all the proceedings in bankruptcy in each case shall, if practicable, be finally adjusted, settled, and brought to a close, by the court, within two years after the decree declaring the bankruptcy....

SEC. 12. If any person, who shall have been discharged under this act, shall afterward become bankrupt, he shall not again be entitled to a discharge under this act, unless his estate shall produce (after all charges) sufficient to pay every creditor seventy-five per cent on the amount of the debt which shall have been allowed to each creditor....

SEC. 14. Where two or more persons, who are partners in trade, become insolvent, an order may be made in the manner provided in this act, either on the petition of such partners, or any one of them, or on the petition of any creditor of the partners; upon which order all the joint stock and property of the company, and also all the separate estate of each of the partners, shall be taken, excepting such parts thereof as are herein exempted; and all the creditors of the company, and the separate creditors of each partner, shall be allowed to prove their respective debts; ... and the sum so appropriated to the separate estate of each partners shall be applied to the payment of his separate debts; and the certificate of discharge shall be granted or refused to each partner, as the same would or ought to be if the proceedings had been against him alone under this act; and in all other respects the proceedings against partners shall be conducted in the like manner as if they had been commenced and prosecuted against one person alone....

SEC. 17. This act shall take effect from and after the first day of February next.

that became effective on February 1, 1842. It was the first bankruptcy law in the United States that permitted a debtor to file a voluntary petition and thereby discharge all his debts by listing and then surrendering virtually all of his assets.[18] (Wearing apparel and necessary household articles of debtor's family not exceeding $300 in value were exempt.) A court-appointed trustee or "assignee" would then take title and liquidate these assets and pay the debtor's creditors according to a set of priorities specified in the act. Appropriately, debts due the United States and bankruptcy administration costs took priority over all other debts.

On April 14, 1842, two full months before the default judgment, Joseph and other Mormons hopeful of finding relief through this act met with Calvin A. Warren. Warren was a Quincy lawyer who had just successfully filed his own petition for bankruptcy and was becoming a leader in the bankruptcy business. Joseph's father had been jailed for debt in New York, so Joseph knew how oppressive debt could become. Still, he expressed some doubt about the new law: "The justice or injustice of such a principle in law, I leave for them who made it, the United States."[19]

Although it was difficult to disentangle Joseph's personal debt from debts incurred on the Church's behalf, when he added them up, his total obligations were just over $73,000.[20] Ultimately, he decided to avail himself of the relief promised by this federal law due to the mobbings and plunderings he had suffered (blamed in part on inaction by the very Congress that had enacted the new bankruptcy law), the necessity of contracting heavy debts for the benefit of his family and friends, the fact that bankruptcy petitions by his own debtors had prevented his collections from them, and the fact that he would otherwise face numerous writs, lawsuits, and probable destitution. Thus on April 18, Joseph rode to Carthage with his brother Hyrum, his clerk Willard Richards, and nine other hopeful petitioners to file with the clerk of the Hancock County Circuit Court on behalf of the Federal District Court in Springfield. The steamboat debt was the first one listed and, after Joseph's

---

18. Oaks and Bentley, "Joseph Smith and Legal Process," 177.

19. *History of the Church*, 4:594.

20. The bankruptcy petition itself has never been found, but see the complete schedule of Joseph's debts, apparently prepared for filing his petition in bankruptcy, in Fawn M. Brodie, *No Man Knows My History: The Life of Joseph Smith, the Mormon Prophet*, 2d ed. rev. (1945; New York: Alfred A. Knopf, 1971), 266.

death, it became the second largest debt in his estate.[21] Additionally, the petition listed assets of nearly twenty thousand dollars.[22]

In spite of the benefits afforded under the bankruptcy law, Joseph still felt obligated to pay other debts. For example, within a few weeks of filing for bankruptcy, Joseph wrote land developer Horace R. Hotchkiss, Joseph's largest creditor, to explain why he had been forced to this step but assured him of his continuing intention to pay the debt in full.[23] By listing the steamboat debt first on his application and assuring other creditors of his continued intent to repay, it appears that Joseph's primary purpose for filing bankruptcy was to relieve himself of the steamboat debt.

Just three weeks after Joseph applied for bankruptcy, the U.S. Treasury Department issued a circular officially discouraging U.S. Attorneys from opposing any bankruptcy applications, consistent with the act's intention of supplying debt relief. Although the Bankruptcy Act of 1841 was repealed in March 1843, the U.S. District Court Clerk for Illinois reported that no bankruptcy discharges had been refused by any court and that only eight of the 1,433 applications had been opposed in Illinois. The low figure was not unusual: nationally only 765 debtors were refused a discharge of their obligations for any reason, with only thirty refused due to fraud.[24] However, Joseph and Hyrum Smith were two of the eight being opposed in Illinois. Treasury Solicitor Charles B. Penrose authorized Justin Butterfield to "take the necessary steps" to oppose them.[25] On October 1, Butterfield filed formal objections seeking to discharge both Smith petitions in Springfield federal court. Handling these affairs for the United States government, Penrose and Robert E. Lee were determined that the steamboat debt must be paid.

---

21. The largest debt was owed to Horace R. Hotchkiss & Co. of New York, the real estate firm from which the Church and Joseph had purchased most of the land for Mormon settlement. Brodie, *No Man Knows My History,* 266. See also Oaks and Bentley, "Joseph Smith and Legal Process," 174, 179.

22. Oaks and Bentley, "Joseph Smith and Legal Process," 177–80. The other nine who filed for bankruptcy at the same time were not involved in the *Nauvoo* case: Samuel H. Smith, Jared Carter, Elias Higbee, John P. Greene, Henry Sherwood, Reynolds Cahoon, Vinson Knight, Arthur Morrison and George Morey. *The Wasp,* May 7, 1842, 3. According to various records, at least 26 Mormons were ultimately discharged in bankruptcy under the 1841 act. See Oaks and Bentley, "Joseph Smith and Legal Process," 180, n. 65.

23. *History of the Church,* 5:6–7, 51–52, 195–96, 382–83.

24. Oaks and Bentley, "Joseph Smith and Legal Process," 180, 189. In practice there were few protections for creditors and unlimited opportunities for fraud by debtors, leading to a hasty repeal of the law only one year after its effective date, on March 3, 1843.

25. Penrose, Letter to Justin Butterfield, August 12, 1842, Treasury Papers. See also Oaks and Bentley, "Joseph Smith and Legal Process," 180–82.

Opposition was largely based on a series of letters John C. Bennett had published in the Springfield, Illinois, *Sangamo Journal*. Bennett was a disaffected Mormon who had been expelled late in May 1842 from his positions as mayor of Nauvoo and counselor to Joseph Smith.[26] On June 11, Judge Pope had issued the default judgment against Joseph Smith and others for nonpayment of the steamboat debt, and that same month Bennett launched a wide range of accusations against Joseph Smith, which Butterfield cited in his letters to the Treasury Solicitor.[27] In this July 4, 1842, letter, Butterfield accused Joseph of hiding assets from his creditors and fraudulently conveying property by recording deeds after the law was passed.

Justin Butterfield. Courtesy Church History Library, The Church of Jesus Christ of Latter-day Saints.

Butterfield took Bennett's claims seriously, even going to Nauvoo and Carthage in September 1842 to examine land records. On October 11, he wrote to the Solicitor of Treasury that he had found enough conveyances to sustain Bennett's accusations of fraud and reported that he had successfully blocked Joseph's bankruptcy petition at the court hearing on October 1. However, Judge Nathaniel Pope ordered these cases to be set over for further hearings in Springfield on December 15.[28]

Butterfield's objections to discharge might have been overcome had Joseph obtained better legal counsel. The bankruptcy law provided that a deed would be "utterly void" if made "in contemplation of bankruptcy," or, "in contemplation of the passage of a bankrupt law" as that would constitute a

---

26. *History of the Church*, 5:12, 18–19; Roberts, *The Rise and Fall of Nauvoo*, 135–40. Bennett apparently was also involved in efforts to extradite Joseph Smith to Missouri to face charges involving the attempted assassination of ex-Governor Boggs (see *History of the Church*, 5:250–51; Stewart, *Joseph Smith: The Mormon Prophet*, 171).

27. John C. Bennett, Letter to the Editor, *Sangamo Journal*, July 9, 1842, 2, and July 15, 1842, 2; Justin Butterfield, Letter to Charles B. Penrose, Solicitor of the Treasury, August 2, 1842, Treasury Papers. See also Oaks and Bentley, "Joseph Smith and Legal Process," 180–85.

28. Justin Butterfield, Letter to Charles B. Penrose, Solicitor of the Treasury, October 11, 1842, Treasury Papers; Objections to discharge of Joseph Smith under Bankruptcy Act of 1841, October 1, 1842, LDS Church Library. See also Oaks and Bentley, "Joseph Smith and Legal Process," 182.

fraud. There is no evidence that Joseph Smith had understood or even heard of the Bankruptcy Act until attorney Calvin A. Warren explained it to him in Nauvoo on April 14, 1842. Thus, the government had the burden to prove that the debtor had contemplated bankruptcy when making the deed. The law also said that any conveyance made "more than two months before the petition is filed"[29] was presumed to be valid and legal.

The main deed in question was a huge transfer of 239 town lots in Nauvoo (about 300 acres), which Joseph as an individual made to himself as a trustee for the Church. That deed of transfer was signed and notarized on October 5, 1841, and thus valid on the date of its execution, long before the law's effective date of February 1, 1842, and well outside the two-month presumption period. However, the deed was not recorded in Carthage until April 18, the same day Joseph filed for bankruptcy. Bennett claimed that it was signed just before the filing, then fraudulently backdated just before it was filed. If this accusation were true, then the deed would have been "deemed utterly void."[30]

Neither Bennett nor Butterfield gave any evidence to support the charge of fictitious backdating. In fact, there is substantial contrary evidence. The October 5, 1841, deed on its face contains sworn statements signed in Nauvoo by two witnesses—Willard Richards and Ebenezer Robinson, an authorized notary and justice of the peace, respectively—proving that the deed was in fact signed on that date.[31] Indeed, perfectly valid deeds were often not officially recorded for long periods of time. That was particularly true because Nauvoo did not have a Registry of Deeds until March 10, 1842.[32] Moreover, during the six months between the signing of the deed and its recording in Carthage, there is no record that Joseph visited Carthage. Therefore, he would have had no opportunity to register the deed without making a special trip on horseback, and at least four of the months would have had notoriously unpleasant weather. Finally, October 5 was the logical date for the deed. It was the last day of LDS General Conference, at which the Quorum of the Twelve had agreed that Joseph should separate Church property from his

---

29. Bankruptcy Act of 1841, chap. 9, sec. 2, 5 Stat., p. 442.

30. Bankruptcy Act of 1841, chap. 9, sec. 2, 5 Stat., p. 442. See also Oaks and Bentley, "Joseph Smith and Legal Process," 176, 182–84.

31. The witnesses were Willard Richards and Ebenezer Robinson, an authorized notary and justice of the peace, respectively. In 1976 this deed was in box 4, fd. 7, LDS Church Library. See Oaks and Bentley, "Joseph Smith and Legal Process," 176.

32. Even after the Nauvoo registry was established on March 10, 1842, it was still the normal practice to record them in the county office in Carthage. Indeed, only two deeds were recorded in Nauvoo before Joseph's April 18, 1842, recording in Carthage. See Bentley, "Joseph Smith's Financial Disasters," 37–38.

own assets and convey to his own ownership enough Church property to support his family.[33]

Initially, Butterfield successfully opposed both Joseph and Hyrum's attempts to be discharged in bankruptcy, but the case was put over to December 15. Once again, Butterfield assured his superiors in Washington, D.C., that he would defeat Joseph Smith's application by causing the allegedly fraudulent conveyances to be set aside, then executing the expected judgment against Joseph's assets. On December 15, however, Butterfield permitted Hyrum to be discharged in bankruptcy and recommended approval of a proposal made by Joseph's representatives in Springfield to settle the entire debt to the United States on the following terms: The note would be paid off in four equal annual installments, secured by a mortgage on real property worth double the amount of the debt.

Why such a change of heart? By this time Butterfield had become Joseph's own lawyer. Soon after the October 1 hearings, Joseph Smith's attorney, Calvin A. Warren, and Joseph's counselor, Sidney Rigdon, engaged Butterfield to oppose Missouri's efforts to extradite Joseph back to that state for the Boggs shooting.[34] Butterfield then persuaded Thomas Ford, the newly elected governor who had just taken office on December 8, 1842, to countermand his predecessor's approval of the extradition and to support Joseph's position. On Butterfield's advice, Joseph allowed himself to be arrested in Nauvoo on December 26, 1842, and the case was successfully tried in Springfield on January 4–5, 1843, before the same Judge Pope in charge of Joseph's bankruptcy matter. In a highly notable habeas corpus decision, Judge Pope granted Joseph a complete release from the extradition order.[35]

To add to the foregoing ironies, Joseph paid Butterfield's fee of $500 with only $50 in cash and the rest with two notes, which Butterfield willingly accepted, thereby evidencing some respect for Joseph's financial integrity.[36]

When Butterfield inquired of Penrose whether the bankruptcy terms were acceptable, Penrose made a prompt counteroffer to Butterfield on January 11, 1842: Joseph must pay one-third of the debt in cash and the reminder in

---

33. *History of the Church*, 4:412–13, 427; Oaks and Bentley, "Joseph Smith and Legal Process," 184–85.

34. Obviously, conflict of interest rules (to the extent that they existed at all) were different then. A modern attorney would not have taken the extradition case, since that would have been contrary to the best interest of Butterfield's existing client, the United States.

35. Oaks and Bentley, "Joseph Smith and Legal Process," 187–88; *History of the Church*, 5:173–79.

36. *History of the Church*, 5:232.

Steamboat *Martha*. Detail of *Independence, the Start of the Santa Fe Trail*, 1842, by John Stobart, available at http://steamboattimes.com/artwork_1.html.

three equal annual installments, to be secured by the same property initially proposed to Butterfield.[37] It is unclear whether Butterfield ever received this letter, since he sent a second inquiry to the Treasury Solicitor on May 25, 1843.[38] There is no record of any further communication on this subject; and on June 27, 1844, Joseph and Hyrum were murdered at Carthage Jail.[39] For the moment it appeared that efforts to collect the steamboat debt or to conclude the bankruptcy matter had passed into history. But this was not to be the final conclusion.[40]

---

37. Charles B. Penrose, Solicitor of the Treasury, Letter to Justin Butterfield, January 11, 1843, Treasury Papers; see also Oaks and Bentley, "Joseph Smith and Legal Process," 188.

38. Justin Butterfield to Charles B. Penrose, Solicitor of the Treasury, May 25, 1843, in *Treasury Papers*; Oaks and Bentley, "Joseph Smith and Legal Process," 188.

39. For an account of the murder and subsequent trial of the accused assassins, see Dallin H. Oaks and Marvin S. Hill, *Carthage Conspiracy: The Trial of the Accused Assassins of Joseph Smith* (Urbana: University of Illinois Press, 1975). Joseph Smith and Justin Butterfield did have several cordial subsequent communications on other subjects. For example, on March 19 and April 2, 1843, Joseph exchanged letters with Butterfield concerning the incarceration of Orrin Porter Rockwell, who was held in a Missouri jail for allegedly shooting ex-Governor Boggs. *History of the Church*, 5:303, 308, 326. Butterfield also visited Nauvoo in October 1843, when Joseph spent considerable time "preparing some legal papers," then "riding and chatting" with Butterfield. *History of the Church*, 6:45–46. Joseph sent letters to Butterfield on other matters in January and May 1844. *History of the Church*, 6:179, 406.

40. On July 4, 1843, one year before Butterfield's stated intention to proceed against Joseph Smith's assets after defeating him in bankruptcy application, the federal circuit court with jurisdiction over the default judgment had sent a federal marshal out with another writ to pursue any assets of the served defendants. On December 18, 1843, the

The Lingering Effects of the Steamboat Debt

It was the same unpaid steamboat debt that wrecked Joseph's efforts to be discharged in bankruptcy in 1842 and ultimately encumbered his estate after his death. In July 1844 Joseph's widow, Emma Smith, was appointed to administer the estate under the jurisdiction of the state probate court. However, she was six months pregnant and soon failed to post the bond required by the court. On September 19, the court revoked her authority as the estate administrator and appointed a Mormon creditor of the estate, Joseph W. Coolidge, to replace her. During his four-year administration, Coolidge sold all available personal property, realizing approximately $1,000 to pay funeral expenses and the costs of estate administration. After Coolidge moved west with the Saints who followed Brigham Young, the court appointed John M. Ferris, another Mormon creditor, as administrator on August 8, 1848. Ferris was much more rigorous in his efforts to identify and prepare for sale the real property to pay more creditors.[41]

Before Ferris could sell off any land, however, the United States under Zachary Taylor's Whig administration took the final step that stifled payment to any other creditors. After conferring with Justin Butterfield (who was then serving in Washington, D.C., as U.S. Commissioner of the General Land Office), U.S. Attorney Archibald Williams in August 1850 filed a twenty-five page complaint, including a long creditor's bill, with the federal circuit court in Springfield to collect the steamboat debt, which by then amounted to $7,870, including costs and interest.[42] He invoked the court's unique powers to act in equity as a chancery court to sell all Illinois properties owned or transferred by Joseph prior to his death.[43] Before it was over, the massive suit named as defendants Emma and all heirs of Joseph Smith, plus more than a hundred others who had acquired land from Joseph. At issue were some 312 town lots and 29 tracts of land—well over 4,000 acres. The court

---

marshal returned the writ with this endorsement: "No property found of the defendants, subject to said execution." The steamboat debt remained unpaid for another nine years.

41. Oaks and Bentley, "Joseph Smith and Legal Process," 189–91.

42. Complete Record of the United States Circuit Court for the District of Illinois, vol. 4, no. 1603, pp. 486–506, June 18, 1841, through July 17, 1852, Federal Records Center, Chicago; hereafter cited as Chancery Records.

43. For more details about "chancery courts with powers of equity," see Bentley, "Joseph Smith's Financial Disasters" 42 and Henry C. Black, "Equity," in *Black's Law Dictionary*, 4th ed. (St. Paul, Minn.: West Publishing, 1951), 634. Here, for example, the remedy being sought was to revoke or set aside all conveyances deemed fraudulent. Since the U.S. Bankruptcy Act of 1841 had long since been repealed and a new bankruptcy law had not been enacted, there was no clear remedy or mechanism for doing that under general common law in America.

transcript is 211 pages in length, by far the longest legal document involving Joseph Smith. The sole basis for the suit was Joseph's alleged conveyances of this land, made in his individual capacity and as trustee for the Church, with intent "to hinder, delay and defraud his creditors"—the same charges first raised by John C. Bennett and Justin Butterfield in 1842.[44] Archibald Williams asked the court to set aside all such conveyances as void and to sell the property to pay off the steamboat debt.[45]

The judge in this case was Thomas Drummond, an experienced state court judge newly appointed to the federal bench, who went on to serve with distinction in that capacity for the next thirty years.[46] Significantly, his resolution of the case said nothing at all about fraud, even though it had been urged for many years. Instead, Drummond applied three legal theories to seize and sell real property that Joseph Smith had once owned. First, Drummond ruled that the June 11, 1842, default judgment that Nathaniel Pope had entered against Joseph Smith and others became a lien against all properties individually owned by Joseph at that time or at any time thereafter, taking precedence over all claims to property acquired from Joseph after that date. It also took precedence over the claims of any family members who inherited property upon Joseph's death. Second, he invoked an 1835 state law that prevented a church from owning more than ten acres.[47] (There is no evidence that Joseph or other Church leaders were ever aware of this limitation.) Third, as a result, all parcels Joseph had owned as sole trustee-in-trust for the Church that exceeded the ten-acre statutory limitation were legally deemed to be his own individual property and therefore subject to foreclosure of the judgment lien.

Following the practice common in such complex equity cases, the court appointed attorney Robert S. Blackwell as a special "master" to inspect properties listed in the complaints, to examine title records for such parcels, and to make recommendations to the court on questions of fact and law. The

---

44. Chancery Records, 492, 495–96, 499, 505, 620.

45. Chancery Records, 504–5. See also Oaks and Bentley, "Joseph Smith and Legal Process," 192–93.

46. The presiding judge, not clearly identified in the chancery records, was not Nathaniel Pope, who had died in January 1850. Rather, newly appointed Thomas Drummond was the judge. See Bentley, "Joseph Smith's Financial Disasters," 42.

47. Chancery Records, 620. Actually, the Illinois law under which Joseph Smith held Church lands as trustee restricted such holdings to no more than five acres. See An Act Concerning Religious Societies, February 6, 1835, Section 1, *[1835] Rev. Laws of Illinois*, 147–48. However, by the time of the chancery court decision, the statutory limitation had been raised to ten acres. Law of March 3, 1845, Chap. 34, section 1, *[1845] Rev. Stat. Ill.* 198. See Oaks and Bentley, "Joseph Smith and Legal Process," 194–95.

judgment lien theory upon which the court ultimately relied first appeared in Blackwell's initial report of December 31, 1850.[48] After receiving that report, the court appointed Charles B. Lawrence as special commissioner to conduct three foreclosure sales after the court approved each of the master's reports and specified the various lands to be sold.[49]

As a result, on April 18, 1851, Lawrence sold 98 lots and six tracts at the Nauvoo House for a total of $2,710.30.[50] At the Carthage Courthouse on November 8, a second sale disposed of 51 lots and 14 tracts for $7,277.75. And finally, on May 3, 1852, four more tracts "with improvements" were sold in Quincy at the Adams County Courthouse for $1,160.35, making a grand total of $11,148.35 in sales proceeds. Over 95 percent of these proceeds came from the sale of properties Joseph had held as trustee-in-trust for the Church.[51]

Who was most harmed by this series of foreclosures and sales? Ironically, it was the estate and successors of General James Adams, a prominent Mormon convert and close friend of Joseph Smith. He had conveyed 1,760 acres to Joseph Smith as trustee, even more ironically, in payment for Adams's half interest in another steamboat, the *Maid of Iowa*. During the public auction at the Carthage Courthouse on November 8, 1851, Adams's land sold for $4,800—representing 43 percent of the total gross sales proceeds.[52]

---

48. Chancery Records, 643, 651–53. Specifically, the court held: "That the said deceased [Joseph Smith] at the time of the renedition [*sic*] of said Judgement and for a long time thereafter was seized in fee of [meaning that he held] the following real estate upon which said Judgement at the time of the death of the said deceased was a lien."

49. Chancery Records, 637–48, 653–54.

50. Chancery Records, 669–74.

51. By the time of the settlement, the Church owned no more than a token amount of the property being sold. No action seems to have been taken against the Church, then based in Utah, to recover losses resulting from the poor title of the land sold by Church trustees prior to the Saint's departure in 1845. Perhaps either warranty deeds were not given, or the prospect of a lawsuit against a far-distant party was simply too burdensome, especially in light of the fact that most affected landowners were able to repurchase their lands for modest sums at the judicial sales. Oaks and Bentley, "Joseph Smith and Legal Process," 198. Incidentally, the United States government acquired land by bidding in part of the debt it was owed without having to put up any cash. As a result, the federal government's name appeared on the title to many Nauvoo properties, mystifying LDS researchers who were unaware of these historic auctions.

52. James Adams died in August 1843. Obituary notice, *Nauvoo Neighbor*, August 16, 1843, 3; *History of the Church*, 5:537. After Joseph's death, the successor Church trustees reconveyed to the executor of Adams's estate the entire 1,760 acres, either in recission of the original arrangement or as a repurchase of Adams's 50 percent ownership in the *Maid of Iowa*. Hancock County Deed Records, Book "N," p. 453; Oaks and Bentley, "Joseph Smith and Legal Process," 197–98.

But the ironies were not yet complete. A claim that would finally take legal priority over the judgment lien was the dower interest of Joseph's widow, Emma.[53] The judge awarded her one-sixth of all cash proceeds realized from the foreclosure sales. She and her second husband, Lewis C. Bidamon, apparently used the proceeds to buy back the Mansion House and other properties at the final foreclosure sale on May 3, 1852.[54] Next to the federal government, which received $7,870.23, the next largest amount ($1,809.41) went to Emma. The remaining $1,468.71 of the $11,148.35 in total proceeds went for legal and court expenses and other administrative costs.[55] The estate assets being exhausted, no other creditors received further payment.

Conclusion

Since his days in Palmyra, Joseph Smith had been persistently accused of being a fraud and a scoundrel. The massive *Nauvoo* debt collection case was just another opportunity for such charges to be leveled against him. Yet in this case, the fraud charge remained unproven. However, more was at stake than Joseph's reputation. Although buying the steamboat *Nauvoo* on credit was not the beginning of his financial woes and was not even his largest debt, it became a critical factor with effects that outlived Joseph himself. The *Nauvoo's* wreck in November 1840 ultimately capsized Joseph Smith's attempts to obtain a discharge in bankruptcy and led to the foreclosure of scores of Nauvoo town lots and outlying parcels previously owned by Joseph or the Church.

This article was originally published as Dallin H. Oaks and Joseph I. Bentley, "Joseph Smith and the Legal Process: In the Wake of the Steamboat Nauvoo," *Brigham Young University Law Review 2, no. 3 (1976): 735–82; in an abbreviated form under the same title in BYU Studies 19, no. 2 (1979): 1–31; and in a modified form as "In the Wake of the Steamboat* Nauvoo: *Prelude to Joseph Smith's Financial Disasters," Journal of Mormon History 35, no. 1 (2009): 23–49.*

---

53. A surviving wife was entitled to a statutory dower interest (one-third) in all real property held by her husband at death. Since a husband took and held real property subject to his wife's dower interest, the dower interest ranked ahead of any subsequent creditor's claim or lien. Oaks and Bentley, "Joseph Smith and Legal Process," 194–95.

54. Emma's dower interest here was an estate for life in one-third of all real estate; but in this case, the judge valued her interest for life as equivalent to an immediate one-sixth of all cash proceeds if Emma would relinquish her dower claim, which she did. Chancery Records, 654–55.

55. Oaks and Bentley, "Joseph Smith and Legal Process," 196–97.

Chapter Fifteen

Serving as Guardian under the Lawrence Estate, 1842–1844

Gordon A. Madsen

Edward Lawrence, a convert to The Church of Jesus Christ of Latter-day Saints from Canada, arrived in Illinois in the winter of 1839–40, the same winter that the Saints were expelled from Missouri. Traveling with him were his wife, Margaret, their six children, his brother John with his family, and others, most of whom, like Edward, had been introduced to the gospel by John Taylor and Almon W. Babbitt. Edward Lawrence bought a farm from William and Amelia Ayers in Lima, Adams County, Illinois, just south of its border with Hancock County.[1] Edward and Margaret had six children: Maria, sixteen; Sarah, thirteen; James, eleven; Nelson, nine; Henry, four; and Julia Ann, three. Margaret was pregnant with their seventh child when Edward died. His exact death date is not known, but he had made his will on November 5, 1839, and it was admitted to probate on December 23, 1839, confirming his death between those two dates. Daughter Margaret was born April 5, 1840.[2]

The primary importance of Edward Lawrence's estate lies in its relevance to the fiduciary integrity of Joseph Smith, who agreed to serve gratuitously as guardian of the Lawrence children. Joseph Smith's actions as guardian have been seen as negligent or even exploitive, based on an 1887 interview

---

1. William and Amelia Ayers to Edward Lawrence, Warranty Deed dated February 15, 1839, recorded July 31, 1839, Deed Book O, 95, Adams County Recorder's Office, Quincy, Illinois.

2. Edward Lawrence, Will, in Adams County Circuit Clerk's Record Archive, 1:44–46 (hereafter cited as Lawrence, Will). The probate file, while incomplete, contains nineteen documents, unpaginated, Adams County Circuit Clerk, Probate Records, box 28, certified copy in my possession (hereafter cited as Lawrence Probate Papers).

of William Law by Wylhelm Wymethal. Law was involved because he signed with Hyrum Smith as one of Joseph's sureties in connection with the administration of the guardianship. But until now, no one has researched the probate records in Adams County to examine this case and these allegations carefully. These recently discovered probate documents allow Joseph Smith's honorable and responsible involvement to be documented, step-by-step, through the legal progress of the estate and guardianship, compelling a significant reappraisal of the accuracy of the Law-Wyl reminiscence that impugns the honesty of Joseph and Emma Smith and others, while denying that Law committed any irresponsible act.[3]

Illinois Probate Law and Edward's Estate

Under the Illinois probate law then in force, when someone died leaving a will, that document was presented to a probate justice of the peace and "admitted" (proved by witnesses to be the genuine last will and testament of the deceased). These witnesses had seen the testator sign the will at the time it was being made and then appeared in court after his death to testify about it. The judge then ordered that letters of administration be issued to the executors named in the will, giving them authority to carry out its provisions.[4] If the deceased person left minor children, the court was required to appoint a guardian for them and whatever property they inherited until they came of legal age (twenty-one for sons and eighteen for daughters), whether or not the will named a guardian.

Edward's will appointed his wife, Margaret, his brother John, and his friend Winslow Farr as executors of his will.[5] An entry at the bottom of the will signed by Andrew Miller, the probate justice of the peace, admitted the will to probate; Joseph Orr and John H. Stockbarger, who had both signed the will as witnesses, testified in person that it was, in fact, Edward's will.[6] Missing from

---

3. I am deeply indebted to Stanley L. Tucker, attorney at law in Carthage, Illinois, who, in the early 1990s, shared with me his copy of the Lawrence guardianship file which he found in the Adams County probate records. Prior to that time, I had searched only the legal records of Hancock County, in which Nauvoo is located.

4. Today "Letters of Administration" relate to the estates of people who die *without* a will; their court-appointed agents are called administrators. The writ issued to executors who carry out the provisions covered by a will is called "Letters Testamentary." In nineteenth-century Illinois, "Letters of Administration" covered all estates, and the terms "executors" and "administrators" were used interchangeably.

5. Lawrence, Will, 45.

6. Lawrence, Will, 46.

the file are the order appointing the three executors and the letters of administration that Miller would have issued to them; but other documents in the file
make it clear that Margaret Lawrence, John Lawrence, and Winslow Farr were,
indeed, appointed on June 4, 1841, as executors and acted in that capacity.

Margaret's appointment has particular significance. Illinois probate law of
that time gave a widow two choices. Within six months after her husband's
death, she had to choose to take what her husband had given her in his will
or reject it and claim a dower interest in the estate. Illinois statutes defined
"dower" as one-third of the husband's personal property and one-third of his
real property for life, meaning that she could occupy, farm, or rent the property but could not mortgage or encumber it in any way that would extend
beyond her lifetime. There was no mandate that she physically occupy the
property, although most widows did. As a practical matter, one-third often
meant occupying the whole real estate unless it could conveniently be
divided ("partitioned," in legal parlance) so that the widow got the home, for
example, and the guardian could manage the remaining two-thirds. Under
Illinois law, after the widow's death, the deceased husband's children or other
heirs would inherit it.[7] If Margaret had claimed a dower, she would have
received her "distribution" (meaning, the one-third of Edward's personal and
real property) while the other two executors would have then turned over
the remaining two-thirds to the court-appointed guardian to manage. The
fact that Margaret served as a co-executor indicates that she chose to take the
inheritance that Edward had granted her in the will.

Executors typically had four principal legal duties: (1) to gather the property owned by the deceased, both real and personal (this duty existed regardless of whether there was a will or whether a will covered all of the property)
and have it appraised by two or more independent, court-appointed appraisers; they could not be heirs or relatives; (2) to notify all creditors of the
deceased (usually by publishing an announcement in a local newspaper) to
present their claims against the deceased by a stated deadline; (3) to pay the
deceased's debts and expenses of the last illness and funeral; and (4) to distribute the remaining estate to the heirs, unless the will provided otherwise.[8]
Edward's will did provide otherwise. He ordered that the estate remain intact
during Margaret's life. It was relatively common for a husband's will to make
other arrangements for the property if his widow remarried, but Edward's
will did not include such a provision.

---

7. *The Public and General Statute Laws of the State of Illinois, 1839* (Chicago: Stephen F.
Gale, 1839), "Wills," sec. 40, p. 696.

8. *The Public and General Statute Laws*, "Wills," secs. 95–125, pp. 710–17.

Edward willed to Margaret "the interest arising from one-third of all my Estate Both Real and personal During her natural lifetime and after the death of my Said wife I do order my said Executors to Divide the Remainder of the Said property and Estate that I have given to my wife as aforesaid Equally amongst all my legal Heirs then living."[9] Thus, by electing to take her bequest as stated in Edward's will, Margaret was entitled to the "interest" of one-third of the estate; this provision did not mean partitioning the estate into thirds with interest from that one-third paid to her, but rather one-third of the "interest" of the whole estate. Since comparatively few estates in rural Illinois were composed of income-producing assets, "interest" was statutorily defined as 6 percent of the total value of the estate, whether or not the estate was income-producing.[10] Thus, Margaret was entitled to an annual payment of 2 percent of the value of the estate until her death.

Edward's will had not named a guardian, and thus the court-appointed guardian of the minor children would serve until the youngest child died or came of age. At that point, the guardian and executors were expected to render an accounting to the court, make a final distribution, and close the estate.[11]

Inventory, Appraisal, and Notice to Creditors

The surviving records in the Lawrence Probate Papers enable us to trace the legal stages, step by step. The first was the inventory and appraisal of Lawrence's estate filed February 18, 1840.[12] It begins by listing livestock (one horse, three cows), a wagon, household furnishings and miscellaneous tools, and ends with twelve promissory notes or mortgages that were owed to Edward at the time of his death, most of them by individuals living in Canada. The total appraised value of the estate is listed as $2,793.76, with these notes and mortgages accounting for $2,615.34.[13]

The next item in the Lawrence Probate Papers is a newspaper clipping headed "Administrator's Notice":

---

9. Lawrence, Will, 44.

10. *The Public and General Statute Laws*, "Interest." sec. 1, p. 343.

11. *The Public and General Statute Laws*, "Interest." sec. 1, p. 343; "Wills," pp. 686–724; "Minors, Orphans and Guardians," pp. 465–69.

12. The court-appointed appraisers were T. G. Hoekersmith, Isaac Wilson, and John C. Wood.

13. Appraisal, February 18, 1840, Lawrence Probate Papers.

> The undersigned having taken out letters of administration on the estate of Edward Lawrence, deceased, late of Adams county Illinois, will attend before the Probate Justice of the Peace at his office in Quincy, in said county, on the first Monday of September 1840, for the purpose of settling and adjusting all claims against said estate. All persons indebted to said estate are requested to make immediate payment to the undersigned.

It was signed by Margaret Lawrence, Winslow Farr, and John Lawrence, as "Administrators of the estate of Edward Lawrence."

Attached to the notice are the certifications by the publishers of the *Quincy Whig* confirming that the notice had been published in the paper for four consecutive weeks, between July 18 and August 8, 1840.[14] Creditors could make their claims by early September, but debtors were asked to make payment immediately. By August, the executors had completed the first two steps of their responsibilities: identifying the heirs (including posthumous daughter Margaret), collecting and appraising the estate assets, and publishing the notice to creditors. A new development, however, frustrated moving to the third and fourth steps—Margaret's marriage to Josiah Butterfield on December 24, 1840.[15] Butterfield, a Mormon living at Bear Creek in Adams County, was a widower. His wife, Polly, had died on September 20, 1840, following an eighteen-month illness and leaving one known child, Josiah Jr., age unknown. The Butterfield-Lawrence marriage thus occurred three months after Polly's death and about a year after Edward's. This union had far-reaching implications for the Lawrence estate's ultimate disposition.

In January or early February 1841, co-executor John Lawrence, filed an undated and untitled petition with the court alleging that Edward's will stated: "And I do further request of my brother, John Lawrence, that he shall act as my agent or Attorney and I do by this, my last will and testament, constitute him, the said John Lawrence, my legal Attorney to collect all moneys due me in the province of Canada."

John contended that Margaret refused to give the notes to him. He also made a more serious accusation: that "Margaret had in her possession at the death of the said Edward money belonging to his estate which she has not accounted for and that she still has the same or has embezzled it." He requested that the court require Margaret and her new husband to appear

---

14. Administrator's Notice, clipping from the *Quincy Whig*, in Lawrence Probate Papers.

15. *Marriages of Adams County, Illinois*, vol. 1: *1825–1860*, 4 vols. (N.p.: Great River Genealogy Society, 1979–83), 1:17.

before Justice Miller and "answer under oath touching the money as afore-said in their or her possession."[16]

On February 11, Justice Andrew Miller held a hearing on this petition. Margaret and Josiah countered that executors are not obliged to answer to their co-executors for their conduct or be required to disclose under oath their conduct in the management of estate affairs. After hearing the evidence and attorneys' argument for both parties,[17] Justice Miller ordered that the Butterfields make such a disclosure under oath. The Butterfields' attorneys announced their intention to appeal.[18] Then, just a week later, on February 18, John Lawrence, Winslow Farr, and Josiah Butterfield filed an "Agreement to Dismiss Appeal," conditioned on the requirement that Margaret and Josiah deliver the promissory notes and the other personal property and money to the court.[19] Although a modern reader would wonder why Josiah, but not Margaret, signed this agreement, a nineteenth-century participant would not because "coverture," the idea that a married woman's civil identity converges with her husband, was then the law in Illinois and most of the other states of the Union.[20] Thus, Margaret could act in her own name as a widow (or, in legal terms, a "feme sole"); but upon remarriage, her identity had been subsumed into Josiah Butterfield's, and he became the new co-executor.

The following day, February 19, a supplemental inventory and appraisal of the assets that Margaret had earlier withheld were filed, adding $1,910.62½ to the value of the estate.[21] Five months later, a bill of sale dated July 7, 1840, totaling $154.56¼ was added to the file, followed nine months later on April 3, 1841, for $177.05. These two bills accounted for the sale of most of the personal

---

16. John Lawrence, untitled and undated petition, Lawrence Probate Papers.

17. Miller's order names "Backenstos and Warren" as the Butterfields' attorneys but does not identify John's attorney. "Backenstos" may well be Jacob B. Backenstos, who by May 1843 had become the clerk of the Circuit Court of Hancock County. There is no record that he ever practiced law in either Adams or Hancock County, however. The 1840 census lists "J. B. Backenstos" as living in Sangamon, Adams County, Illinois. Calvin A. Warren, a resident of Quincy, served as Joseph Smith's attorney in several matters during 1842–43. After the assassinations of Joseph and Hyrum Smith, he represented some of the accused murderers.

18. Order, February 11, 1841, Lawrence Probate Papers.

19. Agreement to Dismiss Appeal, Lawrence Probate Papers. The agreement was signed February 17 and filed February 18, 1841.

20. John Bouvier, *A Law Dictionary Adapted to the Constitution and Laws of the United States of America and of the Several States of the American Union*, 15th ed. (Philadelphia, J. B. Lippincott Company, 1888), s.v. "Coverture."

21. Supplemental Appraisal, February 19, 1841, Lawrence Probate Papers.

property listed in the two appraisals, as the Illinois statute required.[22] A second, undated summary then itemized those sales along with the estate's other assets, showing its final value as $4,155.26½.[23]

Guardianship

A separate responsibility of the court was to appoint a guardian for Edward's seven children, all of whom were under legal age when he died. Minor children whose father had died were classed as "orphans" even if their mother was alive; a father's will could name a guardian but the court would still have to confirm the appointment. When a decedent failed to designate a guardian under Illinois law, children who were age fourteen and older could nominate their own choice for guardian, and the court would appoint that guardian for them.[24] As a widow, Margaret could have been named as that guardian (assuming that the children over fourteen nominated her); but because of her remarriage, she had lost her separate legal identity, and Josiah would have become the children's guardian.

Two of the children were over fourteen: Maria (seventeen) and Sarah (fourteen). Rather than nominate their stepfather or their uncle, John Lawrence, the two girls nominated Joseph Smith as guardian for them and their siblings. Their reasons remain undocumented. Perhaps the friction between Uncle John and their mother made John an unappealing candidate. Josiah and his son had moved into the Lawrence home in Lima, and the adjustment difficulties in stepfamilies are notorious.

These speculations about John Lawrence's and Josiah Butterfield's unsuitability, however, do not explain why the girls chose Joseph Smith. No record seems to suggest any prior acquaintance with or association between any of the Lawrences and Joseph Smith. But Joseph accepted the nomination and was thus injected squarely into the family dynamic.

---

22. *The Public and General Statute Laws*, "Wills," sec. 91, pp. 709–10. "The executor or administrator shall, as soon as convenient, after making the inventory and appraisment, as hereinbefore directed, sell at public sale all the personal property, goods, and chattels of testator ... for the payment of the debts and charges against the estate."

23. Sale Bill #1, July 7, 1840; Sale Bill #2, April 3, 1841, revised summary of assets, n.d., Lawrence Probate Papers.

24. *The Public and General Statute Laws*, "Minors, Orphans and Guardians," sec. 1., p. 465: "The courts of probate, in their respective counties, shall admit orphans, minors, above the age of fourteen years, father being dead, to make choice of guardians, and appoint guardians for such as are under the age of fourteen years, in all cases where such minor shall be possessed of, or entitled to real or personal estate."

Four documents in the Lawrence Probate Papers, all dated June 4, 1841, spell out the next steps. Following the law, the guardian (Joseph) and his two sureties (Hyrum Smith and William Law) first signed a bond which guaranteed that they would "faithfully discharge the office and trust of such guardian" and spelled out their duties: rendering periodic accounts of the guardianship, complying with court orders, and paying to wards at the proper time "all moneys, goods, and chattels, title papers and effects."[25] The bond they posted was in the amount of $7,759.06, $95.98 more than twice the estate value.

Buttressing the bond, as the law required, Hyrum and William filed a supporting affidavit certifying that each of them had a net worth of "more than eight thousand dollars after all their just debts are paid." Next, Justice Miller made the formal appointment. The final piece of paperwork acknowledged delivery of the promissory notes and other estate assets to Smith, for which he signed a receipt at the document's foot.[26] The assets turned over to Joseph totaled $3,831.54.

What happened next is not completely clear. Often wards went with their property to the guardian's home, or the guardian (usually when there were no surviving parents) placed the minors in a foster home. No statutory or customary rules applied, and housing for the wards took a variety of forms almost as disparate as other marital and family connections. In the Lawrence family, as of June 1841, Maria (eighteen), Sarah (fifteen), James (thirteen), and Nelson (eleven) were all out of the Lima home. That fact is documented by a bill dated June 4, 1842, that Josiah Butterfield submitted to Joseph Smith as guardian for Butterfield's "supporting" the three youngest children (seven-year-old Henry, six-year-old Julia Ann, and two-year-old Margaret) for one year beginning June 4, 1841.[27] Had the older siblings remained at Lima, Butterfield would have also included their support in his bill. From the Church's 1842 Nauvoo census, it appears that Maria and Sarah had joined Joseph and Emma's household, although the date of their move to Nauvoo is not documented. James was living with Hyrum Smith. Nelson's

---

25. *The Public and General Statute Laws,* "Minors, Orphans and Guardians," sec. 1., pp. 465–66: "The courts of probate shall take, of each guardian appointed under this act, bond with good security, in a sum double the amount of the minor's estate, real and personal, conditioned as follows."

26. These four documents are the beginning papers in a separate Lawrence Guardianship file, box #28 of the Adams Circuit Court clerk's records (hereafter cited as Lawrence Guardianship file). Certified copy in my possession.

27. Josiah Butterfield to "Joseph Smith, Guardian," Bill for Support, June 4, 1842, Lawrence Probate Papers. This bill is filed with the probate papers rather than the guardianship papers.

whereabouts during this period are unknown, but he was somewhere in the Nauvoo vicinity.[28] It is also unknown whether the new housing arrangement was mutually agreed between the Butterfields, Lawrences, and Smiths, or whether lingering or new friction arose between those older children and their stepfather that prompted the move of all four. In all events, no complaint or motion was made in Judge Miller's court protesting or dissenting from this arrangement.

Managing the Estate and Joseph's Guardianship

Illinois law of the 1840s did not require a guardian to keep estate assets separate from his own property, as modern law requires. However, James Kent's influential *Commentaries on American Law* (1844 edition), notes:

> The guardian's trust is one of obligation and duty, and not of speculation and profit. He cannot reap any benefit from the use of the ward's money. He cannot act for his own benefit in any contract, or purchase, or sale, as to the subject of the trust. If he settles a debt upon beneficial terms, or purchases it at a discount, the advantage is to accrue entirely to the infant's benefit. He is liable to an action of account at common law, by the infant, after he comes of age; and the infant, while under age, may, by his next friend [a relative who is of legal age], call the guardian to account by a bill in chancery.... Every general guardian, whether testamentary or appointed, is bound to keep safely the real and personal estate of his ward, and to account for the personal estate, and the issues and profits of the real estate, and if he make or suffers any waste, sale, or destruction of the inheritance, he is liable to be removed, and to answer in treble damages.

Kent then discusses the general statutory prohibition against selling any of the ward's real property unless authorized by the court, and concludes:

> And if the guardian puts the ward's money in trade, the ward will be equally entitled to elect to take the profits of the trade, or the principal, with compound interest, to meet those profits when the guardian will not disclose them. So, if he neglects to put the ward's money at interest, but negligently, and for an unreasonable time, suffers it to lie idle, or mingles it with his own, the

---

28. Nauvoo Stake, Ward Census, 1842, microfilm of holograph, 49, LDS Church History Library.

court will charge him with simple interest, and in cases of gross delinquency, with compound interest. These principles . . . apply to trustees of every kind.[29]

In short, guardians were prohibited from profiting from the wards' estates and could be removed from guardianship and/or slapped with three-fold punitive damages if they did. They were also enjoined from leaving the estate idle or intermingling it with their own unproductive assets, a lack of action for which they would also be charged with simple or compound interest or the profits attributable to the estate assets. In other words, the sanctions against guardians' self-enrichment or idleness were removal and/or imposition of interest—simple, compound, or treble—depending on the severity of the misconduct or neglect. Those sums would be collected from the bonds posted by the guardians and their sureties at the times of their appointment to serve.

The law also gave guardians broad powers to expend the funds on behalf and for the benefit of their wards, including the expense of their education. Additionally, the same statute obliged guardians to render accounts "from time to time" to the probate court, for adjustment, if necessary. The court had the power to remove and replace a guardian or require him and his sureties to furnish a larger bond as additional security for the guardian's faithful performance.[30]

Without being ordered to do so, Joseph rendered an accounting to the court on June 3, 1843, which showed receipts, expenses, and status of the estate to that date. Figure 1 shows a list of expenses for June 1841 to June 1842. The first three items show efforts to collect the Canadian notes: the first item establishes that "W. & W. Law" collected a note for $705, for which they received a fee of $14.00 ("W. & W. Law" being William Law and his brother Wilson).

---

29. James Kent, *Commentaries on American Law*, 5th ed., 4 vols. (New York: James Kent, 1844), 2:228–31. See also Rowan v. Kirkpatrick, 14 Ill. 1 (1852), and Bond v. Lockwood, 33 Ill. 212 (1864). The Rowan case began in 1844. The Bond case quotes the Rowan decision with approval. Both cases adopt and apply the principles in *Kent's Commentaries*, which were, by Smith's time, widely used by judges and attorneys. *Kent's Commentaries* were the American equivalent and competitor to *Blackstone's Commentaries*. See also the cases summarized in Bouvier, *Law Dictionary*, s.v. "Guardian."

30. *The Public and General Statute Laws*, "Minors, Orphans and Guardians," sec. 7, p. 466. See also secs. 8–11, pp. 466–67. At no time during Smith's lifetime was any petition filed with Probate Justice Miller on behalf of the Lawrence children asking for Smith's removal or for an accounting or increase of the bond.

The second item is a note from a J. Campbell for $500.00 on which no interest could be collected for one year. Joseph therefore took an expense of $30.00. A corroborating receipt reads: "Rec'd. of Joseph Smith a note on J. Campbell of upper Canada for five hundred dollars payable next July, without interest, which when collected we promise to pay to said Joseph Smith or order Nauvoo Ill. Jan. 24th, 1842. W & W. Law."[31]

The third item is a $597.50 note also collected by the Laws. Another receipt likewise confirms that the Law brothers were assigned to collect this note: "Received of Wilson Law Four Hundred and fifty Dollars in part payment of monies collected by said Wilson Law in Canada for which I have claim on said Law. Joseph Smith."[32] This particular receipt apparently refers to item 3, since items 1 through 3 are the only debts in Figure 1 connected to "W & W Law," and would suggest that, of the original $597.50, $450.00 had been collected and paid to Joseph, leaving $147.50 still due. Those entries also indicate that Edward Lawrence's brother John did not act as collector in Canada after all. As discussed below, the remaining $147.50 of this debt was likely never collected in full. The document trail concerning the Canadian collections stops with this itemized list in Joseph Smith's accounting. However, as Figure 2 shows, Joseph increased the value of the estate annually at the statutorily required rate of 6 percent and paid Margaret Lawrence Butterfield her share as though he had possession and use of all the Lawrence assets.

The fourth item in figure 1 shows that Joseph paid a fee pursuant to an order of Judge Miller, and item 5 is the payment of Josiah Butterfield's bill. The next item documents Joseph's payment to Margaret of her annual statutory interest. The remaining entries are for items of clothing from Joseph's Nauvoo store for all of the Lawrence children except daughter Margaret, who was three in 1843. Because Nelson appears on this list, he was presumably living in or near Nauvoo.

Figure 2 further details Joseph's expenses in behalf of the Lawrence children, as well as his summary of the fluctuations in the estate for the previous two years (1841–43). The sum of $3,831.54 was the estate's value when Joseph Smith was appointed guardian. Those entries read:

---

31. W. & W. Law, Receipt, [n.d.], Joseph Smith Collection, LDS Church History Library. "Or order" was a standard legal term meaning that the note's owner—the named payee—could endorse it to a third party; in other words, if Joseph had endorsed this Law receipt to someone else, that third party could collect from Law pursuant to Joseph's "order."

32. Joseph Smith, Receipt to Wilson Law, April 11, 1844, Newel K. Whitney Collection, L. Tom Perry Special Collections, Harold B. Lee Library, Brigham Young University, Provo, Utah.

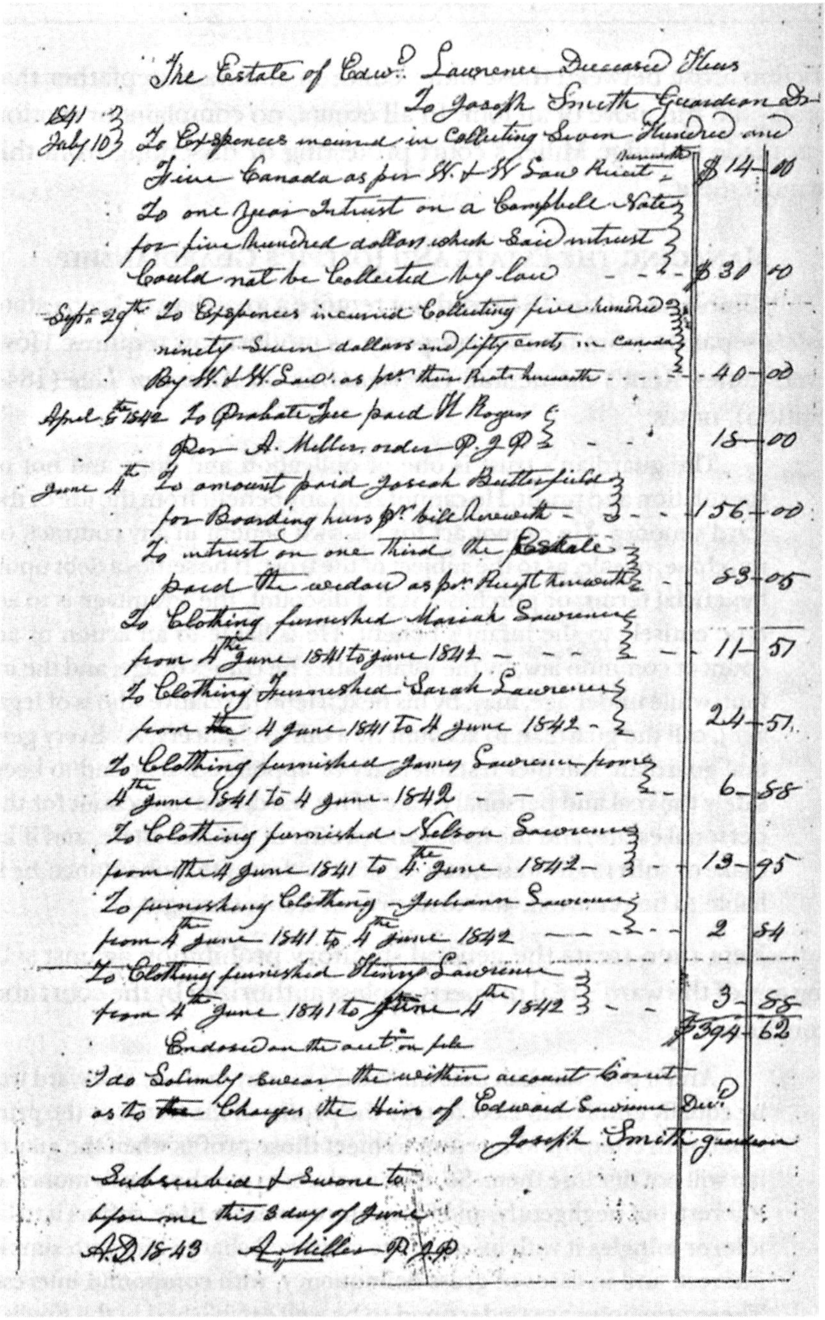

The Estate of Edwd Lawrence Deceased Heirs
To Joseph Smith Guardian Dr

1841
July 10 To Expences incurred in Collecting Seven Hundred and
Five Canada as per W. & W. Law Receipt — $14 00

To one year Intrust on a Campbell Note
for five hundred dollars which Said intrust
Could not be Collected by law — — $30 00

Sept 29th To Expences incurred Collecting five hundred
ninety Seven dollars and fifty cents in Canada
By W. & W. Law. as per their Receipt herewith — 40 00

April 5 1842 To Probate Fee paid W. Rogers
per A. Miller order P. J. P. — — 15 00

June 4 To amount paid Josiah Butterfield
for Boarding hers pr bill herewith — 156 00

To intrust on one third the Estate
paid the widow as per Receipt herewith — 83 05

To Clothing furnished Mariah Lawrence
from 4th June 1841 to June 1842 — — 11 57

To Clothing furnished Sarah Lawrence
from the 4 June 1841 to 4 June 1842 — 24 51

To Clothing furnished James Lawrence from
4th June 1841 to 4 June 1842 — — 6 58

To Clothing furnished Nelson Lawrence
from the 4 June 1841 to 4 June 1842 — 13 95

To furnishing Clothing Juliann Lawrence
from 4 June 1841 to 4 June 1842 — — 2 84

To Clothing furnished Henry Lawrence
from 4th June 1841 to June 4th 1842 — 3 58
$394 62

Endorsed on the auction file

I do Solemly Swear the within account Correct
as to the Charges the Heirs of Edward Lawrence Dcd
                                    Joseph Smith guardian

Subscribed & Sworn to
before me this 3 day of June
A.D. 1843   A. Miller P J P

Figure 1. On June 3, 1843, Joseph Smith voluntarily submitted an accounting of his 1841–42 guardianship, including attempts to collect the debts in Canada and payment to Josiah Butterfield for "boarding" his three young stepchildren.

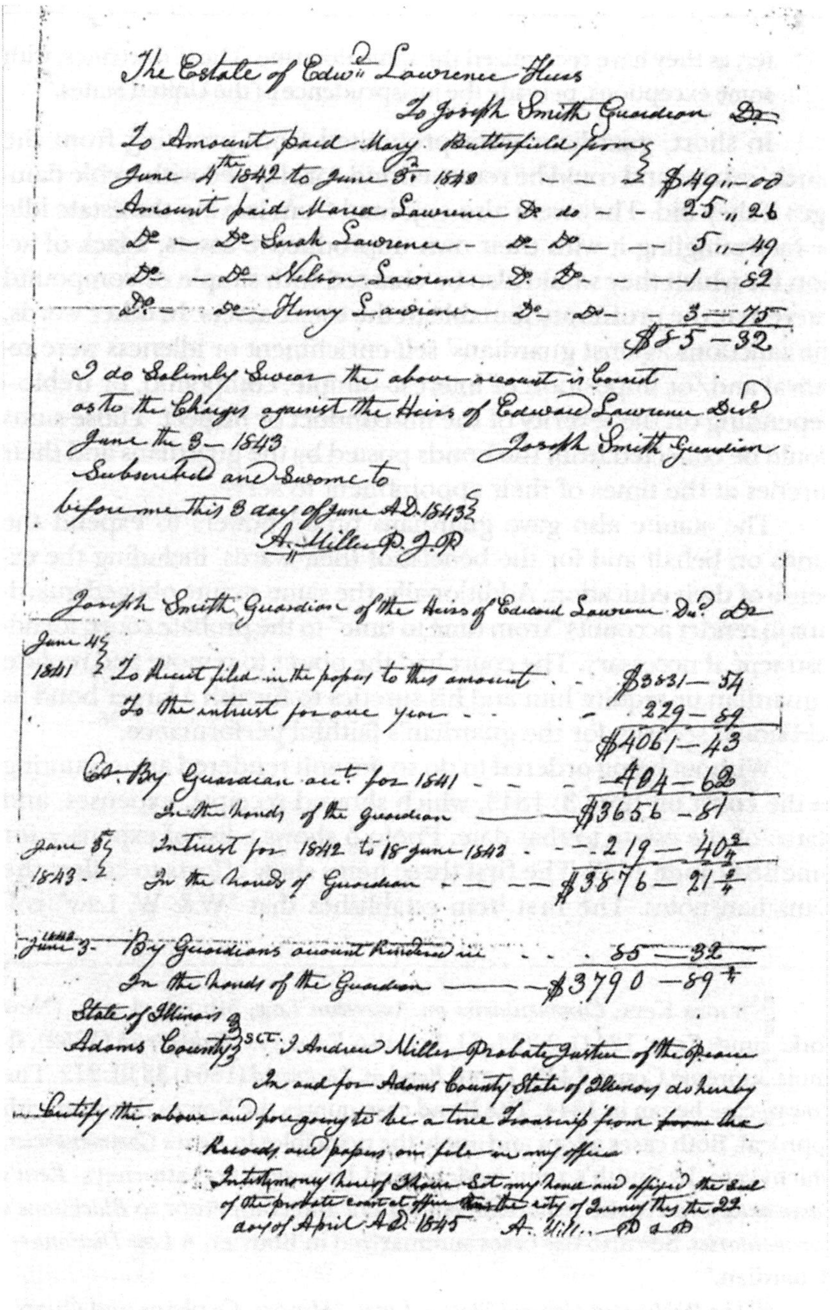

The Estate of Edwᵈ Lawrence Heirs

To Joseph Smith Guardian Dr

To Amount paid Mary Butterfield from
June 4ᵗʰ 1842 to June 3ᵈ 1843 — — $49..00
Amount paid Maria Lawrence Dr do — — 25„26
Do — Do Sarah Lawrence — Do Do — — 5„49
Do — Do Nelson Lawrence Dr Do — — 1„52
Do — Do Henry Lawrence Dr Do — 3—75
$85—32

I do Solemly Swear the above account is correct
as to the Charges against the Heirs of Edward Lawrence Dec'd
June the 3— 1843   Joseph Smith Guardian
Subscribed and Sworn to
before me this 3 day of June A.D. 1843
A. Miller P. J. P.

Joseph Smith Guardian of the Heirs of Edward Lawrence Dr. Dr
June 4ᵗʰ
1841 To Account filed in the papers to this amount — — $3831—54
To the interest for one year — — — 229—59
$4061—43
Cr. By Guardian acct for 1841 — — 404—62
In the hands of the guardian — $3656—81
June 5ᵗʰ Interest for 1842 to 18 June 1843 — — 219—40²⁄₄
1843   In the hands of Guardian — — $3876—21²⁄₄

June 3— By Guardians account Rendered in — — 85—32
In the hands of the Guardian — $3790—89⁴

State of Illinois
Adams County sct. I Andrew Miller Probate Justice of the Peace
In and for Adams County State of Illinois do hereby
Certify the above and foregoing to be a true Transcript from from the
Records and papers on file in my office
In testimony hereof I have Set my hand and affixed the Seal
of the probate court at office in the city of Quincy this the 22
day of April A.D. 1845   A. Miller P. J. P.

Figure 2. On this second page of Joseph Smith's accounting of his 1841–42 guardianship, submitted to the court on June 3, 1843, he enumerates the money paid to or
for the four older children (Maria, Sarah, Nelson, and Henry) and the payment to
Margaret Lawrence Butterfield.

1841	To Recei[p]t filed in the papers to this amount	$3,831.54
	To the interest for one year	229.89
		$4,061.43
	As by Guardian acct. for 1841	404.62[33]
	In the hands of the Guardian	$3,656.81
June 3.	Interest for 1842 to 18 June 1843	219.40¾
1843	In the hands of the Guardian	$3,876.21¾
1843		
June 3	By Guardians account herein in	85.32
	In the hands of the Guardian	$3,790.89¾

These numbers show how a guardian rendered an accounting to the probate court. The estate is enlarged by 6 percent (the legal rate of interest) at the beginning of each year ($229.89 is 6 percent of $3,831.54; $219.40¾ is 6 percent of $3,656.81). The expenses (the sums underlined) are deducted, and the net remaining value of the estate is then used to compute the chargeable interest or enlargement for the following year. Joseph charged himself 6 percent of the full, stated value of the estate, even though its assets (the Canadian notes, originally totaling $1,784) had not been fully collected and likely never were.

Unlike Josiah Butterfield, who billed the estate for boarding Edward's three youngest children, Joseph made no claim against the estate for boarding or supporting Sarah and Maria, nor did Hyrum for James, nor did whoever cared for Nelson. Furthermore, Joseph was entitled by statute to make a claim of 6 percent as compensation for acting as the children's guardian, but he never did.[34]

Among the estate's assets listed by the clerk on other documents pertaining to the Butterfield Estate was a "house in Lima & a Farm," valued at $1,000.

---

33. The $404.62 is $10.00 more than the $394.62 shown in figure 1 as the total expenses for the first year. Was an additional item of $10.00 added to the total? Or was it an error of arithmetic?

34. *The Public and General Statute Laws*, "Wills," sec. 121, p. 718: "Executors and administrators shall be allowed, as a compensation for their trouble, a sum not exceeding six per centum on the whole amount of personal estate, … with such additional allowances for costs and charges in collecting and defending the claims of the estate, and disposing of the same as shall be reasonable." "Minors, Orphans, and Guardians" sec. 14, p. 467 in the same source spells out: "Guardians on final settlement, shall be allowed such fees and compensation for their services as shall seem reasonable and just to the judge of probate, not exceeding what are, or shall be allowed to administrators."

On April 1, 1842, Joseph sold the farm, but not the home, to William Marks for $1,150, a profit to the estate.[35] The deed was signed and acknowledged on April 1, 1842, but was not filed with the county recorder until October 17, 1853—eleven years later. The reconstituted Butterfield household lived in the home until sometime in 1842, when they moved to Nauvoo. There is no record that Joseph sold, rented, or otherwise disposed of the Lima home.

Also a major asset of the Lawrence Estate was the *Times and Seasons*, the Church's official newspaper. At first it was a monthly periodical published by Don Carlos Smith (Joseph's youngest brother) and Ebenezer Robinson (both of whom had learned the printing business under Oliver Cowdery in the Church's printing office at Kirtland). Don Carlos died August 7, 1841, and Robinson continued printing until February 4, 1842, producing also the Nauvoo edition of the Book of Mormon.[36] Then Willard Richards, acting as Joseph's agent, contracted to purchase the printing establishment from Robinson for $6,600. John Taylor and Wilford Woodruff were appointed the new editors, under Joseph's supervision; and over the ensuing months, or perhaps years, Smith paid Robinson in full.[37] While the paper trail is incomplete, Smith invested whatever Lawrence estate funds he ultimately obtained, together with some of his own capital, to finally pay the $6,600.00. He treated the printing operation as an asset of the Lawrence estate. By December 1842, Smith signed a formal five-year lease with Taylor and Woodruff for the printing establishment, including the building in which it was housed.[38] Since the estate's value was $3,790 in June 1843, the difference of $2,810 to make up the $6,600 purchase price of the print shop came from Joseph's personal assets.

Preparing the Proposed Final Accounting

On January 23, 1844, Joseph's principal financial clerk, William Clayton, noted in his journal: "Joseph sent for me to assist in settling with Brother [John] Taylor about the Lawrence Estate." Clayton worked that day on posting

---

35. Book 17 of Deeds, p. 77, Adams County Recorder's Office.

36. Kyle R. Walker, "'As Fire Shut Up in My Bones': Ebenezer Robinson, Don Carlos Smith, and the 1840 Edition of the Book of Mormon," *Journal of Mormon History* 36, no. 1 (Winter 2010): 1–40.

37. Ebenezer Robinson, "Items of Personal History of the Editor," *The Return* 2 (October 1890): 346. The printing establishment consisted of two presses with type, a stereotype foundry, a bindery, and stereotype plates of the Book of Mormon and Doctrine and Covenants, plus incidental equipment and supplies, all of which were itemized in the lease.

38. Lease, December 1, 1842, Joseph Smith Collection.

books and preparing accounts for its settlement.[39] If Clayton finished this summary and accounting, they have not survived. The source that Joseph used for his 1842–43 accountings to the court were "Joseph Smith's Daybook B" and "Joseph Smith's Daybook C"—the running ledgers Clayton and others used to record transactions in Joseph's Red Brick Store in Nauvoo.[40] Presumably, Clayton also used them for his accounting on the Lawrence estate. They cover from the beginning of Joseph's guardianship on June 4, 1841, through January 15, 1844, apparently the last entry Clayton posted. They corroborate the accountings Joseph rendered to the court for the years ending in June 1842 and June 1843, enumerate clothing or other goods that the Butterfields and Lawrence children received from Joseph's store, and include cash payments directly to them, payments of travel expenses, tavern bills, charges from "Yearsleys Store" for Mrs. Butterfield or the Lawrence sisters, and tuition to "Luce's school" for the children.

As noted above, Joseph's accounting for 1842–43 shows an "interest" payment to Margaret Butterfield of $49. The spreadsheets show additional payments amounting to $26.81 dated two days later on June 6, 1843, two days after the 1843 accounting. The 1843 accounting to the court also fails to show a payment to Butterfield for boarding his three youngest step-children, but the later spreadsheet entries show his payments. As of January 1844, Joseph owed Margaret and Josiah Butterfield $272.81 from the estate; but the daybooks show that he actually paid them $319.39—an overpayment of $46.58. The daybooks further show that, between June 1843 and January 1844, Joseph made additional payments, either for or directly to the three younger Lawrence children, of $111.01. For the whole period from June 1841 through January 1844, payments to or for Maria Lawrence totaled $89.78 and those for Sarah amounted to $93.31.

Transferring the Guardianship

After the Apostles returned from their mission to Great Britain in June and July 1841, Joseph Smith transferred many of his Church and business

---

39. George D. Smith, ed., *An Intimate Chronicle: The Journals of William Clayton* (Salt Lake City: Signature Books, 1991), 124–25.

40. "Joseph Smith's Daybook B" and "Joseph Smith's Daybook C," Masonic Lodge Library, Cedar Springs, Iowa. In the 1960s, James L. Kimball received permission to copy all of the entries in both volumes. From them, he extracted all the entries related to the Lawrence estate, Margaret and Josiah Butterfield, and the Lawrence children, and graciously shared them with me. In July 2003, I visited this library and verified all the Lawrence items.

responsibilities to them.[41] By January 23, 1844, as Clayton noted in his journal, Smith began arranging to transfer the Lawrence guardianship to John Taylor, perhaps because Taylor had been associated with the Lawrence family's conversion. Figure 3, the agreement prepared to facilitate that transfer, specified that Taylor,

> for the considerations hereinafter mentioned doth hereby bind himself to assume the Guardianship of the Estate of Edward Lawrence deceased and to free the said Joseph Smith from all liabilities and responsibilities for the same.... And further to obtain and give over to [meaning "take over from"] the said Joseph Smith all obligations, receipts & liabilities now laying [sic] in the hands of the Judge of Probate.[42]

The "considerations" mentioned in this agreement were the printing office, lot, equipment, and supplies, which Joseph had had William W. Phelps, Newel K. Whitney, and Willard Richards appraise on January 23–24. Smith was disappointed at their low evaluation $2,832.[43] Smith had paid Robinson more than double that amount over the previous years and had considered the printing business to be well in excess of the Lawrence estate's value, which by January 1844 amounted to $3,360.49¾.[44] However, neither Smith nor Taylor signed this agreement; and Taylor, though he took some steps to implement it, was overtaken by the rapidly developing events that resulted in Joseph Smith's death six months later.

---

41. Ronald K. Esplin, "Joseph, Brigham, and the Twelve: A Succession of Continuity," *BYU Studies* 21, no. 3 (Summer 1981): 301–41.

42. Agreement, January 24, 1844, in Trustee in Trust Miscellaneous Financial Papers, Joseph Smith Collection. "Trustee in Trust," was the term frequently used to designate "a person in whom some estate, interest, or power in or affecting property of any description is vested [held] for the benefit of another." Bouvier, *Law Dictionary*, "Trustee." It was the statutorily designated title in Illinois to be used by agents or officers of churches who held title or possession of said church's property. Hence, Joseph was listed on Church property as "Trustee in Trust."

43. According to Joseph Smith, Journal, January 23, 1844, LDS Church History Library: "W. W. Phelps, N. K. Whitney and W. Richards prized the printing office & Lot at $1,500— printing apparatus. $950. Binde[r]y, $112. founde[r]y, $270. Total, $2,832." and January 24, "Called at my office about 1 oclock thought the appr[a]isal of the printing office was too low."

44. That figure is the June 1843 accounting total ($3,790.89) minus the daybook expenses paid between June 1843 and January 1844 ($319.39 and $111.01 paid to or for the children). The total presumes that all of the Canadian notes had been collected, which was probably not the case.

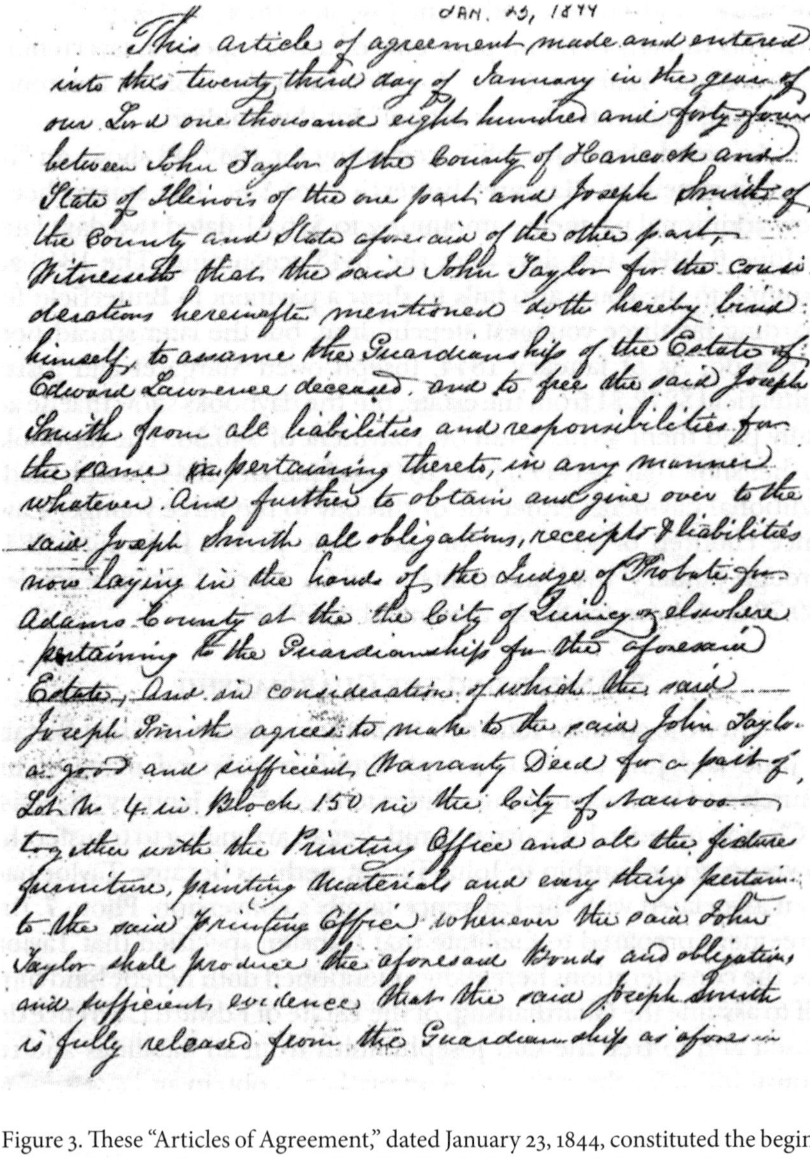

JAN. 23, 1844

This article of agreement made and entered into this twenty third day of January in the year of our Lord one thousand eight hundred and forty four between John Taylor of the County of Hancock and State of Illinois of the one part and Joseph Smith of the County and State aforesaid of the other part, Witnesseth that the said John Taylor for the considerations hereinafter mentioned doth hereby bind himself, to assume the Guardianship of the Estate of Edward Lawrence deceased, and to free the said Joseph Smith from all liabilities and responsibilities for the same pertaining thereto, in any manner whatever. And further to obtain and give over to the said Joseph Smith all obligations, receipts & liabilities now laying in the hands of the Judge of Probate for Adams County at the the City of Quincy or elsewhere pertaining to the Guardianship for the aforesaid Estate, And in consideration of which the said Joseph Smith agrees to make to the said John Taylor a good and sufficient Warranty Deed for a part of, Lot N. 4 in Block 150 in the City of Nauvoo together with the Printing Office and all the fixture furniture, printing Materials and every thing pertaining to the said Printing Office whenever the said John Taylor shall produce the aforesaid Bonds and obligations and sufficient evidence that the said Joseph Smith is fully released from the Guardianship as aforesaid

Figure 3. These "Articles of Agreement," dated January 23, 1844, constituted the beginning steps in transferring the guardianship for the Lawrence children and estate from Joseph Smith to John Taylor, who was purchasing the *Times and Seasons* printing office. The document remained unsigned because the intermediate steps were not taken before Joseph's death in June 1844.

For Taylor to be appointed guardian was a multi-step process that would have required Taylor, plus two new sureties, each of whose net worth was more than $6,720 (twice the $3,360 value of the estate), and probably Joseph Smith as well, to appear in Quincy before Justice Miller to sign the necessary papers. Joseph would have needed, at the same time, to give John a warranty deed for the lot and a transfer document for the printing equipment and supplies. Perhaps the final decision to transfer the guardianship was not made until June 4; but three weeks later, Joseph was dead.

The transfer of the printing operation had its own legal complexities. The firm of Taylor and Woodruff was a partnership publishing the semi-monthly *Times and Seasons* and the weekly *Nauvoo Neighbor*.[45] On March 27, 1844, they dissolved the partnership, and Taylor assumed the lease, previously held jointly, of the printing plant and building.[46] Witnessing this document were Elias Smith, Maria Lawrence, and Sarah Lawrence. It seems reasonable, therefore, that Maria and Sarah understood that the printing enterprise assets constituted the main asset of the estate, as validated by their acting as witnesses. Maria was twenty, and Sarah would turn eighteen two months later.

Litigation

On April 11, 1844, as noted above, Joseph Smith acknowledged receiving $450 as part payment of the money that the Law brothers had collected in Canada and "had claim" for the balance, which the brothers acknowledged. But they refused to pay. On May 2 when Joseph "sent William Clayton to Wilson Law to find out why he refused paying his note, he [Law] brought in some claims as a set-off which Clayton knew were paid, leaving me no remedy but the glorious uncertainty of the law."[47]

---

45. Peter Crawley, *A Descriptive Bibliography of the Mormon Church: Vol. 1, 1830–1847* (Provo, Ut.: BYU Religious Studies Center, 1998), 1:92–94, 218–19.

46. John Taylor, Untitled notice, Nauvoo, March 27, 1844, John Taylor Papers, LDS Church History Library.

47. Joseph Smith Jr., *History of The Church of Jesus Christ of Latter-day Saints,* ed. B. H. Roberts, 2d ed. rev., 7 vols. (Salt Lake City: Deseret Book, 1971), 6:350. None of the quotation appears in Joseph's Nauvoo Journal. However, Clayton wrote on May 2, 1844: President Joseph "desired me to go to [the] Mr. Laws to find out why they refused to pay their note. I went with Moore and asked Wilson what he meant by saying he had got accounts to balance the note. He seemed to tremble with anger & replied that he had demands for his services when he was ordered to call out the Legion to go meet Smith besides money that he had expended at that time. I told him that was a new idea & that Genl Smith had had no intimation of any such thing. Wm Law came in and mentioned $400 which was

Events unfurled rapidly from that point on. Disaffected over both plural marriage and what the Law brothers saw as Joseph's domination, they broke openly with the Church and were excommunicated on April 18, 1844. On May 24, a grand jury in Carthage issued an indictment against Joseph Smith for "Perjury and Adultery" based on testimony by William Law, Robert D. Foster, and Joseph H. Jackson.[48] The indictment named Maria Lawrence as co-respondent (partner) in the adultery charge.[49] Having been forewarned of the coming indictment, Smith, on May 27, rode to Carthage "thinking it best to meet my enemies before the court and have my Indictments investigated." His attorneys, William Richardson, Onias Skinner, and Almon W. Babbitt, pressed the court for an immediate hearing; but the prosecution, claiming that a necessary witness was unavailable, moved the court to grant a continuance to the next term of court. Smith's journal continues, "I was left to give bail to the Shirif at his option & he told me I might go home and he would call and take bail some time."[50] Such a procedure was perfectly acceptable in the nineteenth century, since courts convened only quarterly. An individual who was arrested gave bail to appear at the next term of court and went to jail only if and when he failed to appear and was rearrested.

The consequences of such an indictment were both legally and socially scandalous. Maria Lawrence's reputation would have been publicly damaged, independent of what the reputational consequences might have been to Joseph. She and her sister had been sealed to Joseph on May 11, 1843, nearly two years after the guardianship was created, with Emma's initial consent but later repudiation.[51] Even if this celestial marriage could have been made

---

borrowed of Baily $300 of which I am satisfied was paid, and the other $100 Wm Law said he would pay and give it to help defray the expense of the persecution but he now demands the $100 and some more of the $300." Quoted in James B. Allen, *No Toil nor Labor Fear: The Story of William Clayton* (Provo, Ut.: Brigham Young University Press, 2002), 410–11.

48. See chapter 16 below.

49. People v. Joseph Smith, May 24, 1844, Circuit Court Record, Hancock County, Book D, 128–29.

50. Joseph Smith, Journal, May 27, 1844.

51. Lyndon W. Cook, *Nauvoo Marriages [and] Proxy Sealings, 1843–46* (Provo, Ut.: Grandin Book, 2004), 46–47; Linda King Newell and Valeen Tippets Avery, *Mormon Enigma: Emma Hale Smith,* 2d ed. (Champaign, Ill.: University of Illinois Press, 1994), 143–46; Todd M. Compton, *In Sacred Loneliness: The Plural Wives of Joseph Smith* (Salt Lake City: Signature Books, 1997), 474–80. For plural marriage more generally, see Danel Bachman and Ronald K. Esplin, "Plural Marriage," *Encyclopedia of Mormonism,* 4 vols. (New York: Macmillan Publishing, 1992), 3:1091.

known, it would not have alleviated the scandal—it would have just turned it in another, even more flamboyant, direction.

On the day following Joseph's appearance in Carthage, May 28, 1844, William Law petitioned Probate Justice Miller stating "that he has reason to believe and does believe that the said Joseph Smith who has possession of property to a large amount belonging to said heirs, is in danger of becoming utterly insolvent, if he is not already so." The heirs were in obvious financial jeopardy if this were the case. Law added that in fact "Hiram Smith the co-surety ... has ... been declared a bankrupt under the general bankrupt Law of the United States." He asked Miller to "require from said guardian supplementary security."[52] Although Law did not say so, he was obviously trying to be released from his own liability on the guardian's bond. However, Joseph Smith's death interrupted any action Miller may have taken in response to Law's petition.

On June 4, Joseph met with John Taylor, Almon Babbitt, Hyrum Smith, Willard Richards, Lucian Woodworth, and William W. Phelps and decided to file a counter-suit charging the Laws, Joseph H. Jackson, and two of their associates, Charles A. and Robert D. Foster, with "perjury, slander, etc." The group "counseled Taylor to go in with a prosecution in behalf of—Maria," which he could do once he was confirmed as her guardian. As a necessary accompaniment, Joseph also "Concluded to go to Quincy with—Taylor & give up my Bonds of guardianship etc."[53] That earlier counsel meant that Joseph, after being replaced by Taylor as guardian, could in his own name solely pursue the Laws, Fosters, and Jackson and that Taylor could join in the prosecution as Maria's guardian.[54]

This plan to counter-sue against the Laws and others has some interesting legal aspects. William Law had supplied testimony under oath that led to Joseph's indictment. If the adultery case had gone to trial and the jury had found Joseph not guilty, then Law would have been liable to a criminal charge of perjury and civil liability for slander. Possibly Joseph planned to prove his innocence, not only by his and Maria's denial of sexual intercourse but also by the testimony of a reputable physician who had conducted a physical examination and found that Maria was still a virgin. It would have

52. William Law, Petition to Probate Justice Andrew Miller, May 28, 1844, holograph, Lawrence Guardianship file. "William Law Petition" is written on the wrapper of this letter, but there is no notation of the date on which it was received and filed.

53. Joseph Smith, Journal, June 4, 1844.

54. Even though Maria was then of legal age, the guardianship had not been dissolved because the estate, as required by the will, had to remain intact as long as Margaret lived, so that she could receive her "interest."

been both foolhardy and fruitless for Joseph to have even imagined counter-suing without something of such weight to present at trial. The fact that Maria had lived in the Smith household for a period of time was not of much consequence, since guardians customarily housed their wards under their own roof.

No documents after this date refer to transferring the guardianship to Taylor, probably because the Laws, Fosters, and other dissidents published the first (and only) issue of the *Nauvoo Expositor* on June 7, igniting a firestorm, whose destructive path led directly to the arrest and subsequent deaths of Joseph and Hyrum Smith on June 27.

Post-Martyrdom Events

After the martyrdom of Joseph Smith, John Taylor continued to print the *Times and Seasons*, the *Nauvoo Neighbor*, and other publications until the Mormon exodus from Nauvoo beginning in February 1846. What arrangements he made, if any, with the Butterfields, Maria and Sarah Lawrence, and the younger Lawrence children were not recorded by any of the parties.

Meanwhile, Emma Smith appeared in the Hancock County Probate Court on July 17, 1844, where she was appointed administratrix of Joseph's estate and guardian of her four children, all of whom were minors, ranging from thirteen-year-old Julia to six-year-old Alexander.[55] When some creditors of the estate petitioned the court to raise the limit of her bond as administratrix, she elected to surrender her letters of administration and was succeeded by Joseph W. Coolidge, a neighbor, friend, and a creditor of the estate, on September 19, 1844. Emma continued as the children's guardian.[56]

Emma spent August 30 and September 1, 1844, in Quincy with William Clayton, to settle "the Lawrence business." Justice Miller informed them that a new guardian for the Lawrence children would need to be appointed before making a settlement.[57] At that point, Emma was seven months pregnant.

On September 5, Margaret Lawrence Butterfield, and her two sons, James and Nelson, who were by then over age fourteen, petitioned the Hancock County Probate Court to appoint Almon W. Babbitt as guardian of the five

---

55. Entry, Probate Record, Hancock County, vol. A, 341, microfilm, LDS Family History Library. David Hyrum was born later on November 17, 1844.

56. Entry, Probate Record, Hancock County, vol. A, 356.

57. James B. Allen, *Trials of Discipleship: The Story of William Clayton, a Mormon* (Urbana: University of Illinois Press, 1987), 185 n. 10; also in James B. Allen, *No Toil nor Labor Fear*, 182 n. 11.

minor Lawrence children.[58] (Maria and Sarah had reached their majority.) Babbitt was appointed with a bond set at $5,000; he had four sureties.[59]

Eight months later on May 6, 1845, two events happened that had an impact on the Smiths, Lawrences, and Butterfields. Almon Babbitt submitted a claim to Coolidge of $4,033.87 against Joseph Smith's estate on behalf of the Lawrence heirs. Coolidge approved the claim.[60] On the same day, Mary Fielding Smith petitioned the probate court to be appointed guardian of John, Jerusha, and Sarah, Hyrum's children by his first wife, Jerusha Barden Smith (Jerusha's eldest daughter, Lovina, was married), and her own children, Joseph Fielding and Martha Ann. Her bond was set at $3,000, and her sureties were Robert Pierce and Almon W. Babbitt.[61] By today's standards, at least some of Babbitt's simultaneous functions would be strictly forbidden as conflicts of interest, but it was not an issue in the mid-nineteenth century, in part, perhaps, because his actions were transparently disclosed to the courts.

Four months later, on September 1, Babbitt, acting as guardian for the Lawrence minors, filed a lawsuit against Joseph Smith's estate, Hyrum Smith's estate, and William Law. His goal was to recover whatever assets he could from Joseph's estate, then obtain the remainder from Hyrum's estate and from Law, based on Hyrum's and Law's bond as sureties for Joseph as guardian. Seven weeks later on October 23, Babbitt withdrew the claim ("plaintiff takes a non-suit").[62] Then in January 1846, Babbitt filed a new action against the two estates, adding Maria and Sarah Lawrence as co-plaintiffs with

---

58. Almon Whiting Babbitt had a Church career filled with reverses. Germane to this paper is his mission to Canada in 1837–38 during which he, with John Taylor, was instrumental in converting the Lawrence family. He became an attorney and represented Joseph Smith and the Church before the martyrdom, and the Church and its leaders, including John Taylor, after the martyrdom. Following the Smith murders, he was appointed a trustee with Joseph L. Heywood and John S. Fullmer to dispose of the assets of the Church and of individual Mormons in Illinois as they emigrated west. Andrew Jenson, *LDS Biographical Encyclopedia*, 4 vols. (Salt Lake City: Andrew Jenson History Company, 1901–36), 1:284–86; Wilson Law v. John Taylor, Circuit Court Record, Hancock County, Book D, 178, 228 (May 1845). As noted above, Josiah and Margaret Butterfield and Margaret's three younger children—Henry, Julia Ann, and Margaret—had moved from Adams County to Nauvoo sometime in 1842. Hence, Hancock County had jurisdiction for their probate court petition.

59. Probate Record, Hancock County, vol. A, 352.

60. Probate Record, Hancock County, vol. A, 421.

61. Probate Record, Hancock County, vol. A, 422.

62. Summons, A. W. Babbitt, Guardian, v. William Law et al., Circuit Court Record, Hancock County, Book D, p. 356; photocopy at Perry Special Collections.

himself as guardian for the minor Lawrence children. This time he did not name William Law as a defendant.[63]

When the court next convened on May 19, 1846, it dismissed the September complaint in accordance with Babbitt's October non-suit motion[64] and tried the second case, filed in January. Both Coolidge and Mary Fielding Smith defaulted (failed to appear). After hearing evidence of damages, the court rendered judgment against each estate for $4,275.88 plus court costs.[65] No entry appears in the files of Joseph's estate, Hyrum's estate, or the Lawrence guardianship that Babbitt ever received any payment on these judgments, so he probably did not. He would have been legally bound as guardian to report such payments had they been made.

Babbitt had been present at the meeting on June 4, 1844, when Joseph Smith and John Taylor finalized the decision to transfer the print shop. On becoming guardian, logically he would have pursued those assets by claiming that the Lawrence children had an equitable interest in them. Perhaps he did not because the Apostles, in Nauvoo on August 12, 1844, "voted that the estate of Joseph Smith settle its own debts, and the Church have nothing to do with it." They also voted that John Taylor "hire the printing office & establishment, of the *Nauvoo Neighbor* & *Times & Seasons,* of the Church, and have nothing to do with the Lawrence estate."[66] Although John Taylor was still recovering from the bullet wounds he had received at Carthage some six weeks earlier, he attended this meeting. Even though it was very soon after the Smith brothers' deaths, creditors and ultimately the Hancock County probate and circuit courts were making strenuous efforts to include in Joseph's estate many assets that the Twelve considered to be Church property, including the Nauvoo House, the Mansion House, the Homestead, and numerous lots in Nauvoo that Joseph had sold, both as the Church's Trustee-in-Trust and in his own name. That legal tangle took until 1851 to conclude. The case

---

63. Making Law a judgment debtor was superfluous because of the purpose of these suits, which was a friendly act to both widows. The suits gave each of them a creditor's claim before other creditors filed, both to give the women whatever the suits recovered and perhaps to dissuade other creditors from filing claims. In Mary's case, only a few other small creditors made claims; Babbitt released his claim on that estate to facilitate its sale to the Church's trustees (of which he was one) so Mary could buy the equipment and supplies to travel west.

64. A. W. Babbitt, Guardian, v. William Law et al., May 19, 1846, Circuit Court Record, Hancock County, Book D, 404–5.

65. A. W. Babbitt, Guardian, v. William Law et al., May 19, 1846, Circuit Court Record, Hancock County, Book D, 445–46.

66. Willard Richards, Diary, holograph and typescript, August 12, 1844, LDS Church History Library.

was resolved, however, on issues other than the creditors' assertion that Joseph had defrauded them. The only payments from Joseph's estate went to satisfy the U.S. government's claim relating to the steamship *Nauvoo*, attorneys' fees, court costs, and a negotiated dower interest granted to Emma.[67]

In other words, the Twelve instructed Taylor not to become the Lawrence children's guardian. Almon Babbitt replaced Joseph as guardian on the family's nomination, then sued Joseph's and Hyrum's estates, obtaining judgments of about $4,200 against each. His complaint left John Taylor out of the legal maneuverings and omitted William Law in the later suits, thus freeing Law from his bond as Joseph's surety.

Analysis of William Law's Statement

Now it is possible to detect several inaccuracies in William Law's 1887 interview by Wylhelm Wymethel (W. Wyl).[68]

Maria and Sarah were not, as Law asserted, "worth about $8,000.00 in English gold." Rather, their supposed worth was their potential interest in their father's estate valued only at $3,831.54 and made up primarily of promissory notes which, when delivered to Joseph Smith, they eventually might inherit.[69]

Joseph was not appointed guardian with "help" from the notorious John C. Bennett, but rather because Maria and Sarah had nominated him.

If Law's statement that Smith "naturally put the gold in his pocket" is an accusation that he absconded with the estate assets, the record makes clear that the reverse is true.

---

67. Joseph I. Bentley, "In the Wake of the Steamboat Nauvoo," *Journal of Mormon History* 35, no. 1 (Winter 2009): 41–45.

68. On March 10, 1887, forty-three years after Joseph's death, Wylhelm Ritter von Wymethal, a German doctor/journalist living in Salt Lake City, was writing a series of columns for the *Salt Lake Daily Tribune* that he later published as a book under the name W. Wyl. He asked to interview William Law, then living in Shullsburg, Wisconsin, a request Law declined at least once, but to which he finally agreed. Wyl conducted the interview in person in Shullsburg at the home of Law's son, Thomas. Wyl and Law corresponded prior to the interview; and Wyl printed three of Law's letters, dated January 7, 20, and 27, 1887, in the *Tribune* on July 3, 1887; reprinted in Lyndon W. Cook, *William Law, Biographical Essay—Nauvoo Diary—Correspondence—Interview* (Orem, Ut.: Grandin Book, 1994), 102–11. The interview itself appeared in the July 31, 1887, issue of the *Tribune*; reprinted in Cook, *William Law,* 115–36.

69. Perhaps Law confused this number with the affidavit he signed as surety in which he swore that his net worth exceeded $8,000. He could not possibly, however, have thought that the estate consisted of "English gold." A more likely possibility is that the confusion was Wyl's and the English gold was his invention.

Guardians were legally allowed to co-mingle trust funds with their own, were charged with the value of the estate, and were required to account to the court for the management, receipts, and expenditures, having posted a bond to guarantee faithful performance of duties, all of which Joseph did.

Law's statements that Maria and Sarah were sealed to Joseph Smith[70] and that he, Law, signed on the guardian's bond were correct, but the co-signer was Hyrum Smith, not Sidney Rigdon, nor did these sealings impact Joseph's guardianship functions.

There is no evidence to support Law's assertion that "Babbitt found that Joseph had counted an expense of about $3,000.00 for board and clothing of the girls." The total sums expended from the estate for clothing and educating the two sisters was $89.78 for Maria and $93.31 for Sarah. Babbitt, as successor guardian, had access to the Adams County guardianship file, which he had copied. He knew that Joseph had made no such boarding claim. Thus Law's allegation was a complete fabrication.

The record also refutes Law's statement, "When I saw how things went, I should have taken steps to be released of that bond, but I never thought of it." He both "thought of it" and did indeed "take steps" to be relieved of it.

Law's recital of a confrontation between Babbitt and Emma is suspect for several reasons. When Babbitt became guardian of the younger Lawrence siblings (the "two girls" were already of legal age), Emma Smith had already relinquished her position as administratrix of Joseph's estate and Coolidge had replaced her as the party with whom Babbitt would have needed to contend. The printing establishment, which represented the corpus of the estate, was in John Taylor's possession, not Emma's. The judgments obtained against Joseph's estate were granted by default and may well have been a collusive rather than an adversarial process. Emma owned no real property in Hancock County at the time of Joseph's death, and the court put essentially all of the real property listed in his name into his estate. Emma therefore had no claim to Lawrence estate assets, nor did she have any property that Babbitt could have pursued.

Law's final claim—that he himself had authorized Babbitt to "take hold of all the property left by me in Nauvoo" together with all claims owing Law, and thus as his agent, Babbitt had paid the debt at Law's expense—is also questionable. If payment had been made from any source, Babbitt was legally obligated to report it to the court, but he made no such report.

In comparing the documentary record with the Law interview, made forty-three years after the facts to a writer who was energetically pursuing

---

70. Brian C. Hales, *Joseph Smith's Polygamy,* vol. 2 *History* (Salt Lake City: Greg Kofford Books, 2013), 2:48, 79 n. 58.

an anti-Mormon agenda, Mark Twain's statement seems applicable: "When I was younger I could remember anything, whether it happened or not. But as I grew older, it got so that I only remembered the latter."[71]

Aftermath

What happened to the Butterfields and the Lawrence children is an interesting story in itself, but it lies outside the focus of this article. On August 19, 1846, a promissory note between Babbitt and his fellow trustees acting for the Church, and Babbitt as "Guardian of the Minor heirs of Edward Lawrence deceased" was executed and signed. The trustees borrowed $3,884.61[72] from Babbitt-as-guardian, promising to pay "One day after date." That language made the note immediately negotiable (transferable). Written crossways across it is "Cancelled By new note," meaning that Babbitt did not cash it but kept it until it was cancelled by a new one.[73] Nearly three years later, on July 4, 1849, an unsigned receipt appears to be the final settlement between Babbitt and his co-trustees. Three items are credited to Babbitt: (1) "balance of account on books" in the sum of 3,789.91, (2) "due on note Lawrence Estate" 1248.22, and (3) a promissory note to an individual for $255.97, making a balance due of $5,294.10 "independent of services as Trustee." The receipt adds a note: "There is however some property still in his hands which he is ready to convey over and dispose of to their credit."[74]

---

71. As quoted in Andre Trudeau, *Gettysburg: A Testing of Courage* (New York: Harper-Collins Publishers, 2002), vii. I am indebted to my good friend and colleague Ronald O. Barney for this quotation.

72. Whether this sum represents the price of the print shop and indicates that Slocum took possession before Babbitt's last issues came off the press would be conjecture. One ought to be able to conclude, however, that the print shop brought no less than the $3,884.61 Babbitt loaned to the trustees—which, in turn, suggests that Joseph's disappointment in the 1844 appraisal of the operation was indeed justified and was $33.07 more than the $3,831.54 that Joseph was originally charged with receiving. So Joseph's augmenting the estate and buying the printing establishment, and John Taylor's and A. W. Babbitt's maintaining and reselling it, preserved the principal (corpus) intact; and if Babbitt's loan to the trustees was not all the price he obtained from Slocum, the principal was still larger than the value of the assets originally conveyed to Joseph.

73. Untitled note, Nauvoo, August 19, 1846, signed Almon W. Babbitt, Joseph L. Heywood, and John S. Fullmer, holograph, Nauvoo Trustee papers, 1846–48, LDS Church History Library.

74. Unsigned receipt, July 4, 1849, beginning "Balance of Account on Books...," holograph, Nauvoo Trustee papers, 1846–48, LDS Church History Library.

Obviously, Babbitt was still functioning as guardian of the Lawrence estate when this receipt was made on July 4, 1849. Whether he collected rent or some other payment from Taylor from June 1844 through March 1846 is not documented, but he at least took possession of the print shop without any adverse claim from Taylor. He loaned more than $3,800 from the estate to the Church's trustees (of which he was one) in August 1846, and three years later that debt had been reduced to just over $1,200. While it is unknown when or how Margaret and family made it to Winter Quarters, they departed from it for Utah in 1850. The reduction in the estate had occurred by July 1849; and since Babbitt had been acting as guardian at least through that date, it seems reasonable that the money helped Margaret and her children outfit themselves to cross the plains.

Maria married Almon W. Babbitt on January 24, 1846, as his plural wife and died giving birth to a son, who also died, at Nauvoo.[75] Babbitt was thus not only a guardian but a member of the family, continuing a relationship that had begun as missionary and convert in Canada. Every opportunity for an attachment was present, and plural marriage facilitated a closer union. Ultimately, it is unknown how much money the Lawrence children received from Babbitt.

Conclusion

Thanks to the probate and court records, which are often considered static and somewhat obscured by their legalese, it is possible in some measure to demonstrate what really happened during Joseph Smith's tenure as guardian of the Edward Lawrence estate. Contrary to the negative picture painted by the Law-Wyl interview, the record shows that he performed his duty honorably. He did not claim compensation for service as guardian, and he made no claim for boarding Maria and Sarah; he was more generous in expenditures for and to the children and to the Butterfields than the law required. And finally he took all the steps that time allowed to make an orderly transfer of the guardianship to John Taylor.

This article was condensed from "Joseph Smith as Guardian: The Lawrence Estate Case," Journal of Mormon History 36, no. 3 (2010): 172–211.

---

75. B[enjamin] F. Johnson, Statement, *Deseret Evening News,* August 6, 1897, 5. I am indebted to friend and colleague Jeffery O. Johnson for this reference. See also Cook, *Nauvoo Marriages [and] Proxy Sealings 1843–1846,* 47.

Chapter Sixteen

Invoking Habeas Corpus
in Missouri and Illinois

Jeffrey N. Walker

I. Introduction

Habeas corpus has been referred to as the cornerstone of the common law. Indeed, it is the "Great Writ of Liberty."[1] This article explores the use of this most famous writ during the early nineteenth century and specifically how Joseph Smith used it against those who sought his incarceration.

A writ of habeas corpus is essentially an order directing one who has a person in custody to deliver that person to a court so that the reasons for the incarceration can be independently reviewed. The legal process typically starts with a petition by the prisoner requesting a writ of habeas corpus to a local court authorized to hear the petition. If the local court determines that the petition has merit, it orders the person who has custody of the prisoner, often a sheriff, to bring the prisoner before a court with jurisdiction to hear the writ (as compared to a court with jurisdiction to grant the petition) at a specific time and place. This is referred to as the "return." At the hearing on the writ of habeas corpus, the court determines whether the prisoner is remanded back to jail, allowed to post bail, or discharged and released.[2]

---

1. Eric M. Freedman, *Habeas Corpus: Rethinking the Great Writ of Liberty* (New York: New York University Press, 2001), 1.

2. James Kent, *Commentaries on American Law* (O. Halstead, 1827), 2:22-30; Giles Jacob, *The Law-Dictionary* (I. Riley, 1811), 3:222–31; John Bouvier, *A Law Dictionary, Adapted to the Constitution and Laws of the United States of America and of the Several States of the American Union; with References to the Civil and Other Systems of Foreign Law*, 2 vols. (T. & J. W. Johnson, 1839), 1:454–57.

During Joseph Smith's life (1805–1844), he invoked the habeas corpus laws on several occasions: From seeking review of his incarceration in Liberty Jail to seeking approval for the charter for the City of Nauvoo (which included the right of the municipal court to hear writs of habeas corpus) to seeking review of his arrests during the various extradition efforts to return him to Missouri, Smith developed a keen understanding of the protections that habeas corpus afforded, and he needed that understanding. Joseph Smith believed, and accurately so, that if he were to be jailed in Illinois as he had been in Missouri, he would not survive his incarceration. It was in fact his jailing in Illinois that ended in his murder.

Historians and commentators, however, have almost uniformly assumed or acquiesced that Joseph Smith's use of habeas corpus was unusual and over-reaching.[3] Some critics even assert that such improper use was a catalyst to his death.[4] While it is true that some people in the 1840s were critical of Joseph's use of the right of habeas corpus, and while lawyers in that day still argued about the correct application of this writ in particular cases, the idea that Joseph's use of habeas corpus was not fully within the laws of his day is not supported by careful legal analysis.

II. History of the Writ of Habeas Corpus Leading Up to the Nineteenth Century

The history of habeas corpus predates the Magna Carta of 1215[5] and can be traced to a series of writs from the Middle Ages providing protection from imprisonment unrecognized in law, which had the aggregate effect of the

---

3. See John S. Dinger, "Joseph Smith and the Development of Habeas Corpus in Nauvoo, 1841–44," *Journal of Mormon History* 36 (Summer 2010): 136; Morris Thurston, "The Boggs Shooting and Attempted Extradition: Joseph Smith's Most Famous Case," *BYU Studies* 48, no. 1 (2009): 5, 18–19, 54–56; Glen M. Leonard, *Nauvoo: A Place of Peace, a People of Promise* (Salt Lake City: Deseret Book, 2002), 281, 285; but compare Nate Oman, "Joseph Smith, Justice Frankfurter and the Great Writ," *Times and Seasons,* January 28, 2005, http://timesandseasons.org/index.php/2005/01/joseph-smith-justicefrankfurter-and-the-great-writ/ (accessed December 15, 2012).

4. Robert Flanders, *Nauvoo: Kingdom on the Mississippi* (Urbana: University of Illinois Press, 1965), 99; Thurston, "Boggs Shooting and Attempted Extradition," 55–56.

5. Larry W. Yackle, *Postconviction Remedies* (Rochester, N.Y.: Lawyers Cooperative Pub. Co., 1981), sec. 4, 7–9; St. George Tucker, *Blackstone's Commentaries: With Notes of Reference, to the Constitution and Laws, of the Federal Government of the United States; and of the Commonwealth of Virginia,* 5 vols. (Philadelphia: William Young Birch and Abraham Small, 1803), 3:132; Louis B. Wright, *Magna Carta and the Tradition of Liberty,* ed. Russell Bourne (American Revolution Bicentennial Administration, 1976), 56.

modern writ.[6] The Magna Carta itself makes only an oblique reference to the writ of habeas corpus.[7] This is because the writ had already emerged as the law by the time of the Magna Carta and was thus already a fundamental part of the unwritten common law of the land.

The four hundred years following the Magna Carta saw a growing tension between the rights of the individual and those of the state. The British Parliament codified the common law practice through the enactment of the Habeas Corpus Act of 1679.[8]

Habeas corpus laws traveled across the ocean to the American colonies with the full panoply of English common law and practice. This right was regarded as a fundamental protection guaranteed to each citizen, and historical records confirm that petitions for writs of habeas corpus were filed in colonial America.[9] Indeed, the British restriction of this right was a major cause of the American Revolution.[10] So fundamental was the right of habeas corpus that the Founding Fathers placed it in the Constitution itself.[11]

III. History of the Writ of Habeas Corpus in Nineteenth-Century America

A. Introduction

Historical legal research requires the discipline to not look forward to subsequent events or laws; it is not an exercise to determine whether a judge's or attorney's proposition was subsequently validated, followed, or even cited. The primary historical objective is to determine whether the law was

---

6. See W. S. Holdsworth, *A History of English Law* (Methuen and Co., 1903), 1:95–98; Henry Hallam, *View of the State of Europe during the Middle Ages* (A. C. Armstrong and Sons, 1880), 2:116–19.

7. "No free man shall be seized or imprisoned, or stripped of his rights or possessions, or outlawed or exiled, or deprived of his standing in any other way, nor will we proceed with force against him, or send others to do so, except by the lawful judgment of his equals or by the law of the land."

8. Forsythe, "Historical Origins of Broad Federal Habeas Review Reconsidered," 1095–96.

9. William S. Church, *A Treatise of the Writ of Habeas Corpus including Jurisdiction, False Imprisonment, Writ of Error, Extradition, Mandamus, Certiorari, Judgment, etc. with Practice and Forms VI* (A. L. Bancroft and Co., 1884), 35.

10. The Declaration of Independence, para. 20 (articulating objections to King George III's abuse of his detention power); see generally Allen H. Carpenter, "Habeas Corpus in the Colonies," *American Historical Review* 8 (1902): 18.

11. U.S. Constitution, art. 1, sec. 9.

being properly applied according to the practice and status of the law of that time. It requires an understanding of the judicial system that then existed, the statutes and case law of the time, and the nature of the practice. These understandings are prerequisites to forming any legitimate opinion about the prosecution or defense in a particular historical judicial proceeding.

B. Nineteenth-Century vs. Modern Habeas Corpus Practices

Such a historical understanding is necessary when analyzing the writ of habeas corpus in America's nineteenth century, since many differences exist between the historical and modern use and interpretations. Between 1800 and 1850, there were 906 reported federal and state cases involving the use of habeas corpus (on average, less than eighteen per year).[12] In contrast, today there are an average of more than twenty thousand reported habeas corpus cases each year,[13] with that number rising yearly. While this increase in filings is certainly a result of the dramatic growth in the population in America coupled with the increased size and complexity of the American judiciary, the numbers alone do not tell the whole story.

An even more telling observation of how this fundamental legal vehicle has changed during the past two hundred years emerges when one separates the early nineteenth century cases into the three different phases in which a writ may be sought and compares them to a sampling of such filings today.

Habeas corpus can be sought anytime after an arrest. For purposes of discussion, the application of habeas corpus can be separated into three distinct phases:

(1) postarrest, but prior to indictment;[14]

(2) postindictment, but prior to conviction; and

(3) postconviction.

During any of these three phases of the case, there are three principal outcomes of a petition for habeas corpus. First, the prisoner's petition could be denied and he would be remanded back to jail to await the outcome of the

---

12. The author accessed LEXIS® searching in the all-federal and state courts database using the following search: "habeas w/2 corpus" with date restriction of 1/1/1800 and 12/31/1850. This search found 957 cases. Of the 957 cases, 906 dealt with habeas corpus while the others only made a mention of the writ.

13. Nancy J. King, Fred L. Cheesman II, and Brian J. Ostrom, *Final Technical Report: Habeas Litigation In U.S. District Courts: An Empirical Study of Habeas Corpus Cases Filed by State Prisoners Under the Antiterrorism and Effective Death Penalty Act of 1996* (Nashville, Tenn.: Vanderbilt University Law School, 2007), 9–10.

14. An indictment is the written accusation of a crime found by a grand jury. See Bouvier, *Law Dictionary,* 1:496–98; Black, *Black's Law Dictionary,* 5th ed., 695.

Chart 1. Three Periods in Which a Writ of Habeas Corpus May Be Used

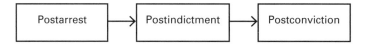

Chart 2. 1800–1850 Use for Writs of Habeas Corpus

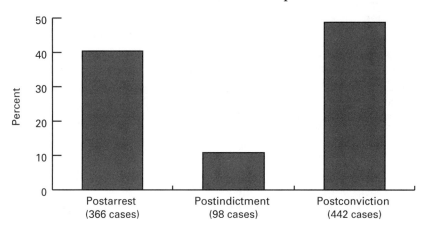

Percentage out of 906 federal and state cases

Chart 3. 2000–2011 Use for Writs of Habeas Corpus

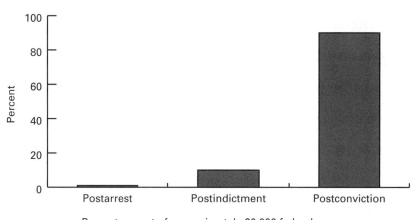

Percentage out of approximately 20,000 federal cases per year

prosecution. Second, the prisoner's petition for release could be denied, but the prisoner would be offered bail pending trial. Third, the prisoner's petition could be granted in full and he would be discharged and released. The process for determining which outcome should result is the central point of discussion of Joseph Smith's use of habeas corpus.

A review of the petitions for habeas corpus reported during the first half of the nineteenth century shows that approximately 40 percent of the writs were filed after arrest but before indictment; approximately 10 percent were filed after indictment but before conviction; and 50 percent were filed after conviction.

In contrast, today less than 1 percent of the habeas corpus cases are filed after arrest but before indictment; approximately 5 percent are filed after indictment but before conviction; and more than 95 percent of the cases are filed after conviction.[15] The change in the timing of habeas corpus use not only highlights differences in the judiciary, but also further underscores the problem of looking at the historical interpretation of habeas corpus through modern lenses.

C. Applying the Writ of Habeas Corpus in Nineteenth-Century America

To properly understand the application of the habeas corpus laws during Joseph Smith's time, we first look at the organization of the court system in that era. Next we consider the applicable legal commentary and case law that defined the use of habeas corpus in the various phases of litigation—from arrest to indictment to conviction—to determine how the application of the writ changed as the case moved through the legal process.

1. How the Nineteenth-Century American Judicial System Encouraged the Use of Habeas Corpus

Engaging in a discussion of Smith's use of habeas corpus first requires an understanding of how the judicial process has evolved over the past two hundred years. One dramatic evolution for purposes of this discussion is the change from a "term-based" court system to a "standing" court system. In the early nineteenth century, with the exception of the most local level of the courts (typically the justices of the peace), a court would be in session only

---

15. See Andrea Lyon, Emily Hughes, Mary Prosser, Justin Marceau, *Federal Habeas Corpus* (Durham, N.C.: Carolina Academic Press, 2010), 5–7; Sara Rodriguez, "Appellate Review of Pretrial Requests for Habeas Corpus Relief in Texas, 32 Tex. Tech. L. Rev. 45 (2000).

twice a year.[16] These terms were most often held in the spring (the May Term, or Spring Term) and the fall (the October Term). In contrast, modern courts, both state and federal, are in session throughout the year. This difference is central to the corresponding change in trends regarding the filing of petitions for writs of habeas corpus.

The term system created a unique situation wherein a person could be arrested for an alleged crime and held until the next term began. For example, if a person were arrested for a crime in November, after the October Term had concluded, his or her charges would not be brought before a grand jury until the May Term began. Moreover, if the charges were not bailable, that person could be held for five or more months, based only on an affidavit or a preliminary hearing. During this period, a prisoner would have both significantly more time and opportunity to seek a review of his or her incarceration by petitioning for a writ of habeas corpus. These long incarceration periods obviously increased incentive to contest the incarceration.

It is during this early phase of the litigation that we see the emergence of an American approach that diverges from the traditional British one. Under British jurisprudence habeas corpus was fundamentally a vehicle to protect against misuse of the judicial process. A review by a court on a writ of habeas corpus under this approach was therefore limited to a consideration of whether the procedural requirements were satisfied. In contrast, under the emerging American approach, while due process considerations remained important, the courts began "looking behind the writ" to review the underlying charges that allegedly supported an arrest and detention.

2. Nineteenth-Century Writs of Habeas Corpus after Arrest but before Indictment ("First Phase")

While the most recognized treatise on habeas corpus was not written until 1858,[17] early commentaries are helpful in assessing the use of habeas corpus. For example, Joseph Chitty's 1819 treatise on criminal law[18] provides

---

16. See *The Revised Statutes of the State of Missouri,* sec. 16 at 169 (1845); An Act Regulating the Terms of Holding the Circuit Courts in this State, in *The Public and General Statutes Laws of the State of Illinois* (Stephen F. Gale, 1839), 180.

17. "There is now but one work [on habeas corpus], to our knowledge, upon the subject, and the first edition of that appeared in 1858, followed by a second in 1876." Church, *Treatise of the Writ of Habeas Corpus,* vii.

18. Joseph Chitty, *A Practical Treatise on the Criminal Law; Comprising the Practice, Pleadings, and Evidence which Occur in the Course of Criminal Prosecutions, Whether by Indictment or Information: with a Copious Collection of Precedents of Indictments,*

a general discussion regarding the propriety of looking behind the writ in ruling on a petition for habeas corpus during this first phase. Chitty's discussion of looking into the underlying factual allegations indicates that it was a common, even expected examination:

> We do not find that the mere informality of the warrant of commitment [a procedural aspect] is, of itself, a sufficient ground for discharging or admitting to bail; ... even though the commitment be regular; the court will examine the proceedings, and if the evidence [the factual aspects] appear altogether insufficient, will admit him to bail; for the court will rather look to the depositions which contain the evidence, than to the commitment, in which the justice may have come to a false conclusion.[19]

Chitty's explanation was further developed in 1827 by James Kent, who authored perhaps the most cited and authoritative treatise on nineteenth-century American law in his *Commentaries on American Law*. Kent traced American jurisprudence's departure from the British common law principle of limited procedural review on a writ of habeas corpus during this first phase of a possible incarceration:

> Upon the return of the *habeas corpus*, the judge is not confined to the face of the return, but he is to examine into the facts contained in the return.... [and] authorizes the judge to re-examine all of the testimony taken before the magistrate who originally committed, and to take further proof on the subject, for he is "to examine into the facts."[20]

Kent's explanation on looking behind the writ in a petition for habeas corpus is further developed in Rollin Hurd's seminal 1858 work, *A Treatise on the Right of Personal Liberty, and on the Writ of Habeas Corpus and the Practice Connected with It with a View of the Law of Extradition of Fugitives,* wherein he conducted a careful analysis of the United States Supreme Court 1807 case *Ex parte Bollman & Swartwout.*[21] This case involved Erick Bollman and Samuel Swartwout's use of habeas corpus to challenge the charges of treason brought

---

Informations, Precedents, and Every Description of Practical Forms, with Comprehensive Notes as to Each Particular Offence, the Process, Indictment, Plea, Defence, Evidence, Trial, Verdict, Judgment, and Punishment (Edward Earle, 1819).

19. Chitty, *A Practical Treatise on Criminal Law*, 87.

20. James Kent, *Commentaries on American Law*, 1st ed. (1827), 2:26. Kent's *Commentaries* was first published in 1827. Fifteen editions have been published, the last in 2002.

21. Ex parte Bollman and Swartwout, 8 U.S. (4 Cranch) 75 (1807).

against them for recruiting persons to participate in Aaron Burr's failed attempt to create a separate nation in the West. Hurd examined how the Supreme Court addressed the use of extrinsic evidence in proving or defending the charge of treason, outside of that evidence presented in the charging pleadings used in the initial arrest.[22]

Hurd noted that the Supreme Court addressed the issue again in the principal Burr case itself, finding,

James Kent. His *Commentaries on American Law* provide an accurate understanding of the law on writs of habeas corpus in nineteenth-century America. Library of Congress.

> The presence of the witnesses to be examined by the committing justice, confronted with the accused, is certainly to be desired; and ought to be obtained, unless considerable inconvenience and difficulty exist in procuring his attendance. An *ex parte*[23] affidavit, shaped perhaps, by the person pressing the prosecution, will always be viewed with some suspicion, and acted upon with some caution; but the court thought it would be going too far to reject it altogether. If it was obvious, that the attendance of the witness was easily attainable, but that he was intentionally kept out of the way, the question might be otherwise decided.[24]

Lastly, William Church's 1884 treatise on the writ of habeas corpus[25] provides some additional clarification. Church provides a summary of how the

---

22. Rollin C. Hurd, *A Treatise of the Right of Personal Liberty and on the Writ of Habeas Corpus and the Practice Connected with It,* (Albany: W. C. Little, 1858), 310–19.

23. *Ex parte* means on the part of one side only.

24. Hurd, *Treatise on the Right of Personal Liberty,* 313 (quoting 1. Burr. Tr. 97).

25. Church, *Treatise of the Writ of Habeas Corpus.*

courts treated the postarrest, but preindictment, petition for habeas corpus during the nineteenth century:

> The decisions on this point may be divided into two classes . . . 1. Those which hold that, upon a commitment regular and valid upon its face, the only open question before a court on the hearing of a return to a writ of habeas corpus is the jurisdiction of the committing magistrate [procedural]; and, 2. Those which hold that not only the proceedings but the evidence taken before the committing magistrate may be examined [factual], and the commitment revised if necessary, or a commitment made *de novo*[26] by the court hearing the matter. . . . The practice set down in the first rule seems to have been followed in many of the states, and is probably supported by a preponderance of authorities; but we consider the second to be the soundest, most in accord with the spirit which gave birth to the writ of habeas corpus, and one from which will flow the greatest and best results of this beneficent writ.[27]

Church recognized the tension between the traditional common law approach (as derived under British precedents), which was that only the form of the writ should be subject for examination, and the more expansive American approach, noted with approval from the United States Supreme Court, which permitted or even required inquiry into the underlying factual predicates.

These legal commentators provide a consistent paradigm to view the use of habeas corpus during the nineteenth century as it evolved from a British model to an American one. This same evolution can be viewed through the courts. For example, in *People v. Martin,*[28] the New York Supreme Court in 1848 confronted the prosecution's position "that the commitment of the magistrate is conclusive upon me, and that I have no right on this return to look beyond the question of its regularity or that if I do look beyond it, I can look only at the depositions taken before the magistrate."[29] The judge confessed that while such an approach appeared consistent with his "reading of [his] boyhood [rather] than of riper years," because of the vital nature of the underlying principals of habeas corpus, he took the time for an "extended" examination, to ensure "an accurate and intimate knowledge of

---

26. *De novo* means from the beginning.

27. Church, *Treatise of the Writ of Habeas Corpus,* 285–86.

28. 2 Edm. Sel. Cas. 28 (N.Y. 1848).

29. 2 Edm. Sel. Cas. 29 (N.Y. 1848).

the properties of this great instrument of personal liberty, the writ of habeas corpus."[30] The judge summarized the law after arrest but before indictment:

> If in custody on criminal process before indictment, the prisoner has an absolute right to demand that the original dispositions be looked into to see whether any crime is in fact imputed to him, and the inquiry will by no means be confined to the return. Facts out of the return may be gone into to ascertain … whether the commitment was not palpably and evidently arbitrary, unjust, and contrary to every principle of positive law or rational justice.[31]

The same court in 1851 acknowledged the continuing fluid development of the American approach of looking behind the writs in *People v. Tompkins,* explaining:

> It was very strenuously urged on the argument of this case, on the part of the public prosecutor, that on habeas corpus the court or officer had no right to go behind the warrant on which the prisoner was detained, and inquire from facts out of the return into the legality of the imprisonment. The effect of this principle would be, that the warrant of a committing magistrate, when legal upon its face, would be conclusive upon the prisoner, and he could have no relief from imprisonment, even if no charge whatever had in fact been preferred against him.… I have examined the subject very carefully, and rejoice to find that there is no authority to shake my previous convictions on this subject.[32]

After reviewing the cases and authority cited by the prosecution advocating only a procedural review [the British approach], the *Tompkins* Court explained:

> Of all the cases which I can find, or to which I have been referred in support of the doctrine contended for in behalf of the prosecution none of them sustain the doctrine, and it is well they do not, for the habeas corpus would be a mockery, whenever a magistrate might please to make the instrument of oppression and false imprisonment formal and regular on its face, and personal liberty

---

30. 2 Edm. Sel. Cas. 28–29 (N.Y. 1848).

31. 2 Edm. Sel. Cas. 38 (N.Y. 1848).

32. 2 Edm. Sel. Cas. 191, 191–92 (N.Y. 1851). Both the New York courts and legislature were leading voices for the development of jurisprudence and policy that would be adopted throughout the other states. James Kent, *Commentaries on American Law* (O. Halstead, 1827), 2:24.

would be at the mercy of ignorance or design, beyond anything yet known to our laws, careless as they too frequently are of freedom in the detail, from the abundance of it in the gross.[33]

A sampling of cases from other jurisdictions involving a postarrest, but preindictment, scenario shows that the courts routinely allowed a substantive analysis of the underlying facts rather than just looking at the procedural formalities.[34] State courts also interpreted the statutory provisions of their respective habeas corpus acts to permit close scrutiny of the factual predicates of the crime.[35]

3. Nineteenth-Century Writs of Habeas Corpus after Indictment but before Conviction (Second Phase)

The American courts' treatment of habeas corpus after indictment in the nineteenth century closely aligns with the traditional English common law. As articulated by the New York Supreme Court in *People v. McLeod,* "Nothing is better settled, on English authority, than that on habeas corpus, the examination as to guilt or innocence cannot, under any circumstances, extend beyond the depositions or proofs upon which the prisoner was committed."[36] This is fundamentally because grand jury testimony is not publicly available to scrutinize. These limitations, however, on review after indictment but before conviction are not applicable when allegations of fraud or perjured testimony are involved. For example, in *United States v. Burr,* one of Aaron Burr's central arguments accepted by the court against the indictments of treason was that they "had been obtained by perjury."[37] Similarly, in *Commonwealth v. Carter,* the Supreme Court of Massachusetts held that its Habeas Corpus Act itself provided for relief after indictment upon showing the prosecutor's "witness is occasioned by fraud," reasoning "that such avoidance is fraudulent, unlawful and collusive, and done or caused with a design

---

33. 2 Edm. Sel. Cas. 194 (N.Y. 1851).

34. See, for example, State v. Doty, 1 Walk. 230 (Miss. 1826); State v. Best, 7 Blackf. 611, 612 (Ind. 1846); In re McIntyre, 10 Ill. (5 Gilm.) 422, 425 (1849); In re Powers, 25 Vt. 261, 269 (1853); Ex parte Mahone, 30 Ala. 49, 50 (Ala. 1857); People v. Stanley, 18 How. Pr. 179, 180 (N.Y. 1859).

35. See, for example, In re Clark, 9 Wend. 212, 220 (N.Y. 1832); Snowden et al. v. State, 8 Mo. 483, 486 (1844).

36. 25 Wend. 483, 568 (N.Y. 1841); see , State v. Mills, 13 N.C., 420, 421-22 (1830); People v. Martin, 2 Edm. Sel. Cas. 28, 31-32 (N.Y. 1848)

37. 25 F.Cas. 55, 70 (D.Va. 1807).

to defeat the claims of justice."[38] As noted by the Arkansas Supreme Court in *Ex parte White,* in a postindictment but pretrial stage:

> The law requires the party to make an affidavit of merits to warrant this court in going behind the indictment, and the affidavit must state such particular facts that, if proven to be false, the affiant [the person who signs an affidavit] could be indicted for perjury: otherwise, the requiring of an affidavit would be a merely idle form.[39]

4. Nineteenth-Century Writs of Habeas Corpus after Conviction (Third Phase)

The nineteenth-century application of habeas corpus after conviction followed more closely the modern application in the same phase: "The writ of habeas corpus was not framed to retry issues of fact, or to review the proceedings of a legal trial."[40] Consequently, postconviction writs of habeas corpus are predominantly limited to constitutional challenges to the charges or procedure of the case and challenges to the implementation of the sentence.[41]

5. Summary

As the foregoing illustrates, these three phases are really parts of a continuum. In a postarrest but preindictment phase, a person is in custody based on a complaint supported at most by an affidavit. In the postindictment but preconviction phase, a person is in custody based on a grand jury finding. Finally, in the postconviction phase, a person is in custody based on the trial itself. At each consecutive phase, there is an increased amount of information supporting the incarceration. The affidavit supporting an arrest does not carry much weight. There is more weight given to an indictment and even more weight yet given to a conviction. Thus, the ability to look behind the writ depends on where the case is heard, with the level of review decreasing or narrowing as the case makes its way through the judicial process.

---

38. 28 Mass. 277, 279 (Ma. 1831).

39. 9 Ark. 223, 226 (1848).

40. Ex Parte Bird, 19 Cal. 130, 131 (1851).

41. See, for example, Stewart's Case, 1 App. Pr. 210, 212 (NY 1820); People v. Martin, 2 Edm. Sel. Cas. 28, 37 (N.Y. 1848).

IV. Joseph Smith's Use of Habeas Corpus

Joseph Smith's first use of habeas corpus was in response to the preliminary hearing before Circuit State Judge Austin A. King in November 1838, which hearing resulted in his incarceration in Liberty Jail. While in the Missouri jail he joined in two petitions for habeas corpus—one in January 1839 to the county judge in Clay County and a second to the Missouri Supreme Court in March 1839. In Nauvoo, Smith was involved in enacting ordinances that articulated the rights extended by the Nauvoo Charter for issuing and hearing writs of habeas corpus. Later, still in Illinois, Smith used the writ of habeas corpus again as a key protection during extradition attempts by the State of Missouri. These events provide a window into his understanding and application of this most important writ.

A. Habeas Corpus in Missouri (1838–1839)

On November 1, 1838, Major General Samuel D. Lucas arrested Joseph Smith and six of his colleagues outside of Far West, Missouri, thereby marking the effective end of the Missouri conflict and the start of a forced exodus by the Mormons from Missouri.[42] More than sixty who were charged with crimes ranging from arson, burglary, and robbery to treason and even murder, joined Smith.[43] Because some of the alleged crimes occurred in Ray County, Missouri, the preliminary hearing (referred to as a Court of Inquiry) was held in Richmond, the

---

42. See Rough Draft Notes of History of the Church, 1838-033 to 036, Church History Library, The Church of Jesus Christ of Latter-day Saints, Salt Lake City; see generally Richard L. Anderson, "Atchison's Letters and the Causes of Mormon Expulsion from Missouri," *BYU Studies* 26, no. 3 (1986): 3–28; Alexander L. Baugh, "A Call to Arms: The 1838 Mormon Defense of Northern Missouri" (PhD diss., Brigham Young University, 1996; Provo, Utah: BYU Studies, 2000); Kenneth H. Winn, *Exiles in a Land of Liberty: Mormons in America, 1830–1846* (University of North Carolina Press, 1989). ch. 4–7.

43. *Document Containing the Correspondence, Orders, &C., in Relation to the Disturbances with the Mormons; and the Evidence Given before the Hon. Austin A. King, Judge of the Fifth Judicial Circuit of the State of Missouri, at the Court-house in Richmond, in a Criminal Court of Inquiry, Begun November 12, 1838, on the Trial of Joseph Smith, Jr., and Others, for High Treason and Other Crimes against the State* (Fayette, Mo.: Boon's Lick, 1841), 19–20, 34 (hereafter cited as Missouri Documents); *Document Showing the Testimony Given before the Judge of the Fifth Judicial Circuit of the State of Missouri, on the Trial of Joseph Smith, Jr., and Others, for High Treason and Other Crimes against That State* (Washington, D.C.: United States Senate, 1841), 119, 132, 140 (hereafter cited as Senate Documents).

county seat of Ray County, before Fifth Circuit State Court Judge Austin King.[44] This hearing lasted two weeks, concluding on November 29, 1838, at which time Judge King found probable cause to charge thirty-four of the defendants. Bail was available for twenty-three of the thirty-four,[45] leaving eleven to be held in custody pending a grand jury, wherein indictments would be considered. Of those eleven, Joseph Smith, Hyrum Smith, Lyman Wight, Alexander McRae, Caleb Baldwin, and Sidney Rigdon were charged with treason and sent to Liberty Jail in Clay County (because no jail existed in either Caldwell or Daviess County, where the alleged crimes had occurred) on December 1, 1838.[46] There they were incarcerated to await a grand jury, which, the October Term having already concluded, would not occur until the 1839 Spring Term, in April.

The Missouri legislature began a review of the matter almost immediately after Judge King bound them over. On December 5, 1838, Governor Boggs provided the Missouri Legislature with a report of the Mormon dispute to support the charges for the incarcerated. The Mormons answered by providing the "Memorial of a Committee to the State Legislature of Missouri in Behalf of the Citizens of Caldwell County" on December 10, 1838.[47] On December 18, 1838, a joint committee of the legislature charged with investigating the Mormon dispute submitted their preliminary findings, concluding that a full investigation lasting several months was necessary, and that their findings should not be made public until after the grand jury had heard the case during the upcoming Spring Term.[48] With the prospects of timely help from the Missouri legislature gone, Joseph Smith and the other prisoners looked to the courts for assistance. Smith recalled,

> Under such circumstances, sir, we were committed to this jail, on a pretended charge of treason, against the State of Missouri, without the slightest evidence to that effect. We collected our witnesses the second time, and petitioned a habeas corpus: but were thrust back again into prison, by the rage of the mob; and

---

44. Austin A. King (1802–1870) was appointed judge of the Fifth Judicial Circuit Court in 1837. He remained on the bench until 1848 when he was elected governor of Missouri. William Van Ness Bay, *Reminiscences of the Bench and Bar of Missouri* (F. H. Thomas and Co., 1878), 153–55.

45. Missouri Documents, 97, 150; Senate Documents, 1.

46. Missouri Documents, 150. Five were bound over for murder arising from the Battle of Crooked River. They included Parley P. Pratt, Norman Shearer, Darwin Chase, Lyman Gibbs, and Maurice Phelps.

47. Rough Draft Notes of History of the Church, 1838-038.

48. Rough Draft Notes of History of the Church, 1838-039; Missouri Documents, 11.

our families robbed, and plundered: and families, and witnesses, thrust from their homes, and hunted out of the State.[49]

Sidney Rigdon prepared an extensive affidavit delineating his experiences in Missouri, including a summary of their efforts for review via this same petition for habeas corpus:

> During the hearing under the habeas corpus, I had, for the first time, an opportunity of hearing the evidence, as it was all written and read before the court. It appeared from the evidence that they attempted to prove us guilty of treason in consequence of the militia of Caldwell County being under arms at the time that General Lucas' army came to Far West. This calling out of the militia, was what they founded the charge of treason upon—an account of which I have given above ... The other charges were founded on things which took place in Davies. As I was not in Davies county at that time, I cannot testify anything about them.[50]

These two accounts provide some useful insights into nineteenth-century application of habeas corpus. Both accounts note that the hearing *included the examination of the evidence,* Joseph Smith noting that they "collected [their] witnesses the second time" (the first being the King hearing), and Rigdon writing that all of the written evidence was "read before the court." These examinations were in accord with the law of looking behind the writ on a petition for habeas corpus when the petition was brought during the first phase (after arrest but before indictment), which was exactly the status of Smith, Rigdon, and their companions.

During this habeas corpus hearing before Clay County Judge Turnham, Alexander Doniphan recruited Peter Burnett,[51] a local attorney, to assist him in representing Smith, Rigdon, and the other prisoners held at Liberty Jail. Burnett's account of this hearing provides some additional details, as well as a flavor of the intensity of the persecution that the Mormons were experiencing. Burnett recorded:

> We had the prisoners out upon a writ of habeas corpus, before the Hon. Joel Turnham, the County Judge of Clay County. In conducting

---

49. Joseph Smith to Isaac Galland, March 22, 1839, Church History Library.

50. Affidavit of Sidney Rigdon, July 2, 1843, Church History Library.

51. For Peter Hardeman Burnett (1807–1895), see Roger D. Launius, "Burnett, Peter Hardeman (1807–1895)," in *Dictionary of Missouri Biography,* ed. Lawrence O. Christensen, William E. Foley, Gary R. Kremer, and Kenneth H. Winn (University of Missouri Press, 1999), 134–35.

the proceedings before him there was imminent peril.... We apprehended that we should be mobbed, the prisoners forcibly seized,
and most probably hung. Doniphan and myself argued the case
before the County Judge ... We rose above all fear, and felt impressed
with the idea that we had a sublime and perilous but sacred duty to
perform. We armed ourselves, and had a circle of brave and faithful
friends armed around us; and, it being cold weather, the proceedings were conducted in one of the smaller rooms in the second story
of the Court-house in Liberty, so that only a limited number, say a
hundred persons, could witness the proceedings...

I made the opening speech, and was replied to by the District
Attorney; and Doniphan made the closing argument. Before he
rose to speak, or just as he rose, I whispered to him: "Doniphan!
Let yourself out, my good fellow; and I will kill the first man that
attacks you." And he did let himself out, in one of the most eloquent and withering speeches I ever heard. The maddened crowd
foamed and gnashed their teeth, but only to make him more and
more intrepid. He faced the terrible storm with the most noble
courage. All the time I sat within six feet of him, with my hand
upon my pistol, calmly determined to do as I had promised him.

The Judge decided to release Sidney Rigdon, against whom
there was no sufficient proof in the record of the evidence taken
before Judge King. The other prisoners were remanded to await
the action of the grand jury of Davis County. Rigdon was released
from the jail at night to avoid the mob.[52]

Burnett's account is consistent with both Smith's and Rigdon's accounts that
Judge Turnham "looked behind the writ" and reviewed the underlying facts.

At the conclusion of this hearing, Judge Turnham ruled that there was not
sufficient evidence to hold Rigdon and released him. While there are several accounts noting Rigdon's release, the basis for the release has remained
largely uncertain. Burnett's account helps to clarify the legal basis, which fits
squarely within the legal parameters of the applicable habeas corpus laws.

Following Rigdon's release in January, but before the grand jury was held
in Daviess County in April 1839, Joseph Smith, his fellow prisoners, and
others sought a second writ of habeas corpus from the Missouri Supreme
Court in a series of documents simply titled "*Petition*," dated March 1839.

---

52. Peter Hardeman Burnett, *Recollections and Opinions of an Old Pioneer* (D. Appleton and Co., 1880), 53–55.

These petitions not only articulated procedural irregularities in the events leading up to their imprisonment in Liberty Jail but also noted irregularities in the underlying factual allegations altogether.[53] They did this in two manners: first, they disputed the factual allegations themselves; and second, they argued that the facts testified of were insufficient to constitute the crime of treason. The Missouri Supreme Court refused to hear these petitions.

A review of the preliminary hearing before Judge King reveals that the treason charge that held Joseph Smith and his colleagues in Liberty Jail can be separated into two categories. The first is the alleged illegal activities that occurred in Daviess County in October 1838. The second category involves various speeches given by Sidney Rigdon in Far West, Caldwell County.

It was these cumulative factual allegations that supported binding these men over for the grand jury and holding them in Liberty Jail until the grand jury would convene.[54]

The law of treason finds its roots in the United States Constitution.[55] The Missouri Constitution directly borrows its language on treason from the United States Constitution. Judicial refinements of the law were defined early in American history through a series of cases arising out of Aaron Burr's failed effort to create a separate nation from Spanish-owned Mexico, which included states west of the Mississippi valley. The most applicable refinement was the affirmation by the United States Supreme Court that treason required an "overt act" to "levy war."[56] Justice Marshall, in the opinion for the *Burr* conspiracy case, held that accessory rules, which make accessories equally guilty as the principal who actually commits the crime, were inapplicable to cases of treason; that is, advising, counseling, advocating, or even assisting in preparing for treasonous actions does not constitute treason.[57]

---

53. Joseph Smith Letter Book, 2:21–24, Joseph Smith collection, Church History Library.

54. They were held in Liberty Jail because the first alleged activities occurred in Daviess County, and since there was no jail in Daviess County, the Liberty Jail the closest. And the speeches were given by Rigdon in Caldwell County, where no jail had been constructed, also leaving Liberty Jail as the closest available jail to hold him. The group of Mormons charged with murder, including Parley P. Pratt, was held in the Richmond Jail pending a grand jury hearing.

55. U.S. Constitution, art. 3, sec. 3: "Treason against the United States, shall consist only in levying War against them, or in adhering to their Enemies, giving them Aid and Comfort. No Person shall be convicted of Treason unless on the Testimony of two Witnesses to the same overt Act, or on Confession in open Court."

56. U.S. Constitution, art. 3, sec. 3.

57. See United States v. Burr, 8 U.S. (4 Cranch) 470, 473 (1807); Ex parte Bollman and Ex parte Swartwout, 8 U.S. (4 Cranch) 75, 126 (1807); see generally David Robertson, *Trial of Aaron Burr for Treason* (James Cockcroft and Company, 1875).

Applying the foregoing rules and factors to the habeas corpus hearing before Judge Turnham is relatively straightforward. As discussed above, if a petition for habeas corpus falls within the first phase (after arrest and before indictment), a judge may look behind the writ to assure that there are sufficient factual allegations to support the charges. While the evidence in the record implicating Joseph Smith, Hyrum Smith, Lyman Wight, Alexander McRae, and Caleb Baldwin would ultimately be insufficient to warrant a conviction, the record does articulate generally that these men were the leaders of or directed various military or riotous actions.[58] Thus apparently Judge Turnham determined that sufficient evidence had been admitted to find that the minimum standard of probable cause was established. Consequently, the judge denied their request to be released from Liberty Jail. It is not clear whether Smith and his colleagues were allowed to affirmatively present additional testimony, although Smith indicates that they had at least prepared to do so.

In contrast, the only evidence implicating Sidney Rigdon was the two speeches he gave in Far West. As Justice Marshall articulated in the *Burr* case, speech alone is insufficient to constitute treason—there must be an actual overt action in levying war; none could be found in the record against Rigdon. As their attorney, Peter Burnett, recounted, "The Judge decided to release Sidney Rigdon, against whom there was no sufficient proof in the record of the evidence taken before Judge King."[59]

This analysis illustrates that courts were allowed, during the period between arrest and indictment, to look behind the procedural niceties of an arrest and resulting incarceration, and examine the underlying facts of the matter. That is exactly what Judge Turnham did for Joseph Smith and his colleagues in hearing their collective petitions for a writ of habeas corpus.

Through these events, Smith became both a student and practitioner in the use of the writ of habeas corpus. He subsequently left Missouri in April 1839, with a growing understanding of the need to protect the right of habeas corpus. This skill became even more evident as he found himself in need of such protection while residing in Illinois.

---

58. This conclusion is based on the testimony given during the Court of Inquiry. For purposes of this analysis such testimony is accepted as true. See Madsen, "Joseph Smith and the Missouri Court Inquiry," 115–19, for a discussion about the chronic problem with the extant testimony of this preliminary hearing to establish treason.

59. Peter Hardman Burnett, *Recollections and Opinions of an Old Pioneer* (D. Appleton, 1880), 55.

B. Habeas Corpus in Illinois under the Nauvoo City Charter

The Nauvoo Charter, granted by the Illinois legislature on December 16, 1840,[60] granted the city council the "power and authority to make, ordain, establish, and execute, all such ordinances, not repugnant to the Constitution of the United States or of this State, as they deem necessary for the peace, benefit, good order, regulation, convenience, and cleanliness, of said city."[61] Under this charter, the Nauvoo City Council had the power to enact laws pertaining to the use of habeas corpus in Nauvoo. The charter also provided for the creation of a court system, as follows:

> Sec. 16: The Mayor and Aldermen shall be conservators of the peace within the limits of said city, and shall have all powers of Justices of the Peace therein, both in civil and criminal cases, arising under the laws of the State:...
>
> Sec. 17:... The Municipal Court shall have power to grant writs of habeas corpus in all cases arising under the ordinances of the City Council.[62]

These sections provided that the mayor and aldermen were "justices of the peace" within Nauvoo and together constituted the "municipal court." The municipal court was the equivalent in some limited situations to the Illinois circuit courts wherein appeals from the justices of the peace could be taken and where original jurisdiction was expanded. Such original jurisdiction expressly extended to the municipal court was the power to grant writs of habeas corpus. While some have viewed this inclusion as unique, two of the five city charters adopted in Illinois before the Nauvoo Charter contained a similar provision.[63]

---

60. For a discussion about the process for obtaining the Nauvoo City Charter, see generally James L. Kimball Jr., "A Wall to Defend Zion: The Nauvoo Charter," *BYU Studies* 15, no. 4 (1975): 492–97; see also B. H. Roberts, *The Rise and Fall of Nauvoo* (Salt Lake City: Deseret News, 1900), 81.

61. "The City Charter: Laws, Ordinances, and Acts of the City Council of the City of Nauvoo," sec. 11 (1840) (hereafter cited as Nauvoo City Charter), Church History Library. Very similar provisions were also incorporated into the Illinois charters of Galena (1839), Springfield (1840), and Quincy (1840). See James L. Kimball, "A Study of the Nauvoo Charter, 1840–1845" (master's thesis, University of Iowa, 1966), 36.

62. Nauvoo City Charter, secs. 16–17.

63. See An Act to Amend an Act, Entitled "An Act to Incorporate the City of Alton," sec. 1, *Incorporation Laws of the State of Illinois Passed by the Eleventh General Assembly, at Their Session Began and Held at Vandalia, on the Third of December, One Thousand Eight Hundred and Thirty-eight* (Vandalia, Ill.: William Walters, 1839), 240; An Act to

The drafting of the Nauvoo charter was undoubtedly influenced by the Mormons' experiences in Missouri and the perceived threat of additional efforts by the Missourians to apprehend Mormon leaders, especially Joseph Smith. Yet its grant of rights to issue writs of habeas corpus cannot be seen as unique. The cumulative effect of these provisions in the charter was the progressive development of ordinances dealing with the rights and uses of habeas corpus. As will be discussed, it appears from these ordinances that the leaders in Nauvoo understood that the charter provided them the right to enact these types of ordinances and that they were restricted only by the contours of the United States Constitution or the Illinois Constitution, whichever was broader. Consequently, these ordinances must therefore be read not only in light of the general law of habeas corpus as understood and applied in the first half of nineteenth-century America, but also in harmony with the broader provisions of the United States and Illinois Constitutions.

C. Missouri's First Effort to Extradite Joseph Smith (June 1841)

In early April 1839, Joseph Smith, Hyrum Smith, Lyman Wight, Alexander McRae, and Caleb Baldwin were taken from Liberty Jail, where they had been incarcerated since early December 1838, to Gallatin, Daviess County, where a grand jury was empanelled at the commencement of the Spring 1839 court term to consider the charges brought against them, including the nonbailable charge of treason. There, after a two-day hearing, they were indicted on several charges. At the close of the grand jury hearing, Judge Thomas Burch granted a request to change venue to Boone County due to the fact that he had been the prosecuting attorney in the preliminary hearing before Judge Austin King. En route to Boone County all of the prisoners either escaped or were released and made their way to Illinois to join the body of the Church.[64]

Sixteen months later, on September 1, 1840, Governor Boggs sent a requisition to Illinois Governor Thomas Carlin seeking the extradition of Joseph

Incorporate the City of Chicago, *Laws of the State of Illinois Passed by the Tenth General Assembly, at Their Special Session, Commencing December 5, 1836, ending March 6, 1837* (Vandalia, Ill.: William Walters, 1837), 75, Sec. 69; An Act in Relation to the Municipal Court of Chicago, and for Other Purposes, *Laws of the State of Illinois Passed by the Tenth General Assembly, at Their Special Session, Commencing July 16, 1837 ending July 22, 1837* (Vandalia, Ill.: William Walters, 1837), 15–16, sec. 1.

64. See Joseph Smith Letter Book 2:6, Joseph Smith collection, Church History Library; see also Jeffrey Walker, "A Change of Venue: Joseph Smith's Escape from Liberty," presented at the Mormon History Association Conference, Sacramento, California, 2007 (copy in possession of author).

Smith and five others to Missouri based on these outstanding indictments. The extradition request was supported by the indictments, of which Governor Boggs had secured certified copies in July 1839.[65] What is not clear is whether Governor Boggs knew that in August 1839 all of these indictments had been dismissed based on a motion by the Boone County prosecuting attorney.[66] The judge in Boone County was Governor Boggs's successor, Thomas Reynolds.

Unfortunately, the resulting arrest warrant issued by Illinois Governor Carlin based on the extradition request of the succeeding Missouri Governor Reynolds for the arrest of Joseph Smith and others is not extant. It apparently was carried to Nauvoo, where the legal officer could not locate Smith or the others listed in it, and the warrant was consequently returned to Governor Carlin.

No further action was taken until Joseph Smith, who was returning to Nauvoo with his brother Hyrum and William Law from a mission in the East, was arrested outside of Quincy, Illinois, on June 5, 1841.[67] Upon arrest, Smith filed a petition for a writ of habeas corpus with Calvin Warren, the master in chancery for the Warren County Circuit Court. Warren granted Smith's petition and issued the writ of habeas corpus. That same evening, Associate Illinois Supreme Court Justice Stephen A. Douglas arrived in Quincy and agreed to hear the writ[68] at the Warren County Circuit Courthouse located

---

65. Thomas C. Burch to James L. Minor, June 24, 1839, Mormon Papers, Missouri Historical Society, St. Louis, Mo.; Indictment [for treason], Gallatin, Missouri, April [11,] 1839, certified copy, 6 July 1839, Joseph Smith Extradition Records, Abraham Lincoln Presidential Library, Springfield, Ill.; Indictment [for burglary], Gallatin, Missouri, April [11,] 1839, certified copy, July 6, 1839, Joseph Smith Extradition Records, Lincoln Presidential Library; Parley Pratt's Indictment [murder], Richmond, Missouri, April 24, 1839, certified copy, July 18, 1839, Joseph Smith Extradition Records, Lincoln Presidential Library.

66. See Circuit Court Record C, Boone County Circuit Court, Columbia, Missouri, 222, 261–62, 280–81, 316–17. Governor Boggs did not send these indictments to Illinois until near the close of his term as governor in December 1840. While this timing is not critical by itself, it becomes more intriguing as a result of Thomas Reynolds becoming the successor governor in Missouri. Prior to being elected governor, Thomas Reynolds was a circuit judge in the state's Second Circuit, which included Boone County that dismissed all of the indictments in August 1840. He, therefore, must have been fully aware that there were no outstanding indictments against any of the men identified in Governor Boggs's requisition made in September 1840. Whether Boggs knew this is uncertain. Circuit Court Record C, Boone County Circuit Court, Columbia, Missouri, 222, 261–62, 280–81, 316–17.

67. "The Late Proceedings," *Times and Seasons*, June 15, 1841.

68. An Act Regulating the Proceeding on Writs of Habeas Corpus, sec. 1, in *The Public and General Statute Laws of the State of Illinois* (Stephen F. Gale, 1839), 322 (hereafter cited as Illinois 1827 Act).

in Monmouth. He scheduled the hearing for the following Monday, June 8, 1841, and after a one-day postponement to allow the state to better prepare, the matter was heard on June 9, 1841.

The hearing started on a procedural matter, as the underlying indictments from the Missouri courts had not been attached to the arrest warrant as required by law. As this procedural irregularity could result in further postponement, both sides stipulated that such indictments existed. Ironically, had Joseph Smith's counsel further investigated this issue, they would have discovered that in fact no indictments existed, all of them having been dismissed in August 1840 by the now-sitting Missouri Governor Reynolds. Notwithstanding this oversight, Joseph Smith's counsel argued that the indictments supporting the requisition from Missouri were obtained by "fraud, bribery and duress." This phraseology closely paralleled the language in the Illinois 1827 Act for summarily ruling on a writ of habeas corpus.[69]

Stephen A. Douglas. While an Associate Illinois Supreme Court Justice, Douglas heard Joseph Smith's writ of habeas corpus over the first extradition attempt, ruling that the arrest itself was invalid. He was a witness for Joseph Smith during the second extradition effort, heard before Federal Judge Nathaniel Pope. Library of Congress.

Joseph Smith's counsel called four witnesses: Morris Phelps, Elias Higbee, Reynolds Cahoon, and George Robinson. The state objected that these witnesses should not be allowed to testify pertaining to the underlying merits of the case because the indictments sufficiently established the facts required at this stage of the litigation. Defense attorney Orville Browning argued for the admissibility of the testimony for more than two hours, concluding his remarks as follows:

> Great God! Have I not seen it? Yes, my eyes have beheld the blood stained traces, and the women and children, in the drear winter, who had travelled hundreds of miles barefoot, through frost and snow, to seek a refuge from their savage pursuers. Twas a scene of horror sufficient to enlist sympathy from an adamantine heart.

---

69. Illinois 1827 Act, sec. 3, 323–24.

And shall this unfortunate man, whom their fury has seen proper to select for sacrifice, be driven into such a savage band, and none dare to enlist in the cause of justice? If there was no other voice under heaven ever to be heard in this cause, gladly would stand alone, and proudly spent my latest breath in defence of an oppressed American citizen.[70]

In the end, Judge Douglas allowed the testimony from these witnesses, as well as several unidentified state witnesses before ruling on the testimony's admissibility.

Judge Douglas delivered his ruling the next morning. He sidestepped the issue as to whether the court could go beyond the indictments, and based his ruling on a narrow procedural issue—the validity of the warrant used to arrest Joseph Smith. It was undisputed that the arrest warrant actually used was the same warrant initially issued by Governor Carlin and returned to him after the legal officer failed to find Joseph Smith in Nauvoo. Douglas held that "the writ once being returned to the executive, by the Sheriff of Hancock County was dead and stood in the same relationship as any other writ which might issue from the Circuit Court and consequently the defendant [Smith] could not be held in custody on that writ."[71] Future Illinois Governor and former Illinois Supreme Court Justice Thomas Ford recorded in his work *History of Illinois* that Smith "was discharged upon the ground that the writ upon which he had been arrested had been once returned, before it had been executed, and was *functus officio*."[72] (*Functus officio* is Latin for "having performed his office." This term is applied to something which once had life and power, but which now has no utility whatsoever.)

While some would argue that Douglas's ruling was solely political move to garner the Mormon vote and lacked legal merit, a review of the doctrine of *functus officio* shows that it was actually the proper legal ruling.[73] Justice Douglas's ruling, while on a technical rather than a substantive basis, was in accord with established law. Accordingly, Joseph Smith was properly discharged.

---

70. "Late Proceedings."

71. "Late Proceedings."

72. Thomas Ford, *A History of Illinois: From its Commencement as a State in 1818 to 1847* (S.C. Griggs and Co., 1854), 266.

73. See Bouvier, *Law Dictionary*, 1:551; Hall v. Hall, 6 G. & L. 386, 411 (Md. 1834); Filkins v. Brockway, 19 Johns. 170, 170-171 (1821).

D. Nauvoo City Council's First Ordinances on Habeas Corpus (July and August 1842)

The Nauvoo City Council's first ordinance regarding habeas corpus was passed on July 5, 1842 (the "July 1842 City Ordinance"). What precipitated the passage of this ordinance is not certain. Yet, it may have been in response to the publishing on July 2, 1842, by the *Sangamon Journal* the first of a series of letters by John C. Bennett, the former mayor of Nauvoo and leading antagonist against the Mormons, especially Smith. This first letter, in part, solicits Governor Reynolds to seek the extradition of Smith "alone" to Governor Carlin and should Governor Carlin issue a writ for the arrest of Smith "in *my hands,* I will deliver him up to justice, or die in the attempt."[74]

The July 1842 City Ordinance provides as follows:

> Sec. 1. Be it, and it is hereby ordained by the city council of the city of Nauvoo, that no citizen of this city shall be taken out of the city by any writs without the privilege of investigation before the municipal court, and the benefit of a writ of habeas corpus, as granted in the 17th section of the Charter of this city. Be it understood that this ordinance is enacted for the protection of the citizens of this city, that they may in all cases have the right of trial in this city, and not be subjected to illegal process by their enemies.[75]

This ordinance is in accord with the Illinois 1827 Act. Section 3 that provides, in pertinent part, for the following rights of the prisoner and responsibilities of the court hearing the writ:

> Sec. 3.... The said prisoner may deny any of the material facts set forth in the return, or may allege any fact to shew, either that the imprisonment or detention is unlawful, or that he is then entitled to his discharge; which allegations or denials shall be made on oath.[76]

The July 1842 City Ordinance, which gives the prisoner the right to investigate the basis for his incarceration and the right to a trial arising from such investigation, does not broaden the right of habeas corpus further than section 3 of the Illinois 1827 Act.

---

74. See *Sangamon Journal,* July 2, 1842.

75. Nauvoo City Council, Minutes, July 5, 1842, Church History Library. This ordinance was published in the *Wasp* (Nauvoo) on July 16, 1842.

76. Illinois 1827 Act sec. 3, 323.

On August 8, 1842, the Nauvoo City Council refined the July 1842 City Ordinance by further delineating the procedures for an investigation.

The following charts compare the August 8 City Ordinance procedures to those provided in the Illinois 1827 Act. The August 8 City Ordinance can be separated into two parts: The first part examines the *process* of the arrest, and the second part examines the *substance* of the charges (looking behind the writ).

1. Challenging the process of the arrest

August 1842 City Ordinance	Illinois 1827 Act
"upon sufficient testimony" (sec. 1)	"by hearing the testimony and arguments" (sec. 3)
"that said writ or process was illegal" (sec. 1)	"second, where, though the original imprisonment was lawful, yet by some act, omission, or event, which has subsequently taken place, the party has become entitled to his discharge" (sec. 3)
"that said writ or process was not legally issued" (sec. 1)	"third, where the process is defective in some substantial form required by law; fourth, where the process, though in proper form, has been issued in a case, or under circumstance where the law does not allow process, or orders for imprisonment or arrest to issue" (sec. 3)
"that said writ or process did not proceed from proper authority" (sec. 1)	"first, where the court has exceeded the limits of its jurisdiction, either as to the matter, place, sum, or person . . . ; fifth, where, although in proper form, the process has been issued or executed by a person either unauthorized to issue or execute the same, or where the person having the custody of the prisoner under such process is not the person empowered by law to detain him" (sec. 3)

2. Challenging the substance of the arrest

August 1842 City Ordinance	Illinois 1827 Act
"fully hear the merits of the case, upon which said arrest was made, upon such evidence as may be produced and sworn before said court" (sec. 1)	"The said prisoner may deny any of the material facts set forth in the return, or may allege any fact to shew, either that the imprisonment or detention is unlawful, or that he is then entitled to his discharge; which allegations or denials shall be made on oath. The said return may be amended by leave of the court or judge, before or after the same is filed, as also may all suggestions made against it, that thereby material facts may be ascertained" (sec. 3)

"and shall have power to adjourn the hearing, and also issue process from time to time, in their discretion, in order to procure the attendance of witnesses, so that a fair and impartial trial and decision may be obtained in every such case." (sec. 1)

"If any person shall be committed for a criminal, or supposed criminal matter, and not admitted to bail, and shall not be tried on or before the second term of the court having jurisdiction of the offence, the prisoner shall be set at liberty by the court, unless the delay shall happen on the application of the prisoner. If such court, at the second term, shall be satisfied that due exertions have been made to procure the evidence for, and on behalf of the people, and that there are reasonable grounds to believe that such evidence may be procured at the third term, they shall have power to continue such case till the third term. If any such prisoner shall have been admitted to bail for a crime other than a capital offence, the court may continue the trial of said cause to a third term, it shall appear by oath or affirmation that the witness for the people of the state are absent, such witnesses being mentioned by name, and the court shewn wherein their testimony is material" (sec. 9)

As these charts demonstrate, section 1 of the August 8 City Ordinance was drafted in accord with corresponding rights and duties found in the Illinois 1827 Act. Thus, in enacting this ordinance, the Nauvoo City Council acted within its rights as granted under section 11 of the Nauvoo Charter.[77]

Section 2 of the August 8 City Ordinance further articulates the duty of the municipal court to assure that the underlying charges were not brought "through private pique, malicious intent, or religious or other persecution, falsehood or misrepresentation;" if so, the prisoner would be "discharged." Similar provisions are found in section 3 of the Illinois 1827 Act.[78] This section provides further evidence that this ordinance was created within the bounds granted under the Nauvoo Charter.

The term "discharged," as used in the August 8 City Ordinance and the Illinois 1827 Act, rendered into modern terminology, means "dismissed without prejudice." This means that should other facts or theories of law be discovered, the person released may be rearrested on the same or different charges arising from the same set of events. Stated another way, the doctrine of "double jeopardy" does not apply to a person discharged (or released) based on a writ

---

77. See Nauvoo City Charter.
78. Illinois 1827 Act, secs. 3,12 at 323–24, 326.

of habeas corpus.[79] The Illinois 1827 Act has a similar provision in section 7,[80] again evidencing the validity of the August 8 City Ordinance.

E. Missouri's Second Extradition Attempt (July 1842)

On May 6, 1842, former Missouri Governor Lilburn W. Boggs was shot at his home in Independence, Missouri.[81] Although serious, the injuries were not fatal.[82] A local citizens committee's initial investigation could find no legitimate suspects.[83] Early insinuations about a possible Mormon involvement gained traction in July 1842 with the published claims of dissident and former Nauvoo mayor John C. Bennett, alleging that Orrin Porter Rockwell, who was in Independence at the time, committed the crime under the direction of Joseph Smith.[84] While there was never any direct evidence implicating either Rockwell or Joseph Smith, Boggs's pivotal role in the displacement of the Mormons from Missouri in 1838 during his governorship made him a supposed target of the Mormons.

Boggs fueled this notion of Mormon involvement with an affidavit dated July 20, 1842, stating that he had information leading him to "believe" that Smith was an accessory before the fact in orchestrating the assassination attempt.[85] Based on this affidavit, Missouri Governor Thomas Reynolds issued

---

79. Kent, *Commentaries*, 2:30–31; see also Ex parte Bollman, 8 U.S. 75, 136-37, 4 Cranch 75 (1807); Gerard v. People, 4 Ill. 362, 363, 3 Scam 362 (1842).

80. Illinois 1827 Act, sec. 7, at 325.

81. William M. Boggs, "A Short Biographical Sketch of Lilburn W. Boggs by His Son," ed. F. A. Sampson, *Missouri Historical Review* 4 (1910): 106–8.

82. His injuries were so serious that several reported them as fatal. These erroneous reports quickly reached Nauvoo. See "Assassination of Ex-Governor Boggs of Missouri," *Wasp*, May 28, 1842, 4; Andrew H. Hedges, Alex B. Smith, and Richard Lloyd Anderson, eds., *Journals, Volume 2: December 1841–April 1843*, vol. 2 of the Journals series of *The Joseph Smith Papers*, ed. Dean C. Jessee, Ronald K. Esplin, and Richard Lyman Bushman (Salt Lake City: Church Historian's Press, 2011), 57 (hereafter cited as *JSP Journals 2*).

83. Citizens of Jackson County to Governor Reynolds, May 13, 1842, Thomas Reynolds, 1840–44, Office of Governor, Record Group 3.7, Missouri State Archives, Jefferson City, Mo; Samuel D. Lucas to Governor Reynolds, May 16, 1842, Thomas Reynolds, 1840–44, Office of Governor, Record Group 3.7, Missouri State Archives.

84. As noted above, Bennett wrote a series of published letters attacking the Mormon leadership, especially Joseph Smith. These letters were published initially in the Springfield newspaper *Sangamo Journal*. See *Sangamo Journal*, July 2, 15, 22, and 29, 1842.

85. Affidavit of Lilburn W. Boggs, July 20, 1842, Lincoln Presidential Library.

a requisition for the extradition of Smith and Rockwell[86] from Illinois to Missouri. As a result of this requisition, Illinois Governor Carlin issued an arrest warrant for Smith and Rockwell.[87] Adams County Sheriff Thomas C. King arrested Smith and Rockwell in Nauvoo on August 8, 1842, on the governor's warrant.

Anticipating that Joseph Smith and Rockwell would petition for a writ of habeas corpus, the Nauvoo City Council convened in the morning of August 8, 1842, and enacted the August 8 City Ordinance.[88]

Both Smith and Rockwell retained Sylvester Emmons as their counsel to prepare and argue their petitions for writs of habeas corpus. The basis for the petition included both procedural claims of the "illegality of the arrest under the Writ issued by Thomas Carlin Governor of this State," as well as factual claims as to "the utter groundlessness of the Charge preferred in said Writ."[89] The municipal court "heard the Petition read, and the reasons addressed by Councilor Emmons upon behalf of the Prisoner, and the nature of the Case, and prayer of the Petition," and granted the petition issuing a writ of habeas corpus for both Joseph Smith and Rockwell.[90] The return was "directed to Thomas C. King, to forthwith bring the body of Joseph Smith before this Court."[91] The minutes of this hearing ended with the court being adjourned "until the first Monday in September next."[92]

Sheriff King left Smith and Rockwell in the custody of the Nauvoo Marshal Dimick B. Huntington.[93] However, Sheriff King took with him the original arrest warrant from Governor Carlin, as well as the writs of habeas corpus granted by the municipal court. Without the arrest warrant, there was no legal basis for Marshal Huntington to keep Smith and Rockwell in custody, and for that reason they were released.[94]

---

86. Discussing Orrin Porter Rockwell's involvement and circumstances connected to these events is beyond the scope of this article. For information see Harold Schindler, *Orrin Porter Rockwell: Man of God, Son of Thunder,* 2d ed. (Salt Lake City: University of Utah Press, 1983), 67–91, 94–102; Richard L. Dewey, *Porter Rockwell, A Biography,* 10th ed. (New York City: Paramount Books, 1996), 49, 50, 55–77.

87. This was done in accord with the Act Concerning Fugitives from Justice, in *The Public and General Statute Laws of the State of Illinois* (Stephen F. Gale, 1839), 318–20.

88. Nauvoo City Council Proceedings (August 8, 1842), MS 3435, Church History Library.

89. *JSP Journals* 2, 181.

90. *JSP Journals* 2, 181.

91. *JSP Journals* 2, 181.

92. *JSP Journals* 2, 181.

93. Law of the Lord, 129, Church History Library.

94. Having the arrest warrant "in hand" was a threshold requirement for detaining a person. See An Act to Regulate the Apprehension of Offenders, and for Other Purposes,

Upon learning of these proceedings, coupled with Rockwell's and Smith's release, Governor Carlin took the position that the municipal court lacked judicial authority to rule on the warrant and that the ordinances passed by the Nauvoo City Council overstepped its legislative authority. Specifically, Governor Carlin contested the interpretation of sections 16 and 17 of the Nauvoo Charter that created the municipal court and articulated its jurisdiction, including its right to grant "writs of habeas corpus in all cases arising under the ordinances of the City Council."[95] Carlin argued that this provision only extended to cases that originated under a violation of a Nauvoo City Council ordinance. Carlin's position was that the underlying charge (accessory before the fact) and the resulting warrant did not arise from a Nauvoo ordinance and therefore was beyond the scope of the municipal court and the city council.

Nauvoo officials, however, argued that these sections must be read in conjunction with section 11 of the Nauvoo Charter that gave the Nauvoo City Council "power and authority to make, ordain, establish, and execute, all such ordinances, not repugnant to the Constitution of the United States or of this State."[96] Nauvoo officials argued that the laws protecting the citizens of Nauvoo (for example, rights pertaining to writs of habeas corpus) were well within the contours of both the U.S. and Illinois Constitutions and therefore fell directly within the jurisdiction of the municipal court and city council.

Most commentators unfortunately miss the legal dichotomy raised by Carlin and the Nauvoo officials. The issue was not whether the July, August, or November ordinances passed by the Nauvoo City Council were in legal accord with state or federal law, but whether the Nauvoo City Council could enact habeas corpus laws that applied to alleged crimes that did not occur in Nauvoo. Therefore, the issue for Carlin was not *how* the Nauvoo Municipal Court handled a petition for a writ of habeas corpus, but rather *whether* it could handle a petition.

The fact that no case or appeal was ever filed in any Illinois court to challenge the legality of any of these ordinances based on the Nauvoo City Council's interpretation of the Nauvoo Charter evidences their validity despite open hostility to the Mormons generally. In the end, the only remedy that was sought was to repeal the Nauvoo Charter itself. These actions in great measure legitimized these ordinances as being in accord with a charter that the Illinois legislature enacted for the operations of Nauvoo.

---

sec. 7, in *Public and General Statutes of the State of Illinois,* 239.

95. Nauvoo City Charter, secs. 16, 17 (1842).

96. Nauvoo City Charter, sec. 11.

Governor Carlin attempted to circumvent the issue of the legality of these ordinances by simply offering a reward for the capture of Smith and Rockwell. Captioned as a "Proclamation," Governor Carlin on September 20, 1842, announced a $200 reward each for the arrest of Smith and Rockwell. The basis of the proclamation was that "the said Rockwell and Joseph Smith resisted the Laws by refusing to go with the officers who had them in custody as fugitives from Justice, and escaped from the custody of said officers."[97] Such a basis is belied by (1) the facts of the petitions for habeas corpus being made by Smith and Rockwell, (2) the proceedings before the Nauvoo Municipal Court granting the writs, (3) the decision of Sheriff King to take the arrest warrants with him when he left Nauvoo to report to Carlin, and (4) the release of Smith and Rockwell by Marshal Huntington based on not having the arrest warrants. Nevertheless, Joseph Smith and Porter Rockwell thereafter went into hiding to avoid being rearrested.

Thomas Ford was elected Illinois governor in November 1842, replacing Thomas Carlin. With this change in administration, a delegation representing Joseph Smith traveled from Nauvoo to Springfield in early December to determine, in part, Governor Ford's disposition regarding the Missouri extradition efforts.[98] After meeting with several prominent attorneys and judges, including Judge Stephen Douglas and Governor Ford, the delegation concluded that if Joseph Smith would voluntarily appear in Springfield, the entire situation could be acceptably resolved. The delegation also met[99] and

---

97. "Proclamation," *Illinois Register,* September 30, 1842.

98. This trip to Springfield had been previously scheduled to hopefully conclude Smith's bankruptcy. Smith and several other prominent Mormon leaders had filed under the newly enacted bankruptcy laws on April 28, 1842. Dallin H. Oaks and Joseph I. Bentley, "Joseph Smith and Legal Process: In the Wake of the Steamboat Nauvoo," *BYU Law Review* (1976): 735–82.

99. Sidney Rigdon had contacted Justin Butterfield through Calvin A. Warren, an attorney who was assisting various Church leaders file under the newly enacted federal bankruptcy laws in October 1842. Rigdon had asked for a more formal opinion. By letter dated October 20, 1842, written from Chicago, where Butterfield lived and practiced law, Butterfield further articulated his legal position. Justin Butterfield to Sidney Rigdon, October 20, 1842, Sidney Rigdon Collection, Church History Library. Butterfield outlined his core argument: "It is not sufficient … that he should be 'charged' with having fled from justice, unless he has actually fled from the state where the office was committed to another state; the governor of this state has no jurisdiction over his persons and cannot deliver him up." Butterfield to Rigdon, October 20, 1842, 2, spelling, grammar and punctuation regularized, emphasis in original.

Butterfield also addresses an apparent concern that the court would not look behind the Reynolds requisition. To this point Butterfield replied: "To this I answer that upon a

retained Justin Butterfield,[100] the United States Attorney for the District of Illinois, to represent Joseph Smith in this matter.[101]

Consistent with the delegation's findings, on December 27, 1842, Joseph Smith, accompanied by a few close colleagues, left for Springfield, arriving on December 30, 1842. Upon their arrival Butterfield's initial efforts were to make sure the niceties of the procedural requirements were satisfied. Wilson Law, a general in the Nauvoo militia, officially "arrested" Joseph Smith pursuant to the September 20 proclamation of Governor Carlin.[102] However, because the arrest warrant that Carlin had previously issued was still in the possession of Sheriff King and it became apparent that getting the arrest warrant in a timely manner might prove difficult, Butterfield recommended seeking a new arrest warrant from Governor Ford. The new warrant could then be used as the legal basis for filing a new petition for a writ of habeas corpus.

The next morning (December 31), Butterfield prepared a petition to Governor Ford for a new arrest warrant. Ford granted the petition and issued the warrant. Butterfield then filed a petition in the United States Circuit Court in Springfield for a writ of habeas corpus to review the arrest the same day.[103] With the filing of the petition, Federal Judge Nathaniel Pope[104] permitted Butterfield

---

writ of habeas corpus the court would be bound to try the question whether Smith fled from justice from Missouri to this state; the affidavit of Mr. Boggs is not conclusive on this point—it may be rebutted that unless Smith is a person who fled from justice, he is not subject to be delivered up under the specific provisions of our own Habeas Corpus Act. He has a right to show the affidavit as false evidence and that the order for his arrest was obtained by false pretenses...." Butterfield to Rigdon, October 20, 1842, 2–3, 5, spelling and punctuation regularized.

100. Justin Butterfield (1790–1855) was appointed in 1841 by President Harrison as the United States District Attorney for the District of Illinois. *Historical Encyclopedia of Illinois*, ed. Newton Bateman and Paul Selby (Munsell Publishing Co., 1918), 1:70. Perhaps his admiration of Daniel Webster was the reason that he often attended court dressed "*a la Webster*, in blue dress-coat and metal buttons, with bluff vest." *History of Sangamon County, Illinois* (Inter-State Publishing Co., 1881), 103. Usher F. Linder, *Reminiscences of the Early Bench and Bar of Illinois* (Chicago Legal News Company, 1879), 87–88.

101. Justin Butterfield to Joseph Smith, December 17, 1842; Law of the Lord, 215; JSP Journals 2 (December 17, 1842), 181–82.

102. JSP Journals 2 (December 27, 1842), 195.

103. Smith's Petition for a Writ of Habeas Corpus issued by Governor Ford, December 31, 1842, Lincoln Presidential Library (spelling regularized).

104. Nathaniel Pope (1784–1850) was appointed by President James Monroe to the federal bench for the District of Illinois in 1819. Paul M. McClelland, *Nathaniel Pope from 1784 to 1850, a Memoir* (Springfield, Ill., 1937); Linder, *Reminiscences of the Early Bench*, 215–17. Paul M. Angle, *Nathaniel Pope 1784–1850—a Memoir* (Privately Printed, 1937).

to address the court. Butterfield articulated the procedural posture of the matter (the requisition from Governor Reynolds, the proclamation of Governor Carlin and the new arrest warrant from Governor Ford), as well as the substantive position of Joseph Smith (that the requisition was flawed because Joseph Smith never fled from Missouri as alleged). He then introduced Joseph Smith to the court, read the petition for a writ of habeas corpus, and requested a trial on the underlying extradition effort and for bail pending the trial.[105] Judge Pope granted the writ of habeas corpus,[106] set bail at $4,000,[107] and scheduled the hearing on the return of the writ for the following Monday, January 2, 1843.

On Monday morning, Joseph Smith was represented before Judge Pope by two attorneys: Justin Butterfield, who lived in Chicago, and Benjamin S. Edwards,[108] who lived in Springfield. Illinois Attorney General Josiah Lamborn represented the state of Illinois.[109]

Lamborn immediately sought a continuance to have additional preparation time for the hearing on the return of the writ. Judge Pope granted the request and moved the hearing to Wednesday, January 4, 1843. Butterfield then moved to file objections to the factual basis of the extradition warrant upon which the writ of habeas corpus was taken. It does not appear that Lamborn objected to the motion. Butterfield's motion was supported by an affidavit of Joseph Smith that noted:

> Joseph Smith being brought up on Habeas Corpus before this Court comes and denies the matter set forth in the return to the same in this, that he is not a fugitive from the justice of the State of Missouri; but alleges and is ready to prove that he was not in the State of Missouri at the time of the Commission of the alleged crime set forth in the affidavit of L. W. Boggs, nor had he been in said State for more than three years previous to that time, nor has he been in

---

105. *JSP Journals* 2 (December 31, 1842), 200–204.

106. Writ of Habeas Corpus ordered by Judge Nathaniel Pope, December 31, 1842, Lincoln Presidential Library, spelling regularized.

107. Section 4 of the Illinois 1827 Habeas Corpus Act required that if bail is admitted, the prisoner (Smith, in this case) "shall enter into recognizance with one or more securities." The record indicates that Judge James Adams and Wilson Law acted as securities for Smith. *JSP Journals* 2 (December 31, 1842), 204.

108. Benjamin S. Edwards (1818–1886). See Linder, *Reminiscences of the Early Bench*, 350–52. See David Herbert Donald, *Lincoln's Herndon: A Biography* (Da Capo Press, 1948), 139–41; *Illinois State Register* (Springfield), February 5, 1886, 7.

109. Josiah Lamborn (1809–1847). See Bateman and Selby, *Historical Encyclopedia of Illinois*, 1:327. *Transactions of the Illinois State Historical Society* (Springfield, Ill.: Phillips Bros., 1903), 218. Linder, *Reminiscences of the Early Bench*, 258–59.

that State since that time—but on the contrary at the time the said alleged assault was made upon the said Boggs as set forth in said Affidavit the said Smith was at Nauvoo in the County of Hancock in the State of Illinois, and that he has not fled from the justice of the State of Missouri and taken refuge in the State of Illinois, as is most untruly stated in the warrant upon which he is arrested and that the matter set forth in the requisition of the Governor of Missouri and in the said Warrant are not supported by oath.

Joseph Smith[110]

The following day, Butterfield drafted two additional affidavits—one to be signed by a group of Mormons and the other by a group of non-Mormons, both affirming Joseph Smith's presence in Nauvoo around the date that Boggs was shot.[111] It appears that these affidavits were prepared to make sure that this evidence became part of the record, as Butterfield probably anticipated the objections from Lamborn. Both of these affidavits were submitted and read into the record at the beginning of the hearing the following day.

On Wednesday, January 4, 1843, the court convened at 9 a.m., all parties being present.[112] The court started by inquiring whether either party had any preliminary motions. Both did. Lamborn had two—the first was a motion to dismiss the issuance of the writ of habeas corpus on the ground that the court had no jurisdiction to hear the matter and the second was effectively a motion in limine (a motion before the trial to resolve evidentiary rulings) to prevent any inquiry into any facts "behind the writ."[113] Butterfield and Edwards countered the two motions, first articulating that the court not only had jurisdiction over this matter but exclusive jurisdiction, because Joseph Smith was in custody "under color of U.S. Law."[114] Concerning Lamborn's second motion, Butterfield argued that the facts were undisputable—Smith

---

110. Affidavit of Joseph Smith, January 2, 1843, Church History Library.

111. See *JSP Journals* 2 (May 7, 1842), 54–55, identifying that Smith was in Nauvoo on the date that Boggs was shot, where he both reviewed the Nauvoo Legion and had dinner with a group of "distinguished Strangers," including Stephen A. Douglas.

112. Numerous accounts report that Judge Pope had several young ladies sit on either side of him at the bench during these proceedings, including his daughters, Butterfield's daughter, and Mary Todd Lincoln, who had recently married Abraham Lincoln. *History of Sangamon County, Illinois*, 103–4; Angle, *Nathaniel Pope 1794–1850*, 56; Isaac Newton Arnold, *Reminiscences of the Illinois Bar Forty Years Ago* (Fergus Printing Co., 1881), 6–7; *JSP Journals* 2 (January 2, 1843), 211–12.

113. *JSP Journals* 2 (January 4, 1843), 216–18.

114. *JSP Journals* 2 (January 4, 1843), 219–20.

could not be a fugitive from a crime that occurred in Missouri when he was in Illinois at the time.[115] Butterfield then had read into the record the two prepared affidavits. The first affidavit, signed by ten Mormons, itemized the times they knew Smith was in Nauvoo, making it impossible for him to have been in Missouri participating in the attempt on Boggs's life.[116]

The second affidavit, signed by Stephen A. Douglas and Jacob Backenstos, confirmed "that [they] were at Nauvoo, in the County of Hancock in this State, on the seventh day of May last, that they saw Joseph Smith on that day reviewing the Nauvoo Legion at that place, in the presence of several thousand persons."[117]

With these preliminary matters heard, open statements were given. Butterfield's opening lines have been recorded in numerous reports and were so poetic and classic that they bear repeating. As reported by a fellow attorney who was present:

> Mr. Butterfield ... rose with dignity and amidst the most profound silence. Pausing, and running his eyes admiringly from the central figure of Judge Pope, along the rows of lovely women on each side of him, he said: "May it please the Court: I appear before you today under circumstances most novel and peculiar. I am to address the 'Pope' (bowing to the Judge) surrounded by angels (bowing still lower to the ladies), in the presence of the holy Apostles, in behalf of the Prophet of the Lord."[118]

Butterfield then argued that the federal court not only had jurisdiction but also had exclusive jurisdiction to hear the return. In support, Butterfield cited *Jack v. Martin,* a New York case involving the return of a slave from Louisiana. The New York Court of Errors held that the state process could not circumvent federal process, noting that "whenever the terms in which a power is granted to Congress, or the nature of the power requires that it should be exercised exclusively by Congress, the subject is as completely taken from the

115. *JSP Journals 2* (January 4, 1843), 222–24.

116. Collaborative Affidavits of Wilson Law, Henry Sherwood, Theodore Turley, Shadrach Roundy, William Clayton, Hyrum Smith, John Taylor, William Marks, Lorin Walker, and Willard Richards, January 4, 1843, Church History Library.

117. Collaborative Affidavits of Stephen A. Douglas, James H. Ralson, Almeron Wheat, J. B. Backenstos, January 4, 1843, Church History Library.

118. Arnold, *Reminiscences of the Illinois Bar,* 3.

state legislature as if they had been expressly forbidden to act."[119] Butterfield opined, "Has not my client, Joseph Smith, the rights of a [slave]?"[120]

Butterfield turned to the second and substantive issue before the court, framing it as follows: "Has the court power to issue Habeas Corpus? It has. Is the return sufficient to hold the prisoner in custody without further testimony? Unless it appears on the testimony that he is a fugitive, it is not sufficient."[121] Butterfield then dissected the affidavit of ex–Missouri Governor Boggs and the requisition from Missouri Governor Carlin, noting that Boggs's affidavit never alleges that Smith was in Missouri when the crime occurred. Next, he cited Carlin's requisition that claimed that Smith was a "fugitive from justice." Butterfield repeated that to qualify as a fugitive Smith had to have "fled" from Missouri, summarising: "Governor Carlin would not have given up his dog on such a requisition."[122]

Butterfield examined the facts supported by the two affidavits previously read into the record that Joseph Smith was in Nauvoo at the time the crime occurred in Missouri as follows: "He [Smith] was at officer's drill until 6 and in the Lodge from 6 to 9 o'clock.... 300 miles off in uniform reviewing the Nauvoo Legion, instead of running away from Boggs in uniform. Judge Douglas partook of the hospitality of General Smith[;] instead of fleeing from Justice, he was dining with the highest court judge in our land."[123]

Butterfield then articulated the established status of the law as to when one could look behind the writ on a return for a writ of habeas corpus stating that "[the] power of Habeas Corpus is pretty well settled." Citing a case involving a conviction for embezzlement, Butterfield noted that on a return for a writ of habeas corpus one "cannot go behind the Judgment. [When a] judgment is not at issue, [one] can go behind the writ."[124]

---

119. Jack v. Martin, 14 Wend. 507 at 535 (N.Y. Court for the Correction of Errors, 1835), quoting Sturges v. Crowninshield, 17 U.S. (4 Wheat.) 122, 193 (1819).

120. *JSP Journals* 2 (January 4, 1843), 220. Butterfield also quoted for the same proposition Priggs v. Commonwealth of Pennsylvania, 41 U.S. 539, 16 Peters 611 (1842). The Priggs court cited to Sturges v. Crowninshield, 17 U.S. (4 Wheat.) 122 (1819).

121. *JSP Journals* 2 (January 4, 1843), 220–21 (spelling and punctuation regularized).

122. *JSP Journals* 2 (January 4, 1843), 222, spelling, grammar, and punctuation regularized.

123. *JSP Journals* 2 (January 4, 1842), 222–23.

124. *JSP Journals* 2 (January 4, 1843), 223, spelling, grammar, and punctuation regularized. Butterfield cited and discussed Ex Parte Watkins, 32 U.S. (7 Pet.) 568 (1833), Ex Parte Burford, 7 U.S. (3 Cranch) 448, 451–52 (1806); In re Clark, 9 Wend. 212, 220–21 (Supreme Court of Judicature of New York, 1832); and the unsuccessful requisition by an Alabama governor to extradite a newspaper publisher in New York for distributing a

Butterfield closed his argument with the following summation:

> That an attempt should be made to deliver up a man who has never been out of the State strikes at all the liberty of our institutions. His fate today may be yours tomorrow. I do not think the defendant ought under any circumstances to be delivered up to Missouri. It is a matter of history that he and his people have been murdered and driven from the state. He had better been sent to the gallows. He is an innocent and unoffending man. The difference is this people believe in prophecy and others do not. Old prophets prophesied in poetry and the modern in prose.[125]

After a short recess, Lamborn made his final argument and the case was submitted to Judge Pope. The judge indicated that the court would issue its opinion at 9:00 a.m. the following day.[126] Willard Richards provides us with a succinct summary of the day's hearing:

> The courtroom was crowded the whole of the trial and the utmost decorum and good feeling prevailed. Esquire Butterfield managed the case very learned and judiciously. Preceded by Esquire Edwards who made some very pathetic allusions to our sufferings in Missouri. Esquire Lamborn was not severe apparently saying little more than the nature of his situation required—and no more than would be useful in satisfying the public mind—that there had been a fair investigation of the whole matter."[127]

The following morning Judge Pope rendered his opinion in open court, ruling in Joseph Smith's favor and discharging him.[128] Pope's written opinion was published in the *Sangamo Journal* on January 19, 1843. Mormon-operated newspapers the *Times and Seasons* and the *Wasp* ran the opinion as well.[129] The opinion was cited in federal and state courts for more than a hundred years.

---

libelous newspaper in Alabama despite having never been in Alabama. *Documents of the Assembly of the State of New-York, Fifty-Ninth Session* (E. Cromwell, 1836), 1:40–51.

125. *JSP Journals* 2 (January 4, 1843), 224, spelling, grammar, and punctuation regularized.

126. *JSP Journals* 2, 225.

127. *JSP Journals* 2, 225, spelling, grammar, and punctuation regularized.

128. *JSP Journals* 2, 233.

129. "Circuit Court of the U. States for the District of Illinois," *Times and Seasons,* January 16, 1843 (three days earlier than the *Sangamo Journal*); "Circuit Court of the United States for the District of Illinois," *Wasp,* January 28, 1843.

The importance of the case was not lost on Judge Pope, who introduced the opinion as follows:

> The importance of this case, and the consequences which may flow from an erroneous precedent, affecting the lives and liberties of our citizens, have impelled the court to bestow upon it the most anxious consideration.... When the patriots and wise men who framed our constitution were in anxious deliberation to form a perfect union among the states of the confederacy, two great sources of discord presented themselves to their consideration; the commerce between the states, and fugitives from justice and labor. The border collisions in other countries had been seen to be a fruitful source of war and bloodshed, and most wisely did not constitution confer upon the national government, the regulation of those matters, because of its exemption from the excited passions awakened by conflicts between neighboring states, and its ability alone to adopt a uniform rule, and establish uniform laws among all the states in those cases.[130]

Pope dismissed Lamborn's argument that there was "greater sanctity in a warrant issued by the governor, than by an inferior officer." Pope poetically responded:

> Magna Charta established the principles of liberty; the habeas corpus protected them. It matters not how great or obscure the prisoner, how great or obscure the prison-keeper, this munificent writ, wielded by an independent judge, reaches all. It penetrates alike the royal towers and the local prisons, from the garret to the secret recesses of the dungeon. All doors fly open at its command, and the shackles fall from the limbs of prisoners of state as readily as from those committed by subordinate officers.[131]

Pope then turned his attention to the second issue before him: Could the factual basis of the moving pleadings be questioned—here the Boggs affidavit and the Reynolds requisition. To answer this question, Pope focused on what "proof" existed to support the extradition. Pope identified that the "proof is 'an indictment or affidavit,' to be certified by the governor demanding the extradition. The return brings before the court the warrant, the demand and the affidavit." Pope concluded that the "affidavit being thus verified,

---

130. Ex parte Smith, 22 F. Cas. 373, 376 (C.C.D. Ill. 1843) (No. 12,968).
131. Ex parte Smith, 22 F. Cas. at 377.

furnished the only evidence upon which the Governor of Illinois could act." He acknowledged that Joseph Smith presented opposing "affidavits proving that he was not in Missouri at the date of the shooting of Boggs." While the state objected to such testimony on the basis that it required looking behind the return, Pope determined that such evidence was unnecessary, "inasmuch as it thinks Smith entitled to his discharge for defect in the affidavit."[132]

The affidavits presented by Joseph Smith all focused on the fact that Smith was not in Missouri when the crime was committed and therefore could not have fled from the justice of Missouri. Pope succinctly reasoned:

> As it is not charged that the crime was committed by Smith in Missouri, the governor of Illinois could not cause him to be removed to that state, unless it can be maintained that the state of Missouri can entertain jurisdiction of crimes committed in other states. The affirmative of this proposition was taken in the argument with a zeal indicating sincerity. But no adjudged case or dictum was adduced in support of it. The court conceives that none can be.[133]

Some commentators have pointed out that the crime of being an accessory was somehow different in the early nineteenth century than it is today and that Smith would not have to be in Missouri to be an accessory today. However, being physically in Missouri is not a requisite then or today to conspire to commit a crime. The issue was not whether Smith had committed a crime, but whether the extradition by Missouri was proper.

Pope then criticized and dismissed the facts asserted in the Boggs affidavit, finding that "beliefs" without facts are insufficient, as are "legal conclusions." Pope simply found that the "affidavit is fatally defective." Pope then, in preparation for the inevitable conclusion, provided a context to his ruling:

> The return is to be most strictly construed in favor of liberty ... No case can arise demanding a more searching scrutiny into the evidence, than in cases arising under this part of the constitution of the United States. It is proposed to deprive a freeman of his liberty— to deliver him into the custody of strangers, to be transported to a foreign state, to be arraigned for trial before a foreign tribunal, governed by laws unknown to him—separated from his friends, his family and his witnesses, unknown and unknowing. Had he an immaculate character, it would not avail him with strangers. Such

---

132. Ex parte Smith, 22 F. Cas. at 377.
133. Ex parte Smith, 22 F. Cas. 378.

a spectacle is appalling enough to challenge the strictest analysis. The framers of the constitution were not insensible of the importance of courts possessing the confidence of the parties.[134]

Pope's ruling was clear and concise: "The affidavit is insufficient—1st. because it is not positive; 2d. because it charges no crime; 3d. it charges no crime committed in the state of Missouri. Therefore, he [Smith] did not flee from the justice of the state of Missouri, nor has he taken refuge in the state of Illinois."[135] Joseph Smith was discharged.

F. Nauvoo City Council's Final Ordinance on Habeas Corpus (November 1842)

The Nauvoo City Council made its final additions to the Municipal Code regarding habeas corpus in November 1842 (the "November 1842 City Ordinance").[136] The November 1842 City Ordinance was the most detailed ordinance passed by the city council regarding writs of habeas corpus. It was this ordinance that some later writers claimed was abusive and overreaching. However, a careful reading of the November 1842 City Ordinance demonstrates that the Nauvoo City Council merely adopted, in substance, the entire Illinois 1827 Act.

Indeed, more than 80 percent of the Illinois 1827 Act was incorporated verbatim by the Nauvoo City Council in the November 1842 City Ordinance. Yet, while the similarities are striking, looking at the differences is crucial. These differences highlight both the sophisticated understanding that the Nauvoo City Council had of the habeas corpus laws, as well as the rights it understood were extended to the city's inhabitants through the Nauvoo Charter.

Section 1 of the November 1842 City Ordinance differs from the Illinois 1827 Act only in that the November 1842 City Ordinance refers to the city of Nauvoo and the Nauvoo Municipal Court (as authorized to hear writs of habeas corpus in section 17 of the Nauvoo Charter) instead of referring to the state of Illinois and the courts of Illinois. The other change in section 1 centered on the process to file a petition requesting a writ of habeas corpus. While the Illinois 1827 Act describes the process, the November City Ordinance provides sample forms to use for a petition.

---

134. *Ex parte Smith*, 22 F. Cas. at 379.
135. *Ex parte Smith*, 22 F. Cas. at 379.
136. Rough Draft Notes of History of the Church, 1842b-015, Church History Library.

Section 2 defines who can file for a petition for a writ of habeas corpus, beyond those arrested for a crime. The November 1842 City Ordinance adds a penalty for violating the provisions of sections 1 and 2.

Sections 3–7 of the November 1842 City Ordinance are materially identical to the corresponding sections in the Illinois 1827 Act, including provisions dealing with the hearings on writs of habeas corpus (sections 3), issues of bail, recognizance, and security (sections 4), procedures for remand (sections 5), second writs of habeas corpus after discharge (sections 6), and procedures for discharge (sections 7).

Section 8 of the November 1842 City Ordinance omitted the corresponding section of the Illinois 1827 Act in its entirety. In the Illinois 1827 Act, this section excluded federal claims, war claims, slavery claims, and high crimes from the act, leaving them to the federal courts. The November 1842 City Ordinance does not include these exclusions. This was done in apparent reliance on section 11 of the Nauvoo Charter. As the Constitution of the United States provided for relief under a writ of habeas corpus for these exclusions, the Nauvoo City Council included them within the scope of its municipal code.

No material differences are found in section 9, with the exception that the November 1842 City Ordinance does not grant as much discretion to the court to delay the resolution of a habeas corpus hearing as does the Illinois 1827 Act.

Section 10 of the Illinois 1827 Act is omitted in the November 1842 City Ordinance. This section deals with the moving of a prisoner from one county to another that would have the impact of delaying or avoiding a trial. As the interest of the Nauvoo City Council was to allow its citizens to have their concerns addressed in Nauvoo, the issue of moving a prisoner out of Nauvoo was apparently deemed unnecessary.

Section 11 of the November 1842 City Ordinance does not include a provision for moving a prisoner to a different jail should an overcrowding issue arise, or moving to a different jail based on a federal law or executive demand. Basically, it said that if prisoners were in Nauvoo, they would stay in Nauvoo until the habeas corpus matter was resolved.

Sections 12–17 of the November 1842 City Ordinance are virtually identical to the corresponding provisions of the Illinois 1827 Act.

Finally, section 18 of the November 1842 City Ordinance differs from the last section of the Illinois 1827 Act in the fact that the Act provided that the supreme and circuit courts shall have power to grant petitions for writs of habeas corpus. The November City Ordinance deleted these provisions, since section 17 of the Nauvoo Charter provides that the "Municipal Court shall have power to grant writs of habeas corpus in all cases arising under the ordinances of the City Council."

As this summary evidence shows, the Nauvoo City Council, under the leadership of Mayor Joseph Smith, adopted a consistent, albeit increasingly detailed, approach to the use of habeas corpus in Nauvoo. This approach is characterized by three guiding principles. First, the Nauvoo Municipal Court was fully vested with the power to grant and hear writs of habeas corpus. Second, the Nauvoo City Council was empowered with the rights to enact ordinances for the city of Nauvoo to the extent permitted by the United States Constitution or the Illinois Constitution, whichever was broader. Lastly, the municipal court had a duty when hearing a writ of habeas corpus to look at both the procedural legality of an arrest and the substantive merits of the underlying charges.

V. Conclusion

Any credible analysis of Joseph Smith's use of the writ of habeas corpus must start with an understanding of the law as it existed and applied in the early nineteenth century. Without this indispensible perspective, the legal theories, arguments, enactments, and actions raised by or for Smith under the rubric of "habeas corpus rights" cannot be properly understood. With this understanding, the actions of the various witnesses, lawyers, clerks, aldermen, council members, sheriffs, and judges involved in Joseph Smith's world make legal sense.

While placing the right of habeas corpus in the United States Constitution itself evidenced the importance that the Founding Fathers placed on this great writ, America's jurisprudence of the writ diverged quickly and distinctively from English law. A central aspect of this evolution was the allowance of an expanded review of the underlying charges allegedly supporting an arrest and detention. The courts often referred to this review as "looking behind the writ." Nineteenth-century legal scholars and practitioners recognized this development and provided useful legal analysis and rules of application. The need for a review of both the procedural and substantive aspects of a case necessarily decreased as a case moved through the system: a person who claimed he was incorrectly arrested could demand looking at both; a need to examine the substance of a detention decreases once a grand jury indicts the accused, absent fraud or bad faith; and if a trial resulted in a conviction, the need to look at the substance of the detention would be only to challenge the trial itself.

This analysis is crucial in understanding how Joseph Smith employed the use of habeas corpus when he was arrested. Critics have argued that Smith attempted to use habeas corpus in an overreaching, even abusive manner. Their critique is principally based on his repeated efforts to have the court look "behind the writ" and determine the legitimacy (or illegitimacy, as he argued) of the underlying charges. Yet these critics have failed to acknowledge that these cases all involved the first phase of the litigation or arose in cases where fraud and bad faith were alleged. In these circumstances, his request to look behind the writ was supported both by the applicable law and the facts.

In the end, it is clear that Joseph Smith and his advisors had a very sophisticated and accurate understanding of the scope and application of the right to habeas corpus in his day. This scope included the important evolution that the writ experienced as it was transformed from an English prerogative writ of the king to a constitutionally based right of all Americans. Upon his return to Nauvoo on June 30, 1843, being under arrest pursuant to a third and final extradition request from the governor of Missouri, and in anticipation of having his petition for a writ of habeas corpus heard the next day, Smith, in speaking to the citizens of Nauvoo, aptly and passionately summarized how he saw the right of habeas corpus: "The Constitution of the United States declares that the privilege of the writ of Habeas Corpus shall not be denied. Deny me the right of Habeas Corpus, and I will fight with gun, sword, cannon, whirlwind, and thunder, until they are used up like the Kilkenny cats."[137]

This article was originally published as part of "Habeas Corpus in Early Nineteenth-Century Mormonism: Joseph Smith's Legal Bulwark for Personal Freedom," BYU Studies Quarterly 52, no. 1 (2013): 4–97. The unabridged version of this article may be found at byustudies.byu.edu.

---

137. Joseph Smith, in *Journal of Discourses*, 26 vols. (Liverpool: F. D. Richards, 1855–86), 2:163, 167. The term "Kilkenny cat" refers to anyone who is a tenacious fighter. To "fight like a Kilkenny cat" refers to an anonymous Irish limerick about two cats that fought to the death and ate each other up so that only their tails were left.

Chapter Seventeen

Defining Adultery under Illinois and Nauvoo Law

M. Scott Bradshaw

The final weeks of the Prophet Joseph Smith's life were busy. Besides the usual press of Church business, Joseph was involved with many things, including reviewing work on the construction of the Nauvoo Temple, selling land, paying debts, making social visits, receiving visits from Indians and dignitaries, attending military training, and coordinating his presidential campaign. He also had to contend with brief bouts of illness affecting both him and Emma, swelteringly hot weather, the defection or removal of highly placed Church and civic leaders, the publication of an anti-Mormon newspaper, and a series of lawsuits and indictments brought against him.[1]

---

1. See generally Scott Faulring, ed., *An American Prophet's Record: The Diaries and Journals of Joseph Smith* (Salt Lake City: Signature Books, 1987); J. Christopher Conkling, *A Joseph Smith Chronology* (Salt Lake City: Deseret Book, 1979); and *A Chronology of the Life of Joseph Smith, BYU Studies* 46, no. 4 (2007). As to legal challenges, the indictments for adultery and perjury are described below in this article. Charges against Joseph before the Municipal Court of Nauvoo brought by Chauncey Higbee were investigated on May 8, 1844. On June 12 and 17, 1844, Joseph was arrested and charged for the destruction of the *Nauvoo Expositor* press; he was discharged both times, later voluntarily travelling to Carthage on June 24, 1844, to face new charges related to the destruction of the Expositor. The next day Joseph and Hyrum were charged with treason, a nonbailable offence. Joseph and his attorneys moved for a change of venue on June 27, out of concern that he would not obtain a fair trial in Carthage. Additionally, at least three civil suits were filed against Joseph in Hancock County during this time. These were *Charles A. Foster v. Joseph Smith, Chauncey Higbee v. Joseph Smith,* and *Alexander Sympson v. Joseph Smith* (discussed below). Two of these were known enemies of Joseph (Foster and Higbee). The third (Sympson), also discussed below, was to be a witness in the adultery trial against

Among the legal challenges that Joseph faced at this time was an indictment for adultery, a charge which arose out of his relationship with Maria
Lawrence,[2] a young English convert to whom Joseph was sealed in Nauvoo
and who lived with Joseph and Emma in their home. Several authors have
assumed that Joseph's plural marriages were entered into in violation of the
law.[3] Indeed, given the conservative social mores of nineteenth century, one
could easily assume that this was the case. However, a study of Illinois law
reveals a different situation. As explained below, Joseph could not have been
properly convicted of adultery under the law of Illinois in 1844. Illinois law
only criminalized adultery or fornication if it was "open." Had Joseph lived to
face trial on this charge, he would have had good reason to expect acquittal
because his relationships with his plural wives were not open, but were kept
confidential and known by a relative few.[4] Given a fair trial on this indictment, Joseph could have relied on several legal defenses.

Joseph. Ironically, all three of these suits were transferred to the court in McDonough
County, Illinois, after the plaintiffs expressed concern that they would not obtain a fair
trial in Carthage. The author discovered them in the Illinois Regional Archives Deposi-
tory collections of Western Illinois University a number of years back; see Circuit Court
files 1844, boxes 190, 196.

2. For background on Maria, and on Joseph's polygamy in general, see Todd Compton,
In Sacred Loneliness: The Plural Wives of Joseph Smith (Salt Lake City: Signature Books,
1997), 473–85; a recent work, Brian C. Hales, *Joseph Smith's Polygamy,* 3 vols. (Salt Lake
City: Greg Kofford Books, 2013), contains considerable information about Maria (see the
index, vol. 2).

3. See for example Compton, *In Sacred Loneliness,* 476–77; Hales, *Joseph Smith's Polygamy,* 2:192–94; 237; and D. Michael Quinn, *The Mormon Hierarchy: Origins of Power* (Salt
Lake City: Signature Books, 1995), 88.

4. For example, Hales, *Joseph Smith's Polygamy,* 1:499, quotes Eliza R. Snow, one of the
women to whom Joseph was sealed: "We women kept secrets in those days." Desdemona
Fullmer reports that she was forbidden to make known to her parents that she had been
sealed to Joseph, as it "would endanger the life of Joseph and also many of the Saints." See
Hales, *Joseph Smith's Polygamy,* 2:3. Emily Dow Partridge recalls that both she and her
sister Eliza were sealed to Joseph, but neither of them knew it initially because "everything
was so secret." See Hales, *Joseph Smith's Polygamy,* 2:13. By the time of Joseph's death, Hales
states that "several hundred Latter-day Saints had been taught about the principle [of
plural marriage] by Joseph Smith or by an authorized representative." See Hales, *Joseph
Smith's Polygamy,* 2:[33]. While the circle of those who knew of the doctrine was substantial, the citizens of Nauvoo overall, and the body of the LDS Church, were not yet aware of
the doctrine. Most of those who knew of the doctrine would not have known who Joseph's
plural wives were. The diaries and correspondence of polygamy insiders from the Nauvoo
years are almost silent on the doctrine. Neither Joseph nor his wives left any contempora-
neous records documenting their experiences.

The Indictment

Joseph's journal records that on May 25, 1844, several LDS brethren informed him that the Hancock County grand jury had preferred two indictments against him. One was said to be for "polygamy or something else" and was based on testimony by William and Wilson Law.[5] The other was for perjury and arose out of unrelated facts.

The first indictment, for adultery, alleged that Joseph had committed adultery with Maria Lawrence and other "women to the jurors unknown." The mention of other women seems to have been as a place holder in the event that evidence later justified expanded charges. The use of the term "women to the jurors unknown" suggests that no other names were available at the time the grand jury drew up the indictment. Under Illinois law of the day, "adultery and fornication" was a crime that was punishable by imprisonment of up to six months.[6]

A charge against Joseph for adultery had previously been issued by the grand jury on May 23, but it was dropped the following day when the state's attorney *pro-tem,* E. A. Thompson, indicated that he would no longer prosecute the indictment. Then that same day, the grand jury issued the charge against Joseph for "adultery and fornication" involving Maria Lawrence and other unnamed women, as well as the one for perjury. These are the charges mentioned in Joseph's journal on May 25.[7]

---

5. Faulring, *American Prophet's Record,* 483; this entry in Joseph's diary seems to have been the basis for the account found in Joseph Smith Jr., *History of The Church of Jesus Christ of Latter-day Saints,* ed. B. H. Roberts, 2d ed., rev., 7 vols. (Salt Lake City: Deseret Book, 1971), 6:405 (hereafter cited as *History of the Church*). Among the men who brought Joseph this news were Edward Hunter and William Marks, both of whom served on the grand jury during this term of court. See Hancock County Circuit Court records, Book D, page (approx.) 100, LDS Family History Library film 0947496. The back of the original indictment has a case caption (People v. Joseph Smith } adultery) with the name of the grand jury foreman, listing William and Wilson Law as witnesses. See indictments of Joseph Smith for adultery and fornication, brought in the May 1844 term of the Hancock County Circuit Court, MS 3464, Archives, The Church of Jesus Christ of Latter-day Saints, Salt Lake City; and faint copies in the Wilford Wood collection, MS 8716, reel 5, file 4-C-b-2, LDS Church Archives.

6. See Criminal Code, section 123, *Revised Laws of Illinois* (Vandalia: Greiner & Sherman, 1833); and Criminal Jurisprudence, section 123, *Revised Statutes of the State of Illinois* (Springfield: William Walters for Walters & Weber, 1845).

7. For the perjury charge, see Hancock County Circuit Court records, Book D, 114, 128, and 166, LDS Family History Library film 0947496. A number of years back, I viewed the original in possession of the Clerk of the Circuit Court for Hancock County in Carthage, Illinois. The Clerk of the Court has this and other valuable legal papers concerning Joseph Smith locked in a box within the records vault.

The perjury charge stemmed from confusion over whether Joseph had sworn an affidavit against a man named Alexander Sympson, who had been accused in a stabbing incident. Joseph believed the perjury charge was entirely baseless, and he vehemently denied having accused Sympson of a crime.[8] According to Joseph, Sympson had even made a public statement clearing Joseph of any involvement in the matter.[9]

On May 27, Joseph and an entourage of friends and guards confidently rode to Carthage, intent on having both indictments "investigated." Three attorneys assisted Joseph in this matter, namely "Messers [William A.] Richardson, [Almon W.] Babbit, and [Onias C.] Skinner,"[10] and although these lawyers "used all reasonable exertion" to have the perjury indictment tried immediately, "the prosecution party was not ready for trial."[11]

This attempt to secure an immediate trial seems to have surprised Joseph's enemies. One county paper known for its anti-Mormon rhetoric (and whose editor was among the accused assassins of Joseph Smith) wrote that "it was the general impression that Joe [Joseph Smith] would never submit to be tried on these indictments." According to this article, "the general opinion appears to be, that he [Joseph] thought to catch his enemies napping, and by a bold stroke, defeat them."[12]

---

8. As reported by Thomas Bullock. See *History of the Church*, 6:409–10. Joseph states that these events occurred "last winter," which could mean either the winter of 1842/43 or the winter of 1843/44. The latter possibility may be more likely. Internet sources containing brief biographical material on Sympson state that he came to Carthage in 1844. Sympson became a prominent man in the area, having a fine house in which Abraham Lincoln reportedly stayed when visiting. Sympson and Lincoln knew each other as boys in Kentucky. See Infobahn Outfitters, "Hancock County Courthouse," http://illinois.outfitters. com/illinois/hancock/courthouse.html; and "The Lincoln Doorway," *Treasures from the Kibbe Museum*, http://kibbe.wordpress.com/2008/06/24/the-lincoln-doorway/).

9. Joseph described this incident during his public remarks on May 26, 1844. See *History of the Church*, 6:401. At the time of Joseph's death, a civil suit by Sympson for slander was pending against Joseph Smith in the McDonough County Circuit Court. This suit arose out of the same facts that resulted in the perjury indictment.

10. See Faulring, *American Prophet's Record*, 485. Richardson and Skinner later were among the lawyers who defended Joseph's accused assassins in their trial for murder. See Dallin H. Oaks and Marvin S. Hill, *Carthage Conspiracy: The Trial of the Accused Assassins of Joseph Smith* (Urbana: University of Illinois Press, 1975), 79, 82–84, 94. Babbitt was a well-known member of the Church who later lobbied the Illinois state government and the U.S. Congress on behalf of the Latter-day Saints. See Andrew Jenson, ed., *LDS Biographical Encyclopedia* (reprint; Salt Lake City: Western Epics, 1971), 1:284–86.

11. See Faulring, *American Prophet's Record*, 485

12. *Warsaw Signal*, May 29, 1844, p. [2].

Court records show that A[lexander] Sympson,[13] R[obert] D. Foster, John Snyder, and J[oseph] Jackson were ordered to come to the court "instanter," or immediately, in connection with the adultery indictment on May 27, 1844.[14] The return notation from Sheriff William Backenstos shows that he read the summons to Sympson, Foster and Jackson; however, Snyder's name is not listed, suggesting that Snyder could not be located that day.

Of the four witnesses, at least two were sworn enemies of the Prophet. Robert Foster was a leading figure in the efforts to organize a dissenting church for disaffected Latter-day Saints. His name is shown among the publishers of the *Expositor* newspaper (published June 7, 1844), which made strong statements about Joseph's plural marriages. Joseph Jackson, another known enemy of Joseph Smith, was seen with a pistol on the day Joseph and his entourage rode to Carthage to have the indictments investigated. While loading his gun, Jackson was reportedly overheard stating he would "have satisfaction" of Joseph and Hyrum.[15] It is unknown why the court thought that Sympson would have anything to say on the topic of Joseph's alleged adultery. He was a newcomer to Nauvoo who was apparently not LDS.

The inclusion of Snyder's name is curious. He was a Latter-day Saint who served missions and assisted with the disposition of LDS properties in Nauvoo after the Exodus. Snyder is listed in the Journal History of the Church on June 28, 1844, as one of the honor guards accompanying the bodies of Joseph and Hyrum back to Nauvoo. He eventually travelled to Utah in 1850, and died in Salt Lake City in 1875, still a faithful member of the Church. After his death in 1875, Snyder was eulogized by John Taylor, further evidence that he was a stalwart member.[16]

---

13. Spelled "Simpson" in *History of the Church*.

14. This subpoena is found in the vault, kept by the Clerk of the Circuit Court for Hancock County in Carthage, Illinois. The Clerk of the Court has this and other valuable legal papers concerning Joseph Smith locked in a box within the records vault.

15. According to a book written by Jackson, the Prophet named two of these men, Foster and Sympson, among his worst enemies and called them a "pack of persecuting d'd rascals," prophesying their destruction. Jackson himself was known to have been a bitter enemy of the Prophet and was said by several Latter-day Saints to have been a counterfeiter, a charge which, ironically, he accused Joseph Smith of in his book. Joseph H. Jackson, *A Narrative of the Adventures and Experience of Joseph H. Jackson, in Nauvoo* (reprint; Morrison, Illinois, 1960), 26 (the original version was published in August 1844, just two months following Joseph's murder); Faulring, *American Prophet's Record*, 484. As to Jackson being a counterfeiter, see *Nauvoo Neighbor Extra*, June 17, 1844.

16. Frank E. Esshom, *Pioneers and Prominent Members of Utah, Comprising Photographs, Genealogies, Biographies: The Early History of the Church of Jesus Christ of Latter-day Saints* (Salt Lake City: Utah Pioneers Book Publishing, 1913), 1173. John Snyder is listed in Early

Notwithstanding the court's summons directed at the four witnesses (and Snyder's apparent unavailability), the efforts of Joseph's attorneys to have the adultery charge investigated did not lead the prosecutor to drop the second charge, as he had done with the initial adultery charge. Court records show that on the day that Joseph went to Carthage, William and Wilson Law were ordered by the court to appear as witnesses before the court for trial on the third Monday of October 1844.[17] Thus, by day's end, the court was making plans for a trial in the fall. Additional subpoenas were issued during the coming weeks, requiring Joseph Smith and other witnesses to appear in court on the third Monday of October.[18] These indictments against Joseph remained on the court's docket until the October term, when they were finally dropped due to the Prophet's death.[19]

Unfortunately, few records exist pertaining to this adultery indictment, and none contain the substance of the testimony against Joseph that was presented to the grand jury. The *History of the Church* provides a few clues, which are found in an account of a public speech that Joseph made in Nauvoo on May 26, 1844. In that speech, Joseph lambasted the Law brothers for their involvement in the adultery suit. Joseph stated that both William and Wilson Law had sworn that Joseph had said that he was guilty of adultery.[20] More will be said about this speech in the section on Joseph's possible legal defenses below.

Otherwise, all that is known of the adultery charge is contained within the wording of the actual indictments, which asserted that Joseph had lived in an open state of adultery and fornication from October 12, 1843, with

---

LDS Membership Data, 1995, Infobases, Inc. The Journal History of the Church housed at the LDS Church History Library contains several entries for Snyder, reporting his death and republishing his obituary. See entry of December 18, 1875. Some sources list Snyder's wife, Mary Heron, as a wife of Joseph Smith. Hales, *Joseph Smith's Polygamy,* 1:460–74, discusses this topic in detail, also providing additional biographical information about John Snyder.

17. See Hancock County Circuit Court records, Book D, Family History Library Film 0947496.

18. See Wilford Wood collection, MS 8716, reel 5, file 4-C-b-2, LDS Church Archives; and "Capias on Indictment," June 22, 1844, stored with the indictments for adultery and fornication, MS 3464, LDS Church Archives. Andrew F. Ehat and Lyndon W. Cook, *Words of the Prophet Joseph Smith* (Salt Lake City: Deseret Book, 1996), 407 n. 21 (entry for May 26, 1844), incorrectly concludes that the case against Joseph was dropped during the May 1844 term of the court.

19. The court's minutes for the October term record: "This day came the state's attorney and suggested the death of the defendant Joseph Smith. Thereupon the court ordered that this suit abate." See Hancock County Circuit Court records, Book D, 166.

20. *History of the Church,* 6:408–12; cited in Ehat and Cook, *Words,* 375–76; see also Ehat and Cook, *Words,* 406 n. 1.

Maria Lawrence and from July 10, 1843, with other women who were "to the jurors unknown."

The earlier indictment (dropped on May 24) exhibits confusion over the dates of the alleged conduct and is difficult to decipher, having numerous insertions and interlineations. It alleges that on January 1, 1844, Joseph lived "with women unknown" to the jurors. It also alleged that Joseph had lived in an open state of adultery with Maria Lawrence on October 12, 1843, this date being written over the date of December 15, 1843. This earlier document as first written did not allege that Joseph lived with Maria or other women on any dates other than the ones expressly alleged, though an insertion of additional wording added that the adulterous conduct occurred "on divers other days & times between that day & the day of finding this indictment."

Illinois Adultery Law

Under Illinois law, enacted in 1833, only open cohabitation of a man and woman not married to each other was punishable by law. The Illinois Criminal Code provided that

> Any man and woman who shall live together in an open state of adultery or fornication, or adultery and fornication, every such man and woman shall be indicted, and on conviction, shall be fined in any sum not exceeding two hundred dollars each, or imprisoned not exceeding six months. This offence shall be sufficiently proved by circumstances which raise the presumption of cohabitation and unlawful intimacy; and for a second offence, such man or woman shall be severely punished twice as much as the former punishment, and for the third offence, treble, and thus increasing the punishment for each succeeding offence: *Provided, however,* That it shall be in the power of the party or parties offending, to prevent or suspend the prosecution by their intermarriage, if such marriage can be legally solemnized, and upon the payment of the costs of such prosecution.[21]

---

21. Criminal Code, section 123, *Revised Laws of Illinois*; see also Criminal Jurisprudence, section 123, *Revised Statutes of the State of Illinois*. It is also possible, though less likely, that the grand jury was acting based upon a Nauvoo city ordinance enacted in May 1842 (discussed below at note 50), which also punished adultery and fornication. If so, indictment by the county court would have been improper; by the terms of Nauvoo's city charter, the city court had exclusive jurisdiction over all offenses arising under the city's ordinances. See An Act to Incorporate the City of Nauvoo, December 16, 1840, section 17. Compare to

The term "open" in this statute is a key element of this crime. The meaning of this term was then and still today is generally understood in law to cover conduct that is "notorious," "exposed to public view," or "visible," and which is "not clandestine."[22] Joseph's relationships with his plural wives did not meet this definition.

As seen in his remarks on May 26, 1844, Joseph never openly acknowledged his marriages to these women; in fact, they seem to have been known only to a limited number of his closest associates, some or all of whom were themselves practicing plural marriage at his instruction. Whatever stories may have circulated occasionally in Nauvoo, it would have been difficult for any witness to tell the grand jury that Joseph "openly" lived with Maria Lawrence in a state of adultery or fornication.

The Illinois statute also provided that the "offense shall be sufficiently proved by circumstances which raise the presumption of cohabitation and unlawful intimacy." In other words, circumstantial evidence could be advanced to raise a presumption of that offense, but construing the statute as a whole, the prosecution would still have needed to show, even by indirect evidence, that the offense was "open." Any presumption would be open to rebuttal by contrary evidence. As the indictments expressly allege that Joseph's conduct was "open," one must wonder if this charge was simply based preliminarily on circumstantial evidence, or perhaps was improperly based on false or overstated testimony.

The fact that only "open" behavior would bring criminal liability for adultery is seen in the wording used in indictments drawn up by prosecutors during this era. Such documents are found in the papers of Stephen A. Douglas and Thomas Ford, men who served during portions of Joseph's Nauvoo years as justices of the Illinois State Supreme Court. Both men earlier served as state's attorneys (prosecutors) and in that capacity had brought adultery charges.

In one case, Douglas brought charges against William S. Holton and Ruth Tanner in 1835 for adultery. This indictment stated that the accused parties "on

---

Illinois divorce law which allowed adultery as a grounds for divorce; however, the cases that involved divorce petitions on this basis do not seemed to have followed any clear standard defining what constituted adultery, focusing rather on proving individual acts of adultery. Divorce law did not require that the conduct be "open" or "notorious." See for example Daniel W. Stowell, ed., Susan Krause, asst. ed., *The Papers of Abraham Lincoln: Legal Documents and Cases*, 4 vols. (Charlottesville: University of Virginia Press, 2008), 1:43–46 [*Wren and Hart et al.*]; and Isaac H. Burch, *The only complete report of the Burch divorce case ... specially reported by the Law Reporter of the New York Daily Times*, electronic resource [Buffalo, NY]: William S. Hein & Co. (2007 [original case in Illinois, 1860]).

22. *Black's Law Dictionary*, 6th ed (St. Paul, Minn.: West Publishing Co., 1990), sv. "open."

the tenth day of June in the year of our Lord one thousand eight hundred and thirty four and for the period of six months preceeding [*sic*] that day at the County aforesaid willfully and unlawfully did live together in an *open* State of Adultery and fornication and did cohabit together as man and wife."[23] This wording shows that Douglas was charging the pair not with a secret relationship that was considered adulterous, but with openly cohabiting as man and wife during a specific time period, thereby committing adultery. One may also contrast the six-month period during which Holton and Tanner were alleged to have cohabited with the much less precise dates and time periods referenced in the adultery indictments drawn up against Joseph. The indictments against Joseph that were drawn up by the grand jury exhibit confusion over the dates, no doubt due to the fact that his conduct was not "open" and public.

Interestingly, Joseph was not the only person charged with adultery at the May 1844 term of the court in Hancock County. In *People v. Mullen,* the state accused Joseph Mullen of committing adultery with one Martha Jolly on May 5, 1844. Attorneys Richardson and Skinner, who represented Joseph in his adultery indictment, also happened to represent Mullen in this matter. They made a motion objecting to this indictment, on the grounds that the adultery "was charged to have been committed upon one day & is not sufficiently charged, the whole indictment is insufficient."[24]

Another example of an early Illinois adultery indictment is found in Thomas Ford's papers. Ford, who was elected governor of Illinois in August 1842, also prosecuted at least one couple for adultery as a state's attorney in the 1830s. This document asserted that the accused parties "did unlawfully live together ... in an open state of adultery."[25] Even though this wording is less specific than seen in the Douglas indictment, it still contains the term "open," showing that Ford too deemed this an essential element of the offense.

The importance of the word "open" to any adultery conviction cannot be overstated. Two Illinois Supreme Court cases in the mid-nineteenth century illustrate this point.[26] Even though these cases were decided after Joseph's death, they nevertheless provide valuable clues as to how the courts likely

---

23. Stephen A. Douglas Papers, SC 415, fd. 1, Illinois State Historical Library, Springfield, Illinois, emphasis supplied. The wording *as man and wife* is not found in the actual wording of the statute, but rather seems to have been inserted by Douglas to bolster the allegation that the two had openly lived together in an improper relationship.

24. Original documents are kept by the Clerk of the Circuit Court for Hancock County in a locked box within the vault.

25. See Thomas Ford papers, SC 513, fd. 1, Illinois State Historical Library.

26. Searles v. The People, 13 Ill. 597 (1852); and Miner v. The People, 58 Ill. 59 (1873).

would have applied the statutory law to Joseph's circumstances, had his case gone to trial in October 1844 as scheduled.

According to the court in the first of these two cases, *Searles v. People* (Illinois, 1852), decided only eight years after Joseph's indictment, the purpose of the state's adultery statute was to "prohibit the *public scandal* and disgrace of the living together of persons of opposite sexes *notoriously* in illicit intimacy, which outrages *public* decency."[27] The court explained that "in order to constitute this crime the parties must dwell together *openly and notoriously,* upon terms as if the conjugal relation existed between them." The courts from several other states also affirmed the same principle, generally holding that "adultery is not indictable unless it is open and notorious."[28] Those and several states in the 1830s had adultery statutes similar to that of Illinois.[29]

---

27. Searles v. The People, 13 Ill. 597, 598 (emphasis added).

28. See *American Digest* (St. Paul: West, 1897), vol. 1, s.v., "Adultery," I, §1[a] (this section cites cases from several states that support this proposition).

29. In addition to Illinois, states with similar statutes using the word "open" include Florida (1824, 1828, 1832), Georgia (1817, 1833), and Iowa (1839). Even clearer, Missouri law spoke of living "in a state of open and notorious adultery ... lewdly and lasciviously," and the New Hampshire (1829) and Wisconsin (1838, 1849) statutes speak of "open gross lewdness and lascivious behavior." The requirement for open conduct would probably have applied in Ohio, where some have suggested that Joseph may have had a plural relationship with a female named Fanny Alger. The Ohio adultery statute (chapter 35, section 24) criminalized only "notorious" cohabitation, providing that "if any married man shall hereafter *desert his wife,* and live and cohabit with any other woman in a state of adultery; or if any married man, *living with his wife,* shall keep any other woman, and *notoriously cohabit* with her in a state of adultery, ... every person so offending shall, on conviction thereof, be fined in any sum not exceeding two hundred dollars, and be imprisoned in the cell or dungeon of the jail of the county, and be fed on bread [and water] only, not exceeding thirty days" (See *Acts of a General Nature, Enacted, Revised, and Ordered to be Reprinted,...* [Columbus: Olmsted and Bailhache, 1831], 149; also in J. R. Swan, *Statutes of the State of Ohio, of a General Nature,...* [Columbus: Samuel Medary, 1841], 244–45). The Ohio statute against fornication of two cohabiting *unmarried* persons did *not* require open conduct. See *Statutes of the State of Ohio* (Cincinnati: Corey and Fairbank, 1835), "Punishment of Offenses," p. 1732, chapter 831, section 25. Given that Joseph was legally married to Emma, the applicability of section 25 is precluded as to Joseph and Fanny. The report of a discussion that took place in the High Council at Far West regarding rumors of Joseph's relationship with a woman other than Emma (likely Fanny Alger) is worth discussing here. Remarks of three of the participants show that they were satisfied that Joseph never confessed to the "crime alleged" (adultery). See Hales, *Joseph Smith's Polygamy,* 1:143. Although the evidence is uncertain, Fanny Alger is believed by many to have been Joseph's first plural wife.

In rendering its decision, the court in *Searles* held to be erroneous an instruction given by the trial court judge to the jury that would have permitted a guilty verdict even in the absence of evidence of a single act of sexual intercourse. While the state's adultery statute provided that the crime would be "sufficiently proved by circumstances which raise the presumption of cohabitation and unlawful intimacy," the court explained that mere suspicions based on circumstances were not sufficient to give rise to the presumption of guilt.

The circumstances under which the alleged crime in *Searles* took place bear some resemblance to those under which Joseph and Maria might have found themselves. The couple in *Searles* lived together—as did Joseph and Maria—in the "same family, but [were] apparently chaste, regularly occupying separate apartments."[30] In light of these facts, the court concluded that for purposes of instructing the jury, "a single instance of illicit intercourse surely would not constitute the crime of living together in an open state of fornication." Whatever the situation was in the *Searles* case, no eyewitness accounts or direct evidence of Joseph's being engaged in conjugal acts with Maria are known to exist.

In the second case, two decades later, *Miner v. People* (Illinois, 1871), the court cited the earlier *Searles* case and was no more inclined to uphold adultery convictions than the court had been in 1852. The court's opinion held that the "familiarities shown on the trial" were insufficient to support the conviction. These "familiarities" included testimony that the allegedly adulterous pair had been seen embracing each other twice—in the defendant's bedroom—and that the two stayed all night in bed on at least two occasions. It was further alleged that the woman, a certain Mrs. Jones, had moved her bed into the defendant's bedroom, where she slept for about three weeks.[31] Even under these facts, the court held that the evidence disclosed no relation between the two that would give rise to liability. Wrote the court, "It barely creates a presumption of illicit intercourse."[32]

Joseph's Possible Legal Defenses against the Charge of Adultery

If the adultery indictment against Joseph had actually gone to trial in October 1844, as scheduled, the Prophet's attorneys might have utilized a number of defenses or tactics on his behalf.

---

30. See Searles v. People, case file 11989, Illinois State Archives, Springfield, Illinois.
31. See testimony in Miner v. The People, case file 4391, Illinois State Archives.
32. Miner v. The People, 58 Ill 59, 60.

1. Not "open" or "notorious." As discussed, Joseph's first line of defense would have been to establish that he and Maria did not "openly" live together in a state of adultery or fornication. His attorneys could have summoned a string of witnesses who would have testified that, although Maria lived in Joseph's home, she was not understood in the community to be his wife, and they were not living openly as man and wife.[33] The presence in the Smith home of Maria and her sister Sarah, as well as of other women, would more likely have been viewed by the community and visitors as an act of kindness (Maria and Sarah were orphans, and Joseph was their guardian) and perhaps as an employment opportunity, allowing the young women to earn their keep.[34]

2. Lack of witnesses. Joseph's attorneys could also have challenged the prosecution to find even one eyewitness to a conjugal act between the two. As the court held in *Searles,* mere suspicions based on circumstances would not be sufficient to establish the case. Actual witnesses to one or more sexual acts

---

33. The date of Joseph and Maria's sealing, and the dates on which she lived in the Smith home may be relevant here. Compton gives the date of Maria's sealing to Joseph as late spring 1843. See Compton, *In Sacred Loneliness,* 475. Van Wagoner estimates the sealing date as late summer or early fall 1843. See Richard S. Van Wagoner, *Mormon Polygamy: A History* (Salt Lake City: Signature Books, 1989), 36. Hales gives the sealing date as May 1843. See table 15.1 in Hales, *Joseph Smith's Polygamy,* 1:428 and discussion in 2:49. Maria and her sister moved in with the Smiths into the Mansion House on August 31, 1843. See Hales, *Joseph Smith's Polygamy,* 1:327. I am not aware of any evidence indicating whether Maria was still living with the Smiths in their home at the time of the indictment (May 24, 1844); however, the indictment specifically alleges that Maria and Joseph lived in an open state of adultery and fornication starting from October 12, 1843, to "the time and the day of finding this indictment." Maria was nineteen at the time of her sealing, her birthday being December 18, 1823. Curiously, the date of October 12 comes up in historical sources and Young family tradition as the date in 1844 when Sarah Lawrence was sealed to Heber C. Kimball and Maria was possibly sealed to Brigham Young. That a sealing to Brigham Young may have occurred was disputed by some early Latter-day Saints. See Compton, *In Sacred Loneliness,* 477, 745. Joseph Smith was guardian of Sarah and Maria Lawrence. See generally chapter 14 above.

34. Hales quotes an anonymous writer who visited Nauvoo in 1843, commenting that "there was no foundation to the report that Joe[seph Smith] kept virgins but that he, as guardian to several orphan girls supported and employed them as servants to do work at his hotel; ... and from what we saw of those orphan girls—we sat at tea with them every meal—they were, I believe, as modest, chaste, and virtuous girls as can be found." This report was published in London in 1844. See Hales, *Joseph Smith's Polygamy,* 2:55. Two of the other girls the writer may have been referring to were Eliza Marie Partridge and Emily Dow Partridge, both of whom were plural wives of Joseph Smith and lived with him for a time in the Mansion House.

would likely have been needed, and it is very doubtful that these existed—otherwise the publishers of the *Expositor* would surely have splashed the names or initials of such witnesses and the details on the pages of the *Expositor.*[35]

Joseph's comments spoken on May 26, 1844, need to be reconsidered in this light. The material quoted below has been cited numerous times by his critics as proof that Joseph publicly denied polygamy while secretly practicing it:

> I had not been married scarcely five minutes, and made one proclamation of the Gospel, before it was reported that I had seven wives.... A man asked me whether the commandment was given that a man may have seven wives; and now the new prophet has charged me with adultery.... Wilson Law also swears that I told him I was guilty of adultery.... I am innocent of all these charges, and you can bear witness of my innocence, for you know me yourselves.... What a thing it is for a man to be accused of committing adultery, and having seven wives, when I can only find one. I am the same man, and as innocent as I was fourteen years ago; and I can prove them all perjurers.[36]

A review of Joseph's remarks in light of the circumstances under which they were spoken shows that Joseph's words were carefully chosen. In this speech, Joseph was specifically reacting to the indictments for perjury and adultery that were presented by the grand jury the day earlier. Thus, when Joseph affirmed during the same speech: "I am innocent of all these charges," he was in particular refuting a claim that he and Maria had openly and notoriously cohabitated, thus committing the statutory offense of adultery. He was also refuting the perjury charge. While the overall tone of Joseph's remarks may seem misleading, it is understandable that Joseph would have taken pains to dodge the plural marriage issue. By keeping his plural marriages in Nauvoo secret, Joseph effectively kept them legal, at least under the Illinois adultery statute.

3. Offering physical evidence to prove Maria's virginity. While this might seem an extreme and grossly embarrassing step, one wonders if Joseph

---

35. Consider John C. Bennett's exposé on Joseph, which besides much information that was patently fanciful or false, contained the initials of alleged plural wives. Some of these initials seem to match with those of women known to have been sealed to Joseph. See John C. Bennett, *History of the Saints; or, an Exposé of Joe Smith and Mormonism* (Boston: Leland and Whiting, 1842).

36. *History of the Church*, 6:410–11.

and even Maria may have been prepared to take such measures.[37] Joseph instructed John Taylor on June 4, to initiate legal action against the Laws and Foster for perjury and slander against Maria.[38] No such suit is known to have been filed, since Joseph was killed three weeks later; however, the mere fact that Joseph planned to bring such a suit suggests that, in Joseph's mind, there was nothing to hide in his relationship with Maria. If there had been a sexual dimension to this particular plural marriage, it is almost unimaginable that Joseph would have wanted to file a lawsuit, knowing that Maria might be put on the witness stand—or even subjected to a gynecological examination. The possibility that Joseph's relationship with Maria Lawrence did not involve intimacy is also plausible given his comments regarding the publication of the *Expositor*: "They make it a criminality for a man to have one wife on earth while he has one wife in heaven."[39] Since the only specific allegation of "criminality" (the adultery indictment) with respect to Joseph's plural marriages concerned Maria Lawrence, this statement by Joseph could be understood as a reference to his spiritual connection, or sealing, with Maria, but perhaps no more.

4. **Challenging the credibility of witnesses who had a poor reputation for truthfulness.** Joseph's lawyers could well have cast doubt on the specifics of opposing testimonies. Indeed, a focus of Joseph's public remarks on May 26, 1844, seems to have been to undermine the reputation of the witnesses against him in the adultery and perjury cases. In this sense, Joseph may have been putting his enemies on notice that any eventual trial on these charges would inevitably involve questions regarding their own reputation for "veracity," or truthfulness. For example, Joseph stated that Jackson, one of the witnesses against him, was guilty of "murder, robbery, and perjury" and that he could "prove it by a half a dozen witnesses."[40]

5. **Excluding testimony based on hearsay.** Especially the Laws' statements that Joseph admitted to adultery could have been challenged. A leading United States Supreme Court case of this era held on the topic of hearsay: "Nothing said by any person can be used as evidence between contending

---

37. Some historians might be perplexed that I even raise such a possibility; however, the facts I cite calling this assumption into question deserve serious consideration. On the other hand, even Brian Hales, who writes from the perspective of a believing Latter-day Saint, assumes that Joseph and Maria's relationship involved intimacy. He bases this on three accounts; however, all of these are secondhand and were recorded at a much later date. See Hales, *Joseph Smith's Polygamy*, 2:386–87.

38. *History of the Church*, 6:427.

39. *History of the Church*, 6:441.

40. *History of the Church*, 6:427.

parties unless it is delivered on oath, in the presence of those parties."[41] While federal legal precedent would not necessarily have been followed by an Illinois state court, the legal reasoning expressed in this case is illustrative of the jurisprudence of the day.[42]

Possible Defenses Based on His Relationship with Maria Being Legal

1. Legal and Protected under Federal and State Constitutional Law. Joseph could also have attempted to invoke his rights of religious liberty, under state or federal law. In his day, it had not yet been decided, as the U.S. Supreme Court would hold in 1879 in *Reynolds v. United States*, that the law can restrict religious conduct that has been found by the legislature to offend public morals.[43] The Illinois Constitution had a broadly worded guaranty of religious freedom that could conceivably have been read by the state's judiciary to extend protection to religiously based polygamy. In 1844, this guaranty provided:

> That all men have a natural and indefeasible right to worship Almighty God according to the dictates of their own consciences; that no man can of right be compelled to attend, erect or support any place of worship, or to maintain any ministry against his consent; that no human authority can in any case whatever control or interfere with the rights of conscience; and that no preference shall ever be given by law to any religious establishments or modes of worship.[44]

Recognizing the breadth of this state constitutional provision as it stood in 1844, Illinois adopted a new constitution in 1869 that introduced a number of changes in the clause governing religious liberty, including wording specifically intended to give the state authority to prohibit Mormon

---

41. Ellicott v. Pearl, 35 U.S. 412, 437(1836).

42. See generally S. M. (Samuel March) Phillipps, *A treatise on the law of evidence: to which is added the Theory of presumptive proof, &c.*, 1st American from the 2nd London ed. by John A. Dunlap (New-York, 1816); *The Making of Modern Law* (Gale, Cengage Learning, 2013), http://galenet.galegroup.com.proxlaw.byu.edu/servlet/MOML?af=RN&ae=F105 -003815&srchtp=a&ste=14 (accessed February 14, 2013); and Simon Greenleaf, *A Treatise on the Law of Evidence*, 3 vols. (Boston, 1842–53), vol. 1.

43. Reynolds v. United States, 98 U.S. 145 (1879).

44. Illinois Constitution (1818), Art. VIII, Sect. III.

polygamy[45] or other religiously-based practices that might be deemed offensive. Comments by certain delegates to the 1869 Illinois Constitutional Convention show that there was a concern that the Mormon practice of plural marriage could be protected under the state constitution. Borrowing wording from the New York Constitution, the Illinois Constitution then could not "be construed to ... excuse acts of licentiousness, or justify practices inconsistent with the peace or safety of the State."[46]

2. Defenses under Nauvoo City Ordinances on Religious Societies, Adultery, and Marriage. Joseph might have claimed rights of freedom of religion in 1844 under a Nauvoo City ordinance that was approved on March 1, 1841, less than a month after the Nauvoo Charter went into force, and only a month before Joseph is known to have entered into the first of his Nauvoo plural relationships.[47] Entitled "An Ordinance in Relation to Religious Societies,"[48] this ordinance provided that all religious sects and denominations, including "Mohommedans," were to have "free toleration" and "equal privileges" in Nauvoo. Given that polygamy is permitted under Islam, one

---

45. I discovered this fact by reading the published report of the debates held during the 1869 Illinois Constitutional Convention, which show that Mormon polygamy was specifically discussed. Several delegates expressed support for changes in the wording of the Illinois constitution in order to protect the state from what they viewed as extreme forms of worship, including Mormon polygamy. These delegates feared that the more liberal wording of the earlier constitution (in force in Joseph's day) might actually protect practices such as polygamy. One such delegate was Thomas J. Turner. In comments addressed to the convention delegates, Turner stated: "This section [Article II, Section III of the Illinois Constitution (1870)] secures the people of the State, in the free exercise of their religious professions and worship, without discrimination. It also provides that liberty of conscience shall not excuse acts of licentiousness or practices inconsistent with the peace, safety and morality of the State. The pagan world is full of religion ... Mormonism is a form of religion 'grant it, a false religion' nevertheless, it claims to be the true Christian religion ... [d]o we desire that the Mormons shall return to our State, and bring with them polygamy?" See *Debates and Proceedings of the Constitutional Convention of the State of Illinois, Convened at the City of Springfield, Tuesday December 13, 1869* (Springfield, April 29–30, 1870), 1561; see also similar comments by another delegate, George R. Wendling in *Debates and Proceedings*, 1565–66, available online at: http://www.idaillinois.org/cdm/compoundobject/collection/isl2/id/12546.

46. Illinois Constitution (1870), Art. II, Sec. III at http://archive.org/stream/constitution ofooilli#page/4/mode/2up/search/3.

47. According to the chronology prepared by Compton, all of Joseph's Illinois plural marriages occurred after this date, the first having occurred on April 5, 1841, when he married Louisa Beaman. Compton lists two marriages he believes may have occurred prior to this date and not in Illinois, one to Fanny Alger, and another to Lucinda Pendleton.

48. *History of the Church*, 4:307; Dinger, *Nauvoo City and High Council Minutes*, 17.

could easily argue that the mention of "Mohammedans" was intended to bring plural marriage within the scope of Nauvoo's ordinance on religious toleration. Comments that Joseph made during a sermon in 1841 support this interpretation. Joseph Lee Robinson's autobiography, published in 1853, provides this interesting recollection:

> While speaking to the people in that place he [Joseph Smith] supposed a case, he said suppose we send one of our elders to Turkey or India or to a people where it is lawful to have several wives. Where they practiced polygamy and suppose he should say to them your laws are not good, you should put away your plural wives. What would they do to him? They would kick him out of their realm. Said he, what right has he to speak against their laws and usages. Said he, God doesn't care what laws they make if they will live up to them. What shall they preach? Said he, they shall preach the gospel and nothing but the pure gospel and some will believe and be baptized.

Discussing what the hypothetical LDS elder would say to the Turk or Indian who embraces the gospel and wishes to gather to Zion with his wives, Joseph further stated:

> He shall say, yes, brother, there is a land of Zion where Saints of God are required to gather to. Then, said he, to the elder, I have five wives and I love one equally as well as I do the other and now what are the laws in that land? Can I bring my five wives there and enjoy them there as well as I can here? Said the prophet, yes the laws in Zion are such that you can bring your wives and enjoy them here as well as there, the elder shall say to his brother.[49]

Robinson gives the date of this sermon as "fall 1841," which would mean that it followed the adoption of the Nauvoo ordinance on religious liberty by perhaps six months. The only "Zion" to which foreign converts would have been required to gather in 1841 was Nauvoo or surrounding communities. Thus, this reference to the laws of Zion may be understood as a reference to Nauvoo, or perhaps to the State of Illinois. This reference seems to suggest

---

49. Oliver Preston Robinson and Mary Robinson Egan, eds., *The Journal of Joseph Lee Robinson Mormon Pioneer*, 41–42; available at www.boap.org/LDS/Early-Saints/, cited in Hales, *Joseph Smith's Polygamy*, 1:246–47.

that Joseph believed that the laws of Nauvoo and possibly Illinois would not reach polygamy.[50]

One would not normally expect that a city ordinance could grant rights of religious freedom; however, the Nauvoo Charter granted broad authority for the municipal government to enact ordinances. Section 11 of that document provided that:

> The city council shall have power and authority to make, ordain, establish and execute all such ordinances, not repugnant to the Constitution of the United States or of this State, as they may deem necessary for the peace, benefit, good order, regulation, convenience and cleanliness of said city.[51]

Joseph's lawyers might have pointed out that any Nauvoo city ordinance was authorized, so long as it was not "repugnant" to the Illinois State Constitution and served to promote the peace and good order of the city—even if it varied from the usual Illinois statutes or laws. An examination of the wording in the charters for other Illinois municipalities of this era shows that this clause was unique and probably granted Nauvoo unusually expansive powers. The charters for Illinois *towns* often stipulated that ordinances must not contradict state *law* or the state and federal constitutions. On the other hand, the charters for *cities* sometimes contained wording similar to Section 11 of the Nauvoo Charter, but unlike in this charter, such wording was inevitably linked to a specific list of enumerated powers. Thus, these cities could pass ordinances that would contradict state law, but only covering a prescribed range of topics.[52] Nauvoo's powers, by comparison, seem to have

---

50. Joseph was a member of the city council at this time (see *History of the Church*, 4:295) and personally presented this ordinance to the city council for consideration (*History of the Church*, 4:306), so we may presume that the ordinance reflected his thinking.

51. "The City Charter: Laws, Ordinances, and Acts of the City Council of the City of Nauvoo," sec. 11 (1840) (hereafter cited as Nauvoo City Charter), Church History Library.

52. A comparison between Nauvoo's powers under its charter with the powers of other Illinois towns and cities is instructive. Towns in Illinois were often incorporated by the General Assembly under the terms of a standard charter empowering the town to establish ordinances on a defined range of topics "not inconsistent with the laws, or the constitution" of Illinois. See Incorporations, section 5, An Act to Incorporate the Inhabitants of Such Towns as May Wish to be Incorporated (passed 12 Feb. 1831), *Revised Laws of Illinois* (1833), 382. Under the terms of this standard charter, town ordinances could not contradict state law. On the other hand, some cities had broader legislative powers. For example, Springfield could pass ordinances within a prescribed range of topics, even if these ordinances contradicted state law, as long as the ordinances were not "repugnant to, nor inconsistent with" the U.S. or Illinois constitutions. See An Act to Incorporate the City

been intentionally crafted to be broader. Given the Saints' recent history of persecution in Missouri which had culminated in the infamous "extermination order" by Governor Boggs, Nauvoo's city authorities would have had more than ample reason to establish the broadest possible legal basis for religious freedom in Nauvoo.

---

of Springfield, *Laws of the State of Illinois Passed by the Eleventh General Assembly, at Their Special Session, Began and Held at Springfield on December 9, 1839* (Vandalia, Ill.: William Walters, 1840), art. V, sec. 36.

The Nauvoo Charter provided even broader powers than granted to Springfield. Section 11 provided that the "city council shall have power and authority to make, ordain, establish and execute all such ordinances, not repugnant to the Constitution of the United States or of this State, as they may deem necessary for the peace, benefit, good order, regulation, convenience and cleanliness of said city." The Nauvoo Charter included Springfield's powers by reference in section 13, but those were treated as being supplemental. See the full text of these sections in chapter 12 above. Thus, Nauvoo's powers were not limited to the same list granted to Springfield.

Compare Springfield and Nauvoo's municipal powers to those of Quincy. The charter for the city of Quincy, also passed in February 1840, originally stated that Quincy was to have the power to "make all ordinances which shall be necessary and proper for carrying into execution the powers specified in this act so that such ordinance be not repugnant to nor inconsistent with the constitution of the United States or of this State" (passed February 3, 1840, see section [41]); however, the legislature pared back Quincy's authority the following year. On January 7, 1841, the General Assembly of Illinois amended the Quincy Charter to clarify that the city council "shall pass no ordinance contrary to, or which in any way conflicts with, the laws of the United States or of this State, and any such ordinance which the city council may have passed, shall be void and of no effect." See An Act to Amend an Act Entitled An Act to Incorporate the City of Quincy (approved January 7, 1841), 12th General Assembly, 1st Sess., 1840, sec. 5. Interestingly, the General Assembly amended the Springfield Charter the next month, but in doing so left intact the broader enabling clause. See An Act to Amend An Act to Incorporate the City of Springfield, February 27, 1841, 12th General Assembly, 1st Sess., 1840. Thus, Springfield and Nauvoo could pass ordinances that contradicted state law, but Quincy could not (Springfield within the defined range of topics, and Nauvoo as long as the ordinance was, as provided in section 11, for "the peace, benefit, good order, regulation, convenience and cleanliness of said city"). Seen in this context of legislative awareness and intent, it seems almost certain that the General Assembly in fact intended to grant Nauvoo the very broad powers claimed here. Agreeing, a Hancock County history (Nauvoo was located in Hancock County) notes the breadth of municipal authority granted under the Nauvoo Charter: "Except as to constitutional questions the city of Nauvoo possessed all legislative power, or, to say the least, its ordinances and proceedings were not to be rendered invalid by reason of being repugnant or inconsistent with the laws of the state." Charles J. Scofield, ed., *History of Hancock County,* vol. 2 of *Historical Encyclopedia of Illinois,* ed. Newton Bateman, Paul Selby, and J. Seymour Currey (Chicago: Munsell, 1921), 717, 835.

Since Nauvoo had adopted its own adultery ordinance on May 17, 1842, Joseph's lawyers might also have argued that the circuit court lacked jurisdiction to bring a charge of adultery against Joseph outside of Nauvoo on the grounds that Nauvoo—where the offense allegedly occurred— had jurisdiction. This enactment banned the keeping and frequenting of brothels or houses of ill-fame; adultery and fornication were also punishable, the penalty for violations being stipulated as imprisonment for six months and a fine ranging from five hundred to fifty thousand dollars.[53]

It is likely that city authorities intended their ordinances to replace the state law when the two covered the same topics and the alleged offenses arose within Nauvoo. According to Section 17 of the charter, the mayor's court was to have "exclusive jurisdiction in all cases arising under the ordinances" of the city.[54] Joseph's lawyers might have argued that any trial for adulterous conduct that allegedly took place in Nauvoo would have to be tried in

---

53. The timing of the adoption of this ordinance is very curious. The ordinance itself was signed by John C. Bennett as mayor, yet he resigned his office as mayor that very day, on May 17, 1842. See "Letter from General Bennett," *Sangamon Journal*, July 8, 1842, p. 2. A note that Joseph sent to the Church's clerk, James Sloan, also on that same day, instructed him to "permit Gen. Bennett to withdraw his Name from the Church Records, if he desires to do so, and this with the best of feelings towards you and General Bennett." See Joseph Smith Papers, MS 155, box 2, fd. 5, LDS Church Archives. That same day Bennett also appeared before alderman Daniel H. Wells and swore an affidavit that Joseph had never taught him "that illicit intercourse with females, was under any circumstances, justifiable." Bennett reiterated his belief in Joseph's virtue before the city council two days later. See *Times and Seasons* 3 (July 1, 1842). Bennett is said to have been a seducer of a number of females in Nauvoo and to have kept a brothel. See Andrew F. Smith, *The Saintly Scoundrel: The Life and Times of John Cook Bennett* (Urbana: University of Illinois Press, 1997), 80–114. Bennett does not appear to have ever been prosecuted in Nauvoo for this offense. See foreword by Morris S. Thurston in John S. Dinger, *The Nauvoo City and High Council Minutes* (Salt Lake City: Signature Books, 2011).

54. If this was indeed the council's intent, it would not have been the only instance when this body acted to supplant state law in a significant way. In March 1843, the city council passed an ordinance making gold and silver the only legal tender in the city. See "An Ordinance Regulating Currency," March 4, 1843, in Proceedings of the Nauvoo City Council, 167–68, LDS Church Archives. In public comments spoken a few days prior to the adoption of this ordinance, Joseph explained that this law was needed so that the city would not be governed by a state law "making property a lawful tender for payment of debts." Joseph implied that this state law was unconstitutional and explained to the Saints that without a law on the same subject, the city would be governed by the state law; Joseph also justified the Nauvoo ordinance on other grounds. His comments, recorded in *History of the Church*, 5:289, show several arguments that could support a claim that this ordinance was for "the benefit" of the city.

Nauvoo, under the city adultery ordinance, and of course, if the couple were considered married under the laws of Nauvoo, their relationship would not be considered adulterous under the law in Nauvoo.

Thus, the Nauvoo City Council ordinance on marriage, enacted on February 17, 1842, might have further helped shield Joseph and Maria from prosecution, particularly if the State had brought bigamy charges (which never occurred).[55] This ordinance was based on the Illinois statute regarding marriage (see fig. 1), but it made several important changes as well. Like Illinois law in general, it allowed males over the age of 17, and females over the age of 14, to contract for marriage. The Nauvoo ordinance also followed the Illinois law in allowing "any persons … wishing to marry" to go before any regular minister or other authorized person to "declare their marriage, in such manner and form as shall be most agreeable," but it allowed marriages to be performed by the city mayor (who was Joseph Smith) and the aldermen, to take place without a marriage license or the issuance of a marriage certificate, without any notification of the public, and by filing a record of the marriage only with the city recorder, rather than with the clerk of the county commissioner's office.[56]

---

55. An Illinois newspaper of the day commented on these Nauvoo ordinances. This paper stated, "To carry on the pantomime the wise body called the 'Mayor and Alderman of the City of Nauvoo,' has passed a series of ordinances, some of them of rather a whimsical character, others of a conflicting nature. One, in relation to marriages, ordinances that boys of the age of 17 may be joined in wedlock to girls of 14, and that too without licenses." *Davenport Gazette*, February 15, 1844, in Dale L. Morgan, *News Clippings from Iowa and Illinois, 1841–1849* (Burlington, Wisc.: John J. Hajicek, 1992). The editors misquote the age requirements for marriage under the Nauvoo ordinance and seemed unaware that, with respect to marriage age, the Nauvoo ordinance retained the requirements of state law.

56. "An Ordinance Concerning Marriages," February 17, 1842, in Proceedings of the Nauvoo City Council, 1841–45, MS 3435, LDS Church Archives. See sidebar. The next day, February 18, the Nauvoo City Council passed an ordinance establishing a registry of deeds in Nauvoo. According to *History of the Church*, 4:516, Joseph prophesied in this setting that no judge would set aside this law. Among the several unusual features of the Nauvoo marriage law was the omission of a provision in the state's law banning interracial marriage. The Nauvoo marriage enactment did not go unnoticed by Governor Ford, who himself commented on its adoption in his *History of Illinois*, and at least one of the newspapers in the region noted its provisions. Nevertheless, under the broad wording of the Nauvoo Charter, this exercise of the council's authority was probably sound. As with the freedom of religion ordinance, so long as the City Council deemed this ordinance of "benefit," etc., to the city, and its provisions were not "repugnant" to the state and federal constitutions, it would have been presumptively valid. Thomas Ford, *A History of Illinois, from Its Commencement as a State*, ed. Milo Milton Quaife (reprint; Chicago: Lakeside Press, 1946), 160.

Figure 1. Illinois Marriage Statute (approved February 14, 1827)

SEC. 1. *Be it enacted by the people of the State of Illinois, represented in the General Assembly,* That all male persons over the age of seventeen years, and females over the age of fourteen years, may contract and be joined in marriage: *Provided,* in all cases where either party is a minor, the consent of parents or guardians be first had, as is hereinafter required.

SEC. 2. All persons belonging to any religious society, church, or denomination, may celebrate their marriage according to the rules and principles of such religious society, church, or denomination; and a certificate of such marriage, signed by the regular minister, or if there be no minister, then by the clerk of such religious society, church, or denomination, registered as hereinafter directed, shall be evidence of such marriage.

SEC. 3. Any persons wishing to marry, or be joined in marriage, may go before any regular minister of the gospel, authorized to marry by the church or society to which he belongs, any justice of the supreme court, judge of any inferior court, or justice of the peace, and celebrate or declare their marriage, in such manner and form as shall be most agreeable. And such minister of the gospel, justice of the supreme court, judge, or justice of the peace, shall make a certificate of such marriage, and return the same, with the license, to the clerk of the county commissioners' court, who issued such license, within thirty days after solemnizing such marriage; and the clerk, after receiving such certificate, shall make a registry thereof, in a book to be kept by him for that purpose only; which registry shall contain the Christian and sur-names of both the parties, the time of their marriage, and the name of the person certifying the same: and said clerk shall, at the same time, endorse on such certificate, that the same is registered, and the time when; which certificate shall be carefully filed and preserved, and the same, or a certified copy of the registry thereof, shall be evidence of the marriage of the parties.

SEC. 4. No person shall be joined in marriage as aforesaid, unless their intention to marry shall have been published at least two weeks previous to such marriage, in the church or congregation to which the parties, or one of them, belong; or unless such persons have obtained a license, as herein provided.

SEC. 5. In all cases when publication of such intention to marry has not been made, as before described, the parties wishing to marry shall obtain a license from the clerk of the county commissioners' court of the county where such marriage is to take place; which license shall authorize any regular minister of the gospel, authorized to marry by the church or society to which he belongs, any justice of the supreme court, judge, or justice of the peace, to celebrate and certify such marriage; but no such license shall be granted for the marriage of any male under twenty-one years of age, or female under the age of eighteen years, without the consent of his or her father, or if he be dead or incapable, of his or her mother or guardian, to be noted in such license. And if any clerk shall issue a license for the marriage of any such minor, without consent as aforesaid, he shall forfeit and pay the sum of three hundred dollars, to the use of such father, mother, or guardian, to be sued for and recovered in any court having cognizance thereof: and for the purpose of ascertaining the age of the parties, such clerk is hereby authorized to examine either party, or other witness, on oath.

Sec. 6. If any clerk shall, for more than one month, refuse or neglect to register any marriage certificate which has been, or may hereafter be delivered to him for that purpose, (his fee therefor being paid,) he shall be liable to be removed from office, and shall moreover pay the sum of ___ hundred dollars to the use of the party injured, to be recovered by action of debt in any court having cognizance of the same.

Sec. 7. If any minister, justice of the supreme court, judge, or justice of the peace, having solemnized a marriage, or clerk of any religious society, as the case may be, shall not make return of a certificate of the same, as required, within the time limited, to the clerk of the commissioners' court of the county in which such marriage was solemnized, he shall forfeit and pay one hundred dollars for each case so neglected, to go to the use of the county, to be revered by indictment. And if any minister of the gospel, justice of the supreme court, judge, or any other officer or person, except as herein before excepted, shall solemnize and join in marriage any couple without a license as aforesaid, he shall, for every such offence, forfeit and pay one hundred dollars to the use of the county, to be recovered by indictment.

Nauvoo City Ordinance on Marriages (passed February 17, 1842)

Sec. 1. *Be it Ordained by the City Council of the City of Nauvoo,* That all Male Persons over the Age of seventeen years, and Females over the Age of fourteen years, may contract and be joined in Marriage: Provided in all Cases where either Party is a Minor, the consent of Parents or Guardians be first had.

Sec. 2. Any Persons as aforesaid wishing to Marry, or be joined in Marriage, may go before any regular Minister of the Gospel, Mayor, Alderman, Justice of the Peace, Judge or other Person authorized to Solemnize Marriages in this State, and Celebrate or declare their Marriage, in such manner and form as shall be most agreeable; either with or without License.

Sec. 3. Any Person solemnizing a Marriage as aforesaid shall make return thereof to the City Recorder, accompanied by a recording Fee of Fifty Cents, within thirty days of the Solemnization thereof, And it is hereby made the Duty of the Recorder to keep an accurate Record of all such Marriages. The Penalty for a Violation of either of the Provisions of this Ordinance shall be twenty Dollars, to be recovered as other Penalties or Forfeitures.

3. Countering a Charge of Bigamy. It is worth noting that Joseph was never charged with bigamy. It is unknown why he was not. Quite likely, the evidentiary challenges would have been very onerous. The State would have had to prove the existence of both marriages (i.e. with Emma and Maria) in some way, such as by producing marriage certificates or actual witnesses to the ceremonies. The prosecutor could also rely on "such evidence as is admissible to prove a marriage in other cases,"[57] but that would probably

---

57. Criminal Code, section 121, *Revised Laws of Illinois*; and Criminal Jurisprudence, section 121, *Revised Statutes of the State of Illinois*. This statute provided, "Bigamy consists in the having of two wives or two husbands at one and the same time, knowing that the former husband or wife is still alive. If any person or persons within this State, being married, or who shall hereafter marry, do at any time marry any person or persons, the former husband or wife being alive, the person so offending shall, on conviction thereof, be punished by a fine, not exceeding one thousand dollars, and imprisoned in the penitentiary, not exceeding two years. It shall not be necessary to prove either of the said marriages by the register or certificate thereof, or other record evidence; but the same may be proved by such evidence as is admissible to prove a marriage in other cases."

Although the wording of this law first mentions "two wives or husbands," the subsequent language ("marry any person or persons") would have been sufficient to reach third and subsequent marriages. An illustration of how a prosecutor might have used the bigamy law is seen in an indictment for bigamy at the May 1843 term of the Hancock County Circuit Court of Jordon P. Hendrickson (sometimes spelled Jordan; see Hancock County Court Records, Book C, 458). The indictment later that year alleged that Hendrickson had married four women in different years, his first wife still living and undivorced from him. Curiously, this particular man was a member of the Church, though he was not a close associate of the Prophet and there is no evidence that these bigamous marriages were entered into with the Church's sanction. In fact, charges were brought against him before the Nauvoo High Council in February 1843 for one such bigamous marriage and for neglecting that wife (see Dinger, *Nauvoo City and High Council Minutes*, 458, spelling the name Hendrixson). County court records show that this man never stood trial for these crimes; summons repeatedly returned by the sheriff show that he could not be located for trial. Other cases involving adultery or bigamous marriages are recorded in Dinger, *Nauvoo City and High Council Minutes*, for example 444, 445.

Bigamy laws had historically been intended under Anglo-American jurisprudence to reach and include polygamy. Sources linking bigamy and polygamy include James Kent, *Commentaries on American Law*, 2d ed., vol. 2 (New York, 1832), pt. 5, pp. 80–81; Joel Prentiss Bishop, *Commentaries on the Law of Marriage and Divorce and Evidence in Matrimonial Suits* (Boston, 1852), ch. 1, secs. 201–203; and William Blackstone, *Commentaries on the Laws of England*, ed. John Wendell (New York, 1854), vol. 1, ch. 15, sec. 1; however, at least one authority wrote that bigamy, "in its proper signification, is said to mean only being twice married, and not having a plurality of wives at once. See William Oldnall Russell, *A Treatise on Crimes and Misdemeanors*, Charles Sprengel Greaves, ed., 7th American ed., 2 vols. (Philadelphia, 1853), 1:186 n. a.

have required proof of open behavior typical of married couples. As discussed above, the law governing marriage in Nauvoo did not require marriage licenses or public notices of marriages; and given the privacy of Joseph's plural sealings, circumstantial proof of such marriages would have been difficult to obtain. The fact that Joseph was the legal guardian of Maria could also have explained and undercut circumstantial evidence that the State otherwise might have presented in establishing the existence of a marriage to Maria, such as the fact that she resided in Joseph's home.[58]

Conclusion

In any prosecution under the Illinois adultery statute, Joseph would have had every reasonable expectation of acquittal. His conduct did not fit the crime with which he had been charged. The wording of the adultery statute, case law, and actual indictments from the nineteenth century indicate strongly how Illinois courts would have interpreted and applied the law. Joseph could also have mounted a credible defense using the State's constitutional guaranty of freedom of religion. It is likely not coincidental that the first of Joseph's many plural marriages in Nauvoo came only a month after the passage of the ordinance on religious toleration, which assured even "Mohommedans" free toleration and equal privileges in Nauvoo. This ordinance, along with others passed by the Nauvoo City Council, would have helped legitimize plural marriages within the confines of the City of Nauvoo. The adoption of those ordinances at a time when Joseph served as a member of the Nauvoo City Council and later as mayor suggests that Joseph was already working to ensure the legality of Nauvoo plural marriage for himself and his followers.

---

58. Presumably, the Law brothers would have wanted the grand jury to present a bigamy charge against Joseph, if possible. The fact that such a charge was not brought against Joseph suggests that there was either not enough evidence to bring the charge, or that the city ordinances and constitutional defenses mentioned above presented enough complications that the charge was not brought at that time.

Any conviction for bigamy or other serious crime would have rendered Joseph an "infamous person" under Illinois law, and this would have meant that Joseph would have been forever "rendered incapable of holding any office of honor, trust, or profit, of voting at any election, of serving as a juror, and of giving testimony," Criminal Code, section 164, *Revised Laws of Illinois,* 229; or he could have been "exclude[d] from the privilege of electing or being elected," Illinois State Constitution, art. 2, sec. 30. Joseph, thus, would have been ineligible to serve as mayor of Nauvoo, as lieutenant general of the city's militia following a bigamy conviction, as a guardian, or as a trustee of Church assets.

Joseph's apparent concern for working within the law to ensure the legality of plural marriage in Nauvoo may surprise some people. Historian D. Michael Quinn, for example, has used Joseph's performance of marriages in Ohio and the subsequent practice of plural marriage in Nauvoo in part to extrapolate a broader principle: namely, that Joseph was guided by "theocratic ethics" and chose to disregard civil law whenever it did not serve his purpose.[59] Several other writers, influenced by Quinn's conclusions, have borrowed this term in describing Joseph's approach to ethics and legal matters. In view of legal and historical evidence presented here and elsewhere, however, it is now clear that sweeping, negative characterizations of Joseph's legal ethics based on his approach to marriage are in need of reevaluation.[60]

---

59. Quinn, *Origins of Power,* 88.

60. See my previous article on Joseph's performance of marriages in Ohio. M. Scott Bradshaw, "Joseph Smith's Performance of Marriages in Ohio," *BYU Studies* 39, no. 4 (2000): 23–68.

Chapter Eighteen

Legally Suppressing the *Nauvoo Expositor* in 1844

Dallin H. Oaks

The suppression of the *Nauvoo Expositor* by the Mormons in Nauvoo, Illinois, in 1844 has interest for historians because it was the first in a series of events that lead directly to the murder of the Mormon prophet, Joseph Smith.[1] The effect of the suppression of this anti-Mormon newspaper on the non-Mormon elements in the vicinity was explosive. In the neighboring cities of Warsaw and Carthage, citizens in mass meetings declared the act revolutionary and tyrannical in tendency and resolved to hold themselves ready to cooperate with their fellow citizens in Missouri and Iowa "to exterminate, utterly exterminate the wicked and abominable Mormon leaders" and to wage "a war of extermination ... to the entire destruction, if necessary for our protection, of his adherents."[2] Thomas Ford, then governor of Illinois, called the event a violation of the Constitution and "a very gross outrage upon the laws and the liberties of the people."[3] Even B. H. Roberts, a Mormon historian, conceded that "the procedure of the city council ... was irregular; and the attempt at legal justification is not convincing."[4]

This article will assess those judgments by examining the legal basis of some of the charges the *Expositor* made against the leading citizens of Nauvoo and

1. See H. Smith, *The Day They Martyred the Prophet* (1963); Gayler, "The 'Expositor' Affair—Prelude to the Downfall of Joseph Smith," *Northwest Missouri State College Studies* 25 (February 1, 1961): 3.

2. J. Smith, *History of the Church of Jesus Christ of Latter-day Saints,* 6:464 (2d ed. 1950) (hereafter cited as *History of the Church*).

3. *History of the Church,* 6:534.

4. Roberts, *A Comprehensive History of the Church of Jesus Christ of Latter-day Saints,* 2:231–32 (1930).

the legal implications of the suppression of the newspaper by those citizens. Before this is done, however, it will be helpful to review some facts that put the event in historical perspective.

Historical Background

After successively fleeing or being driven from their homes and property in Lake County (Ohio), Jackson County (Missouri), and Clay, Daviess, and Caldwell counties (Missouri), the Mormon people gathered along the Illinois bank of the Mississippi River about forty miles north of Quincy. There, in winter 1839, they commenced to build the city of Nauvoo. Under the leadership of their prophet and president, Joseph Smith, the Mormons obtained a generous city charter, erected substantial homes and public buildings, obtained a charter for a university, and initiated trading and some manufacturing.

By 1844, Nauvoo was the largest and one of the most prosperous cities in Illinois. But events already in progress were soon to prove its downfall. Some citizens were jealous of Nauvoo's prosperity, others were hostile to the curious religion of a majority of its inhabitants, and many were suspicious of the political power of its leaders.[5] Each of these sore spots was aggravated by events in the first six months of 1844. At this time Joseph Smith was mayor of the city of Nauvoo, ex officio chief justice of the municipal court, and lieutenant general of the Nauvoo Legion, a large body of state militia organized pursuant to the Nauvoo City Charter. Prominent church officers and members filled most of the other positions of leadership in the city and legion.

Antipathy toward the union of religious, civil, and military authority in Nauvoo was sharpened by Hyrum Smith's candidacy for the legislature from Hancock County and by Joseph Smith's announced candidacy for President of the United States. These enmities, engendered by political controversies and local commercial rivalries between Saint and Gentile, were further magnified by religious and personal animosities. The religious turmoil was given such a sensational focus in 1843–1844 by several new doctrines that the Prophet was reportedly introducing, especially polygamy, that historians are fond of characterizing these conditions as combustible materials awaiting only a spark to set them aflame to work death and destruction.[6]

---

5. Berry, "The Mormon Settlement in Illinois," in *Transactions of the Illinois State Historical Society for the Year 1906*, at 88 (1906), and Gayler, "The Mormons and Politics in Illinois 1839–1844," *Illinois State Historical Society Journal* 49 (1956).'

6. E.g., Nibley, *Joseph Smith the Prophet* 518 (1946); *History of the Church*, 6:xxxvii.

The spark came in the wrecking of the *Nauvoo Expositor*, a newspaper established in Nauvoo by anti-Mormons and suppressed by the city authorities on June 10, 1844, three days after its first issue. Francis M. Higbee, one of the newspaper's proprietors, promptly made a complaint before a justice of the peace in Carthage, the Hancock County seat, against Joseph Smith, the city council, and other leading citizens for committing a riot while destroying the *Expositor* press.[7] The Carthage justice issued a "writ" (an arrest warrant) ordering state officers to "bring them before me or some other justice of the peace" to answer the charges.[8]

When Joseph Smith and his associates were arrested on this warrant on June 12 in Nauvoo, he proposed to go before any justice of the peace in Nauvoo, but the constable insisted on what seems to have been his legal right to take the prisoner before the issuing justice in Carthage.[9] Exercising the broadest range of habeas corpus jurisdiction authorized by the Nauvoo Charter and Illinois law, the municipal court held what amounted to a preliminary hearing on the guilt or innocence of the prisoner. After hearing testimony on this question, the court decided that Joseph Smith had acted under proper authority of the Nauvoo City Council in destroying the *Expositor* (referring to both the newspaper and the press), that his orders were executed without noise or tumult, that the proceeding resulting in his arrest was a malicious prosecution by Francis M. Higbee, that Higbee should, therefore, pay the costs of the suit, and that Joseph Smith should be honorably discharged from the accusations and from arrest.[10] On the following morning, Joseph Smith took his seat as chief justice of the municipal court, and the court proceeded to consider the habeas corpus petitions of Joseph's codefendants on the same charges of riot. After hearing testimony, the court ordered that these defendants also be honorably discharged and that Francis M. Higbee pay the costs. Thereupon, execution was issued against Higbee for the amount.[11]

---

7. *History of the Church*, 6:453.

8. *History of the Church*, 6:453.

9. The Illinois statutes on this subject provided that the warrant should direct the officer to bring the prisoner "before the officer issuing said warrant, or in case of his absence, before any other judge or justice of the peace," Ill. Rev. Stat. §3, at 220 (1833), or "before the judge or justice of the peace who issued the warrant, or before some other justice of the same county." Ill. Rev. Stat. §7, at 222 (1833). Under these provisions, and under the language of the warrant itself, text accompanying note 8 supra, the constable would have had authority to take the prisoners before a justice of the peace in Nauvoo. But he was not compelled to do so, and returning them to the Carthage justice was probably the normal practice.

10. *History of the Church*, 6:456–58.

11. *History of the Church*, 6:461.

To the non-Mormons of Hancock County, these actions of the municipal court, which were of questionable legality if interpreted to have the significance that the Nauvoo authorities assigned to them, added the insult
of defiance to the injury of riot and gave substantial impetus to the furious citizens' groups who met in nearby Warsaw and Carthage and called for
"extermination."[12]

As the week progressed, the magnitude of the crisis became increasingly
apparent. In a letter dated June 16, Joseph Smith advised Governor Ford of
sworn information he had received that an attempt was going to be made
to exterminate the Mormons by force of arms. He also placed the Nauvoo
Legion at the governor's service to quell the insurrection and asked the governor to come to Nauvoo to investigate the situation in person. On June 18,
before any reply had been received from Ford, Joseph Smith declared the city
of Nauvoo under martial law in view of the reports of mobs organizing to
plunder and destroy the city.[13]

Perhaps because of the rising tide of resentment against the Mormon leaders, and perhaps because of some doubts about the legality of the municipal court's action on the riot charges, the Nauvoo authorities consulted the
state circuit judge Jesse B. Thomas. He advised them that in order to satisfy the people they should be retried before another magistrate who was
not a member of their faith.[14] This advice clearly explains the fact that on
Monday, June 17, a citizen named W. G. Ware signed a complaint for riot in
the destruction of the *Expositor* against Joseph Smith and the other parties
named in the Higbee complaint. Daniel H. Wells, a non-Mormon justice of
the peace residing near Nauvoo, thereupon had the defendants arrested and
brought before him for trial.[15] After hearing numerous witnesses and counsel for both prosecution and defense, Wells gave the prisoners a judgment of
acquittal.[16]

This second trial was no more satisfactory to the anti-Mormons than the
first. During the remainder of the week there were reports of mobs forming
around Nauvoo and charges of violence on each side. The Nauvoo Legion
began entrenching the city against attack.[17] On Saturday, June 22, Governor Ford sent a rider to Joseph Smith with a letter declaring that nothing
short of trial before the same justice by whom the original writ was issued

---

12. *History of the Church,* 6: 463–65.
13. *History of the Church,* 6:480, 97.
14. *History of the Church,* 6:498, 592.
15. *History of the Church,* 6:487.
16. *History of the Church,* 6:488–91.
17. *History of the Church,* 6:504–24, 528, 531–31.

Daniel H. Wells. Courtesy Church History Library.

would "vindicate the dignity of violated law and allay the just excitement of the people." Joseph Smith's reply reminded the governor that the defendants had already been tried and acquitted by a justice of the peace for the riot offense, so that a second trial would rob them of their constitutional right not to be twice put in jeopardy of life and limb for the same offense. Joseph also expressed willingness to stand another trial, but reluctance to rely on the governor's promise of physical protection because he felt that the governor could not control the mob.[18]

On Sunday, June 23, a posse sent by the governor arrived in Nauvoo to arrest the Prophet, but was unable to find him. He had crossed the river to Montrose, Iowa, during the night, contemplating a flight to the West. He returned to Nauvoo that evening, however, and sent the governor a message offering to give himself up on the following day in reliance on the governor's pledge of protection.[19]

On Tuesday morning, June 25, in Carthage, Illinois, Joseph and Hyrum Smith voluntarily surrendered themselves to the constable who had attempted to bring them to Carthage on the original riot warrant. That afternoon the prisoners were taken before a Carthage justice of the peace, Robert F. Smith, who was also the captain of the Mormon-hating Carthage militia, and not the justice who had issued the original writ. At this preliminary hearing, the justice fixed five hundred dollars bail for each defendant on the riot charge, which was paid. Almost immediately thereafter, however, the two brothers were arrested on another warrant sworn out by a private citizen on a dubious charge of treason against the state of Illinois for having declared martial law in Nauvoo.[20]

---

18. *History of the Church*, 6:536–40.
19. *History of the Church*, 6: 48–50.
20. Ford, *History of Illinois*, 337 (1854); *History of the Church*, 6:561–62.

This second arrest had unfortunate consequences for the prisoners. Because the charge of treason was non-bailable,[21] they were compelled to remain in the custody of the constable. The prisoners were hustled into the Carthage County jail by the constable and militia under Robert F. Smith's command, pursuant to a mittimus (a warrant of commitment to prison) which recited that they had been examined on the treason charge but that trial had been postponed by reason of the absence of a material witness— none other than Francis M. Higbee.[22] The statement in the mittimus was false; the examination had not been held; and the prisoners were thus committed for treason without an opportunity to be heard on the charges.

On the following day, Wednesday, June 26, the prosecution sought to remedy the defect in the mittimus by again bringing the prisoners before Robert F. Smith for examination on the treason charge. None of the defendants' witnesses were present, however, so the defendants requested a one-day continuance (until June 27) and subpoenas for witnesses in Nauvoo, which the court granted. Later that evening Robert F. Smith changed the return day on the subpoenas to June 29, thus assuring that the defendants would be imprisoned without a hearing at least until that day.

On the morning of June 27, Governor Ford released most of the 1,200 to 1,300 militiamen then under arms in Carthage. But instead of ordering them to march to their homes for dismissal, he disbanded them in or near Carthage. To guard the prisoners at the jail, Ford selected the Carthage Grays, the company commanded by Robert F. Smith that had been so notorious for their uproarious conduct and for their threats toward the prisoners.[23] With a few remaining troops the Governor then marched to Nauvoo, where he delivered a speech berating the inhabitants for civil disobedience.

Shortly after five o'clock on the afternoon of Thursday, June 27, a mob of about a hundred men with blackened faces, apparently composed largely of members of the disbanded militia,[24] overcame the token resistance of the militia guards and shot Joseph and Hyrum to death in their room in the jail. Two fellow prisoners survived to record the brutal details.[25] This concluded the chain of events set in motion by the destruction of the *Nauvoo Expositor*.

---

21. The Illinois Constitution, art. VIII, §13 (1818).
22. *History of the Church*, 6:567–70; *History of the Church*, 7:85.
23. *History of the Church*, 6:606–607.
24. See *History of the Church*, 7:143–46.
25. *History of the Church*, 6:616–22.

The *Nauvoo Expositor* and Its Charges

Nauvoo citizens had been notified of the coming of the *Expositor* by a pro-spectus issued May 10, 1844. Sylvester Emmons, a non-Mormon member of the Nauvoo City Council, was named editor, and William and Wilson Law, Francis and Chauncey Higbee, Robert and Charles Foster, and Charles Ivins signed as publishers. The prospectus declared that a part of the newspaper's columns would be devoted to advocating free speech, religious tolerance, unconditional repeal of the Nauvoo Charter, disobedience to political reve-lations, hostility to any union of church and state, censure of gross moral imperfections wherever found, and, "in a word, to give a full, candid, and succinct statement of FACTS AS THEY REALLY EXIST IN THE CITY OF NAUVOO." The publishers further declared their intent to "use such terms and names as they deem proper, when the object is of such high importance that the end will justify the means."[26]

The first and only issue of the *Nauvoo Expositor,* the four-page issue of Friday, June 7, 1844, was more sensational than distinguished.[27] While the paper contained a short story, some poetry, a few news items (mostly copied from eastern newspapers), and a scattering of ads, it was principally devoted to attacking Joseph and Hyrum Smith and their unnamed associates in the Church and in the city government. With "lame grammer and turgid rheto-ric" that John Hay termed dull or laughable,[28] the paper assailed the Mormon leaders on three fronts: *religion, politics,* and *morality.* A summary of the most prominent charges will be set forth here as a basis for the discussion to follow.

Religion: The religious items are all contained in a "Preamble, Resolu-tions and Affidavits, of the Seceders from the Church at Nauvoo," which, an editor's note explains, is included in order to give the public the facts about the schism in The Church of Jesus Christ of Latter-day Saints.[29] This lengthy document commenced with an affirmation that the gospel as originally taught by Joseph Smith is true and that its pure principles would invigorate, ennoble, and dignify man. However, it proclaimed that Joseph Smith was a fallen prophet who had introduced many doctrines that were "heretical and

---

26. *History of the Church,* 6:444.

27. The excerpts from the *Nauvoo Expositor* that appear in the text were taken from an original copy in the Illinois State Historical Library at Springfield, Illinois.

28. Oaks explores the validity of these claims in more detail in his original article. See pp. 877–85.

29. *Nauvoo Expositor,* June 7, 1844, p. 1, col. 5. The "Preamble," "Resolutions," and "Affi-davits" were reprinted in the *Salt Lake Tribune,* October 6, 1910, 4; the "Preamble" and "Resolutions" were quoted at length in the *Deseret Evening News,* December 21, 1869.

damnable in their influence."[30] It denounced Joseph and Hyrum Smith and other unnamed officials as apostates from the doctrine of Jesus because they had "introduced false and damnable doctrines into the Church, such as a plurality of Gods above the God of this universe, and his liability to fall with all his creations; the plurality of wives, for time and eternity; the doctrine of unconditional sealing up to eternal life, against all crimes except that of shedding innocent blood."[31] The "Resolutions" also proposed that all persons presently preaching false doctrines come and make satisfaction and have their licenses renewed,[32] which was presumably a bid for allegiance to the church recently organized by the seceders.

Politics: At the political level, the principal complaint was the Mormon leaders' attempts to unite church and state. Various editorial notes and news articles described these attempts and the "Resolutions" condemned them.[33] There were three specific complaints.

First, the "Preamble" speaks vaguely of "examples of injustice, cruelty and oppression" accomplished by "the inquisitorial department organized in *Nauvoo,* by Joseph and his accomplices."[34] If suffered to persist, the paper predicted, this inquisition "will prove more formidable and terrible to those who are found opposing the iniquities of Joseph and his associates, than even the Spanish Inquisition did to heretics as they termed them."[35]

Second, an "Introductory" by the editor bitterly protested the Nauvoo authorities' use of the writ of habeas corpus to defy the law by inquiring into the guilt or innocence of prisoners and by releasing prisoners arrested or held in custody pursuant to the authority of the United States or the state of Illinois.[36]

The third complaint related to the political candidacies of Joseph and Hyrum. Excerpts from Joseph's letter to Henry Clay and from his *Views on the Powers and Policy of the Government of the United States* were quoted and ridiculed.[37] The "Resolutions" of the seceders submitted that this bid for political power was not pleasing to God,[38] and an open letter to the citizens of Hancock County by Francis M. Higbee argued that the citizens of the

---

30. *Nauvoo Expositor,* June 7, 1844, p. 1, col. 6.
31. *Nauvoo Expositor,* June 7, 1844, p. 2, col. 3.
32. *Nauvoo Expositor,* June 7, 1844, p. 2, col. 4.
33. *Nauvoo Expositor,* June 7, 1844, p. 2, col. 4.
34. *Nauvoo Expositor,* June 7, 1844, p. 2, col. 3.
35. *Nauvoo Expositor,* June 7, 1844, p. 2, col. 3.
36. *Nauvoo Expositor,* June 7, 1844, p. 2 col. 6.
37. *History of the Church,* 6:207–8, 376–77.
38. *Nauvoo Expositor,* June 7, 1844, p. 2, col. 4.

county should not support the Smiths, citing the candidates' alleged immoralities, Joseph's being under indictment for adultery and perjury, the candidates' defiance of the law by using habeas corpus to rescue fugitives from justice, and the dangerous tendencies of their attempts for civil power.[39]

Morality: The third and most pervasive theme was the alleged immorality of Joseph and his associates, of whom Hyrum was the only one specifically named. Some of these charges related to financial affairs or vague implications of murderous conduct. Most concerned sexual behavior.

The "Resolutions" of the seceders from the Church made serious charges of misuse of Church funds. The general charges of knavery were also numerous, varied, and unrestrained. Higbee's letter about the political candidates said Joseph was "one of the blackest and basest scoundrels that has appeared upon the stage of human existence since the days of Nero, and Caligula" and urged that the community "support not that man who is spreading death, devastation and ruin throughout your happy country like a tornado."[40]

"It is a notorious fact," the "Preamble" continues, as its charges begin to get specific, "that many females in foreign climes … have been induced, by the sound of the gospel, to forsake friends, and embark upon a voyage … as they supposed, to glorify God … But what is taught them on their arrival at this place?" They are soon visited and told that there are great blessings in store for the faithful and that "brother Joseph will see them soon, and reveal the mysteries of Heaven to their full understanding." Later, the "harmless, inoffensive, and unsuspecting creatures" are requested to meet brother Joseph or some of the Twelve Apostles at some isolated spot. There, the "Preamble" alleges, the faithful follower of Joseph is sworn to secrecy upon a penalty of death and then told that God has revealed

> that she should be his [Joseph's] Spiritual wife; for it was right anciently, and God will tolerate it again: but we must keep those pleasures and blessings from the world, for until there is a change in the government, we will endanger ourselves by practicing it— but we can enjoy the blessings of Jacob, David, and others, as well as to be deprived of them, if we do not expose ourselves to the law of the land. She is thunderstruck, faints, recovers, and refuses. The Prophet damns her if she rejects. She thinks of the great sacrifice, and of the many thousand miles she has traveled over sea and land, that she might save her soul from pending ruin, and

---

39. *Nauvoo Expositor*, June 7, 1844, p. 3, col. 4.
40. *Nauvoo Expositor*, June 7, 1844 p.3 col. 5.

replies, God's will be done, and not mine. The Prophet and his devotees in this way are gratified.[41]

The "Preamble" then goes into a lengthy and detailed description of the injured feelings, the broken health, and the eventual untimely death of those "whom no power or influence could seduce, except that which is wielded by some individual feigning to be God."[42] One of the most often repeated themes in the *Expositor* was the promise that future issues would be unrestrained in their exposure. The editor's "Introductory" declared:

> We intend to tell the whole tale and by all honorable means to bring to light and justice, those who have long fed and fattened upon the purse, the property, and the character of injured innocence;—yes, we will speak, and that too in thunder tones, to the ears of those who have thus ravaged and laid waste fond hopes, bright prospects, and virtuous principles, to gratify an unhallowed ambition.[43]

The foregoing summary is representative of the worst that the *Expositor* had to offer. Comment on this material will follow a review of the Nauvoo authorities' reaction to the paper.

The Reaction to and Suppression of the *Expositor*

The first issue of the *Expositor* produced a furious reaction from the citizens of Nauvoo, which, as one observer reported at the time, "raised the excitement to a degree beyond control, and threatened serious consequence."[44] Joseph Smith later gave this explanation to the governor:

> [C]an it be supposed that after all the indignities to which we have been subjected outside, that this people could suffer a set of worthless vagabonds to come into our city, and right under our own eyes and protection, vilify and calumniate not only ourselves, but the character of our wives and daughters, as was impudently and unblushingly done in that infamous and filthy sheet?

41. *Nauvoo Expositor,* June 7, 1844, p. 2, col. 1.

42. *Nauvoo Expositor,* June 7, 1844, p. 2, col. 1.

43. *Nauvoo Expositor,* June 7, 1844 p. 3 col. 1.

44. *History of the Church,* 6:470. See generally Roberts, *Comprehensive History,* 2:229 (1930); *History of the Church,* 6:446.

There is not a city in the United States that would have suffered such an indignity for twenty-four hours.

Our whole people were indignant, and loudly called upon our city authorities for redress of their grievances, which, if not attended to they themselves would have taken the matter into their own hands, and have summarily punished the audacious wretches, as they deserved.[45]

The temper of the times suggests that the prospect of mob action against the *Expositor* press was real and not merely speculative. One historian has said that there were sixteen instances of violence in Illinois between 1832 and 1867 to presses or editors who dared to express highly controversial views contrary to those generally held in the community.[46] The editors of the *Expositor* did not openly advocate mob action, but that possibility did not remain unnoticed. The editors posed the following rhetorical question:

[W]ill you bring a mob upon us? In answer to that, we assure all concerned, that we [the editors] will be among the first to put down anything like an illegal force being used against any man or set of men.... [But] if it is necessary to make a show of force, to execute legal process, it will create no sympathy in that case [for the Mormons] to cry out, we are mobbed.[47]

On Saturday, June 8, 1844, the day following issuance of the *Expositor,* the Nauvoo City Council met for a total of six and a half hours in two sessions in which they discussed the character and conduct of the various publishers of the *Expositor.* The council then adjourned until Monday, June 10, when it met for an additional seven and a half hours, dedicating much of its attention to reviewing the *Expositor* itself.[48]

During this Monday meeting, Mayor Joseph Smith expressed a concern that what the opposition party was trying to do by the paper was to destroy the peace of Nauvoo, excite its enemies, and raise a mob to bring death and

45. *History of the Church,* 6:581.

46. Davis, *The Story of the Church,* 335–36 (6th ed. 1948). One of these cases involved the destruction of the *Alton Observer,* public meetings and outroar, violent harrangues, the secret organization of an abolitionist society, and an armed nighttime mob attack resulting on October 26, 1837, in two deaths, including that of the publisher, Elijah P. Lovejoy, in an Illinois town on the Mississippi River. Ford, *History of Illinois,* 234–38 (1854).

47. *Navuoo Expositor,* June 7, 1844, p. 2, col. 5.

48. *History of the Church,* 6:430, 432.

destruction upon the city.[49] He argued that the paper was "a nuisance—a greater nuisance than a dead carcass," and urged the council to make some provision for removing it.[50] (This was not the first time that the city council had been urged to exercise the power given in its legislative charter "to declare what shall be a nuisance, and to prevent and remove the same.")[51]

Joseph's concern about the *Expositor* was echoed by some and supported by others throughout the deliberations. Hyrum Smith announced himself in favor of declaring the *Expositor* a nuisance.[52] Councilor John Taylor said that no city on earth would bear such slander and that he was in favor of active measures. He read from the United States Constitution on freedom of the press and concluded: "We are willing they should publish the truth; but it is unlawful to publish libels. The *Expositor* is a nuisance, and stinks in the nose of every honest man."[53]

After the mayor read the provisions of the Illinois Constitution on the responsibility of the press for its constitutional liberties,[54] Councilor Stiles read Blackstone's definition of and comments on abatement of nuisances and declared himself in favor of suppressing any more slanderous publications. Others likewise supported abating the *Expositor* as a nuisance.[55] Hyrum Smith stated that the best way to suppress it was to smash the press and pi (scatter) the type.[56]

Not all council members agreed. Councilor Warrington, a non-Mormon, considered the proposed action rather harsh. He suggested assessing a heavy fine for libels and then proceeding to quiet the paper if it did not cease publishing libels. Hyrum Smith replied that, in view of the financial condition of the publishers, there would be little chance of collecting damages for libels. Other aldermen and councilors said there was no reason to suppose that the publishers would desist if fined or imprisoned and that it was unwise "to give them time to trumpet a thousand lies."[57]

Finally, at about 6:30 P.M. on Monday, June 10, the council came to a decision. It resolved that the issues of the *Nauvoo Expositor* and the printing office from whence it issued were "a public nuisance . . . and the Mayor is instructed

---

49. *History of the Church*, 6:438, 442.

50. *History of the Church*, 6:441.

51. Ill. Laws 1840, §13 at 54–55. See also *History of the Church*, 4:442, 444.

52. *History of the Church*, 6:445.

53. *History of the Church*, 4:442, 444.

54. *History of the Church*, 4:442, 444.

55. *History of the Church*, 6:445.

56. *History of the Church*, 6:445.

57. *History of the Church*, 6:446.

to cause said printing establishment and papers to be removed without delay, in such manner as he shall direct." The mayor promptly ordered the marshal to "destroy the printing press from whence issues the *Nauvoo Expositor,* and pi the type of said printing establishment in the street, and burn all the *Expositors* and libelous handbills found in said establishment."[58] He also ordered the Nauvoo Legion to be in readiness to execute the city ordinances if the marshal should need its services.

By eight o'clock that evening, the marshal had made a return to the order.[59] Accompanied by a large crowd of citizens and by a number of the militia, he had proceeded to the *Expositor* office, destroyed the press, and scattered the type as ordered.

According to the criminal charges soon filed against the principals in this action, the manner of execution of the council's order constituted a riot. This crime was committed when two or more persons did an unlawful act "with force or violence against the person of another" or did a lawful act "in a violent and tumultuous manner."[60] At the two subsequent trials for riot, numerous witnesses, including several visitors from cities outside Illinois, testified without significant contradiction that the whole transaction was accomplished quietly and without noise or tumult.[61] The marshal demanded the press, Higbee refused, the marshal opened the door (one witness said he ordered it "forced," another said "a knee was put against it," another named a man who had opened it; several said there was little or no noise or delay at its opening), Higbee left the premises unhindered, and seven to twelve men went inside and carried out the press and type. Except for one minor deviation, all witnesses also agreed that there was no violence, and that nothing was destroyed or damaged that did not pertain to the press.[62]

An Evaluation of the *Expositor's* Charges

The legality of the council's action in suppressing the *Expositor* depends upon the inflammatory nature of the charges in the *Expositor* and the reaction which the city councilors could therefore reasonably conclude that they were likely to produce in the community and the surrounding areas.

---

58. *History of the Church,* 6:448.
59. *History of the Church,* 6:448.
60. Ill. Rev. Stat. §117, at 197 (1833).
61. *History of the Church,* 6:456–58, 488–91.
62. *History of the Church,* 6:456–58, 488–91.

The *Expositor*'s general complaints about the union of the authority of church and state in Nauvoo were essentially true. Notwithstanding the presence of non-Mormons on the city council, the dominance of Mormon Church leaders in every branch of government in the city and legion was beyond question. In protesting this condition, in urging its readers to vote against Joseph and Hyrum Smith in their election contests, and even in advocating repeal of the Nauvoo Charter, the *Expositor* was performing the traditional function of a free press. The name-calling accompanying the *Expositor*'s political advocacy was pretty rough, but not particularly unique in view of the prevailing style of political commentary of that day.[63] However offensive this aspect of the newspaper's copy may have been to the individuals in power, it offered no conceivable justification for harassment, much less suppression.

The *Expositor*'s most specific complaints against Joseph's and Hyrum's political conduct or their qualifications for office were the charges that they had defied the law by using the writ of habeas corpus: (a) to release prisoners held in the custody of state or federal authorities and (b) to try the guilt or innocence of parties who applied for the writ. An evaluation of these charges requires a discussion of the habeas corpus law in Illinois in 1844.

Honored as the "highest safeguard of liberty," the writ of habeas corpus was the command by which a court or judge required a person who had another in custody to produce the prisoner and explain the cause of his detention.[64] In Illinois during the Nauvoo period, the law of habeas corpus was the common law, as modified by the Illinois Habeas Corpus Act of 1827 and supplementary legislation. These laws authorized the writ of habeas corpus to be issued by the Illinois Supreme Court, by various circuit courts, or by any of the judges of these courts or the masters in chancery.[65] In addition—and this was the source of contention—the legislative charter of the city of Nauvoo gave its municipal court "power to grant writs of habeas corpus in all cases arising under the ordinances of the city council."[66] The *Expositor*'s complaint related to several instances where the Nauvoo court had issued this writ to bring before it prisoners in the custody of state or federal officers, held hearings on the prisoners' guilt or innocence, and ordered them discharged.

---

63. See, e.g., Mott, *American Journalism* 237, 255, 263, 310 (3d ed. 1941); Mott, *A History of American Magazines, 1741–1850*, 159–60 (1930); *Truth's Advocate* and *Monthly Anti-Jackson Expositor*, January–October, 1821 (Cincinnati newspaper).

64. Oaks, *Habeas Corpus in the States—1776–1865*, 32 *University of Chicago Law Review* 243 (1965).

65. Ill. Rev. Stat. §1, at 322 (1833) (Habeas Corpus Act of 1827); Ill. Laws 1834–35, §2, at 32.

66. Ill. Laws 1840, §17, at 55.

The legality of this action will be considered first from the standpoint of the special problems involved in issuing the writ for a federal prisoner. Courts that had ruled on the matter prior to 1844 were practically unanimous in the opinion that state courts had the power to issue the writ of habeas corpus for persons held by federal officers. In 1858, a leading authority on habeas corpus law declared: "It may be considered settled that state courts may grant the writ in all cases of illegal confinement under the authority of the United States."[67] Among the cases relied upon were recent decisions by the supreme courts of Ohio and Wisconsin holding that the courts of those states had properly issued their writs of habeas corpus for prisoners arrested by federal officers or tried, convicted, and imprisoned by federal courts.[68] It was not until 1859, when the Supreme Court of the United States reversed the Wisconsin judgment in the leading case of *Ableman v. Booth*,[69] that it was established that persons held in federal custody could not be freed by a writ of habeas corpus issued by a state court. Consequently, there was nothing in federal statutory or state common law that forbade a court like Nauvoo's that the state had authorized to issue the writ of habeas corpus from issuing the writ for a federal prisoner. It is equally true, however, that there was nothing to prevent a state from voluntarily forbidding its courts to interfere with the custody of federal prisoners.

Since the city of Nauvoo derived its authority from state law, the question whether the municipal court had jurisdiction over state prisoners was simply a question whether the legislature had given the court that authority in the Nauvoo City Charter. The relevant charter provision, giving the municipal court "power to grant writs of *habeas corpus* in all cases arising under the ordinances of the city council," might have been read narrowly so that the court would have power to issue the writ only in those cases where the prisoner was confined by the authority of the city of Nauvoo.

The habeas corpus provision could also be read more broadly to give the court power to investigate any confinement, state or federal, within the city of Nauvoo that was in violation of the terms of a valid ordinance of the city of Nauvoo. During summer and fall 1842, when Missouri was striving feverishly to extradite Joseph Smith, the Nauvoo authorities relied on this later interpretation to enact an ordinance which provided that whenever any person should be "arrested or under arrest" in Nauvoo he could be brought before

---

67. Hurd, *Habeas Corpus*, 166 (1858).

68. In the Matter of Collier, 6 Ohio St. 55 (1856); *In re* Booth & Rycraft, 3 Wis.157 (1855); *In re* Booth, 3 Wis.1 (1854).

69. 62. U.S. (21 How.) 506 (1859).

the municipal court by a writ of habeas corpus. The court was thereupon required to "examine into the origin, validity and legality of the writ of process under which such arrest was made."[70] Since this portion of the ordinance does not seem to have exceeded the council's charter authority to make ordinances "as they may deem necessary for the peace, benefit, good order, regulation, convenience and cleanliness of said city,"[71] it probably offers a valid basis for the issuance of the writ of habeas corpus if the broader construction of the charter's habeas corpus powers is the correct one.

Governor Ford conceded that the officials of Nauvoo "had been repeatedly assured by some of the best lawyers in the State who had been candidates for office before that people, that it [the municipal court] had full and competent power to issue writs of habeas corpus in all cases whatever."[72] The foregoing discussion shows that their advice had considerable support in the law of that time. The better construction of the charter provision gave the municipal court authority to issue its writ of habeas corpus for any confinement within the limits of the city—state or federal—that was in violation of any valid ordinance of the city council. The *Expositor's* first criticism of the Nauvoo court's habeas corpus actions was, therefore, legally unjustified.

The *Expositor's* second complaint about the Nauvoo writ of habeas corpus—that the Nauvoo authorities defied the law by using habeas corpus to try the guilt or innocence of parties who applied for the writ—was also unfounded. These complaints concern instances wherein individuals held under warrants of arrest in Nauvoo were given a writ of habeas corpus to bring them before the municipal court, which held a hearing upon their cases and gave them discharges.[73]

But it is apparent that this action and most, if not all, of the others complained of were perfectly legal uses of the writ of habeas corpus. Under Illinois law, typical of the state law of that period, a person who had been arrested was promptly taken before a judicial officer—typically a justice of the peace—for an examination to determine "the truth or probability of the charge exhibited against such prisoner or prisoners, by the oath of all witnesses attending."[74]

---

70. *History of the Church,* 6: 88.

71. Ill. Laws 1840, §11, at 54.

72. Ford, *History of Illinois,* 325 (1854). See *History of the Church,* 5:466–68, 471–73.

73. Joseph Smith's journal notes the following instances: *History of the Church,* 5:461–74 (Joseph Smith released from Governor's extradition warrant); *History of the Church,* 6:418–22 (Jeremiah Smith released from custody of two different federal marshals acting under writs issued by federal district judge). The court also used the writ to free persons seized under civil process. *History of the Church,* 6:80, 286.

74. Ill. Rev. Stat. §3, at 221 (1833).

The judicial officer would hear the evidence and then decide whether to commit the prisoner to jail to await trial or action of the grand jury, admit him to bail, or discharge him from custody. Although based upon evidence of guilt or innocence, the decision at the examination was only preliminary. If discharged, the prisoner could still be rearrested if additional evidence was secured. If held in jail or admitted to bail, he could still prove his innocence at his trial.

One might wonder if it would have been an abuse of the writ of habeas corpus to use it to consider questions of guilt or innocence, for one important role of habeas corpus was to determine whether the arrest warrant was free from any formal defects and perhaps whether the warrant had been based on sufficient written evidence.[75] But several states, including Illinois, assigned a broader role to habeas corpus, as explained in this passage from a Philadelphia lawyer's 1849 book on habeas corpus:

> There is, however, an engraftment upon its use, as we derived this writ from the English law, which seems to have grown into strength in America, in some of the States by judicial decision, and in others by express statutory enactment, viz.: the hearing the whole merits and facts of the case upon habeas corpus, *deciding* upon the guilt or rather upon the *innocence* of the prisoner, and absolutely discharging him without the intervention of a jury, where the court is of opinion that the *facts* do not sustain the criminal charge.[76]

In Illinois this approach was embodied in the statutory provision that permitted a petitioner for habeas corpus to "allege any facts to shew, either that the imprisonment or detention is unlawful, or that he is then entitled to his discharge," and empowered the court or judge to "proceed in a summary way to settle the said facts, by hearing the testimony ... and dispose of the prisoners as the case may require."[77] Under these provisions, an Illinois prisoner who had been arrested under a warrant issued by a justice of the peace[78] could validly use a writ of habeas corpus to obtain a judicial review of his case, including a hearing at which he could present witnesses or other evidence and a judicial determination of his guilt or innocence (to the limited extent of discharging him if he was clearly innocent, or holding him in

---

75. Church, Habeas Corpus §§234–35 (1884); Oaks, *supra* note 106, at 258–60.

76. Ingersoll, *History and the Law of the Writ of Habeus Corpus,* 39–40 (1849).

77. Ill. Rev. Stat. §3, at 324 (1833).

78. Ill. Rev. Stat. §3 at 324 (1833).

custody or admitting him to bail if there was probable cause to believe that he had committed the charged offense). The Nauvoo Municipal Court may have erred in its application of these principles, and some of its members seem to have misapprehended the significance of the discharge—considering it a final adjudication of innocence that would preclude any further arrest or trial—but the power that the court exercised was clearly authorized by law, not in defiance of it.

The *Expositor's* charges about abuse of the writ of habeas corpus have provided the occasion for a discussion of the municipal court's use of this ancient and honored remedy. It is readily apparent that, even though the *Expositor's* charges of abuse of the writ were not well founded, the whole subject was well within the area of political controversy. There was nothing in the *Expositor's* political copy that gave the authorities of Nauvoo any legal basis whatever for the suppression of the newspaper.

The same can be said of the *Expositor's* charges that Joseph Smith was teaching false religious doctrines, notably polygamy. Since the Illinois Constitution provided that "no human authority can in any case whatever control or interfere with the rights of conscience; and that no preference shall ever be given by law to any religious establishments or modes of worship,"[79] the teachings of religion could not properly be the concern of any civil authority. Consequently, the doctrinal controversy in the *Expositor* offered no conceivable basis for suppressionary action by city authorities.

Probably the most provocative portions of the *Expositor* were the claims that Hyrum Smith was a "base seducer, liar and perjurer" and the charges that Joseph Smith had spread "death, devastation and ruin," that he had committed fraud in handling Church monies, and that he was guilty of practicing whoredoms and had engaged in numerous seductions, which were said to have caused the untimely death of the women involved.

Volumes have been written about the truth or falsity of these and similar charges relating to the character of the Mormon leaders.[80] For present purposes it is unnecessary—even if it were possible—to resolve the conflicts between their detractors and defenders. Whether the charges were true or false, they were malicious, scandalous, and defamatory.[81] In view of the Mormons' undoubted affection for their leaders, the virulent attacks upon

---

79. Ill. Const. art. VIII, §3 (1818).

80. *E.g.,* Brodie, *No Man Knows My History* (1945); Evans, *Joseph Smith—An American Prophet* (1933); O'Dea, *The Mormons* (1957).

81. Defamation, which includes libel and slander, consists of an attempt by words or pictures to blacken a person's reputation or to expose him to hatred, ridicule, or contempt. Prosser, Torts §92, at 574, §96, at 630 (2d ed. 1955).

them had a tendency to provoke retaliatory mob action against the newspaper by the citizens of Nauvoo. The councilmen also feared that the first and subsequent issues of the *Expositor* would arouse mobs of anti-Mormons to come to Nauvoo to drive out its citizens. Subsequent events, notably the mob murder of Joseph Smith and the eventual expulsion of the Mormons from Nauvoo by armed mobs, suggest that these fears were not groundless. Each of these aspects of the *Expositor's* charges was a legitimate concern of the city government and a possible basis for its suppressionary action.

The Legality of the Suppression

Governor Ford and subsequent commentators have made three objections to the legality of the council's action in suppressing the *Expositor*. First, the council had gone beyond its legislative powers of defining a nuisance by general ordinance and had entered upon the judicial prerogative of passing judgment on individual acts, all without notice, hearing, or trial by jury. Second, a newspaper, however scurrilous or libelous, cannot be legally abated or removed as a nuisance. Third, the council's action violated the state constitutional provision insuring the liberty of the press.[82] These points will be discussed in that order.

The Council's Power to Abate Nuisances. So far as municipal government law is concerned, Governor Ford's insistence that "the Constitution abhors and will not tolerate the union of legislative and judicial power in the same body of magistracy"[83] was totally without merit. The concept of separation of legislative, executive, and judicial authority, so vital in our federal government, has relatively little application at the municipal level. The blend of legislative and executive authority inherent in the mayor-council form of government was and is familiar. Less common, but by no means unique, was the combination of executive, legislative, and judicial powers established by the Illinois General Assembly in the Nauvoo Charter. The city council was composed of the mayor, four aldermen, and nine councilors.[84] This was the lawmaking body, whose legislative authority expressly included the power (invoked in the destruction of the *Expositor*) "to make regulations to secure the general health of the inhabitats [*sic*], to declare what shall be a nuisance, and to prevent and

---

82. These are the main problems identified by Governor Thomas Ford. Ford, *History of Illinois*, 325–27 (1854); *History of the Church*, 6:534–35.

83. *History of the Church*, 6:535.

84. 8 Ill. Laws 1840, §6, at 53. A complete copy of the Nauvoo Charter also appears in Gregg, *The Prophet of Palmyra*, 463–71 (1890), and in *History of the Church*, 4:239–48.

6 May 1844

State of Illinois
City of Nauvoo

To the Honorable Municipal
Court in and for the City of Nauvoo —
The undersigned Your Petitioner most respectfully
represents that he is an inhabitant of said city
Your Petitioner further represents that he is
under arrest in said City and is now in the custody
of one John D. Parker Deputy Sheriff of the County
of Hancock & State of Illinois — that the said
Parker holds your Petitioner by virtue of a
writ or Capias ad respondendum issued by
the Clerk of the Circuit Court of the County of
Hancock in the State of Illinois at the instance
of one Francis M. Higbee of said county requiring
Your Petitioner to answer the said Francis M. Higbee
of a Plea of the Case Damage five Thousand Dollars —
Your Petitioner further represents that the proceed
ings against your petitioner him are Illegal —
that the said warrant of arrest is informal, and
not of that Character which the Law recognises
as valid, that the said writ is wanting
and Deficient in the plea therein contained
that the charge or Complaint which your
Petitioner is therein contained required to answer
is not a that of known to the Law —
Your Petitioner further avers that the

Petition of Joseph Smith for a writ of habeus corpus filed with the Nauvoo Municipal Court to quash an arrest warrant served on Joseph Smith based on a complaint of slander raised by Francis M. Higbee. Church History Library.

said Writ does not Disclose in any way or Manner any Whatever any Cause of Action Which Matter your Petitioner most Respectfully Submits for your Consideration — together with a copy of the said Warrant of Arrest which is hereunto attached.

Your Petitioner further States that this proceeding has been instituted against him without any Just or Legal Cause and further that the said Francis M. Higbee is actuated by no other motive than a desire to persecute and harass your Petitioner for the base purpose of gratifying feelings of revenge which without any cause the said Francis M. Higbee has for a long time been fostering and Cherishing —

Your Petitioner further states that he is not guilty of either Charge preferred against him or of any act against him by which the said Francis M. Higbee could have any Charge Claim or demand Whatever against your Petitioner —

Your Petitioner further states that he verily believes that another object the said F. M. Higbee had in instituting this proceeding was and is to throw your Petitioner into the hands of his Enemies that he might the better carry out a Conspiracy which has for some time

remove the same."[85] The judicial authority was vested in the individuals who were mayor and aldermen. As a group, they comprised the municipal court. In addition, the mayor had exclusive jurisdiction in all cases arising under city ordinances, and he, with the various aldermen, had all the powers of justices of the peace within the limits of the city, both in civil and in criminal cases arising under state law.[86]

The traditional function of legislative power is to enact general legislation to define what constitutes a crime, leaving it to the judiciary to determine whether individual acts or conditions come within that definition. Therefore, Governor Ford criticized the Nauvoo City Council for assuming both legislative and judicial functions by declaring particular property to be a nuisance and simultaneously ordering its abatement without first laying the matter before a court. In his conference with the governor in Carthage, Joseph Smith undertook to justify this action on the ground that the council represented both legislative and judicial powers:

> I cannot see the distinction that you draw about the acts of the
> City Council, and what difference it could have made in point of
> fact, law, or justice, between the City Council's acting together
> or separate, or how much more legal it would have been for the
> Municipal Court, who were a part of the City Council, to act sep-
> arate, instead of with the councilors.[87]

There are two reasons Joseph Smith's argument was not well founded and the council's action cannot be justified on the basis of the judicial powers of some of its members. First, judicial power cannot be validly exercised without notice to interested parties and an opportunity for them to be heard. The owners and publishers of the *Expositor* were not given notice or hearing. Second, the Nauvoo Charter guaranteed "a right to a trial by a jury of twelve men in all cases before the municipal court,"[88] and there was, of course, no jury trial prior to the suppression.

Joseph Smith was on sounder ground, however, in the original explanation he gave of the *Expositor* suppression as simply an exercise of the council's legislative authority to abate nuisances.[89] The destruction or removal (abatement) of nuisances was one of those classes of acts that the common

---

85. Ill. Laws 1840, §13 at 54–55.

86. Ill. Laws 1840, §§16–17, at 55.

87. *History of the Church*, 6:584–85.

88. Ill. Laws 1840, §17, at 55.

89. *History of the Church*, 6:538.

law permited without the interposition of judicial power. Blackstone, whose definitive work on the common law was studied by the councilors to determine the legality of their proposed action, states that certain nuisances may be abated by the aggrieved party without notice to the person who committed them.[90] The leading American case on summary abatement at this time was an 1832 decision by the highest court of the state of New York concerning the right of the city of Albany to pass an ordinance declaring a structure in its harbor to be a public nuisance and directing its officers to abate it by destruction (without any judicial proceedings).[91] The court held that the municipality's proposed action was a valid exercise of its common law powers and of the police power conferred by its statutory authority to abate nuisances and that no judicial hearing was required.

Blackstone and this same New York case were the principal authorities followed by the Illinois Supreme Court in 1881 in a nuisance-abatement case.[92] There the court held that a municipality's charter authority to abate nuisances permitted it to pass a valid ordinance ordering its marshal (without any judicial proceedings) to remove a roof that did not conform to fire regulations from a private home and destroy it, without any liability for damages. Similarly, in a later case the Illinois Supreme Court said that a municipality (whose charter powers to abate nuisances were practically identical to those of Nauvoo) could properly provide by ordinance that a certain house infected with smallpox germs be summarily abated by burning, if the circumstances were such that less drastic measures were not feasible.[93]

From the authorities discussed above it appears that the first objection to the Nauvoo Council's action—that it wrongly failed to use or that it improperly exercised judicial powers—was without foundation. If the *Expositor* was a nuisance, and if it was the sort of nuisance that permitted summary abatement, the council's legislative powers sufficed to justify the action taken. These two qualifications will be discussed next.

Abatement of Newspapers as a Nuisance. The common law defined a nuisance as any unreasonable, unwarranted, or unlawful use of property, or any improper, indecent, or unlawful personal conduct that produced material annoyance, inconvenience, discomfort, or injury to others or their property.[94] Nuisances were private when they affected particular individuals, and

---

90. 2 Blackstone, *Commentaries*, 4–5 & n.6 (Am. ed. from 18th Eng. ed. 1832).

91. Hart v. Mayor of Albany, 9 Wend. 571 (N.Y. Ct; Err. 1832).

92. 9 King v. Davenport, 98 Ill. 305, 311 (1881).

93. Sings v. City of Joliet, 237 Ill. 300, 86 N.E. 663 (1908).

94. 1 Wood, Nuisances §1 (3d ed. 1893).

public when their effect was general. Under this definition, if the *Expositor* was a nuisance at all it could have been classified as both a public and a private nuisance, since its inflammatory language not only injured private individuals but were also of such a scandalous and provocative character as to be of concern to the community at large. A party injured by a private nuisance could sue to obtain damages or to compel its removal. The commission of a public nuisance was punishable as a crime. In addition, in certain circumstances private individuals could abate private nuisances and private individuals or public officials could abate public nuisances.[95] There seems to have been considerable basis from which a person acting in 1844 could have concluded that a publication devoted to malicious, scandalous, and defamatory matter likely to provoke mob action could be abated as a nuisance.

The passage of Blackstone's *Commentaries* referred to by the Nauvoo city councilors in their deliberations on what measures should be taken against the *Expositor* reads as follows:

> (6) … As to private nuisances, they also may be abated.… So it seems that a libellous print or paper, affecting a private individual, may be destroyed, or, which is the safer course, taken and delivered to a magistrate. 5 Coke, 125, b. 2 Camp. 511.[96]

The basis for the statement in footnote six—the passage specifically relied on by the councilors[97]—is the classification as a private or public nuisance of whatsoever has a deleterious influence upon the morals, good order, or well being of society. For example, in a case decided in 1854, the Illinois Supreme Court gave its opinion that obscene books, prints, and pictures could be categorized as a public nuisance because they were hurtful and injurious to the public morals, good order, and well-being of society.[98]

Authorities suggest three bases for the characterization of the *Expositor* and its individual issues as a nuisance. The safety and good order of the community were threatened by the *Expositor:* (1) because the reaction of an outraged citizenry threatened the annihilation of the newspaper and perhaps the injury of its publishers by mob action in the city; (2) because its continuance might incite mob action by anti-Mormons in the surrounding areas against the city and its inhabitants; and (3) because of their scurrilous, defamatory,

---

95. Wood, Nuisances §2 at 941–70 (3d ed. 1983).

96. 2 Blackstone, *Commentaries,* 4–5 & n.6 (Am. ed. from 18th Eng. ed. 1832).

97. *History of the Church,* 6:445, 538, 581; see note 148 supra.

98. See Goddard v. President of Jacksonville, 15 Ill. 589, 594 (1854); 2 Russell, *Crimes 1731* (8th ed. 1923).

and perhaps obscene character, the individual newspapers were offensive to public morals. In view of the law discussed previously, particularly the statement in Blackstone, the combination of these three considerations seems to have been sufficient to give the Nauvoo City Council considerable basis in the law of their day for their action in characterizing *the published issues* of the *Nauvoo Expositor* as a nuisance and in summarily abating them by destruction.

The characterization of the printing press as a nuisance, and its subsequent destruction, is another matter. The common law authorities on nuisance abatement generally, and especially those on summary abatement, were emphatic in declaring that abatement must be limited by the necessities of the case, and that no wanton or unnecessary destruction of property could be permitted. A party guilty of excess was liable in damages for trespass to the party injured. This principle was illustrated by an Illinois court shortly after the *Expositor* affair.

The Illinois Supreme Court rendered an opinion[99] in an action for damages for trespass against a citizen who had broken into a saloon, smashed glasses, boxes, and beer kegs, and had torn down the building on the pretext of abating a public nuisance. The court affirmed the saloon keeper's right to recover damages from the intruder. Even if the house were a public nuisance, the court said, "neither the common law nor the statute has authorized individuals or communities to tear down and destroy the buildings in which such unlawful business is pursued, nor does either permit the courts, on conviction, to have such buildings destroyed or abated."[100]

The principle applied in this case was that set forth in Blackstone's discussion of nuisances, which the council studied and used as authority for its abatement ordinance.[101] This case makes clear that there was no legal justification in 1844 for the destruction of the *Expositor* printing press and type as a nuisance. Its libelous, provocative, and perhaps obscene output may well have been a public and a private nuisance, but the evil article was not the press itself but the way in which it was being used. Consequently, those who caused or accomplished its destruction were liable for money damages in an action of trespass.

Constitutional Guarantee of Free Press. It was not the destruction of private property without compensation that caused Joseph Smith and his associates to be condemned for the *Expositor* affair. The principal complaint

---

99. Earp v. Lee, 71 Ill. 193 (1873).
100. Earp v. Lee, 71 Ill. 193 (1873).
101. 2 Blackstone, *Commentaries*, 4–5 & n.6 (Am. ed. from 18th Eng. ed. 1832).

would have been the same if the council had silenced the paper by a court order, by jailing the editor, or by padlocking the premises. The most important legal aspect of the *Expositor* suppression—the one that served to enrage public opinion, disenchant sympathetic historians, and offend the sensibilities of modern students—is the charge that the action violated the freedom of the press.

The major modern bulwark of the free press, the first amendment to the United States Constitution, had no application to the suppression of the *Nauvoo Expositor*. By its terms, the First Amendment only restricts the action of the federal government, and it was not until long after the Fourteenth Amendment was adopted in 1868 that the free-press guarantees became applicable to the agencies of state authority.[102] Therefore, the only constitutional free-press guarantees relevant to the *Expositor* suppression are those that were embodied in the Illinois Constitution.

The pertinent provision of the Illinois Constitution of 1818, then in effect, was section 22 of the Declaration of Rights:

> The printing presses shall be free to every person, who undertakes to examine the proceedings of the General Assembly or of any branch of government; and no law shall ever be made to restrain the right thereof. The free communication of thoughts and opinions is one of the invaluable rights of man, and every citizen may freely speak, write, and print on any subject, being responsible for the abuse of that liberty.[103]

The constitutional status of the abatement of the *Expositor* as a nuisance depends on the meaning to be drawn from these words in 1844. Since the Illinois Supreme Court had given no opinion on the meaning of the above provision by 1844, it is necessary to examine the history of the free-press guarantees and the meaning ascribed to comparable language in neighboring states.[104]

Although the Illinois free-press provision seems to have been copied from the guarantees previously adopted by Kentucky, Ohio, and Indiana,[105] this particular phraseology was apparently first used in the Pennsylvania

---

102. *E.g., Near v. Minnesota ex rel.* Olson, 283 U.S. 697, 707 (1931).

103. Ill. Const. art VIII, §22 (1818), reprinted in Ill. Rev. Stat. at 46 (1833).

104. See generally Duniway, "The Development of Freedom of the Press in Massachusetts," *Harvard Historical Studies* no. 12 (1906): 141; Schofield, *Essays on Constitutional Law and Equity,* 510–71 (1921); Kelly, "Criminal Libel and Free Speech," *Kansas Law Review* 6 (1958): 295.

105. Levy, *Preface* to *Legacy of Suppression* at vii (1960).

Constitution of 1790.[106] Because there seems to have been no early interpretive litigation in any of the first three states, the meaning that the Pennsylvania courts read into this provision is, therefore, of the greatest significance.

The first judicial opinion on the meaning of the general phrases later embodied in the Illinois Constitution came in a 1788 Pennsylvania case, which held that they simply meant that every citizen had a right to investigate the conduct of public officials "and they effectually preclude any attempt to fetter the press by the institution of a *licenser*."[107] This view that the great general guarantees of a free press were simply a precaution against reinstitution of the historic prior restraints or censorships on publication was reiterated by James Wilson, a renowned lawyer and Justice of the United States Supreme Court, who drafted the 1790 Pennsylvania Constitution.

> What is meant by the liberty of the press is that there should be no antecedent restraint upon it; but that every author is responsible when he attacks the security or welfare of the government, or the safety, character and property of the individual.[108]

The Illinois Constitution also said that the editor should be "responsible for the abuse of that liberty." The usual form of responsibility was a civil action for damages or a state prosecution for criminal libel, particularly seditious libel, which consisted broadly of criticism of the form, officers, or acts of government. Such prosecutions were relatively common, especially at the turn of the nineteenth century.[109] The temper of the times is revealed by an 1805 Pennsylvania case. The defendant was indicted for seditious libel for statements in a weekly paper that were alleged to have been intended to bring the independence of the United States and the constitution of Pennsylvania into hatred and contempt, to excite popular discontent against the government, and to scandalize the characters of revolutionary patriots and statesmen. When the defendant urged the constitutional freedom of the press in defense, the Pennsylvania court gave this exposition of the meaning of the constitutional provision that was the prototype of the Illinois free-press guarantee:

> There shall be no licenses of the press. Publish as you please in the first instance without control; but you are answerable both to the community and the individual, if you proceed to unwarrantable lengths. No alteration is hereby made in the law as to

---

106. Anthony, *The Constitutional History of Illinois* 39 (1891).
107. Respublica v. Oswald, 1 Dall. 319, 325 (Pa. 1788).
108. Levy, *Legacy of Suppression,* 201–2 (1960). (Emphasis omitted.)
109. Levy, *Legacy of Suppression,* 176–309 (1960).

private men, affected by injurious publications, unless the discussion be *proper for public information*. But "If one uses the weapon of truth wantonly, for disturbing the peace of families, he is guilty of a libel."[110]

The cases decided before 1844 do not provide a definitive answer to the question whether the Illinois free-press guarantee would have permitted an agency of the state to use its nuisance-abatement powers to suppress a newspaper which was publishing material that offended the public's sense of decency or threatened the public peace or welfare. They do hold that the only purpose of the general free-press language was to prevent formal prior restraints upon publication, such as licensing and censorship.[111] They also show great judicial sympathy for stern repressive measures in the enforcement of the criminal libel and civil damage laws against newspaper editors who abused their privileges. Although the succeeding century was relatively free from litigation interpreting the free-press guarantees, the available evidence demonstrates that the nineteenth-century interpretation of constitutional provisions like that of Illinois laid far more emphasis on the "responsibility" of the press than on its "freedom."

The Illinois free-press guarantees would not have been an obstacle if the Nauvoo authorities had brought criminal prosecutions against the *Expositor* publishers for an abuse of the liberty of the press. A prosecution for criminal libel for the attacks on the city officials or a prosecution for unlawful assembly for the paper's efforts to incite violence would both have been feasible under Illinois laws then in effect.[112] The arrest and jailing of the editor and publishers might have stilled the *Expositor*. The same effect might also have been produced by suing these parties for damages for libel, obtaining judgment, and then satisfying the judgment by levying upon and selling the press. A third alternative, a suit for an injunction against the publication of the newspaper, was not feasible as a practical matter.

Two factors distinguish these alternatives from the method (abatement by destruction) used by the council. First, it can be argued that the destruction of the press was a prior restraint with respect to later issues of the *Expositor*, and, therefore, illegal under the predominant purpose of the free-press provision. Although admittedly forceful, this argument falls short of being

---

110. Respublica v. Dennie, 4 Yeates 267, 269–70 *(Pa.* 1805). (Emphasis added.)

111. Beman, *Censorship of Speech and the Press*, 208–9 (1930); 2 Cooley, *Constitutional Limitations*, 883 (8th ed. Carrington 1927); Vance, "Freedom of Speech and of the Press," *Minnesota Law Review* 2 (1918): 239, 248.

112. Ill. Rev. Stat. §120, at 172 (1833); Ill. Rev. Stat. §115, at 196 (1833).

conclusive, for the free-press provision can be read to prohibit only licensing measures that allow the state to prevent *initial* publication of the writer's efforts. The constitutional provision clearly did not prevent criminal punishment, or civil attachment, even though either of these remedies could easily suppress subsequent writings. In numerous other instances, legislative bodies have imposed, and courts have approved, restraints prior to publication.[113] With the exception of avowed licensing measures, the prohibition against prior restraints, it seems, was relative and not absolute, and it is by no means obvious that the "prior restraint" rationale forbade what was done at Nauvoo.

Second, in a criminal prosecution or in a civil action for damages or an injunction, there is an interposition of judicial power between the party who desires to stop the newspaper and the application of the force that brings about that result. There was no such use of judicial power at Nauvoo. This is an important distinction to a people who believe in a rule of law. Nevertheless, there are circumstances in which the use of private property can be curtailed, forbidden, or, where necessary, even destroyed by the government or by private individuals without invoking judicial power. The summary abatement of nuisances, the theory on which the council proceeded, is one such example.

In sum, the action of the Nauvoo City Council in suppressing an opposition newspaper may have been the earliest example of official action of this type (in a day when mobs were not infrequently employed for the same purpose), but subsequent history shows that such official acts of suppression were not unique. The most striking example, because of its similarity to the events in Nauvoo, occurred in September 1927 when a weekly newspaper, the *Saturday Press*, was established in Minneapolis by Howard A. Guilford and J. M. Near. Its avowed mission was to furnish an exposé "of conditions AS THEY ARE in this city."[114] The various issues of the newspaper charged in brutally frank language that the *Twin City Reporter* and various city officials were in league with or part of the gangsters who controlled gambling, bootlegging, and racketeering in Minneapolis and linked them to various instances of blackmail, murder, and assault. The police chief was attacked for graft, neglect of duty, and companionship with gangsters; the county attorney was accused of failure to take corrective measures against known centers of vice; the mayor was castigated for inefficiency and dereliction of duty.[115]

---

113. See Note, *Previous Restraints Upon Freedom of Speech*, 31 Colum. L. Rev. 1148, 1151–55 (1931).

114. Record, p. 15, Near v. Minnesota *ex rel.* Olson, 283 U.S. 697 (1931) [hereinafter cited as Record].

115. Record, pp. 57–58, 96.

Minnesota at this time had a unique statute providing that any person who was engaging in publishing or circulating a malicious, scandalous, and defamatory newspaper was guilty of a nuisance and could be enjoined.[116] On November 21, two days after the ninth issue of the *Saturday Press,* the county attorney filed a complaint under the above statute alleging that the *Saturday Press* was largely devoted to malicious, scandalous, and defamatory articles and asking for an injunction to abate the nuisance.[117] The trial judge promptly issued an order restraining Guilford and Near from any further circulation of existing issues and from producing or publishing any further issues of the *Saturday Press.*[118] Two weeks later, the judge issued an opinion upholding the constitutionality of the Minnesota legislation and denying defendants' motion to dismiss the action.[119] Later, after a consideration of the evidence, the judge reaffirmed this conclusion and entered an order that the nuisance be abated and that defendants Guilford and Near be permanently enjoined from further publication or sale of the *Saturday Press* or any other malicious, scandalous, or defamatory newspaper.[120]

Twice this case was appealed to the Minnesota Supreme Court, and twice that court—without dissenting voice—affirmed the trial judge, holding that the suppressive action did not offend the constitutional guarantee of a free press.[121] The court rested on three main findings.

First, the Minnesota Supreme Court concluded that a newspaper, which exhibited "a continued and habitual indulgence in malice, scandal, and defamation," could validly be characterized as a nuisance within the meaning of the statute "since it annoys, injures, and endangers the comfort and repose of a considerable number of persons."[122] Second, the court ruled that, in declaring such a business to be a public nuisance, the statute was a legitimate exercise of the police power of the state:

> The distribution of scandalous matter is detrimental to public morals and to the general welfare. It tends to disturb the peace of the community. Being defamatory and malicious, it tends to provoke assaults and the commission of crime.[123]

---

116. Minn. Laws 1925, ch. 285, §1, at 358.
117. Record, pp. 4, 7.
118. Record, p. 1.
119. Record, p. 336.
120. Record, p. 360.
121. Record, p. 360.
122. State v. Guilford, 174 Minn. 457, 459 (1928).
123. State v. Guilford, 174 Minn. 457, 461–62 (1928).

Finally, the court ruled that the action taken did not offend the liberty of the press guaranteed by the Minnesota Constitution (a provision similar to Illinois'),[124] which simply "meant the abolition of censorship and that governmental permission or license was not to be required."[125] The court's opinion on what the freedom of the press did mean is worth reproducing at length.

> It was never the intention of the Constitution to afford protection to a publication devoted to scandal and defamation. He who uses the press is responsible for its abuse.... It is the liberty of the press that is guaranteed—not the licentiousness. The press can be free and men can freely speak and write without indulging in malice, scandal, and defamation; and the great privilege of such liberty was never intended as a refuge for the defamer and the scandalmonger.... A business that depends largely for its success upon malice, scandal, and defamation can be of no real service to society.
>
> It is not a violation of the liberty of the press or of the freedom of speech for the Legislature to provide a remedy for their abuse.... Indeed, the police power of the state includes the right to destroy or abate a public nuisance. Property so destroyed is not taken for public use, and therefore there is no obligation to make compensation for such taking. 6 R.C.L. 480, §478. The rights of private property are subservient to the public right to be free from nuisances which may be abated without compensation. 12 C. J. 1279, §1085. The statute involved does not violate the due process of law guarantee.[126]

Although the reaction of the nation's press to this decision was predictably intense, the ruling also had strong support, including the immediate endorsement of the Minnesota Legislature, which rejected an attempt to repeal the law by an 86 to 30 margin.[127]

Ultimately, the United States Supreme Court reversed this Minnesota judgment by a bare 5 to 4 majority in *Near v. Minnesota*,[128] the first case where the United States Supreme Court struck down the action of a state

---

124. Minn. Const. art. 1, §3.
125. 174 Minn. at 462, 219 N.W. at 772.
126. 174 Minn. at 462, 463–65.
127. Beman, *Censorship of Speech and the Press supra* note 180, at 321.
128. 283 U.S. 697 (1931).

for violating the freedom of the press. Interestingly, the Supreme Court did not find that the state practice constituted a prior restraint in the traditional sense. Rather, the practice was stricken in reliance upon an expanded concept of the free-press guarantees (made applicable to the states by the Fourteenth Amendment) as also forbidding other restraints on publication which, like the Minnesota statute, comprised "the essence of censorship."[129] Four dissenting justices, who adhered to the traditional definition, would have sustained the suppression.

The Minnesota opinion in the *Near* case stands at a turning point in the law of free speech. It was preceded and decisively influenced by the suppressionist philosophy that guided the action of numerous state authorities in the nineteenth century and even extended its effects into the twentieth century. It was followed by the enlightened liberalism of our own day, when the freedom of the press is so jealously guarded that we are able to forget that not many years have elapsed since lawyers and judges united in attempts to suppress and hold responsible the publications whose scandalous and provocative character were thought to have caused that freedom to be forfeited through abuse.

The facts that led to the suppression of the *Saturday Press* and the *Nauvoo Expositor* are strikingly similar, and the legal theories upon which each was suppressed are practically identical. The method of abatement—by destruction or by injunction—was different, but the end results and the consequences of the action so far as a free press was concerned were equivalent. The reasoning of the Minnesota opinion was a justification not only of what was done in Minneapolis, but also of what was done over eighty years earlier in Nauvoo. If the *Saturday Press,* like the *Nauvoo Expositor,* had been printed in 1844 (when there was no Fourteenth Amendment), this state court judgment abating a newspaper as a nuisance would have remained unchallenged.

The crucial issue to the legality of the *Expositor's* suppression under the Illinois Constitution was whether the rule that the editor shall be "responsible for the abuse of that liberty" is limited to the prospect of civil damages and criminal penalties or whether it also includes the risk that the publication will be suppressed as a nuisance.

There was no direct precedent in 1844 to support the use of nuisance-abatement powers to suppress a newspaper like the *Expositor,* but there was no direct authority against such use either. Subsequent history shows that other government officials also undertook to exercise suppressionist powers beyond the conventional damage or criminal action, and some even found

129. 283 U.S. 697 (1931).

high judicial approval for the use of the nuisance device. Once the Nauvoo City Council had concluded that its nuisance-abatement powers extended to the abatement of newspapers publishing scandalous or provocative material, it would be unrealistic to have expected them to observe limitations that were not articulated clearly in any constitution, statute, or court decision of their day. To charge them with a willful violation of the Illinois free-press guarantees, one must overlook the suppressionist sentiments of the age in which they lived and attribute to them a higher devotion to the ideals of a free press than was exhibited from 1928 through 1931 by eight justices of the Minnesota and United States Supreme Courts.

Conclusion

A historian friendly to the people of Nauvoo has called the suppression of the *Nauvoo Expositor* "the grand Mormon mistake."[130] That its consequences were disastrous to the Mormon leaders and that alternative means might better have been employed cannot be doubted. Nevertheless, the common assumption of historians that the action taken by the city council to suppress the paper as a nuisance was entirely illegal is not well founded. Aside from damages for unnecessary destruction of the press, for which the Nauvoo authorities were unquestionably liable, the remaining actions of the council, including its interpretation of the constitutional guarantee of a free press, can be supported by reference to the law of their day.

This article was originally published as "The Suppression of the Nauvoo Expositor," Utah Law Review 9 (1965): 862–903.

---

130. Durham, "A Political Interpretation of Mormon History," *Pacific Historical Review* 13 (1944): 136, 140.

Legal Chronology of Joseph Smith

The first occurrence of each case is marked in ***bold italics.***

1805

Joseph Smith Jr. was born to Lucy Mack Smith and Joseph Smith Sr. • Dec. 23, 1805. Sharon, VT.

1814

Jesse Smith files his protest objecting to changes in the orgnization of his local congregation. • Nov. 18, 1814, Tunbridge, VT. [**Discussed in ch. 4**]

1818

Joseph Smith Sr. v. Hurlbut: Joseph Smith Sr. and Alvin Smith executed a promissory note to pay Jeremiah Hurlbut $65.00 in grain for the purchase of two horses. • Mar. 27, 1818. Palmyra, NY. [**Discussed in ch. 3**]

Joseph Smith Sr. v. Hurlbut: Joseph Smith Sr. created a list of damages sustained by "fraud or ducet" when he and Alvin Smith had purchased two deficient horses from Jeremiah Hurlbut. • May–July 1818. Palmyra, NY.

Joseph Smith Sr. v. Hurlbut: Joseph Smith Sr. and Alvin Smith transferred $53.00 in "crops on the ground" to Hurlbut. • Aug. 10, 1818. Palmyra, NY.

1819

Joseph Smith Sr. v. Hurlbut: Joseph Smith Sr. and Alvin Smith filed suit against Hurlbut in the Justice Court seeking damages for deficient horses they had bought from Hurlbut. • Jan. 12, 1819. Palmyra, NY.

Joseph Smith Sr. v. Hurlbut: Constable D. Uandee served the summons to Jeremiah Hurlbut. • Jan. 13, 1819. Palmyra, NY.

Joseph Smith Sr. v. Hurlbut: JS appeared as a credible witness before Justice of the Peace Abraham Spear. The jury found for the Smiths and awarded them damages of $40.78. • Feb. 6, 1819. Palmyra, NY.

Joseph Smith Sr. v. Hurlbut: An arrest warrant was issued to Sheriff P. P. Bates, commanding him to take Joseph Smith Sr. and Alvin Smith before the

Court of Common Pleas in Canandaigua on "the third Tuesday of May next" [May 18, 1819] to answer Hurlbut in a plea of trespass. • Feb. 7, 1819. Palmyra, NY.

Joseph Smith Sr. v. Hurlbut: Jeremiah Hurlbut appealed the decision against him to the Ontario County Court of Common Pleas. • Feb. 8, 1819. Palmyra, NY.

Joseph Smith Sr. v. Hurlbut: Effectively setting the jury verdict aside, the Court of Common Pleas ordered the sheriff to collect evidence about the amount of damages sustained. • May 18, 1819. Canandaigua, NY.

1820–25

JS received his First Vision. • Spring 1820. Manchester, NY.

The angel Moroni visited JS three times in the night in the Smith family log home, telling JS about the gold plates (the Book of Mormon) and the Lord's divine mission for him. • Sept. 21–22, 1823. Manchester, NY.

JS's brother Alvin died at age 25. He had been ill with "bilious colic" and was given a dose of calomel, which may have killed him. • About Nov. 19, 1823. Palmyra, NY.

Stoddard v. Smith Sr.: Stoddard filed suit against Joseph Smith Sr. for unpaid carpentry work on the frame home. • Feb. 18, 1824. Manchester, NY.

The Joseph Smith Sr. family home and 99.5-acre farm were sold to Lemuel Durfee, who kept the Smiths as tenants. • Dec. 20, 1825. Manchester, NY.

1826–28

People v. Smith: On a complaint brought by Peter Bridgeman, JS was charged with being a disorderly person and brought before Justice of the Peace Albert Neely. JS was acquitted. • Mar. 20, 1826. South Bainbridge, NY. [**Discussed in ch. 4**]

Stoddard v. Smith Sr.: Joseph Smith Sr. had confessed judgment to Stoddard for $66.59. The judgment was satisfied on this day. • Apr. 19, 1826. Manchester, NY.

Smith v. Worden: JS and Hyrum Smith hired the firm of Howell & Hubble, presumably as legal counsel, in an action against Sylvester Worden. The balance the Smiths owed to Howell & Hubble is recorded as $8.62 with interest beginning on that date. • June 20, 1826. Ontario County, NY.

JS was married to Emma Hale by Justice of the Peace Zachariah Tarble. • Jan. 18, 1827. South Bainbridge, NY.

JS received the gold plates from the angel Moroni on the hill where they were buried. • Sept. 22, 1827. Manchester, NY.

JS completed the translation of the book of Lehi. Martin Harris took the 116 manuscript pages to Palmyra, New York, to show selected members of his family as bound by covenant. • June 14, 1828. Harmony, PA.

JS arrived at his father's farm and learned from Martin Harris that the 116 manuscript pages of the book of Lehi had been lost. • About July 1, 1828. Manchester, NY.

Smith v. Worden: In the Supreme Court of Ontario County, a writ of collection was returned by Deputy George Smith of Wayne County, New York. The sheriff was given a writ of execution on Sylvester

Worden's property. No more information has been found. • Nov. 25, 1828. Ontario County, NY.

1829

JS incurred a $200 debt by purchasing ("articling") a small home and land from his father-in-law, Isaac Hale. • Apr. 6, 1829. Harmony, PA.

JS began dictating the translation of the Book of Mormon to Oliver Cowdery. • Apr. 7, 1829. Harmony, PA.

Martin Harris's wife, Lucy Harris, at least threatened to sue JS in an attempt to prove that he had never had the gold plates and intended to defraud credulous people. No documents from this action have survived. • May/June 1829. Palmyra, NY.

Richard R. Lansing, clerk for the Northern District Court of New York, entered JS's copyright application for the Book of Mormon. • June 11, 1829. Utica, NY. [Discussed in ch. 5]

JS was present as the Three Witnesses were shown the plates by the angel Moroni. • About June 20, 1829. Fayette, NY.

JS showed the Eight Witnesses the gold plates. • About June 24, 1829. Palmyra, NY.

Egbert B. Grandin published the title page of the Book of Mormon as a "curiosity" in the Wayne Sentinel. • June 26, 1829. Palmyra, NY.

JS received Doctrine and Covenants 19, a revelation to Martin Harris concerning repentance and the Atonement of Jesus Christ. Martin was commanded to pay the debt that he had contracted with the printer for the publication of the Book of Mormon. • Summer 1829. Palmyra, NY.

State v. Smith: A legal action was brought by the state of Pennsylvania against JS and Oliver Cowdery. • Summer 1829. Harmony, PA.

Martin Harris mortgaged his farm in order to assure payment to Egbert B. Grandin of $3,000 to print 5,000 copies of the Book of Mormon. • Aug. 25, 1829. Fayette, NY.

1830

Joseph Smith v. Cole: Abner Cole published selections from the Book of Mormon in his newspaper, *The Reflector,* that he took without permission from the E. B. Grandin & Co. press where both his newspaper and the Book of Mormon were being printed. The matter was arbitrated, and Cole ceased publishing any such selections. • Jan. 1830. Palmyra, NY. [Discussed in ch. 5]

JS and Martin Harris enter into an agreement regarding proceeds from the sale of the Book of Mormon. • Jan. 16, 1830. Palmyra, NY.

A revelation was given authorizing agents to go to Canada to try to publish the Book of Mormon there, which would protect its copyright "upon all the face of the earth" under British law. • Jan.–Feb. 1830. Manchester, NY.

JS officially organized the Church of Christ in Peter Whitmer Sr.'s home. • Apr. 6, 1830. Fayette, NY. [Discussed in ch. 6]

Doctrine and Covenants 20, the Articles and Covenants of the Church, was finalized. • Apr. 10, 1830. Fayette, NY.

People v. Smith: JS was tried and discharged by Justice of the Peace Joel Noble on charges of being a disorderly person for claiming that he could discover lost goods. • About June 30, 1830. South Bainbridge, Chenango County, NY.

People v. Smith: JS was re-arrested and taken to Broome County to be tried again on the charge of being a disorderly person before Justice of the Peace Joseph Chamberlin. JS was acquitted again. • About July 1, 1830. Broome County, NY.

Noble v. Joseph Smith: JS executed a promissory note to pay George H. Noble $190.95 to enable JS on April 6, 1829, to purchase 13 acres from Isaac Hale and the home where he and Emma had been living and where he had translated much of the Book of Mormon. • Aug. 25, 1830. Harmony, PA.

Noble v. Smith: An amicable judgment was entered in favor of George H. Noble to secure his creditor rights for the $190.95 owed to him by JS. Jesse Lane was Justice of the Peace as well as notary on the deed, filed with Court of Common Pleas in Montrose, Pennsylvania. It was satisfied in full June 3, 1831. • Aug. 26, 1830. Susquehanna County, PA.

Noble v. Smith: A transcript from the papers of Justice of the Peace Lane was filed and entered in the Susquehanna Court of Common Pleas. • Aug. 31, 1830. Susquehanna County, PA.

JS received Doctrine and Covenants 28, a revelation to Oliver Cowdery, in response to Hiram Page's professed revelations, directing that no one was to receive revelation for the Church except the Prophet. • About Sept. 20, 1830. Fayette, NY.

1831

During the third conference of the Church, which was held at the Peter Whitmer Sr. home, JS received Doctrine and Covenants 38, a revelation calling the Saints to gather in Ohio. • Jan. 2, 1831. Fayette, NY.

A revelation titled "The Law" is given to JS in two parts: verses 1–72 on Feb. 9 and verses 73–93 on this date. • Feb. 23, 1831. Kirtland, OH.

Copley v. Smith: Church members were forced to leave Leman Copley's farm and "pay sixty dollars damage for fitting up his houses and planting his ground." • June 1831. Thompson, OH.

Noble v. Smith: Plaintiff's acknowledgement that judgment had been satisfied was filed with the court • June 4, 1831. Susquehanna County, PA.

JS received Doctrine and Covenants 57, a revelation concerning the building up of Zion in Independence, Missouri. • July 20, 1831. Independence, MO.

JS received Doctrine and Covenants 58, a revelation regarding obeying the laws of the land and the commandments of God. • Aug. 1, 1831. Jackson County, MO.

JS received Doctrine and Covenants 64, a revelation containing the Lord's law of forgiveness and the promise "he that is tithed shall not be burned." • Sept. 11, 1831. Kirtland, OH.

1832

A mob violently tarred and feathered JS and Sidney Rigdon at the John Johnson home. No legal action was brought by JS. • Mar. 24, 1832. Hiram, OH.

Johnson v. Williams: John Johnson brought an action for trespass against those who tarred and feathered JS and Sidney Rigdon. It was tried before Justice of the Peace Aaron Williams and appealed to Court of Common Pleas. The judgment was affirmed. • After Mar. 24, 1832. Ravenna, OH.

JS preached at a Sabbath meeting the day after he had been tarred and feathered. He also baptized three people that afternoon. • Mar. 25, 1832. Hiram, OH.

Joseph Murdock Smith, adopted son of JS and Emma Smith, died as a result of exposure during the violence. • Mar. 29, 1832. Hiram, OH.

1833

JS received Doctrine and Covenants 89, a revelation containing the dietary code known as the Word of Wisdom. • Feb. 27, 1833. Kirtland, OH.

JS attended a council to hear the ecclesiastical appeal of Doctor Philastus Hurlbut ("Doctor" was his first given name). His excommunication from the Church was upheld two days later. • June 21, 1833. Kirtland, OH.

Doctor Philastus Hurlbut returned to Kirtland from Palmyra and vicinity, seeking information to prove that the Book of Mormon was a work of fiction and that JS was not an honest man. He began to lecture on his findings and threatened the life of JS. • Dec. 1833. Kirtland, OH.

State of Ohio v. Hurlbut: JS filed a complaint against Hurlbut alleging that Hurlbut had threatened to kill him. • Dec. 21, 1833. Kirtland, OH. [**Discussed in ch. 7, 10**]

State of Ohio v. Hurlbut: An arrest warrant was issued for Hurlbut, returnable before Painesville Justice of the Peace William Holbrook. • Dec. 27, 1833. Kirtland, OH.

1834

State of Ohio v. Hurlbut: The hearing was postponed until Jan. 13, 1834. Hurlbut was transferred from Constable Stephen Sherman's custody to the custody of Painesville Constable Abraham Ritch. • Jan. 6, 1834. Kirtland, OH.

State of Ohio v. Hurlbut: JS and his brethren prayed for success in the upcoming hearing. • Jan. 11, 1834. Kirtland, OH.

State of Ohio v. Hurlbut: A preliminary hearing was held before Justice of the Peace William Holbrook. Sixteen witnesses gave testimony concerning the alleged threat. JS testified on at least two of the three days. Hurlbut was represented by James A. Briggs, and JS by Benjamin Bissell. The court ordered Hurlbut to post a recognizance bond of $200 to keep the peace and to appear before the Geauga County Court of Common Pleas during its Mar. 31, 1834 term. • Jan. 13–15, 1834. Painesville, OH.

State of Ohio v. Hurlbut: JS thanked the Lord for deliverance from Doctor Philastus Hurlbut and petitioned him for success in the upcoming trial. • Jan. 28, 1834. Kirtland, OH.

State of Ohio v. Hurlbut: JS appeared at the Geauga County Court of Common Pleas in Chardon, Ohio. As several cases were to be heard that day, *State v. Hurlbut* did not come up for several days. • Mar. 31, 1834. Kirtland, OH.

State of Ohio v. Hurlbut: While preparing subpoenas for witnesses at Ezekiel Rider's home, JS prophesied that the Lord would not allow Hurlbut to prevail in court against him. • Apr. 1, 1834. Chardon, OH.

State of Ohio v. Hurlbut: The trial began. • Apr. 2–3, 1834. Chardon, OH.

Johnson v. Remonstrance: JS testified before the Geauga County Court of Common Pleas on John Johnson's application to obtain a tavern license. The license was granted at a fixed rate of $6 per year. • Apr. 5, 1834. Chardon, OH.

State of Ohio v. Hurlbut: The trial continued. Seventeen prosecution witnesses testified. Four witnesses testified for the defense. Judge Matthew Birchard ruled that JS had sufficient cause to file the complaint and Hurlbut was required to post $200 recognizance, to pay $112.59 in court costs, and to keep the peace for six months. Hurlbut never fulfilled the obligation. • Apr. 7–9, 1834. Chardon, OH.

State of Ohio v. Hurlbut: Sheriff Jabez Tracy attempted to apprehend Hurlbut to require him to satisfy the judgment, but Hurlbut was not found. • Apr. 16, 1834. Chardon, OH.

While on the Zion's Camp march, JS received word that Daniel Dunklin, governor of Missouri, would not fulfill the expectation to reinstate the Saints to their lands in Jackson County, Missouri. • June 15, 1834. Chariton River, MO.

Elder Sylvester Smith had accused JS of criminal conduct during the journey to and from Missouri during the Zion's Camp march but confessed that his accusation was false and asked JS for forgiveness. • Aug. 11, 1834. Kirtland, OH.

JS wrote instructions to the high council of the Church in Missouri and urged them to sign a petition to Governor Daniel Dunklin of Missouri requesting his protection. • Aug. 16, 1834. Kirtland, OH.

The Kirtland High Council read and adopted resolutions concerning JS's conduct toward Sylvester Smith, saying that

JS was "worthy of [their] esteem and fellowship." • Aug. 23, 1834. Kirtland, OH.

During a special council assembled for the ecclesiastical trial of Sylvester Smith, JS was cleared of Sylvester Smith's false accusations arising out of the Zion's Camp march. • Aug. 28, 1834. Kirtland, OH.

Lake v. Smith: A summons, with Dennis Lake as plaintiff, was served on JS by Constable J. Ames. Lake alleged that JS had promised him a lot of land in Missouri if he would march with Zion's Camp, which Lake had done. • Nov. 24, 1834. Geauga County, OH. [**Discussed in ch. 10**]

Lake v. Smith: The parties and their attorneys attended a Justice of the Peace court before Justice of the Peace J. C. Dowen. Proofs and allegations were heard, and court was adjourned until Dec. 4, 1834. • Nov. 28, 1834. Geauga County, OH.

State of Ohio v. Hurlbut: A writ of collection was issued against Hurlbut and delivered to Sheriff Jabez Tracy per William Graham. • Dec. 2, 1834. Geauga County, OH.

Lake v. Smith: Judgment was rendered in favor of plaintiff Dennis Lake for $63.67 in addition to $8.04 for the costs of the suit. JS appealed the case to the Geauga Court of Common Pleas. • Dec. 4, 1834. Geauga County, OH.

Lake v. Smith: A certified transcript of the Justice of the Peace court case judgment was filed at the Geauga Court of Common Pleas. Ebenezer Jennings signed a bail bond before Justice of the Peace J. C. Dowen for the appellant (defendant), JS, in the amount of $150. • Dec. 10, 1834. Geauga County, OH.

State of Ohio v. Hurlbut: Orders were entered to seize Hurlbut's property for resale to satisfy the judgment of *State v. Hurlbut*. No property was found. • Dec. 12, 1834. Kirtland, OH.

1835

State of Ohio v. Hurlbut: A writ of execution was issued and delivered to Sheriff Jabez Tracy. It was returned to the court on Mar. 29, 1836, with "Nothing made." • Feb. 1835. Geauga County, OH.

State of Ohio v. Hurlbut: The writ of collection that was delivered per William Graham was returned. No property had been found. • Mar. 31, 1835. Geauga County, OH.

State of Ohio v. Smith: A warrant was issued against JS on the oath of Granden [Grandison] Newel leveling charges of assault and battery of Smith's brother-in-law Calvin W. Stoddard. The warrant was returned the same day as Constable Samuel Brown arrested JS, who was held for bail until the next day. • Apr. 21, 1835. Geauga County, OH. **[Discussed in ch. 10]**

State of Ohio v. Smith: The parties appeared by their attorneys in Justice of the Peace Court before Justice of the Peace Lewis Miller. The charge was sustained; JS was ordered to post bail in bonds of $200 and to appear at Court of Common Pleas. • Apr. 22, 1835. Geauga County, OH.

State of Ohio v. Smith: A transcript of the proceedings of the case was given to lawyer Reuben Hitchcock, the prosecuting attorney for this case in the Court of Common Pleas. • Apr. 25, 1835. Geauga County, OH.

Lake v. Smith: Lake's declaration was filed (action of assumsit) stating that JS was indebted to Lake for $800 as of Nov. 21, 1834, consisting of $200 for labor performed, $200 for the use of property, and two $200 loans made to JS. JS responded on the same day that no such promise was given. • May 7, 1835. Geauga County, OH.

Lake v. Smith: The parties appeared in court. JS entered a plea of non assumpsit. Jurors were sworn. Before the jury deliberated the facts of the case, the court ruled that Lake had failed to provide evidence in support of his claim—requiring the court to order a nonsuit of the case. The court ordered Lake to pay JS $25.64 for his costs of the suit and also to pay $10.86 to the court for its costs. • June 16, 1835. Geauga County, OH.

State of Ohio v. Smith: JS was brought before the Court of Common Pleas on a bill of indictment for assault and battery against Calvin W. Stoddard. The court found Smith not guilty. • June 16, 1835. Chardon, OH.

Lake v. Smith: A writ of collection (*fieri facias*) was issued and forwarded to Sheriff Jabez Tracy by Peter Thompson. It was returned on Oct. 20, 1835, "wholly unsatisfied." • June 29, 1835. Chardon, OH.

The assembled body of the Church voted unanimously to accept the first edition of the D&C containing an appendix with the declaration of belief now contained in D&C 134 regarding governments and laws in general and "On Marriage." • Aug. 17, 1835. Kirtland, OH.

JS met with the high council and, through the voice of the Spirit, decided to petition Missouri Governor Daniel Dunklin to restore lands to the Saints who had been driven off. • Sept. 24, 1835. Kirtland, OH.

JS met with the high council and acted in defense of and pleaded for mercy for those who had been accused of offenses against the Church. • Sept. 29, 1835. Kirtland, OH.

Lake v. Smith: Sheriff Jabez Tracy reported to the court that he was unable to recover any costs from Lake. • Oct. 20, 1835. Geauga County, OH.

JS solemnized the marriage of Newel Knight and Lydia Goldthwaite Bailey • Nov. 24, 1835. Geauga County, OH. [**Discussed in ch. 8**]

1836

JS filed certificates of marriage in the Geauga County probate court. • Feb. 22, 1836. Chardon, OH.

JS prepared elders' licenses to send to Medina County in order for them to obtain licenses to perform marriages, since the court in Geauga County had refused. • Mar. 21, 1836. Kirtland, OH.

JS dedicated the Kirtland Temple. • Mar. 27, 1836. Kirtland, OH.

State of Ohio v. Hurlbut: Leman Copley confessed to JS that he had testified falsely against JS in this case. • Apr. 1, 1836. Kirtland, OH.

Scribner v. Smith: Sidney Rigdon, JS, and Oliver Cowdery purchased 200 lbs. of lead pipe from merchant Jonathan F. Scribner for $790.91, due on Oct. 16, 1836. • June 16, 1836.

Newbould v. Rigdon, Smith, and Cowdery: The three defendants executed a six-month promissory note for $287.32 to pay for merchandise they purchased in Buffalo. • June 17, 1836. Geauga County, OH.

Kelley v. Rigdon, Smith, and Cowdery: Reynolds Cahoon, Jared Carter, and Hyrum Smith (operating as the firm of Cahoon, Carter & Co.) had executed

a promissory note for $2,014.74 to pay John Ayers (who assigned it to A. C. Demerrit who assigned it to Hezekiah Kelley), payable in six months. JS, Sidney Rigdon, and Oliver Cowdery (most likely operating as Rigdon, Smith & Cowdery) assumed the obligation. • June 18, 1836. Kirtland, OH.

Barker for use of Bump v. Smith and Cowdery: JS and Oliver Cowdery executed a promissory note to pay William Barker $621.32 in money or Missouri land by Sept. 1, 1836. • July 7, 1836. Kirtland, OH.

Rigdon, Smith, and Cowdery for use of Smith v. Woodworth: Eli Woodworth signed a note for $5.88 to pay Sidney Rigdon, JS, and Oliver Cowdery. • Sept. 19, 1836. Geauga County, OH.

Smith for use of Hitchcock and Hitchcock v. Cheney: Cheney was indebted to the plaintiff for $400 for work, money, goods, and merchandise. • Sept. 22, 1836. Geauga County, OH.

Lake for use of Quin v. Millet, Smith, and Smith: Artemus Millet, JS, and Hyrum Smith borrowed $50 from Cyrus Lake, payable four months later. Lake assigned the obligation to Christopher Quin Jr. • Sept. 26, 1836. Kirtland, OH.

Smith for use of Granger v. Smalling and Coltrin: John Coltrin and Cyrus Smalling signed a promissory note for $500 to pay Julius Granger and JS. • Sept. 30, 1836. OH.

Samuel and Sabrina Canfield executed a promisory note payable to JS for $500 for the purchase of parts of lots 29, 41, and 42 in Kirtland, which note he held for four weeks. • Oct. 1, 1836. OH.

Wright v. Whitney and Johnson: Sidney Rigdon, JS, Oliver Cowdery, Newel K. Whitney, and John Johnson signed two promissory notes for $500 each to pay Justus Wright. • Oct. 3, 1836. OH.

Holmes and Holmes v. Smith and Cahoon: Lory and Charles Holmes sold three parcels of land in Kirtland township to JS and Reynolds Cahoon for $12,000. • Oct. 5, 1836. OH.

Stannard v. Young, Pratt, and Smith: JS, Brigham Young, and Parley P. Pratt purchased a farm from Claudius Stannard just outside of Chester, Ohio (south of Kirtland) for $6,914.93, payable $1,000 that day and $2,000 within sixty days, which amounts were paid (possibly by way of Kirtland Safety Society notes), with $1,000 due each October 3 for the next four years (which payments were not paid). • Oct. 11, 1836. Geauga Co., OH.

Stannard v. Young and Smith: Brigham Young and JS signed a promissory note for $235.50 to pay Claudius Stannard and also for "goods sold and delivered amount appearing to be due $250." • Oct. 11, 1836. Kirtland, OH.

Eaton v. Smith: JS and Oliver Cowdery signed a promissory note to Winthrop Eaton for $1,150. The note was to be satisfied in Kirtland Safety Society notes in six months. • Oct. 11, 1836. New York City, NY.

Martindale v. Smith, Whitney, Cahoon, and Johnson: JS, Newel K. Whitney, Reynolds Cahoon, and Luke Johnson executed a promissory note for $5,000 to pay Timothy Martindale, payable on Jan. 1, 1837. • Oct. 11, 1836. Kirtland, OH.

Bailey, Keeler, and Remsen v. Smith and Cowdery: JS and Oliver Cowdery signed a promissory note to pay to Bailey, Keeler, & Remsen for items purchased, in the amount of $1,804.94. The note was due in July 1837. • Oct. 12, 1836. Kirtland, OH.

Scribner v. Smith: Action to collect $796.65 from Sidney Rigdon, JS, and Oliver Cowdery. • Oct. 19, 1836. OH.

Holmes v. Dayton, Slitor, and Smith: Hiram Dayton, Truman Slitor, and JS issued a promissory note for $208.30 to pay Ezra Holmes, payable Jan. 1, 1837. • Nov. 16, 1836. Kirtland, OH.

Cahoon, Carter and Co. v. Avery: Avery signed a promissory note for $24.50. • Dec. 2, 1836. Kirtland, OH.

Patterson and Patterson v. Cahoon, Carter, Smith, Rigdon, Cowdery, and Smith: Reynolds Cahoon, Jared Carter, and Hyrum Smith (operating as the firm of Cahoon, Carter & Co.) and Sidney Rigdon, Oliver Cowdery, and JS (operating as the firm of Rigdon, Smith & Cowdery) executed a promissory note to pay Gardner & Patterson $596.46, payable at the Bank of Geauga on Jan. 14, 1837. • Dec. 14, 1836. Geauga County, OH.

1837

Bank of Geauga v. Smith, Whitney, and Rigdon: JS, Newel K. Whitney, and Sidney Rigdon obtained a loan from the Bank of Geauga for $3,000, payable in 45 days. • Jan. 22, 1837. Kirtland, OH.

Rounds qui tam v. Smith: A writ of summons was issued against JS. He was ordered to appear before the Geauga Court of Common Pleas on Mar. 21, 1837, to answer Samuel D. Rounds and the State of Ohio; $1,000 damages. The writ stated that on Jan. 4, 1837, JS acted "as an officer of a Bank not incorporated by law of this State and denominated 'The Kirtland Safety Society Anti Banking Co.' contrary to the Statute in such case made and provided." • Feb. 9, 1837. Geauga County, OH. [**Discussed in ch. 9**]

Seymour and Griffith v. Rigdon and Smith: JS and Sidney Rigdon signed three promissory notes—two for $20, and one for $7—to pay John S. Seymour and Thomas Griffith. • Feb. 10, 1837. Kirtland, OH.

State of Ohio v. Auken: JS had been subpoenaed to appear in the Portage County Court of Common Pleas and testify as a character witness for John Alford, a prosecution witness. JS did not appear and was charged with contempt of court. • Feb. 14, 1837. Portage County, OH.

Martindale v. Smith: Timothy Martindale filed suit against JS and his other co-obligators under a promissory note, alleging damages of $7,500. • Feb. 16, 1837. Geauga County, OH.

Martindale v. Smith: JS and his co-defendants filed a $10,000 bail bond with Warren Parrish, Hyrum Smith, Oliver Cowdery, and Vinson Knight as sureties. The case was continued until the next term. • Feb. 22, 1837. Geauga County, OH.

Rounds qui tam v. Smith: Plaintiff's attorney R. Hitchcock filed a writ asserting the defendant's failure to incorporate by law the Kirtland Safety Society Anti-Banking Co., and sued for $1,000—one half for the state of Ohio and the other half for the plaintiff. • Mar. 1837. Geauga County, OH.

Bank of Geauga v. Smith: Defendants owed the Bank $4,000, and promised to pay the money on request. • Mar. 2, 1837. Kirtland, OH.

Seymour and Griffith v. Rigdon and Smith: JS and Sidney Rigdon signed a fourth promissory note with John S. Seymour and Thomas Griffith for $100. • Mar. 9, 1837. Kirtland, OH.

Millet for use of Smith v. Woodstock: Willard Woodstock made a bill to A. Millet for $1.85, payable when drawn. • Mar. 9, 1837. OH.

Usher v. Smith: Moses Usher obtained a judgment before Justice of the Peace Ariel Hanson against JS for $35.70 plus court costs. • Mar. 15, 1837. Kirtland, OH.

Martindale v. Smith: JS appeared before the Court of Common Pleas to enter special bail. • Mar. 21, 1837. Geauga County, OH.

Bank of Geauga v. Smith: The bank sued JS and his co-obligators in the Court of Common Pleas. • Mar. 22, 1837. Kirtland, OH.

Kelley v. Rigdon: Hezekiah Kelley sued JS and his co-obligors in the Court of Common Pleas on the promissory note assigned to Kelley claiming damages of $3,000. • Mar. 22, 1837. Geauga County, OH.

Bank of Geauga v. Smith: Sheriff Abel Kimball endorsed the writ and arrested the defendants two days later. • Mar. 24, 1837. Kirtland, OH.

Bank of Geauga v. Smith: JS and his co-defendants posted a bail bond of $8,000 with Vinson Knight and Ira Bond as sureties. The case was continued until the next term. • Mar. 24, 1837. Kirtland, OH.

Holmes v. Dayton: Ezra Holmes filed a suit against JS and his co-obligors in the Court of Common Pleas to collect on a promissory note, claiming damages of $500. • Mar. 28, 1837. Geauga County, OH.

Patterson and Patterson v. Cahoon: George A. H. Patterson and John Patterson filed a suit against Cahoon, Carter & Co., and Rigdon, Smith & Cowdery to collect on a promissory note claiming damages of $1,000. • Mar. 28, 1837. Geauga County, OH.

Patterson and Patterson v. Cahoon: Copies of the writ were left with Reynolds Cahoon, Jared Carter, Hyrum Smith, JS, and Sidney Rigdon. Oliver Cowdery was not found. The case was continued until the next term. • Mar. 29, 1837. Geauga County, OH.

State v. Auken: A writ of *capias ad testificandum* (to give evidence) was issued and delivered to Sheriff George Wallace. Attachment was returned May 7, 1837. • Mar. 30, 1837. Portage County, OH.

State of Ohio v. Smith: JS was ordered to appear and respond to charges of contempt of court for failing to appear pursuant to a subpoena in the case of *State v. Auken.* • Apr. 7, 1837. Portage County, OH. **[Discussed in ch. 10]**

State of Ohio v. Smith: JS personally appeared in court and filed his answer to the writ issued Mar. 30, 1837, at the Portage Court of Common Pleas. JS stated that he had attended court on Feb. 16, 1837, but that Alford, the prosecuting witness, was absent. Since JS was summoned to sustain the character of Alford, JS was informed on Feb. 16 that he "would not be wanted." • Apr. 9, 1837. Portage County, OH.

Bump v. Smith: JS signed a promissory note for $854.28 to pay to M. C. Davis, JS's gunsmith, singing teacher, and bodyguard. Davis transferred the note to Jacob Bump, who sued in the Justice Court. • Apr. 11, 1837. Kirtland, OH.

Bailey and Reynolds v. Smith: JS, along with Sidney Rigdon, Hyrum Smith, Edmund Bosley, and John Johnson issued a promissory note to John W.

Howden. Howden later endorsed the note to Nathaniel P. Bailey and Henry J. Reynolds for $825; the note was for "goods sold and delivered, money had & received &c." • Apr. 13, 1837. Geauga County, OH.

Boynton and Hyde v. Smith: JS, along with Sidney Rigdon, Edmund Bosley, John Johnson, and Hyrum Smith, executed a promissory note to pay John W. Howden $825 with interest five months from date. The note was later assigned to Ray Boynton and Harry Hyde. • Apr. 13, 1837. Geauga County, OH.

State of Ohio on complaint of Newel v. Smith: Grandison Newell made a complaint before Justice of the Peace Edward Flint claiming that "he has just cause to fear and did fear, that Joseph Smith Jr. would kill him or procure other persons to do it." A warrant was issued for JS the same day. • Apr. 13, 1837. Geauga County, OH. **[Discussed in ch. 10]**

Martindale v. Smith: Plaintiff by his attorney Hitchcock filed his declaration with Geauga Court of Common Pleas clerk D. D. Aiken. The declaration stated the indebtedness: $5,000 on Oct. 11, 1836; $6,000 on Feb. 20, 1837; $7,500 on Apr. 25, 1837. • Apr. 24, 1837. Geauga County, OH.

Newbould v. Rigdon, Smith, and Cowdery: Rigdon, JS, and Cowdery were arrested. A bail bond was subsequently posed by Martin Harris and five others. • Apr. 25, 1837. Geauga County, OH.

Patterson and Patterson v. Cahoon: The plaintiffs filed their declaration at the Geauga Court of Common Pleas. The declaration stated the intent of the defendants was to pay Gardner and Patterson $596.46 one month after date of execution, which was Dec. 14, 1836. By Mar. 1, 1837, the defendants had incurred a further debt of $800 for work and merchandise Gardner and Patterson had sold to them. • Apr. 29, 1837. Geauga County, OH.

State v. Auken: JS appeared before the Court of Common Pleas. His defense against the charge of not appearing was that he appeared on Feb. 16 instead of Feb. 14, 1837, because he understood he was to appear on the 16th. The court dismissed the contempt charges on the condition that JS paid the court costs of $4.70. • May 8, 1837. Portage County, OH.

Foster v. Johnson, Johnson, Smith and Smith: Luke and Lyman E. Johnson signed a promissory note to pay William Foster by Dec. 1, 1838. At some time the note was endorsed by Hyrum and JS. • May 15, 1837. Kirtland, OH.

State of Ohio on complaint of Newel v. Smith: Constable George Lockwood returned with JS to the Justice of the Peace Court. JS was not ready for his trial, so the case was continued until June 3, 1837. • May 30, 1837. Geauga County, OH.

State of Ohio on complaint of Newel v. Smith: Constable George Lockwood returned to court with JS. The Court heard witnesses, and JS was recognized to the amount of $500 and was to appear at the next Court of Common Pleas. • June 3, 1837. Geauga County, OH.

State of Ohio on complaint of Newel v. Smith: JS was brought before the Court of Common Pleas. The court, upon hearing the evidence, discharged him at the cost of the state. • June 5, 1837. Kirtland, OH.

Kelley v. Rigdon: The case was tried before the Court of Common Pleas, where the court entered judgment against the defendants in the amount of $2,083.47 and court costs of $10.53. • June 5, 1837. Kirtland, OH.

Martindale v. Smith: All parties appeared before the court and settled the matter by mutual agreement. • June 5, 1837. Kirtland, OH.

Patterson and Patterson v. Cahoon: JS and his co-defendants failed to appear after being requested three times to come to court. A default judgment was entered against them. The plaintiffs were awarded $610.37 in damages and court costs of $11.50. • June 5, 1837. Kirtland, OH.

Holmes v. Dayton: JS and his co-defendants did not appear. A default judgment was entered against them in the amount of $183.30 and court costs of $11.50. • June 5, 1837. Geauga County, OH.

Bank of Geauga v. Smith: The parties appeared in court and informed the court that the case had been settled. The defendants were assessed court costs of $11.20. • June 5, 1837. Kirtland, OH.

Eaton v. Smith: Winthrop Eaton, by his attorneys Andrews & Foot, filed a writ of *capias ad respondendum* at the Geauga Court of Common Pleas. Sheriff Abel Kimball was to have JS and Oliver Cowdery before the Court of Common Pleas to answer Eaton's plea of assumpsit; damages were $2,000. • June 6, 1837. Geauga County, OH.

Underwood v. Rigdon: Four plaintiffs, who had been employed as engravers for the printing of Kirtland Safety Society notes, summon sixteen defendants seeking payment for services rendered. • June 9, 1837. Geauga County, OH.

Eaton v. Smith: JS appeared at the Geauga County Court of Common Pleas in response to a writ of capias respondendum issued on June 6, 1837, in connection with Eaton's assumpsit case against him and Oliver Cowdery. • June 9, 1837. Geauga County, OH.

Smith for use of Hitchcock and Hitchcock v. Cheney: Plaintiffs by their attorney Reuben Hitchcock filed a writ of summons against Elijah Cheney to answer an assumpsit plea. • June 9, 1837. Geauga County, OH.

Commercial Bank of Lake Erie v. Cahoon, Smith, and Young: Reynolds Cahoon, JS, and Brigham Young signed a promissory note to pay the Commercial Bank of Lake Erie for $1,225 payable in three months. • July 3, 1837. Geauga County, OH.

Underwood v. Rigdon: Plaintiffs file their declaration seeking $1,643.63 plus costs. • July 7, 1837. Geauga County, OH.

Lake for use of Quin v. Millet: Christopher Quin Jr. sued Artemus Millet, JS, and Hyrum Smith to collect on a $50 obligation that was assigned to him by Cyrus Lake, plus accrued interest. • July 8, 1837. Geauga County, OH.

Newbould v. Rigdon, Smith, and Cowdery: Plaintiff filed his declaration for the amount due on the promissory note plus $400 for additional goods sold. • July 8, 1837. Geauga County, OH.

Lake for use of Quin v. Millet: A trial was held before the Justice Court in Kirtland and Justice of Peace Oliver Cowdery. The defendants did not appear, and a default judgment was entered in favor of Quin in the amount of $52.39 and $0.60 in court costs. • July 12, 1837. Kirtland, OH.

Holmes v. Dayton: The judgment was satisfied. • July 15, 1837. Geauga County, OH.

Bank of Geauga v. Smith: The court costs were paid. • July 15, 1837. Geauga County, OH.

Bailey v. Smith: B. Graham requested that Lord Sterling secure payment on the Smith and Cowdery note "by security or otherwise." Graham found that the note due on July 15 was protested at Cleveland then returned. Graham ordered the note forwarded to Sterling, requesting Sterling pursue the best course to secure it. • July 18, 1837. OH.

Millet and Joseph Smith v. Woodstock: Willard Woodstock failed to appear in the justice court and a judgment on his promissory note was rendered in favor of Artemis Millet for use of JS in the amount of $1.87 plus $0.40 in court costs. • July 20, 1837. Kirtland, OH.

Cahoon, Carter and Co. for use of Smith v. Draper: JS obtained a summons against Marvin C. Draper for payment of a promissory note made payable to Cahoon, Carter & Co. for $4.49 and it was returned "served by copy." • July 22, 1837. Geauga County, OH.

Cahoon, Carter and Co. for use of Smith v. Draper: JS brought his action of debt against Marvin C. Draper before Oliver Cowdery, Justice of the Peace. The defendant did not appear, and the case was continued until Aug. 19, 1837. • July 25, 1837. Geauga County, OH.

Barker for use of Bump v. Smith and Cowdery: Second Sheriff Abel Kimball was ordered to bring JS and Oliver Cowdery before the Geauga Court of Common Pleas to answer an assumpsit plea of Barker for use of Bump; damages of $1,000 were found. • July 26, 1837. Geauga County, OH.

Seymour and Griffith v. Rigdon and Smith: John S. Seymour and Thomas Griffith filed a suit on a promissory note dated Feb. 10 and Mar. 9, 1837, with face value of $150. They also filed a writ of capias against Sidney Rigdon and JS. Rigdon and Smith were arrested by Second Sheriff Abel Kimball and held in custody until Seymour and Griffith requested their release. • July 27, 1837. Kirtland, OH.

On their journey to visit the Saints in Canada, JS, Sidney Rigdon, and Thomas B. Marsh were detained all day in Painesville, Ohio, because of malicious lawsuits. Regarding *Barker for use of Bump v. Smith and Cowdery,* Second Sheriff Kimball arrested JS and Oliver Cowdery and took Smith's bail bond. Anson Cook, William Earl, and Vinson Knight acted as sureties. • July 27, 1837. Painesville, OH. [**Discussed in ch. 10**]

Six lawsuits were heard the same day. • July 27, 1837. Painesville, OH.

Rigdon, Smith, and Cowdery for use of Smith v. Woodworth: Sidney Rigdon, JS, and Oliver Cowdery brought suit against Eli Woodworth for not paying the note. Both parties appeared without process. The defendant claimed a set-off of book account for $3.50, and testified to his account. The balance was struck and judgment rendered against defendant for $1.68, plus court costs of $0.58. • July 31, 1837. Kirtland, OH.

Cahoon, Carter and Co. v. Avery: Arvin Avery failed to appear in justice court, and a judgment was rendered in favor of Cahoon, Carter & Co. for use of JS in the amount of $7.89. Avery had signed a promissory note dated Dec. 2, 1836, for $24.50. • Aug. 5, 1837. Kirtland, OH.

Allen v. Granger (originally *Allen v. Smith, Cowdery, Knight, Orton, Cahoon*): Justice of the Peace Frederick G. Williams rendered a judgment against JS, Oliver Cowdery, Vinson Knight, Roger Orton, and Reynolds Cahoon being the Kirtland Steam Company for $23, with

$1.31½ court costs. • Aug. 8, 1837. Chardon, OH.

State of Ohio vs. Smith [Joseph Smith Sr.] et al. Joseph Smith Sr. and 18 others including JS's brothers William, Samuel, and Don Carlos, were charged with riot and assault and battery on the complaint of Warren Parrish. Parrish and others, armed with pistols and Bowie knives, attempted to take possession of the Kirtland Temple. Joseph Sr. and the 18 other named defendants removed them. Justice of the Peace Oliver Cowdery discharged all defendants. • August 15, 25, and 26, 1837. Kirtland, OH. [**Discussed in ch. 10**]

Usher v. Smith: An order vacating the court record *(scire facias)* was issued to Constable B. H. Phelps, returnable on Aug, 24, 1837, at 10 a.m. Moses Usher also signed judgment over to Oliver Granger by receipt on the transcript. The Justices Court received $0.59 from Granger. • Aug. 17, 1837. Kirtland, OH.

Usher v. Smith: Judgment was entered against JS for the amount of $36.60 plus court costs when he did not appear before the Justice of the Peace. • Aug. 24, 1837. Kirtland, OH.

Halsted, Haines & Co. v. Granger: JS signed as surety along with twenty-nine other people for a $2,251.77 promissory note. In a separate matter, JS and others signed two additional promissory notes to Halsted, Haines & Co. on this date—one for $2,323.66 and another for $2,395.57. • Sept. 1, 1837. Kirtland, OH.

Boynton and Hyde v. Smith: JS became further indebted to Ray Boynton and Harry Hyde, who received John W. Howden's $825 note by assignment, for $1,200 total debt owed. • Sept. 1, 1837. Geauga County, OH.

Bailey v. Smith: Plaintiff's attorney Lord Sterling directed an instruction (precipe) to the Geauga Court of Common Pleas clerk, requesting he issue a summons returnable at the next court term for $1,804. • Sept. 7, 1837. Geauga County, OH.

State of Ohio v. Ritch: Justice of the Peace Oliver Cowdery issued a warrant against Abram Ritch, upon oath of JS, to constable B. H. Phelps for "unlawful oppression by color of office." JS claimed that Ritch had criminally misused his office as constable. • Sept. 12, 1837. Kirtland, OH. [**Discussed in ch. 10**]

State of Ohio v. Ritch: The warrant was returned concerning defendant Abram Ritch. Subpoenas were granted for several people including JS. The defendant pled not guilty to the charges. • Sept. 14, 1837. Geauga, County, OH.

Rigdon, Smith, and Cowdery for use of Smith v. Woodworth: Execution was issued to Constable J. Markell. • Sept. 15, 1837. OH.

Bailey, Keeler, and Remsen v. Smith and Cowdery: JS, Reuben Hedlock, Sidney Rigdon, John Gould, and Vinson Knight signed three promissory notes for $609.18 each to pay Bailey, Keeler and Remsen 12, 18, and 24 months from date. • Sept. 26, 1837. Geauga County, OH.

Bump v. Smith and Smith: JS and Samuel H. Smith signed a promissory note to pay Ebenezer Jennings $43, sixty days after this date. • Sept. 27, 1837. Kirtland, OH.

Oliver Granger became JS's and Sydney Rigdon's agent and held a power of attorney on their behalf to settle their business affairs in Kirtland after their departure. • Sept. 27, 1837. Kirtland, OH.

Underwood v. Rigdon: Defendants file their answer and plea. • Oct. 1837. Geauga County, OH.

Wright v. Whitney and Johnson: A writ commanding the sheriff to take the defendant and hold him responsible to answer the complaint *capias ad respondendum* was issued against Sidney Rigdon, JS, Oliver Cowdery, Newel K. Whitney, and John Johnson. They were commanded to appear at the Geauga Court of Common Pleas on Oct. 24 to answer Justus Wright's assumpsit plea. • Oct. 11, 1837. Geauga County, OH.

Wright v. Whitney and Johnson: Recognizance of special bail was entered into by Newel K. Whitney, John Johnson, Heman Hyde, and Jacob Bump for $3,000 each, stating that if Whitney and Johnson were condemned in the suit, the four above mentioned would pay costs. • Oct. 24, 1837. Geauga County, OH.

Seymour and Griffith v. Rigdon and Smith: Seymour and Griffith dropped their suit started on July 27, and Rigdon and Smith were awarded costs of $1.11 in the Court of Common Pleas before Judge Van R. Humphrey. • Oct. 24, 1837. Geauga County, OH.

Barker for use of Bump v. Smith and Cowdery: The plaintiff discontinued his suit, and defendants recovered against the plaintiff $1.27 in costs. The plaintiff paid his own costs of $4.92. • Oct. 24, 1837. Geauga County, OH.

Rounds qui tam v. Smith: The court issued a judgment for the plaintiff of $1,000 in *qui tam* case (regarding notes that lost all value when the Kirtland Safety Society failed). • Oct. 24, 1837. Geauga County, OH.

Smith for use of Hitchcock and Hitchcock v. Cheney: Defendant was demanded three times to defend suit, but defaulted. Plaintiff recovered against defendant for use of Hitchcock & Hitchcock a sum of $213.92 damages plus court costs of $9.79. The defendant was ordered to pay his own costs of $0.76. Execution was issued. • Oct. 24, 1837. Geauga County, OH.

Newbould v. Rigdon, Smith, and Cowdery: The case was settled out of court by mutual agreement of the parties and discountinued, with the defendants being assessed the court costs. • Oct. 24, 1837. Geauga County, OH.

Bailey and Reynolds v. Smith: Nathaniel P. Bailey and Henry J. Reynolds sued JS and the other signers of the note and sought a writ of *capias ad respondendum* against JS and the other signers of the note for damages of $1,200. Second Sheriff Abel Kimball and Deputy J. A. Tracy attempted to serve the writ but could not find any of the defendants within their jurisdiction. The case was continued until the next term of court in April of the following year. • Oct. 25, 1837. Geauga County, OH.

Rounds qui tam v. Smith: Jurors Guy Wyman, Caleb E. Cummings, John A. Ford, William Coafts, David Smith, George Patchin, Ira Webster, Stephen Hulbert, William B. Crothers, Jason Manley, Joseph Emerson, and Thomas King found the defendant indebted to the plaintiff for $1,000. The plaintiff was to recover against the defendant $1,000 plus costs. A bill of exceptions was signed by Van R. Humphrey, Daniel Kerr, Storm Rosa, and John Hubbard, stating that JS was a director in the "society," and assisted in issuing paper or bills, thus making "him an 'officer' within the meaning of the statute." • Oct. 25, 1837. Geauga County, OH.

Holmes v. Smith: A writ of summons was issued against JS and Reynolds Cahoon commanding them to appear before the Court of Common Pleas in Chardon to answer Lory & Charles Holmes' assumpsit plea. • Oct. 25, 1837. Geauga County, OH.

Scribner v. Smith: Scribner requested a writ of summons against Sidney Rigdon, JS, and Oliver Cowdery. The suit was brought to recover goods and money advanced amounting to $850. • Oct. 26, 1837. OH.

Commercial Bank of Lake Erie v. Cahoon, Smith, and Young: A writ of summons was issued against Reynolds Cahoon, JS, and Brigham Young to answer to the president, directors, and company of the Commercial Bank of Lake Erie, to the amount of $2,000. Suit brought on July 1837 default note. • Oct. 26, 1837. Geauga County, OH.

Boynton and Hyde v. Smith: Boynton and Hyde obtained a writ of summons against JS for failure to fulfill the promissory note, and left a copy with Emma Smith, because JS was absent from home that day. • Oct. 26, 1837. Geauga County, OH.

Stannard v. Young and Smith: Summons were issued for Brigham Young and JS to appear before the Geauga Court of Common Pleas to answer Stannard's assumpsit plea and make payment of the note. • Oct. 28, 1837. Geauga County, OH.

Rounds qui tam v. Smith: A writ of collection (*fieri facias*) was issued and delivered to Sheriff Abel Kimball. • Nov. 6, 1837. Geauga County, OH.

Stannard v. Young and Smith: The plaintiff, by his attorney Lord Sterling, filed his declaration, citing the failure of the defendants to pay $235.50, which was overdue as of Oct. 3, 1837. • Dec. 4, 1837. Geauga County, OH.

Foster v. Johnson: On plaintiff's complaint, a summons was issued to Constable J. Markell. It was served on Luke Johnson, Hyrum Smith, and JS the same day. Lyman Johnson was not found. • Dec. 18, 1837. Geauga County, OH.

Foster v. Johnson: The parties were scheduled to appear, but the defendants did not appear. Judgment was rendered against the defendants for $9.02 debt plus $1.05 for the cost of suit. Lyman Cowdery posted bail for the defendants. • Dec. 23, 1837. Kirtland, OH.

1838

Bump v. Smith: The plaintiff issued a writ to take (*writ of capias*) to constable Luke Johnson, which was returned endorsed by the defendant (*cepi corpus*). Judgment was rendered for $100 debt plus $1.09 for the cost of suit. • Jan. 1, 1838. Kirtland, OH.

Allen v. Granger: The defendants failed to appear, and a judgment of $20.57½ plus $0.64 for the cost of the suit was rendered against them. • Jan. 8, 1838. Kirtland, OH.

Foster v. Johnson: William Foster authorized Justice of the Peace Warren A. Cowdery to transfer the judgment to J. W. and W. W. Oakley. • Jan. 11, 1838. Geauga County, OH.

Martindale v. Smith: The court costs were paid. • Jan. 11, 1838. Geauga County, OH.

JS and Sidney Rigdon fled Kirtland to escape mob violence. They arrived in Far West, Mo., in March. • Jan. 12, 1838. Kirtland, OH.

Lake for use of Quin v. Millet: Christopher Quin Jr. received the amount of the judgment. • Jan. 15, 1838. Geauga County, OH.

Wilder v. Rounds: Sheriff Abel Kimball served notice regarding property levied under a writ of execution issued from the Geauga Court of Common Pleas, including some hay located in a barn that JS had occupied, claimed by Harvey Strong and Joseph Wilder. • Jan. 16, 1838. Kirtland, OH.

Wilder v. Rounds: The parties appeared before the court, and the jury ruled in favor of Joseph Wilder and Harvey Strong. • Jan. 18, 1838. Geauga County, OH.

Allen v. Granger, Smith, Cowdery, Carter, Knight, Orton, and Cahoon: The execution returned $9.25 but no further property was found against which to levy court costs. • Jan. 24, 1838. Geauga County, OH.

Spencer v. Cahoon, Carter, Smith, Smith, Rigdon, and Smith: On November 9, 1835, the Kirtland Temple building committee incurred a $50 debt to William Spencer, payable "when called for." When this action was commenced six defendants were named, including JS, but the court determined that only Cahoon, Carter, and Hyrum Smith were members of the committee and discharged the others. • Jan. 25, 1838. Geauga County, OH.

Allen v. Granger, Smith, Cowdery, Carter, Knight, Orton, and Cahoon: $5.41 of the judgment was received. • Jan. 26, 1838. Geauga County, OH.

Smith for use of Granger v. Smalling and Coltrin: JS obtained from the county clerk a writ requiring the sheriff to find the defendant and then to require him to answer the complaint (*capias ad respondendum*) against John Coltrin and Cyrus Smalling for failure to pay a $500 promissory note for services provided by Julius Granger. • Feb. 28, 1838. Geauga County, OH.

Holmes and Holmes v. Smith and Cahoon: In the Court of Common Pleas in Geauga County the plaintiffs sued on two promissory notes of $5,000 each. A default judgment was rendered for $10,071. • About Mar. 1838. Geauga County, OH.

Stannard v. Young, Pratt, and Smith: Having initiated a suit against JS, Brigham Young, and Parley P. Pratt, the day before the case was scheduled to be heard, the parties settled. Apparently some additional payment was made and the farm returned. • Apr. 2, 1838. Geauga Co., OH.

Rounds qui tam v. Smith: The writ of collection (*fieri facias*) was returned. Sheriff Abel Kimball had levied another writ in favor of the same plaintiffs against Sidney Rigdon upon properties sold for $604.50 and another property sold for $111.75. This matter remained unsettled until after JS's death, when the judgment was revived and satisfied. • Apr. 3, 1838. Geauga County, OH.

Wright v. Whitney and Johnson: The defendant, being demanded to appear at court three times, did not come and made default. The plaintiff recovered against Whitney and Johnson his damages of $1,055.31, plus costs ($11.51). Defendants pay own costs ($1.89). Execution was issued to collect on judgment. • Apr. 3, 1838. Geauga County, OH.

Holmes and Holmes v. Smith and Cahoon: The defendants, having been called to appear, made default. The plaintiffs recovered in full against the defendants $10,071.48, plus $10.38 costs. • Apr. 3, 1838. Geauga County, OH.

Stannard v. Young and Smith: The defendants made default, and the plaintiff recovered damages of $256.40, plus costs of $10.44. Execution was issued to collect on the same. • Apr. 3, 1838. Kirtland, OH.

Bailey and Reynolds v. Smith: The case was settled on the condition that plaintiffs pay the court costs of $2.50 and that the defendants recovered their costs of $0.60. The court issued an execution order for the plaintiffs to collect on the judgment. On June 4, 1838, plaintiffs discontinued this suit. • Apr. 3, 1838. Kirtland, OH.

Commercial Bank of Lake Erie v. Cahoon, Smith, and Young: The parties appeared in court, and the cause was settled and costs were paid. Plaintiffs' costs were $4.26; defendants' costs were $4.51. • Apr. 3, 1838. Geauga County, OH.

Boynton and Hyde v. Smith: JS did not appear in court and was judged to be in default. Boynton and Hyde were awarded $881.15 in damages and $11.15 in costs. • Apr. 3, 1838. Geauga County, OH.

Smith for use of Granger v. Smalling and Coltrin: The defendant was released after posting bail. The case was continued. • Apr. 3, 1838. OH.

JS and Sidney Rigdon attended the High Council by invitation and filled in as councilors in an ecclesiastic appeals case. • Apr. 28, 1838. Far West, MO.

Foster v. Johnson: J. W. and W. W. Oakley received judgment in full. • May 8, 1838. Geauga County, OH.

JS attended the ecclesiastical trial of William E. McLellin and Dr. McCord before the bishop's court. Both were excommunicated. • May 11, 1838. Far West, MO.

JS and other leaders left Far West to visit the north counties for the purpose of establishing land claims for the gathering of the Saints in Caldwell and Daviess counties. • May 18, 1838. Far West, MO. **[Discussed in ch. 11]**

Allen v. Granger, Smith, Cowdery, Carter, Knight, Orton, and Cahoon: An appeal was brought by plaintiff Allen in the Geauga County Court of Common Pleas seeking to recover $23 debt from Granger, who claimed he did not owe the debt. Allen discontinued the suit and was ordered to pay his own and Granger's costs of $8.50. • June 4, 1838. Kirtland, OH.

JS attended circuit court and received a visit from Judge Austin A. King. • July 31, 1838. Far West, MO.

JS went with a group of about 15 brethren to Colonel Lyman Wight's in Gallatin, Missouri, and met with the Saints who had been beaten while trying to vote. • Aug. 7, 1838. Far West, MO.

JS met with the Justice of the Peace Adam Black, who gave a written agreement to the Saints to uphold the law. • Aug. 8, 1838. Daviess County, MO.

JS and other Saints met with a citizens committee from Millport, Missouri, and entered into a covenant of peace with them. JS then rode to Far West. • Aug. 9, 1838. Adam-ondi-Ahman, MO.

JS was chased by "evil designing men" on his journey back to Far West from the Grand River and upon arrival was informed of a writ for his arrest for a complaint brought by Adam Black. • Aug. 13, 1838. Far West, MO.

JS told Sheriff William Morgan of Daviess County that he wished to be tried in Caldwell County according to the law. • Aug. 16, 1838. Far West, MO.

JS met with various inhabitants of Caldwell County, who had formed themselves into "Agricultural Companies." • Aug. 20, 1838. Far West, MO.

JS visited with a man from Livingston County, Missouri, who gave him reports of a growing mob in Daviess County. • Sept. 2, 1838. Far West, MO.

JS engaged Generals David R. Atchison and Alexander W. Doniphan as his lawyers. • Sept. 4, 1838. Far West, MO.

JS's hearing at the home of Waldo Littlefield before Judge Austin A. King could not proceed because of the absence of Adam Black, the plaintiff. • Sept. 6, 1838. Daviess County, MO.

In a hearing in John Raglin's home, Adam Black claimed his life had been threatened by Church members, and JS was required to post a $500 security bond despite the lack of evidence against him. • Sept. 7, 1838. Daviess County, MO.

JS received news that a mob planned to attack Adam-ondi-Ahman, Missouri. • Sept. 8, 1838. Far West, MO.

A mob was frustrated in its attempts to attack Adam-ondi-Ahman, Missouri, but the mobbers continued to send taunting reports of tortured prisoners to JS and the Saints, trying to provoke them to commit the first act of violence. • Sept. 9, 1838. Far West, MO.

JS received a report that citizens from Daviess County, Missouri, had sent a letter to Governor Lilburn W. Boggs, filled with lies and falsehoods about the Saints in Missouri. • Sept. 12, 1838. Far West, MO.

JS was at home with illness when Lilburn W. Boggs, governor of Missouri, issued orders to General David W. Atchison of the state militia to march into Daviess and Caldwell counties in Missouri and assist in the apprehension of certain Church leaders. • Sept. 18, 1838. Far West, MO.

A committee of the Church related to JS that they had entered into an agreement with a mob to purchase the lands of all of those citizens wishing to leave Daviess County. • Sept. 26, 1838. Far West, MO. [**Discussed in ch. 11**]

An armed mob held the Saints in De Witt under siege for a period of days, during which time JS saw several of the brethren die from starvation. • Oct. 9, 1838. De Witt, MO.

JS preached about the scripture "Greater love hath no man than this, that he lay down his life for his brethren" and requested the support of all who would stand by him to meet on the public square the next day. • Oct. 14, 1838. Caldwell County, MO.

JS traveled to Adam-ondi-Ahman with a militia company of about a hundred men under the command of Colonel George M. Hinkle to protect the Saints from the Daviess County mob. • Oct. 15, 1838. Far West, MO.

Halsted, Haines and Co. v. Granger: William H. Halsted and others requested a writ of summons against Jared Carter and others to appear at the Geauga Court of Common Pleas to answer an assumpsit plea of Halsted, Haines, and Co. • Oct. 15, 1838. Geauga County, OH.

Lilburn W. Boggs, governor of Missouri, issued an extermination order which stated, "The Mormons must be treated as enemies and must be exterminated or driven from the state." • About Oct. 27, 1838. Jefferson City, MO. [**Discussed in ch. 11**]

About 3,500 mob members and Missouri militia approached Far West, acting on orders from Governor Lilburn W. Boggs. • Oct. 30, 1838. Far West, MO.

A mob from Livingston County, MO, attacked the Mormon settlement at Haun's Mill, killing seventeen Mormons. • Oct. 30, 1838. Haun's Mill, Caldwell County, MO.

Colonel George M. Hinkle, on the pretense that the hostile militia surrounding Far West desired a truce, escorted JS and other Church leaders to a supposed parley with militia officers. Instead, the men were taken prisoner and marched to the enemy camp on Goose Creek. • About Oct. 31, 1838. Far West, MO.

At Goose Creek camp, officers of the Missouri militia held a court martial and sentenced JS, his brother Hyrum Smith, and others to be shot at 9:00 a.m. that morning, but General Alexander W. Doniphan refused to carry out the sentence. • Nov. 1, 1838. Caldwell County, MO. [**Discussed in ch. 12**]

JS's wife and children wept as the guards thrust them away with their swords and took the Prophet under heavy guard toward Independence, Missouri. • Nov. 2, 1838. Far West, MO.

Smith for use of Granger v. Smalling and Coltrin: In the Geauga County Court, an action was brought against a promissory note for $500 signed Sept. 30, 1836, by John Coltrin and Cyrus Smalling for service performed by Julius Granger. The defendants counterclaimed against JS for $2,000 allegedly owed for "various goods and merchandise" as well as $1,500 for Kirtland Safety Society notes, an "unauthorized bank paper." In a jury trial, the defendants recovered their costs of $23.24 and the plaintiffs paid their own costs of $5.31. • Nov. 6, 1838. Geauga County, OH.

Smith for use of Granger v. Coltrin: Lawyers for JS and Julius Granger gave notice of intent to appeal the case. • Nov. 8, 1838. Geauga County, OH.

Colonel Sterling Price chained JS and the other prisoners together in an old vacant house. • Nov. 9, 1838. Richmond, MO.

State of Missouri v. Joseph Smith and others: On the first day of JS's hearing before Judge Austin A. King, a group of armed men was sent out to obtain witnesses. • Nov. 12, 1838. Richmond, MO. [**Discussed in ch. 12**]

Over forty witnesses appeared at court and testified against JS. • Nov. 13, 1838. Richmond, MO.

All of the witnesses requested by JS and many of his brethren were arrested, thrown in prison, and prohibited from testifying. • Nov. 18, 1838. Richmond, MO.

The preemption rights of the Saints lapsed while many were unjustly detained in preliminary hearings. Some of their lands were purchased by their Missouri enemies. • Nov. 23, 1838. [**Discussed in ch. 11**]

After being abused and enduring an unjust preliminary hearing, JS and five of the other brethren were committed to Liberty Jail in Liberty, Missouri, by Judge Austin A. King. • Nov. 29, 1838. Richmond, MO.

Heber C. Kimball and Alanson Ripley were appointed by the brethren in Far West, Missouri, to visit JS and the others in Liberty Jail "as often as circumstances would permit." • About Dec. 1, 1838. Far West, MO.

Halsted, Haines, and Co. v. Granger: The plaintiffs, by their attorneys, Perkins and Osborn, filed their declaration in the Geauga County Court of Common Pleas clerk's office, citing the defendants'

failure to pay the promissory note and claiming damages totaling $3,000. • Dec. 17, 1838. Geauga County, OH.

Emma Smith visited her husband, JS, in Liberty Jail. • Dec. 20, 1838. Liberty, MO.

JS spent Christmas Day imprisoned in Liberty Jail. • Dec. 25, 1838. Liberty, MO.

1839

All six inmates in Liberty Jail petitioned Judge Joel Turnham for a writ of habeas corpus. Only Sidney Rigdon's was granted because of insufficient evidence against him. He was released that night and was pursued but succeeded in arriving in Illinois. • Feb. 1839. Liberty, MO. [**Discussed in ch. 12**]

After much rude treatment in jail and lack of due respect from the law, JS considered escaping from Liberty Jail and received a confirmation that he and the brethren could go that night if they all assented. Lyman Wight objected, however, so they delayed the attempt. • Feb. 7, 1839. Liberty, MO.

After JS's failed escape attempt, local citizens gathered outside of Liberty Jail and threatened to kill JS and his fellow inmates. JS prophesied that he and his friends would be kept safe. • Feb. 8, 1839. Liberty, MO.

Smith v. McLellin: William E. McLellin was summoned to appear before the Clay County Circuit on the first day of the next term. While JS was imprisoned in Liberty Jail, he sued McLellin for trespass and accused him of stealing some personal items. • Mar. 6, 1839. Liberty, MO.

In the Geauga County Court of Common Pleas, a suit was brought "for goods sold and delivered and work and labor done by plaintiffs as engravers for the defendants." Judgment for plaintiffs for $1,644.63 plus $20.92 costs. Defendants gave notice of intent to appeal. The amount due was satisfied in full by A. W. Babbitt, because the other defendants Samuel Parker, Warren Smith, Hiram Clark, and Andrew Allen were "not found" in the county. • Mar. 10, 1839. Geauga County, OH.

Still in prison, JS predicted his own release in a letter and sent a petition to the justices of the Supreme Court of Missouri for a writ of habeas corpus or in the alternative for a writ of change of venue. The peition was denied. • Mar. 15, 1839. Liberty, MO.

From jail JS dictated a seventeen-page letter to the Saints, who had found refuge in Quincy, Illinois, and elsewhere, after they had been driven from Missouri. The letter included what is now known as Doctrine and Covenants 121, 122, and 123. • Mar. 20, 1839. Liberty, MO.

JS was sent with other prisoners by a arduous route from Liberty to Gallatin, Daviess County, where the alleged crimes had occurred. • Apr. 6, 1839. Liberty, MO.

JS arrived in Daviess County on Monday after being transferred from Liberty Jail and was turned over to Sheriff William Morgan and his guard. • Apr. 8, 1839. Daviess County, MO.

JS's two-day trial commenced before a drunken grand jury and judge. • Apr. 9, 1839. Gallatin, MO.

JS spent the day in court as witnesses were examined. He petitioned for a change of venue. • Apr. 10, 1839. Gallatin, MO.

State of Missouri v. Smith et al. (Daviess Co. Circuit Court): JS was indicted for treason by a Daviess County grand jury. Judge Thomas Burch agreed to a change of venue to Boone County, Missouri. • Apr. 11, 1839. Gallatin, MO.

JS and other prisoners left the home of Judge Josiah Morin en route to Boone County, under a strong guard, for trial there. • Apr. 12, 1839. Millport, MO.

JS and the other prisoners escaped from their guards while en route to Boone County. Although Sheriff Morgan later denied it, there is evidence to support the claim that the sheriff aided the prisoners in their escape. The Missourians rode Morgan on a rail. • Apr. 15, 1839. Chariton Co., MO.

Halsted, Haines and Co. v. Granger and Carter: JS had signed as surety along with twenty-nine others guaranteeing a promissory note from Halsted, Haines & Co. on Sept. 1, 1837. The defendants, having been requested three times to attend court, failed to appear. The plaintiff recovered damages of $2,337.35 plus costs of $17.24. The defendants were ordered to pay their own costs of $0.77. JS and others had signed two additional promissory notes to Halsted Haines & Co. on Sept. 1, 1837—one for $2,323.66 and the other for $2,395.57. These two promissory notes were not located and have no connection with this court case. • Apr. 16, 1839. Kirtland, OH.

Underwood v. Rigdon: Court hears evidence and finds defendants liable, and defendants give notice of intent to appeal the judgment. • Apr. 16, 1839. Geauga County, OH.

JS arrived at Quincy, Illinois, after escaping from Missouri and was reunited with his wife Emma. • Apr. 22, 1839. Quincy, IL.

Underwood v. Rigdon: Six parcels of land are levied to pay the judgment, but not sold at this time for lack of bidders. • May 20, 1839. Geauga County, OH.

Missouri Governor Lilburn Boggs requested certified copies of the treason indictments against JS. • June 24, 1839. Independence, MO.

Coe v. Smith: The case was heard in the Geauga County Court of Common Pleas, for goods sold and delivered in the amount of $900. A pre-judgment attachment against JS's property was attempted, but no service of process was served on JS, so the case was stricken from the calendar. Coe was ordered to pay costs. • June 25, 1839. Kirtland, OH.

Sheriff William Morgan filed a statement that JS and the other prisoners had escaped without the "connivance, consent, or negligence" of Morgan and the other officers. • July 6, 1839. Daviess Co., MO.

Nauvoo High Council: Five members of the high council voted to have JS go to Washington D.C. Two members voted against. • Oct. 21, 1839. Nauvoo, IL.

Sidney Rigdon and Joseph Smith v. William Smith: A writ for collection of a judgment against William Smith for $2,000 was returned by the sheriff since no property of the defendant could be found in the county. The plaintiffs paid the court costs. • Nov. 12, 1839. Kirtland, OH.

JS consulted with the Illinois congressional delegation about how to get the Church's petition for redress brought before the United States Congress. • Dec. 7, 1839. Washington D.C.

Missouri v. Gates: The case accusing JS and several other Mormons of treason was dismissed from the Daviess County Circuit Court because the accuseds were no longer in the state. • Dec. Term, 1839. Daviess County, MO.

1840

On his way home from a fruitless visit to Washington, D.C., to seek redress for injustices the Saints suffered in Missouri, JS proclaimed the iniquity and insolence of Martin Van Buren, the president of the United States, with whom he had visited. • Early Mar. 1840. Between Washington, D.C., and Nauvoo, IL.

Nauvoo High Council: Trial held regarding the dispute between John Hicks and John Green surrounding a stolen horse. Green was found innocent of the theft and Hicks ordered to make peace by publishing the outcome of the case in the *Times & Seasons.* • May 2, 1840. Nauvoo, IL.

Nauvoo High Council: JS requested that the High Council relieve him from his duties in connection with the City Plot and acting as Clerk so that he could focus more of his attention on the translation of the Bible and Ancient Egyptian Records. The High Council granted his request and placed Henry G. Sherwood in his stead. • June 20, 1840. Nauvoo, IL.

State v. Auken: Feri facias was issued by Sheriff Dewey. It was returned on Nov. 7, 1840, satisfied. • July 1, 1840. Ravenna, OH.

JS met with the Nauvoo Stake high council in his office to discuss John Patten's charges against Elijah Fordham for unchristian conduct, slander, theft, and attempted murder. It was concluded that the two "had better be reconciled without an action, or vote of the Council, and henceforth live as brethren." • Aug. 17, 1840. Nauvoo, IL.

State of Missouri v. Smith et al. (Boone Co. Circuit Court): The Boone County prosecuting attorney filed a *nolle prosequi* (meaning the prosecutor intended to proceed no further) in the treason case against JS. This was a dismissal without prejudice, meaning the prosecutor was free to later change his mind. When these charges were revivied in 1842, the State of Missouri began again with a new indictment by a new grand jury. • Aug. Term, 1840. Boone County, MO.

State of Missouri v. Smith et al. (Boone Co. Circuit Court): Lilburn W. Boggs, former governor of Missouri, demanded the extradition of JS as a fugitive from justice. Missouri Governor Thomas Reynolds, successor to Boggs, initiated extradition proceedings against JS and others by sending a requisition to Illinois Governor Thomas Carlin. • Sept. 1, 1840. Independence, MO. [**Discussed in ch. 16**]

Nauvoo High Council: Charges brought against Almon Babitt by JS for accusing him of extravagant purchases and claims while in Washington D.C. Several were appointed to speak on the case. JS withdrew the charges the next day. • Sept. 5, 1840. Nauvoo, IL.

JS and Hyrum Smith and three others purchased ⅚ of a steamboat (renamed the *Nauvoo*) and other river equipment from Robert E. Lee, agent for the United States Army Corps of Engineers. • Sept. 10, 1840. Quincy, IL. [**Discussed in ch. 14**]

JS's father, Joseph Smith Sr., died. • Sept. 14, 1840. Nauvoo, IL.

Underwood v. Rigdon: Lands sold to Gilbert Granger at county courthouse. • Sept. 14, 1840. Geauga County, OH.

Scribner v. Smith: The plaintiff defaulted, and the defendants recovered against him their costs of $2.25; plaintiff paid his own costs of $7.85. No docket fee was taxed by agreement of the parties. • Oct. 20, 1840. Kirtland, OH.

Nauvoo High Council: Charges brought a week earlier against William Gregory for slander, pilfering, and stealing were heard. Evidences were heard and the charges sustained. Gregory made confession to the satisfaction of the Council. • Oct. 24, 1840. Nauvoo, IL.

Nauvoo High Council: John Huntsman was found guilty of destroying certain bargains that would have benefitted the Church. • Oct. 31, 1840. Nauvoo, IL.

Hibbard for use of Hungerford and Livingston v. Miller: George Miller and JS were summoned to appear before Justice of the Peace Samuel Marshall on a complaint of Davidson Hibbard for failure to pay $85.81. • Nov. 27, 1840. Hancock County, IL.

Nauvoo High Council: Robert D. Foster was accused of slandering the authorities of the church and for other unchristianlike conduct and evidences were heard. • Nov. 28, 1840. Nauvoo, IL.

Smith v. Holladay: JS and Hyrum Smith and others brought an action against river pilots Benjamin and William Holladay for wrecking the steamboat *Nauvoo*. They claimed $2,000 in damages and $1,000 in lost profits. This case was dismissed in May 1841. • Nov. 30, 1840. Carthage, IL. [**Discussed in ch. 14**]

Hibbard for use of Hungerford and Livingston v. Miller: The defendants failed to appear. The plaintiff recovered their demands plus court costs. • Dec. 5, 1840. Hancock County, IL.

Nauvoo High Council: JS presided at the ecclesiastical trial of Dr. Robert D. Foster for "slandering the authorities of the Church, profane swearing, etc." Evidences were heard most of this day and all of the next. • Dec. 12–13, 1840. Nauvoo, IL.

State v. Auken: Clerk William Coolman Jr. received $6.04 from Sheriff Dewey. • Dec. 14, 1840. Ravenna, OH.

Hibbard for use of Hungerford & Livingston v. Miller: Justice of the Peace Marshall created a copy of the judgment for the Hancock County Circuit Court. • Dec. 14, 1840. Carthage, IL.

The city of Nauvoo was granted its charter from the state of Illinois, making it an official city with various government rights and protections. The document was signed by Governor Thomas Carlin and Secretary of State Stephen A. Douglas. Abraham Lincoln supported the charter. • Dec. 17, 1840. Nauvoo, IL. **[Discussed in ch. 13]**

Nauvoo High Council: Trial of Robert D. Foster was concluded by submitting it to the First Presidency who acquitted him of the charges, which action the Council unanimously sustained. • Dec. 20, 1840. Nauvoo, IL.

Hibbard for use of Hungerford & Livingston v. Miller: The Hancock County Circuit Court issued an injunction suspending all proceedings in this case in the Justice of the Peace Court. • Dec. 21, 1840. Carthage, IL.

Hibbard for use of Hungerford & Livingston v. Miller: Sheriff Abernathy served a *supersedeas* (a type of surety bond that the court required from an appellant who wanted to delay payment of a judgment until the appeal was over). • Dec. 23, 1840. Carthage, IL.

State v. Auken: George Kirkum received $2.64 from Clerk William Coolman in satisfaction of his fees. • Dec. 29, 1840. Ravenna, OH.

1841

State v. Auken: Sheriff George Wallace received $2.98 from Clerk William Coolman for his fees. • Jan. 5, 1841. Ravenna, OH.

William Law was called to the First Presidency, replacing Hyrum Smith. • Jan. 19, 1841. Nauvoo, IL.

Smith v. Guthrie: JS and his partners sold a sixth-part of the steamboat *Nauvoo* to Edwin Guthrie for $1,226.06. • Jan. 25, 1841. Fort Madison, IA.

JS appointed sole trustee-in-trust for the Church, executed in Nauvoo and recorded in Carthage on Feb. 8. This authorized JS to acquire or convey all properties for the Church. • Feb. 2, 1841. Carthage, IL.

At a meeting organizing the city council of Nauvoo, JS gave the opening prayer, presented bills concerning the University of Nauvoo and the Nauvoo Legion, and was sworn in as a member of the council. • Feb. 3, 1841. Nauvoo, IL.

JS attended a court martial organizing the Nauvoo Legion and was elected lieutenant general. • Feb. 4, 1841. Nauvoo, IL.

Nauvoo High Council: Charges against John P. Green for abuse of lent money and unchristian-like conduct toward Jacob Ulrich were settled by the president (apparently JS), who structured an agreement regarding repayment. Charges were also sustained against Theodore Turley for unchristian-like sexual conduct with women and non-repayment of moneys received. The president then determined that in order to retain his membership in the church Turley would need to acknowledge his wrongdoing before the Council and a public congregation. • Feb. 6, 1841. Nauvoo, IL.

Nauvoo City Ordinance: Mandated city councilmen to attend all meetings, subject to a two-dollar fine upon absence without excuse. • Feb. 8, 1841. Nauvoo, IL.

Nauvoo City Ordinance: Unanimously prohibited all persons and establishments within the city of Nauvoo from dispensing whiskey in quantities smaller than one gallon, or other alcoholic beverages in quantities less than one quart, without a medical prescription. • Feb. 15, 1841. Nauvoo, IL.

Nauvoo City Ordinance: Transferred all powers over the educational system in Nauvoo to the City Council. • Feb. 22, 1841. Nauvoo, IL.

JS and others incorporated the Nauvoo House Association and Nauvoo Agricultural & Manufacturing Association. • Feb. 23, 1841. Nauvoo, IL.

Nauvoo City Ordinance: Divided Nauvoo into four wards and set forth City Council representation for those wards. • Mar. 1, 1841. Nauvoo, IL.

Nauvoo City Ordinance: Required all surveyed tracts of land within Nauvoo to be plotted and laid out into city lots corresponding with the original survey of Nauvoo. • Mar. 1, 1841. Nauvoo, IL.

Nauvoo City Ordinance: Aimed to protect the constitutional right of free speech by allowing peaceable assembly in public meetings without riot, rebellion, or disturbance of the peace, on pain of fine and imprisonment. • Mar. 1, 1841. Nauvoo, IL.

Nauvoo City Resolution: Called for all nuisances along the river to be removed by the City Supervisor. • Mar. 1, 1841. Nauvoo, IL.

At the Nauvoo City Council meeting, JS presented a bill for an ordinance allowing "free toleration and equal privileges" to all religious sects and denominations and banning the "ridiculing, abusing or depreciating another for his religion" or disturbing any religious meeting. • Mar. 1, 1841. Nauvoo, IL.

George Miller reported to JS that John C. Bennett had a history of adultery. JS took no action at this time. • Mar. 2, 1841. Nauvoo, IL.

Nauvoo City Ordinance: Established a one-dollar fine for any owner of a dog who molests any person, horse, or cattle. • Mar. 29, 1841. Nauvoo, IL.

Nauvoo High Council: A charge against Alonson Brown for theft of Church funds was partially sustained, and Brown was forgiven as he had confessed and repented. • Mar. 30, 1841. Nauvoo, IL.

JS married Louisa Beamon as his first plural wife in Nauvoo. The marriage is performed by J. B. Noble, JP. • Apr. 5, 1841. Nauvoo, IL.

Sweeney v. Miller: JS and Hyrum Smith, Peter Haws, and George Miller (operating as Miller, Smith, Smith, & Haws) signed a $58 note for repairs to the steamboat *Nauvoo* to be "payable in sixty days." • Apr. 16, 1841. Nauvoo, IL.

Hibbard for use of Hungerford and Livingston v. Miller: Justice of the Peace Samuel Marshall created a certified transcript of the proceedings from his docket book for the Hancock County Circuit Court. • Apr. 26, 1841. Carthage, IL.

Nauvoo City Resolution: Allowed any person to kill any dogs running at large which molest any person, horses, or cattle. Also established a fine of twenty dollars for any person who keeps an unspayed female dog. • May 1, 1841. Nauvoo, IL.

Singley v. Rigdon: JS was summoned to testify in a circuit court case regarding a promissory note that was allegedly already paid. The defendant recovered costs from the plaintiff. • May 3, 1841. Carthage, IL.

Ebenezer and Elender Wiggins signed an agreement with JS to sell their 232 acres, excepting the house, in exchange for "one of the best city lots in Nauvoo" and $100 in goods. • May 14, 1841. Nauvoo, IL.

Smith v. Hinkle: George Miller swore an affidavit stating that George Hinkle owed JS $1,500 for property that he had taken in Missouri in 1838 when JS was incarcerated in Liberty Jail. • May 14, 1841. Fort Madison, IA.

Nauvoo High Council: Approved the purchase of the Stone School House property for $1,000 payable over 18 years. A petition by Ebenezer Black for rebaptism into the Church was accepted. • May 28, 1841. Nauvoo, IL.

JS had an agreeable meeting with Illinois Governor Thomas Carlin in Quincy. Apparenlty no mention was made of the outstanding requisition from Missouri seeking JS's extradition on treason charges. • June 4, 1841. Quincy, IL.

JS was appointed guardian of the heirs of Edward Lawrence. Hyrum Smith and William Law signed JS's Guardian's Bond as sureties. • June 4, 1841. Quincy, IL. **[Discussed in ch. 15]**

Missouri v. Joseph Smith. JS was arrested by Sheriff Thomas King of Adams County on a warrant from Illinois Governor Thomas Carlin and was charged as a fugitive from justice. JS returned to Quincy and obtained a writ of habeas corpus from Charles A. Warren, Master in Chancery. Judge Stephen A. Douglas, who happened to be in town, set the hearing on the writ for June 8 in Monmouth. • June 5, 1841. Bear Creek, IL. **[Discussed in ch. 16]**

JS and his guards traveled from Quincy to Nauvoo. Sheriff Thomas King had taken sick and was nursed in JS's home. • June 6, 1841. Nauvoo, IL.

Missouri v. Joseph Smith. JS, Sheriff Thomas King, his posse, and a substantial retinue of JS's bodyguards started very early in the morning for the court hearing in Monmouth, Illinois, 75 miles distant. • June 7, 1841. Nauvoo, IL.

Missouri v. Joseph Smith. JS arrived at Monmouth to stand trial before Judge Stephen A. Douglas and found the public stirring with curiosity. • June 8, 1841. Monmouth, IL.

Missouri v. Joseph Smith. JS stood trial and was represented by a cadre of lawyers: Orville H. Browning, Charles A. Warren, Sidney B. Little, James H. Ralston, Cyrus Walker, and Archibald Williams. Browning was particularly eloquent in defense of Smith. • June 9, 1841. Monmouth, IL.

Missouri v. Joseph Smith. Judge Stephen A. Douglas ruled that the writ was invalid and discharged JS. • June 10, 1841. Monmouth, IL.

JS made a patriotic speech to the Nauvoo Legion troops in which he declared his willingness to lay down his life in defense of the United States. • July 3, 1841. Nauvoo, IL.

Nauvoo High Council: Heard an appeal from a bishop's court regarding a business dispute and unchristian conduct, and Shermon Gilbert was told to acknowledge that he had acted wrongly and unwisely. • July 4, 1841. Nauvoo, IL.

Smith v. Hinkle: JS, through his attorneys, filed his declaration, claiming Hinkle was indebted to him for books, horses, and personal property valued at $1,500. • Aug. 1, 1841. Fort Madison, IA.

JS received a letter from his brother William Smith regarding the Hotchkiss land purchase in Nauvoo. • Aug. 5, 1841. Nauvoo, IL.

It was announced at a conference of the Church that Saints will be disfellowshipped if they sell lots to immigrants in competition with sales by Church agents. • Aug. 16, 1841. Nauvoo, IL.

JS responded to a letter from Horace R. Hotchkiss regarding the purchase of the land that JS called "a deathly sickly hole." That swampy land would be drained and settled as a major portion of Nauvoo. • Aug. 25, 1841. Nauvoo, IL.

Nauvoo City Resolution: Called for the City Recorder to procure a seal for the City of Nauvoo. • Sept. 4, 1841. Nauvoo, IL.

Nauvoo High Council: The High Council resolved no longer to handle any business of a temporal nature and to transfer all debts and temporal business to the First Presidency. • Sept. 22, 1841. Nauvoo, IL.

JS sent the deputy sheriff of Adams County a statement detailing his total costs of $685 due to his arrest and trial while in the sheriff's custody. • Sept. 30, 1841. Nauvoo, IL.

Most Church real property was deeded to JS as sole trustee in trust. • Oct. 5, 1841. Nauvoo, IL.

Smith v. Cowdery: The case was continued for the first of six times. • Oct. 16, 1841. Carthage, IL.

Nauvoo City Resolution: Declared several houses in Nauvoo to be removed as nuisances. • Oct. 16, 1841. Nauvoo, IL.

Nauvoo City Ordinance: Provided for an appeal process for any decision of the Mayor or Aldermen starting with the Municipal Court. • Nov. 13, 1841. Nauvoo, IL.

Nauvoo City Ordinance: Required that any vagrant, disorderly person, person found drunk in the streets, person without a fixed place of residence, or person guilty of profane or indecent language be confined to labor for ninety days and be fined up to five hundred dollars or be imprisoned for up to six months. • Nov. 13, 1841. Nauvoo, IL.

JS presented and passed a bill at the Nauvoo City Council meeting for "an Ordinance in relation to Hawkers, Peddlers, Public Shows, and Exhibitions, in order to prevent any immoral or obscene exhibition." • Nov. 26, 1841. Nauvoo, IL.

Nauvoo City Ordinance: Established that if any person fired a gun or pistol idly in the night have the gun confiscated and pay a fine not exceeding fifty dollars. • Nov. 27, 1841. Nauvoo, IL.

Nauvoo City Ordinance: Prohibited hawkers and peddlers from working without proper license. It established a ten to fifty dollar fee for its violation. • Nov. 27, 1841. Nauvoo, IL.

JS instructed that all donations for the building of the temple should be received by his hands, not by the Building Committee. • Dec. 11, 1841. Nauvoo, IL.

The First Presidency instructed the immigrating Saints to remove from Warsaw, Illinois, to Nauvoo immediately to avoid economic conflicts there. • Dec. 13, 1841. Nauvoo, IL.

JS commenced unpacking merchandise on the second floor of his new Red Brick Store. • Dec. 14, 1841. Nauvoo, IL.

William Wightman delivered to JS, as sole trustee in trust, a deed for all of the unsold lots in the town of Ramus, Illinois. • Dec. 16, 1841. Nauvoo, IL.

Nauvoo City Resolution: Recommended that all Nauvoo citizens subscribe to the "New York Weekly Herald" and thanked its editor for his contributions. • Dec. 18, 1841. Nauvoo, IL.

1842

JS opened his new Red Brick Store on Water Street, near competing stores owned by Amos Davis and William & Wilson Law. • Jan. 5, 1842. Nauvoo, IL.

Boosinger v. Cowdery: George Boosinger sued Oliver Cowdery and JS and Hyrum Smith for nonpayment of loan evidenced by a promissory note signed in Tallmage, Ohio, on May 26, 1836. These court proceedings were signed by Austin King, Feb. 28, 1842. • Jan. 8, 1842. Caldwell County, MO.

Boosinger v. Smith: The plaintiff sued JS, Oliver Cowdery, Sidney Rigdon, and Hyrum Smith for nonpayment on another loan evidenced by a second promissory note signed in Kirkland, Ohio, on May 23, 1836. These court proceedings were also signed by Austin King on Feb. 28, 1842. • Jan. 8, 1842. Caldwell County, MO.

JS was elected Vice Mayor of Nauvoo City. A resolution called for a complete "Plot [plat] of the City" to be procured for use of the Council. Rules of order for the Council were adopted, including the duties of the mayor, vice mayor, recorder and marshal; the order of business, decorum, debate, amending, and voting. A meeting schedule was set, with compensation of two dollars per day for attendance and fines for unexcused absences. • Jan. 22, 1842. Nauvoo, IL.

Nauvoo City Resolutions: Transferred the business of the burying ground to the standing Committee on Public Grounds, and established a road labor tax to be assessed at three days during the year of 1842. This labor tax applied to male citizens between twenty-one and fifty years of age. If they neglected to help maintain city streets, they were fined one dollar per day. • Feb. 12, 1842. Nauvoo, IL.

Nauvoo City Ordinance: Required an individual to obtain a license before auctioning off real or personal property within the city and imposed a fine of twenty five dollars per lot sold without an appropriate license. • Feb. 12, 1842. Nauvoo, IL.

Nauvoo City Ordinance: Established that any male over seventeen years old, and any female over fourteen years old could contract and be joined in marriage as long as they attained the appropriate license and the marriage was solemnized by one with authority. Resolutions called for a tax of one half of one percent on all taxable property in the city, and established a fund for the poor of the City using any surplus Council funds. • Feb. 17, 1842. Nauvoo, IL.

Smith v. Shearer: JS entered a complaint before Justice of the Peace Ebenezer

Robinson against Thomas J. Shearer for unlawful possession of 100 acres of land belonging to Smith. • Feb. 18, 1842. Nauvoo, IL.

JS spoke to the City Council about the Nauvoo Charter and the Registry of Deeds. He expressed his confidence in the privileges afforded by the Nauvoo charter. • Feb. 18, 1842. Nauvoo, IL.

Smith v. Shearer: Subpoenas were issued for witnesses by order of the defendant. • Feb. 21, 1842. Nauvoo, IL.

Smith v. Shearer: The summons for jury was returned. JS recovered and obtained restitution of the property. Shearer was ordered to pay Smith's costs of $18, which included the cost of the writ of restitution. • Feb. 26, 1842. Nauvoo, IL.

Nauvoo City Resolutions: Established that if any person's property is subjected to a sheriff's, marshal's, or constable's sale, they will have the privilege to redeem the sale by paying the principal and fifteen percent on the principal within thirty days of the sale. Required parents to keep their children at home on Sundays or pay a five dollar fine for every offense. Required the owners of any "carrion" who had died to remove the animal from the city bounds and to bury it three feet under the ground. • Mar. 5, 1842. Nauvoo, IL.

Nauvoo City Ordinances: Established the position of a Sealer of Weights and Measures whose duty it was to enter every store, shop, and market every six months and examine the scales, weights, and measures to ensure they are working properly. Several fines imposed for improper equipment use or failure to comply with this ordinance. Appointed "a City Register whose duty it [was] to record all deeds" and other instruments of writing presented to him. Fees for

recording established. • Mar. 5, 1842. Nauvoo, IL.

City of Nauvoo v. Davis: JS charged Amos Davis with "indecent and abusive language" toward JS the day previous. Mayor John C. Bennett presided and a jury convicted Davis, and he appealed to the Circuit Court of Hancock County. • Mar. 10, 1842. Nauvoo, IL.

JS was made Master Mason "on sight" by Abraham Jonas in Nauvoo Masonic Lodge. •Mar. 15, 1842. Nauvoo, IL.

Smith v. Hinkle: Hinkle's lawyers, Chapman and Mudd, received a copy of interrogatories, which was subsequently filed in Lee County District Court. • Apr. 6, 1842. Burlington, IA.

Nauvoo City Ordinance: Required each tavern or ordinary eating place within the city of Nauvoo to have appropriate licensure. In order to obtain the licensure the owner was required to allow six freeholders within his ward examine the premises and approve of its condition. Fees and punishments for failure to comply with this ordinance were established. • Apr. 9, 1842. Nauvoo, IL.

JS and others met with attorney Calvin A. Warren to consider declaring bankruptcy under the new federal law made effective Feb. 1, 1842. • Apr. 14, 1842. Nauvoo, IL.

Applications for bankruptcy were filed by JS and Hyrum Smith, along with several other Church leaders. • Apr. 18, 1842. Carthage, IL. **[Discussed in ch. 14]**

Smith v. Hinkle: Nauvoo Mayor John C. Bennett was appointed to gather depositions from subpoenaed witnesses. • Apr. 18, 1842. Nauvoo, IL.

Smith v. Hinkle: Mayor Bennett gathered depositions from 16 witnesses. The

cost for taking the depositions was $13. •
Apr. 22, 1842. Nauvoo, IL.

Nauvoo City Ordinances: Established
that all bricks made in the city of Nauvoo had to comply to a particularized
mold size and established penalties for
failure to comply. Required each store
or grocery owner to obtain appropriate
licensure from the City Council before
operating business. • Apr. 22, 1842. Nauvoo, IL.

The Nauvoo City Council passed its first
business licensing ordinance. • Apr. 29,
1842. Nauvoo, IL.

Smith v. Hinkle: The jury members were
sworn. Plaintiff was awarded $200 dam-
ages. • Apr. 29, 1842. Fort Madison, IA.

JS administered the first Nauvoo endow-
ments to nine men in his Red Brick Store.
• May 4, 1842. Nauvoo, IL.

Sweeney v. Miller: Sweeney recovered
judgment against JS, Hyrum Smith, and
Peter Haws for $58.97 in damages plus
the cost of suit. • May 5, 1842. Carthage,
IL.

Former Missouri Governor Lilburn W.
Boggs was shot and seriously wounded
at his home. For several days he was not
expected to live. • May 6, 1842. Independence, MO.

During a mock battle of the Nauvoo
Legion, John C. Bennett asked JS to take
a station in the rear of the cavalry without his guards. JS felt Bennett may have
been plotting to kill him. • May 7, 1842.
Nauvoo, IL.

Nauvoo City Ordinances: Prohibited
brothels within the city of Nauvoo and
declared them public nuisances, imposing a penalty from $500 to $50,000 on
those keeping them. Made all adultery

and fornication "which can be proved"
punishable by six month prison and
fines in the same amounts. "The individual's own acknowledgment shall be
considered sufficient evidence." JS spoke
strongly in favor of this ordinance. Also
repealed previous ordinances in relation to hawkers, peddlers, public shows,
exhibitions, auctions, taverns, ordinar-
ies, stores and groceries." • May 14, 1842.
Nauvoo, IL.

JS spoke at a meeting and told the assembly that Boggs had been murdered. Soon
thereafter rumors began circulating,
fanned by Mayor John C. Bennett, that
Orrin Porter Rockwell had been the
shooter and that he had been ordered or
encouraged to do so by JS. • May 15, 1842.
Nauvoo, IL.

Nauvoo City Resolution: Accepted the
resignation of Mayor John C. Bennett
and thanked him for his service. JS was
elected mayor by a vote of 18–1. • May 19,
1842. Nauvoo, IL.

Robert D. Foster was charged before
a special council with abusing the city
marshal and Samuel H. Smith. JS labored
to get Foster clear. • May 20, 1842. Nauvoo, IL.

Nauvoo High Council: Charges brought
by George Miller against Chauncey Higbee for unchaste and unvirtuous conduct
with women, teaching them that it was
right to have free intercourse if it was kept
secret, and that JS had authorized him to
practice these things. Higbee was expelled
from the Church, the same to be published in the *Times & Seasons.* Another
charge was brought against Robert Foster
for unchristianlike conduct and the failure to pay a debt. Foster was acquitted
and the parties reconciled. • May 21, 1842.
Nauvoo, IL.

JS wrote a letter to the Quincy *Whig* denying any involvement in the Boggs affair. He wrote, among other things, "My hands are clean, and my heart pure, from the blood of all men." • May 22, 1842. Nauvoo, IL.

Nauvoo City Resolution: Created the office of coroner and appointed Samuel H. Smith as such. • May 23, 1842. Nauvoo, IL.

State v. Higbee: In an action brought by JS before Justice of the Peace Ebenezer Robinson, Chauncy L. Higbee was charged with slandering and defaming the character of JS. • May 24, 1842. Carthage, IL.

Smith v. Shearer: The writ of restitution was returned; no property was found belonging to Shearer. • May 24, 1842. Nauvoo, IL.

Truman Gillet swore on June 18, 1844, that on June 1, 1842, he heard Missouri men plotting to kidnap JS. They implicated William Law. • June 1, 1842. Nauvoo, IL.

U.S. v. Miller: A default judgment was entered by U.S. District Court Judge Nathaniel Pope against JS and Hyrum Smith and others for $5,212 regarding their promissory note to Robert E. Lee for the purchase of the steamboat *Nauvoo*. No property was found of the defendants subject to execution. • June 11, 1842. Springfield, IL.

Illinois Governor Thomas Carlin commissions JS as Justice of the Peace by virtue of his being mayor for Nauvoo. • June 13, 1842. Springfield, IL.

City of Nauvoo v. McGraw: William H. McGraw was brought before the Nauvoo Mayor's Court (over which JS presided) for breach of ordinance by selling spirituous liquors. The execution of sentence was stayed on appeal to the Nauvoo Municipal Court. • July 5, 1842. Nauvoo, IL.

Nauvoo City Ordinances: Required an investigation before the Nauvoo Municipal Court before any citizen of the city be taken out of the city by any writs, and extended the benefit of a writ of habeas corpus to all citizens of the city. Required that any individual wishing to put on a public show or exhibition attain a license, costing fifty dollars and that any public show or exhibition be consistent with standards of good morals and decency. • July 5, 1842. Nauvoo, IL. [**Discussed in ch. 16**]

Nauvoo Legion Court Martial: JS attended court martial this day. • July 5, 1842. Nauvoo, IL.

Nauvoo City Ordinances: Called for the appointment of several auctioneers and required them to take an oath before commencing their duties. Required that all laws and ordinances by the City Council be inserted into the book of law which was currently being printed. • July 12, 1842. Nauvoo, IL.

In re John C. Bennett: JS took affidavits of Daniel Wells regarding John C. Bennett. • July 12, 1842. Nauvoo, IL.

In re John C. Bennett: JS attended meeting regarding Orson Pratt and alleged sexual involvement of John C. Bennett with Sarah Pratt, Orson Pratt's wife. • July 15, 1842. Nauvoo, IL.

Missouri v. Joseph Smith. Former Missouri Governor Lilburn W. Boggs executed an affidavit stating that he had good reason to believe that JS was accessory before the fact in the attempt on Boggs's life. • July 20, 1842. Independence, MO. [**Discussed in ch. 16**]

Missouri v. Joseph Smith. Missouri Governor Thomas Reynolds issued a requisition to Illinois Governor Thomas Carlin for the extradition of JS and Orrin Porter Rockwell in connection with the Boggs assault. • July 22, 1842. Independence, MO.

Nauvoo City Resolution: Upheld the character of JS, and organized petitions to the Governor not to issue a writ against JS • July 22, 1842. Nauvoo, IL.

Parker v. Foster: The case, in Nauvoo Mayor's Court, was heard before JS as mayor and Justice of the Peace, for action of debt on a $55 promissory note. A judgment was issued by JS. The plaintiff recovered $55.47 to fulfill the debt and $1.45 in costs. • July 25, 1842. Nauvoo, IL.

State v. Little: Edwin Little was charged in Nauvoo with assault and battery on William Seely. The execution was issued by JS. The Plaintiff recovered $5 as damages and $0.93¾ costs. • July 25, 1842. Nauvoo, IL.

Gray v. Allen: JS paid James Gray $237 for the balance of judgment ($695) recovered in this case. • July 25, 1842. Carthage, IL.

State v. Tubbs: A warrant was issued against Silas Tubbs on suspicion of stealing a cow from JS's yard. Tubbs was discharged the following day for lack of evidence. • July 26, 1842. Nauvoo, IL.

City of Nauvoo v. McGraw: William McGraw and James White were charged in Nauvoo Mayor's Court for breach of ordinance by selling spirituous liquors. The execution was issued by JS. The city of Nauvoo recovered $25 debt and $3 in court costs. The defendants appealed to the Nauvoo Municipal Court. The defendants failed to appear and default judgment was granted to the city plus court costs. • Aug. 2, 1842. Nauvoo, IL.

City of Nauvoo v. Thompson: William Thompson was charged in Nauvoo Mayor's Court with disorderly conduct. A warrant and summons were issued by JS. Thompson entered into recognizance to keep the peace for one year. • Aug. 2, 1842. Nauvoo, IL.

Nauvoo City Ordinance: Refined the ordinance of July 5, 1842 by establishing that whenever a person is brought before the Nauvoo Municipal Court on the basis of a writ of habeas corpus, the court has powers to examine the origin, validity, and legality of the writ of process under which the arrest was originally made. If the writ of process appears to be illegal or unfounded, the Court will discharge the prisoner from the arrest. • Aug. 8, 1842. Nauvoo, IL.

Missouri v. Joseph Smith. JS was arrested by Adams County Sheriff Thomas King on a charge of being "an accessory to an assault with intent to kill" ex-governor Lilburn Boggs of Missouri and was placed under custody of the city marshal after the Nauvoo Municipal Court issued a writ of habeas corpus. King returned to Quincy for further instructions from Governor Thomas Carlin. When King returned, Smith had gone into hiding. • Aug. 8, 1842. Nauvoo, IL.

JS held a private council after dark with his wife Emma, his brother Hyrum, William Law, Wilson Law, and a few others at the lower end of an island in the river between Nauvoo and Montrose, Iowa. His legal position was discussed and lawyers were soon retained to represent him in both Iowa and Illinois. • Aug. 11, 1842. Mississippi River.

JS's wife, Emma Smith, eluded detection by the sheriff while taking a carriage to visit her husband, who was in hiding. • Aug. 13, 1842. Nauvoo, IL.

JS heard multiple reports that sheriffs, officers, and a militia were on their way to take him captive. In a letter to Wilson Law, JS wrote that the proceedings against him were "a farce . . . gotten up unlawfully and unconstitutionally . . . by a mob spirit." • Aug. 14, 1842. Nauvoo, IL.

In a letter to his wife Emma, JS considered the possibility of escaping with her and "20 or 30 of the best men we can find" to the Wisconsin pine country, and "then we will bid defiance to the world, to Carlin, Boggs, Bennett, and all their whorish whores, and motly [sic] clan, that follow in their wake." JS discouraged Emma from visiting Carlin, whom he considered to be "a fool," but said she could write him if she wished. • Aug. 16, 1842. Nauvoo, IL.

JS's wife Emma encouraged him to change his hiding spot immediately, and they accordingly traveled together to Carlos Granger's place. • Aug. 18, 1842. Nauvoo, IL.

JS had a meeting with his brother Hyrum and four others where they discussed the proceedings against him. • Aug. 20, 1842. Nauvoo, IL.

In a letter addressed to "All the Saints in Nauvoo," JS wrote that his enemies pursued him "without cause, and have not the least shadow, or coloring of justice, or right on their side." • Sept. 1, 1842. Nauvoo IL.

JS received a report that the sheriff was on his way to Nauvoo with a posse. • Sept. 2, 1842. Nauvoo, IL.

JS escaped out the back door of his home from Deputy Sheriff Pitman and others who had come to arrest him. • Sept. 3, 1842. Nauvoo, IL.

Copeland v. Brown: Asa Copeland sued Albert Brown in Nauvoo Mayor's Court for Brown's failure to pay Copeland $44.37½ for work and labor. The summons was issued by JS, Mayor. • Sept. 5, 1842. Nauvoo, IL.

Harwood v. Brown: James Harwood sued Albert Brown in Nauvoo Mayor's Court for Brown's failure to pay Harwood $44.06 for work and labor. • Sept. 5, 1842. Nauvoo, IL.

Nauvoo City Ordinance: Allowed the Municipal Court to make returnable forthwith any writs of habeas corpus that it had issued. • Sept. 9, 1842. Nauvoo, IL.

JS remained in hiding the entire day and returned home at night. • Sept. 10, 1842. Nauvoo, IL.

Missouri v. Joseph Smith. Governor Thomas Carlin, acknowledging the inability of his state law enforcement officers to capture JS, issued a "proclamation" setting forth the legal basis for issuing the arrest warrants for Smith and Orrin Porter Rockwell, reciting that they had "resisted the laws by refusing to go with the officers who had them in custody," and offering a reward of $200 for their apprehension. • Sept. 20, 1842. Quincy, IL.

Nauvoo City Ordinances: Called for the election of a Notary Public for the City of Nauvoo. Legalized the immediate killing of any animal or dog that may be rabid, and established a one thousand dollar fine against the owner of a rabid animal. Gave authority to the Municipal court to issue writs of attachment against persons who may commit a contempt of the court. • Sept. 26, 1842. Nauvoo, IL.

In the matter of Joseph Smith: Authorized by Treasury Solicitor Charles B. Penrose, U.S. Attorney Justin Butterfield filed formal objections in federal district court, based upon allegations of fraud, seeking to block the discharge of both JS and Hyrum's bankruptcy petitions. The pleading is captioned, "Objections to his Discharge." Butterfield was successful in blocking the discharge, but Judge Nathaniel Pope ordered the cases be set over for further hearings on Dec. 15. • Oct. 1, 1842. Springfield, IL.

Jacob Bump Administrator for the Estate of Stannard v. Brigham Young and Joseph Smith: Jacob Bump revived a judgment that Claudius Stannard had obtained on a promissory note signed in Oct. 1836 by JS and Brigham Young for $250. Handled in the Geauga Court of Common Pleas, the sheriff eventually levied and auctioned four of JS and Emma's properties to satisfy the debt. The properties remained unsold, however, for lack of bidding. • Oct. 4, 1842. Kirtland, OH.

Smith v. Guthrie: Judgment awarded to Guthrie, who recovered costs from the plaintiffs. • Oct. 10, 1842. Fort Madison, IA.

Nauvoo City Ordinance: Established that whenever less than a quorum of the City Council was present, the remaining members could send a Marshal to retrieve absent members, and subject them to a fine. • Oct. 22, 1842. Nauvoo, IL.

Nauvoo City Ordinance: Established the taxation of all lands within the City of Nauvoo, excluding City lands, or Church lands, and for stud horses, asses, mules, horses, mares, cattle, clocks, watches, carriages, wagons, carts, and money in loans, stock, or trade. It called for the appointment of an Assessor and Collector to insure that these taxes were paid, and it established fines for non-payment. • Oct. 31, 1842. Nauvoo, IL.

JS, acting as Justice, issued writs and affidavits in order to clear up problems with fraud and irregularity at the Nauvoo Post Office. Sidney Rigdon was the postermaster; later, JS replaced him. • Nov. 8, 1842. Nauvoo, IL.

Nauvoo City Ordinance: Outlined the right of an imprisoned individual to apply for a writ of habeas corpus and the rights of the Municipal Court to grant or reject that application. • Nov. 14, 1842. Nauvoo, IL.

State v. Daniel Brown and Thomas S. Edwards (Nauvoo Mayor's Court): The defendants were charged with felony theft of lumber; execution of the judgment issued by JS. • Nov. 15, 1842. Nauvoo, IL.

Ex parte George Brown: On habeas corpus (Nauvoo Municipal Court): Petition for writ of habeas corpus on charges of larceny. Brown posted $200 bail, and case was heard before the Hancock County Circuit Court. • Nov. 21, 1842. Nauvoo, IL.

Nauvoo City Ordinance: Established that any slaughterhouse within one half mile of any dwelling house be declared a public nuisance and be removed. If the owner refused to remove the nuisance he would be fined one hundred dollars for every week he continues to use the establishment. • Nov. 26, 1842. Nauvoo, IL.

JS held a trial at his house that lasted all day concerning the unequal distribution of provisions among those working on the Nauvoo Temple. • Nov. 28, 1842. Nauvoo, IL.

City of Nauvoo v. Hunter: JS submitted a complaint to alderman and Justice of the Peace William Marks, claiming that Thomas J. Hunter had breached Nauvoo's "ordinance concerning vagrants and disorderly persons" when stating JS was an imposter and swindler. JS claimed the accusations injured his moral and religious character. • Nov. 28, 1842. Nauvoo, IL.

City of Nauvoo v. Hunter: Thomas J. Hunter pled guilty in Nauvoo Municipal Court to charges of slandering JS and was discharged. Hunter was fined $10 for contempt. • Nov. 29, 1842. Nauvoo, IL.

City of Nauvoo v. Davis: Amos Davis's appeal from the Nauvoo Municipal Court conviction of "abusive and ridiculous language" was reversed by the Circuit Court. Chauncey Higbee was Davis's attorney and Robert D. Foster signed his appeal bond. • Nov. 30, 1842. Nauvoo, IL.

JS purchased the printing plant and *Times and Seasons* from Ebenezer Robinson for $6,600.00 using $3,790.00 of the Lawrence Estate funds and $2,810.00 of his own. He appointed John Taylor and Wilford Woodruff as co-Editors of the *T&S* and entered a five year lease with Taylor and Woodruff for the presses, etc., and the building which housed them. • Dec. 1, 1842. Nauvoo, IL.

Dana v. Brink: JS sat as a judge (Nauvoo Mayor's Court) in the case that charged William B. Brink with committing malpractice while delivering Charles A. Dana's wife's baby. • About Dec. 1842. Nauvoo, IL.

A delegation was dispatched by JS to visit Springfield to sound out the new Illinois governor, Thomas Ford, on the possibility of dismissing the outstanding warrant for Smith's arrest. Governor Ford said that while he was sure the writ was illegal, he did not believe he had the authority to interfere with the acts of the former governor. • Dec. 2, 1842. Nauvoo, IL.

City of Nauvoo v. Hunter: Nauvoo Municipal Court Clerk James Sloan created a copy of the case proceedings for the Hancock County Circuit Court. • Dec. 5, 1842. Nauvoo, IL.

City of Nauvoo v. Davis: Amos Davis was charged with the use of indecent language and behavior toward Ira S. Miles on Dec. 3, 1842. Hyrum Smith, Lyman E. Johnson, Andrew M. Gravel, and JS were subpoenaed as witnesses. The case was taken to Nauvoo Municipal Court, where Davis claimed he was unable to receive a fair and impartial trial because of Mayor JS, and requested a change of venue regarding this action as well as charges against Davis for slandering Miles, assaulting William Walker, and selling liquor in small quantities. • Dec. 6, 1842. Nauvoo, IL.

City of Nauvoo v. Hunter: Sheriff William Backenstos served an injunction to Constable Dimick Huntington and Nauvoo Municipal Court clerk James Sloan, requesting suspension of the case. Thomas Hunter and surety Harmon Wilson filed an appeal bond for $100. • Dec. 7, 1842. Carthage, IL.

Missouri v. Joseph Smith. JS's delegation at Springfield, Illinois, swore an affidavit that he was in Illinois on May 6, the day of the assassination attempt of the former governor of Missouri, Lilburn W. Boggs. • Dec. 14, 1842. Nauvoo, IL.

Hyrum Smith was discharged in bankruptcy by Judge Nathaniel Pope. U.S. Attorney Justin Butterfield attempted to settle JS's bankruptcy application. This matter was still unresolved when he was martyred. • Dec. 15, 1842. Springfield, IL.

City of Nauvoo v. Anderson: Burr Anderson, Edwin Cutler, and Joseph Hamilton were brought before the Nauvoo Mayor's Court for breach of ordinance by disorderly conduct ("indecent behavior and conduct") toward Robert Ivins. The execution was issued by JS. The city of Nauvoo recovered $15 in debt and $8.81 in court costs. • Dec. 16, 1842. Nauvoo, IL.

City of Nauvoo v. Clements: Albert Clements and Nathan Tener [or Tanner] were brought before the Nauvoo Mayor's Court for breach of ordinance by disorderly conduct ("assault and battery") toward Adah Clements. Execution and recognizance was issued by JS. The city of Nauvoo recovered $20 in debt and $5.31 in court costs. Clements and Tener entered into recognizance to keep the peace for six months. • Dec. 17, 1842. Nauvoo, IL.

Missouri v. Joseph Smith. Thomas Ford, governor of Illinois, wrote JS a letter advising him to submit to the law and come to Springfield to have his extradition case heard. Justin Butterfield, U.S. Attorney for Illinois, also encouraged JS to come to Springfield and assured him that he would represent him. • Dec. 17, 1842. Nauvoo, IL.

City of Nauvoo v. Clements (Nauvoo Mayor's Court): For breach of ordinance by disorderly conduct ("slanderous and abusive language") toward the wife, son, and daughter of Duncan McArthur. City of Nauvoo recovered $5 in debt and $3.62½ in court costs (Albert Clements on Dec. 22 1842); $1 in debt and $2.62½ in court costs (Henry Tener on Dec. 20, 1842); in addition, $0.66 in debt and $0.25 in court costs (Henry Tener on Apr. 4, 1843). • Dec. 20 and 22, 1842 Nauvoo, IL.

Canfield v. Morey: In Nauvoo Mayor's Court, on a suit on account, JS issued summons for the defendant and witnesses as mayor and Justice of the Peace. Nothing further is known about this case. • Dec. 26, 1842. Nauvoo, IL.

Missouri v. Joseph Smith. JS voluntarily surrendered to Wilson Law, general of the Nauvoo Legion, on charges relating to the Boggs assault. • Dec. 26, 1842. Nauvoo, IL.

Ex parte Smith. JS appeared before Judge Nathaniel Pope of the U.S. District Court in Springfield and posted bail in connection with Missouri's extradition demand relating to the Boggs assault. • Dec. 31, 1842. Springfield, IL.

1843

JS accepted the offer of Representatives Hall to provide Sunday services there while awaiting his hearing in District Court. Orson Hyde and John Taylor delivered the sermons. • Jan. 1, 1843. Springfield, IL.

Missouri v. Joseph Smith. JS appeared in a packed federal court in connection with Missouri's extradition demand. Judge Nathaniel Pope continued the hearing at the request of Attorney General Josiah Lamborn to allow more time to fully prepare. • Jan. 2, 1843. Springfield, IL.

Ex parte Smith. JS appeared in district court in connection with Missouri's extradition demand. Attorney General Josiah Lamborn argued for the State of Missouri and Benjamin Edwards and U.S. Attorney Justin Butterfield argued on behalf of Smith. Judge Nathaniel Pope took the matter under submission. • Jan. 4, 1843. Springfield, IL. [**Discussed in ch. 16**]

Ex parte Smith. Judge Nathaniel Pope delivered his opinion that the Boggs affidavit, upon which Missouri's extradition requisition was based, was fatally defective in that it was vague, contained conclusions of law, and presented insufficient facts to show that Smith was a fugitive from Missouri law. Pope therefore discharged Smith. • Jan. 5, 1843. Springfield, IL.

JS went to see Judge Nathaniel Pope in the morning. The judge wished him well and hoped he would no longer be persecuted. Then JS visited Governor Ford, who signed an executive order rescinding Governor Carlin's earlier order for JS's arrest. • Jan. 6, 1843. Springfield, IL.

Nauvoo City Ordinances: Prescribed the way in which elections were to be conducted in Nauvoo. Specially divided the city into eight wards as voting precincts and designated the first Monday of February, every two years, as Election Day. Any white male over the age of twenty-one, who has resided in Nauvoo sixty days preceding the election was allowed to vote. Set the salaries of the City Council and Municipal Court judges and the fees for the Alderman, Marshal, jurors, witnesses, arbitrators, and coroners. • Jan. 14, 1843. Nauvoo, IL.

JS attended a large public meeting at his house on the day proclaimed by Brigham Young and the apostles for fasting, praise, and thanksgiving due to JS's deliverance from oppression. In the evening, JS heard a land case involving Robert D. Foster. • Jan. 17, 1843. Nauvoo, IL.

On their sixteenth wedding anniversary, JS and Emma hosted at their home some 74 guests at an all-day gala dinner and celebrated his recent court victory in Springfield. • Jan. 18, 1843. Nauvoo, IL.

Nauvoo City Ordinance: Required the burial of a person at least six feet under ground and with the approval and help of the Sexton and set the Sexton's fees for a burial service. • Jan. 30, 1843. Nauvoo, IL.

State v. Goddard: In Nauvoo Mayor's Court, Stephen H. Goddard, William F. Cahoon, and William W. Riley petitioned the court for a writ of habeas corpus. The warrant was issued on oath of Josiah Simpson for charges of assault. Affiants claimed the writ was "informal and insufficient." • Feb. 4, 1843. Nauvoo, IL.

JS was re-elected mayor of Nauvoo. • Feb. 6, 1843. Nauvoo, IL.

State v. Olney: Oliver Olney and Newel Nurse were brought before Nauvoo Mayor's Court on charges of burglary and larceny of Moses Smith's store. The goods were ordered to be returned to Moses Smith. Nurse was discharged. Oliver Olney held to bail for $5,000 to appear at the Hancock County Circuit Court. • Feb. 10, 1843. Nauvoo, IL.

At a city council meeting, JS reproved the judges of elections for closing the polls at six o'clock when many still wished to vote. • Feb. 11, 1843. Nauvoo, IL.

JS publicly chastised Robert D. Foster for selling lots and building the big "Mammoth Hotel" in uptown Nauvoo in competition with Church lot sales and the Church's Nauvoo House hotel. This was a major grievance against JS for the Fosters (and Laws), who considered JS as having an unjust monopoly and engaging in unfair competition • Feb. 21, 1843. Nauvoo, IL.

Nauvoo City Ordinance: Established a market on Main Street to be run by the city and JS as mayor to contract with any person to receive goods and complete the market-house building. • Feb. 25, 1843. Nauvoo, IL.

City of Nauvoo v. Davis: Documents relating to this court case (abusive and ridiculous language) were sent to the Hancock County Circuit Court. • Feb. 27, 1843. Nauvoo, IL.

City of Nauvoo v. Hunter: JS's complaint and affidavit and Henry G. Sherwood's notification of summons were filed at the Hancock County Circuit Court. • Feb. 28, 1843. Carthage, IL.

Dana v. Brink: The plaintiff recovered $99 plus costs, but the case was appealed to the Nauvoo Municipal Court. • Mar. 2–3, 1843. Nauvoo, IL.

Nauvoo City Ordinance: Required any payment of city taxes, debts, and fines imposed under the ordinances of the city to be paid in gold and silver coin only and set forth fines for attempting to pass counterfeit or paper currency. • Mar. 4, 1843. Nauvoo, IL.

JS spent most of the morning in the office in "cheerful conversation" with Willard Richards and others. About noon he lay down on the writing table with his head on a pile of law books and said, "Write and tell the world I acknowledge myself a very great lawyer; I am going to study law, and this is the way I study it." He then fell asleep. • Mar. 18, 1843. Nauvoo, IL.

JS settled all debts to Robert D. Foster with a promissory note. • Mar. 20, 1843. Nauvoo, IL.

Jacob Bump Administrator for the Estate of Stannard v. Brigham Young and Joseph Smith: Collection order returned to the court with no assets having been found. • Mar. 28, 1843. Geauga Co., OH.

JS received a letter from former United States senator Richard M. Young of Quincy, Illinois, containing a bond for a quarter section of land. • Mar. 25, 1843. Nauvoo, IL.

JS moved his office to the Red Brick Store. He was so insulted by Josiah Butterfield (stepfather of the two Lawrence heirs who were later sealed to JS), that he kicked Butterfield "out of the house, across the yard and into the street." • Mar. 28, 1843. Nauvoo, IL.

As mayor, JS rendered judgment against Robert D. Foster for nonpayment of his debt. • Mar. 29, 1843. Nauvoo, IL.

Webb v. Rigby: After deciding the case, JS fined defense attorney O. C. Skinner for insulting a witness and for contempt of court. • Mar. 30, 1843. Nauvoo, IL.

State of Illinois v. Jonathan Hoopes and Lewis Hoopes: JS sat with several brethren in the municipal court on a writ of habeas corpus and discharged Jonathan and Lewis Hoopes. • April 4, 1843. Nauvoo, IL.

Dana v. Brink: When the case was heard on appeal from the Nauvoo Mayor's Court, Chief Justice JS and his Associate Justices found that the right of appeal did not lie with their court. • Apr. 13 and 19, 1843. Nauvoo, IL.

City of Nauvoo v. Driggs: Execution on goods of Samuel Driggs. Plaintiff recovered $9.43¾ in costs. • Apr. 26, 1843. Nauvoo, IL.

Nauvoo City Ordinance: Prohibited any swine running at large within the city, imposing a fine of five dollars upon the owner of any swine that did so, and established that any unclaimed or unidentified swine be taken to the Marshal's office in order to determine the owner's identity. • May 12, 1843. Nauvoo, IL.

Dana v. Brink: The defendant appealed the case to the Hancock Circuit Court by *certiorari* bond. After a series of continuances and a motion to arrest judgment, the plaintiff recovered of the defendant $75 plus costs in May 1844. • May 15, 1843. Carthage, IL.

City of Nauvoo v. Hunter: Hunter made a motion to dismiss the suit. • May 16, 1843. Carthage, IL.

JS dined with Judge Stephen A. Douglas and prophesied that the judge would aspire to the presidency of the United States but that if he ever turned against the Saints, he would feel the hand of the Almighty. • May 18, 1843. Carthage, IL.

City of Nauvoo v. Hunter: The motion for dismissal was sustained. The defendant recovered his costs. • May 23, 1843. Carthage, IL.

City of Nauvoo v. Davis: The County Circuit Court affirmed the convictions of Dec. 2, 1841, for the liquor sales and assault violations but reversed the conviction of Davis's allegded slander against JS. • May 24, 1843. Nauvoo, IL.

City of Nauvoo v. Simpson (Nauvoo Municipal Court): Execution issued by clerk James Sloan. No property was found on which to levy as of July 3, 1843. • May 26, 1843. Nauvoo, IL.

In the Red Brick Store, JS and Emma Smith were sealed for eternity. • May 28, 1843. Nauvoo, IL.

State of Missouri v. Smith (Daviess Co. Circuit Court): A Daviess County grand jury indicted JS for alleged treason arising out of 1838 activities. • June 1843. Gallatin, MO.

Nauvoo City Ordinances: Gave JS the authorization and license to run a ferry service across the Mississippi using the *Maid of Iowa,* which he had previously purchased a part interest in. Called for the immediate extermination of any animal that had been "bitten or worried" by a rabid animal and imposed a fine of one thousand dollars upon the owner. Also allowed for the killing of any dog found more than twenty rods from their masters, within city limits. • June 1, 1843. Nauvoo, IL.

JS rendered to Probate Justice of the Peace Andrew Miller his first accounting as Guardian of the Lawrence children and Estate. • June 3, 1843. Quincy, IL.

State of Missouri v. Smith: A letter was sent from Missouri to Illinois Governor Thomas Ford, informing him that JS had been indicted for treason. A special agent, Joseph Reynolds, was sent to apprehend JS. • June 10, 1843. Independence, MO.

State v. Dayley: On oath of JS, a warrant was issued for James Dayley and James McMellin for riot. The defendants were discharged for want of evidence on June 17, 1843. • June 13, 1843. Nauvoo, IL.

State of Illinois v. Smith (Sangamon Co. Circuit Court): Illinois Governor Thomas Ford issued an arrest warrant for JS in connection with the new Missouri treason charge. • June 17, 1843. Springfield, IL.

Nauvoo City Ordinance: Specifically listed the tolls for the passage of various persons, wagons, carriages, and animals across the Mississippi by use of the ferry. • June 20, 1843. Nauvoo, IL.

JS was arrested by Sheriff Joseph H. Reynolds of Jackson County, Missouri, and Constable Harmon T. Wilson of Carthage, Illinois, while JS and Emma were visiting at the home of Emma's sister. Reynolds and Wilson had passed themselves off as Mormon missionaries when inquiring about JS's whereabouts. • June 23, 1843. Near Dixon, IL.

Ex parte Joseph Smith (Ninth Circuit Court, Lee Co.): Although Joseph Reynolds and Harmon Wilson sought to prevent JS from obtaining legal counsel, they were unsuccessful. Smith obtained a writ of habeas corpus, returnable before Judge John D. Caton at Ottawa, Illinois. Cyrus Walker, candidate for U.S. Representative, agreed to serve as Smith's lawyer only after securing his promise to vote for him. • June 24, 1843. Dixon, IL.

Ex parte Joseph Smith: Joseph Reynolds and Harmon Wilson attempted to prevent JS from addressing the local citizens but were rebuked by David Town, "an aged gentleman." • June 26, 1843. Paw Paw Grove, IL.

JS and his entourage returned to Dixon and obtained a second writ of habeas corpus, this one "returnable before the nearest tribunal in the Fifth Judicial District authorized to hear and determine writs of habeas corpus." • June 26, 1843. Dixon, IL.

JS, still in custody of Joseph Reynolds and Harmon Wilson, who were in turn in the custody of the sheriff of Lee County, was joined by members of the Nauvoo Legion and, shedding tears of joy, said, "I am not going to Missouri this time. These are my boys." • June 27, 1843. Fox River near Genesseo, IL.

JS consulted with his lawyers and told them that Nauvoo was the nearest place where writs of habeas corpus could be heard and determined. They agreed and the party, including Joseph Reynolds and Harmon Wilson, turned toward Nauvoo. • June 29, 1843. Near Monmouth, IL.

Nauvoo City Ordinances: Required all strangers entering Nauvoo to give their names, former residence, and what intent they have in being in Nauvoo. Also gave authorities the right to ask whether any of these persons had recently been exposed to any contagious disease or diseases from whence they came. Prohibited citizens of Nauvoo from keeping any animal confined within the City for the purpose of "increasing the passions or ferocity of said animal" or endangering any passer-by. States that only animals such as cows, calves, sheep, goats, and harmless and inoffensive dogs may run at large in the city. Established that if any person swam or bathed in the public waters in Nauvoo and exposed themselves to public view in a state of nudity, they would be fine three dollars for the first offense and charged under the Ordinance Concerning Vagrants and Disorderly Persons for the second offense. • June 29, 1843. Nauvoo, IL.

JS and more than a hundred members of the Nauvoo Legion rode into Nauvoo, where JS was greeted with a band and processional. • June 30, 1843. Nauvoo, IL.

Missouri v. Joseph Smith: JS petitioned the Nauvoo Municipal court for a writ of habeas corpus to quash a warrant issued by Governor Thomas Ford on charges of treason against Missouri. • June 30, 1843. Nauvoo, IL.

Ex parte Joseph Smith (Nauvoo Municipal Court): After a hearing on the return of habeas corpus pertaining to JS's arrest on the Missouri charge of treason, the Nauvoo Municipal court ordered Smith be discharged "for want of substance in the warrant ... as well as upon the merits of the case." • June 30, 1843. Nauvoo, IL.

JS preached in a grove near the Nauvoo Temple concerning traitorous thoughts harbored by some in Nauvoo who professed to be Saints. • July 16, 1843. Nauvoo, IL.

JS told Democratic candidate for the U.S. Congress Joseph P. Hoge that the latest habeas corpus case was "the 38th vexatious lawsuit against me for my religion." • July 24, 1843. Nauvoo, IL.

JS, insulted by Hancock Co. tax collector Walter Bagbee, struck him, knocking him to the ground. JS asked Daniel H. Wells to allow him to plead guilty to Assault and Battery and pay a fine. Wells refused, saying in his opinion the blow was justified. JS went to Justice of the Peace Aaron Johnson, who took the plea and JS paid the fine. • Aug. 1, 1843. Nauvoo, IL.

JS preached to the Saints about politics and the current elections. • Aug. 6, 1843. Nauvoo, IL.

JS preached a sermon honoring Judge Elias Higbee, who had died on June 8, 1843. • Aug. 13, 1843. Nauvoo, IL.

JS received a letter written by Mr. J. Hall of Independence, Missouri, "breathing hard things against us as a people," which he forwarded along with some additional remarks to Illinois Governor Thomas Ford. • Aug. 21, 1843. Nauvoo, IL.

JS as mayor "fined Stephen Wilkinson for selling spirits without a license." JS heard rumors that people in Carthage, Illinois, were raising a mob to drive the Mormons from the state. • Aug. 22, 1843. Nauvoo, IL.

JS read a letter from former Illinois Governor Thomas Carlin written to Sidney Rigdon attempting to clear Rigdon of rumors that he had used his influence "to have JS arrested and delivered to the Missourians." JS called Carlin's letter "evasive" and "a design to hide the truth," but wondered who could have been "concerned in a conspiracy" to deliver him to Missouri. • Aug. 27, 1843. Nauvoo, IL.

State v. Joseph Smith: JS was charged with forgery. • About Sept. 1843. Nauvoo, IL.

JS appointed William W. Phelps, Henry Miller, and Hosea Stout to work with Illinois Governor Thomas Ford to obtain public firearms for the Nauvoo Legion. • Sept. 11, 1843. Nauvoo, IL.

JS had William W. Phelps reply to a recent letter from Illinois Governor Thomas Ford and send him "a copy of the resolutions passed at the meeting of the mobocracy at Carthage." • Sept. 19, 1843. Nauvoo, IL.

Schwartz v. Smith: JS was summoned to appear in circuit court for unlawfully withholding possession of a tract of land from William, Edward, Isabella, Eliza, Horatio, Josiah, Hiram, and Elizabeth Schwartz. • Oct. 1, 1843. Carthage, IL.

State v. Drown: On a habeas corpus petition in the Nauvoo Municipal Court, Charles Drown challenged an arrest on warrant for perjury. The petition for habeas corpus claimed Drown was innocent of crime and was not discharged after his case was heard before Justice of the Peace Leonard E. Harrington. With JS serving as chief judge, execution was issued against goods and chattels of Drown and Bathrick for $24.37½ each, plus costs of court. • Oct. 11, 1843. Nauvoo, IL.

Schwartz v. Smith: JS was provided a copy of the Schwartz's declaration, with instruction to appear at the Hancock County Circuit Court to plead. If Smith failed to appear, the plaintiffs would recover possession of the land. • Oct. 14, 1843. Carthage, IL.

From the speaker's stand east of the Nauvoo Temple, JS preached about the Constitution of the United States, the Bible, and Nauvoo's economy. • Oct. 15, 1843. Nauvoo, IL.

JS received $300 from Orson Spencer to pay to Robert D. Foster. • Oct. 30, 1843. Nauvoo, IL.

Elders Willard Richards and John Taylor spent the day helping JS write letters to presidential candidates about protection of Mormon rights. These letters were sent to John C. Calhoun, General Lewis Cass, Hon. Richard M. Johnson, Hon. Henry Clay, and U.S. President Martin Van Buren. Calhoun, Clay, and Cass responded to JS's queries, but their answers were considered unsatisfactory. • Nov. 4, 1843. Nauvoo, IL.

JS suggested petitioning Congress for a grant to build a canal around the Mississippi River rapids or a dam to turn the water to the city for mills and other machinery. • Nov. 23, 1843. Nauvoo, IL.

State v. Finch: John M. Finch petitioned the Nauvoo Municipal Court for a writ of habeas corpus. Finch had been charged with larceny for allegedly stealing a clothes brush belonging to Amos Davis. The petition for habeas corpus claimed warrant was illegal and did not conform to the laws of the state of Illinois. Finch was discharged by the court. • Nov. 24, 1843. Nauvoo, IL.

JS and the brethren prepared a "memorial" for Congress that included an account of their history and grievances with the state of Missouri. • Nov. 28, 1843. Nauvoo, IL.

At a city council meeting, JS suggested petitioning Congress to have Nauvoo placed under the protection of the United States government. • Dec. 8, 1843. Nauvoo, IL.

JS sent an affidavit to Thomas Ford, governor of Illinois, reporting conditions surrounding the recent kidnapping of Daniel Avery, allegedly by John Elliott and Levi Williams—both later implicated in the murder of JS. • Dec. 11, 1843. Nauvoo, IL.

JS received a letter from Thomas Ford, governor of Illinois, in which Ford claimed he had no place to interfere in individual crimes committed against the Saints in the Avery matter and that punishment belonged to the judicial power and not to the executive. • Dec. 14, 1843. Nauvoo, IL.

JS signed a "Memorial to Congress for redress of losses and grievances in Missouri" and prophesied that if Congress would not hear the petition, the administration in power would be broken up. • Dec. 16, 1843. Nauvoo, IL.

State v. Eagle: On a complaint of JS, John Eagle was charged with robbery and assault with the intent to kill Richard Badham. The defendant was discharged for want of evidence. The case was heard before Justices of the Peace Aaron Johnson and Robert D. Foster. • Dec. 22, 1843. Nauvoo, IL.

Orrin Porter Rockwell appeared at JS's Christmas party, having just been released from jail for nine months in Missouri. He warned JS of a traitor close to both him and to his enemies in Missouri. • Dec. 25, 1843. Nauvoo, IL.

JS pronounced a blessing on the Nauvoo police and offered to pay twice the amount of any bribe offered to them for information about the briber. He also told police he suspected that a Brutus, a Judas, a pretended friend, was helping Missourians try to kidnap and harm him. • Dec. 29, 1843. Nauvoo, IL.

1844

JS wrote a letter to Thomas Ford, governor of Illinois, relative to the kidnapping of certain Saints who were falsely imprisoned in Missouri. • Jan. 1, 1844. Nauvoo, IL.

At city council meetings, William Law complained that JS tried to have city police put him and William Marks "out of the way" as traitors. After interviewing thirty police and others (including Francis Higbee), Law and Marks pledged full devotion to JS. JS warned Higbee to "hold his tongue" lest JS disclose some private matters that Higbee would prefer kept hidden. JS later suspected that William Law and William Marks were "absolutely traitors." • Jan. 3 and 5, 1844. Nauvoo, IL.

JS interviewed William Law in the street and dropped him from the First Presidency. Later, on June 8, Hyrum Smith testified that William had confessed to Hyrum that he had committed adultery. • Jan. 8, 1844. Nauvoo, IL.

JS received a long letter from Francis Higbee, "full of bombast" but not denying any of JS's charges against him. Higbee threatened to sue JS. • Jan. 10, 1844. Nauvoo, IL.

Nauvoo City Ordinance: Emphasized the idea that the foregoing ordinances and resolutions of the City Council of Nauvoo should never be construed to prevent justice, but only to aid and assist

civil officers in ensuring justice. • Jan. 10, 1844. Nauvoo, IL.

City of Nauvoo v. Higbee: In Nauvoo Municipal Court an affidavit of Orson Pratt claimed Francis M. Higbee offered slanderous and abusive language to JS, mayor. At a council hearing for Higbee, JS forgave Higbee for writing his slanderous letter on Jan. 10. Both pledged eternal friendship to the other. • Jan. 16, 1844. Nauvoo, IL.

State v. Simpson: On complaint of JS, Alexander Simpson was suspected of robbery and attempted murder of Richard Badham. Simpson was discharged for want of evidence. • Jan. 17, 1844. Nauvoo, IL.

JS gave a lecture on the Constitution of the United States and on the candidates for the presidency of the United States. • Jan. 19, 1844. Nauvoo, IL.

JS instructed William Clayton to prepare final accounting to the Probate Justice of the Peace in order to transfer the Lawrence guardianship to John Taylor. On the same day Articles of Agreement to effect the transfer were prepared, but never signed by JS or Taylor. • Jan. 23, 1844. Nuavoo, IL.

The Church apostles voted unanimously that JS should be a candidate for president of the United States. JS dictated the main points of his pamphlet, *Views on the Powers and Policy of the Government of the United States.* • Jan. 29, 1844. Nauvoo, IL.

Presiding over the Municipal Court as chief judge, JS spent the whole day listening to different city wards present their tax lists; then he remitted the taxes of the widows and poor. • Feb. 5, 1844. Nauvoo, IL.

JS reported to architect William Weeks that he had seen in vision the pattern for the Nauvoo Temple, which had been under construction since Apr. 1841. • Feb. 5, 1844. Nauvoo, IL.

JS prayed that the Saints would be delivered from the harassment of Thomas Reynolds, governor of Missouri. • About Feb. 7, 1844. Nauvoo, IL.

JS met with his brother Hyrum Smith and the Twelve Apostles to consider ways to promote the interests of the general government. • Feb. 7, 1844. Nauvoo, IL.

At a political meeting in the assembly room above the Red Brick Store, JS gave his reasons for running for the office of president of the United States. • Feb. 8, 1844. Nauvoo, IL.

City of Nauvoo v. Withers: In Nauvoo Mayor's Court, an affidavit of Jacob Shumaker was entered against William Withers for assault. • Feb. 9, 1844. Nauvoo, IL.

Nauvoo City Ordinance: Repealed the previous "Ordinance Regulating the Currency." • Feb. 12, 1844. Nauvoo, IL.

At a city council meeting, JS signed the Memorial to Congress, a document outlining the afflictions of the Saints in Missouri, and he blessed Orson Pratt to prosper in presenting the memorial before government officials in Washington, D.C. • Feb. 12, 1844. Nauvoo, IL.

Davis v. Smith: Proceedings occurred in connection with *State v. John M. Finch*, on habeas corpus, in the Nauvoo Municipal Court. Defendants JS, Orson Spencer, and John P. Green were to bring papers dealing with the imprisonment of John M. Finch. The case was dismissed at defendants' costs on Oct. 21, 1844, due to the death of JS. • Feb. 23, 1844. Carthage, IL.

JS prophesied at a temple block prayer meeting that within five years the Saints would be out of the power of old enemies. • Feb. 25, 1844. Nauvoo, IL.

City of Nauvoo v. Bostwick: In Nauvoo Mayor's Court an affidavit of John Scott claimed O. F. Bostwick conversed with him about Bostwick's belief that Hyrum Smith had acquired spiritual wives and about Bostwick's allegations that there were several prostitutes in Nauvoo. Bostwick was convicted of slander. • Feb. 26, 1844. Nauvoo, IL.

City of Nauvoo v. Bostwick: JS deplored Francis Higbee's appeal to Carthage of Higbee's client's (Orsimus Bostwick's) conviction for slandering Hyrum Smith, as an attempt to "stir up the mob and bring them against us." • Feb. 26, 1844. Nauvoo, IL.

The first meeting was held at William Law's home to organize a conspiracy to destroy the Smiths. It was later reported by Dennison Harris and Robert Scott, who lived there. • Feb. 26, 1844. Nauvoo, IL.

JS held a council with the First Presidency, the Twelve Apostles, the temple committee, and others, emphasizing the importance of finishing the Nauvoo Temple and having it paid for. • Mar. 4, 1844. Nauvoo, IL.

JS proposed James Arlington Bennet as his vice-presidential running mate. • Mar. 4, 1844. Nauvoo, IL.

JS denounced the use of legal appeals to Carthage in a speech to a general assembly. • Mar. 7, 1844. Nauvoo, IL.

Russell v. Smith et al. (Lake Co. Court of Common Pleas): The Lake County Court of Common Pleas entered a default judgment for $16,409.61 against JS and others in a mortgage foreclosure action regarding debts in Ohio. • Mar. 12, 1844. Kirtland, OH. [**Discussed in ch. 10**]

Conspiracy meetings (involving the Higbees, Laws, and Fosters) were described in affidavits by Abiathar Williams and M. G. Eaton. Also, Robert D. Foster claimed that JS had tried to seduce Mrs. Foster. • Mar. 15, 1844. Nauvoo, IL.

Robert D. Foster's wife denied to JS, Alexander Neibaur, and William Clayton that JS had ever tried to seduce her or ever commit any immoral act or preach the plurality of wives. She later changed her story after being threatened by her husband. • Mar. 23, 1844. Nauvoo, IL.

Simpson v. Smith: Alexander Simpson filed a declaration that JS's charges of robbery, attempted murder, and felony against him had tarnished his reputation. [See *State v. Simpson,* Jan. 17, 1844.] Smith entered a plea of not guilty. The plaintiff granted a change of venue to McDonough County on May 23, 1844. • Mar. 28, 1844. Carthage, IL.

JS prepared a written message for United States president John Tyler, requesting permission to enlist a hundred thousand men to help protect Americans seeking to settle in Oregon and other areas within United States territory, and to help provide security for the independent republic of Texas. • Mar. 30, 1844. Nauvoo, IL.

JS investigated a robbery of the Keystone Store, where some of the aforementioned conspiracy meetings had been held. • Mar. 30, 1844. Nauvoo, IL.

State v. Greene: JS and the Municipal Court discharged John P. Greene, Andrew Lytle, and Jonathan Lytle, three city policemen on a writ of habeas corpus after being arraigned on Chauncey L.

Higbee's complaint of false imprisonment. Higbee was charged with costs for bringing a "vexatious and malicious suit." • Apr. 3, 1844. Nauvoo, IL.

JS had an interview with eleven visiting Indians "who wanted counsel." • Apr. 4, 1844. Nauvoo, IL.

JS was served with notice from Amos Davis to produce the docket and other papers for the Circuit Court in a Davis appeal. • Apr. 9, 1844. Nauvoo, IL.

State v. Colton: Andrew Colton (arrested on charge of perjury) appeared on a habeas corpus petition in the Nauvoo Municipal Court claiming that Colton was refused the right to move to another court for a "legal impartial & just examination," and was required to give $200 bail to appear at the Hancock Co. Circuit Court. Execution for $15.03¾ costs. • Apr. 13, 1844. Nauvoo, IL.

JS and other Church leaders excommunicated William, Jane, and Wilson Law and Robert D. Foster for unchristianlike conduct. • Apr. 18, 1844. Nauvoo, IL.

JS as mayor fined Augustine Spencer for assaulting his brother Orson Spencer. Charles A. Foster, Robert D. Foster, and Chauncey L. Higbee were also fined for resisting marshal John Greene while he was arresting Augustine Spencer on JS's orders. Higbee and Charles Foster were also fined for threatening JS with a pistol at the mayor's office. When the pistol was seized by JS and Joseph Coolidge, Robert D. Foster tried to interfere. Because Charles Foster was restrained and jailed, he sued JS, Joseph Coolidge, and John Greene. • Apr. 26, 1844. Nauvoo, IL.

City of Nauvoo v. Foster. JS issued a warrant against Robert D. Foster for slandering Willard Richards. In turn, Foster accused JS "with many crimes." JS tried to settle but when Foster refused, JS "shook his garments" against Foster. • Apr. 26, 1844. Nauvoo, IL.

Brigham Young cursed Foster from the stand and the people cried "Amen." • Apr. 28, 1844. Nauvoo, IL.

The Reformed Church was organized at Wilson Law's home, with William Law as president and Wilson Law as a counselor, Robert D. Foster and Francis M. Higbee as apostles, and Keokuk hotelier Charles Ivins as bishop. This church's apparent purpose was to destroy the Smiths and take control of Nauvoo. • Apr. 28, 1844. Nauvoo, IL.

William and Wilson Law were dropped from the Nauvoo Legion and the Masonic Lodge. • Apr. 29, 1844. Nauvoo, IL.

Higbee v. Smith (Hancock Co. Curcuit Court): Francis Higbee sued JS in Carthage for being slandered before the Nauvoo City Council on Jan. 5, 1844, as a thief, fornicator, whoremaster, murderer, adulterer, and perjurer, with a "rotten stinking [venereal] disease" that kept JS from coming near him; also claiming that JS had urged other young people in Nauvoo to stay away from him. The warrant issued for the arrest of JS in the Hancock County Circuit Court reads: "to answer Francis M. Higbee of a plea of the Case damages the sum of five thousand dollars." Higbee "prayed" for $5,000 in damages against JS. $5,000 was paid in bail. • May 1, 1844. "Nauvoo, IL."

JS could not collect his July 2, 1843, debt from Wilson Law, because Law tried to offset his debt with claims JS had already been paid. Thus, JS said there was no other "remedy but the glorious uncertainty of the law." • May 2, 1844. Nauvoo, IL.

The Nauvoo Municipal Court received notice of appeals from the Nauvoo Mayor's court for cases against Augustine Spencer, Chauncy L. Higbee, Robert D. Foster, and Charles Foster. • May 2, 1844. Nauvoo, IL.

Phelps assignee of Smith v. Law: The case regarded two promissory notes to JS, dated Jan. 24, 1842, which were subsequently assigned to W. W. Phelps on Jan. 1, 1843. Plaintiff took nonsuit, and defendant recovered of plaintiff his costs on May 21, 1845. • May 4, 1844. Nauvoo, IL.

JS addressed a large company of friends at his home on the Saints' course of dealings with the national government. • May 5, 1844. Nauvoo, IL.

Higbee v. Smith: An arrest warrant was served on JS based on the slander complaint of Francis M. Higbee, but JS filed for a writ of habeas corpus from the Nauvoo Municipal Court. • May 6, 1844. Nauvoo, IL.

A printing press was purchased from Abraham Jonas by William Law, the Fosters, and the Higbees, publishers of the new *Nauvoo Expositor,* and arrived at the law office of Robert D. Foster. • May 7, 1844. Nauvoo, IL.

Ex parte Smith (Nauvoo Municipal Court): writ of habeas corpus was granted by the Nauvoo Municipal Court dismissing the charges brought by Higbee with costs assessed against him. • May 8, 1844. Nauvoo, IL.

Higbee v. Smith: JS went before the municipal court (Newel K. Whitney, presiding). The defendant was discharged after nine witnesses proved Francis Higbee's immorality and that his sole motive was to "throw JS into the hands of his enemies ... to carry out a conspiracy ... against his life." Also, the arrest writ was found to be illegal and the complaint was deficient. Higbee was ordered to pay costs; the case was appealed to the Hancock Circuit Court, the venue was changed to the McDonough County Circuit Court, and the case was dismissed. • May 8, 1844. Nauvoo, IL.

Smith v. Street: JS and Hyrum Smith and others sued Charles and Marvin Street and Robert F. Smith as co-purchasers of the steamboat *Nauvoo* for nonpayment of their 1840 promissory notes for $4,000 payable to the plaintiffs. • May 8, 1844. Carthage, IL.

State of Missouri v. Smith: A Lee County jury awarded JS $40 in damages plus court costs against constables Harmon Wilson and Joseph Reynolds for abuse and illegal imprisonment of JS during the third extradition attempt in July 1843. • May 9, 1844. Dixon, IL.

Higbee v. Smith: The case was based again on a complaint for slander arising out of JS's statements to the Nauvoo City Council on Jan. 5. JS allegedly claimed Higbee was guilty of theft, fornication, adultery, and perjury, was a whoremaster, and possessed venereal disease. He "forbid" women from associating with Higbee. Much like the case filed on May 1 and dismissed May 8, 1844, on habeas corpus. The case was transferred on Aug. 14, 1844, to McDonough County and later dismissed there at the plaintiff's cost. • May 10, 1844. Carthage, IL.

Foster v. Smith: Charles A. Foster filed his declaration, charging JS and Joseph W. Coolidge with false imprisonment. Foster allegedly intervened in the attempt by Orrin Porter Rockwell and John P.

Greene to arrest Augustine Spencer for breach of peace. A change of venue was granted to the McDonough Circuit Court. • May 10, 1844. Carthage, IL.

U.S. v. Jeremiah Smith: Jeremiah Smith Sr. petitioned the Nauvoo Municipal Court for a writ of habeas corpus sworn before Chief Judge JS. Jeremiah Smith claimed the warrant for his arrest did not divulge charges known by the law ("obtain money under false pretences") and requested a fair investigation. Execution made on goods and chattels of T. B. Johnson, $7.75 in court costs. • May 16, 1844. Nauvoo, IL.

JS was nominated as a U.S. presidential candidate for the National Reform Party at the Illinois state convention. • May 17, 1844. Nauvoo, IL.

JS and other Church leaders excommunicated Francis M. Higbee, Charles Ivins, and two others. • May 18, 1844. Nauvoo, IL.

Bostwick v. Smith: This case was consolidated with *City of Nauvoo v. Bostwick*. The defendants, Hyrum Smith and John P. Greene, were to provide the Hancock Circuit Court with the proceedings of *City of Nauvoo v. Bostwick* from the Nauvoo Mayor's Court. The case was dismissed at plaintiff's costs. • May 20, 1844. Carthage, IL.

Smith v. Street: The case was dismissed at the plaintiffs' cost. • May 22, 1844. Carthage, IL.

State v. Smith: A grand jury indicted JS for perjury based on Robert D. Foster's oath that JS had sworn a complaint to arrest Alexander Simpson for theft and assault of a Brother Richard Badham outside Nauvoo. (See *State of Illinois v. Simpson,* Jan. 17, 1844.) JS was so irate that he sent Orrin Porter Rockwell and Justice of the Peace Aaron Johnson to have Foster indicted for perjury. They arrived too late and the jury "had risen." • May 23, 1844. Carthage, IL.

JS prophesied to his brother Hyrum that their enemies would lie about Hyrum the same as they had about JS. • May 23, 1844. Nauvoo, IL.

State v. Smith: A grand jury indicted JS for adultery and fornication with Maria Lawrence "and other diverse women," based on William and Wilson Law's testimony. JS considered suing him for perjury and slander on behalf of Maria Lawrence. Dropped the following day when the state's attorney *pro-tem* indicated that he would not prosecute the indictment. • May 23, 1844. Carthage, IL. [**Discussed in ch. 17**]

State v. Smith: Grand jury issued an indictment against Joseph for "adultery and fornication" involving Maria Lawrence and other unnamed women, as well as the one for perjury. The suit abated on Oct. 21, 1844, on account of death of JS.• May 24, 1844. Carthage, IL. [**Discussed in ch. 17**]

JS, accompanied by about twenty friends attended the circuit court in answer to the perjury and adultery indictments against him and some other cases. While in Carthage, JS learned of a plot to kill him en route to court and took extra defensive precautions to ensure his safety. • May 27, 1844. Carthage, IL.

Bostwick v. Smith: Defendant moved to have the case dismissed, and the motion was granted. • May 27, 1844. Carthage, IL.

U.S. v. Jeremiah Smith: Chief Judge JS and the municipal court discharged Jeremiah Smith on a habeas corpus writ despite a federal arrest for alleged fraud. The U.S. was ordered to pay costs. JS tried to arrest the U.S. agent for disturbing the peace by threatening to bring federal troops into Nauvoo to seize the defendant and defy the court. • May 30, 1844. Nauvoo, IL.

City of Nauvoo v. Foster: The breach of ordinance case was appealed from the Nauvoo Municipal Court. A motion to dismiss the suit was entered. • June 3, 1844. Carthage, IL.

JS met with Hyrum, John Taylor and others. Concluded to go to Quincy and "give up my Bonds of guardianship, etc." so that Taylor as new Guardian on behalf of Maria Lawrence and JS in his own right could pursue Perjury and Slander actions against the Laws and Foster. • June 4, 1844. Nauvoo, IL.

The first issue of the *Nauvoo Expositor* appeared, attacking the political powers in Nauvoo and specifically JS and Hyrum Smith. • June 7, 1844. Nauvoo, IL.

Nauvoo City Ordinance: Established the duties of the City Attorney of Nauvoo to advise the officers within Nauvoo, to prosecute in all cases for breaches of Nauvoo City Ordinances, and to collect fines. Also established a salary of one hundred dollars annually for his services. • June 8, 1844. Nauvoo, IL.

Nauvoo City Ordinance: Provided that if any person or persons should write or publish any false statement or libel against another citizen for the "purpose of exciting the public mind against the chartered privileges, peace, and good order of the city" or should slander another, they would be deemed disturbers of the peace and fined up to five hundred dollars, and imprisoned for up to six months. • June 10, 1844. Nauvoo, IL.

After extensive deliberations and consultation of legal authorities, the City Council ordered the town police and Nauvoo Legion to suppress the *Expositor* as a nuisance. They opened a locked door with "not more than one thump" and removed the press, then smashed the press, burned all papers, and "pied" (scattered) the type in Mulholland Street. No other property was destroyed. Francis M. Higbee had said, "this city is done the moment a hand is laid on the press." Also, "you may date their downfall from that very hour and in 10 days, no Mormon will be left in Nauvoo." • June 10, 1844. Nauvoo, IL. [**Discussed in ch. 18**]

JS wrote a proclamation that was published in the *Nauvoo Neighbor* regarding the promulgation of false statements injurious to the people of Nauvoo. • June 11, 1844. Nauvoo, IL.

State v. Smith: Based on a complaint filed by Francis M. Higbee in Carthage, Illinois, JS and the city council and participating police were arrested by a Carthage constable and charged with riot for destruction of the *Nauvoo Expositor*. JS went before the Nauvoo Municipal Court with George W. Harris presiding on Justice Aaron Johnson's writ of habeas corpus and was acquitted. Thomas Sharp and the *Warsaw Signal* urged "war and extermination" against the Mormon leaders. • June 12, 1844. Nauvoo, IL.

State v. Hyrum Smith et al.: Presiding over the Nauvoo Municipal Court, JS discharged all of the other sixteen defendants in the *Expositor* matter. Francis Higbee was assessed all of the court costs for malicious prosecution. JS received a report that a mob of about three hundred was assembled at Carthage, Illinois, and was ready to attack Nauvoo. • June 13, 1844. Nauvoo, IL.

JS dictated a letter to Illinois Governor Thomas Ford explaining the destruction of the *Nauvoo Expositor* printing press. • June 14, 1844. Nauvoo, IL.

Foster v. Smith et al. At the urging of presiding judge Jesse Thomas from Carthage, all seventeen defendants in the *Expositor* case were arrested again on a complaint by W. G. Ware of Carthage and tried before Justice of the Peace Daniel H. Wells, a non-Mormon. After a full day's trial, all defendants were acquitted on the merits. The *Warsaw Signal* called for the extermination of all Latter-day Saints in Illinois. • June 17, 1844. Nauvoo, IL.

Truman Gillett Jr. gives an affidavit that William Law had been involved in a plot to abduct JS in June 1842, but Gillett had discounted the tale until learning of Law's later misdeeds. • June 18, 1844. Nauvoo, IL.

JS declared martial law and stood in full military uniform on the frame of a building to give his final address to the Nauvoo Legion. • June 18, 1844. Nauvoo, IL.

JS met the Nauvoo Legion at the front of his home and gave orders to have a picket guard posted on all the roads leading out of the city, to have all the powder and lead in the city secured, and to have all the arms put into use. • June 19, 1844. Nauvoo, IL.

JS prepared for the defense of Nauvoo against the growing mob. He appealed to Governor Thomas Ford and even to U.S. President John Tyler, wrote letters telling those on missions to come home immediately, and advised his brother Hyrum Smith to take his family on the next steamboat to Cincinnati, Ohio. Hyrum refused to leave his brother. Robert D. Foster wrote to warn Amos Davis "to keep his eyes open, as we learn that consecration law will soon commence on him." • June 20, 1844. Nauvoo, IL.

JS wrote a letter to Illinois Governor Thomas Ford explaining the difficulties in Nauvoo and asking Ford to visit. Governor Ford addressed his reply to the mayor (JS) and the Nauvoo City Council and concluded that the destruction of the *Nauvoo Expositor* was a violation of the laws protecting freedom of the press in the United States. • June 21, 1844. Nauvoo, IL.

State v. Hyrum Smith et al.: Governor Ford and Jesse Thomas, Presiding Judge of the Illinois Fifth Judicial Circuit, urged that yet another trial of the *Expositor* case should be held, this time in Carthage on appeal to the Hancock County Circuit Court. With the promise of full protection pledged by Governor Ford, JS and Hyrum Smith decided to go voluntarily to Carthage, Illinois, for the hearing. • June 23, 1844. Nauvoo, IL.

State v. Hyrum Smith et al.: All seventeen defendants rode to Carthage, finding the town in turmoil. • June 24, 1844. Carthage, IL.

State v. Hyrum Smith et al.: In the morning, Thomas Ford, governor of Illinois, paraded JS and Hyrum Smith through the unruly ranks of the troops assembled by his orders from the surrounding counties. JS and the other defendants were arraigned before Justice of the Peace Robert F. Smith, also Captain of the Carthage Grays. On motion by Chauncey L. Higbee, the case was postponed until October, because Francis Higbee, a key witness, had failed to appear. All the defendants posted bail, even in excessive amounts, and the case was continued to the October Term. • June 25, 1844. Carthage, IL.

State v. Joseph and Hyrum Smith: In the courtroom, JS and Hyrum Smith were served writs charging them with treason, a nonbailable offense, for placing Nauvoo under martial law on June 18, 1844. Despite there having been no hearing on that new charge, the defendants were taken to the Carthage Jail that evening under protective custody. The two treason complaints against JS and Hyrum were apparently signed by Augustine Spencer and Henry Norton, respectively. John Taylor called them "two worthless fellows not worth 5 cents between them." Governor Ford speculated that the charges of treason were based on declaring martial law in Nauvoo and resisting the "posse comitatus." • June 25, 1844. Carthage, IL.

State v. Joseph and Hyrum Smith: In court, JS moved for a change of venue on the charge of treason brought against him. JS had two lawyers, Woods and Reid; the state had five. The motion was denied, and the case was continued until noon the next day, allowing time to bring witnesses to Carthage. They were taken back to jail, where JS had an extensive interview with Governor Thomas Ford. Again Ford promised JS and the other prisoners full protection. The hearing was changed to June 29, apparently without consulting the defendants. • June 26, 1844. Carthage, IL.

JS prepared a list of witnesses regarding the charge of treason to give to Cyrus Wheelock. Governor Ford took the most neutral troops away from Carthage for a visit to Nauvoo, leaving the Carthage Greys to guard the jail. The last letter written by JS was an urgent request for legal services from O. H. Browning. While in protective custody at Carthage Jail, JS and Hyrum Smith were both shot and killed by an armed mob. After their deaths, the treason cases causing the Smiths' incarceration were dismissed. • June 27, 1844. Carthage, IL.

Smith v. Cowdery: The suit was dismissed from the Hancock County Chancery Court for want of prosecution. • June 29, 1844. Carthage, IL.

Emma appeared in the Hancock County Probate Court and was appointed administratrix of JS's estate, and guardian of her four children. • July 17, 1844. Hancock County, IL.

City of Nauvoo v. Foster: The case was appealed from the Nauvoo Municipal Court. • July 26, 1844. Carthage, IL.

Foster v. Smith: Plaintiff's attorney Almon W. Babbitt made a motion to require Foster to post a Cost Bond because he was insolvent. • Aug. 26, 1844. Carthage, IL.

Emma Smith and William Clayton went to Quincy to consult with Justice Miller regarding what should be done about the Lawrence guardianship. He advised that a final accounting and new Guardian needed to be filed and appointed respectively. • Aug. 31 and Sept. 1. Quincy, IL.

People v. Williams 1: Twenty-three grand jurors, who would hear evidence against the accused assassins, were designated by the county commissioners. Despite Latter-day Saints comprising approximately half of the population, not one grand juror was a Mormon. • Sept. 5, 1844. Hancock Count, IL.

Almon Babbittt appointed legal guardian of the five Lawrence children. • Sept. 5, 1844. Hancock County, IL.

Dana v. Brink: Precipe was filed requesting a copy of the May 16, 1843, certiorari bond. Brink persists in failing to pay the bond or damages. • Sept. 17, 1844. Carthage, IL.

Joseph W. Coolidge succeeded Emma as administrator of JS's estate. • Sept. 19, 1844. Hancock County, IL.

People v. Williams 1: Murray McConnell, appointed as special agent to gather evidence, began issuing warrants for the arrest of those suspected of being involved in the murders. • Sept. 22, 1844. Hancock County, IL.

Charles Ivins, William Law, Wilson Law, Chauncey Higbee, Francis Higbee, Robert Foster, Charles Foster v. Edward Hunter, Orson Spencer, John P. Greene, Stephen Markham, Alpheus Cutler & Joseph W. Collidge: Ivins with the Laws, Fosters, and Higbees, sued for civil damages resulting from the destruction of the *Expositor* printing press. • Sept. 1844. Carthage, IL.

City of Nauvoo v. Foster: In a full jury trial, all remaining defendants were acquitted of riot and destruction of property by the County Circuit Court in its October term. • Oct. 1844. Carthage, IL.

People v. Williams 1: After being relentlessly pursued by Governor Ford's forces, Defendants Sharp and Williams surrender themselves. • Oct. 1, 1844. Carthage, IL.

People v. Williams 1: Defendants Sharp and Williams avoid a preliminary hearing to determine probable cause, and with it the possibility of being held without bail, by entering into an agreement with the prosecution. They waived the right to a hearing in exchange for being able to go free upon posting a relatively small bail. • Oct. 2, 1844. Quincy, IL.

Charles Ivins, William Law, Wilson Law, Chauncey Higbee, Francis Higbee, Robert Foster, Charles Foster v. Edward Hunter,

Orson Spencer, John P. Greene, Stephen Markham, Alpheus Cutler & Joseph W. Collidge: Three promisory notes totaling $625 were delivered by seven LDS property owners in settlement of this case. The notes were ultimately paid by Hiram Kimball in May 1849 after further litigation. • About Oct. 5, 1844. Carthage, IL.

Dana v. Brink: Suit is dismissed at plaintiff's costs. • Oct. 19, 1844. Carthage, IL.

City of Nauvoo v. Foster: Plaintiff's attorney moved that the suit be dismissed and defendant recovered costs from the plaintiff. • Oct. 21, 1844. Carthage, IL.

People v. Williams 1: After presenting the names of approximately sixty persons for indictment in the murders of JS and Hyrum Smith, two separate signed indictments were filed against nine defendants: John Wills, William Voras, William N. Grover, Jacob C. Davis, Mark Aldrich, Thomas C. Sharp, Levi Williams, Gallaher, and Allen. • Oct. 26, 1844. Carthage, IL.

1845

People v. John C. Elliott: Arrested in Nauvoo for the murder of JS and Hyrum Smith. Three Nauvoo Justices of the Peace found probable to support the charge, and sent him to the Carthage jail to await the May grand jury. • Feb. 11, 1845. Nauvoo, IL.

People v. Benjamin Brackenbury: Arrested, accused of testifying falsely about Levi Williams being on horseback in Carthage during the murders. • Mar. 10, 1845. Carthage, IL.

Reid v. Smith: Payment in case of charge of riot and treason by the state of Illinois. • Apr. 1845.

Almon Babbitt submitted a claim of $4,033.87 against the estate of JS, on behalf of the Lawrence heirs. Coolidge approved the claim. • May 6, 1845. Hancock County, IL.

People v. Williams 1: Trial convened for five indicted assassins, Levi Williams, Thomas C. Sharp, Mark Aldrich, Jacob C. Davis, and William N. Grover. • May 19, 1845. Carthage, IL.

People v. John C. Elliott: John C. Elliott was accused of murdering JS. The grand jury refused to indict. • May 1845. Carthage, IL.

People v. Williams 1: All of the defendants were acquitted for the murder of JS and Hyrum Smith. • June 1845. Carthage, IL.

Smith v. Emmons: Suit was brought on an attested debt of $22.75. Sylvester Emmons was subpoenaed on June 22, 1844. Lucien Woodworth and Eliza Partridge were also subpoenaed. • June 7, 1845. Nauvoo, IL.

Sweeney v. Miller: JS, Guy C. Sampson (Sweeney's attorney), transferred judgment to Sheriff William Backenstos of Nauvoo, who collected from the Church trustees. Backenstos later transferred the May 5, 1842, judgment to the Church Trustees Almon W. Babbitt, Joseph L. Heywood, and John S. Fullmer on Apr. 4, 1846. • Aug. 14, 1845. Carthage, IL.

Almon W. Babbitt, Guardian for heirs of Edward Lawrence v. William Law, Joseph Coolidge: Almon W. Babbitt, acting as guardians for the Lawrence heirs, filed suit against the estates of JS and Hyrum Smith, and against William Law (based on Hyrum and Law's bond for JS as guardian). • Sept. 1, 1845. Hancock County, IL. [**Discussed in ch. 16**]

Almon W. Babbitt, Guardian for heirs of Edward Lawrence v. William Law, Joseph Coolidge: Babbitt withdrew his claim. • Oct. 23, 1845. Hancock County, IL.

In speaking of the martyrdom of JS, Robert D. Foster told Abraham Hodge: "I haven't seen one moment's peace since that time. . . . The thought of meeting Joseph and Hyrum Smith at the bar of God is more awful to me than anything else." • Nov. 2, 1845. Nauvoo, IL.

1846

Almon W. Babbitt, Guardian for heirs of Edward Lawrence v. Smith and Coolidge: Babbitt filed a new action, adding Sarah and Maria Lawrence as co-petitioners. Babbitt filed only against the estates of JS and Hyrum. • Jan. 1846. Hancock County, IL.

Almon W. Babbitt, Guardian for heirs of Edward Lawrence v. Smith and Coolidge: The case was tried. Mary Fielding Smith and Joseph Coolidge failed to appear. After hearing evidence of damages, judgment was rendered against each estate for $4,275.88 plus court costs. It does not appear that Babbit made any effort to execute on the judgments. • May 19, 1846. Hancock County, IL.

1848

John M. Ferris was appointed administrator of JS's estate, following the appointments of Emma Smith (in July 1844) and of Joseph Coolidge (on Sept. 19, 1844). • Aug. 8, 1848. Carthage, IL.

1850

United States v. Smith: The United States brought actions against the estate of JS and 104 defendants for nonpayment of the 1840 debt to Robert E. Lee for the purchase of the steamboat *Nauvoo*. No fraud was found, but foreclosures were permitted by Judge Thomas Drummond against nearly 4,000 acres originally owned by JS. Four public sales were conducted locally through July 17, 1852. • Aug. 19 and Dec. 4, 1850. Springfield, IL.

Lawyers and Judges
in the Legal Cases of Joseph Smith

Because of his frequent and varied encounters with the law, Joseph Smith relied heavily on lawyers for legal advice and representation in court. Serious consequences often rested on the outcomes of these cases, so it was vital that Joseph select competent, trustworthy lawyers. Choosing an attorney in Joseph's day was not easy. Attorneys on the frontier were often young and not well established. The Mormon cause was usually unpopular, and non-Mormon attorneys sometimes worried that they would be stigmatized and lose business if they associated with Mormons. Additionally, having been driven from one place to another, the Mormons were impoverished yet often forced to pay significant legal fees for the best lawyers. Nearly all of those who represented Joseph and his people went on to become highly successful professionals, and many would later hold high local and national political offices. This appendix includes biographical sketches of the lives of the lawyers with whom Joseph interacted, both for and against him, and of some of the judges Joseph appeared before, as well as a number of legal advisors with whom he consulted. Although a few of these were Mormons, most were not. By giving information about their professional careers, this appendix aims to provide a better context for Joseph's legal world.

ADAMS, James (1783–1843). Adams was born in Simsbury, Connecticut. He moved to New York and served in the militia as ensign, lieutenant, captain, and major and as brigadier general in the War of 1812. In 1812 he settled at Springfield, Illinois, and became a pioneer attorney of Sangamon County, where he was referred to as General Adams. He served with the Illinois militia in the Winnebago War in 1827 and the Black Hawk War in 1831–32 and in 1839 became Worshipful Master of Springfield Masonic Lodge. Adams converted to the LDS faith around 1836 but probably first met Joseph Smith in

1839 in Springfield. He became a regent of the University of Nauvoo in 1840. In 1841 he became a probate judge at Springfield. He was ordained a high priest by Hyrum Smith in 1841, served as branch president in Springfield in 1842, and was ordained a patriarch by Joseph Smith. He was elected probate judge of Hancock County in 1843 and died of cholera the same year.

Power, John. *History of the Early Settlers of Sangamon County, Illinois,* 76. Springfield, Illinois, 1876.

Smith, Joseph, Jr. *History of The Church of Jesus Christ of Latter-day Saints,* ed. B. H. Roberts, 4:20; 5:527–28; 6:510. 2d ed., rev., 7 vols. Salt Lake City: Deseret Book, 1971.

Walgren, Kent L. "James Adams: Early Springfield Mormons and Freemasons." *Journal of the Illinois State Historical Society* 75 (Summer 1982): 121–36.

Church Historian's Press. "James Adams." The Joseph Smith Papers, http://josephsmithpapers.org/person/adams-james (accessed November 21, 2013).

ATCHISON, David Rice (1807–1886). Atchison was one of the first attorneys in northwest Missouri. He was educated at Transylvania University in Kentucky, one of the best institutions in the west at the time. Atchison continued his education by working two years as a clerk in the office of a former Kentucky senator, Judge Jesse Bledsoe, then set out to practice on his own and in about 1830 moved to Missouri. Atchison's first of many interactions with the Mormons came in 1833, when a mob forced them to leave Jackson County and destroyed Mormon homes and shops. After consulting with Joseph Smith, Bishop Edward Partridge and W. W. Phelps retained Atchison, along with Alexander Doniphan, Amos Rees, and William Wood. The attorneys were initially reluctant to represent the Mormons and asked for a substantial $1,000 retainer, which was a burdensome amount for the Mormons. Their actions were largely unsuccessful, both in pressing for criminal charges and recovering civil damages. Atchison was the commanding officer of third division of the Missouri state militia during the Mormon conflict in 1838. Interestingly, command of the army that was to carry out Governor Boggs's extermination order in October 1838 could have been given to Atchison. Boggs, however, gave command to another, likely because of Atchison's reputation as friendly to the Mormons. Joseph's earlier appreciation for Atchinson cooled as a result of his Liberty Jail imprisonment. In March of 1839 Joseph wrote to castigate the Missouri mobbers and politicians, noting that "General Atchinson has proved himself as contemptible as any of them." Atchison was elected to the Missouri legislature in 1834, and in 1841 he was appointed by Governor Thomas Reynolds as a circuit court judge. He served as a U.S. senator for eleven years (1843 to 1855), acting as President Pro-tem for six years. As a strong pro-slavery advocate, Atchinson was influential in framing the Kansas-Nebraska Act of 1854, being himself a slave owner.

Anderson, Richard L. "Atchison's Letters and the Causes of Mormon Expulsion from Missouri." *BYU Studies* 26, no. 3 (1986): 3–28.

"Atchison, David Rice." *American National Biography.* New York: Oxford University Press, 1999.

Atchison, Theodore. "David R. Atchison, a Study in American Politics." *Missouri Historical Review* 24 (July 1930): 502–15.

Parrish, William E. *David Rice Atchison of Missouri: Border Politician.* University of Missouri Press, 1961.

BABBITT, Almon Whiting (1812–1856). Babbitt, baptized about 1830, had a tumultuous relationship with the Church. He became a member of Zion's Camp in 1834 and served in many Church callings including as a member of Zion's Camp, a missionary, a seventy in 1835, president of the Kirtland Stake in 1841, president of the Ramus, Illinois, branch in 1843, and a member of the Council of Fifty. However, he was subject to formal church discipline a number of times, being disfellowshipped at least four times. Babbitt was an attorney by profession and served as counsel for the Church on several occasions. In particular Babbitt remained in Nauvoo in 1844 to take charge of the Mormon property after the Saints had been expelled. His signature is found on the document that ultimately surrendered the city of Nauvoo. The day before Joseph Smith was killed in Carthage Jail, Joseph sent a message asking Babbitt to represent him in the expected trial, to which Babbitt told the messenger, "You are too late, I am already engaged on the other side." Babbitt also had an expansive political history, first serving as a delegate to Congress for the provisional State of Deseret in 1849, and later as secretary and treasurer of the Utah Territory in 1852. Babbitt was excommunicated in May of 1854. He was killed in an attack in Nebraska Territory in 1856, ostensibly at the hands of hostile Indians.

Anderson, Gary. "Almon W. Babbitt and the Golden Calf." In *Regional Studies in Latter-day Saint Church History: Illinois,* ed. H. Dean Garrett, 35–54. Provo, Utah: Brigham Young University, 1995.

Church Historian's Press. "Babbitt, Almon Whiting." The Joseph Smith Papers, http://josephsmithpapers.org/person/almon-whiting-babbitt (accessed July 2, 2013).

Omer, Greg, W. Whitman, and James L. Varner. *Neither Saint nor Scoundrel: Almon Whiting Babbitt—Territorial Secretary of State.* N.p.: PublishAmerica, 2008.

BIERCE, Lucius Verus (1801–1876). Bierce was an attorney, military general, and politician in Ohio. He served as district attorney and county prosecuting attorney in Portage County, Ohio. He was brigadier general in the Ohio militia and commander in chief of the Patriot army during Patriot War in Upper Canada, 1837–1839. He was elected as mayor of Akron numerous times and then as Ohio state senator. Bierce first met Joseph Smith in April

1834 and had a respectful relationship with the Prophet from that time forward. In particular, Bierce counseled Joseph personally regarding the numerous charges brought against Joseph by Grandison Newell.

Church Historian's Press. "Bierce, Lucius Verus," The Joseph Smith Papers, http://josephsmithpapers.org/person?name=Lucius+Verus+Bierce.

Bierce, L. V. *Historical Reminiscences of Summit County,* Akron, Ohio: Canfield, 1854.

Doyle, William B. *Centennial History of Summit County, Ohio, and Representative Citizens.* Chicago: Biographical Publishing, 1908.

BISSELL (BISSEL), Benjamin (1805–1878). Bissel was a well-respected lawyer and judge in Ohio who represented the Church on various important occasions. James Briggs, the opposing lawyer in the Hurlbut series of cases, described Bissel as "the consummate practitioner of the art of legal defense." Similarly, Justice Dallin of the Ohio Supreme Court called Bissel "one of Ohio's ablest lawyers."Bissel began practicing law around 1830 in Geauga County, Ohio. He defended Joseph in a variety of cases, including in 1834 against Doctor Philastus Hurlbut, who threatened Joseph's life. In 1835, Joseph blamed Bissel for not telling the Smiths (Hyrum, Samuel, and Don Carlos) how to provide documentation to avoid fines for not performing military duty. Bissel assisted Joseph in escaping the hands of a mob in 1837. Bissel went on to become an Ohio state senator in 1839–40 and was instrumental in creating Lake County, Ohio. In 1837 he formed the law firm Bissell & Axtell, with Salmon B. Axtell, and practiced with Axtell until 1842. He served as an Ohio circuit judge from 1842 until 1857. Oliver Cowdery began his study of law under Bissel's tutelage in Ohio in 1838.

Church Historian's Press. "Bissell (Bissel), Benjamin." The Joseph Smith Papers, http://josephsmithpapers.org/person/benjamin-bissell-bissel (accessed July 2, 2013).

Jessee, Dean C., Mark Ashurst-McGee, and Richard L. Jensen, eds. *Journals, Volume 1: 1832–1839,* vol. 1 of the Journals series of *The Joseph Smith Papers,* ed. Dean C. Jessee, Ronald K. Esplin, and Richard Lyman Bushman, 75. Salt Lake City: Church Historian's Press, 2008.

Riddle, A. G. *History of Geauga and Lake Counties, Ohio: With Illustrations and Biographical Sketches of Its Pioneers and Most Prominent Men,* 30. Evansville, Ind.: Unigraphic, 1973.

Walker, Jeffrey N. "Oliver Cowdery's Legal Practice in Tiffin, Ohio." In *Days Never to Be Forgotten: Oliver Cowdery,* ed. Alexander L. Baugh, 295–326. Provo, UT: Religious Studies Center, Brigham Young University, 2009.

BROWNING, Orville Hickman (1806–1881). Browning was a Kentucky legislator and veteran of the Black Hawk War. He later moved to Illinois, where he served in the Illinois Senate and House of Representatives. He was well respected in the legal community; one colleague noted that Browning was "perhaps the ablest speaker in the State." In 1841, Browning, along with Charles A. Warren, Sidney B. Little, James H. Ralston, Cyrus Walker, and Archibald Williams, represented Joseph Smith in an extradition hearing, despite personal threats against Browning. His two-hour final remarks brought Judge Stephen Douglas and others to tears and was described as "one of the most eloquent speeches ever uttered by mortal man in favor of justice and liberty." On the day of his assassination, Joseph's last piece of recorded writing was addressed to Browning, requesting his services. Browning was subsequently part of the legal team that successfully defended the five men charged with the assassination of Joseph and Hyrum Smith. Following Douglas's untimely death in 1861, Browning was appointed to fill his U.S. Senate seat. In 1866, President Andrew Johnson appointed Browning Secretary of the Interior, where he served for three years. Browning served briefly as Attorney General and launched an unsuccessful campaign for appointment to the U.S. Supreme Court.

Baxter, Maurice G. *Orville H. Browning, Lincoln's Friend and Critic.* Bloomington, Indiana: University Press, 1957.

"Browning, Orville Hickman." Biographical Directory of the United States Congress, http://bioguide.congress.gov/scripts/biodisplay.pl?index=b000960 (accessed July 2, 2013).

"History of Joseph Smith." *Millennial Star* 18 (August 30, 1856): 551.

Pease, Theodore Calvin, and James G. Randall, eds. *The Diary of Orville H. Browning, 1850–1881.* 2 vols. Springfield, Ill.: Illinois State Historical Society, 1927–33.

BURCH, Thomas (also BIRCH) (ca. 1807–1839). Burch was likely born in Tennessee. He began law practice in 1831 at Richmond, Ray County, Missouri, and then served as circuit attorney for Ray County in 1838. He was appointed judge of the Eleventh Judicial Circuit later the same year. On April 9, 1839, Burch presided over the grand jury proceedings for Joseph Smith and the Mormon leaders at Gallatin, Daviess County. Joseph later described: "Our trial commenced before a drunken grand jury, Austin A. King, presiding judge, as drunk as the jury; for they were all drunk together." (The reference to King is undoubtedly a mistake; Hyrum Smith later correctly explained that "Birch, who was the district attorney, the same man who had been one of the court martial when we were sentenced to death, was now the circuit judge of that pretended court." Hyrum also maintained that the members of the grand jury were all participants "at the massacre at Haun's Mills.") Sometime before the proceedings, the Missouri State legislature amended its venue statute, which allowed the Mormons to challenge Burch's continuing role, since he had previously served as prosecuting attorney for the state at the earlier hearing in Richmond presided over by Judge Austin King. As a result, Joseph and the others obtained a change of venue to Boone County. During the trip to Boone County they were allowed to escape, possibly with the secret encouragement of Judge Burch.

Church Historian's Press. "Burch, Thomas." The Joseph Smith Papers, http://josephsmithpapers.org/person/burch-thomas (accessed November 16, 2013).

Smith, Joseph, Jr. *History of The Church of Jesus Christ of Latter-day Saints,* ed. B. H. Roberts, 3:421–23. 2d ed., rev., 7 vols. Salt Lake City: Deseret Book, 1971.

BURNETT, Peter H. (1807–1895). Burnett was a self-educated attorney who was admitted to the Missouri bar in 1839. That same year Burnett defended Joseph Smith in the grand jury hearing in Daviess County, where Joseph and others were indicted for treason, arson, and robbery. The hearing was very hostile, as a mob within the courtroom was armed and angry. Burnett and other attorneys for Smith armed themselves in self-defense. Burnett promised to "kill the first man that attack[ed]." During the hearing Burnett requested a change of venue to Boone County. While in transit to the new venue, the defendants were assisted in their escape to Illinois by the sheriff who was escorting them. Of the Prophet Joseph, Burnett said that he "was more than an ordinary man" and that even in the face of a mob, Joseph had the ability to tell his story and convince people. Burnett left Missouri in 1843, when he organized a wagon train and traveled to Oregon, where he later served in the Territorial Legislature of Oregon and on the Oregon Territorial Supreme Court. In 1848 he and his family moved to California in search of gold. In 1849 Burnett was elected the first governor of the State of California, serving until 1851. After resigning from office, Burnett served as a justice of the California Supreme Court from 1857 to 1858, as a member of the Sacramento City Council, and as president of the Pacific Bank of San Francisco.

Burnett, Peter Hardeman. *Recollections and Opinions of an Old Pioneer.* New York: D. Appleton and Co., 1880.

Launius, Roger D. "Burnett, Peter Hardeman (1807–1895)." In *Dictionary of Missouri Biography,* ed. Lawrence O. Christensen et al., 134–35. Missouri: University of Missouri Press, 1999.

Melendy, H. Brett. *The Governors of California: From Peter H. Burnett to Edmund G. Brown.* Georgetown, Calif.: Talisman Press, 1965.

BUTTERFIELD, Justin (1790–1855). Butterfield was a respected Illinois attorney with a quick wit. He practiced law in New York and Louisiana before moving to Illinois. In Chicago, Butterfield became a leader of the local bar and was appointed federal district attorney in 1841 for the District of Illinois.

One colleague noted that Butterfield was "one of the most learned, talented, and distinguished members of the Bar." Another colleague commented that he "was one of the ablest, if not the very ablest lawyer we have ever had at the Chicago Bar. He was strong, logical, full of vigor and resources." Butterfield first met Joseph Smith in 1841, when the then–Solicitor of the Treasury, Charles B. Penrose, asked Butterfield to collect a debt Joseph owed to the U.S. government. The debt was incurred when Joseph, along with his brother Hyrum and others, purchased a steamship and executed a promissory note to cover the purchase price. Unfortunately, the steamship soon ran aground. Joseph sought to recover the cost from the steamship captain, whom he believed intentionally damaged the ship, and the remaining owners. However, when they could not be located, the balance of the promissory note fell upon Joseph. Eventually a default judgment was entered. Prior to entry of the default judgment, Joseph filed for bankruptcy. Butterfield opposed Joseph's bankruptcy, claiming Joseph had fraudulently conveyed land to hide it from creditors. Even though it was rare to prevail on a bankruptcy opposition, Butterfield petitioned for a hearing on the matter. Yet Butterfield was subsequently lenient and prepared a plan to settle the debt, which he recommended to solicitor General Penrose. The note was paid in full by Smith's estate in 1852.While awaiting a response from Penrose, Butterfield represented Joseph in another case. Joseph was implicated in the attempted assassination of Missouri Governor Lilburn W. Boggs. The State of Missouri filed an extradition requisition in July 1842, and Joseph went into hiding to avoid it. The requisition claimed Smith was an accomplice in Boggs's attempted murder and claimed he had fled from justice. Because Joseph was not in Missouri at the time of the attempted assassination, Butterfield consulted with Illinois Supreme Court Justices, who assured him that Joseph could not be extradited under existing law. At Butterfield's suggestion, Joseph turned himself in and at the extradition hearing Butterfield and his co-counsel, Benjamin Edwards, successfully persuaded Judge Nathaniel Pope to refuse the extradition order. Butterfield's speech included a remark that he appeared on behalf of the Prophet, with the attendance of Apostles, before the Pope (Judge Nathaniel Pope), and in the presence of angels (women present in the court, including Mary Todd Lincoln). After Butterfield's representation of Joseph ended, they maintained an amicable relationship. Professionally, Butterfield went on to serve as the United States Commissioner of the General Land Office from 1849 to 1852.

Butterfield, Justin, to Charles Penrose, December 17, 1842. National Archives, Records of the Solicitor of the Treasury, Record Group 206, Part I (1841–52), microfilm copy at Church History Library, Salt Lake City.

Church Historian's Press. "Butterfield, Justin." The Joseph Smith Papers, http://josephsmithpapers.org/person/justin-butterfield (accessed July 3, 2013).

History of Sangamon County, Illinois. Chicago: Inter-State Publishing Co., 1881.

"Justin Butterfield's Defence of Joe Smith." *Central Law Journal* 2 (1875): 776.

Linder, Usher F., and Joseph Gillispie. *Reminiscences of the Early Bench and Bar of Illinois*, 87–88. Chicago: Chicago Legal News Company, 1879.

Oaks, Dallin H., and Joseph I. Bentley. "Joseph Smith and Legal Process: In the Wake of the Steamboat Nauvoo." *BYU Law Review* (1976): 735–82.

"Opening in Joe Smith's Case." *New Orleans Daily Picayune*, February 24, 1842.

Palmer, John M., ed. *The Bench and Bar of Illinois*, 1:2, 181; 2:613–614. Chicago: Lewis Publishing Company, 1899.

Thurston, Morris A. "The Boggs Shooting and Attempted Extradition: Joseph Smith's Most Famous Case." *BYU Studies* 48, no. 1 (2009): 5–56.

Wilson, John M. *Memoir of Justin Butterfield.* Chicago: Chicago Legal News Co., 1880.

CHAMBERLAIN, Joseph P. (c. 1795–1857). Chamberlain was born in New York, where he served as postmaster, sheriff, justice of the peace and farmer. By 1823 he was living in Bainbridge, Chenango County, New York. Chamberlain served as Justice of the Peace at a trial held for Joseph Smith in Chenango County in 1830.

Hayes, Carlton J.H. *Story of Afton: A New York Town on the Susquehanna.* Afton, N.Y.: Afton Free Library, 1976, p. 16.

Smith, James Hadden. *History of Chenango and Madison Counties, New York: with Illustrations and Biographical Sketches of Some of its Prominent Men and Pioneers*, 117–19, 144, 154. Syracuse, N.Y.: D. Mason and Co., 1880.

COWDERY, Oliver (1806–1850). Cowdery was Joseph Smith's principal scribe in translation of Book of Mormon in 1829, and was one of the Three Witnesses of the Book of Mormon. He led missionaries through Ohio and to Missouri, 1830–31, and assisted William W. Phelps in conducting church's printing operations at Jackson County, Missouri, 1832–33. In 1833 Cowdery moved to Kirtland, where he was a member of United Firm, Literary Firm, and Kirtland High Council. He edited Kirtland continuation of *The Evening and the Morning Star,* the *LDS Messenger and Advocate,* and the *Northern Times.* On October 2, 1835, Joseph Smith gave Oliver a blessing which stated: "Behold, he shall be a choice lawyer in Israel, both pertaining to the law of God and also the law of the land; for he shall have understanding in these matters." He was appointed assistant president of church in 1834 and elected Justice of the Peace in Kirtland in 1837. The same year he moved to Far West, Caldwell County, Missouri, where he was excommunicated in 1838. He then returned to Kirtland and briefly practiced law before relocating to Tiffin, Seneca County,

Ohio, where he continued law practice and held political offices from 1840 to 1847, when he moved to Elkhorn, Wisconsin Territory. He requested and received readmission to the LDS Church in Kanesville, Iowa, in 1848.

> Church Historian's Press, "Oliver Cowdery," The Joseph Smith Papers, http://josephsmithpapers.org/person/cowdery-oliver (accessed December 5, 2013).
>
> "Blessing for Oliver Cowdery, 2 October 1835," The Joseph Smith Papers, http://josephsmithpapers.org/paperSummary/blessing-for-oliver-cowdery-2-october-1835 (accessed December 5, 2013).

DAVIDSON, James (1779–1847). Along with another farmer, John Reed, Davidson represented Joseph Smith in two 1830 New York cases brought in South Bainbridge and Colesville, accusing Joseph of being a disorderly person. After Joseph established a branch of the Church, an element of the Bainbridge community became enraged, and Josiah Stowell's wife's nephew, Peter Bridgman, a Methodist exhorter, pressed charges against Joseph claiming he was a disorderly person who had defrauded his uncle. Immediately following Joseph's discharge in Bainbridge, similar charges were brought in Colesville. Joseph was completely exonerated in both cases.

> Church Historian's Press. "Davidson, James." The Joseph Smith Papers, http://josephsmithpapers.org/person?name=James+Davidson (accessed December 5, 2013).
>
> Vogel, Dan. *Early Mormon Documents*, 4:121–25. 5 vols. Salt Lake City: Signature, 1996.
>
> Smith, Joseph, Jr. *History of the Church of Jesus Christ of Latter-day Saints*, ed. B. H. Roberts, 1:89–96. 2d ed., rev. 7 vols. Salt Lake City: Deseret Book, 1971.

DONIPHAN, Alexander William (1808–1887). Doniphan was a highly respected attorney in the northwestern Missouri region. At Augusta College he was trained in the art of public discourse. After graduating, Doniphan began his study of law by apprenticing in the office of Martin P. Marshall, nephew of Supreme Court Justice John Marshall. After two years and at only twenty years old, Doniphan was admitted to the Kentucky and Ohio bars to practice law. He soon moved to Missouri, drawn by the excitement of a rough country in need of lawyers. Doniphan had many interactions with the Mormons and the Prophet Joseph Smith. He first represented a number of Church leaders in 1833 when he, along with David Atchison, Amos Rees, and William Wood were hired to represent the Mormons in an effort to recover losses from mob violence in Jackson County. The attorneys pressed for criminal prosecution of the mob leaders as well as monetary reimbursement for a few of the victims of the mob action. As a member of the state legislature Doniphan was also instrumental in the formation of Caldwell County, which was intended as a safe haven for the Mormons who had been driven out of Jackson County. In 1838, as tensions began to rise between the Mormons and non-Mormons in western Missouri, Doniphan acted as a liaison in attempting to resolve the conflict. The Mormon leaders eventually turned themselves in, and, after an illegal court martial, the general of the Missouri militia ordered the Mormon leaders be executed. In a show of great courage, Doniphan rebuked the general and refused to carry out the order. From Nov. 12 to 29, 1838, Doniphan and Amos Rees represented Joseph Smith and others in the Richmond Court of Inquiry before Judge Austin King. Although Doniphan's closing remarks were powerful and widely cited for years following, Joseph and the others were bound over for trial and detained in Liberty Jail. In 1843 Doniphan represented Porter Rockwell, who, was along with Joseph Smith, had been accused of the attempted assassination of Governor Lilburn Boggs. Doniphan was successful in his representation, and Rockwell was acquitted. Doniphan had an extensive military career and served as a brigadier general in the state militia and as a colonel in the U.S. Army during the Mexican American War of 1846. He was elected to the Missouri state legislature in 1836, 1840, and 1854.

Dawson, Joseph G. *Doniphan's Epic March: The 1st Missouri Volunteers in the Mexican War.* Lawrence: University Press of Kansas, 1999.

Dawson, Joseph G., III. "American Civil-Military Relations and Military Government: The Service of Colonel Alexander Doniphan in the Mexican War." *Armed Forces & Society* 22, no. 4 (1996): 555–72.

Elliot, R. Kenneth. "Alexander William Doniphan." Clay County Archives and Historical Library, http://claycountyarchives.org/index.php/resources/history/89-alexander-william-doniphan (accessed July 3, 2013).

Launius, Roger D. *Alexander William Doniphan: A Portrait of a Missouri Moderate.* Missouri: University of Missouri Press, 1997.

DOUGLAS, Stephen Arnold (1813–1861). Douglas was a lawyer, judge, and politician who was born in Vermont and moved to Jacksonville, Illinois, in 1833. He served as attorney general of Illinois (1835–36); state representative, (1836–41); Illinois secretary of state (1840–41); state supreme court justice (1841–42); U.S. representative (1843–4) and U.S. senator (1847–61). Douglas visited with Joseph in Nauvoo in May 1841 and enjoyed a close relationship with the Mormons during Joseph's life. As Associate Justice of the Illinois Supreme Court, Douglas conducted a hearing on Joseph Smith's first habeas corpus petition in June of 1841 in response to Missouri's extradition effort, ruling that the warrant used to arrest the prophet was invalid. At a dinner with Douglas in Carthage in 1843, Joseph prophesied: "Judge, you will aspire to the presidency of the United States; and if you ever turn your hand against me or the Latter-day Saints, you will feel the weight of the hand of the Almighty upon you; and you will live to see and know that I have testified the truth to you; for the conversation of this day will stick to you through life." In a political speech in 1857 Douglas castigated the Mormons for their "treasonable, disgusting and bestial practices." Douglas was subsequently defeated by Abraham Lincoln for the US presidency in 1860 and died of typhoid fever on June 3, 1861.

Church Historian's Press. "Douglas, Stephen A." The Joseph Smith Papers, http://josephsmithpapers.org/person/stephen-arnold-douglas (accessed November 15, 2013).

Smith, Joseph, Jr. *History of The Church of Jesus Christ of Latter-day Saints,* ed. B. H. Roberts, 3:372. 2d ed., rev. 7 vols. Salt Lake City: Deseret Book, 1971.

"Douglas, Stephen Arnold." *Encyclopædia Britannica.* 11th ed. 1911.

DOWEN, John C. (1796–1885). Dowen was a farmer and Justice of the Peace who was born in New York. In June of 1832 he moved to Kirtland, Geauga County, Ohio. He was a member of the Methodist church and elected Justice of the Peace in 1833 and 1836. Acting on Joseph Smith's complaint, Dowen issued the December 27, 1833, warrant for Doctor Philastus Hurlbut, who was charged with threatening to kill or injure Joseph. Dowen subsequently served as a witness for Hurlbut during the preliminary hearing in which Hurlbut was ordered to post a recognizance bond to keep the peace and pay court costs.

Grua, David W. "Joseph Smith and the 1834 D. P. Hurlbut Case," *BYU Studies* 44, no. 1 (2005): 33–54.

Dowen, John C. "Statement of J. C. Dowen." In "Arthur B. Deming's *Naked Truths about Mormonism II.*" Dale R. Broadhurst, *Uncle Dale's Readings in Early Mormon History,* http://www.sidneyrigdon.com/dbroadhu/CA/natr1988.htm#120088-1c2 (accessed December 5, 2013).

"Brigham Young (1801–1877)." Autobiography from Eldon Jay Watson, ed., "Manuscript History of Brigham Young, 1801–1844," fall of 1834. Available at V. W. Smith, Book of Abraham Project, http://www.boap.org/LDS/Early-Saints/MSHBY.html (accessed December 5, 2103).

EDWARDS, Benjamin Stephenson (1818–1886). Edwards was the son of Ninian Edwards, Illinois governor and senator. He graduated from Yale in 1838 and studied law the following year with Stephen T. Logan, one of the most distinguished lawyers in Illinois and one-time partner with Abraham Lincoln. Together with Justin Butterfield, Edwards represented Joseph Smith in the extradition hearings of 1843 in Illinois. He was a delegate to the Illinois Constitutional Convention in 1862, elected circuit judge of Springfield Circuit in 1869, and served as president of the Illinois State Bar Association.

Church Historian's Press. "Edwards, Benjamin Stephenson." The Joseph Smith Papers, http://josephsmithpapers.org/person?name=Benjamin+Stephenson+Edwards (accessed July 8, 2013).

"Edwards, Benjamin Stephenson." *Historical Encyclopedia of Illinois and History of Sangamon Volume 2—Biographical.* Chicago: Munsell Publishing Company, 1912.

Linder, Usher F., and Joseph Gillispie. *Reminiscences of the Early Bench and Bar of Illinois,* 350–52. Chicago: Chicago Legal News Company, 1879.

Palmer, John, ed. *The Bench and Bar of Illinois: Historical and Reminiscent,* 1:190. Chicago: Lewis Publishing, 1899.

EMMONS, Sylvester (1808–1881). Emmons was a lawyer and newspaper publisher who was born in New Jersey. He moved to Philadelphia in 1831 and then to Illinois in 1840, where he was admitted to the bar in Hancock County in May of 1843. The same year he was elected to the Nauvoo City Council despite being a non-Mormon. In 1842 Joseph Smith and Orrin Porter Rockwell retained Emmons to represent them to prepare and argue petitions for a writ of habeas corpus before the Nauvoo Municipal Court in response to Missouri's second extradition attempt. In 1844 Emmons, having become disaffected, became the editor of the *Nauvoo Expositor.* Emmons subsequently appeared as counsel for the state during the legal proceedings which resulted in Joseph and Hyrum being held without bail on a charge of treason in the Carthage Jail. That same year he moved to Beardstown, Cass County, Illinois, where he edited the *Beardstown Gazette* from 1844 to 1852 and served as county circuit clerk for nine years. In 1849 he was appointed postmaster of Beardstown. He served as mayor of Beardstown for two terms; was Master in Chancery for several terms, and was police magistrate and Justice of the Peace. He was a member of the Methodist Church.

Church Historian's Press. "Emmons, Sylvester." The Joseph Smith Papers, http://josephsmithpapers.org/person/sylvester-emmons (accessed October 7, 2013).

William Henry Perrin, ed. *History of Cass County, Illinois.* Chicago: O. L. Baskin & Co. Historical Publishers, 1882. Available at http://www.rootsweb.ancestry.com/~ilcass/Perrin/biographies/emmons.s.txt2 (accessed November 12, 2013).

Hedges, Andrew H., Alex B. Smith, and Anderson Lloyd Richard, eds. *Journals, Volume 2: December 1841–April 1843,* vol. 2 of the Journals series of *The Joseph Smith Papers,* ed. Dean C. Jessee, Ronald K. Esplin, and Richard Lyman Bushman, 75. Salt Lake City: Church Historian's Press, 2011.

GORDON, John A. Gordon represented Joseph in a suit against William McLellin in Missouri, 1838. On a few occasions, Gordon also visited Joseph in Liberty Jail.

HIGBEE, Elias (1795–1843). Higbee was never formally a lawyer, but was a judge. Higbee joined the Church in 1832 and suffered during the Missouri persecutions. He later became the presiding judge of Caldwell County, Missouri. He served a mission to Missouri, Illinois, Indiana, and Ohio in 1835. Higbee assisted the Prophet in general legal matters and traveled with Joseph in 1839 to Washington, D.C., to seek reparations from President Van Buren for the Missouri mob depredations. He was the father of Francis M. and Chauncey L. Higbee, lawyers and excommunicated Mormons who were identified as members of the mob that killed Joseph and Hyrum Smith.

Church Historian's Press. "Higbee, Chauncey Lawson." http://josephsmithpapers. org/person?name=Chauncey+Lawson+Higbee (accessed July 8, 2013).

Church Historian's Press. "Higbee, Elias." The Joseph Smith Papers http://joseph smithpapers.org/person?name=Elias+Higbee (accessed July 8, 2013).

Church Historian's Press. "Higbee, Francis Marion." The Joseph Smith Papers http://josephsmithpapers.org/person?name=Francis+Marion+Higbee (accessed July 8, 2013).

HOLBROOK, William (1781–1865). Born in Connecticut, Holbrook was a Justice of the Peace and farmer. He moved to Geauga County, Ohio, about 1811 and to Painesville township by 1820, where he operated a mercantile business in partnership with Solomon Kingsbury. He served as Justice of the Peace in Painesville from at least 1831 to 1834. Holbrook was one of two justices who conducted the 1834 preliminary hearing to consider Joseph Smith's complaint against Doctor Philastus Hurlbut for threatening Joseph Smith's life.

Grua, David W. "Joseph Smith and the 1834 D. P. Hurlbut Case." *BYU Studies* 44, no. 1 (2005): 33–54.

"Obituary for William Holbrook." *Painesville Telegraph*, September 28, 1865, 3.

HUGHES, Andrew S. Hughes served as a consultant for the attorneys who represented Joseph Smith and others at Gallatin, Missouri, in 1839. He also visited Joseph at Liberty Jail.

The History of Clinton County, Missouri: Containing a History of the County, Its Cities, Towns, etc., 434–35. St. Joseph, Mo.: National Historical Company, 1881.

HUMPHREY, Van Rensselaer (1800–1864). Humphrey was a teacher, lawyer and judge born in Goshen, Connecticut. He was a teacher at age seventeen and admitted to the bar in 1820. In June 1821 he moved to Hudson, Summit County, Ohio, where he was elected Hudson Township Justice of the Peace in 1824. He was elected to the Ohio House of Representatives in 1828 and 1829. Humphrey was elected by the Ohio Legislature and served as President Judge of the Court of Common Pleas for the Third Judicial District from 1837 to 1844. He was appointed by the Ohio governor as a presiding judge (1844), served as mayor of Hudson (1851–52), district elector for the

Whig Party (1852), and Ohio delegate to the Democratic National Convention (1864).

Doyle, William B., James F. Caccamo, and Brianna L. Caccamo. *Centennial History of Summit County, Ohio and Representative Citizens,* 262. Mt. Vernon, Ind.: Windmill Publications, 1993. Reprint of Chicago: Biographical Pub. Co., 1908.

Lane, Samuel Alanson. *Fifty Years and Over of Akron and Summit County (Ohio),* 1080. Akron, Ohio: Beacon Job Department, 1892.

Perrin, William Henry. *History of Summit County: With an Outline Sketch of Ohio,* 236. Chicago: Baskin and Bettey, 1881.

KING, Austin Augustus (1802–1870). King was born in Sullivan County, Tennessee. In 1830 King moved to Missouri, where he practiced law at Columbia, Boone County, in partnership with John B. Gordon. He was elected to the state legislature as a Jacksonian Democrat from Boone County, 1834 and 1836. In 1837 he moved to Richmond, Missouri, where he was appointed circuit judge in northwestern Missouri by Governor Lilburn W. Boggs. Between 1837 and 1848, King served as judge of Missouri's Fifth Judicial Circuit, consisting of the counties of Clinton, Ray, Caldwell, Clay, Daviess, Carroll, and Livingston. According to Hyrum Smith, in November 1838, King participated in an illegal court martial at Far West which sentenced Joseph and other Church leaders to be executed. He subsequently presided at a court of inquiry or preliminary hearing for Joseph Smith and other Mormons at Richmond where he committed them to jail pending a grand jury hearing to be held in March 1839. On January 24, 1839, Joseph petitioned the Missouri legislature from Liberty Jail in which he charged Judge King of prejudice against the Mormons as a result of his brother-in-law's death during the earlier Jackson County conflict, as well as other evidence of bias demonstrated at the court of inquiry. This likely played a role in prompting enactment of a change to the Missouri venue statute, which allowed the prisoners to obtain a change of venue to Boone County. During their transfer to Boone County, Joseph and his fellow prisoners were allowed to escape, at the probable direction of King. King subsequently served as governor of Missouri in 1848–52 and represented Missouri in the U.S. Congress in 1863–65.

Bay, William Van Ness. *Reminiscences of the Bench and Bar of Missouri,* 153–55. F. H. Thomas and Co., 1878.

Church Historian's Press. "King, Austin." The Joseph Smith Papers, http://josephsmithpapers.org/person/austin-augustus-king (accessed November 14, 2013).

Madison, Gordon A., "Joseph Smith and the Missouri Court of Inquiry: Austin A. King's Quest for Hostages," *BYU Studies* 43, no. 4 (2004): 93–136.

Smith, Joseph, Jr. *History of The Church of Jesus Christ of Latter-day Saints,* ed.
B. H. Roberts, 3:372. 2d ed., rev. 7 vols. Salt Lake City: Deseret Book, 1971.

LAMBORN, Josiah (1809–1847). As attorney general, Lamborn represented
the State of Illinois in Joseph Smith's 1841 habeas corpus hearings in Illinois.
He was a gifted but troubled attorney. One colleague, W. F. Linder, noted,
"Intellectually, I know of no man of his day who was his superior. He was
considered by all the lawyers who knew him as a man of the tersest logic."
On multiple occasions he engaged in debates against Stephen Douglas and
Abraham Lincoln. Illinois Supreme Court Justice Theophilus Smith said he
"knew of no lawyer who was his equal in strength or force of argument." From
1840 to 1843, he served as Illinois Attorney General and appeared before the
Supreme Court forty-six times and was known as "one of the most untiring
yet merciless prosecutors that ever lived." The latter part of his term as prosecutor, however, was marked with corruption. As Usher Linder, who subsequently served as Illinois Attorney General, noted, Lamborn "was wholly
destitute of principle, and shamelessly took bribes from criminals prosecuted under his administration." After the 1841 trial, Lamborn commented
that Joseph was "a very good looking, jovial man." In 1844, Lamborn was
appointed special prosecutor in a feeble and remarkably unsuccessful effort
to prosecute the Carthage assassins of Joseph and Hyrum.

> Church Historian's Press. "Lamborn, Josiah." The Joseph Smith Papers, http://
> josephsmithpapers.org/person/josiah-lamborn (accessed July 8, 2013).
> Doyle, Cornelius J. "Josiah Lamborn, Attorney General of Illinois, 1840–1843."
> Speech given at White Hall, Illinois, May 30, 1927. Copy of transcript available
> in *Journal of the Illinois State Historical Society* 20 (1927): 185–200.
> *History of Sangamon County, Illinois,* 104. Chicago: Inter-State Publishing Co., 1881.
> *Josiah Lamborn: Memorial Exercises by Greene County Bar at White Hall, Illinois,
> May 30, 1927.* White Hall, Ill.: Press of White Hall Register-Republican, 1927.
> Linder, Usher F. *Reminiscences of the Early Bench and Bar of Illinois,* 350–52. Chi-
> cago: Chicago Legal News Company, 1879.
> Oaks, Dallin H., and Marvin S. Hill. *Carthage Conspiracy: The Trial of the Accused
> Assassins of Joseph Smith.* Illinois: University of Illinois Press, 1979.
> *People v. Lamborn,* 2 Ill. 123 (1834).

LANE, Jesse (1800–1881). Lane was born in Cannonsville (later in Tompkins), New York. He moved to Harmony (later in Oakland), Susquehanna
County, Pennsylvania, by 1823. In 1825 he was appointed Justice of the Peace
in Harmony and was also the owner of a sawmill and gristmill from 1825
to 1841. He also operated a storehouse in partnership with Nathan S. Williams. He moved to Wilmington, Delaware, by 1843, where he was a lumber

merchant. He served as a director of the Mechanics' Bank in 1859 and the National Bank of Wilmington & Brandywine in 1866. As Justice of the Peace, Lane witnessed the indenture or deed from Isaac and Elizabeth Hale to Joseph Smith for the purchase of thirteen acres and buildings in Harmony Township on August 25, 1830. On the 31st of the same month, Lane also signed the judgment in a consent case between George H. Noble and Joseph Smith for $190.95, which was satisfied the following year.

Church Historian's Press. "Jesse Lane." *The Joseph Smith Papers*, http://joseph smithpapers.org/person/jesse-lane (accessed November 21, 2013).

Mackay, Michael Hubbard, ed. *Documents, Volume 1: July 1828–June 1831, 167–71.* Vol. 1 of the Documents series *of The Joseph Smith Papers,* ed. Dean C. Jessee, Ronald K. Esplin, and Richard Lyman Bushman. Salt Lake City: Church Historian's Press, 2013.

LEONARD, Abiel (1797–1863). Leonard was born in Vermont and educated at Dartmouth College, originally intending to be a minister, but then changing his course of study to law. Because of failing eyesight he was forced to abandon his formal studies. In 1816 he commenced studying law in the offices of Gould and Gill of Whiteboro, New York, and was admitted to the bar there in 1818. In 1819 at age twenty-two, he arrived at St. Louis and then walked to Franklin, Missouri, where he taught school and began a legal practice before moving to Fayette. While in Franklin he was goaded into a duel in which he killed his opponent, for which he was disbarred and disenfranchised. However, in response to public outcry, his rights were restored at the following session of the legislature. In Fayette he became known as a leader of the bar and was well known throughout central Missouri. In 1823 he was appointed state's attorney, and in 1834 he was elected to the state legislature. In 1855 he was appointed to the Missouri Supreme Court, where a colleague said of him: "While I have known others to excel him as an orator, I have known none who could excel him in the argument of a law question ... he was the ablest lawyer I have known." On February 13, 1834, A. Sidney Gilbert wrote to Leonard confirming Parley P. Pratt's earlier meeting with Leonard, who agreed to represent the Church in prosecuting claims for damages against certain Jackson County residents. Gilbert also confirmed that Rees, Atchison, Doniphan and Williams were agreeable to Leonard's involvement.

Bay, W. V. N. *Reminiscences of the Bench and Bar of Missouri,* 356–70. St. Louis: F. H. Thomas and Co., 1878.

"History, 1838–1856, volume A-1 [23 December 1805–30 August 1834]," p. 426. The Joseph Smith Papers Project, http://josephsmithpapers.org/paperSummary/ history-1838-1856-volume-a-1-23-december-1805-30-august-1834?p=432

Shoemaker, Floyd A. *Missouri and Missourians: Land of Contrasts and People of Achievements,* 1:632. Chicago: Lewis Publishing Co., 1943.

LITTLE, Sidney B. Little represented Joseph Smith in 1841 together with Orville Hickman Browning, Charles A. Warren, James H. Ralston, Cyrus Walker, and Archibald Williams before Judge Stephen Douglas in Joseph's 1841 extradition hearing in Illinois.

Gregg, Thomas. *History of Hancock County, Illinois: Together with an Outline of the History of the State and a Digest of State Laws,* 1:413. Lacrosse, Wisc.: Brookehaven Press, 2001.

"The Late Proceedings." *Times and Seasons* 2 (June 15, 1841): 447.

MASON, Charles. Charles Mason was a prominent figure in early Iowa history. When the Iowa territory was formed out of the Wisconsin territory, Mason was made chief justice of the Supreme Court of the Territory of Iowa. He served as chief justice through statehood until June 11, 1847, after which he resumed the practice of law. In 1841, Joseph Smith located and sued former Mormon militia commander George Hinkle in Iowa, alleging Hinkle broke into Joseph's house and stole property and forced Emma and their children from the home during the mob depredations at Far West. The case is notable in that sixteen depositions on written interrogatories were taken before Nauvoo Mayor John C. Bennett. Following a jury trial before Judge Mason on April 29, 1842, an award was entered against Hinkle for $200 and court costs.

Iowa Official Register, 342. Iowa: Iowa General Assembly, Legislative Services Agency, 2009–10.

Morris, Eastin. *Reports of Cases Argued and Determined in the Supreme Court of Iowa,* 1:viii. Iowa City, Iowa: Silas Foster, 1847.

The History of Des Moines County, Iowa, 649. Chicago: Western Historical Company, 1879.

MORIN, Josiah (1791–1885). Morin was a pioneer settler of Millport, in present-day Daviess County, Missouri, in 1831. He was appointed county judge of Daviess County in 1837, and attended the court hearing at Gallatin, Daviess County, for Joseph Smith, Hyrum Smith, Lyman Wight, Caleb Baldwin, and Alexander McRae, April 9–11, 1839. After they were granted change of venue to stand trial in Columbia, Boone County, Missouri, Joseph Smith and his party stayed April 14–15, 1839, in home of Judge Morin, who was sympathetic to the Mormon cause. He later moved to Jackson County, Missouri, ca. 1842; to what later became Oregon Territory in 1846; to El Dorado County, and to Green Valley, Sonoma County, California, 1850.

NEELY, Albert (1798–1857). Born in New York, Neely was a merchant, postmaster, and Justice of the Peace. He was elected vestryman of the Protestant Episcopal Church in South Bainbridge, Chenango County, New York, in 1825 and commissioned Justice of the Peace the same year. He also may have been South Bainbridge's first postmaster. In March 1826, Neely presided over Joseph Smith's trial on charges of being a disorderly person. He was elected Boone County commissioner in 1844, and moved to Chicago, Illinois, by June 1850, where he died.

> Madsen, Gordon A. "Joseph Smith's 1826 Trial: The Legal Setting." *BYU Studies* 30, no. 2 (1990): 91–108.
>
> Smith, James H. *1784 History of Chenango and Madison Counties, of New York, with Illustrations and Biographical Sketches of Some of Its Prominent Men and Pioneers*, 176. Syracuse, New York: D Mason and County, 1880.
>
> Vogel, Dan, comp. and ed. *Early Mormon Documents*, 4:95, 108, 127–28, 226, 239–40, 257–65. 5 vols. Salt Lake City: Signature Books, 1996.

NOBLE, Joel King (1789–1874). Born in Connecticut, Noble moved to Cambridge, Washington County, New York, by August 1800; to Windsor, Broome County, by August 1820; and Colesville, Broome County, New York, by 1822. Noble was elected Justice of the Peace in 1828, 1832, and 1835. Noble was one of three Justices of the Peace who presided over a court of special sessions which tried Joseph and acquitted Joseph a second time in 1830 for being a disorderly person.

> Bushman, Richard Lyman, with Jed Woodward. *Joseph Smith: Rough Stone Rolling*, 116–17. New York: Alfred A. Knopf, 2005.
>
> County Clerk. "Certificates of Election" (Broome County, New York). In "Certificates of Election and Register of Civil Officers, 1821–1885," *Certificates of Election and Register of Civil Officers, 1821–1885*, 42, 74, 102. Salt Lake City: Filmed by the Genealogical Society of Utah from original records in the Broome County Courthouse, 1969.
>
> "Mormonism." *New England* (Boston) *Christian Herald*, November 7, 1832, 22–27.

OSBORN, Salmon S. (1804–1904). Osborn represented Joseph Smith in multiple suits in Ohio. He was an attorney and bank executive. In 1828 he opened a law office with R. Gidding in Chardon, Geauga County, Ohio. He moved to Painesville in 1833 and formed the law firm of Perkins & Osborn with William L. Perkins in Painesville in 1834. He was elected Cashier at First National Bank of Painesville in 1849 and remained there until at least 1870.

PAINE, J. C. [Possibly Ira C. Paine (1805–1883).] Paine represented Joseph Smith in Ohio. He was an attorney, judge, and Justice of the Peace in

Painesville, Geauga (now Lake) County, Ohio. Ira Paine practiced law in Ohio from 1830 to 1847, when he moved to Wisconsin.

PERKINS, William Lee (1799–1882). Perkins was a lawyer and politician born in Connecticut, where he studied law and was admitted to the Hartford bar in 1824. He moved to Painesville, Geauga County, Ohio, in 1828, where he continued to practice law. In 1834 he and Salmon S. Osborn formed the law firm of Perkins & Osborn, which represented Joseph Smith in Ohio. He was Lake County Prosecuting Attorney in 1840 and served in the Ohio senate from 1843 to 1847. He was mayor of Painesville, beginning in 1853, and Lake County Prosecuting Attorney again from 1859 to 1863.

PHELPS, William Wines (1792–1872). Phelps was a writer, teacher, printer, newspaper editor, publisher, postmaster, and ultimately lawyer. He first obtained a copy of the Book of Mormon and met Joseph Smith in 1830 but was not baptized until June 10, 1831, at Kirtland. He was appointed church printer in 1831 and after moving to Jackson County, Missouri, Oct. 1831, he became editor of *The Evening and the Morning Star* and *Upper Missouri Advertiser.* In 1833 he was in the midst of printing the Book of Commandments when his printing office was razed by a mob. After being exiled from Jackson County, he moved to Clay County, where he was appointed to Missouri High Council presidency. He returned to Kirtland and served as Joseph Smith's scribe and helped compile the Doctrine and Covenants and first Latter-day Saint hymnal in 1835. He subsequently returned from Kirtland to Clay County, where he resumed duties with Missouri presidency in 1836. He was excommunicated in 1838, but reconciled with the Church and was rebaptized in 1841. A prolific hymn writer, Phelps served a mission to the eastern U.S., was appointed assistant Church historian, and was recorder of Church licenses. In Nauvoo, Illinois, Phelps assisted John Taylor in editing *Times and Seasons* and *Nauvoo Neighbor.* He was elected to the Nauvoo City Council and was a member of the Council of Fifty. In Utah he helped draft the constitution for Utah Territory, was admitted to the Utah territorial bar in 1851, and was a member of the territorial legislative assembly from 1851 to 1857. On March 9, 1843, Joseph wrote in his diary: "Bro[ther] Phelps you shall know law, and understand law and you shall be a lawyer in Israel and the time shall come when I shall not need say thus is the law for you shall know the law."

Church Historian's Press, "William Phelps," The Joseph Smith Papers, http://josephsmithpapers.org/person/phelps-william (accessed December 5, 2013)

Faulring, Scott H., ed. *An American Prophet's Record: The Diaries and Journals of Joseph Smith,* 328–29. Salt Lake City: Signature Books, 1987.

POPE, Nathaniel (1784–1850). Pope was the U.S. District Judge for Illinois who presided over Joseph Smith's January 1843 habeas corpus hearing in Springfield. He was born in Louisville, Kentucky, and graduated from Transylvania University in 1806. He moved first to the St. Genevieve District, Louisiana Territory (later in St. Genevieve County, Missouri) and then to Kaskaskia, Illinois Territory, in 1809. He served as secretary of the Illinois Territory (1809–17); as territorial delegate to U.S. Congress (1817–18) and as register of land office at Edwardsville, Illinois Territory (1818–19). Pope was appointed to the federal bench by President James Monroe and served as U.S. district judge for Illinois from 1819 to 1850.

> Angle, Paul McClelland. *Nathaniel Pope from 1784–1850, a Memoir.* Springfield, Ill., 1937.
>
> Church Historian's Press. "Pope, Nathaniel." The Joseph Smith Papers, http://josephsmithpapers.org/person/nathaniel-pope (accessed November 10, 2013).

RALSTON, James Henry (1807–1864). Ralston was born in Bourbon County, Kentucky, and served in Black Hawk War in 1832. He was a member of Illinois House of Representatives (1836–38), circuit judge in 1837, and a member of Illinois Senate from 1840 to 1844. In the Mexican War he was captain and assistant quartermaster. By 1850 he had moved to California, where he became a member of California's first state senate. Ralston later moved to Utah Territory (later in Nevada Territory), ca. 1860 and lived at Austin, Nevada Territory, by 1863. He assisted Orville Browning, Sidney B. Little, Cyrus Walker, and Archibald Williams in Joseph Smith's 1841 extradition hearing before Judge Stephen A. Douglas. On August 31, 1841, Calvin A. Warren wrote Joseph Smith requesting a loan for "Judge Ralston" and him.

> Church Historian's Press. "Ralston, James Henry." The Joseph Smith Papers, http://josephsmithpapers.org/person/james-henry-ralston (accessed November 21, 2013).
>
> "Letter from Calvin A. Warren, 31 August 1841," http://josephsmithpapers.org/paperSummary/letter-from-calvin-a-warren-31-august-1841 (accessed November 21, 2013).
>
> Snyder, J. F. "Forgotten Statesmen of Illinois: James Harvey Ralston." In *Transactions of the Illinois State Historical Society for the Year 1908*, 13:215–32. Illinois: Illinois State Journal Co., State Printers, 1909.
>
> Young, Kevin R. "Ralston, James Harvey." In *Handbook of Texas Online*, Texas State Historical Association, http://www.tshaonline.org/handbook/online/article/fra55 (accessed July 8, 2013).

REED, John Savage (ca. 1785–1878). Reed was a farmer and layman/lawyer in Bainbridge, New York, who first met Joseph Smith in 1823 when the eighteen-year-old Joseph arrived in Bainbridge. Reed and James Davidson were hired by Joseph Knight to defend Joseph in the Bainbridge and Colesville disorderly person cases in 1830. Reed visited Nauvoo during May 1844 as a delegate from Chemung County, New York, to elect Joseph Smith as United States president, and related his experiences in defending Joseph during the early New York trials. In 1861, an elderly Reed wrote to Brigham Young recounting his legal defense of Joseph Smith: "i beli(e)ve to this Day that God was on his side to diliver him from those wicked sons of bitc(h)es, for that Boy Joseph sat thare aparently as unconcarned as if he was in his one (own) farthers house and when a hard witness woold com(e) upon the stand I wood say to him that our case Looked bad he said with a smile upon his countanance, i shall be cleared(:) de your duty and fear not.'" Reed also commented on his own performance, stating, "but I had not stood long uaon the floor before the corrt before my tung was Loosed from the reff of my mouth and it did came to me and has ever sence that time inspired By that god that stood by that bo(u)ndless Boy to clear and deliver him from the <h>and of the Devil(.)"

Bushman, Richard Lyman, with Jed Woodward. *Joseph Smith: Rough Stone Rolling,* 116–17. New York: Alfred A. Knopf, 2005.

Reed, John S., to Brigham Young, December 6, 1861. Brigham Young Collection, Church History Department, Salt Lake City.

"Some of the Remarks of John S. Reed, Esq., as Delivered before the State Convention." *Times and Seasons* 5 (June 1, 1844): 549–51.

Vogel, Dan, comp. and ed. *Early Mormon Documents,* 4:121–25. 5 vols. Salt Lake City: Signature Books, 1996.

Smith, Joseph, Jr. *History of The Church of Jesus Christ of Latter-day Saints,* ed. B. H. Roberts, 1:89–96. 2d ed., rev. 7 vols. Salt Lake City: Deseret Book, 1971.

REES, Amos (1800–1886). Rees moved to Missouri by 1830 and represented Joseph and others along with attorneys Atchison, Doniphan, and Wood to recover damages for mob actions taken against the Mormons in Jackson County in 1833. He was the resident prosecuting attorney for Clay County, 1831–34; and for Missouri fifth judicial circuit, 1831–37. Rees was a major in the militia in 1838 in Ray County, Missouri. Despite his legal representation of Joseph Smith, Rees was antagonistic towards the Mormons. He and Wiley C. Williams presented Governor Boggs with exaggerated tales of Mormon conflicts with Missourians, and their reports ultimately resulted in Governor Boggs issuing his infamous extermination order in 1838. Notwithstanding, Rees, along with Alexander Doniphan, Andrew Hughes, and Peter Burnett, represented Joseph and several others in the Richmond Court of Inquiry before Judge Austin King in November 1838. In April 1839, Rees and Burnett represented Joseph Smith and other Church leaders at the Grand

Jury hearing in Gallatin, Missouri, where Joseph and others were indicted for treason, arson, and burglary.

Church Historian's Press. "Rees, Amos." The Joseph Smith Papers, http://joseph smithpapers.org/person?name=Amos+Rees.

Roberts, B. H. *The Missouri Persecutions*. Salt Lake City: George Q. Cannon and Sons, 1900.

REEVES, Lewis R. (1817–1854). Reeves, born in Trumbull County, Ohio, moved to Fort Madison as a young man. He practiced law in Fort Madison, Lee County, Iowa Territory, gaining a reputation as one of the ablest lawyers in the county. Reeves represented Joseph Smith with Alfred Rich under the partnership of Rich & Reeves, in *Smith v. Hinkle,* filed in the District Court for the Iowa Territory, in Lee County, on May 14, 1841. He moved to Keokuk County, Iowa Territory, by 1850 and shortly thereafter formed a partnership with Samuel F. Miller, who subsequently became a Justice of the U.S. Supreme Court. The law firm Reeves & Miller was considered one of the finest firms in the territory. Reeves died unexpectedly in 1854.

Stiles, Edward H. *Recollections and Sketches of Notable Lawyers and Public Men of Early Iowa,* 329–30. Des Moines: Homestead, 1916.

Hall, Timothy L. *A Biographical Dictionary: Supreme Court Justices,* 141. New York: Facts on File, 2001.

Ross, Michael A. *Justice of Shattered Dreams: Samuel Freeman Miller and the Supreme Court during the Civil War Era,* 20–21. Baton Rouge: Louisiana State University Press, 2003.

The Supreme Court Historical Society Quarterly 11 (1993): 10.

Fairman, Charles. *Mr. Justice Miller and the Supreme Court, 1862–1890,* 18–19. Cambridge: Harvard University Press, 1939.

REID, Hugh T. (1811–1874). Reid was a farmer, lawyer, land developer, railroad owner, and operator. He graduated from Indiana College in 1837 and was admitted to the Indiana Bar in 1839. He practiced law in Fort Madison, Lee County, Iowa. In June 1844, Reid and James Woods represented Joseph and Hyrum in the final hearings that resulted in their imprisonment and subsequent murders at Carthage Jail.

REYNOLDS, Thomas (1796–1844). Reynolds was born in Kentucky and admitted to the bar there in 1817 before he was twenty-one years old. In his early twenties he moved with his family to Springfield, Illinois, where he served as the clerk of Illinois House of Representatives (1818–22), member of the house (1826–28), and as chief justice of the Illinois Supreme Court (1822–25). He moved to Fayette, Missouri, ca. 1829, where he practiced law and served as the editor for the local newspaper. In 1832 he was elected to the Missouri General Assembly and served as speaker of the house. On January 25, 1837, he was appointed by Governor Lilburn W. Boggs as judge of the Second Judicial Circuit of Missouri, which included Boone County. In August 1840, Judge Reynolds dismissed the outstanding indictments against Joseph Smith and five others. Reynolds was elected governor in 1849, succeeding Boggs. As governor, Reynolds issued a requisition for the extradition of Joseph Smith, which resulted in the habeas corpus hearing before Judge Nathaniel Pope the following year. Reynolds committed suicide in the executive mansion ten months before his term expired.

Church Historian's Press. "Reynolds, Thomas." The Joseph Smith Papers, http://josephsmithpapers.org/person/thomas-reynolds (accessed November 15, 2013).

Livingstone, William G. "Historical Notes: The Thomas Reynolds Confusion." *Journal of Illinois Historical Society* 54 (Winter 1961): 423–30.

RICH, Alfred (?-1842). Rich was born in Kentucky and studied law under W. W. Southworth in Covington, Kentucky. He moved to Fort Madison, Lee County, Iowa Territory, by 1838, where he became the district attorney. Described as eccentric, gifted, and very bright, Rich taught school in Fort Madison. In 1839 he was elected to the Iowa Territorial Legislature. He ran for Congress in 1840 and 1841 as a Whig candidate, losing both times. Rich died as a young man in the spring of 1842 of consumption. Rich represented Joseph Smith with Lewis R. Reeves under the law partnership of Rich & Reeves, in *Smith v. Hinkle*, filed in the District Court for the Iowa Territory, in Lee County, on May 14, 1841. This case was tried on April 22, 1842, shortly before Rich's death.

Parvin, Theodore. *The Early Bar of Iowa*, 4, 9–10 n. 1, 14–15. Iowa City, Iowa: State Historical Society, 1894.

Portrait and Biographical Album of Louisa County, Iowa, 601, 622. Chicago: Acme, 1889.

Shaffer, John R. *Annual Report of the Board of Directors of the Iowa State Agricultural Society*, 345. Des Moines: Geo. E. Roberts, 1889.

Fairall, Herbert S. *Manual of Iowa Politics*, 1:11–13. Iowa City: Republican Publishing Co, 1884.

Stiles, Edward H. *Recollections and Sketches of Notable Lawyers and Public Men of Early Iowa*, 324–26. Des Moines: Homestead, 1916.

ROLLINS, James S. (1812-1888). Rollins was born in Richmond, Kentucky and attended Washington College (now Washington and Jefferson College) in Pennsylvania. He graduated from Indiana University in 1830, when his family moved to Boone County, Missouri. He read law in the Columbia office of Abiel Leonard for two years and then in 1832 enlisted in the Black Hawk War with the rank of major. After the war he entered law school at the University of Transylvania in Lexington, Kentucky, graduating in 1834. The same year he was admitted to the bar and began practicing in Columbia. Rollins assisted Alexander Doniphan and Amos Rees as attorneys for the Mormons for the November 1838 Court of Inquiry before Judge Austin King in Richmond. Rollins was elected a representative to the Missouri state legislature in 1838, 1840, and 1854 and as senator in 1846. As a representative Rollins was instrumental in establishing the University of Missouri at Columbia. He was elected to Congress in 1860 and again in 1862. He was a substantial slave-holder who was nonetheless a Unionist who voted for most war measures in Congress. Rollins played a key role in the passage of the Thirteenth Amendment to the Constitution, which abolished slavery.

"Rollins, James Sidney." Biographical Directory of the United States Congress, http://bioguide.congress.gov/scripts/biodisplay.pl?index=R000412 (accessed November 12, 2013).

Wood, James M. "James Sidney Rollins of Missouri: A Political Biography." PhD diss., Stanford University, 1951.

Smith, William Benjamin. *James Sidney Rollins.* New York: De Vinne Press, 1891.

Launius, Roger D. *Alexander William Doniphan: Portrait of a Missouri Moderate,* 66. Columbia: University of Missouri Press, 1997.

RYLAND, John F. (1797–1873). Ryland was a teacher, farmer, lawyer, judge. He was born in Virginia, but moved to Kentucky in 1809 where he attended Forest Hill Academy in Washington County (later in Marion County). Licensed as a lawyer in Kentucky before 1819, Ryland moved to Franklin, Missouri, in 1819 to begin his law practice, and was admitted to the circuit court in Lexington, Missouri, in 1823. He was appointed judge of Missouri's Sixth Judicial Circuit in 1830 and served on the Missouri Supreme Court from 1848 to 1857. During the 1833 conflict in Jackson County, Ryland at least twice refused the Mormons' request for peace warrants. At the July 1836 term of the Ray County Circuit Court, Ryland tried W. W. Phelps and Bishop Edward Partridge's civil suits for damages against those who admitted to having destroyed Phelps's printing press and office and tarred and feathered Bishop Partridge. Ryland found the defendants culpable for the acts, but awarded Phelps a judgment of only $750 and Bishop Partridge "a peppercorn and one penny."

Church Historian's Press. "Ryland, John F." The Joseph Smith Papers, http://josephsmithpapers.org/person/john-f-ryland (accessed November 16, 2013).

Firmage, Edwin Brown, and Richard Collin Mangrum. *Zion in the Courts: A Legal History of the Church of Jesus Christ of Latter-day Saints, 1830–1900,* 66, 69–70. Urbana: University of Illinois Press, 1988.

Ray County Circuit Court. July 1836, Book A, pp. 236–38, 249–50.

Garr, Arnold K., and Clark V. Johnson, eds. *Regional Studies in Latter-day Saint Church History, Missouri,* 245, 298. Provo, Utah: Department of Church History and Doctrine, Brigham Young University, 1994.

SKINNER, Onias C. (1817–1877).

Skinner was a sailor, schoolteacher, preacher, farmer, lawyer, and railroad president. Born in Oneida County, New York, he moved to Hancock County, Illinois, by 1841. As a lawyer, he both represented and opposed Joseph Smith. Beginning in 1841, when he was only twenty-three years old, Skinner performed some general legal work for Joseph. However, just three years later, in 1844, he took a leading role in the anti-Mormon Warsaw, Illinois, meeting where a resolution was drafted that recommended the Mormon extermination or expulsion from Illinois. A few weeks after the Warsaw meeting, Skinner was appointed as special counsel to prosecute Joseph Smith and others in a preliminary treason hearing. He was Illinois Governor Thomas Ford's aide-de-camp during the Mormon persecutions in Illinois. Skinner, along with Chauncey L. Higbee, Thomas Sharp, Sylvester Emmons, and Thomas Morrison, all represented the State during the hearings that led to Joseph and Hyrum's imprisonment and subsequent murder at Carthage Jail. Later in 1844, after Joseph and Hyrum's assassination, Skinner was part of the defense team in the trial of the accused assassins. Skinner served as an Illinois State Legislator from 1848 to 1850. In 1851 he was elected a circuit judge for the Fifth Judicial Circuit. He was a justice of the Illinois Supreme Court from 1855 to 1857. Abraham Lincoln appeared before him during that time in approximately thirty-eight cases. Skinner took part in the Illinois State Constitutional Convention in 1870.

Gregg, Thomas. *History of Hancock County, Illinois,* 1:411. Chicago: Charles C. Chapman, 1880.

Palmer, John, ed. *The Bench and Bar of Illinois: Historical and Reminiscent,* 1:54; 2:876. Chicago: Lewis Publishing, 1899.

Smith, Joseph, Jr. *History of The Church of Jesus Christ of Latter-day Saints,* ed. B. H. Roberts, 6:596. 2d ed., rev. 7 vols. Salt Lake City, Deseret Book, 1971.

State of Illinois. "Onias C. Skinner: Previous Illinois Supreme Court Justice." Illinois Courts, http://www.state.il.us/court/SupremeCourt/JusticeArchive/Bio _Skinner.asp (accessed July 9, 2013).

Wilcox, David F., ed. *Quincy and Adams County: History and Representative Men,* 149. Chicago: Lewis Publishing Company, 1919.

SMITH, Robert F. Smith was a Methodist minister, justice of the peace, and captain of the Carthage Greys Militia. On June 25, 1844, Governor Thomas Ford maintained that only a state trial would calm the furor over the destruction of the *Nauvoo Expositor.* Joseph and fifteen others therefore received guarantees of safety and presented themselves before Justice of the Peace Smith in Carthage, where they were freed on bail pending the October term of the Circuit Court. However, before they could leave, Joseph and Hyrum were immediately jailed on a writ issued by Smith on a charge of treason, which was a nonbailable offense. On June 1844, Governor Ford met with the prisoners and then disbanded all the militia companies, except the hostile Carthage Greys, who were left to guard the jail while Ford traveled to Nauvoo. After Ford's departure, the discharged Warsaw militia company and others attacked the jail. The Carthage Greys gave only token resistance; they had loaded their weapons with gunpowder but no bullets. The mob then stormed the jail, murdering Joseph and Hyrum.

> Smith, Joseph, Jr., *History of The Church of Jesus Christ of Latter-day Saints,* ed. B. H. Roberts, 6:561–74. 2d ed., rev. 7 vols. Salt Lake City, Deseret Book, 1971.

STILES, George Philander (1816–1885). Born in New York, Stiles operated a law office from at least 1842–43, in Nauvoo, Illinois, and was for a time Nauvoo City Attorney. He was ordained a Seventy by 1846 and served as first lieutenant, Nauvoo Legion. By 1850 he had moved to Pottawattamie County, Iowa, eventually settling in Council Bluffs, being elected Council Bluffs City Attorney in 1853. He was appointed Associate Justice of Utah Territory in 1854, and assigned as Associate Justice of Third District of Utah Territory. In 1856 he was excommunicated, and subsequently moved to Washington, D.C., and then to Ohio, after which he served as a first lieutenant in the Civil War, mayor of Cardington Twp., and a member of the Bar in Morrow County. By 1880 he had moved back to Washington, D.C., where he worked as a clerk in the Treasury. Stiles appeared as a lawyer for Joseph Smith and other Nauvoo authorities in the Justice Court proceeding before Daniel H. Wells on June 17, 1844, in which the defendants were all discharged.

> Smith, Joseph, Jr., *History of The Church of Jesus Christ of Latter-day Saints,* ed. B. H. Roberts, 6:488–91. 2d ed., rev. 7 vols. Salt Lake City, Deseret Book, 1971.

THOMAS, Jesse B. (1806–1850). Thomas was born in Lebanon, Ohio. After studying law at Transylvania University in Lexington, Kentucky, he settled in Edwardsville, Illinois. By 1830 Thomas was serving as secretary to the Illinois State Senate. Four years later he served a partial term in the Illinois House of Representatives for Madison County before being appointed Attorney General, a post he held for a single year. From 1837 through 1839, he was a circuit court judge based in Springfield. His circuit included New Salem, where he heard cases argued by Abraham Lincoln. When Stephen A. Douglas gave up his seat on the Illinois Supreme Court in 1843 after being elected to Congress, Governor Thomas Ford appointed Thomas as Douglas's successor. After retiring from the Supreme Court in 1848, he moved first to Galena and then to Chicago, where he died in 1850. Following Joseph's acquittal before the Nauvoo Municipal Court on charges of riot arising from the destruction of the *Expositor,* the Nauvoo authorities consulted with Judge Thomas, who advised them that in order to satisfy their critics they should be retried before a non-Mormon magistrate. Accordingly, Joseph and other Nauvoo leaders submitted to a second hearing before nonmember Nauvoo Justice of the Peace Daniel H. Wells, who acquitted them.

Bateman, Newton, Paul Selby, Frances M. Shonkwiler, and Henry L Fowkes. *Historical Encyclopedia of Illinois,* 521. Chicago: Munsell Publishing Company, 1908.

Linder, Usher F., and Joseph Gillespie. *Reminiscences of the Early Bench and Bar of Illinois,* 261–64. Chicago: Chicago Legal News, 1879.

Smith, Joseph, Jr. *History of The Church of Jesus Christ of Latter-day Saints,* ed. B. H. Roberts, 6:498. 2d ed., rev. 7 vols. Salt Lake City: Deseret Book, 1971.

THOMPSON, Robert Blashel (1811–1841). Thompson was not an attorney, but more of a legal philosopher. Parley P. Pratt baptized Thompson a member of the Church in 1836. While he never represented Joseph or the church in court, he did assist in various transactional matters. In 1839 Thompson, Almon Babbitt, and Erastus Snow were appointed to be a traveling committee charged with obtaining all the libelous reports and publications that had been circulated against the Church. In 1840, Thompson assisted Elias Higbee in drafting a petition to Congress for a redress of the grievances against the Mormons in Missouri. Later, in January 1841, Joseph Smith received a revelation that Thompson was to assist the Prophet in drafting religious proclamations to the kings, presidents, and governors of earth. Thompson served as a scribe and clerk of the Church and died in Nauvoo.

Church Historian's Press. "Thompson, Robert Blashel." The Joseph Smith Papers, http://josephsmithpapers.org/person/robert-blashel-thompson (accessed July 9, 2013).

Jenson, Andrew. *Latter-day Saint Biographical Encyclopedia: A Compilation of Biographical Sketches of Prominent Men and Women in The Church of Jesus Christ of Latter-day Saints,* 1:284. 4 vols. Salt Lake City: Andrew Jenson History, 1901–36.

Smith, Joseph, Jr. *History of The Church of Jesus Christ of Latter-day Saints,* ed. B. H. Roberts, 3:283–84, 345; 4:191–97, 237, 250–51, 411. 2d ed., rev. 7 vols. Salt Lake City: Deseret Book, 1971.

TURNHAM, Joel (1783–1862). Turnham was a farmer and judge who was born in Virginia and moved to Kentucky by 1810. He served in the War of 1812 in the Kentucky militia. By 1822 he had moved to Clay County, Missouri, where he served as Clay County court judge, 1827–30, 1838–44, and 1854–56. He built a tobacco warehouse at Liberty Landing (later Liberty) in 1830–31. Turnham was the judge who heard the habeas corpus petitions by Joseph and other Church leaders in 1839 when Sidney Rigdon alone was released. According to Hyrum Smith's Affidavit presented to the Nauvoo Municipal Court in July at 1843, Judge Turnham visited the prisoners in Liberty Jail in the evening following the hearing and apologized for keeping them in jail, knowing they were innocent but fearing mob violence if he had released them.

> Burnett, Peter Hardeman. *Reflections and Opinions of an Old Pioneer,* 53–55. D. Appleton and Co., 1880.
> Church Historian's Press. "Joel Turnham." The Joseph Smith Papers, http:// josephsmithpapers.org/person/turnham-joel (accessed November 21, 2013).
> Smith, Joseph, Jr. *History of The Church of Jesus Christ of Latter-day Saints,* ed. B. H. Roberts, 3:264, 421. 2d ed., rev. 7 vols. Salt Lake City: Deseret Book, 1971.

WALKER, Cyrus (1791–1875). Walker represented Joseph Smith in 1841 along with Orville Hickman Browning, Charles A. Warren, Sidney B. Little, James H. Ralston, and Archibald Williams before Judge Stephen Douglas in an extradition hearing in Illinois. Walker agreed to represent Joseph only after securing Joseph's vote in his race for the U.S. House of Representatives.

> "Cyrus Walker, Esquire." Melissa's World, http://www.beadles.org/mcdonough -county-illinois-history/cyrus-walker-esquire/ (accessed July 9, 2013).
> "History of Joseph Smith." *Millennial Star* 18 (August 30, 1856): 551.
> Palmer, John, ed. *The Bench and Bar of Illinois: Historical and Reminiscent,* 2:736– 39. Chicago: Lewis Publishing, 1899.

WARREN, Calvin Averill (1807–1881). Warren was one of the attorneys who represented Joseph Smith through his 1841 bankruptcy hearings and then after Joseph's death. Interestingly, Warren also acted as defense attorney for Joseph's accused assassins during the same time period. He was identified by Jacob Backenstos as one of the mob that killed Joseph and Hyrum. On August 31, 1841, Warren wrote Joseph Smith requesting a loan to purchase land in Warsaw.

> Church Historian's Press. "Warren, Calvin Averill." The Joseph Smith Papers, http:// josephsmithpapers.org/person/calvin-averill-warren (accessed July 9, 2013).
> "The Late Proceedings." *Times and Seasons* 2 (June 15, 1841): 447.

Oaks, Dallin H., and Marvin S. Hill. *Carthage Conspiracy: The Trial of the Accused Assassins of Joseph Smith*, 85. Illinois: University of Illinois Press, 1979.

Smith, Joseph, Jr. *History of The Church of Jesus Christ of Latter-day Saints,* ed. B. H. Roberts, 4:594. 2d ed., rev. 7 vols. Salt Lake City: Deseret Book, 1971.

"Warren, Calvin A." In *Historical Encyclopedia of Illinois,* ed. Newton Bateman and Paul Selby, 577. Chicago: Munsell Publishing, 1900.

WARREN, Charles A. Warren assisted Orville Hickman Browning, Sidney B. Little, James H. Ralston, Cyrus Walker, and Archibald Williams before Judge Stephen Douglas in the extradition hearing in Illinois in 1841.

WELLS, Daniel H. (1814–1891). Wells was a farmer, teacher, ferry operator, lumber merchant, manager of a nail factory, Justice of the Peace, politician and LDS apostle. Born in Oneida County, New York, Wells moved to Marietta, Ohio, around 1832 and to Commerce (later Nauvoo), Illinois in 1834. As non-Mormon, Wells served as Justice of the Peace, alderman, school warden, regent of University of Nauvoo, and commissary general in the Nauvoo Legion. On June 10, 1844, Wells was a member of the Nauvoo City Council which ordered the suppression of the *Nauvoo Expositor.* Following Joseph Smith's arrest for riot, Joseph was acquitted by the Nauvoo Municipal Court. In the face of rising resentment, the Nauvoo authorities consulted with state circuit judge Jesse B. Thomas, who advised that in order to satisfy the people, they should be retried before another magistrate who was not a member of their faith. Accordingly, on June 17, Joseph and other leaders submitted to a retrial before Daniel Wells as Justice of the Peace residing near Nauvoo. After hearing numerous witnesses and counsel for both prosecution and defense, Wells granted a judgment of acquittal. In 1846 Wells was baptized into LDS church and played a leading role in the Battle of Nauvoo. He migrated to Salt Lake City in Brigham Young's pioneer company in 1848. Wells subsequently served as attorney general for the provisional state of Deseret, a member of legislative council, and was ordained an Apostle and appointed second counselor in First Presidency by Brigham Young in 1857. He afterwards served as president of territorial legislative council, president of the European mission, president of the Manti temple and counselor to the Quorum of the Twelve.

Church Historian's Press. "Wells, Daniel Hanmer." The Joseph Smith Papers, http://josephsmithpapers.org/person/daniel-hanmer-wells (accessed November 16, 2013).

Oaks, Dallin H. "The Suppression of the Nauvoo Expositor." *Utah Law Review 9* (1965): 865–66.

WILLIAMS, Archibald. Williams represented Joseph Smith along with Orville Hickman Browning, Charles A. Warren, Sidney B. Little, James H. Ralston, and Cyrus Walker in the 1841 extradition hearing before Judge Stephen Douglas.

City of Quincy Lincoln Bicentennial Commission. "Archibald Williams." Building on Lincoln's Legacy in Quincy and Adams County, Illinois, http://www.lincolndouglasquincydebate.com/html/williams.html (accessed July 9, 2013).

The Lincoln Institute. "Archibald Williams." Mr. Lincoln and Friends, http://www.mrlincolnandfriends.org/inside.asp?pageID=121 (accessed July 9, 2013).

Livingston, John. "Hon. Archibald Williams of Quincy Illinois." In *Portraits of Eminent Americans Now Living with Biographical and Historical Memoirs of Their Lives and Actions*, 2:679–80. New York: Cornish, Lamport and Co., 1853.

WILLIAMS, John R. During the Austin King Court of Inquiry in Richmond, the Mormon defendants hired Williams and others to assist in their defense.

LeSueur, Stephen C. *The 1838 Mormon War in Missouri*, 212. Columbia: University of Missouri Press, 1987.

WOOD, William Thomas (1809–1902). Along with Doniphan, Atchison, and Rees, one of the first attorneys who agreed to represent the Mormons in the reparation efforts following the 1833 Jackson County mob attacks. He received legal training while working as a court clerk for Clay County in 1829. He later became a Circuit Court Judge in Lexington, Missouri. In 1886, Wood wrote a lengthy letter to the *Liberty Tribune* responding to an article highly critical of Clay County people and officials which had been published in the Salt Lake Evening News. Wood branded the article "false and reckless" and purported to give the facts surrounding the Saints' early settlement in Clay County, the creation and settlement of Caldwell County, the Austin King Court of Criminal Inquiry, the Liberty Jail incarceration, and what he termed the "kindness and generosity" shown the Mormons by the people of Clay County. Inter alia, Wood acknowledged his early representation of the Mormons with Atchison, Doniphan and Rees, and his subsequent engagement by the state during the King hearing. He claimed: "I was never an attorney against them (the Mormons) in any of their suits or controversies in the courts, except in this one instance of giving my aid to the circuit attorney on their examining trial before Judge King, and went into that with but little faith that the prosecution could be made successful." Wood claims it was the testimony he heard during the hearing which caused him to believe the Mormons were "dangerously unfriendly to our Government and to the law of the land; and if for the next quarter of a century they increase as rapidly as in the last quarter, they will cost the government and country untold amount in money and blood."

Church Historian's Press. "Wood, William Thomas." The Joseph Smith Papers, http://josephsmithpapers.org/person?name=William+Thomas+Wood.

Clark, Charles. "W. T. Wood." KansasBogusLegislature.org, http://kansasbogus legislature.org/mo/wood_w_t.html (accessed July 9, 2013).

"Death of Judge William T. Wood." *Lexington News,* May 15, 1902, 3.

Wood, William T. "Mormon Memoirs." *Liberty Tribune,* April 9, 1886.

WOODS, James W. (1800–1886). Woods was born near Boston, Massachusetts, and moved to Virginia in 1824 before being admitted to the bar in 1827 in Lewisburg, Virginia. In 1833 he moved to Wisconsin Territory and settled in what later became Burlington, Iowa, where he practiced law and served as the City Solicitor in 1837. Together with Hugh T. Reid, Woods represented Joseph and Hyrum during the Carthage *Expositor* riot charges in June 1844. He later gave an account of the events surrounding Joseph and Hyrum's murders, published in the *Times and Seasons* (July 1, 1844). Woods was later Secretary of the Iowa State Senate and Clerk of Iowa Supreme Court.

YOUNG, Richard Montgomery (1798–1861). Young was the judge in Illinois who presided over the trial of the accused assassins of Joseph Smith in 1844. Earlier, as a legislator, he was instrumental in the formation of the Nauvoo Charter. He also acted as a character reference in Joseph's acquisition of the steamship *Nauvoo.* He also sold a tract of land in Nauvoo to Joseph Smith as Trustee-in-Trust for the Church. He served as U.S. Senator for Illinois from 1837 to 1843 and was commissioned a justice of the Illinois Supreme Court in 1843. In 1847 he was appointed commissioner of the General Land Office at Washington, D.C., and later served as clerk of the U.S. House of Representatives from 1850 to 1851.

Church Historian's Press. "Young, Richard M." The Joseph Smith Papers, http://josephsmithpapers.org/person/richard-m-young (accessed July 9, 2013).

Crossley, Frederick B. *Courts and Lawyers of Illinois,* 1:232–33. Chicago: American Historical Society, 1916.

Palmer, John, ed. *The Bench and Bar of Illinois: Historical and Reminiscent,* 1:42–43; 2:875. Chicago: Lewis Publishing, 1899.

Snyder, J. F. "Forgotten Statesman of Illinois: Richard M. Young." *Transactions of the Illinois State Historical Society for the Year 1906* (January 1906): 302–27.

"Young, Richard Montgomery." In *Historical Encyclopedia of Illinois,* ed. Newton Bateman and Paul Selby, 603–4. Chicago: Munsell Publishing, 1900.

Glossary of
Early Nineteenth-Century Legal Terms

The nineteenth-century legal terms in this glossary appear at least once in the preceding volume. This glossary draws primarily on Bouvier's Law Dictionary (1839). Original wordings have been modified for clarity and brevity, while remaining true to the historical definitions.

Adjudge: To declare, to announce formally.

Administrator: A person appointed by a court to manage the estate of a deceased person who died without a will. An administrator had the authority to take possession of the deceased's estate, to collect debts, and to represent the deceased in all matters related to his or her property. An administrator also had the authority to pay the debts of the deceased and was entitled to compensation for services.

Affidavit: A written oath or affirmation sworn or affirmed to before an officer of the court. It differed from a deposition in that a deposition could be cross-examined by the opposing party, whereas an affidavit could not.

Answer: The name of the document used by the defense to answer the plaintiff's "bill" or "information." It contained statements of facts (not arguments), and confessions or denials of material accusations of the bill.

Appeal: The act by which a party submitted an inferior court's decision to a higher court for review.

Appellant: The party who initiated the appeal.

Appellee: The party in a suit that has been appealed who did not initiate the appeal.

Application: The act of making a request, the paper on which the request is written, or the use or disposition of a thing (as "the application of purchase money"). The term was often used regarding trusts and property law.

Appurtenances: Rights, privileges, easements, or improvements that belonged to and passed with a piece of property.

Arbitration: A type of dispute resolution in which litigants attempted to solve a dispute through investigation and determination by one or more persons selected to resolve the dispute and grant an award, rather than engaging in a judicial proceeding. The decision of the third-party arbitrator was binding.

Assault: An attempt or threat to violently hurt another. When an injury was inflicted, it amounted to a battery. There were two kinds of assault: simple and aggravated. Simple assault occurred when there was no intention to do injury. This was punishable by a fine and imprisonment. Aggravated assault occurred when there was an intention to do harm as well as an intention to perform an additional crime. For example, if a man fired his pistol at another and missed, the man would have been charged with aggravated assault with intent to murder.

Assign: (1) To transfer a right over to another, as in "to assign an estate," (2) To appoint, as in "Justices are assigned to keep the peace," (3) To set forth or point out, as in "to assign false judgment."

Assignment: The transfer of all kinds of property (real, personal, mixed) from one person to another. Technically, it was restricted to only those transfers which involved terms of years (transfers for a specified period of time). But in regular parlance, the term was used for any transfer of property. When making an assignment, the words "assign, transfer, and set over" were the proper terms to use in deeds. However, "grant, bargain, and sell" or similar phrases were also accepted. Furthermore, the deed by which an assignment was made was also called an "assignment."

Assumpsit: See *"Writ of Assumpsit"* below.

Attachment: See *"Writ of Attachment"* below.

Bail: A surety or collateral meant to insure that a party would appear in court. The persons who posted this surety were also called "bail." Furthermore, the term was applied to the security given by a defendant in order to obtain a stay of execution. The term *Special Bail* referred to a surety posted by one or more persons on behalf of another that he or she will appear at a certain time and place to answer charges against him or her.

Bail Bond: Occurred when the defendant and other individuals (usually two or more) became bound to the sheriff for the amount equal to the demanded bail as assurance that the defendant would appear in court. A bail bond could only be issued when the defendant was arrested or in the custody of the sheriff.

Bailiff: An officer of the court who was given administrative authority over lands and goods for the benefit of another.

Battery: The crime or tort of intentionally or recklessly causing offensive physical contact or bodily harm. This included striking another individual, or even spitting in one's face.

Bill: A written complaint issued by the complainant in a Court of Chancery. The complaint included the names of the parties in the suit, a statement of the facts from the complainant's point of view, the allegations which the complainant made in connection with the facts, and a prayer for relief.

Bill of Indictment: A written accusation presented before a grand jury accusing one or more individuals with a misdemeanor or a felony. If the grand jury was satisfied that the accused should be tried, it returned the bill with the words "true bill" written on it. If the grand jury was not satisfied, it would write "ignoramus" on it.

Bind Over: The act of holding someone on bail in order for them to appear in court at a later date. A person may also be bound over, or kept on bail, to act in a certain fashion, such as being bound over for good behavior or to keep the peace. This latter type of bail was often referred to as a Recognizance.

Body Politic: (1) A group of individuals organized under a single government authority; (2) When referring to a corporation, the members of such a corporation.

Bona Fide: Latin for "with good faith." The law required transactions to be made in good faith. If one party did not act in good faith, the contract could be voided at the pleasure of the injured party.

Bond: An obligation where one "obliges" to pay a certain sum of money by a specified date or after the occurrence of a specified activity. Bonds were also used as ways to ensure the good behavior of an individual. A surety (the person posting the bond) would place a bond to ensure that person's performance in accordance with the law.

Capias: Latin for "thou mayest take." A writ issued commanding an officer to take the body of the person named therein or to arrest that person. Also called a writ of capias.

Cause Continued: An order of a court to have the case continued or postponed until the next term.

Chancery, Court of: Also known as Courts of Equity. There was a distinction between courts of "law" and courts of "chancery" (or equity). During medieval times, the courts of law were the only courts used in England, through which the king enforced his laws. By the thirteenth century, the courts of law gradually froze the types of cases that they would hear and the procedure governing how they would hear them, which caused the procedure to become very technical. Another way for plaintiffs to seek relief was through petitioning directly to the king, who had discretionary judicial powers based on his mercy or conscience. In time, these petitions became so numerous that the king delegated authority to hear them to his chancellor, a high-ranking official of the king's court who was originally a spiritual advisor. Before long the Chancery (the king's secretarial department) resembled a judicial body and became known as the Court of Chancery. The Court of Chancery developed rules about what types of cases they could hear, and the procedures governing the court. In time, they became as complex and technical as the Courts of Law. Courts of Chancery migrated with the settlers to the United States and became an essential part of American law. Eventually courts of Chancery and Courts of Law were merged, but that was after Joseph Smith's time.

Color of Office: This term referred to wrongs committed by an officer under the pretended authority of his office.

Common Law: The body of law derived from judicial decisions rather than law expressed by the legislative branch through a written statute or law.

Complainant: The party, in a Court of Chancery, that made a complaint.

Complaint: The allegation made by the accusing party that was filed with the court, requesting the offender be punished according to the law.

Consideration: The reason that moved the contracting party to enter into the contract, or the compensation that was paid for the performance of a contract.

Consignment: The goods or property sent from one or more people in one place (the consignors) to one or more people who are in another place (consignees).

Constable: An officer, often popularly elected, who was charged with maintaining the peace in the area over which he had responsibility.

Contempt: The willful disregard or disobedience of a public authority. Each court of justice had the power to punish all those who disobeyed its rules, processes and for disturbed the proceedings.

Coverture: The legal theory under which a wife was viewed as being merged with her husband. In coverture, the wife, generally, could make no contracts without the express or implied consent of her husband.

Credit: (1) The arrangement for a deferred payment of a loan, the terms governing such an arrangement, and the time allowed for the payment. (2) The reputation a person had for repaying their debts, although in the 1830s credit was connected with an individual's social position. (3) The right-hand column in an accounting book which contained entries due to a creditor (the opposite of debit).

Debt, Action of: The name of an action used for the recovery of a debt.

Declaration: A document filed by the plaintiff in a Court of Law (as opposed to Chancery) that set forth the facts from the view of the plaintiff, named the parties, and requested the court to find in his or her favor.

Default: (1) Failure to do something that was required (such as the failure to pay back a loan); (2) Failure to defend an issue at court. If a defendant, for example, did not attend court on the day of his or her case, the court assumed that their absence meant he or she did not contest the charges. The court entered a default judgment against them.

Demurrer: A plea in a response to an allegation. It admitted the truth of the allegation, but at the same time asserted that it was not sufficient as a cause of action. If the court found the allegations insufficient, the court could dismiss the case.

Discharge: The act by which an individual who was in confinement under some legal process or accusation was set at liberty.

Discontinue: An act by the plaintiff to terminate his or her cause of action.

Docket: A formal record of judicial proceedings.

Empannel: To form a jury by summoning and selecting members.

Engrossed: (As in an "engrossed bill") A bill in a written form ready for final passage, or the form in which it was passed by one house of a legislature.

Ex parte: An action usually taken at the request of only one of the parties to an action, or to indicate that one party did not receive notice of the action. Usually used in emergencies.

Equity, Court of: See *"Chancery, Court of"* above.

Error, Writ of: A writ issued from a superior court to an inferior one (for example, from the Court of Common Pleas to a Justice of the Peace Court) commanding the latter to send up the record of the case at issue.

Esquire: An unofficial title of respect, having no precise significance. It did apply to men in the field of law, but not only to them.

Execution, Stay of: A term during which no execution could be issued on a judgment.

Executor: An individual appointed, as set forth by a will, to manage the estate of a deceased person.

Fieri Facias: Latin for "cause to be made," The name of a writ issued by a court commanding the sheriff to levy property belonging to a party against whom there was a judgment in order to pay off his or her creditor(s).

For the Use of: For the benefit or advantage of another. Thus, where an assignee is obliged to sue in the name of his assignor, the suit was entitled "A for the use of B v. C."

Grand Jury: A body of between twelve and twenty-four men summoned by the court to determine whether an indictment should be given charging an individual with a crime.

Grantee: The party to whom land was granted.

Grantor: The party who granted land.

Hands and Seals: A legal instrument with "hands and seals" or under "hand and seal" was signed and sealed by the parties named to certify the document.

Habeas corpus: Latin for "you have the body." The writ was employed by a court to grant an opportunity to discern whether or not imprisonment was lawful. It required the one who held the prisoner to bring the prisoner in front of the court so the court could make a determination of lawfulness.

Indictment: A written accusation found by a Grand Jury that charged an individual for a crime.

Injunction: A court order that either commanded or prevented an action.

Instrument: A writing that contained an agreement.

Judgment: The decision or sentence of the law given by a court as the result of proceedings instituted therein.

Jurisdiction: (1) The authority given to a judge to decide certain issues and to carry his sentence into execution; (2) The area over which a judge had authority. Jurisdiction can be original (the right to hear a case from its inception), or appellate (the right to hear a case that has already been decided to look for legal defects).

Justice of the Peace: A public officer possessing judicial powers with the responsibility of preventing breaches of the peace and punishing those who violated the law. They were elected by the people and were commissioned by the executive. In some states they held their offices for life dependant on good behavior, while others served for a limited period.

Law, Court of: There was a distinction between courts of "law" and courts of "chancery" (or equity). During medieval times, the courts of law were the only courts used in England through which the king enforced his laws. In order to be heard before a court of law, the petitioner's case had to fit certain fact patterns. These fact patterns corresponded to various "writs" (see "*writ*" below), which the petitioner would apply for. If the court granted the writ, then a case would begin. Over time, the rules of the courts of law became so technical that legitimate causes were denied on minute details. Thus arose the court of chancery. See "*Chancery, Court of*" above.

Leave to Amend: Time granted by a court to a party in order to amend a plea that had been submitted.

Levy: The seizure by a court of money or property belonging to a party in order to pay off a judgment issued against them.

Libel: A defamatory statement made in a fixed medium such as writing.

Lien: A judgment placed upon a piece of property belonging to a debtor that ordered the property to be sold to satisfy the creditor.

Lis Pendens: Latin for "pending quarrel or dispute" (1) A pending suit; (2) Written notice of a pending suit; (3) The principle that the filing of a suit constitutes notice of the claim asserted.

Litigant: One engaged in a suit.

Mayor's Court: The name of a court established in cities where the mayor, recorder, and aldermen served as officers. These courts generally had jurisdiction over offenses committed within city boundaries and over matters that were given to them by statute (often contained within the city charter).

Mens Rea: Latin for "guilty mind." *Mens rea* described the state of mind at the time that an act was committed. If the defendant had sufficient *mens rea* required by common law or statute he or she could be convicted.

Misdemeanor: An offense, inferior to a felony, that was punishable by imprisonment or fine.

Mittimus: Latin for "we send." A writ from a Justice of the Peace that directed a gaoler (or jail keeper) to receive and keep safely a person charged with an offence until the prisoner was delivered by due course of law.

Mortgage: A conveyance of land by a debtor to a creditor as security for the repayment of a sum of money the debtor had borrowed from the creditor.

Mortgagee: The party who provided the money for a mortgage.

Mortgagor: The party who entered into a mortgage.

Motion: An application by one of the parties to a court in order to obtain some court order.

N. B. (Nota Bene): Latin for "note well," "observe carefully." Take special notice.

Non Assumpsit: The name of a plea to the declaration of assumpsit.

Non Suit: The name of a judgment given against a plaintiff when he or she was unable to prove his or her case, or when he or she abandons the case altogether.

Notary or Notary Public: An officer appointed by the executive of the state who attested deeds, agreements, and other instruments in order to give them authenticity. They also certified copies of agreements and other instruments.

Notice: The information given of some act done, usually in writing.

Oath: A declaration made according to law, before a competent tribunal or officer, to tell the truth.

Orator: In a Court of Chancery, an orator is the party that filed the bill.

Overrule: To annul, to make void.

Petition: An instrument of writing containing a prayer from the person presenting it (the petitioner) for the redress of some wrong or for the grant of some favor.

Plaintiff: The party who initiated a lawsuit. Plaintiffs would ask the court, through a declaration, to perform a specific writ against a defendant. Over time, each writ developed certain criteria that had to be met in the declaration and in the plea (or answer) by the defendant.

Preliminary Hearing: In a criminal matter, a hearing held to determine wether or not there is enough evidence to prosecute the case. The hearing serves the same purpose in state court that a grand jury proceeding serves in federal court.

Prior restraint: A governmental suppression of speech or a publication prior to its actual expression. During the twentieth century the Supreme Court of the United States deemed such restraints to violate the First Amendment as applied to the federal government and the states.

Probable Cause: Reasonable grounds to suspect that a person has committed a crime.

Process: The process, through a writ, mandate, etc., by which a cause is brought before a court.

Promissory Note: A written, unconditional, promise to pay a disclosed sum of money at a future date. Promissory notes were also used as a form of currency and were exchanged from one person to another.

Quit Claim: Transferring of land without including any warranties or assurances as in quit claim deed.

Receipt: A written acknowledgment from a seller indicating that he or she had received the money or thing that had been bargained for.

Recognizance: An obligation given to an individual commanding him or her to do some court-required act, usually accompanied by bail.

Record: *noun*—A written memorial made by a public officer. Often found in deeds. *verb*—The act of making a record.

Replevin: The name of an action for the recovery of goods and chattels.

Respondent: In a Court of Chancery, a respondent was the party responding to a bill, complaint, or other proceeding in court.

Seal: An impression upon a wafer or some other substance that was capable of being impressed.

Security: (1) An instrument that certified the performance of a contract; (2) A designated person who guaranteed that someone else would perform a certain action and becomes liable, usually by paying some amount of money, if that person did not perform.

Scire Facias: A judicial writ that was founded on some record that required the defendant to "show cause why the plaintiff should not have the advantage" of the record.

Seizure: The act of taking possession of property belonging to a person against whom there is a judgment in order to pay the sum of money indicated within that judgment.

Serve (Service): To deliver a copy of a summons to the house of the party, to the party personally, or to read it to the party.

Sheriff's Sale: In order to execute on a lien against a person's property, sheriffs sold the land at an auction, also called a Sheriff's Sale.

Slander: A defamatory statement made through speech or some other transitory medium.

Special Session, Court of: A court comprised of three justices who gathered to try an individual who was accused of certain offenses.

Statute of Limitations: A fixed period wherein a case could be brought before a court.

Subpoena: A document that commanded a witness to appear and give testimony before a court on the date and time mentioned, under which failure to comply would result in a penalty therein mentioned.

Summons (writ of): A document prepared by the court that summoned an individual to come to court, typically to answer the complaint of the plaintiff, stand trial, be a witness, or be a member of a jury.

Supersedeas: A writ or bond that suspended a judgment creditor's power to execute the judgment.

Surety: A person who promised to pay a sum of money or to carry out a certain performance for another person who is also bound for the same thing.

Testate: Dying after having made a will.

Testimony: The statement made by a witness under oath.

Trust: A right, title, or interest (held in a court of equity) in real or personal property that was distinct from its legal ownership. For example, Joseph Smith held certain pieces of property in trust for the Church, which meant that he did not actually own the property, but managed it on behalf of the Church.

Trustee: The person to whom an estate has been conveyed in trust.

Truster: The party who created a trust.

Use: Or "usury," another word for "interest."

Venue: The county from which the jury was selected.

Verdict: The unanimous decision made by a jury on the matters submitted to them during the course of the trial.

Ward: (1) An infant placed by authority of law under the care of a guardian; (2) A district within a city; (3) To watch during the day time (ex. it was the duty of all police officers to keep ward over their districts).

Warrant: A writ issued by a justice of the peace directing a constable to arrest a person named within the warrant and bring him or her before that or some other court.

Warrantee Deed: A deed containing warranties. Also spelled as Warranty Deed.

Wit (to wit): A common legal way of saying "that is to say," "namely," etc.

Witness: One who is sworn in and relates their knowledge of the facts that are at issue during a case.

Writ: A mandatory precept that was issued by the authority of the state (or sovereign) that ordered the defendant to do something therein mentioned. There were several different kinds of writs.

Writ, Return of: The sheriff was often ordered to deliver writs to the parties named therein. He was also ordered to return the original copy of the writ to the court with the means whereby he had served the parties written on the back. This was called the "return of the writ."

Writ of Assumpsit: To apply for a writ of assumpsit, an issue had to involve a contract that was made verbally, or in writing, but not under seal. Traditionally, formal agreements like the transfer of land or other large contracts were accepted in court only after the seals of the parties were attached to the documents. Therefore, the writ of assumpsit came to take the place of all those agreements that did not have the formality of a seal, but at the same time, gave some consideration.

Writ of Attachment: (1) A writ requiring the sheriff to apprehend an individual who was accused of a contempt of court and to bring that person before the court; (2) This was also the writ which commanded the sheriff to seize any property, belonging to the defendant, in whatever hands they may be found, to satisfy the demands of the plaintiff against him. The writ was always issued before a judgment and in that way differed from an execution. It was issued on an oath or affirmation, made by a creditor or someone on his behalf confirming the truth of the debt and the facts surrounding the case.

Writ of Error: The writ through which a party could send a case to an appellate court in order for an alleged error to be corrected.

Writ of Execution: The writ that put in force the sentence of the judge.

Writ of Process: A writ that forced the defendant to appear in court, either by arresting him, or by seizing his property, etc.

Writ of Replevin: (1) The name of a writ issued for the recovery of moveable goods. (2) The wrongful detention of moveable property.

Writ of Trespass: A writ through which a party may have sued for damages that were committed against the person or his or her property.

Contributors

M. Scott Bradshaw is senior corporate counsel in private practice for major multinational corporations. He received a BA in 1986 and a JD in 1989, both from Brigham Young University, and received an MA in European Union Law in 2011 from King's College of London. He has practiced law for thirteen years, including two years in the Moscow offices of Baker & McKenzie and a recent assignment in China. His practice focuses on issues concerning food and drug, international transactions, and compliance programs.

Joseph I. Bentley is a past international chair of the J. Reuben Clark Law Society, chair of the Council for Mormon Studies at Claremont Graduate University, and is serving as a volume editor in the Legal and Business Records series of the Joseph Smith Papers Project. He received his bachelor's degree from BYU in 1965 and his JD degree from the University of Chicago in 1968. He joined the law firm of Latham and Watkins, where he practiced real estate law until 2003.

David W. Grua is a historian and curator at the Church History Museum in Salt Lake City. He has a PhD in American history, with specialties in the American West and Native America, from Texas Christian University. His publications have appeared in *BYU Studies Quarterly, Mormon Historical Studies, Federal History,* and other peer-reviewed venues.

James L. Kimball Jr. earned his BS in history from the University of Utah and master's in history at the University of Iowa, where he wrote his thesis about the Nauvoo Charter. He taught in the Seminary and Institute programs of the LDS Church, including stints at West High (Salt Lake City), Oregon State University, and the University of Washington. He worked for the Historical Department of The Church of Jesus Christ of Latter-day Saints for more than twenty-five years as a librarian, archivist, and supervisor of the Archives Search Room. He passed away August 26, 2012.

Gordon A. Madsen earned a BS in 1954 and JD in 1957 from the University of Utah. He has practiced as an assistant district attorney, Third Judicial District, Utah; assistant attorney general, Utah; served as a member Utah House of Representatives; in private law for fifty-six years; and is a senior coeditor for the Joseph Smith Papers Legal and Business Records series.

Elder Dallin H. Oaks is a graduate of Brigham Young University in 1954 and of the University of Chicago Law School in 1957. He practiced law and taught law in Chicago. He was president of Brigham Young University from 1971 to 1980 and a justice of the Utah Supreme Court from 1980 until his resignation in 1984, when he accepted a call as an Apostle in The Church of Jesus Christ of Latter-day Saints.

David Keith Stott has practiced corporate law for four years at a private law firm in New York City and London. He specializes in mergers and acquisitions and capital markets. He graduated from the J. Reuben Clark Law School in 2009, where he was executive editor of the *BYU Law Review.*

Nathaniel Hinckley Wadsworth is an attorney at Rowley Chapman & Barney in Mesa, Arizona. He received a BA in 2003 from Brigham Young University and a JD in 2006 from the J. Reuben Clark Law School at Brigham Young University. For seven years he has been a commercial litigator.

Jeffrey N. Walker earned a BS from Western Michigan University in 1985 and a JD from Brigham Young University in 1988. He has practiced law for twenty-five years, mostly in Utah. He is series manager and a coeditor on the Joseph Smith Papers Legal and Business Records series and a member of the editorial board. He is also managing editor of *Mormon Historical Studies* and a trustee of the Mormon Historic Sites Foundation.

John W. Welch is the Robert K. Thomas University Professor of Law at the J. Reuben Clark Law School, Brigham Young University. He earned a bachelor's degree in history and a master's degree in Greek and Latin at BYU and a JD at Duke University. He practiced in the tax department of O'Melveny & Myers in Los Angeles. He is editor in chief of BYU Studies and is a consulting scholar on the Joseph Smith Papers Legal and Business Records series.

Index

A

Ableman v. Booth, 441
An Act for Determining Differences by Arbitration, 108
An Act for Supporting Ministers of the Gospel, 43
An Act for the Support of the Gospel, 41–42, 43
An Act Regulating Marriages, 163, 170–72
An act to prohibit the issuing and circulating of authorized bank paper, 197–201, 207–8, 210–11
An Act to Provide for the Incorporation of Religious Societies, 116, 118–20
Act to regulate judicial proceedings where banks and bankers are parties, and to prohibit bank bills of certain descriptions, 198–201, 208
Adams, James, 327, 515
adultery, 407–26
Aldrich, William, 264
appeal, cases having an, 231, 231–32
arbitration, between JS and Abner Cole, 108–12
Arkansas Supreme Court, 369
arson, 230
Atchison, David Rice, 516
Avard, Sampson, 278–79, 291

B

Babbitt, Almon W., 348, 349, 350–53, 354–56, 404, 517
Bailey, Calvin, 161–62
Bailey, Lydia Goldthwaite, 158–59, 161–63, 166
Baldwin, Caleb, 275, 280, 290, 371, 375
Bank of Monroe, 190, 192
banking, 180–82, 192, 196
bankruptcy, 315–28
Bankruptcy Act of 1841, 315–20
Baptist Church, 131, 132
Benjamin Bissel v. Joseph Smith Sr. et al., 230
Bennett, John C., 298, 301, 321, 381, 384
Benton, A. W., 91
Bierce, Lucius Verus, 517
bigamy, 161–62, 424
Birchard, Matthew, 151, 153, 156–57, 174–75
Bissell, Benjamin, 145, 147, 230, 518
Blackwell, Robert S., 326
Boggs, Lilburn W., 293–94, 315, 377–78, 384
Bollman, Erick, 283, 364
Book of Mormon, copyright for, 93–112
Boynton, Ray, 236
breach of contract, 313
Bridgeman, Peter, 71, 85
Briggs, James A., 147
Brown, Rufus, 86

Browning, Orville H., 379, 518
Brunson, Seymour, 173
Burch, Thomas, 377, 519
Burnett, Peter H., 372–73, 375, 520
Burr, Aaron, 282–88
Butterfield, Josiah, 333–44, 350–51
Butterfield, Justin, 313, 320–24, 388–93, 520
Butterfield, Margaret Lawrence. *See* Lawrence, Margaret

C

Cahoon, William, 163, 165, 169
Caldwell County, Missouri, 253–56
Calhoun, John C., 30, 31
Carlin, Thomas, 377–79
Chamberlain, Joseph P., 91, 522
Chitty, Joseph, 363–64
The Church of Jesus Christ of Latter-day Saints
    not incorporated, 113–39
    motto of, 19–20
church and state, relationship between, 39–40
Church, William, 365–66
Clark, John B., 261, 272, 293–94
Clayton, William, 343–44
Cleminson, John, 279
Cole, Abner, 94, 106–12
collection, of judgment, 222–23
Commonwealth v. Carter, 368
Constitution. *See* U.S. Constitution
Coolidge, Joseph W., 325, 350–51
copyright, 93–112
Copyright Act of 1790, 96, 97–98
corporations, religious, 116–20
court of chancery, 325
court of common pleas
    cases brought before, 65–70, 150–54, 156–58, 204–20, 228–29, 231, 232, 237
    issued licenses to perform marriages, 156
court of general sessions, definition of, 78
court of inquiry, 261, 273–82, 370–71
court of special sessions
    cases brought before, 80–84, 92
    definition of, 77
Cowdery, Oliver, 106–8, 115, 123, 133, 190, 522

Cravens, Jon, 265–66, 266–67

D

Davidson, James, 91, 523
Daviess County, Missouri, 253–70
De Zeng, Philip, 72, 73, 78–79, 81
Declaration of Independence, 3
Des Moines rapids, 309–10
disestablishmentarianism, 39–40
disorderly person, 72, 74–75
Doctrine and Covenants
    statement in, on marriage, 165–67
    statements in, on government, 6–14
Dogberry, Obadiah, 107
Donaldson v. Beckett, 95
Doniphan, Alexander W., 253, 523
Douglas, Stephen A., 300, 378–80, 408, 524
Dowen, John C., 144, 151–52, 231–32, 525
dower, 328, 331
Drummond, Thomas, 326
due process, 276–78
Dunklin, Daniel, 258
Durfee, Jabis, 264, 265, 266–67
Durfee, Perry, 264

E

Edwards, Benjamin S., 389, 525
Emmons, Sylvester, 385, 433, 526
Episcopal Church, 131, 132
Ewing, Finis, 258
Ex parte Bollman & Swartwout, 282–83, 364
Ex parte White, 369
executors, 330–31
Expositor. See Nauvoo Expositor
extermination order, 260

F

Ferris, John M., 325
Ford, Thomas, 27, 34, 387, 388, 409, 430–31
Foster, Charles A., 349, 433
Foster, Robert D., 348, 349, 405, 433
functus officio, 380

G

Gallatin, 290

Geauga County, Ohio, 173–75
George Metcalf Paymaster of 1st Brigade, 2nd Regiment, 9 Division Ohio Militia v. Samuel H. Smith, 231
Gibbs, Nancy Miranda, 163, 165
Gordon, John A., 526
Grandin, Egbert B., 104, 106
Granger, Oliver, 225, 237–40
guardian, 335–38

H

habeas corpus. *See* writ of habeas corpus
Hamilton, Alexander, 16
Hanson, Arial, 231
Hatch, Ebenezer, 91
Haws, Peter, 311–12, 314
hearing, preliminary. *See* court of inquiry
Higbee, Chauncey L., 433, 527
Higbee, Elias, 526
Higbee, Francis M., 429, 527
Hinkle, George M., 292
Hitchcock, Reuben, 203, 207
Hobbes, Thomas, 15
Holbrook, William, 144–45, 147–48, 527
Holcomb, Henry, 244
Holladay, Benjamin, 312–13
Holladay, William, 312–13
Hotchkiss, Horace R., 320
Howe, Eber D., 154
Hughes, Andrew S., 527
Humphrey, Van R., 204, 213, 527
Huntington, Dimick B., 385
Hurd, Rollin, 364–65
Hurlbut, Doctor Philastus, 141–54, 228
Hurlbut, Jeremiah, 51–70
Hyde, Orson, 185, 189

I

Illinois Constitution, 415–16, 438, 444, 452–53
Illinois Habeas Corpus Act of 1827, 381–84, 396–97, 440
Illinois state legislature, 299–301
Illinois Supreme Court, 409–11
incorporation, of churches, 116–28
interlocutory judgment, 69
Ivins, Charles, 433

J

Jackson, Andrew, 248
Jackson, Joseph H., 348, 349, 405
Jackson County, Missouri, 252
Jackway, William, 67
Jacobsen v. Massachusetts, 18
Jenkins, John, 52
Johnson, John, 193
joint stock company, 186–87
jury trial, cases having, 62–70, 157–58, 215–18, 237, 242
justice court
    cases brought before, 59–64, 91, 144–50, 229–31, 232
    definition of, 59, 76

K

Kelly, Hezekiah, 236
Kent, James, 337, 364
Kimball, Abel, 205, 223–24
King, Austin A., 261, 272–82, 371, 528
King, Thomas C., 385
Kingsbury, Horace, 201, 213
Kirtland Safety Society, 179–226, 240, 242
Kirtland Temple, 228, 230, 237, 244
Knight, Joseph, Sr., 91
Knight, Newel, 158–59, 161–63, 166

L

Lake, Dennis, 231
Lake v. Smith, 231
Lamborn, Josiah, 389–90, 529
Land Act of 1787, 249
lands
    associated with JS's bankruptcy, 321–28
    public, sale of, 247–70
    sold to pay Church debts, 237–38
    sold to pay judgments, 222–25
Lane, Jesse, 529
Lansing, Richard Ray, 93, 100
law, common, definition of, 94
law, statutory, definition of, 94
Law, William, 330, 336, 348, 349, 351, 353–55, 406, 433
Law, Wilson, 347, 349, 388, 406, 433
Lawrence, Charles B., 327
Lawrence, Edward, 329

Lawrence, John, 329–35, 333–34
Lawrence, Margaret, 329–35, 339, 344, 350
Lawrence, Maria, 348, 356, 407, 412, 414–15
lawsuit, procedure for, in Ohio, 241–42
Lee, Robert E., 311, 312, 313
Leonard, Abiel, 530
libel, 453–54
Little, Sidney B., 531
Little, Sidney H., 299, 300
Lucas, Samuel D., 271
Lynch, Mark, 288–89

M

Magna Carta, 359
Marks, William, 225
marriage, 155–77, 421–22, 422–23
Marshall, Charles, 72
Marshall, John, 17, 283–84, 286
Martin Harris, 103
Mason, Charles, 531
Massachusetts Supreme Court, 368
Mathews, Stephen, 150
McMaster, Mr., 85
McRae, Alexander, 275, 280, 290, 371, 375
mens rea, 87
Methodist Church, 128, 130
Miller, Andrew, 334, 350
Miller, George, 311
Miller, Henry W., 311
Miner v. People, 411
Minnesota Supreme Court, 456
Missouri Constitution, 280
mittimus, 432
mobs, 260, 437
Moore, John, 299
Morin, Josiah, 531
Morse, Charles, 236–37
mortgages, 50, 237, 241, 332

N

Nauvoo, charter of, 297–307, 376–77, 416, 440, 418
Nauvoo (steamboat), 309–15
Nauvoo City Council, 381–84, 385, 386, 396–98, 437, 445, 448, 455
Nauvoo Expositor, 33, 429, 433–59
Nauvoo High Council, 297

Near v. Minnesota, 457
Neely, Albert, 71–73, 75–76, 78, 80–85, 88, 89, 532
Newell, Grandison, 189, 202, 224–26, 229, 243, 244–45
New York Court of Errors, 391
New York Supreme Court, 66, 366, 368
Noble, Joel K., 92, 532
nuisance, 438, 448–51, 454–58

O

Ohio v. Doctor Philastus Hurlbut, 141–54, 228
Ontario Court of Common Pleas, 59, 65, 67, 68
An Ordinance in Relation to Religious Societies, 416–17
Osborn, Salmon S., 208, 532

P

Paine, J. C., 532
Panic of 1837, 192
Parks, H. G., 259
Parrish, Warren, 194, 201, 213, 230
Patten, David W., 290
Pearsall, Emily, 72
Pearsall notes, 83, 84–86, 87, 88, 89
Peck, Reed, 290
Pennsylvania Constitution, 453
Penrose, Charles B., 313, 320
People v. Babcock, 86
People v. C. & L. Sands, 87
People v. Lynch, 288–89
People v. Martin, 366
People v. McLeod, 368
People v. Mullen, 409
People v. Tompkins, 367
Perkins, William, 208, 533
petition for redress, 21–22
Phelps, Morris, 278
Phelps, William W., 349, 533
Pope, Nathaniel, 314, 321, 323, 388–96, 534
Pratt, Parley P., 274, 277
preemption, 249–51, 257–70
Pre-emption Act of 1830, 249, 257
Presbyterian Church, 127–30
press, freedom of, 452–59

probate, 244, 330–31
probate court, 325, 329–30, 338, 349, 350
promissory note, 232
    of Joseph Smith in Kirtland, 232–36
    from Smiths to Hurlbut, 52, 53–54
    for steamboat, 312
    to Lawrence estate, 332, 339, 355
property. *See* lands; mortgages
publishing, 111–12
Purple, William D., 71
Purple notes, 83, 84–86, 88

Q

Quinn, D. Michael, 159

R

Ralston, James Henry, 534
Rawle, William, 17
recognizance, 79–80, 274
redress, 21–22
redress petitions, 263–65
Reed, John S., 91, 92, 534
Reed, Nathaniel C., 200, 201
Rees, Amos, 268, 535
Reeves, Lewis R., 536
Reid, Hugh T., 536
Reynolds, Thomas, 378, 384, 536
Rich, Alfred, 537
Richards, Willard, 264, 343, 349
Richardson, William, 299, 348, 404, 409
Rigdon, Sidney
    accused of treason, 275, 276–77, 371,
        372, 375
    charged with operating unchartered
        bank, 201–22, 242
    dealings of, with Oliver Granger, 239
    denied license to perform marriages,
        156–58, 173–76
    obtained writ of habeas corpus, 295
    performed marriages, 164
    property of, sold for collection, 223–24,
        243
rights, due process, 276–78
rights, preemption, 247–70
riot, 429, 439
Ritch, Abram, 229–30
Robinson, Ebenezer, 343

Rockwell, Orrin Porter, 384–87
Rollins, James S., 537
Rounds, Samuel D., 201–5, 242
Rounds v. Smith, 201–21
Russell, Alpheus C., 241
Ryland, John F., 538

S

Saturday Press, 455–58
Searles v. People, 410–11
Skinner, Onias C., 348, 404, 409, 539
Smith, Alvin, 52, 53, 59, 68–69
Smith, Don Carlos, 343
Smith, Emma, 244, 325, 328, 350, 354
Smith, Frederick, 65, 69
Smith, Hyrum
    accused of treason, 275, 280, 290, 292
    alleged immorality of, 435
    charged with treason, 371, 375, 431–32
    confronted Cole regarding copyright
        infringement, 106–8
    filed counter-suit against Laws, Fosters,
        and Johnson, 349
    filed for bankruptcy, 315, 320, 323
    martyrdom of, 432
    on Missouri persecutions, 259, 260, 295
    as surety for steamboat purchase, 311
    as surety in guardianship, 336
    worked for Hurlbut, 55–56
Smith, Jesse, 40–50, 103
Smith, Joseph, Jr.
    accused of being accomplice in assas-
        sination attempt, 24
    accused of death threat, 229
    activities for Kirtland Safety Society,
        183, 184, 185, 190, 193, 194
    alleged immorality of, 435
    appeared as witness, 62–64, 70, 147–48,
        228, 229
    attempts to extradite, 323, 377–80,
        384–96
    began process of transferring guard-
        ianship, 344–47
    campaigned for presidency, 31, 434
    charged as disorderly person, 71–75,
        80–92
    charged with adultery, 402–26

Smith, Joseph, Jr. *(cont.)*
  charged with assault and battery,
    228–29
  charged with being accomplice in
    assassination attempt, 315
  charged with committing a riot while
    suppressing *Expositor* press, 429
  charged with operating unchartered
    bank, 201–22, 242–43
  charged with perjury, 403–4
  charged with perjury and adultery, 348
  charged with treason, 27, 271–95, 371–
    75, 431–32
  cited for contempt, 229
  collection cases against, 233–43, 234
  collection efforts against, 221–22, 225
  as co-owner of steamboat, 311–14
  copyright of, 93–112
  estate of, in Illinois, 350–53, 354
  estate of, in Ohio, 244
  exempted from fine for failure to
    appear at militia muster, 231–32
  filed action for "oppression by color of
    office," 229
  filed complaint against Hurlbut for
    death threat, 141–54, 228
  filed counter-suit against Laws, Fosters,
    and Jackson, 349
  filed for bankruptcy, 315–28
  finances of, 311–28, 336–53
  forclosure on mortgage held by, 241
  as glass looker, 75
  as guardian of Lawrence estate, 335–56
  held office, 23
  invested in Kirtland Safety Society, 184
  justified suppressing *Expositor* press,
    448
  legal chronology of life of, 461–514
  martyrdom of, 432
  and Nauvoo Charter, 298, 302
  organized Church, 113–39
  performed marriages, 158–73
  plural marriage of, 348
  purchased *Times and Seasons*, 343
  redress petition of, to Congress, 263
  statements by, regarding the Constitu-
    tion, 6–38

  visited Jesse Smith while recuperating
    from leg surgery, 44
  worked for Hurlbut, 55–56
Smith, Joseph, Sr.
  charged with riot and assault and bat-
    tery, 230
  filed suit against Hurlbut, 53–70
  moved to Palmyra, 51–52
  organized Adam-ondi-Ahman, 256
  as witness in JS disorderly person trial,
    85
Smith, Lucy Mack, 106
Smith, Mary Fielding, 351
Smith, Robert F., 312, 431–32, 540
Smith, Samuel H., 231–32
Snow, Erastus, 137
Snyder, Adam W., 299
Snyder, John, 405
society, religious, 125–32
Spears, Abraham, 53, 54, 59, 61, 63
*State of Ohio on complaint of Newell v.
  Smith*, 229
State of Ohio v. Ritch, 229
State of Ohio v. Smith (1835), 228
State of Ohio v. Smith (1837), 229
*State of Ohio v. Smith [Joseph Smith Sr.]
  et al.*, 230
*State of Ohio v. Zebedee Coltrin, Lyman
  Sherman, John Sawyer, Harlow Red-
  field, and Willard Woodstock*, 230–31
Statute of Anne, 95
Stiles, George Philander, 540
Stoddard, Calvin, 228
Story, Joseph, 17
Stowell, Arad, 85
Stowell, Horace, 85
Stowell, Josiah, 85, 88
Street, Charles, 312
Street, Marvin, 312
Swartwout, Samuel, 364
Swift, John, 52
Sympson, Alexander, 404, 405

T

tax, on behalf of religion, 42, 43
Taylor, John, 343, 345, 347, 349, 350, 352–53,
  414

Temple Committee, 228, 233
  collection cases against, 235, 236–37
Thomas, Jesse B., 430, 540
Thompson, Jonathan, 85
Thompson, Robert B., 298, 541
threats, 144–54
Tice, Solomon, 67
Times and Seasons, 343, 352
treason, 280–95, 374
trespass, 237
trustees, 118–25
Turney, Daniel, 300
Turnham, Joel, 372–73, 375, 542
Tuttle, Daniel S., 72

U

United States v. Burr, 368
U.S. Army Corps of Engineers, 311
U.S. Constitution, 1–38, 248, 280, 284–85,
  286, 438
  copyright under, 96
  First Amendment, 3–4, 452
  Fourteenth Amendment, 458
  LDS revelations mentioning, 6–8
  Preamble, 9–18
U.S. Supreme Court, 364–65, 414, 457

V

Van Wagoner, Richard S., 160
*Views of the Powers and Policy of the
  Government of the United States* by
  Joseph Smith, 9, 32–33

W

Walker, Cyrus, 542

Walters, Wesley P., 72, 79–83
Warren, Calvin A., 319, 322, 323, 378, 542
Warren, Charles A., 543
Washington, Bushrod, 106
Wells, Daniel H., 430, 543
Wheaton v. Peters, 99, 106
Whitmer, David, 136
Whitney, Newel K., 201, 213
Whitney, Samuel, 151, 152
Wight, Lyman, 275, 280, 290, 291, 371, 375
will, of Edward Lawrence, 330–32
Williams, Archibald, 325, 326, 544
Williams, Frederick G., 201, 213
Williams, John R., 544
Wilson, James, 453
witness, credible, 51, 62–63
Wood, William Thomas, 544
Woodruff, Wilford, 343
Woods, James W., 545
Woods, Sashel, 260, 265–66, 266–67
Woodworth, Lucian, 349
writ of capias ad respondendum, 65
writ of fieri facias, 222–23
writ of habeas corpus, 27, 357–99, 434,
  440–44
writ of inquiry, 69
writ of trespass, 61, 65

Y

Young, Richard M., 311, 545
Younger, Joseph, 264

Z

Zion's Camp, 231